THE OLIVER WENDELL HOLMES DEVISE
HISTORY OF THE SUPREME COURT
OF THE UNITED STATES

General Editor: STANLEY N. KATZ

VOLUME I, *Antecedents and Beginnings to 1801*, by Julius Goebel, Jr.

VOLUME II, *Foundations of Power: John Marshall, 1801–15*, by George L. Haskins and Herbert A. Johnson

VOLUMES III–IV, *The Marshall Court, 1815–35* by G. Edward White

VOLUME V, *The Taney Period, 1836–64*, by Carl B. Swisher

VOLUME VI, *Reconstruction and Reunion, 1864–88, Part One*, by Charles Fairman

VOLUME VII, *Reconstruction and Reunion, 1864–88, Part Two*, by Charles Fairman

SUPPLEMENT TO VOLUME VII, *Five Justices and the Electoral Commission*, by Charles Fairman

VOLUME VIII, *Troubled Beginnings of the Modern State, 1888–1910*, by Owen M. Fiss

VOLUME IX, *The Judiciary and Responsible Government, 1910–21*, by Alexander M. Bickel and Benno C. Schmidt, Jr.

VOLUME X, *Constitutional Rights and the Regulatory State, 1921–30*, by Robert C. Post

VOLUME XI, *The Crucible of the Modern Constitution, 1930–41*, by Richard D. Friedman

THE
Oliver Wendell Holmes
DEVISE

HISTORY OF
THE SUPREME COURT
OF THE UNITED STATES

VOLUME VIII

THE OLIVER WENDELL HOLMES DEVISE

History of the

SUPREME COURT

of the United States

VOLUME VIII

Troubled Beginnings of the Modern State, 1888–1910

By Owen M. Fiss

Macmillan Publishing Company
NEW YORK

Maxwell Macmillan Canada
TORONTO

Maxwell Macmillan International
NEW YORK • OXFORD • SINGAPORE • SYDNEY

Macmillan Publishing Company
866 Third Avenue, New York, NY 10022

Maxwell Macmillan Canada, Inc.
1200 Eglinton Avenue East, Suite 200, Don Mills, Ontario M3C 3N1

Macmillan, Inc., is part of the Maxwell Communication Group of Companies.

Library of Congress Catalog Card Number: 78-30454

Printed in the United States of America

printing number
1 2 3 4 5 6 7 8 9 10

Library of Congress Cataloging-in-Publication Data
(Revised for v. 8)

History of the Supreme Court of the United States.

At head of title: The Oliver Wendell Holmes Devise.
Includes bibliographical footnotes and indexes.
Contents: v. 1. Antecedents and beginnings to
1801, by J. Goebel, Jr.—v. 2. Foundations of power,
John Marshall, 1801–15, by G.L. Haskins and
H.A. Johnson.—[etc.]—v. 8. Troubled beginnings
of the modern state, 1888–1910, by Owen M. Fiss.
1. United States.—Supreme Court—History.
2. United States.—Permanent Committee for the
Oliver Wendell Holmes Devise.
KF8742.A45H55   347.73′26′09   78-30454
                                347.3073509

ISBN 0-02-541360-0 (v. 2)

To

Irene Sherman Fiss

for the dreams we lived together

Many historians assert that the
French failed at Borodino because
Napoleon had a cold in his head. . . .

Leo Tolstoy, *War and Peace*

Contents

Illustrations

FOLLOWING PAGE 204

Cartoon from Puck, *1904, dramatizing Standard Oil's influence over government*

William Howard Taft as circuit court judge, 1892–1900; Taft during his service in the Philippines, 1900–1904

William Howard Taft on the day of his inauguration as president, March 4, 1909, with President Theodore Roosevelt

Cartoon of the Roosevelt administration's position on railway regulation, shortly before Congress passed the Hepburn Act of 1906

A photograph of the bakery involved in Lochner v. New York

Associate Justice Louis D. Brandeis

A photograph of the laundry involved in Muller v. Oregon; *Josephine Goldmark, publication secretary of the National Consumers' League and sister-in-law of Louis D. Brandeis*

Cartoon advocating temperance, 1894

FOLLOWING PAGE 268

Two newspaper front pages announcing the explosion of the U.S. man-of-war Maine, *February 17, 1898*

Two cartoons on the Spanish-American War, 1898

Associate Justice Edward Douglass White

A photograph of a certificate of residence required by the Geary Act of 1892

Front page of The Rocky Mountain News, *June 25, 1905, leading to a contempt citation that was the subject of* Patterson v. Colorado

Albion Tourgée

Associate Justice Henry Billings Brown; Associate Justice John Marshall Harlan

A photograph of a march in New York City, 1917, organized by the recently formed National Association for the Advancement of Colored People

Foreword

THE *History of the Supreme Court of the United States* is being prepared under the auspices of the Permanent Committee for the Oliver Wendell Holmes Devise with the aid of the estate left by Mr. Justice Oliver Wendell Holmes, Jr. Mr. Justice Holmes died in 1935 and the Permanent Committee for the Devise was created by Act of Congress in 1955. Members of the Committee are appointed by the President of the United States, with the Librarian of Congress, an *ex officio* member, as Chairman. The present volume is the eighth in the series. The Committee hopes to complete the history expeditiously while maintaining the high quality of the scholarship. The volumes in the Holmes Devise *History of the Supreme Court of the United States* bring to this subject some of the best legal scholarship of the decades since Mr. Justice Holmes' death. We hope that, when completed, the series will widen and deepen our understanding of the Supreme Court and bring honor to the memory of one of its great Justices.

James H. Billington
LIBRARIAN OF CONGRESS

PERMANENT COMMITTEE FOR
THE OLIVER WENDELL HOLMES DEVISE

(TERMS OF EIGHT YEARS EXCEPT FOR INITIAL APPOINTMENTS)

Charles T. McCormick	1956–58	(two-year term)
Edward S. Corwin	1956–60	(four-year term)
George L. Haskins	1956–58	(six-year term, but resigned 10/7/58)
Virgil M. Hancher	1956–64	
Frederick D. G. Ribble	1958–66	
Ethan A. H. Shepley	1959–67	
Nicholas Kelley	7/8/60–7/22/60	
Jefferson B. Fordham	1961–69	
Harry H. Ransom	1964–72	
Herbert Wechsler	1966–74	
Robert G. McCloskey	1967–69	
J.A.C. Grant	1970–78	
Alfred H. Kelly	1970–78	
Philip B. Kurland	1975–83	
Charles A. Wright	1975–83	
Stanley N. Katz	1976–84	
Paul J. Mishkin	1979–87	
Gerhard Casper	1985–93	
Richard B. Morris	1985–93	
Robert H. Bork	1990–98	
Arlin M. Adams	1991–99	

Editor's Foreword

Although this is now the second volume in the Holmes Devise series for which I have taken full editorial responsibility, it is the first for which I have not had the moral support of my co-editor, Paul Freund. Paul's death in 1992 has deprived the world of constitutional scholarship of its most distinguished member, and the Holmes Devise of its memory and its scholarly conscience. I should like to record here my personal and professional debt to Paul, an acknowledgment that places me among hundreds of fortunate legal scholars and lawyers.

It is fitting that this volume should be the work of Owen M. Fiss. Owen was one of Paul Freund's most distinguished constitutional law students, though I think it unlikely that Owen had yet identified himself as a student of legal history. Owen and I were colleagues at the University of Chicago Law School in the 1970s, where we co-taught a seminar on antebellum race and law with our beloved friend, the late Harry Kalven, Jr. As a historian, I take pleasure in putting in the record that our very proper dean, Phil C. Neal, listed the course in the catalogue as *Government Regulation of Race Relations in the United States* to avoid the imputation that the Law School was promoting chattel slavery. It gives me great pleasure to think that history no longer needs such a disguise in American law schools!

Owen Fiss's volume follows along the new path opened for the Holmes Devise by G. Edward White in his Marshall Court volume. It is a tightly organized, highly interpretive, and monographic approach. It serves, I think, not only to provide an accurate record of the United States Supreme Court at the turn of the twentieth century but also to make available a readable account of the function of the Court in American life. Fiss challenges the accepted interpretations of many of the most famous Supreme Court opinions in this period, especially that of the *Lochner* case. Above all, he provides a fresh approach to the political orientation of the Court, rejecting the simplistic notion of crude conservatism that has for too long stigmatized a creative bench. I believe that Owen has produced the benchmark study of the Fuller Court.

Owen M. Fiss is the Sterling Professor of Law at the Yale Law School. A Harvard Law graduate, he clerked first for then Judge Thurgood Marshall on the United States Court of Appeals for the 2nd Circuit, and subsequently for Justice William J. Brennan of the United States Supreme Court. He has also served in the Civil Rights Division of the Justice Department and as professor of law at the University of Chicago. As any of his students will tell you, Owen is also one of the best—and most demanding—law teachers in this country. Working with him on this book has been an unusual pleasure for me.

Stanley N. Katz

Troubled Beginnings
of the
Modern State, 1888–1910

PART ONE

The Legacy of Negative Examples

CHAPTER I

Legitimacy and History

T HE TWO-HUNDRED-YEAR HISTORY of the Supreme Court has been
divided among a dozen or more chief justices. Each segment has
achieved a separate identity, each bears the name of the chief justice, and
each is referred to as a "Court." Each Court has been graded, and some
have been deemed great, others mediocre, some quite dismal. By all
accounts, the Court over which Melville Weston Fuller presided, from
1888 to 1910, ranks among the worst.

In its day the Fuller Court was the subject of heated criticism, and
it became an issue in the presidential election of 1896. The controversy centered on two decisions announced in the spring of 1895: *Pollock v. Farmers'
Loan & Trust Co.*,[1] which invalidated the federal income tax, and *In re
Debs*,[2] which sustained the use of a federal court injunction to break a massive strike centered in Chicago. The attack on the Court in the 1896 election
was led by the Democratic-Populist candidate, William Jennings Bryan,
and was embodied in two planks in his platform: One called for an income
tax; the other denounced "government by injunction."[3] The more general
charge, often only insinuated but sometimes made explicit, was that the
Court had become an instrument of the propertied classes, dedicated to
stopping the masses in their effort to curb, through either self-help or legislation, the abuses of big business.

This first attack on the Fuller Court was largely unsuccessful. Bryan
gained control of the Democratic Party and, as the leader of the party for
much of the next decade or so, forged alliances that caused the party to
move to the left and fixed its character for much of the twentieth century.[4]
But Bryan lost the election of 1896 in a most decisive fashion. The principal
issue in the election was not the Court but the monetary standard,[5] and as

---

[1] 157 U.S. 429 (1895); 158 U.S. 601
(1895).
[2] 158 U.S. 564 (1895).
[3] Kirk H. Porter and Donald B. Johnson, comps., *National Party Platforms,
1840–1976*, rev. ed. (Urbana: University of Illinois Press, 1978), 1: 98–99.

[4] James L. Sundquist, *Dynamics of
the Party System: Alignment and
Realignment of Political Parties in the
United States*, rev. ed. (Washington,
D.C.: Brookings Institution, 1983),
152–59.
[5] Ibid., 153–56.

the campaign moved from the convention hall to the streets less and less emphasis was placed on the Court. Overall, Bryan's attack on the Court was a liability. The image his opponents successfully projected, vividly captured by a front-page cartoon in *Harper's Weekly*, was that under Bryan the Court would be staffed by the most notorious and feared leaders of the left.[6]

During the first decade of the twentieth century, as Fuller's chief justiceship drew to a close, the Court once again became the subject of broad public attack. Now the criticism was voiced by members of the progressive movement. Their theme was similar to Bryan's earlier charges: The judicial power was being used to thwart the will of the people and to advance the interests of the propertied classes. This time, however, critics focused on liberty of contract rather than on the income tax decision or the labor injunction. The most notorious decision of that decade was *Lochner v. New York* (1905),[7] which invalidated, under the rubric of liberty of contract, a state statute that placed a sixty-hour ceiling on the workweek of employees of bakeries.

Lochner did not, however, stand alone. The Court also invalidated legislation protecting union activity,[8] applied the Sherman Antitrust Act to a labor-organized boycott,[9] enjoined the enforcement of statutes regulating the rates of railroads,[10] and held unconstitutional a federal statute establishing new standards of liability for work-related injuries on railroads.[11] The Court upheld the Roosevelt administration's effort to block the blatant scheme of J. P. Morgan and James Hill to merge two competing rail lines but did so only grudgingly.[12] Theodore Roosevelt, a leading voice of progressivism, ended his presidency in 1908 with an address to Congress strongly critical of the Court.[13]

His successor, William Howard Taft, also a Republican but less enamored of progressive reform, did not share Roosevelt's view of the Court. Though he expressed disappointment with those justices who he

---

[6] *Harper's Weekly*, Sept. 12, 1896. The cartoon was captioned, "On a Populistic Basis—A Forecast of the Consequence of a Popocratic Victory to the Supreme Court of the United States."

[7] 198 U.S. 45 (1905).

[8] Adair v. United States, 208 U.S. 161 (1908).

[9] Loewe v. Lawlor (Danbury Hatters Case), 208 U.S. 274 (1908).

[10] *Ex parte* Young, 209 U.S. 123 (1908).

[11] The Employers' Liability Cases, 207 U.S. 463 (1908).

[12] Northern Sec. Co. v. United States, 193 U.S. 197 (1904).

[13] Fred L. Israel, ed., *The State of the Union Messages of the Presidents, 1790–1966* (New York: Chelsea House, 1966), 3: 2307–2316. In this, his eighth and final annual message to Congress, which was read to the Congress on December 8, 1908, Roosevelt characterized the Court as sometimes arrogating to itself "functions which properly belong to the legislative bodies," ibid., 2313, and referred to the Court's decision in the *Employers' Liability Cases* as "a very slovenly piece of work," ibid., 2315.

thought were well past retirement age, Taft, a major figure in the legal establishment, was no critic of the Court as an institution. Nonetheless, outside the White House, criticism of the Court spread. The 1911 decisions in the *Standard Oil* and *American Tobacco* cases,[14] firmly establishing that the Sherman Act did not proscribe all restraints of trade but only "unreasonable" ones, fueled such criticism, and the Court once again became the subject of a presidential election. The 1912 election was for the progressives what 1896 had been for the populists—an occasion for a broad-based political and social movement to express its anger and disappointment with the Court. This time, however, the criticism carried greater depth and persuasiveness.

In 1912 the Court was defended by the incumbent Taft, firm in his belief in the integrity of the judicial power and its claim to supremacy. The principal critic of the Court was Theodore Roosevelt, who sought to return to the presidency, this time on the Progressive ticket. Roosevelt had ended his previous term as president by denouncing the Court; he repeated this theme in his 1912 campaign and went one step further. He endorsed the popular recall of judicial decisions as a check upon abuses of the judicial power, although, anxious to give the appearance of moderation, he limited his proposal to state judicial decisions.[15] The Democratic candidate, Woodrow Wilson, also a progressive, was even more restrained and opposed recall of judicial decisions. But Wilson proposed statutes that promised to revise, and thus limit, many of the decisions of the Court. Upon his victory he pressed, mostly successfully, for their enactment.

One such measure, the Clayton Act of 1914,[16] placed procedural limitations on the labor injunction. That statute also reversed the *Danbury Hatters Case* of 1908[17] by exempting organized labor from antitrust laws. In addition, the Clayton Act responded to the 1911 "rule of reason" cases by proscribing such anticompetitive practices as price discrimination, tying

---

[14] Standard Oil Co. v. United States, 221 U.S. 1 (1911); United States v. American Tobacco Co., 221 U.S. 106 (1911).

[15] Stephen Stagner, "The Recall of Judicial Decisions and the Due Process Debate," *Am. J. Legal Hist.*, 24: 257 (1980). State judicial decisions holding a state statute in conflict with either the state or federal constitution were to be subject to popular recall, although Roosevelt added, "If [the court's judgment] is sustained, well and good. If not, then the popular verdict is to be accepted as final, the decision is to be treated as reversed, and the construction of the constitution definitely decided—sub-

ject only to action by the Supreme court of the United States." *Chicago Tribune*, Feb. 22, 1912. Two years earlier, in his call for a "New Nationalism" in a speech at Osawatomie, Kansas, Roosevelt had declared that, in order to ensure to the public the power to regulate property, the federal courts should be made subsidiary to Congress and to the president, who would become the "steward of the public welfare." George E. Mowry, *The Era of Theodore Roosevelt, 1900–1912* (New York: Harper Bros., 1958), 271–72.

[16] 38 Stat. 730 (1914).

[17] See above, note 9.

5

contracts, and interlocking directorships. It also strengthened the enforcement mechanism of the Sherman Act. It created the treble damage action. The Federal Trade Commission Act,[18] also passed in 1914, established a new administrative agency to curb unfair business practices. In another domain, but also in response to the Court's decisions, Congress had enacted the Webb-Kenyon Act one year earlier. That measure effectively curtailed Supreme Court decisions denying states the power to regulate the importation of liquor.[19] During this same period two constitutional amendments, the first since the aftermath of the Civil War, were passed. One provided for the direct election of senators (the Seventeenth), while the other (the Sixteenth) spoke more directly to the Court. Adopted in 1913, the Sixteenth Amendment legitimated the income tax and thus reversed the result in *Pollock*.

The criticism of the Court implicit in all these measures and in Wilson's 1912 victory (or, more precisely, in Taft's defeat) was not confined to the political arena but extended throughout the culture. It found strong support in the legal academy, particularly in the work of the prominent Harvard scholar Roscoe Pound, who denounced the work of the Court as excessively mechanistic and divorced from changing economic and social realities.[20] A number of progressive economists, especially Richard Ely and John Commons, also threw their support behind maximum hour laws and other similar measures that the Court had declared invalid as an infringement of liberty of contract.[21] Charles Beard, the political scientist and historian at Columbia, struck a more radical note. In 1913 he published *An Economic Interpretation of the Constitution of the United States*, which threw the very source of judicial authority into question by depicting the original Constitution as the work of a propertied elite trying to further their own narrow interests.[22] Most of the critics of the judiciary during this early phase of progressivism charged the Court with abuse of power, but Beard's

---

[18] 38 Stat. 717 (1914).

[19] 37 Stat. 699 (1913). In addition, in 1910 Congress passed the Mann-Elkins Act, 36 Stat. 539, which established the Commerce Court to review ICC orders, as a way of curbing aggressive review by the ordinary courts. Section 17 of that Act, enacted in response to *Ex parte Young*, required a panel of three judges, of whom one had to be a justice of the Supreme Court or a circuit court judge, to issue federal court injunctions against state legislation. See Chapter 7.

[20] See, e.g., his articles "Mechanical Jurisprudence," *Colum. L. Rev.*, 8: 605 (1908), and "Liberty of Contract," *Yale*

L.J., 18: 454 (1909).

[21] See, e.g., John R. Commons and John B. Andrews, *Principles of Labor Legislation* (New York: Harper & Bros., 1916), 95–132, and Richard T. Ely, *Property and Contract in Their Relations to the Distribution of Wealth* (New York: Macmillan, 1914), 2: 651–79.

[22] *An Economic Interpretation of the Constitution of the United States* (New York: Macmillan, 1913). See also his book *The Supreme Court and the Constitution* (New York: Macmillan, 1912) and his article "The Supreme Court— Usurper or Grantee?," *Pol. Sci. Q.*, 27: 1 (1912).

work suggested an even more disquieting possibility: The Court might be acting as an instrument of class justice even when interpreting the Constitution correctly.

The progressive critique of the Court had one further resource to draw on: the dissent by Oliver Wendell Holmes, Jr., in *Lochner v. New York*.[23] Over the years that dissent has become one of the most famous opinions in the entire history of the Supreme Court. Even in its day it was of great significance, for it provided the progressives with a critique of the Court from within. In so using Holmes's dissent, critics were able to draw upon the prestige of its author, who, only in his third year on the Supreme Court, already had achieved considerable fame. Prior to his appointment to the Supreme Court, Holmes had been a justice and then chief justice of the Supreme Judicial Court of Massachusetts. Before that, he was a professor at Harvard Law School, an editor of an influential legal periodical, and the author of some of the most important jurisprudential works of the time, including *The Common Law* and "The Path of the Law."[24] Holmes's circle of acquaintances, even during this early period, was staggering, without equal in his time or ours. His *Lochner* dissent possessed a rhetorical power and sweep that served the critics of the Court well.

Fuller died in 1910—just as the criticism of the Court gained a new momentum—but his death did not signal, much less cause, either a change in doctrine or an abatement of the attacks. The struggle between Court and society persisted. There were, of course, some modifications in the Court's stance in the years following Fuller's death, as the nation experienced increased industrialization, urbanization, world war, labor unrest, and new waves of immigration, and as influential progressives were appointed to the Court—first Charles Evans Hughes in 1910, and then Louis D. Brandeis in 1916. For the most part, however, the body of doctrine created by the Fuller Court, epitomized by *Lochner*, stood. It was inherited by Fuller's successor, Edward Douglass White, who had served as an associate justice under Fuller and was appointed to the chief justiceship in 1910 by Taft; it was also inherited by Taft, who succeeded White as chief justice in 1921. The criticism of the Court that was rooted in Holmes's dissent in *Lochner*, and now an integral part of the progressive movement, grew in the years following Fuller's death, but it did not cause either the White or Taft Court to reverse course.

The break with *Lochner* finally came in the 1930s. Confronted with the Great Depression, President Franklin Roosevelt managed to enact into

---

[23] 198 U.S. at 74–76.
[24] *The Common Law* (Boston: Little, Brown, 1881); "The Path of the Law," *Harv. L. Rev.*, 10: 457 (1897). Once on the

Supreme Court, Holmes's scholarly contributions virtually ceased; presumably he found another outlet for his views.

law a program of state intervention far more extensive than any that had gone before. Although the Court was now led by the progressive Charles Evans Hughes (who had left the Court in 1916 to pursue his political ambitions but returned in 1930 as chief justice), its first response to Roosevelt's economic recovery program was negative: The Court clung to the jurisprudence of *Lochner* and invalidated several early New Deal measures. In 1935 the Court held unconstitutional the suspension of the gold clause in government bonds,[25] the Railroad Retirement Act,[26] and the "hot oil" provision of the National Industrial Recovery Act,[27] and then, later that year, declared the National Industrial Recovery Act itself unconstitutional.[28] As a result, the antagonism between the political and judicial branches intensified, and in 1937, at the beginning of his second term, Franklin Roosevelt made explicit a threat only alluded to by Bryan in 1896: the appointment to the Court of persons who were sympathetic to his political program.

Unlike Bryan, Roosevelt spoke from the White House and with great popular support, but his desire to appoint like-minded individuals to the Court was frustrated by the low turnover rate of justices during his first term in office. In response, he proposed an increase in the size of the Court in order to provide opportunities for the new appointments needed to obtain a majority—his infamous court-packing plan.[29] As it turned out, however, this controversial and unpopular plan was never implemented. Because of a change in the position of Justice Roberts (the "switch in time that saved nine"[30]) and the retirement of Justice Van Devanter, the conflict between the Court and the political branches came to an end. In 1937 the Court assumed a new stance,[31] implicitly acknowledging the supremacy of the legislative branch and repudiating *Lochner* and all that it stood for.

---

[25] Perry v. United States, 294 U.S. 330 (1935).

[26] Railroad Retirement Bd. v. Alton R.R., 295 U.S. 330 (1935).

[27] Panama Refining Co. v. Ryan, 293 U.S. 388 (1935).

[28] A. L. A. Schechter Poultry Corp. v. United States, 295 U.S. 495 (1935).

[29] On February 5, 1937, Roosevelt sent Congress his plan for reorganizing the federal judiciary, which he claimed was hobbled by a deficiency of personnel. His plan was to empower the president to add a new judge to a federal court in the event that a federal judge who had served for ten years or longer did not retire or resign within six months after his seventieth birthday. There was, however, a limit to the number of judges the president could appoint: no more than six new justices to the Supreme Court and forty-four judges to the lower courts. *The Public Papers and Addresses of Franklin D. Roosevelt*, vol. 6 (New York: Macmillan, 1941), 51–66. See also William E. Leuchtenburg, *Franklin D. Roosevelt and the New Deal, 1932–1940* (New York: Harper & Row, 1963), 232–33.

[30] This phrase was coined by Thomas Reed Powell. See John P. Roche, *Sentenced to Life* (New York: Macmillan, 1974), 268, note 105.

[31] See West Coast Hotel Co. v. Parrish, 300 U.S. 379 (1937) (sustaining a state minimum wage law for women), and NLRB v. Jones & Laughlin Steel Corp., 301 U.S. 1 (1937) (upholding the National Labor Relations Act).

Chapter I: *Legitimacy and History*

I

For almost two decades the so-called settlement of 1937 remained unquestioned. *Lochner* lay buried in peace. Reinforced by economic recovery and victory in World War II, the attachment to the settlement of 1937 and its vision of government power grew steadily, as though the entire social order depended on it. Moreover, those who had participated in the formulation or implementation of the political programs of the 1930s began to fill positions of leadership within the legal profession, both in the bar and the academy. Three of the most important justices of the modern period—Hugo Black, William O. Douglas, and Felix Frankfurter—owed their appointments largely to their roles in the New Deal. In 1954, however, a momentous case placed new strains upon the settlement of 1937: *Brown v. Board of Education.*[32]

In that decision the Supreme Court, under the leadership of Earl Warren, declared racially segregated public education unconstitutional. Nearly all forms of official racial segregation were brought within the sweep of that ruling, and by the mid-1960s the Court's commitment to racial equality was broadened into a concern with equality in general. In a series of decisions, the Supreme Court intervened to protect the poor, just as it had done for blacks.[33] Similarly, it invalidated a law prohibiting the sale of contraceptives[34] and thus laid the constitutional foundation for upholding the claims of the women's movement that culminated in *Roe v. Wade.*[35] The Court sought also to give substance to the constitutional ideal of equality by announcing a one-person–one-vote rule to govern apportionment of electoral districts.[36] Equality was the Court's principal concern but not its only one. The Court also sought to reform civil and criminal procedures,[37] expand the frontiers of freedom of speech,[38] and build a sturdier wall between church and state.[39] All of this occurred at the expense of many state statutes and even some federal ones, which were either invalidated or narrowly construed.

---

[32] 347 U.S. 483 (1954).

[33] See, e.g., Harper v. Virginia Bd. of Elections, 383 U.S. 663 (1966). See generally Frank I. Michelman, "On Protecting the Poor Through the Fourteenth Amendment," *Harv. L. Rev.*, 83: 7 (1969).

[34] Griswold v. Connecticut, 381 U.S. 479 (1965).

[35] 410 U.S. 113 (1973).

[36] Reynolds v. Sims, 377 U.S. 533 (1964).

[37] See, e.g., Mapp v. Ohio, 367 U.S. 643 (1961); Miranda v. Arizona, 384 U.S. 436 (1966); Goldberg v. Kelly, 397 U.S. 254 (1970); and Gideon v. Wainwright, 372 U.S. 335 (1963).

[38] See, e.g., New York Times Co. v. Sullivan, 376 U.S. 254 (1964), and Brandenburg v. Ohio, 395 U.S. 444 (1969). See generally Harry Kalven, Jr., *A Worthy Tradition: Freedom of Speech in America*, ed. Jamie Kalven (New York: Harper & Row, 1988).

[39] Engel v. Vitale, 370 U.S. 421 (1962).

The substantive values propounded by the Court in the 1960s differed radically from those of the Court at the turn of the century. While the Fuller Court was committed to protecting liberty and the idea of limited government, the Warren Court was primarily committed to promoting equality, knowing full well that extensive governmental intervention and sometimes a curtailment of liberties, like freedom of association or whom to hire, would be required. The relationship between constitutional edict and the status quo also differed for the two Courts. At the turn of the century the legislative and executive branches were agents of change and the Court the force of resistance. During the 1960s the roles switched, and the Court became the impetus for change. The Warren Court mandated a change of the status quo, either by direct judicial decree or, alternatively, by gently prodding various legislative and executive agencies to reverse their long-standing policies and to undo entrenched social practices.

Although these differences between the Warren and Fuller Courts were important, there was also a similarity that for many seemed even more significant: Both shared a common conception of the judicial function. Each Court viewed itself as the guardian of a public morality that was anchored in and made authoritative by the Constitution. The Equal Protection Clause was for the Warren Court what the Due Process Clause had been for the Fuller Court; the First Amendment was the functional equivalent of the Commerce Clause. Each was perceived as a mandate for the most vigorous judicial action.

Thus comparisons with *Lochner* were frequently made to reproach the Warren Court.[40] How, critics asked, could the Warren Court's activism be distinguished from that represented by *Lochner*, which, as all agreed, was an error of colossal proportions? Some scholars sought to answer this question by confining *Lochner* to the domain of social and economic policies, arguing that on matters of principle deference to the legislature was inappropriate. Others sought to defend the Warren Court by distinguishing property rights from human rights, arguing that it was appropriate for the Court to intervene for purposes of protecting the latter but not the former. But both of these arguments presupposed categories that were far from self-defining or self-justifying. What, for example, is the difference between a "policy" and a "principle"? What is the difference between a "property right" and a "human right"? Why is a "human right," as opposed to a "property right," more appropriately protected by the judiciary? A decision invalidating a state statute restricting employment opportunities for blacks might be seen as expressive of the "principle" of racial equality and as protective of a "human right"; it also might be seen as furthering an "economic

---

[40] See, e.g., the dissenting opinion of Justice Black in Griswold v. Connecti-   cut, 381 U.S. 479, 514–15 (1965).

and social policy" or as an effort to protect the "property" black workers might have in their capacity to work.

More recently some commentators have sought to distinguish *Lochner* and *Brown*, and thus to embrace the activism of the Warren Court while honoring the settlement of 1937, by emphasizing the political vulnerability of the various groups on whose behalf the Warren Court intervened. Blacks, in contrast to the economic groups protected by the Fuller Court, suffered unique disadvantages in electoral politics: They were few in number, unable to form effective coalitions, and sometimes even disenfranchised. This line of argument had its roots in the reference to "discrete and insular minorities" in footnote four of the *Carolene Products* case[41]—generally regarded as part of the settlement of 1937—and has achieved great currency in the modern period. It accounted for the great success of John Ely's book, *Democracy and Distrust*, which was a defense of the Warren Court's activism within the terms of the settlement of 1937.[42] Ely accepted legislative supremacy but created a broad exception for laws that corrupted or distorted the political process or adversely affected groups who were unable to participate fully and fairly in that process. He focused on the political vulnerability of blacks and explained how it was possible both to embrace *Brown* and reject *Lochner*.

In the end, Ely's explanation, and others that followed the lead of *Carolene Products*, were less than fully satisfactory. For one thing, they did not adequately distinguish certain Fuller Court precedents, such as the decision invalidating the 1894 income tax. The tax fell on only 2 percent of the population, and though that particular minority possessed considerable economic power, it might have suffered a vulnerability at the polls by force of numbers alone sufficient to warrant special judicial solicitude. Moreover, political vulnerability could not explain the strong exercise of the judicial power by the Warren Court on behalf of the press, which surely was not lacking in political power. There was also some question whether the poor could be considered a "discrete and insular minority" and thus whether it was appropriate to move from race to class, as the Warren Court did, in defining the egalitarian crusade.[43] Finally, contrary to what might be expected from a theory emphasizing political vulnerability, the Warren Court did not confine itself to correcting the imperfections of the political process but also conferred substantive benefits on disadvantaged groups. Massive disenfranchisement and the special vulnerability of blacks in the political process may have warranted judicial intervention, but under the

---

[41] United States v. Carolene Prods. Co., 304 U.S. 144 (1938).

[42] *Democracy and Distrust: A Theory of Judicial Review* (Cambridge: Harvard University Press, 1980).

[43] But see Bruce A. Ackerman, "Beyond *Carolene Products,*" *Harv. L. Rev.*, 98: 713 (1985).

theory stemming from *Carolene Products* it remains unclear why the intervention took the form that it did.

For these reasons, the familiar lawyerly arguments used to distinguish the activism of *Brown* and *Lochner* collapsed, and *Lochner* continued to be used to impeach the activism of the Warren Court. It was as though the Fuller and Warren Courts were locked in a dialectic across history, *Lochner* acting as a negative example for the Warren Court. Oddly enough, however, in time the dialectic took a new turn and began to reverse itself. As *Brown* became more fully absorbed into the national political and legal culture and assumed an almost axiomatic quality, *Lochner* began to appear in a new light. Those who, like myself, took *Brown* as their starting point, began to wonder whether *Lochner* was in fact mistaken. To us *Lochner* at first appeared as a limit on *Brown*, but over time *Brown* appeared as an invitation to reexamine the settlement of 1937, to wonder whether the use of the judicial power affirmed by *Lochner* and by the other decisions of the Fuller Court was in fact illegitimate.

This work takes up that invitation. As a historical essay, it cannot resolve the question of legitimacy directly or fully; that question can be answered only by identifying and examining the normative premises that underlie decisions such as *Lochner*. History can, however, make us appreciate more fully the conditions that produced *Lochner* and thus enable us to see the legacy of the Fuller Court for what it truly is. It can prepare us finally to confront the ghost of *Lochner*.

II

My method is to return to the words of the justices, to their public utterances, and to place them in a conceptual framework and historical context that render them meaningful. This book is not an apology (I hope), but rather an attempt to bring the work of the Fuller Court out into the light. To many, especially to the generation of lawyers schooled in the New Deal, *Lochner* and the legacy of the Fuller Court strike an odd and discordant note. They seem out of step with the rest of our judicial history. My claim is that this is a misunderstanding and that the Fuller Court should be understood as an institution devoted to liberty and determined to protect that particular constitutional ideal from the social movements of the day.

In this endeavor I labor uneasily against a scholarly tradition that treats all the talk of liberty by the Fuller Court as mere camouflage or subterfuge and insists that Fuller and his colleagues were simply using their power to further class interests. This view, echoing much of the political criticism voiced about the Court in the presidential elections of 1896 and 1912, has been advanced in our own day, notably by two scholars, Arnold

Chapter I: *Legitimacy and History*

Paul[44] and Alan Westin.[45] They depict the decisions of the Court invalidating the income tax and limiting the Sherman Act as rationalizations of class interests. They read *Debs*'s validation of the labor injunction similarly. Focusing on the privileged or elite backgrounds of the justices and the pro-business character of their decisions, Westin and Paul discount the seemingly neutral reasons that the justices gave in justifying their decisions and treat them as mere rhetoric. These two scholars addressed the early phase of the Fuller Court, specifically the years immediately preceding the election of 1896, but their work has been taken to cover the entire period of Fuller's tenure. Westin and Paul have given us the standard account of the Fuller Court and, as a criticism, it has become an important part of the progressive tradition that so disparages that phase of the history of the Supreme Court.

Initially, it should be noted that the Westin and Paul accounts are at odds with a more recent interpretation of facts and circumstances surrounding the legislative measures that were invalidated or curbed by the Court at the turn of the century. According to the interpretation offered by Gabriel Kolko, these measures were not expressions of a populist or reformist spirit, as Paul or Westin or other progressive historians would have it; instead, in Kolko's words, they represented the "triumph of conservatism."[46] The legislature intervened in economic affairs, Kolko has argued, at the behest not of the people but of big business, which sought to use state power to "rationalize competition," or, to put the point less abstractly, to moderate the discipline of the market. According to this view, antitrust, to take one prominent example, was not a populist attack on business but a sophisticated and complicated strategy that enabled a politician such as Theodore Roosevelt to wave the reform banner high while keeping his ties to the business community intact.

Revisionist accounts of the politics of the 1890s and 1900s such as Kolko's are supported by fragmentary manuscript sources. The most striking is Attorney General Richard Olney's (in)famous statement concerning the value of the Interstate Commerce Commission to the railroads: "It thus

---

[44] See Arnold M. Paul, *Conservative Crisis and the Rule of Law: Attitudes of Bar and Bench, 1887–1895* (Ithaca: Cornell University Press, 1960; repr. Gloucester, Mass.: Peter Smith, 1976), and "David J. Brewer," in Leon Friedman and Fred L. Israel, eds., *The Justices of the United States Supreme Court, 1789–1969: Their Lives and Major Opinions* (New York: Chelsea House, 1969), 2: 1515–34.
[45] "The Supreme Court, the Populist Movement, and the Campaign of 1896,"

J. Politics, 15: 3, 30–39 (1953).
[46] *The Triumph of Conservatism: A Reinterpretation of American History, 1900–1916* (New York: Free Press, 1963). See also his *Railroads and Regulation, 1877–1916* (Princeton: Princeton University Press, 1965), which treats railroads specifically. Subsequently, Kolko's theory, part of the New Left, found a home on the New Right, in Chicago economics. See George J. Stigler, "The Theory of Economic Regulation," *Bell J. Econ. & Mgmt. Sci.*, 2: 3 (1971).

becomes," he wrote to Charles E. Perkins, president of the Burlington Railroad, "a sort of barrier between the railroad corporations and the people and a sort of protection against hasty and crude legislation hostile to railroad interests. . . . The part of wisdom is not to destroy the Commission, but to utilize it."[47] But such overt archival evidence for the revisionist interpretation is rare.

Kolko can also be criticized for limiting his investigation to regulatory measures implemented at the federal, rather than the state, level; misunderstanding both the economics of the railroad industry and the characteristics of the market economy during the period; relying too heavily on material drawn from railroad trade journals; and focusing too exclusively on the relations between big business and government at the expense of such other aspects of the progressive reform agenda as maximum hour or child labor laws.[48] Nevertheless, Kolko's hypothesis is a sobering antidote to Westin and Paul, for it rests on a highly credible theoretical claim, that the power possessed by big business is likely to extend to politics as well as the marketplace.

In this view, politics is not an autonomous sphere of activity, but one that reflects the distribution of wealth and power prevailing in the social and economic spheres. Regulation is likely to be acquired by, rather than

---

[47] Letter from Olney to Perkins, Dec. 28, 1892, Richard Olney Papers, Letterbook, Library of Congress Manuscript Division. See the discussion of this exchange in Matthew Josephson, *The Politicos, 1865–1896* (New York: Harcourt, Brace, 1938), 525–26.

[48] See Herbert Hovenkamp, "Regulatory Conflict in the Gilded Age: Federalism and the Railroad Problem," *Yale L.J.*, 97: 1023–25 (1988); Barton J. Bernstein and Allen J. Matusow, eds., *Twentieth-Century America: Recent Interpretations*, 2d ed. (New York: Harcourt Brace Jovanovich, 1972), 17–19; and Thomas K. McGraw, "Regulation in America: A Review Article," *Bus. Hist. Rev.*, 49: 164–71 (1975) for useful summaries of the critiques of Kolko's work. Hovenkamp does not dismiss Kolko's hypothesis altogether but instead suggests, using the theory of natural monopoly, that the capture of public instruments by certain private firms, specifically the railroads, was not necessarily antithetical to the public interest. Other scholars have found Kolko's hypothesis less persuasive on the whole, notably Albro Martin in *Enterprise Denied: Origins of the Decline of American Railroads, 1897–1917* (New York: Columbia University Press, 1971) and in "The Troubled Subject of Railroad Regulation in the Gilded Age—A Reappraisal," *J. Am. Hist.*, 61: 339–71 (1974), and also Robert U. Harbeson, "Railroads and Regulation, 1877–1916: Conspiracy or Public Interest?," *J. Econ. Hist.*, 27: 230–42 (1967). Both these historians dispute Kolko's assertions about the nature and sources of progressive reform of railroads. Martin argues that regulation, by interfering with the market economy, undermined rather than benefited the rail industry, and Harbeson, like Hovenkamp, argues that by no means can it be assumed that "regulation favored the railroads at the expense of shipper and consumer interests." Ibid., 230. Still other historians contest Kolko's claims by suggesting that business interests were not unified in their support of regulation nor did they even share a consensus in their approach to implementing it. See, e.g., Edward A. Purcell, Jr., "Ideas and Interests: Businessmen and the Interstate Commerce Act," *J. Am. Hist.*, 54: 561–63 (1967).

imposed on, big business; if it is, we must pause before accepting the instrumental hypothesis of Westin and Paul. It is not at all clear, for example, how a decision of the Supreme Court curbing or limiting the Interstate Commerce Act could be understood as an instrument of class justice, or as a means of furthering the interests of the railroads, as Westin and Paul contend, if, in fact, the Act had been promoted and perhaps even sought by the railroads.

The instrumental hypothesis advanced by Westin, Paul, and others working within the progressive tradition is also at odds with a more complete account of the Court's behavior. While it is supported by some of the decisions of the Fuller Court, such as *Lochner* (overturning a maximum hours statute for bakers), *Pollock* (invalidating the income tax), *Debs* (sustaining the labor injunction), and *United States v. E. C. Knight Co.*[49] (refusing to apply the Sherman Act to the Sugar Trust), other decisions contradict it. Among the counterexamples are the decisions that sustained maximum hours legislation for miners and women[50] and a whole string of decisions that applied the Sherman Act to big business.[51] Indeed, throughout the period under examination, the 1895 decision in *E. C. Knight*, which figures centrally in both Westin's and Paul's accounts (perhaps because it was rendered contemporaneously with *Pollock* and *Debs*) is the only noteworthy instance in which the Court refused to apply the Sherman Act to business.

The instrumental hypothesis also fails to take adequate account of dissenting voices on the Court. *Debs* was a unanimous decision. So was *Reagan v. Farmers' Loan & Trust Co.*,[52] which upheld the power of a federal court to restrain enforcement of "unreasonable and unjust" rates set by a state railroad commission. But in almost all the other cases, including *Lochner*, *Pollock*, and *E. C. Knight*, the Court was divided, some of the justices dissenting in the most emphatic terms. The class or social backgrounds of the dissenters were not in any obvious way distinguishable from those of the justices in the majority. Complicating the picture further, the justices were by no means consistent in their positions by the standard of instrumentalism. Some who filed dissents that contradict the instrumental hypothesis later switched sides and joined majority decisions that are used to support the same hypothesis. Justice Harlan, for example, dissented in *Lochner*, but later became the author of the Court's opinion in *Adair v. United States*,[53] which invalidated on liberty of contract grounds a federal statute seeking to protect union organization. Conversely, some justices

---

[49] 156 U.S. 1 (1895).

[50] Holden v. Hardy, 169 U.S. 366 (1898) (miners); Muller v. Oregon, 208 U.S. 412 (1908) (women).

[51] See, e.g., United States v. Trans-Missouri Freight Ass'n, 166 U.S. 290 (1897); United States v. Joint Traffic Ass'n, 171 U.S. 505 (1898); Addyston Pipe & Steel Co. v. United States, 175 U.S. 211 (1899); and Northern Sec. Co. v. United States, 193 U.S. 197 (1904).

[52] 154 U.S. 362 (1894).

[53] 208 U.S. 161 (1908).

who joined decisions used to support the instrumental hypothesis also joined decisions at odds with it. For example, Justice Peckham, the author of *Lochner*, also wrote the majority opinion in the first important cases to apply the Sherman Act to big business.

Admittedly, a historian inclined to agree with Westin and Paul could try to rescue the instrumental hypothesis by emphasizing divisions or disagreements within the ruling class. The ruling class might, for example, be divided over the best strategy for dealing with the income tax, outright invalidation versus a reluctant validation. The latter might be accepted as a minimal concession to egalitarian demands, which in turn might assure the long-term protection of entrenched wealth. Such explanations are tenable abstractly, but they shed little light on the shift of a justice's position from one case to another. Why would Harlan take the confrontational tack in *Adair* and a more conciliatory one in *Lochner* if there was nothing more to his position than a desire to preserve capitalism? Why would Peckham, if moved only by considerations of class justice, apply the Sherman Act to big business yet invalidate the maximum hours law in *Lochner*? Divisions in the ruling class are possible; disagreements over the correct strategy for achieving an agreed-upon goal are perhaps to be expected; but we are not given any independent reason for believing that the split of justices in any one case, or the shift of a single justice from one case to the other, turned on divisions within the ruling class or on differences concerning the best strategy for preserving a privileged position. The explanation appears concocted to sustain the theory.

Nor are we given any reason for believing why complex and even contradictory data—for example, a decision applying the Sherman Act against business—should be taken as more sublime evidence supporting the instrumental hypothesis. At best, we are invited to imagine why big business might, through a complicated reasoning process, favor such a decision, even though it at first appears against its interest. This method of proceeding is not without support. It may sometimes make sense to work backward—to construct plausible explanations from outcomes—but what is not tenable is to change the backward inference from decision to decision to decision. The Court's refusal to apply the antitrust laws to big business (as in *E. C. Knight*) might suggest that the judicial power had become an instrument of class justice; but then the application of the antitrust laws against big business (as in *Joint Traffic*) must be taken as a denial of that hypothesis, not as a strategic instance of class justice, that is, as a minimal concession to preserve the overall system.

For all these reasons, I find it difficult to reconcile the instrumental hypothesis with the varied positions of individual justices and the overall pattern of decisions of the Court during this period. Depicting the decisions as efforts by the justices to protect big business from populist attack is as much in conflict with the specifics of judicial behavior as it is with the revisionist view of the political facts. Too many decisions and too many votes remain unexplained. I also believe, contrary to Westin and Paul, that greater weight must be given to what the justices said in defense of their actions in opinions, in off-bench lectures and comments, and even in private correspondence. The justices' opinions might be, as instrumentalists suggest, mere camouflage, an attempt to convince the public that their decisions were founded not on class interests but on reasons of general principle. Once again, the possibility of such contrivance cannot be denied as an abstract matter, but in this context such an interpretation of the justices' action rings hollow. We are given no independent reason for believing that the justices were speaking strategically and that the stated (or public) reason differed from the real reason. All that is offered in support of the claim is the contradiction between the stated reason and the reason initially hypothesized for the decision under the instrumental theory.

A strategic reading of the justices' opinions is also strained by the consistency and continuity of the justices' statements. There is virtually no difference between what the justices said in their opinions and what they said in less guarded moments before bar groups, in professional journals likely to be read only by members of their class, or in correspondence with their personal friends and professional acquaintances. Moreover, their official utterances on the bench occurred so often and over such a sustained period—for some justices we are dealing with a tenure of twenty years or more—that it is almost impossible to believe that what they said was all a charade. As E. P. Thompson acknowledged in qualifying the instrumentalism of his own Marxism, it is hard for anyone to play a role for so long and so consistently without becoming the character portrayed.[54]

Those inclined toward the instrumental hypothesis might concede that the reasoning offered by the justices in their opinions was not crafted to mislead, at least not on any conscious level. They might nonetheless try, in one last attempt, to rescue the instrumental view by insisting that the reasons themselves were determined by class interests. While the "neutral" and "universal" reasons given for the judicial action were genuinely believed by those who wielded power—the stated reasons *were* the real reasons—those reasons were, at a deeper level, neither "neutral" nor "universal" but rather shaped by the interests of the ruling class.[55] The justices in

---

[54] See E. P. Thompson, *Whigs and Hunters: The Origin of the Black Act* (New York: Pantheon Books, 1975), 258–69, esp. 263–65.

[55] See generally Quintin Hoare and Geoffrey Nowell Smith, eds. and trans., *Selections from the Prison Notebooks of Antonio Gramsci* (New York: International Publishers, 1971); David Forgacs, ed., *An Antonio Gramsci Reader* (New York: Schocken Books, 1988); Joseph V.

Femia, *Gramsci's Political Thought: Hegemony, Consciousness, and the Revolutionary Process* (New York: Oxford University Press, 1981); Eugene D. Genovese, *Roll, Jordan, Roll: The World the Slaves Made* (New York: Pantheon, 1972), 25–49; and T. J. Jackson Lears, "The Problem of Cultural Hegemony: Problems and Possibilities," *Am. Hist. Rev.*, 90: 567 (1985).

Lochner, to take the preeminent example, may have genuinely struggled over the meaning of the constitutional ideal of liberty, but that ideal itself, so instrumentalists might now argue, was shaped by class interests that operated in the background and at a deeper level. In this view class interests were the structural determinants of the ideal of liberty.

So reformulated, the instrumental hypothesis has its greatest appeal. Like any human activity, law cannot achieve a full autonomy but must reflect the interests of those who shape it. In this reformulation, however, where interests operate once or twice removed (since they are the structural determinants of constitutional ideals), all the power has been drained from the instrumental hypothesis as a way of explaining or characterizing the Fuller Court as a discrete historical phenomenon. The instrumentalism no longer resides in *Lochner*, or in *Pollock*, *Debs*, or *E. C. Knight*, but in the concept of liberty itself, or for that matter in all constitutional ideals. Moreover, the instrumentalism that remains is not precisely what Paul or Westin and the other progressives had in mind. Prevailing notions of liberty may have reflected the special economic and social conditions of nineteenth-century America and the interests and vision of those who shaped constitutional ideals for that period, but it cannot be presumed that those who had the most decisive power in 1900—people like the Rockefellers, the Morgans, or the Fricks—had been in control throughout the century. The members of the ruling class shifted as did their interests. Also, we should not assume that the interests of the less powerful—say the journeyman worker or small farmer, or perhaps the idealistic or eloquent politician—played no role in this shaping process. That role might have been less decisive than that of the economic elite, but any role would be sufficient to stop the reduction of ideal to interest implicit in the instrumental critique. What emerged from the shaping process might have been 5 percent journeyman worker and 95 percent big business, but we can never be certain what to attribute to whom.

The autonomy that law can rightfully claim, therefore, is largely a function of the complicated and varied character of the processes that bring law into being. It is a function of our inability to sort those processes out with any specificity or to trace general ideals, or any part of them, to a well-defined set of interests (economic or otherwise). In that sense, the autonomy of the law arises not from the fact that it is unconnected to social structure but from the fact that it is *too* connected. To say that law is autonomous is thus to acknowledge that life is complicated and our knowledge limited. It is also a way of saying that the relationship between law and economic or social interests proceeds in both directions. Just as law may be shaped in some indeterminate way by the interests of the participants in the process that brings it into being, law also has the power and capacity to define and shape the interests of those participants.

18

Chapter I: *Legitimacy and History*

In enforcing the antitrust laws against railroad cartels and proclaiming that such state intervention was necessary to further the ideal of liberty, the justices may have given expression to a conception of liberty that might (somehow) be traceable to the interests of those who decisively shaped the legal system during the nineteenth century. It is equally true, however, that when the justices took this action, they also defined the interests of the owners of the railroads, or at least those who for a host of reasons—some idealistic, some materialistic—were committed to liberty and the rule of law. Whatever their materialistic interests initially might have dictated about the enforcement of the Sherman Act, over time it became true, simply by virtue of what the Court did and what it said, that to be for liberty and for the Court was to be for antitrust.

III

Autonomy is not validity. To free oneself from the instrumental critique and the reductionism that it implies is not necessarily to free oneself of the ghost of *Lochner*. To demonstrate, as I will try, that for the most part the work of the Fuller Court had a coherence and an inner logic—that it should be understood not as an exercise of class justice but as an attempt to explicate and protect the constitutional ideal of liberty—is not to validate that work. The question of validity remains, and as a consequence, even at the end, *Lochner* might continue to be a powerful reminder of how the judicial power might be misused.

The question of validity remains outside the scope of this book. At this point, however, I would like to underscore one distinction that bears on that question and that might add some perspective on what is to follow. It is foreshadowed by some of the lawyerly techniques described earlier that have been used to cordon off *Lochner* and to protect *Brown*. I am referring to the distinction between the role of the Supreme Court and the substance of the Court's doctrine. *Lochner* stands for both a distinctive body of constitutional doctrine and a distinctive conception of judicial role: One could reject one facet of *Lochner* and accept the other. *Lochner* may be illegitimate and an error, but once we see clearly what it was trying to do, we may wish to criticize its substantive values and yet leave unimpeached its conception of role—which it shared in common with *Brown*.

The Court's conception of role in *Lochner* and *Brown* was premised on a belief that there is a fundamental distinction between law and politics. Politics is will. The legislative and executive branches are charged with the duty of giving expression to the preferences or desires of the people. The Supreme Court, on the other hand, in both *Lochner* and *Brown* defined its function in terms of reason. The Court owed its primary duty to a set of values it saw enshrined in the Constitution and gave itself the task of protecting those values from encroachment by the political branches. The justices believed that the Constitution embodies a set of values that exists apart from, and above, ordinary politics and that their duty was to give, through exercise of reason, concrete meaning and expression to these values.

It is this image of the Court as the guardian of the transcendent values of society that inspires the "activist" epithet often applied to both the Fuller and Warren Courts. The justices controlling each of these Courts saw themselves located in a historical period in which those values were threatened and which therefore called for action on their part that was equal in intensity and scope to the character of the perceived threat. In other respects, however, the two Courts diverged, for their activism differed substantively. For the Warren Court, the organizing value was equality, and the perceived threat to that value was ingrained in the status quo (previously created in part by the political branches and perpetuated by the inaction of those institutions). The judicial power was used, above all, to eliminate the caste structure that so scarred America. For the Fuller Court, however, the overriding commitment was to liberty. The threat that the Court perceived arose not from the established order but from the changes that were then taking place in America. The activism of Melville Fuller, in contrast to Earl Warren's, was a method of resistance, a way of coping with new forms of social and political organization and activity.

Sometimes these changes occurred outside the arena of formal politics, through, for example, the emergence of new forms of collective activity in industry and labor. Sometimes the Court was confronted with new uses of the legislative power, both at the federal and local level. Here I have in mind statutes to regulate rates, the Sherman Antitrust Act, the income tax law, maximum hours statutes, prohibition laws, and various measures protecting the safety and organizing activities of workers. Sometimes the threat was tied to the emergence of a new institution of government, such as the administrative agency charged with policing immigration or the railroads. And sometimes the justices were confronted with new forms of state power required by imperialist ventures such as the Spanish–American War of 1898 and the acquisition of the Philippines and Puerto Rico.

In all these instances, the Supreme Court or a majority of the justices perceived a threat to liberty and used the power at its disposal to protect that value. In some instances the Court responded by legitimating and reinforcing the work of the political branches when, as in *Debs*, these branches in fact resisted social change. In other instances, as in *Lochner* and *Pollock*, the Court checked and curbed the other branches when the new exercises of power were seen as threatening liberty. In still others, this initial impulse was complicated by other factors or countervalues, and the protection of liberty was thus less complete.

Chapter I: *Legitimacy and History*

It may be asked whether the conception of liberty that informed and structured the Fuller Court's work was adequate for its purposes. This book will define and describe that conception of liberty, at least as it was understood at the turn of the century, and thus reveal many of its limitations. But to conclude that, measured against some abstract constitutional standard, the Court's conception of liberty was inadequate does not necessarily impeach the way the Court understood its role. The settlement of 1937 may have to be reopened in order to preserve the basic analytic distinction between role and doctrine or substance and procedure. One very plausible view is that the failure of the Fuller Court lay not in the Court's understanding of its place in the American political system but in its attachment to a conception of liberty that consisted almost entirely of a demand for limited government. Under this hypothesis, one may, with perfect consistency (though not without a touch of bravado), remain attached to *Brown* and its robust use of the judicial power to further the ideal of equality, yet be happy that *Lochner* lies dead and buried.

CHAPTER II

The Identity of the Institution

MELVILLE WESTON FULLER was appointed chief justice in 1888 and died in office in 1910, and as is customary, his name is often used to identify that twenty-two-year segment of Supreme Court history. Yet it is wrong to infer from this practice that Fuller exercised the leadership role in a way that gave the Court of his time its special character. The use of his name stands on a wholly different plane from that of Marshall, Taney, or Warren.

Fuller had an inauspicious beginning.[1] At the time of his appointment to the Supreme Court he was a mildly successful lawyer in Chicago. He had served as president of the Illinois Bar Association and had handled one case, involving the Chicago lakefront,[2] that ultimately went to the Supreme Court. But he had no stature in the national bar. He was, and always remained, active in Democratic politics, and once served in the Illinois legislature. President Cleveland knew Fuller personally, and saw, too, the special significance of Chicago for the nation at that time. The site of the Haymarket Riot of 1886, Chicago was the hub of the national rail system, the location of the nation's principal stockyards, the frontier of industrial America, and the home of many new literary figures.[3] Appropriately, Chicago would be chosen as the site for the spectacular Columbian Exposition of 1893. In a similar spirit, President Cleveland first offered the position of

---

[1] For an admiring account of Fuller's life, see Willard L. King, *Melville Weston Fuller: Chief Justice of the United States, 1888–1910* (New York: Macmillan, 1950; repr. Chicago: University of Chicago Press, 1967).

[2] The Lake Front Case involved an 1883 suit by the State of Illinois against the City of Chicago to reclaim the entire lakefront held by the Illinois Central and other railroads under certain statutes and ordinances. Fuller, representing the city in the lower court, argued that the lakefront belonged to the city rather than the state by virtue of the city's riparian rights. Fuller's position was sustained by the circuit court and ultimately by the Supreme Court. Illinois v. Illinois Cent. R.R., 33 F. 730 (C.C.N.D. Ill. 1888), aff'd sub nom. Illinois Cent. R.R. v. Illinois, 146 U.S. 387 (1892). Fuller, who was on the Court by the time it decided the case, did not participate. See the discussion of the case in King, *Melville Weston Fuller*, 95.

[3] See generally the marvelous account by Larzer Ziff, *The American 1890s: Life and Times of a Lost Generation* (New York: Viking Press, 1966).

Chapter II: *The Identity of the Institution*

chief justice to a state court judge in Illinois.[4] When he turned it down, Cleveland turned to Fuller, not because of any particular achievement, intellectual or professional, on Fuller's part, but because (as is so often the case in presidential appointments) he wanted someone from a particular area of the country, and had confidence, stated in the most general terms, in the appointee's ability and integrity.[5]

As chief justice, Fuller enjoyed the normal prerogatives of office, and he even looked the part. He had the usual ceremonial duties to perform. He probably controlled the agenda of the conference and the order in which cases were discussed, and, of course, he knew that order could sometimes determine outcome. He allocated the justices to the circuits. He also had the power to assign opinions and thus to determine who would speak for the Court (there is some slight evidence that Fuller exercised that power even when he was not in the majority[6]). The justices were then, as today, vitally interested in their opinion-writing assignments, for these assignments in large part determined how they spent their time and how they were to be regarded by the public in their day and in history. The associate justices sometimes wrote to Fuller complaining of their assignments, asking for additional or more important cases,[7] but there is no evidence that he abused this prerogative or used it as a patronage system. He used his power evenhandedly. Still, it was inevitable that, simply by virtue of his rights as chief justice and his concomitant power to assign opinions, Fuller played an important role in shaping the law. For the Supreme Court, perhaps more than any other tribunal, the particular words of the opinion have almost

---

[4] Judge John Scholfield of the Illinois supreme court was Cleveland's first choice. He declined for personal reasons, as he had done earlier when offered a district court judgeship. See King, *Melville Weston Fuller*, 106–107.

[5] Ibid., 111.

[6] In Downes v. Bidwell, 182 U.S. 244 (1901), discussed in Chapter 8, it appears Justice Brown was assigned the task of writing the opinion of the Court (though he eventually failed to obtain a majority or for that matter any other support). It was not clear who made that assignment, but presumably it was Fuller, who voted to dissent. Gray voted the same way as Brown, and he would have had the seniority to make the assignment, but given his position it is likely that he would have been inclined toward White.

On another occasion, Fuller asked Holmes to write the majority opinion in a case in which Fuller had been in the minority when the conference voted.

The opinion had initially been assigned to Brewer, but he died shortly thereafter. See Fuller to Holmes, May 19, 1910, Holmes Papers, Harvard Law School Library Manuscript Division ("I am compelled to ask you if you can write this case—The vote was Lurton & C.J. to affirm & Day, Holmes, McKenna, White, Brewer and Harlan to reverse."). When the case was announced, Holmes indeed was the author of the opinion, but there were by then no dissenters. Dozier v. Alabama, 218 U.S. 124 (1910).

[7] See, e.g., Field to Fuller, Mar. 7, 1896, Fuller Papers, Library of Congress Manuscript Division, returning a memorandum of assignment in which no cases were assigned to Field. Field wrote: "I do not know, and shall not ask the reason, why no cases have been assigned to me within the last two months." See also King, *Melville Weston Fuller*, 224.

as much status as the decision, and these words are largely in the control of the justice who happens to be the author of the Court's opinion.

A chief justice also has important liaison duties to perform with the other branches of government, and Fuller was fully attentive to these. In one instance, in which he was assisted by Justice Horace Gray, Fuller worked with congressional leaders to curb the backlog of cases that had accumulated on the Court's docket.[8] The result was the Circuit Court of Appeals Act of 1891,[9] a statute that broke the stalemate that had stymied efforts at court reform since the Civil War.[10] Unfortunately, the problem of backlog did not disappear—indeed, it persists to this day—but the 1891 legislation nonetheless made a lasting and important contribution to the federal judicial structure. It created the intermediate courts of appeals, essentially moving the federal judiciary from a two-tier system (trial courts and the Supreme Court) to a three-tier one (trial courts, appellate courts, and the Supreme Court).[11] The 1891 Act also laid the foundations for the certiorari jurisdiction of the Supreme Court.

---

[8] Fuller was interested in this problem even before his appointment to the Court. In his presidential address to the Illinois State Bar Association in 1886, Fuller called attention to the large number of cases on the Supreme Court docket. King quotes him as saying on that occasion, "From less than 300 cases in 1858, there are [now] over 1,300 cases on the calendar." King, *Melville Weston Fuller*, 97. By the time Fuller was appointed chief justice there were 1,571 cases on the docket. Ibid., 148.

[9] 26 Stat. 826 (1891). Fuller played a skillful role in this enactment. In January 1890 he gave a dinner in honor of the newly appointed justice, David Brewer. Among the guests were several powerful members of the Senate Judiciary Committee, where several bills to relieve the Supreme Court's docket were pending. Some weeks later the Committee sent the bill to the chief justice for the comments of the justices. Fuller asked Justice Gray to make a report on the bills, and, with the unanimous consent of the justices, Gray recommended, among other things, the establishment of intermediate circuit courts of appeals. The Act was finally passed early in 1891. See King, *Melville Weston Fuller*, 150–51.

[10] See Felix Frankfurter and James M. Landis, *The Business of the Supreme Court: A Study in the Federal Judicial System* (New York: Macmillan, 1928), 69–102.

[11] Portions of the two-tier system remained. Section 5 of the 1891 statute, for example, provided a right of direct review by the Supreme Court in all capital or otherwise infamous criminal cases, in all final decrees and sentences in prize cases, and in all cases involving constitutional, treaty and jurisdictional issues. Similarly, the Expediting Act of 1903 allowed direct review in antitrust cases, which were then viewed as of almost constitutional significance. See Chapter 5. The Criminal Appeals Act of 1907 allowed direct appeals by the United States in cases in which an indictment or count was dismissed on grounds that involved a construction of the Constitution or a federal statute or following a special plea in bar when the defendant had not been put in jeopardy. The Mann-Elkins Railroad Act of 1910, enacted in response to *Ex parte* Young, 209 U.S. 123 (1908), provided for direct review of interlocutory orders enjoining the enforcement of unconstitutional state laws. See Chapter 7. It also allowed direct appeals from the Commerce Court, which was then established to review orders of the Interstate Commerce Commission, but was abolished in 1913. On the Commerce Court, see George E. Dix, "The Death of the Commerce Court: A Study in Institutional Weakness," *Am. J. Legal Hist.*, 8: 238–60 (1964), and Frankfurter and Landis, *Business of the Supreme Court*, 153–74.

Chapter II: *The Identity of the Institution*

Originally, certiorari was conceived in rather narrow terms, to give the Supreme Court access to a relatively trivial category of cases (those for which the judgments of the new appellate courts would be final, namely diversity, patent, revenue, criminal, and admiralty cases).[12] Soon, however, it evolved into a discretionary jurisdiction, which allowed the Court to pick and choose the cases it wanted to hear. The framers of the 1891 Act thought that with regard to those cases that otherwise would be finally decided by the courts of appeals, the writ would be issued only for the purpose of achieving nationwide uniformity. But in the very first decision on this matter, *Lau Ow Bew*,[13] the Court broadened the discretion nearly to its present boundaries. In deciding which cases it should review on writ of certiorari, the Supreme Court was permitted, so the opinion said, to consider the "gravity and importance" of a case. Fuller wrote the opinion.

Either because of his involvement in the formulation and enactment of the statute, or because he believed it was his principal duty as chief justice to ensure the smooth and continuous flow of work, Fuller took it upon himself to write most of the opinions that construed the 1891 Act.[14] Almost

---

[12] Section 6 of the Act provided: "And excepting also that in any such case as is hereinbefore made final in the circuit court of appeals it shall be competent for the Supreme Court to require, by certiorari or otherwise, any such case to be certified to the Supreme Court for its review and determination with the same power and authority in the case as if it had been carried by appeal or writ of error to the Supreme Court." 26 Stat. at 828. The cases in which the judgments of the circuit courts of appeals were final were those "in which the jurisdiction is dependent entirely upon the opposite parties to the suit or controversy, being aliens and citizens of the United States or citizens of different States; also in all cases arising under the patent laws, under the revenue laws, and under the criminal laws and in admiralty cases. . . ." Ibid.

The 1891 Act did not provide for new appellate judges. The new circuit courts of appeals were to be staffed by one Supreme Court justice and two circuit court judges; district court judges would serve as substitutes of last resort. Prior to the 1891 Act, the circuit courts, which had original jurisdiction over diversity, federal question, and any other cases not reserved exclusively to the district courts, acted as an appellate tribunal of the district courts.

[13] 141 U.S. 583, 587 (1891). For the decision on the merits, see Lau Ow Bew v. United States, 144 U.S. 47 (1892).

[14] See, e.g., *In re* Woods, 143 U.S. 202 (1892) (unanimous) (the Court should grant certiorari only when questions of "gravity and general importance" are presented in order to guarantee sound jurisprudence and uniformity of decision); *In re* Heath, 144 U.S. 92 (1892) (unanimous) (the 1891 Act does not incorporate the District of Columbia statutes governing appeals from the District's supreme court to the Court); Colorado Cent. Consol. Mining Co. v. Turck, 150 U.S. 138 (1893) (unanimous) (whether or not a court of appeals judgment is final will depend solely on the basis for a plaintiff's original complaint); Carey v. Houston & Tex. Cent. Ry., 150 U.S. 170 (1893) (unanimous) (the Court will grant a direct appeal or writ of error raising jurisdictional and constitutional questions only if the jurisdictional question challenges the jurisdiction of the lower court in the case at bar and the constitutional question was raised at trial and controlled its outcome); *In re* Lennon, 150 U.S. 393 (1893) (unanimous) (following *Carey*, and adding that habeas corpus petitioners do not have a right to direct review by the Court); Maynard v. Hecht, 151 U.S. 324 (1894) (unanimous) (before the

invariably these decisions were unanimous, and somewhat arcane. Likewise, Fuller wrote most of the other decisions that shaped the bounds of Supreme Court jurisdiction during this period.[15]

These contributions, not to be slighted, are characteristic of his tenure as chief justice. Fuller was respected by his colleagues, but only for his personal qualities and his administrative competence, not his legal acuity or

---

Court can grant an otherwise proper appeal or writ of error on a jurisdiction question, the lower court must certify it); Moran v. Hagerman, 151 U.S. 329 (1894) (unanimous) (same); Borgmeyer v. Idler, 159 U.S. 408 (1895) (unanimous) (whether or not a court of appeals judgment is final will depend solely on the basis for a plaintiff's original complaint); United States v. American Bell Tel. Co., 159 U.S. 548 (1895) (unanimous) (while the courts of appeals have final jurisdiction over patent law cases in general, the Court must review those cases in which the federal government seeks to enforce the patent laws); The Three Friends, 166 U.S. 1 (1897) (unanimous, except for a Harlan dissent that did not challenge the Court's jurisdiction holding) (the Court can grant a writ of certiorari in an admiralty case to a court of appeals that threatens to dismiss a libel since the petition for the writ leads automatically to dismissal, which is final); Huguley Mfg. Co. v. Galeton Cotton Mills, 184 U.S. 290 (1902) (unanimous) (if a party relies only on diversity of citizenship jurisdiction in a circuit court and later appeals that court's decision to a court of appeals, the latter's decision is final, even if issues arose in the circuit court over which the Court would have had exclusive jurisdiction if they had been the basis for the original complaint); Cary Mfg. Co. v. Acme Flexible Clasp Co., 187 U.S. 427 (1903) (unanimous) (a party that goes to a court of appeals waives any right to direct Supreme Court review of a circuit or district court judgment); and Hutchinson, Pierce & Co. v. Loewy, 217 U.S. 457 (1910) (unanimous) (courts of appeals have final jurisdiction in trademark cases). In one case involving the 1891 Act, in which Fuller did not participate, the responsibility of speaking for the Court fell to Justice Gray (see above,

note 9). American Constr. Co. v. Jacksonville, Tampa & Key W. Ry., 148 U.S. 372 (1893). Recognizing that the Court should grant certiorari only for questions of "peculiar gravity and general importance," *American Construction* held that certiorari can be granted in a case in a court of appeals prior to judgment, provided a danger of "extraordinary inconvenience and embarrassment" exists. Ibid., 383–84. Justice Gray also ruled that the Judiciary Act of 1789 authorized the Court, as at common law, to issue writs of certiorari, even though that power was not exercised before.

[15] See, e.g., *In re* Rice, 155 U.S. 396 (1894) (unanimous) (the Court does not have to grant a writ of prohibition on a jurisdictional question when there is another legal remedy, the question is doubtful or depends on facts not in the record, or a stranger applies for the writ; and a writ of mandamus cannot substitute for an appeal or writ of error, even if the latter are not available); United States v. Rider, 163 U.S. 132 (1896) (unanimous) (the 1891 Act repeals an old statute permitting circuit courts to certify their divisions of opinion on questions of law in criminal cases to the Court, particularly when final jurisdiction over a case rests with a court of appeals); *In re* Huguley Mfg. Co., 184 U.S. 297 (1902) (unanimous) (the Court does not have to grant a writ of prohibition on a jurisdiction question when there is another legal remedy, the question is doubtful, or the question depends on facts not in the record, and a writ of mandamus cannot substitute for an appeal or writ of error); and United States v. Dickinson, 213 U.S. 92 (1909) (unanimous) (the Court's certiorari jurisdiction is not intended to replace appeals and writs of error to correct mere errors).

depth. On returning home from Fuller's funeral, Holmes, one of the chief justice's greatest admirers, put an edge on the matter:

> The Chief died at just the right moment, for during this last term he had begun to show his age in his administrative work, I thought, and I was doubting whether I ought not to speak to his family, as they relied upon me. He died in the same place and with the same quiet as his wife a few years before. And so ends a great career. He was not a great writer, but he carried off the business of the Court, the specific work of a Chief, with promptness, decision, [and] good humor. . . . I suspect that it would be easier to get a man who wrote as well as Marshall than to get one who would run the Court as well as Fuller. He loved me and I shall miss him as long as I sit on the Bench.[16]

Praised as he was by Holmes, and presumably others, as a good administrator and decent person, it is equally true that he was not in any way the source of the ideas that gave this Court its place in history. In the realm of ideas, he was just one more vote.

During his twenty-year tenure, Fuller wrote few of the major opinions of the Court. For the most part, his majority opinions did not divide the justices, address the great issues of the day, nor in any way give the Court its special character. The principal exceptions were *Pollock v. Farmers' Loan & Trust Co.* (1895),[17] *United States v. E. C. Knight Co.* (1895),[18] the early decisions involving state prohibition laws,[19] and finally, the *Danbury Hatters Case* (1908).[20] It is of some significance that, with the exception of the last, all of Fuller's major opinions came in the early years of his tenure, that is, before the 1896 election; he wrote only one major opinion of the Court in the last fifteen years of his chief justiceship. Even when a case implicated basic institutional values of the Court—as when a state prisoner whose habeas petition was pending before the Court was lynched—Fuller turned to others, in this instance Holmes, to speak for the Court.[21] For his entire career, only one dissent, in the *Insular Cases* of 1901,[22] could be considered significant.

---

[16] Holmes to Baroness Moncheur, July 14, 1910, Harvard Holmes Papers.

[17] 157 U.S. 429 (1895); 158 U.S. 601 (1895).

[18] 156 U.S. 1 (1895).

[19] Leisy v. Hardin, 135 U.S. 100 (1890); *In re* Rahrer, 140 U.S. 545 (1891).

[20] Loewe v. Lawlor, 208 U.S. 274 (1908).

[21] United States v. Shipp, 203 U.S. 563 (1906). However, Fuller did write for the Court in a later opinion upholding contempt judgments against some of the *Shipp* defendants. United States v. Shipp, 214 U.S. 386 (1909).

[22] Downes v. Bidwell, 182 U.S. 244, 347 (1901). See generally Chapter 8. Some might also include Fuller's dissent protesting the confiscation by the federal government of the property of the Mormon Church as a way of enforcing the ban on polygamy. Late Corp. of the Church of Jesus Christ of Latter Day Saints v. United States, 136 U.S. 1, 66 (1890).

Holmes's correspondence mentions regular Sunday morning visits with Fuller during the last several years of Fuller's chief justiceship,[23] and it seems likely that Holmes was assisting Fuller in the performance of his managerial duties, such as assigning cases. Moreover, a reading of Fuller's opinions, especially when compared with those of the justices, such as Brewer and Peckham, who so often voted the same way, suggests a very good reason why he rarely assigned himself the task of speaking for the Court in the great cases of the day. Fuller would not have been doing the Court or himself a service. The issue was not simply one of rhetorical style, elegance, vividness, or clarity of exposition, though his opinions lacked these qualities. The issue was instead one of logical structure. His writings suggest that he was not fully in command of the central ideas that so characterized the time. Fuller was in no position to lead.

I

In terms of intellectual leadership, then, the death of Chief Justice Waite in 1888 and Cleveland's decision to fill the vacancy with Fuller had no intrinsic importance for the life of the Court. The change was just another fortuity of the law. It did, however, take on a certain symbolic significance because, as it turned out, Fuller's appointment marked the beginning of a period in which the Court was reconstituted by a number of appointments made by President Cleveland and President Harrison. Between 1888 and 1896 these two presidents appointed a group of six justices that controlled the Court for almost twenty years. Even more significantly, this group included the two justices who I consider to be the intellectual leaders of the Fuller Court: David Brewer and Rufus Peckham.

Waite's death in 1888 marked the end of the post–Civil War Court. Within a few years, the great judicial figures who had dominated that period of Supreme Court history were gone from the Court. Samuel Miller died in 1890, Joseph Bradley in 1892, and Stephen Field left in spirit, if not body, around that time. Field was a formidable presence in the Court during the post–Civil War era, notable for his dissents in two of the major decisions

---

[23] Holmes to Leslie Scott, Oct. 13, 1907, Harvard Holmes Papers ("I shall begin my Sunday calls on the Chief today though I ill can spare the time. He is old and relies up[on] my doing it."); Holmes to Pollock, Mar. 7, 1909, Mark DeWolfe Howe, ed., *Holmes–Pollock Letters: The Correspondence of Mr. Justice Holmes and Sir Frederick Pollock, 1874–1932* (Cambridge: Harvard University Press, 1941), 1: 152 ("Now I must make my Sunday call on the Chief Justice.").

of the time, the *Slaughter-House Cases* and *Munn v. Illinois.*[24] But his intellectual powers waned considerably during the 1890s, almost to the point of senility. He did not write a single major opinion for the Court during that period, and in fact he wrote to Fuller bitterly complaining about the absence of assignments.[25] The opinions he did write, in concurrence or in dissent, had an eerie, somewhat idiosyncratic, erratic, and highly emotional quality. Sometimes it seemed as though he were grappling with another case, as in the *Income Tax Cases*, where he saved his passion for a diatribe on the impact of the 1894 statute on salaries of judges.[26] Harlan commented that Field acted "like a mad man" during the income tax controversy.[27] In another instance, Field launched a bitter attack on the Court that is traceable to a dispute over the content of a headnote.[28] Once he went so far as to devise and promote his own court-packing plan,[29] and one of his personal fiascos forced the Court to consider issues relating to the power of the United States to protect federal judges.[30] While riding circuit, Field had managed to cast aspersions on the character of a woman, leading to an

---

[24] Slaughter-House Cases, 83 U.S. (16 Wall.) 36, 83 (1873) (Field, J., dissenting); Munn v. Illinois, 94 U.S. 113, 136 (1877) (Field, J., dissenting). On Field generally, see Charles W. McCurdy, "Stephen J. Field and the American Judicial Tradition," in Philip J. Bergan, Owen M. Fiss, and Charles W. McCurdy, *The Fields and the Law: Essays* (San Francisco: United States District Court for the Northern District of California Historical Society; New York: Federal Bar Council, 1986), 5–18; and "Justice Field and the Jurisprudence of Government–Business Relations: Some Parameters of Laissez-Faire Constitutionalism, 1863–1897," *J. Am. Hist.*, 61: 970 (1975).

[25] See above, note 7. For a discussion of the limited nature of Field's contribution during Fuller's years, see Owen M. Fiss, "David J. Brewer, The Judge as Missionary," in Bergan, Fiss, and McCurdy, *Fields and the Law*, 53–63.

[26] 157 U.S. at 604–606 (Field, J., concurring).

[27] Letter from Harlan to his sons James and John, May 24, 1895, quoted in David G. Farrelly, "Justice Harlan's Dissent in the Pollock Case," *S. Cal. L. Rev.*, 24: 175, 179 (1951).

[28] For a look at Field's antics in this episode, see Alan F. Westin, "Stephen J. Field and the Headnote to O'Neil v. Vermont: A Snapshot of the Fuller Court at Work," *Yale L.J.*, 67: 363 (1957).

[29] Field's dissatisfaction with the outcome of Fong Yue Ting v. United States, 149 U.S. 698 (1893) (upholding a statute requiring the registration of alien Chinese laborers) culminated in a court-packing plan described in a letter from Field to Don M. Dickinson, a high-ranking government lawyer: "As a general rule it would be dangerous to increase the bench for the purpose of correcting a bad decision, but where that decision goes to the very essentials of Constitutional Government, the question of an increase of the bench may properly be considered and acted upon." Field to Dickinson, June 17, 1893, Dickinson Papers, Library of Congress Manuscript Division. See Chapter 10.

[30] *In re* Neagle, 135 U.S. 1 (1890). See also A. Russell Buchanan, *David S. Terry of California, Dueling Judge* (San Marino, Calif.: Huntington Library, 1956), 210–30.

armed assault on him by the woman's husband, a former chief justice of the California supreme court. Throughout the nineties, Field's colleagues hoped for his resignation; some drafted his letter of resignation, and Harlan and Brewer (Field's nephew) personally urged him to resign, which he finally brought himself to do in 1897.[31]

Aside from Justice Field, only two other justices from the post–Civil War Court, Gray and Harlan, continued to sit through the 1890s. Gray began the practice of using law clerks, first paying them from his own funds, later using funds appropriated by Congress in the mid-1880s for "legal stenographers." From 1886 to 1919, each justice had a "legal stenographer," but it was Gray (and later his successor, Holmes) who used this position in the way it is used today.[32] Either for reasons linked to that practice or personal to the man, Gray's opinions are marked by great erudition, containing thorough, scholarly summaries of all the relevant cases, English and American, state and federal. On the other hand, it is fair to say that they lack any distinctive perspective or judicial position. It is not clear what Gray stood for, and thus it is difficult to gauge his impact on either the intellectual or ideological profile of the Court during this period.[33]

In contrast, John Marshall Harlan was a most striking figure. When he left the bench in 1911, he ended a career on the Court that spanned more than thirty years. He provided an element of continuity with the post–Civil War Court and also made important and highly visible contributions to the work of the Court during Fuller's tenure. Lawyers today remember his dissents, particularly in *Plessy v. Ferguson*[34] and perhaps also in *Lochner v. New York*,[35] *Pollock*,[36] and *E. C. Knight*,[37] as well as in the 1911 antitrust cases that announced the "rule of reason."[38] (To return the compliment

---

[31] In an unsuccessful first attempt to convince the aging justice to resign, Harlan reminded Field of the time, years before, when Field had been sent on a similar mission to deal with the elderly Justice Grier. Field, never one to make such a job easy, reportedly shot back, "Yes! And a dirtier day's work I never did in my life!" Carl B. Swisher, *Stephen J. Field: Craftsman of the Law* (Washington: Brookings Institution, 1930; repr. Hamden, Conn.: Archon Books, 1963), 444. See also Charles Evans Hughes, *The Supreme Court of the United States* (New York: Columbia University Press, 1928), 75–76; King, *Melville Weston Fuller*, 224.

[32] Chester A. Newland, "Personal Assistants to Supreme Court Justices: The Law Clerks," *Or. L. Rev.*, 40: 299, 301–306 (1961).

[33] On Justice Gray, see generally Robert M. Spector, "Legal Historian on the United States Supreme Court: Justice Horace Gray, Jr., and the Historical Method," *Am. J. Legal Hist.*, 12: 181 (1968).

[34] 163 U.S. 537, 552 (1896) (Harlan, J., dissenting).

[35] 198 U.S. 45, 65 (1905) (Harlan, J., dissenting).

[36] 157 U.S. at 652 (Harlan, J., dissenting); 158 U.S. at 638–86 (Harlan, J., dissenting).

[37] 156 U.S. at 18 (Harlan, J., dissenting).

[38] Standard Oil Co. v. United States, 221 U.S. 1, 82 (1911) (Harlan, J., concurring in part and dissenting in part); United States v. American Tobacco Co., 221 U.S. 106, 189 (1911) (Harlan, J., concurring in part and dissenting in part).

Chapter II: *The Identity of the Institution*

Harlan once paid Field, Charles Evans Hughes, then one of his colleagues, complained that Harlan acted in a "most unseemly" manner in the 1911 antitrust cases.[39]) But it is hard to think of Harlan as a leader of his brethren, either in propounding the organizing ideas of the Court or in constructing majorities. He had friendly ties to Fuller, yet had little influence with the group of justices who dominated the Court during this period. The historical image of Harlan as "the great dissenter" overstates the case, for as we will see, Harlan adopted and approved many of the doctrines that prevailed in those days; he was as deeply committed to the idea of limited government as the next justice. But the image is correct insofar as it suggests that he was something of a loner.

With the exception of the three carry-over justices—the senile Field, the pedantic Gray, and the independent-minded Harlan—the Supreme Court of the 1890s and early 1900s was constituted by a group of justices chosen by Grover Cleveland and Benjamin Harrison: Melville Fuller, David Brewer, Henry Brown, George Shiras, Edward White, and Rufus Peckham.[40] Cleveland was a Democrat and Harrison a Republican, but their politics were virtually indistinguishable—business-oriented and conservative. Their judicial appointments reflected their politics and sailed through the Senate.

At the time of his nomination, a pamphlet was written and circulated criticizing Fuller, particularly his position on slavery and the Civil War. He was accused of betraying the Union cause.[41] This attack turned out,

---

[39] David J. Danelski and Joseph S. Tulchin, eds., *The Autobiographical Notes of Charles Evans Hughes* (Cambridge: Harvard University Press, 1973), 170 ("He went far beyond his written opinion, launching out into a bitter invective, which I thought most unseemly."). Others were equally displeased with Harlan's performance in *Standard Oil*. President Taft wrote his daughter, "Harlan concurred in the judgment but delivered a nasty, carping and demagogic opinion, directed at the Chief Justice and intended to furnish La Follette and his crowd as much pabulum as possible." Taft to Helen Taft, May 16, 1911, W. H. Taft Papers, Library of Congress Manuscript Division.

[40] Samuel Blatchford, a final carry-over justice appointed by President Arthur in 1882, served until 1893. His impact on the Fuller Court was slight, although he did write for the Court in two of the early rate regulation cases, Chicago, M. & St. P. Ry. v. Minnesota,

134 U.S. 418 (1890), and Budd v. New York, 143 U.S. 517 (1892). See Chapter 7. In addition, Lucius Q. C. Lamar and Howell Jackson were among the justices appointed by Presidents Cleveland and Harrison, but they served for short periods. In fact, the early 1890s was a period of constant turnover: There was a replacement every year. By 1896 the personnel had stabilized.

[41] Specifically, he was criticized for, among other things, his introduction of a bill in the Illinois legislature, after the issuance of the Emancipation Proclamation, to ratify an amendment to the Constitution that would have prohibited interferences with slavery. He was also criticized for supporting a bill against permitting soldiers in the field to vote and for supporting a resolution favoring a peace convention at Louisville. "The War Record of Melville W. Fuller," Fuller Papers, Library of Congress. See King, *Melville Weston Fuller*, 116.

however, to be nothing more than a minor embarrassment, and Fuller was easily confirmed. Cleveland also had some difficulty filling the position to which White was finally appointed, but only because he ran afoul of the rule of senatorial courtesy.[42] This, too, was a relatively trivial incident, tied to a long-standing feud within the Democratic Party of New York, and reflected Grover Cleveland's political ineptitude more than dissatisfaction with his initial choices. Aside from these two instances, none of the other Cleveland-Harrison appointees had any difficulty being confirmed by the Senate. Evidently, their views were well in keeping with the conservative politics of both the White House and Senate. In the case of four of the appointees, there can be no doubt on this score, for they came before the Senate with a public record that clearly revealed where they stood on the issues of the day: White was a senator, and Brewer, Peckham, and Brown were judges.

Of this group of six Cleveland-Harrison appointees, two stood out: David J. Brewer and Rufus W. Peckham. Brewer was born of missionary parents in Asia Minor and educated in the northeastern United States (at Wesleyan, Yale, and, after clerking in the office of his uncle, David Dudley Field, at the Albany Law School).[43] Then, like his other uncle, Stephen J. Field, he moved west, apparently to seek gold in Pike's Peak. That endeavor proved unsuccessful, and in the late 1850s he settled in Leavenworth, Kansas. Before his appointment to the Supreme Court of the United States in 1890, Brewer served with distinction first on the Kansas supreme court (1870–1884) and then on the federal circuit court (1884–1890).

Before being appointed to the Supreme Court, Rufus Peckham had served for about a decade on the New York Court of Appeals, probably one of the most prominent tribunals in the country. Unlike Brewer, however, he hardly had much of a formal education. Son of a distinguished Albany family, at seven he was enrolled in the Albany Academy (the school of Learned Hand and Herman Melville), where he remained until shortly after

---

[42] Carl A. Pierce, "A Vacancy on the Supreme Court: The Politics of Judicial Appointment, 1893–94," *Tenn. L. Rev.*, 39: 555 (1972). The vacancy was created by the death of Justice Blatchford in 1893. Cleveland tried twice to fill the vacancy, and when rebuffed, took the safer strategy of nominating a senator.

[43] For valuable background on Brewer, see Lynford A. Lardner, "The Constitutional Doctrines of Justice David Josiah Brewer" (Ph.D. diss., Princeton University, 1938). See also Michael J. Brodhead, "Justice David J.

Brewer: A Voice for Peace on the Supreme Court," *Sup. Ct. Hist. Soc'y Y.B.*, 93 (1985); D. Stanley Eitzen, "David J. Brewer, 1837–1910: A Kansan on the United States Supreme Court," *Emporia St. Res. Stud.*, vol. 12, no. 3 (1964); and Robert E. Gamer, "Justice Brewer and Substantive Due Process: A Conservative Court Revisited," *Vand. L. Rev.*, 18: 615 (1965). See also Fiss, "David Brewer, The Judge as Missionary," in Bergan, Fiss, and McCurdy, *Fields and the Law*, 53–63.

his sixteenth birthday, when he left in the middle of the academic year without graduating. Peckham studied with a tutor in Philadelphia, traveled in Europe, and finally turned to the law. He apprenticed in the Albany law firm of his father (also Rufus) and then followed his father's footsteps: He was elected district attorney, a state trial judge, and a judge of the Court of Appeals. His brother, Wheeler H. Peckham, had been nominated to the Supreme Court by Cleveland in 1894 for the seat that finally went to White. In the confirmation fight over Wheeler, Senator Hill, a Democrat from New York who headed the opposition, said that he would have no objection to "the other Peckham."[44] Cleveland got the point. When another vacancy occurred in 1895, only a year later, President Cleveland turned back to New York and this time chose Rufus.

Both Peckham and Brewer are relatively unknown today, obscured by such grand figures of the law as Harlan and Holmes, and to some extent Field, but in their time they were prominent judicial figures, especially important for the role they played on the Fuller Court. They were its intellectual leaders, influential within the dominant coalition and the source of the ideas that gave the Court its sweep and direction. These ideas were neither unique nor original to Brewer or Peckham (indeed, no justice in American history could claim or even would want to claim such originality), but Brewer and Peckham gave these ideas their fullest and perhaps most authoritative expression.

Time and time again, Chief Justice Fuller turned to either Brewer or Peckham to write the opinion of the Court in a major case. Brewer wrote *In re Debs*,[45] *Reagan v. Farmers' Loan & Trust Co.*,[46] *Muller v. Oregon*,[47] and *Hodges v. United States*.[48] Peckham wrote the first cases to apply the antitrust laws to business[49] and spoke for the Court in *Lochner* and *Ex parte Young*.[50] Brewer and Peckham did not always secure a majority, but even in dissent their views were central. They set the terms of the debate, and,

---

[44] Quoted in "Mr. Justice Peckham," *Law Notes*, 13: 168 (1909). Additional details of Peckham's life and his schooling can be found in L. B. Proctor, "Rufus W. Peckham," *Albany L.J.*, 55: 286 (1895), and in his Albany Academy registration card (on file with author). For the most comprehensive account of Peckham's work see the trio of articles by another son of Albany, William F. Duker: "Mr. Justice Rufus W. Peckham: The Police Power and the Individual in a Changing World," *B.Y.U. L. Rev.*, 1980: 47; "The Fuller Court and State Criminal Process: Threshold of Modern Limitations on Government,"

B.Y.U. L. Rev., 1980: 275; and "Mr. Justice Rufus W. Peckham and the Case of *Ex Parte Young*: Lochnerizing *Munn v. Illinois*," *B.Y.U. L. Rev.*, 1980: 539. On Holmes's impression of Peckham, see Chapter 7, note 31.
[45] 158 U.S. 564 (1895).
[46] 154 U.S. 362 (1894).
[47] 208 U.S. 412 (1908).
[48] 203 U.S. 1 (1906).
[49] United States v. Trans-Missouri Freight Ass'n, 166 U.S. 290 (1897); United States v. Joint Traffic Ass'n, 171 U.S. 505 (1898); Addyston Pipe & Steel Co. v. United States, 175 U.S. 211 (1899).
[50] 209 U.S. 123 (1908).

as in the cases of *Budd v. New York*[51] and *Holden v. Hardy*,[52] over time their dissenting positions often achieved majority status. Of the two, Brewer was the more eloquent, and he frequently defended his position and the Court's off the bench. Apparently, he also had the closer personal relationship with the chief justice. At Brewer's death, Fuller referred to him as "one of the most lovable of them all."[53]

Brewer and Peckham could generally count on the support of the other Cleveland-Harrison appointees (Fuller, Shiras, Brown, and White). Field was also a reliable ally. Conventional wisdom, largely traceable to Frankfurter's writings,[54] is to read the important decisions of this period, such as *Lochner*, as "simply" writing into law Justice Field's dissent in the *Slaughter-House Cases*. That view seems to me a gross oversimplification, but the fact remains that Brewer and Peckham invariably could turn to Field, senile or not, for another vote. Moreover, Field's resignation in 1897 had no appreciable impact on the alignments. William McKinley—who won the 1896 election and thus succeeded Cleveland—appointed the like-minded Joseph McKenna as Field's replacement. Like Field, McKenna was a Californian. He previously had served as a federal judge and as a congressman. He was appointed attorney general by President McKinley with the understanding that he would fill Field's seat on the Court as soon as Field stepped down, an arrangement apparently worked out with Field's support.[55]

As for the other carry-over justices, Brewer and Peckham could not count on Harlan in putting together their majorities. Harlan shared their

---

[51] 143 U.S. 517, 548 (1892). Brewer's dissent came to fruition in Reagan v. Farmers' Loan & Trust Co., 154 U.S. at 398.

[52] 169 U.S. 366, 398 (1898). Their dissenting position became the majority's view in *Lochner*.

[53] "Proceedings on the Death of Mr. Justice Brewer," 218 U.S. vii, xv (1910). A footnote reads: "These remarks were delivered on the last day that Mr. Chief Justice Fuller presided over the court. October Term, 1909, adjourned the same day, and during vacation the Chief Justice died at his summer home in Sorrento, Maine, on July 4, 1910." Ibid. The tie was there from the beginning. In a letter to his wife dated January 13, 1891, Fuller chatted about his colleagues and, referring to Brewer, commented:

He said he was rather prejudiced against me (which I did not know) when he came but he became at once one of the warmest friends and then

a variety of complimentary things. (But you seem to have captured them both at once.) Brown told him that *he* knew better than to have any prejudice against me. Brown really warmed up. I was amused and rather pleased. Brewer is a great favorite with me.

Fuller Papers, Chicago Historical Society.

[54] See Frankfurter's articles "Mr. Justice Holmes and the Constitution," *Harv. L. Rev.*, 41: 121, 141–43 (1927), and "The Constitutional Opinions of Justice Holmes," *Harv. L. Rev.*, 29: 683, 690–91 (1916).

[55] Swisher, *Stephen J. Field*, 444; James F. Watts, Jr., "Joseph McKenna," in Leon Friedman and Fred L. Israel, eds., *The Justices of the United States Supreme Court, 1789–1969: Their Lives and Major Opinions* (New York: Chelsea House, 1969), 3: 1719, 1725–26.

attachment to individual liberty and often joined their most important opinions (for example, Brewer's opinions in *Debs* and *Reagan* and Peckham's antitrust opinions in *Trans-Missouri, Joint Traffic,* and *Addyston Pipe*), but for the most part Harlan had to be treated as an independent and highly unpredictable force. He was not led by Brewer or Peckham, nor for that matter by anyone else. On the other hand, Justice Gray, who served on the Court until 1902, seemed ideologically inclined toward Brewer and Peckham. The Fuller Court, then, was composed of a group of seven or eight justices who largely shared the same basic premises and outlook: Brewer and Peckham, the leaders, and then Fuller, Shiras, Brown, White, Field/McKenna, and possibly Gray. Such homogeneity has been seen rarely in the Court's history.

This bloc remained in power for most of the twenty-two years of Fuller's chief justiceship. Of the Cleveland-Harrison appointees, only Shiras and Brown left the Court before 1910. Theodore Roosevelt, who was in the White House when those vacancies occurred, appointed William Day in 1903 to replace Shiras and William Moody in 1906 to replace Brown. At the time of Day's appointment, Roosevelt was president as a result of McKinley's assassination and looked to appoint someone who could fairly be considered as McKinley's man. Day, who served as McKinley's secretary of state and was appointed by McKinley to serve on the Sixth Circuit, did not constitute a break with the past. Moody, however, was Roosevelt's own attorney general and his appointment did modify the hegemony of the Cleveland-Harrison group, but only marginally.

The truly decisive break came with Roosevelt's appointment in 1902 of Oliver Wendell Holmes, Jr., to replace Gray. Holmes was already a great figure in American law. His position in a number of labor cases that arose while he was on the Massachusetts high court provoked some protests by big business over his nomination (which he characteristically brushed off[56]), but that aside, his appointment to the Supreme Court of the United States was an important public event, something of a judicial coronation. Justice Brown described it as a "topping off."[57]

Holmes had no taste for the outlook or the framework of the Cleveland-Harrison appointees. His appointment was to have great significance for the work of the Court over time, but his immediate impact—and this cannot be stressed too strongly—was not great. For the first decade of the twentieth century, his role was that of the prophet: He laid the foundations

---

[56] Holmes to Pollock, Aug. 13, 1902, *Holmes–Pollock Letters,* I: 103–104 ("The President has offered me a place on the U.S. Supreme Court which I shall accept—subject to confirmation by the Senate. There have been powerful influences against me, because some at least of the money powers think me dangerous, wherein they are wrong.").

[57] Brown to Holmes, Sept. 14, 1902, Harvard Holmes Papers ("I congratulate you upon this pleasant 'topping off' of your judicial career.").

for the future but was largely ignored by those with whom he shared power. He secured a place in history for his dissent in *Lochner*, but this was a dissent no other justice joined. Like Justice Harlan, he represented an independent force within the Court, but he seems to have been even more alienated than Harlan from the basic coalitions and the intellectual mainstream of the Court in the early 1900s. It is not surprising that an intense rivalry developed between Holmes and Harlan; it was as though they were competing for the accolade of "the great dissenter." It is also not surprising that, with the exception of Fuller and to a slightly lesser extent White,[58] Holmes had no close relationships with any of the other justices. In all his voluminous correspondence, he barely mentioned them. It is almost as though he ignored those at hand and lived through the mails.

Fuller died in 1910. Many of the themes and doctrines established in the preceding twenty years continued thanks to stare decisis, the fortuities of the appointments process (the political forces that produced the original Cleveland-Harrison bloc did not disappear from the national stage), and the fact that some of the earlier appointees, like Justices White, Day, and McKenna, continued to sit. The year 1910 was important, however, because just as the progressive movement was gaining momentum and achieving greater success on the national political scene, the Court's leadership changed. Here I am not referring to the death of Fuller—he was no leader and in any event was replaced immediately, for reasons perhaps not completely to President Taft's credit,[59] by Edward White, another justice also appointed to the Court by Cleveland and an integral member of the governing coalition. I am referring instead to the odd coincidence that Brewer and

---

[58] See, e.g., Holmes to Mrs. Gray, Jan. 4, 1903, Harvard Holmes Papers ("I like my brethren. The C.J. is most amicable and efficient. I have talked much with White—a fertile mind and charming man."); Holmes to Wigmore, Dec. 21, 1905, Harvard Holmes Papers ("There is a good deal of loneliness in the midst of much society here, although I find great companionship with White, a very able man who somewhat ruins his great powers by defective expression when he writes, and although I have most affectionate relations with the C.J. and very pleasant ones with the rest."). Over time, the relationship with White seems to have cooled somewhat. See, e.g., Holmes to Baroness Moncheur, May 16, 1912, Harvard Holmes Papers ("The Chief [White] and I are apt to agree (with an occasional sharp differ-

ence) but our interests are so remote from each other that the sense of companionship is not as great as I could wish. The speculative side, which is what I think of most, doesn't interest him.").

[59] Taft relied on White's opinion in the state prohibition cases (see Chapter 9) and must have liked White's position on the issue of colonialism (see Chapter 8). White's capacity to form fusion positions for the Court, as in the *Insular Cases*, also must have worked to his benefit. But there were aspects of White's approach, especially manifest in his dissent in *Northern Securities*, that were probably too rigid and formalistic for Taft. Thus one is inclined to put at least some store in the speculation of certain commentators that Taft wanted to appoint someone who in all likelihood

Chapter II: *The Identity of the Institution*

Peckham—the true leaders of the Court—both died just months before Fuller.[60] Without Brewer and Peckham on the Court to formulate and expound the ideas that gave this segment of the Court's history its distinctive character, the Fuller Court came to an end. It is almost as though Fuller could not go on without them.

II

We can see in the 1890s and early 1900s the emergence of the trends that so dominated the first part of the twentieth century. The country was becoming increasingly urbanized; the number of immigrants, particularly from the southern and eastern parts of Europe, was growing; and so was the role of manufacturing in the economy.[61] The rail industry had almost reached maturity[62] and the forms of communication and transportation that mark modern life—the telephone and the car[63]—were nearly at hand. All these developments—increased urbanization, industrialization, and immigration—served as a backdrop for this period of Supreme Court history but did not constitute the specific social context within which the Fuller Court acted and forged its identity. That identity instead arose from the Court's confrontation with three specific political and social developments: populism, imperialism, and progressivism.

The early 1890s was a period of radical politics in America, during which basic aspects of social structure were called into question. At issue was nothing less than capitalism and the social relationships that it implied.

---

would leave the position soon, thereby creating a vacancy for Taft himself when he left the White House. See, e.g., David H. Burton, *William Howard Taft in the Public Service* (Malabar, Fla.: Robert E. Krieger, 1986), 122. For contrasting views emphasizing more political and policy motives for the appointment, see Merlo J. Pusey, *Charles Evans Hughes* (New York: Macmillan, 1952), 1: 280–81, and Bickel and Schmidt, *Judiciary and Responsible Government*, 37–39, 59–64.

[60] Justice Moody left the Court in the same year because of illness. Justice Harlan died the following year.

[61] See generally Samuel P. Hays, *The Response to Industrialism, 1885–1914* (Chicago: University of Chicago Press, 1957); Harold G. Vatter, *The Drive to Industrial Maturity: The U.S. Economy, 1860–1914* (Westport, Conn.: Green-

wood Press, 1975); Bernard A. Weisberger, *The New Industrial Society* (New York: John Wiley & Sons, 1969); Paul Boyer, *Urban Masses and Moral Order in America, 1820–1920* (Cambridge: Harvard University Press, 1978); and Thomas J. Archdeacon, *Becoming American: An Ethnic History* (New York: Free Press, 1983).

[62] See Stuart Leuthner, *The Railroaders* (New York: Random House, 1983).

[63] See H. M. Boettinger, *The Telephone Book: Bell, Watson, Vail and American Life, 1876–1976* (Croton-on-Hudson, N.Y.: Riverwood, 1977), and Jean-Pierre Bardou, Jean-Jacques Chanaron, Patrick Fridenson, and James M. Laux, *The Automobile Revolution: The Impact of an Industry*, trans. James M. Laux (Chapel Hill: University of North Carolina Press, 1982).

Communism, socialism, and even anarchism were debated as viable alternatives as the growing gap between laborers and wealthy capitalists intensified class conflict. The period also spawned important utopian literature, above all Edward Bellamy's novel *Looking Backward, 2000–1887* (1888), a celebration of the ownership of industry by the national government.[64] This book managed to sell more copies than any other in America in the nineteenth century save *Uncle Tom's Cabin* and *Ben Hur*,[65] but even the most generous reading suggests that its popularity could hardly be due to its literary qualities. The key must have been its political vision. The book gave rise to a journal and even a network of political clubs to advance Bellamy's plan of "nationalism."

People also seemed prepared to give practical force to their political commitments. The Knights of Labor, the first mass organization of American workers, reached its height from the late 1870s through the mid-1880s. During this period, suggests historian Leon Fink, the Knights "helped to sustain a national debate over the social implications of industrial capitalism."[66] When the Knights collapsed in the late 1880s, the casualty of efforts to transform itself into a politically based workers' movement, laborers sought new forms of organization and in the early 1890s confronted capitalism in massive, bitter, and often violent ways.

One stirring example was the Homestead Strike of 1892, which was marked by Alexander Berkman's attempted assassination of Henry C. Frick, chairman of the Carnegie Steel Company, and the deployment of troops and Pinkertons by the Carnegie interests to break the strike.[67] The struggle between organized labor and capital also erupted in the Pullman Strike of 1894. Eugene Debs and the American Railway Union managed to obstruct the rail system of the nation and federal troops were called out to restore order.[68] At the time, strikes like Homestead and Pullman seemed

---

[64] *Looking Backward, 2000–1887* (Boston: Ticknor, 1888; repr. New York: New American Library, 1960). See also Henry Demarest Lloyd's *Wealth Against Commonwealth* (New York: Harper & Bros., 1894) and Henry George's *Progress and Poverty* (San Francisco: Wm. M. Hinton, 1879). See generally John L. Thomas, *Alternative America: Henry George, Edward Bellamy, Henry Demarest Lloyd and the Adversary Tradition* (Cambridge: Harvard University Press, 1983).

[65] See Erich Fromm's Foreword to Bellamy, *Looking Backward*, v.

[66] Leon Fink, *Workingmen's Democracy: The Knights of Labor and American Politics* (Urbana: University of Illinois Press, 1983), xiii, 32–33. See also Joseph G. Rayback, *A History of American Labor*, rev. ed. (New York: Macmillan, 1966), 173–84.

[67] See Arthur G. Burgoyne, *The Homestead Strike of 1892* (Pittsburgh: Rawsthorne, 1893; repr. Pittsburgh: University of Pittsburgh Press, 1979); Leon Wolff, *Lockout: The Story of the Homestead Strike of 1892: A Study of Violence, Unionism and the Carnegie Steel Empire* (New York: Harper & Row, 1965); and Samuel Yellen, *American Labor Struggles* (New York: Harcourt, Brace, 1936; repr. New York: Arno Press, 1969), 72–100.

[68] See Chapter 3.

more like revolutionary agitation than the kind of collective activity that later was to characterize the American Federation of Labor led by Samuel Gompers. Indeed, looking back, the 1886 Haymarket Riot in Chicago served as an appropriate prelude to this volatile period.[69] As police officers sought to close down a protest meeting, a bomb, allegedly thrown by anarchists, exploded. The police fired into a crowd of three thousand workers and in the ensuing violence both police officers and civilians were killed.

The intense and sometimes bitter struggles of the early and mid-1890s took place under severely depressed conditions, in which prices fell and unemployment rose—in 1894 unemployment was as high as 30 percent, maybe 50 percent in manufacturing and construction. This was then the Great Depression of the nineteenth century. It was, moreover, a time when the national government was not inclined to provide any relief—as Jacob Coxey of Ohio learned. He proposed a $500 million relief program that would put the unemployed to work building national roads. When Congress failed to respond affirmatively to this idea, Coxey decided to send "a petition to Washington with boots on." Coxey's army—five hundred workers, students, and sympathizers—marched on Washington in 1894, only to be met with arrests and beatings, but no legislation.[70]

As these events were occurring in industrial America, farmers gave life to a new social movement, populism. In his book *Democratic Promise* (1976),[71] Lawrence Goodwyn describes in vivid detail the notions and methods that gave populism its distinctive cast: the grass-roots organization, the experiential rather than theoretical basis of the political culture, the centrality of the ethic of cooperation rather than competition. Forced from their land by creditors, a number of southern farmers set out for Texas and tried to set up an economic system that would keep them free of the provision merchant. The result was the establishment of cooperatives to buy farm equipment and sell crops. These organizations grew into the Texas Farmers' Alliance, then the National Farmers' Alliance. The Alliance soon broadened into the People's Party, a political party with strongholds in the South and West. Together, these developments constituted the populist movement.

Populism was at its inception and at its heart an agrarian movement centered around farmers' cooperatives, but the political activities of American farmers influenced and reinforced the radicalism that was developing

---

[69] See Paul Avrich, *The Haymarket Tragedy* (Princeton: Princeton University Press, 1984).

[70] See Carlos A. Schwantes, *Coxey's Army: An American Odyssey* (Lincoln: University of Nebraska Press, 1985), and Donald L. McMurry, *Coxey's Army: A Study of the Industrial Army Movement of 1894* (Boston: Little, Brown, 1929; repr. Seattle: University of Washington Press, 1968).

[71] *Democratic Promise: The Populist Moment in America* (New York: Oxford University Press, 1976).

39

in the industrial centers of the nation. I use the term "populism" to refer to the radical political movements of the early 1890s, both agrarian and industrial, because all these movements, like populism proper, questioned the competitive premises of the capitalist structure. For all of them cooperation, not competition, was to be both the central dynamic and the central ethic of production.

The election of 1896 marked the eclipse of the populist movement. The People's Party was absorbed into more traditional politics and overwhelmed by the organizational imperatives of the Democratic Party.[72] Even domesticated, however, the threat it posed to the established order was too much for the electorate. In 1896 the voters rejected the populist political challenge by defeating Bryan and the Democrats. They elected McKinley, and in so doing endorsed the continuation of the conservative politics of Cleveland and Harrison. Stability and prosperity returned, and, as the twentieth century approached, Americans began to contemplate the future and to ponder the nation's place in the world. The question arose whether America should follow the European example and acquire a colonial empire.[73]

As early as 1893, Frederick Jackson Turner's announcement that the frontier had closed[74] led many business leaders to conclude that the recent spate of depressions in which production outpaced consumption, and the accompanying labor unrest, could be avoided only by seizing new territory. Prominent Protestant ministers such as Josiah Strong added their voices to the call for geographic expansion, which they saw as an opportunity to Christianize the world. Strong and others also hoped to deter the spread of Roman Catholicism and socialism abroad, which in their minds posed a threat at home with the influx of immigrants. In the political realm, fig-

---

[72] Ibid., 426–514.

[73] See generally Robert L. Beisner, *Twelve Against Empire: The Anti-Imperialists, 1898–1900* (New York: McGraw-Hill, 1968; repr. Chicago: University of Chicago Press, 1985); Richard Hofstadter, "Manifest Destiny and the Philippines," in Daniel Aaron, ed., *America in Crisis* (New York: Alfred A. Knopf, 1952), 173; Walter LaFeber, *The New Empire: An Interpretation of American Expansion, 1860–1898* (Ithaca: Cornell University Press, 1963); Ernest R. May, *American Imperialism: A Speculative Essay* (New York: Atheneum, 1968); Ernest R. May, *Imperial Democracy: The Emergence of America as a* *Great Power* (New York: Harcourt, Brace & World, 1961); Julius W. Pratt, *Expansionists of 1898: The Acquisition of Hawaii and the Spanish Islands* (Baltimore: Johns Hopkins Press, 1936); and William Appleman Williams, *The Tragedy of American Diplomacy*, rev. ed. (New York: Dell, 1972).

[74] Turner took up and popularized the "closing of the frontier" thesis (apparently first formulated by the superintendent of the Census) in his seminal paper, "The Significance of the Frontier in American History," reprinted in Turner's *The Frontier in American History* (New York: Henry Holt, 1920), 1–38.

ures such as Theodore Roosevelt and Richard Olney insisted that America's mission was to bring democratic institutions and a civilized culture to the world.

In 1898 the United States discovered the satisfaction of wielding its military might abroad when it sent troops to assist Cuban rebels in overthrowing the Spanish regime. The result was the Spanish–American War of 1898. This "splendid little war," as the encomium suggests, was a short and highly successful military adventure that culminated in the acquisition of Spanish territories in the Caribbean (Puerto Rico) and the Pacific (the Philippines).[75] The United States also annexed Hawaii that year. It was generally assumed that these territories, like Alaska (acquired in the late 1860s), would not become states within the foreseeable future, but would be held as "colonies," with all that term implied: economic domination and political disenfranchisement.

Not everyone supported such international forays. Anti-imperialists objected that by creating a subject class, colonization of foreign lands violated the democratic principles of self-determination and consent of the governed that America embodied. They feared that the acquisition of foreign lands would require the establishment of a large standing army and would increase the power of the central government, jeopardizing the liberties of Americans. Imperialism was debated with intensity and great fanfare—in the Court, in the Congress, and in the nation at large—and was a major issue in the presidential election of 1900. It dominated the Court's docket for two years (the 1900 and 1901 terms) and then virtually disappeared. A bloody insurrection in the Philippines in the early 1900s[76] and the experience of the English in South Africa at roughly the same time[77] made the difficulties of governing colonies all too apparent. Americans seemed to lose their taste for empire, at least in the European form.

The drive to acquire new territories gave way to a program to consolidate existing possessions. Expansionism was transformed into a program to support the entrepreneurial adventures of the emerging multinational corporations. This transformation was exemplified by the construction of the Panama Canal, which secured for the United States political hegemony

---

[75] See Lewis L. Gould, *The Spanish–American War and President McKinley* (Lawrence: University Press of Kansas, 1982), and David F. Trask, *The War with Spain in 1898* (New York: Macmillan, 1981).

[76] See Stanley Karnow, *In Our Image: America's Empire in the Philippines* (New York: Random House, 1989), 106–195.

[77] See Thomas Pakenham, *The Boer War* (London: Weidenfeld & Nicolson, 1979), and Byron Farwell, *The Great Boer War* (London: Allen Lane, 1977).

in the Americas while spurring new economic growth.[78] Roosevelt sought security for national economic interests and freedom from European intervention in the Americas but disavowed any intention to establish new colonies.[79] By 1905 imperialism appeared before the Court as nothing more than a social movement now at an end—maybe not forever, but at least for the time being.

The nation's attention, previously focused on imperialistic forays, turned inward. Moralistic concerns that had long been part of American culture gained prominence and found expression in the temperance movement and concerted programs to outlaw lotteries, obscenity, and prostitution. But, once again, it was primarily economics and the problems of a maturing capitalism that dominated the politics of the early 1900s. Some traces of the radicalism of the earlier period remained. The Socialist Party of America, led by Eugene Debs, emerged as a viable political organization able to obtain a significant percent of the popular vote.[80] The Industrial Workers of the World, the "Wobblies," also appeared as a militant alternative to Gompers's American Federation of Labor.[81] Talk of class antago-

---

[78] See David McCullough, *The Path Between the Seas: The Creation of the Panama Canal, 1870–1914* (New York: Simon & Schuster, 1977), and Lewis L. Gould, *The Presidency of Theodore Roosevelt* (Lawrence: University Press of Kansas, 1991), 91–99. Far from a new expression of acquisitive imperialism, the Hay-Bunau-Varilla Treaty of 1903 was the culmination of a long history of the United States' efforts to control the Isthmiad passage. The Canal served specific strategic and economic interests of the United States, distinguishing Panama from other nations in South and Central America. Conversely, Washington then had little interest in the affairs of Panama outside the protection of the Canal. While the treaty reserved to the United States the right to intervene in Panama's internal affairs if they threatened operation of the Canal (a prerogative exercised in 1908, 1912, and 1918 and as recently as December 1989), Roosevelt expressly disavowed any intention of acquiring the newly declared sovereign state. On October 18, 1904, he wrote to Taft, then secretary of war:

We have not the slightest intention of establishing an independent colony in the middle of the State of Panama,

or of exercising any greater governmental functions than are necessary to enable us conveniently and safely to construct, maintain and operate the canal, under the rights given us by the treaty.

Elting E. Morison, ed., *The Square Deal (1903–1905)*, vol. 4 of *The Letters of Theodore Roosevelt* (Cambridge: Harvard University Press, 1951), 986. The president further declined to establish naval bases in the Canal zone. See Walter LaFeber, *The Panama Canal: The Crisis in Historical Perspective*, updated ed. (New York: Oxford University Press, 1989), 44.

[79] Theodore Roosevelt, annual messages to Congress, Dec. 6, 1904, and Dec. 5, 1905, reprinted in Hermann Hagedorn, ed., *The Works of Theodore Roosevelt* (New York: Charles Scribner's Sons, 1925) 17: 250–310, 315–400. See also Gould, *Presidency of Theodore Roosevelt*, 175–76.

[80] Nick Salvatore, *Eugene V. Debs: Citizen and Socialist* (Urbana: University of Illinois Press, 1982), 220–302.

[81] See Melvyn Dubofsky, *We Shall Be All: A History of the Industrial Workers of the World*, 2d ed. (Urbana: University of Illinois Press, 1988).

nism that so marked the early 1890s again surfaced.[82] But neither this talk nor the idea of class struggle gave the early 1900s its distinctive character or directly affected the agenda of the Supreme Court. That role was played instead by the progressive movement.

The progressive movement first achieved national prominence during the administration of Theodore Roosevelt, but its antecedents can be found at both the state and national levels.[83] The Sherman Antitrust Act of 1890,[84] for example, and the 1887 statute establishing the Interstate Commerce Commission might be regarded as progressive measures.[85] The progressive movement also persisted beyond 1910 and Fuller's death. Its name was used by Roosevelt in the election of 1912 (he ran as the Progressive Party candidate), and progressives were instrumental in the enactment of the Clayton Act[86] and the Federal Trade Commission Act,[87] the establishment of the Federal Reserve System,[88] the adoption of the Sixteenth Amendment, and in fact the entire pattern of early-twentieth-century regulatory measures that culminated in the New Deal. The years 1900 to 1910 were thus neither the beginning nor the end of progressivism, but they were nonetheless an especially important formative period for the movement. It was a time when progressivism became the dominant political and social movement on the national scene, challenging the established order and thereby shaping the agenda and work of the Court.

Progressivism, in contrast to populism and the radicalism of the early 1890s, did not contemplate significant alteration of the existing social structure. It accepted the market and private ownership of capital as the basic mechanism for ordering socioeconomic relations. Progressivism was a "reform" movement and sought to use law, principally statutes, as the instrument of progress, but the reforms urged were of an incremental nature. While populists sought to supplant the competitive market with cooperative enterprises, progressives were content to curb the "excesses" and "abuses" of the market at the margins. On the traditional account—

---

[82] See, e.g., John R. Commons, "Is Class Conflict in America Growing and Is It Inevitable?," *The Square Deal*, 4: 29 (1908) (address delivered before the American Sociological Society, December 1906).

[83] See, e.g., Boyer, *Urban Masses*, 189–292; Robert W. Cherny, *Populism, Progressivism, and the Transformation of Nebraska Politics, 1885–1915* (Lincoln: University of Nebraska Press, 1981); David P. Thelen, *Robert M. La Follette and the Insurgent Spirit* (Boston: Little, Brown, 1976); and James

Edward Wright, *The Progressive Yankees: Republican Reformers in New Hampshire, 1906–1916* (Hanover, N.H.: University Press of New England, 1987).

[84] Act of July 2, 1890, Ch. 647, 26 Stat. 209.

[85] Act of Feb. 4, 1887, Ch. 104, 24 Stat. 379.

[86] Act of Oct. 15, 1914, Ch. 323, 38 Stat. 730.

[87] Act of Sept. 26, 1914, Ch. 311, 38 Stat. 717.

[88] Federal Reserve Act, Ch. 6, 38 Stat. 251 (1913).

assumed by historians who follow Paul and Westin—progressives sought to mitigate the harshness and caprices of that system for the benefit of consumers and workers;[89] for a revisionist such as Kolko,[90] they sought to protect businessmen from the discipline of the market ("ruinous competition"). On either account, progressives sought to preserve the market, only with the edges trimmed.[91]

Progressives accepted the employment relationship that lay at the heart of the capitalist system. They viewed labor as a commodity to be bought and sold on the market and sought only to regulate that market at the margins. They pressed for statutes that prohibited employers and workers from contracting for hours in excess of a certain specified maximum (the sixty-hour week). They also pressed for the enactment of laws that prohibited certain vulnerable groups (such as children) from entering the market altogether. These were perceived as incidental intrusions. For the most part, the market was accepted as the basic determinant of the working relationship. The market for consumer goods and services was equally respected by progressives. Only on occasion, and then only under the most exceptional circumstances (as in the case of railroad regulation or the prohibition of liquor), did progressives ever contemplate an interference with the normal exchange relationship.

Theodore Roosevelt's so-called trust-busting of the early 1900s represented the more general and typical program of progressivism.[92] This program raised the deepest and most far-reaching constitutional questions of the day—antitrust was for the early 1900s what the civil rights movement was for the 1960s and the Warren Court—but it did not contemplate a repudiation or even a significant modification of the market. Antitrust was ameliorative. It sought to preserve and enhance the functioning of markets by prohibiting destructive conduct, like price-fixing or monopolization. Ironically, self-interest served as the essential dynamic of the market, but if allowed to operate without restraint, it could also lead to practices that

---

[89] See, e.g., Robert H. Wiebe, *The Search for Order, 1877–1920* (New York: Hill & Wang, 1967), 164–95. On Paul and Westin, see Chapter 1, text accompanying notes 44 and 45.

[90] See Chapter 1, text accompanying note 46.

[91] On the diversity of historians' interpretations of progressivism, see Daniel T. Rodgers, "In Search of Progressivism," *Rev. Amer. Hist.*, vol. 10, no. 4, 113–32 (1982). See also David M. Ken-

nedy, ed., *Progressivism: The Critical Issues* (Boston: Little, Brown, 1971), vii–xiv.

[92] See Lewis L. Gould, *Reform and Regulation: American Politics From Roosevelt to Wilson*, 2d ed. (New York: Alfred A. Knopf, 1986), and Sean Dennis Cashman, *America in the Gilded Age: From the Death of Lincoln to the Rise of Theodore Roosevelt*, 2d ed. (New York: New York University Press, 1988), 340–68.

would destroy the market. Holmes, no friend of antitrust laws, described the Sherman Act as requiring one to fight, but not to win.[93]

III

Populism, imperialism, progressivism. These were the dominant social and political movements of the 1890s and the early 1900s, shaping the cultural and political life of the nation and defining the agenda of the Court.[94] The identity of the Court at the turn of the century was forged largely by the reaction of the justices—or, more specifically, by the response of the bloc of Cleveland-Harrison appointees led by Brewer and Peckham—to the various constitutional issues raised by these movements.

There were many such issues, and, as will be detailed, each of these movements had its own distinct sources of support and its own agenda. The differences are important. Yet all three movements brought to the fore the single issue that unified the Court's work: the scope of government power. Populism and the labor agitation of the early 1890s, for example, tested the authority of the state to maintain order and to preserve the conditions necessary for the exercise of liberty. These radical movements also sought to use state power to bring about a redistribution of wealth. Progressivism eschewed such redistributive ambitions; it promised to save the market and the values it furthered, but nonetheless encouraged the state to intervene in economic affairs in a manner and magnitude that appeared to represent a break with the past. New questions about state power also emerged from the imperialist ventures spurred by the Spanish-American War and embraced by the American people in the election of 1900. In wondering whether "the Constitution follows the flag," the Court tried to determine whether the very exercise of the power needed to maintain a colonial empire was compatible with the constitutional ideal of liberty. Such exercises of state power were taken for granted in Europe, but were difficult to reconcile with the American commitment to limited government.

The justices of the Cleveland-Harrison bloc obviously did not believe that people should be free to do whatever they wished—they viewed this

---

[93] Holmes to Mrs. Gray, July 28, 1915, Harvard Holmes Papers ("I also think I rather mortified [Mr. Beveridge], when I had expressed an opinion that the Sherman Act was an imbecile performance, by not knowing that he had stuck up for the Trusts for years. We always get on well. His talk interests me and he was tickled when I summed up the statute as a command that you must fight but must not win.").

[94] See generally William F. Swindler, *Court and Constitution in the Twentieth Century: The Old Legality, 1889–1932* (Indianapolis: Bobbs-Merrill, 1969), 3–131.

conception of liberty as a form of anarchism. They understood the need for order and control and for the state to monopolize the means of force. Their commitment was to "ordered liberty," a phrase Justice Cardozo later coined[95] to denote a middle area lying somewhere between anarchism and absolutism. The justices' understanding of that middle area and thus the role of the state was shaped by an intellectual tradition that grounded the state in a social contract. This tradition originated in the late seventeenth and eighteenth centuries, particularly in the work of John Locke,[96] although it was interpreted and reinterpreted throughout the nineteenth century to account for the formation of the nation state, the transformation of the economy, and the emergence of a new political culture. Although the justices argued over the meaning of the Constitution, not over John Locke or the work of any other political theorist, nevertheless the social contract tradition constituted the intellectual structure that rendered their differences and divisions coherent. Contractarianism ultimately shaped their conception of liberty as the summum bonum of the Constitution and as the value threatened by all that they saw around them.

Social contract theories posit a sharp distinction between the social and the political. The social sphere consists of all those activities of individuals that are connected to their happiness or well-being. The political sphere, on the other hand, refers to the activities that relate to the state—its

---

[95] See Palko v. Connecticut, 302 U.S. 319, 325 (1937).

[96] John Locke, *Two Treatises of Civil Government* (London: J. M. Dent & Jars, 1962). For the historical context of Locke, see John Dunn, *The Political Thought of John Locke: An Historical Account of the Argument of the "Two Treatises of Government"* (Cambridge: Cambridge University Press, 1969). See also Neal Wood, *The Politics of Locke's Philosophy: A Social Study of "An Essay Concerning Human Understanding"* (Berkeley: University of California Press, 1983). In recent years, the long-standing view, advanced by such scholars as Richard Hofstadter, *The American Political Tradition and the Men Who Made It* (New York: Alfred A. Knopf, 1948), and Louis Hartz, *The Liberal Tradition in America: An Interpretation of American Political Thought Since the Revolution* (New York: Harcourt, Brace, 1955), which took Locke as central for understanding the political ideology of the American revolution and the founding period, has been challenged. In time a revisionist account arose, culminating in the work of J. G. A. Pocock, *The Machiavellian Moment: Florentine Political Thought and the Atlantic Republican Tradition* (Princeton: Princeton University Press, 1975), which sought to introduce an element of civic republicanism. A book that pushes the pendulum in the opposite direction is Isaac Kramnick, *Republicanism and Bourgeois Radicalism: Political Ideology in Late Eighteenth-Century England and America* (Ithaca: Cornell University Press, 1990). For an important summary of this debate and a review of that book, see Gordon S. Wood, "The Virtues and the Interests," *The New Republic*, Feb. 11, 1991, 204: 32. For a more general statement of Wood's contribution to this debate, see Gordon S. Wood, *The Creation of the American Republic, 1776–1787* (Chapel Hill: University of North Carolina Press, 1969).

creation, use, and control. The social contract tradition not only insisted on a distinction between these two spheres but also assumed a priority of the social over the political. This is implied by the story concerning the origins of the state usually associated with the tradition, whereby people existing in a "state of nature" deliberate and then decide to create the state to serve their interests.

The priority implied by this story is normative, not just temporal. The implication is that even without a state, people can achieve a measure of happiness through the pursuit of self-interest and the formation of exchange relationships. As a result, the market, growing from the social realm, is treated as the basic ordering mechanism of society and the state as a derivative or supplemental institution. The state is an artificial creation, not part of the social order nor responsible for it. The state is an instrument, created to serve certain discrete ends that exist prior to and independent of it. Its duty is to facilitate exchange in the social realm by protecting property rights, among others, and to bring to an end those activities—for example, outbursts of violence or fraud—that prevent individuals from engaging in exchange or otherwise fully realizing their own ends.

Themes implicit in the social contract tradition—privileging the social over the political and confining the state to the task of facilitating exchange relationships—were reflected in social Darwinism, a late-nineteenth-century social theory rooted in the work of an Englishman, Herbert Spencer[97] (it was he, not Darwin, who coined the phrase "the survival of the fittest") and finally immortalized by Holmes's dissent in *Lochner* ("The Fourteenth Amendment does not enact Mr. Herbert Spencer's *Social Statics*"[98]). Spencer's ideas did not represent a new departure for American political thought—as Richard Hofstadter acknowledged, they "were imported into the Republic long after individualism had become a national tradition"[99]—but they achieved great currency in American intellectual circles at the turn of the century, especially through the work of William Graham Sumner, a professor of sociology at Yale.

Drawing on Spencer and a number of other theorists, including Adam Smith, Sumner extolled competition as both good and natural and denounced state intervention aimed at relieving the rigors of the competitive process. Declared Sumner:

---

[97] On social Darwinism in general, see Richard Hofstadter, *Social Darwinism in American Thought*, rev. ed. (New York: George Braziller, 1959), 51–66; A. J. Beitzinger, *A History of American Political Thought* (New York: Dodd, Mead, 1972), 403–410; and Alan Pendleton Grimes, *American Political Thought* (New York: Henry Holt, 1955), 303–311.

[98] 198 U.S. at 75.

[99] Hofstadter, *Social Darwinism*, 50.

If . . . the state enters as an agent into the industrial or social relations of its own subjects, it becomes the greatest and worst of all monopolies, the one best worth having under one's control, the best prize of base struggles, and the most powerful engine by which some men may exploit others.[100]

He openly spoke about "the glory of the United States"[101] and looked to the free market to produce a nation in which the fittest would survive and, indeed, flourish.

While social contract theory, like social Darwinism and its economic counterpart, the theory of laissez-faire,[102] placed limits on the activities of the state, it also sought to legitimate the state by grounding its authority in the people acting as a collectivity. As we shall see in examining the issues of colonialism and protective legislation for women, as well as issues more on the margin of the Court's agenda, like immigration and racial equality, membership in the authorizing collectivity—the constitutional community—was then defined to exclude certain groups. That community nonetheless remained the ultimate source of authority, both legitimating and controlling the power of the state.

Those operating within the social contract tradition recognized that the state might fail in its assigned tasks. There was a risk that the state would not exercise the power at its disposal, or not act when it should, for example to protect property rights or to prevent outbursts of violence. Conversely, there was another and, for adherents of the tradition, even greater threat, namely, that the state might exceed its authority. The apparatus of the state might be seized by groups who wished to use it for purposes of altering or transforming the social order, for example by interfering with exchange relationships or by taking the wealth of some and giving it to others. To

---

[100] Albert Galloway Keller and Maurice R. Davie, eds., *Essays of William Graham Sumner* (New Haven: Yale University Press, 1934), 240. See also William Graham Sumner, *What Social Classes Owe to Each Other* (New York: Harper & Bros., 1883; repr. Caldwell, Idaho: Caxton Printers, 1961), and *Folkways: A Study of the Sociological Importance of Usages, Manners, Customs, Mores, and Morals* (New York: Dover, 1906).

[101] Keller and Davie, *Essays of William Graham Sumner*, 2: 142.

[102] Grimes, *American Political Thought*, 305. See also Herbert Hovenkamp, "The Political Economy of Substantive Due Process," *Stan. L.*

Rev., 40: 379 (1988). For alternative accounts of the intellectual and cultural sources of the Court's doctrine in this period, see Charles W. McCurdy, "The Roots of 'Liberty of Contract' Reconsidered: Major Premises in the Law of Employment, 1867–1937," in *Sup. Ct. Hist. Soc'y Y.B.*, 20, 20–23 (1984); William E. Nelson, "The Impact of the Antislavery Movement upon Styles of Judicial Reasoning in Nineteenth Century America," *Harv. L. Rev.*, 87: 513 (1974); and Michael Les Benedict, "Laissez-Faire and Liberty: A Re-Evaluation of the Meaning and Origins of Laissez-Faire Constitutionalism," *Law & Hist. Rev.*, 3: 293–95 (1985).

Chapter II: *The Identity of the Institution*

guard against this contingency, techniques had to be found that simultaneously placed limits on the power of the state and that were consistent with the democratic aspiration that made the consent of the people the source of state authority. The solution lay in the idea of contract. Consent may be the ultimate source of legitimacy for the state, but that to which the people gave their consent—a contract—is not open to constant revision. It is fixed once and for all. Naturally enough, the Constitution became this contract, and it was the Constitution that the Fuller Court drew upon in defining the bounds of the modern state.

PART TWO

Class Conflict and the Supreme Court

CHAPTER III

Debs *and the Maintenance*
of Public Order

T HE ALBANY of William Kennedy's *Ironweed* was run down, full of
character but a city of back streets and alleys, waiting to be restored.
In the 1890s things were different. The city glistened. Albany was then one
of the most important cultural, economic, and political centers of the
nation. It was the home of two important national legal institutions, the
New York Court of Appeals and the famed Albany Law School. It was
in Albany that Justice Brewer delivered a speech that provides a key to
understanding the *Debs* case[1] and much of the Supreme Court's work of
the early 1890s. Its message: America was at the edge of revolution.[2]

The occasion was the annual meeting of the New York State Bar Association. The date was January 1893, about a year and a half before the Pullman Strike and the beginning of the *Debs* litigation. The speech contained
a sprinkling of the kind of legal analysis that the audience might have
expected from a Supreme Court justice. Brewer argued against labor arbitration and rate regulation, and in favor of permanent tenure and a fixed
salary for the judiciary. The larger themes, however, were introduced in a
different key. Brewer gave an assessment of his times, speaking with an
almost religious passion that overwhelmed the genteel legal argumentation.

He began by identifying the essence of civilization, those attributes
which "differentiate the civilized man from the savage": knowledge, morality, and the possession of property. A man's civilization was, according to
Brewer, determined by "that which he knows, that which he is, and that
which he has."[3] It was the last of these that most concerned Brewer because
property was the one attribute of civilized man "within the reach of others."[4] It was the most vulnerable.

---

[1] *In re* Debs, 158 U.S. 564 (1895).
[2] "The Nation's Safeguard," in New
York State Bar Association, *Proceedings
of the New York State Bar Association*

(New York: Stumpf & Steurer, 1893),
37–47.
[3] Ibid., 37.
[4] Ibid., 38.

By "property" Brewer did not mean the meager possessions of the savage ("a bow and arrow for his means of support—a canoe and a horse for his travel—and sea-shells for his jewels"[5]). For Brewer, the property of civilization was the accumulated wealth of capitalism, "the magnificence and luxuriousness which surround our lives."[6] This wealth, moreover, benefited all: "And the potency of civilization is that it accumulates all that the earth produces, and pours it round and into the homes of its children."[7] Brewer acknowledged the inequalities in the distribution of wealth but saw this as inevitable: "It is the unvarying law, that the wealth of a community will be in the hands of a few."[8] He also saw this unequal distribution as just: "The large majority of men are unwilling to endure that long self-denial and saving which makes accumulation possible; they have not the business tact and sagacity which brings about large combinations and great financial results."[9]

Although he was willing to accept inequalities in the distribution of wealth as both natural and just, Brewer also recognized that "the many"[10] or "the multitudes"[11] would not abide that judgment. They would often seek the property of "the few."[12] Brewer's principal concern was not with common thieves, for religious and societal mores against ordinary theft remained unquestioned; rather, he focused, as did the social contract tradition of which he was part, on the power of "the multitudes" to endow their taking with political and legal legitimacy. He saw this power of the democracy as posing the greatest danger to property and thus to civilization. This danger was manifest, Brewer thought, in two popular movements of the day. One was the effort to use the power of legislation to regulate prices even to the point of depriving the owners of a fair rate of return. For him this was tantamount to a confiscation: "[I]t robs property of its value."[13] The other movement of which Brewer spoke—more relevant for understanding *Debs*—was unionization.

Unionization took place outside the lawmaking process. It represented a form of self-help. It also contained a democratic element. Unionization was a means of joining together to promote common goals. As Brewer saw it:

> Labor organizations are the needed and proper complement of capital organizations. They often work wholesome restraints on the greed, the unscrupulous rapacity which dominates much of capital; and the fact that they bring together a multitude of tiny forces, each helpless in a solitary struggle with capital, enables labor to secure its just rights.[14]

---

5 Ibid.
6 Ibid.
7 Ibid.
8 Ibid., 39.
9 Ibid.

10 Ibid., 41.
11 Ibid., 39.
12 Ibid., 41.
13 Ibid., 41.
14 Ibid., 42.

Chapter III: *The Maintenance of Public Order*

Brewer's point, of course, was not to celebrate organized labor but rather to attack its excesses. He decried "the improper use of labor organizations to destroy the freedom of the laborer, and control the uses of capital."[15] In this charge, Brewer was not referring to the typical union demands for ceilings on the number of hours worked and standardized wages, although he did mention these derisively in passing. He was instead referring to a more dramatic form of organizational activity—the mass strike, "the assumption of control over the employer's property, and blocking the access of laborers to it."[16] This appropriation occurred, Brewer claimed, largely through the power of the picket line:

> When a thousand laborers gather around a railroad track, and say to those who seek employment that they had better not, and when that advice is supplemented every little while by a terrible assault on one who disregards it, every one knows that something more than advice is intended. It is coercion, force; it is the effort of the many, by the mere weight of numbers, to compel the one to do their bidding.[17]

This "effort of the many" was for Brewer itself a form of coercion or violence, tantamount to a taking of the property of the employer. It also constituted an interference with the employee's freedom to contract for his personal services and in that sense was a taking of the employee's property. Brewer went on to link these various takings of property to grosser, more universally condemned forms of violence: assault and murder. The Homestead Strike of 1892, with all its violence and cruelty, was still fresh in the memory of those who heard his speech.[18] Brewer drew on those memories to establish the connection between the mass strike and physical violence: "Weihe, the head of a reputable labor organization, may only open the door to lawlessness; but Berkman, the anarchist and assassin, will be the first to pass through; and thus it will be always and everywhere."[19]

At this point in his speech, Brewer raised the stakes. Having first identified the coerciveness inherent in the mass strike and explained how it constituted an appropriation of property, and having then suggested how that activity could naturally lead to the kind of physical violence everyone abhors, he proceeded to move his audience to a near apocalyptic vision—that mass strikes were not minor or discrete disturbances of the status quo

---

[15] Ibid., 40.
[16] Ibid.
[17] Ibid.
[18] On the Homestead Strike, see Chapter 2, note 67.
[19] "Nation's Safeguard," 40. William Weihe was president of the Amalgamated Association of Iron and Steel Workers during the Homestead Strike and was known as a conservative who abhorred labor strife. During the strike, Alexander Berkman, a Russian-born anarchist, attempted to assassinate Henry Frick, chairman of the board of Carnegie Steel.

but instead threatened the entire social order. They had the quality of the extraordinary and the revolutionary. Referring to the Homestead Strike, he reminded his audience that pending in the Pennsylvania courts was "an inquiry as to whether this disturbance of social order did not amount to treason."[20]

Near the end of his speech, Brewer dramatically altered his tone. He added a personal note: "While preparing this address I had a dream."[21] His dream was one familiar to anxious lecturers: He could not decipher his text and was forced to extemporize. He mentioned (or fabricated) the dream to wake the audience and to alert them to the importance of what was soon to follow. It was a warning:

> Who does not perceive that the mere fact of numbers is beginning to assert itself? Who does not hear the old demagogic cry, "*Vox populi vox Dei*" (paraphrased to-day, "the majority are always right"), constantly invoked to justify disregard of those guaranties which have hitherto been deemed sufficient to give protection to private property?[22]

Brewer then proceeded to denounce "the black flag of anarchism, flaunting destruction to property, and, therefore [the] relapse of society to barbarism."[23] There also loomed, he said, "the red flag of socialism, inviting a redistribution of property which, in order to secure the vaunted equality, must be repeated again and again at constantly decreasing intervals."[24] And with an apparent reference to the movement to nationalize industry spawned by Bellamy's utopian novel, *Looking Backward*, Brewer spoke of that "colorless piece of baby-cloth, which suggests that the State take all property and direct all the life and work of individuals as if they were little children."[25]

In the end, Brewer was sustained by a spirit approaching religious faith. He was optimistic about the capacity of social institutions—particularly the courts, insulated as they were from the pressure of "the multitudes"—to guide and control the changes taking place in America and to preserve the public order. But the element of alarm that soon would animate his opinion in *Debs* was unmistakable: "Who does not see the wide unrest that fills the land; who does not feel that vast social changes are

---

[20] Ibid. "Treason" meant treason against the State of Pennsylvania, as defined by a Civil War statute to be "levy[ing] war against the same, or . . . adher[ing] to the enemies thereof. . . ." Act of Mar. 31, 1860, Public Law No. 385, as reprinted in The Homestead Case, 1 Pa. D. 785, 789 (1892).

[21] "Nation's Safeguard," 46.
[22] Ibid.
[23] Ibid., 47.
[24] Ibid.
[25] Ibid. On *Looking Backward, 2000–1887*, see Chapter 2, text accompanying notes 64 and 65.

impending, and realize that those changes must be guided in justice to safety and peace or they will culminate in revolution?"[26]

I

Hysterical? Maybe. But the social unrest that characterized the 1880s and 1890s suggests that Brewer had cause for alarm. The long hours, low pay, and unhealthy working conditions of industrial workers; the huge disparity between their standard of living and that of their employers; and the frequent downturns in the economy, including depressions in 1873 and 1893 that each lasted four years, all provided fertile soil for conflict between capital and labor.[27] Strikes abounded: In 1886 alone there were 1,400, involving over 9,800 establishments and nearly 500,000 workers.[28] The figures for the next year were even higher. The violence that marked many of these confrontations was epitomized by the Haymarket Riot in 1886, in which police fired at rallying workers after a bomb exploded in their midst;[29] the Homestead Strike in 1892 (which Brewer evoked in his mention of Berkman), in which Pinkerton detectives and laborers met in bloody battle; and the frequent confrontations between authorities and loosely organized bands of unemployed workers, the best known of which was Coxey's Army.[30]

The depression of 1893 was particularly severe, comparable to the Great Depression of the 1930s. In 1894 unemployment rose to an average of approximately 30 percent in the nonagricultural labor force and may have climbed as high as 50 percent in manufacturing and construction.[31] At the beginning of this downturn, the company that manufactured Pullman sleeping cars announced an austerity measure. It reduced wages between 17 and 40 percent but refused to lower the rent on company-owned housing. The workers responded in May 1894 by calling for a strike. Soon the dispute broadened. The American Railway Union, meeting in Chicago, voted to authorize a "sympathetic strike," an action that today we would call a secondary boycott. The resolution required union members to stop handling any train with Pullman cars unless the company would consent

---

[26] "Nation's Safeguard," 46.

[27] See Chapter 2.

[28] Commissioner of Labor, *3d Annual Report, 1887, Strikes and Lockouts* (Washington, D.C.: Government Printing Office, 1888), 12. See generally Nell Irvin Painter, *Standing at Armageddon: The United States, 1877–1919* (New York: W. W. Norton, 1987).

[29] See Chapter 2.

[30] On Coxey's Army, see Chapter 2, text accompanying note 70. Fear of social unrest and a growth of volunteer militias led to the building of many new armories during this period. See Robert M. Fogelson, *America's Armories: Architecture, Society and Public Order* (Cambridge: Harvard University Press, 1989).

[31] Robert Higgs, *Crisis and Leviathan: Critical Episodes in the Growth of American Government* (New York: Oxford University Press, 1987), 84–85.

to arbitration. Management refused. The union's deadline passed and in the closing days of June 1894, the strike began.[32]

Coordinating the collective action was Eugene Debs, then head of the American Railway Union. His center of operations was Chicago, but the union had a national following, with some 150,000 members in 465 locals. While Chicago bore the brunt of the strike, its effect was felt nationwide, in part thanks to the coordinated action of locals throughout the country, but more generally because Chicago was the hub of the national rail system. Some sixty thousand workers went on strike in Chicago and in the region to the south and the west. The trains of the nation ground virtually to a halt, and with them so did the shipment of the nation's vital supplies, including food, fuel, and livestock.[33] The dispute with Pullman had escalated into a paralysis of the rail system, and with that turn of events, the strike acquired a transcendent significance. The government responded with all its might and all its resources.[34]

On July 2, 1894, soon after the strike began, Attorney General Richard Olney managed to obtain an ex parte injunction from a federal court against the continuation of the strike. The order barred Debs from issuing commands to the officers and members of the American Railway Union and ordered all those who had notice of the injunction to stop interfering with the operation of the rail system. When the injunction was first read to the mobs on the tracks in Chicago, it was greeted with jibes, cheers, and groans—and continued resistance. Issuing the injunction was, to use an analogy attributed to Debs's counsel, as effective as "read[ing] a writ of injunction to Lee's army."[35] The United States marshal had hastily recruited hundreds of deputies, and had them at hand when he read the injunction to the mob, but he knew that he did not have the force to clear the tracks. On that very day he telegraphed for troops.

---

[32] See generally Almont Lindsey, *The Pullman Strike: The Story of a Unique Experiment and of a Great Labor Upheaval* (Chicago: University of Chicago Press, 1942). For accounts less sympathetic to Debs and the strikers, see Allan Nevins, *Grover Cleveland: A Study in Courage* (New York: Dodd, Mead, 1958), and Samuel Yellen, *American Labor Struggles* (New York: Harcourt, Brace, 1936; repr. New York: Arno Press, 1969).

[33] Higgs, *Crisis and Leviathan*, 94.

[34] The government operations were directed by the attorney general, Richard Olney, and a special government attorney, Edwin Walker. Both Olney and Walker were successful corporate lawyers, naturally with close ties to the railroads. In fact, Walker had represented the railroad association just the week before the strike. See Nick Salvatore, *Eugene V. Debs: Citizen and Socialist* (Urbana: University of Illinois Press, 1982), 131; Lindsey, *Pullman Strike*, 154; and John W. Leonard, ed., *Who's Who in America, 1899–1900* (Chicago: A. N. Marquis, 1899), 760.

[35] 158 U.S. at 597. The U.S. Reports does not indicate which of Debs's counsel, Clarence Darrow, S. S. Gregory, or Lyman Trumbull, made this argument, but from newspaper accounts it is almost certain that it was Darrow. See, e.g., "Debs Case Is Closed," *Inter Ocean*, Mar. 27, 1895, p. 5, col. 1.

Chapter III: *The Maintenance of Public Order*

The situation had escalated and Debs responded accordingly:

> The first shot fired by the regular soldiers at the mobs here will be the signal for a civil war. I believe this as firmly as I believe in the ultimate success of our course. Bloodshed will follow, and 90 per cent. of the people of the United States will be arrayed against the other 10 per cent. And I would not care to be arrayed against the laboring people in the contest, or find myself out of the ranks of labor when the struggle ended. I do not say this as an alarmist, but calmly and thoughtfully.[36]

While the full-scale "civil war" that Debs prophesied did not materialize, the confrontation between the government and the working people that he feared did.[37] When the federal troops arrived, crowds responded by stoning, tipping, looting, and burning railroad cars. Strikers misplaced switches and detached and derailed cars and engines.[38] Two thousand cars were destroyed and twenty people died.[39] To restore order, the government deployed almost two thousand regular army troops from Kansas, Nebraska, Michigan, and New York and deputized an additional five thousand men as marshals.

Unlike the injunctions that restrained railway strikes in the 1870s and 1880s,[40] the Pullman injunction was predicated on the recently promulgated Sherman Antitrust Act.[41] The attorney general also used the power conferred on him by the Sherman Act to prosecute criminally those who participate in conspiracies to restrain trade.[42] A federal grand jury was convened while the strikers flouted the injunction, and on July 10 the principal officers of the American Railway Union, including Debs, were indicted and arrested for violating the Sherman Act. Debs quickly made bail, but the

---

[36] *New York Times*, July 5, 1894, p. 2, col. 3. The statement was made to a reporter of the United Press, and ran in the *New York Times* under the headline, "Debs Wildly Talks Civil War. First Shot from Soldiers, He Says, Will Cause Revolution."

[37] Salvatore, *Eugene V. Debs*, 134.

[38] United States Strike Commission, *Report on the Chicago Strike of June–July 1894*, S. Exec. Doc. No. 7, 53d Cong., 3d Sess., XLV (1895). Contemporary witnesses differ on the level of participation in the rioting by strikers, some arguing that they played little to no role, others claiming that the strikers instigated the destruction. Compare the testimony of Police Officer Nicholas Hunt, ibid., 385, with that of N. D. Hutton, reporter for the *Chicago Tribune*,

ibid., 399.

[39] Higgs, *Crisis and Leviathan*, 95.

[40] See William E. Forbath, *Law and the Shaping of the American Labor Movement* (Cambridge: Harvard University Press, 1991), 66–79. The first federal injunctions against "sympathetic strikes" were issued by federal courts that held bankrupt railroad lines in receivership. Before passage of the Sherman Act, some courts construed the Interstate Commerce Act of 1887 as authority for enjoining boycotts that affected interstate rail traffic.

[41] Sherman Antitrust Act, Ch. 647, Sect. 4, 26 Stat. 209, 209 (1890). The injunction is reprinted in United States v. Debs, 64 F. 724 (C.C.N.D. Ill. 1894) at 726–27.

[42] Sherman Antitrust Act, Sect. 1.

momentum of the strike had been broken. Then, on July 17, the circuit judge signed a warrant for Debs's arrest for disobeying the July 2 injunction. This time Debs turned himself in and decided against making bail. He explained: "The poor striker who is arrested would be thrown in a cell. We are no better than he."[43] The government lawyer in charge of the case had another explanation: Debs either was attempting to make himself a martyr or was simply exhausted.[44] Either way, the strike was effectively over. On July 18 Pullman announced that its shops would soon reopen and on the nineteenth the grand jury was disbanded.

Debs was convicted of criminal contempt for disobeying the July 2 injunction and in December 1894 was sentenced to six months' imprisonment. During that same winter, Debs was also tried on the criminal conspiracy charge under the Sherman Act, but the trial came to a halt when a juror became ill, and the jury was discharged. A year later, in the spring of 1896, a nolle prosequi was entered in the record, ending the prosecution. The reasons for that action are not known. Almont Lindsey, the author of the standard history of the strike, is willing to believe the boast of Clarence Darrow, Debs's lawyer, that the jury was eleven to one for acquittal and has argued that the prosecutor was "convinced of the futility" of going forward.[45] But there is another, equally plausible, explanation: By the time the nolle prosequi had been filed, the Supreme Court had affirmed the injunction and Debs's conviction for criminal contempt and had thereby legitimated the overall strategy of the federal government; Debs had served the contempt sentence; the threat posed by Debs and his union had already passed. The battle had been won.

II

Although the Pullman Strike began in a rather ordinary way, it quickly led to a disruption of the national rail system that seemed to fulfill Brewer's deepest fears. The events in Chicago provoked a coordinated response by all the branches of the federal government—the president, the attorney general, a federal equity court, a federal grand jury, the United States marshals, and the army. Even the Congress made an appearance, so to speak, in the form of the Sherman Act—the statutory basis of both the injunction and the criminal proceeding initiated by the attorney general. It was therefore not at all surprising that the Supreme Court's opinion

---

[43] *Chicago Times*, July 18, 1894, p. 1, col. 5.
[44] Walker to Olney, July 20, 1894, in *Appendix to the Annual Report of the* *Attorney-General of the United States for the Year 1896* (Washington, D.C.: Government Printing Office, 1896), 91–93.
[45] Ibid., 303–304.

turned out to be no ordinary one but rather, in essence, a disquisition justifying massive intervention by a government that found itself in "the throes of rebellion or revolution."[46] The opinion was written by Justice Brewer and, to note one of its most remarkable features, the decision was unanimous. On few other occasions did the justices reach such complete agreement.

Eugene Debs sought review in the Supreme Court of his criminal contempt conviction by means of a writ of habeas corpus. According to the standard rule, the Court was not to determine whether the injunction that Debs had disobeyed was appropriately issued; as stressed by Olney in his argument before the Supreme Court, the only issue open for review was whether the circuit court had jurisdiction.[47] Accordingly, the Court formulated the question before it in jurisdictional terms. But this was only a formal gesture, and the Court did not confine itself to this technical question. Rather, it tried to explain why the injunction itself was a proper exercise of judicial power.

In a similar spirit, the Supreme Court reached for the broadest possible grounds for its decision. The circuit court had found ample authority for its action in the Sherman Act, which prohibited conspiracies in restraint of trade and authorized the attorney general to enforce that prohibition through injunctive proceedings.[48] But the Supreme Court declined to follow the circuit court's example and instead decided to rest its decision on constitutional grounds. There were, perhaps, certain strategic advantages to this choice of law. The Court might have thought it inappropriate to apply the Sherman Act to organized labor when just four or five months prior, in the *E. C. Knight* case, it had declined to apply the statute to the Sugar Trust.[49] It is also possible that the Court wanted to rest the injunction on grounds less vulnerable to legislative revision. But to my mind it is more plausible that the choice of law, like the Court's unwillingness to confine itself to a narrow review of the question of jurisdiction, reflected a conscious desire to reach beyond the technical requirements of the case in order to define the powers of the state in the constitutional design. The events in Chicago raised profound questions about the constitutional sys-

---

[46] 158 U.S. at 597.

[47] *Inter Ocean*, Mar. 27, 1895, p. 5, col. 1. For the general rule see, e.g., *In re Sawyer*, 124 U.S. 200 (1888). The Court in *Sawyer* understood jurisdiction expansively to mean not only the authority to adjudicate but also "equity jurisdiction"—the authority to employ an equitable remedy. *Debs* used the rubric of jurisdiction but went even further than *Sawyer*. While the *Sawyer* Court suggested that the adequacy of legal remedies did not go to the question of "equity jurisdiction," Brewer's opinion nonetheless addressed the adequacy issue.

[48] 64 F. 724 (C.C.N.D. Ill. 1894).

[49] United States v. E. C. Knight Co., 156 U.S. 1 (1895).

tem and called for answers that were couched in the highest terms of generality.

For Brewer and the other justices, the Pullman Strike required government intervention to maintain the public order. Such preservation of order was the most important function of the government under the social contract tradition. In his Albany speech, Brewer identified security as "the chief end of government,"[50] and security seemed to be precisely what was at issue in Chicago. One of Debs's counsel before the Court, Clarence Darrow, did not allay Brewer's fears. In fact, his brief defiantly reinforced them, in much the same way Debs had done when he warned of civil war.

Darrow's brief was a remarkable document.[51] In it he spoke about the rise of the factory system and the need for collective action on the part of the workers. Collective action—specifically, the strike and the sympathetic strike—was, he argued, labor's only source of strength.[52] Darrow also described the basic antagonism between labor and capital, and acknowledged that violence would probably—not just possibly—accompany strikes.[53] Darrow concluded the brief with a moving portrayal of the reality and unfortunate inevitability of such conflict and violence:

> Strikes are deplorable, and so are their causes. All men who engage in them hope for a time when better social relations will make them as unnecessary as any other form of warfare will some day be. But under the present conditions of industrial life, with the present conflicting interests of capital and labor, each perhaps blindly seeking for more perfect social adjustments, strikes and lockouts are incidents of industrial life. They are not justified because men love social strife and industrial war, but because in the present system of industrial evolution to deprive workingmen of this power would be to strip and bind them and leave them helpless as the prey of the great and strong. It would be to despoil one army of every means of defense and aggression while on the field

---

50 "Nation's Safeguard," 39.

51 See Chapter 11 for a comparison with Darrow's performance in the *Turner* case.

52 Brief and Argument for Petitioners at 78, *In re* Debs, 158 U.S. 564 (1895).

53 He wrote:
[I]f it were conceded that violence generally followed strikes, it would by no means follow that a great body of men would not have the right to lay down the tools and implements of their trade to better the conditions of themselves and their fellow-men, although growing out of [such action] violence, bloodshed and crime would surely come. As violence and bloodshed frequently follow strikes, so do they frequently follow lockouts and reductions of wages, but these facts are not sufficient to deprive men of their free moral agency and make their acts subject to the control of courts.
Brief and Argument for Petitioners at 95–96.

of battle, and in the presence of an enemy with boundless resources and all the equipment of warfare at their command.[54]

Darrow realized that some concession to the principle of public order was necessary, but he sought to confine that concession to the minimum: the criminal prosecution of those who actually committed acts of violence. Since these prosecutions would fall to the states, Darrow's scheme had the effect of excluding the federal government completely. Darrow was also careful to guard against vicarious responsibility: "If it is lawful for men to organize, and in accordance with the organization to cease to labor, they can not be regarded as criminals because violence, bloodshed or crime follows such a general strike."[55] The argument explicitly presupposed the legality of the strike, and to support that premise Darrow quoted extensively from Justice Harlan's circuit court opinion in *Arthur v. Oakes*,[56] in which the right to strike was linked with the right to quit work, inviolable under common law and even more emphatically under the Thirteenth Amendment.

The image Darrow offered was of two clashing armies, labor and capital. He portrayed government as a neutral third force, which could intervene only in the most narrow and circumscribed manner to punish, after the fact, specific acts of violence defined in the most elemental sense. In contrast, the starting point for the justices, as suggested in Brewer's Albany speech and the *Debs* opinion itself, was entirely different. Government was not to stand by as a neutral bystander and watch "civilization" destroyed by the warring factions. It had a right and even a duty to preserve the public order, even if that meant intervening on behalf of one side or the other and doing so in a preemptive manner. Change was, of course, possible, but change had to come through the methods and procedures prescribed by the constitutional system itself.

Darrow's overall strategy was to separate the violence from the strike and confine the coercive power of the state to dealing with the violence.

---

[54] Ibid., 96. In his biography, Nick Salvatore puts Debs's position in more conciliatory terms: "That Debs never intended to lead a revolution in 1894 is quite clear . . . Debs lashed out at the corporation for *its* revolutionary transformation of American society." Salvatore, *Eugene V. Debs*, 134. According to Salvatore, Debs rejected the ethic of survival of the fittest and wished to curb the predatory behavior of corporations and to return to workers their dignity and self-respect. Ibid., 63–64, 129. Debs viewed mass strikes not as a threat to individual freedoms, as Brewer did, but rather as a means of democratizing the economy and thereby restoring social harmony. Ibid., 124–25.

[55] Brief and Argument for Petitioners at 95.

[56] 63 F. 310 (7th Cir. 1894).

For Brewer, this separation was impossible. As the Albany speech revealed, he saw mass picketing itself not as a legitimate element of industrial life but as a form of violence—an interference with the freedom of others to work and an appropriation of property. The predicate for intervention was violence, but since Brewer saw coercion and appropriation as forms of violence, and since both were present in Pullman, the strike could be prohibited: In order to preserve the public order, Eugene Debs could be restrained from persuading others to strike and from exercising a leadership role in the strike.

To be precise, the labor injunction legitimated by *Debs* did not embrace all strikes, but only those that created "forcible obstructions." As Brewer put it, "The right of any laborer, or any number of laborers, to quit work was not challenged. The scope and purpose of the bill was only to restrain forcible obstructions. . . ."[57] Although the injunction seemed to be limited by context, labor rightly feared that this limitation would prove meaningless. Brewer and the other justices would probably have acknowledged that a rule cast in terms of "forcible obstructions" would tend to inhibit workers from exercising their right to strike, but they would have also insisted that such a rule would not "strip and bind" the working men and leave them "helpless." They were still free to pursue their interests through other, more formal means, such as legislation or adjudication:

> A most earnest and eloquent appeal was made to us in eulogy of the heroic spirit of those who threw up their employment, and gave up their means of earning a livelihood, not in defence of their own rights, but in sympathy for and to assist others whom they believed to be wronged. We yield to none in our admiration of any act of heroism or self-sacrifice, but we may be permitted to add that it is a lesson which cannot be learned too soon or too thoroughly that under this government of and by the people the means of redress of all wrongs are through the courts and at the ballot-box, and that no wrong, real or fancied, carries with it legal warrant to invite as a means of redress the cooperation of a mob, with its accompanying acts of violence.[58]

In consigning labor to the courts and the ballot box, Brewer must surely have been aware of the difficulties that lay ahead. Capital was no more likely to capitulate in the legislatures or the courtrooms of the nation than it had in the streets. But Brewer remained unmoved—leaving us to wonder whether his stance stemmed from his attachment to the established order, or from his high estimate of the magnificence of his civilization, or from his desire to preserve the public order at all costs, or even possibly a combination of all three.

---

[57] 158 U.S. at 598.   [58] Ibid., 598–99.

III

The difficulty of *Debs*, both then and now, does not arise from any doubt as to the correctness of Brewer's plea, stated in the most general terms, on behalf of public order. Such a plea would always receive acceptance in the law, at least by any judge who took seriously his sworn duty to uphold the Constitution. The intellectual challenge posed by the *Debs* case arose because it was the national rather than the state government that restored order and because the national government had used the injunction as part of its overall strategy for doing so. To justify this course of action, Brewer drew from three different political and legal sources: the Commerce Clause, the Civil War, and public nuisance doctrine. His opinion was something of a tour de force.

I have spoken of the social contract tradition in America as though there were only one contract, but in truth there might well have been two: the first legitimating the states; the second, concretized by the Constitution, creating the national government. While in the first instance the people conferred upon the states the power to act as policemen, in the second the states authorized the national government to pursue more specialized and circumscribed ends. The problem confronting the justice sitting down to write *Debs* was that the maintenance of order was not one of the ends that the Constitution assigned to the federal government. Security, Brewer's "chief end of government," was a traditional function of the states.

In 1894, the governor of Illinois was John Peter Altgeld, who was identified with labor and more radical causes.[59] Shortly before the Pullman Strike, he had commuted the death sentences of some of those convicted of the Haymarket bombings. Although he was prepared to deploy state law enforcement resources against actual violence, and four thousand state troops were in fact mobilized, Altgeld was not in the least inclined to enforce the broader prohibitions of the injunction nor to request the assistance of the federal government in pursuing this objective. In fact, he protested federal intervention in the Chicago crisis at every turn, and as a result the federal government had to proceed without his cooperation and over his objection. Washington felt that Altgeld's response was insufficient and that federal intervention was necessary. But the question of authority remained: A default of the state did not by itself confer on the national government authority to intervene. A central constitutional tenet of the nineteenth century—accepted by Brewer and all the others—was that the national government did not have a police power, and the perceived inade-

---

[59] See Harry Barnard, *"Eagle Forgotten": The Life of John Peter Altgeld* (Indianapolis: Bobbs-Merrill, 1938), and Ray Ginger, *Altgeld's America: The Lincoln Ideal versus Changing Realities* (New York: Funk & Wagnalls, 1958).

quacy of a state's exercise of its police power did not necessarily work a transfer of that power to the national government.

Brewer's task, then, was to identify in the Constitution specific ends—not just the maintenance of order—that had been entrusted to the national government and that were threatened by the Chicago disturbance. Clearly, one such end was the operation of a national postal system. This was mentioned by Brewer, but to rely on that as the basis of the federal intervention seemed like relying on the Sherman Act—a theory inappropriate for the occasion, trivializing all that was involved. Brewer turned to the Commerce Clause, which, in the nineteenth century, had a wholly different stature than it does today.

The Commerce Clause confers upon Congress the power to regulate commerce among the states, but it has been read to encompass much more: as creating a common market or economic union within the United States. At the time of *Debs*, the Commerce Clause was seen as embodying a principle—often referred to today as the "dormant" Commerce Clause—that nullified state laws that interfered with the free flow of commerce. It did not require a congressional enactment to become fully operative. State laws interfering with the free flow of interstate commerce were prohibited by the Commerce Clause itself. Although the roots of the dormant Commerce Clause reached back to the Marshall Court and most notably to a dictum in *Gibbons v. Ogden*,[60] the principle achieved a very special prominence in the late 1880s and early 1890s, when it was used by the Supreme Court to invalidate, for example, state rate regulations[61] and state prohibition laws.[62]

The "forcible obstruction" that Brewer referred to as the proper subject of the *Debs* injunction was the obstruction of the free flow of commerce among the states. As we have seen, this obstruction was caused by the American Railway Union and the strikers, a circumstance that created something of a problem, because the precedents regarding the dormant Commerce Clause concerned interferences with the free flow of goods by states rather than private organizations. Justice Brewer did not try to find state action in Illinois's refusal to clear the tracks but instead solved the problem by asking a question he thought could have only one answer: "If a State with its recognized powers of sovereignty is impotent to obstruct interstate commerce, can it be that any mere voluntary association of individuals within the limits of that State has a power which the State itself does not possess?"[63]

---

[60] 22 U.S. (9 Wheat.) 1 (1824). See also Brown v. Maryland, 25 U.S. (12 Wheat.) 419 (1827).
[61] Wabash, St. L. & Pac. Ry. v. Illinois, 118 U.S. 557 (1886). See Chapters 7 and 9.
[62] Leisy v. Hardin, 135 U.S. 100 (1890). See Chapter 9.
[63] 158 U.S. at 581.

Chapter III: *The Maintenance of Public Order*

The issue in *Debs* was not whether the action of the American Railway Union should be declared "unconstitutional," as a state statute might be, on the theory that it obstructed the free flow of commerce. Rather, the question was whether it was proper for the attorney general to seek an injunction against the obstruction and for the courts to grant that relief. The emphasis on the precise remedial question before the Court did not relieve Brewer of the obligation to ground the right allegedly being protected by the suit—that of free passage—in the Constitution, or to explain why the right was protected from interferences by private entities such as the American Railway Union. But the focus on remedy did enable Brewer to supplement his constitutional analysis with judge-made law regarding public nuisance. He was able to fuse equity and constitutional law in order to finesse the state action problem.

Equity allowed an attorney general to bring a suit to abate a public nuisance—for example, to remove a boulder lying across a highway. The mobs that roamed the Chicago tracks in 1894, like the boulder removed by the public nuisance doctrine, were, in Brewer's eyes, obstructing the nation's highways. The problem was, however, that equity was surrounded and thus circumscribed by a number of doctrines—maxims—that tended to limit the applicability of the public nuisance rule.

One maxim held, as Brewer noted, "that equity only interferes for the protection of property, and that the government has no property interest."[64] Brewer was quick to add that a "sufficient reply is that the United States have a property in the mails,"[65] but in the final analysis he did not want to restrict the government's ability to seek an injunction in that way. He instead appeared willing to repudiate the maxim. Like the decision not to confine review to jurisdictional defects and the decision not to rest the injunction on the Sherman Act but on the Commerce Clause itself, Brewer sought a more general foundation for the standing of the United States:

> Every government, entrusted, by the very terms of its being, with powers and duties to be exercised and discharged for the general welfare, has a right to apply to its own courts for any proper assistance in the exercise of the one and the discharge of the other, and it is no sufficient answer to its appeal to one of those courts that it has no pecuniary interest in the matter. The obligations which it is under to promote the interest of all, and to prevent the wrongdoing of one resulting in injury to the general welfare, is often of itself sufficient to give it a standing in court.[66]

Brewer was not unmindful of the need to impose some limits on the power of the attorney general to initiate injunctive proceedings, but he shied away

---

[64] Ibid., 583.
[65] Ibid.

[66] Ibid., 584.

from defining those limits in terms of property rights. Rather, he insisted that "the wrongs complained of [be] such as affect the public at large" and that they not involve "private controversy between individuals."[67] He also required that the wrongs regard "matters which by the Constitution are entrusted to the care of the Nation, and concerning which the Nation owes the duty to all the citizens of securing to them their common rights."[68]

A second maxim denied equity courts the power to enjoin a crime, and in response to that Brewer wrote:

> Something more than the threatened commission of an offense against the laws of the land is necessary to call into exercise the injunctive powers of the court. There must be some interferences, actual or threatened, with property or rights of a pecuniary nature, but when such interferences appear the jurisdiction of a court of equity arises, and is not destroyed by the fact that they are accompanied by or are themselves violations of the criminal law.[69]

At first reading, this passage seems to repudiate what Brewer had said earlier about the standing of the attorney general, namely, that it arose from his duty to protect, not property rights, but the public welfare. There is, however, no contradiction. Whether or not the attorney general could demonstrate that a property interest was threatened, the property of others might be threatened and that would be sufficient to establish equity jurisdiction—a jurisdiction that would not be defeated by the mere presence of an overlapping criminal jurisdiction.

A third and closely related maxim limits the jurisdiction of equity to situations where the ordinary processes of law fail. "It is well settled," he wrote, "that, as a general rule, equity will not interfere, where the object sought can be as well attained in the ordinary tribunals."[70] This maxim must have been particularly troubling to Brewer, because only several months earlier a special sensitivity to the unique aspects of the contempt power had led him to object to a congressional scheme that used the courts in enforcing subpoenas of the Interstate Commerce Commission.[71] Under that scheme, the equity court could issue an order compelling compliance and punish disobedience of that order through contempt.

In that earlier case, Brewer dissented and complained because no showing had been made as to why the ordinary legal route—a prosecution

---

[67] Ibid., 586.
[68] Ibid.
[69] Ibid., 593.
[70] Ibid., 591, quoting Attorney General ex rel. Gloucester City v. Brown, 24 N.J. Eq. 89, 91–92 (1873).
[71] ICC v. Brimson, 154 U.S. 447 (1894). Brewer's dissent was not filed in time for inclusion with the rest of the volume, so it is printed at 155 U.S. 3.

for violating a statutory obligation to comply with an ICC subpoena—would have been inadequate. The majority was apparently willing to allow Congress the discretion to choose between equity and the criminal law, but Brewer feared that the scheme chosen would compromise the ideal of judicial independence. The courts would become a mere instrument of congressional policy. Brewer also objected to the arrangement because it entailed a derogation of certain procedural guarantees like trial by jury. These guarantees would be available to those prosecuted in an ordinary court of law for violating a criminal statute but not in a contempt proceeding, and thus were indirectly protected by the maxim that denied equity the power to intervene "where the object can be as well attained in the ordinary tribunals."

For Brewer, then, the power of the court to grant an injunction in *Debs* could not rise from the fact that the attorney general thought it necessary, or from the fact that Congress, in the Sherman Act, actually authorized such relief. There had to be something more, some special circumstance, independently assessed by a court, that would justify supplanting the more ordinary method (such as a criminal prosecution) for dealing with the violence expected from the strike. Brewer scrupulously insisted on this point, yet found in the events on the tracks in Chicago in 1894 that special circumstance: "If ever there was a special exigency, one which demanded that the court should do all that courts can do, it was disclosed by this bill. . . ."[72]

The "special exigency" that Brewer spoke of in *Debs* arose from two interrelated factors. One was the vastness and importance of the interests threatened by the disturbance—if not the public order itself, then surely the operation of the nation's rail system, whose continued functioning was vital to the health of the national economy.[73] The threat to these interests made it imperative for courts to do all they could. It also made it inappropriate for the government to rely exclusively on such after-the-fact legal remedies as criminal prosecution, which must await the harm or a good measure of it before the actual proceeding is begun. To rely exclusively on such retrospective remedies requires a certain patience and discipline, more than one could demand of the executive: "Have the vast interests of the nation in interstate commerce, and in the transportation of the mails,

---

[72] 158 U.S. at 592.

[73] On the importance of the railroads, see Alfred D. Chandler, Jr., comp. and ed., *The Railroads—The Nation's First Big Business: Sources and Readings* (New York: Harcourt, Brace & World, 1965), 21–43; Albert Fishlow, *American Railroads and the Transformation of the Antebellum Economy* (Cambridge: Harvard University Press, 1966); and Robert William Fogel, *Railroads and American Economic Growth: Essays in Econometric History* (Baltimore: Johns Hopkins Press, 1964).

no other protection than lies in the possible punishment of those who interfere with it? To ask the question is to answer it."[74]

The second special circumstance that rendered the criminal law inadequate (and that distinguished *Debs* from the ICC subpoena case) was the risk of jury nullification—that a jury would acquit even though a violation was proved. Every criminal prosecution poses such a risk; indeed, that may be the very point of the jury trial right and a reason for strictly limiting equity. What Brewer emphasized in *Debs*, however, were the unusual circumstances in Chicago—arguably absent in the ICC case—that made the risk of jury nullification especially great and especially unpalatable:

> If all the inhabitants of a State, or even a great body of them, should combine to obstruct interstate commerce or the transportation of the mails, prosecutions for such offenses had in such a community would be doomed in advance to failure. And if the certainty of such failure was known, and the national government had no other way to enforce the freedom of interstate commerce and the transportation of the mails than by prosecution and punishment for interference therewith, the whole interests of the nation in these respects would be at the absolute mercy of a portion of the inhabitants of that single State.[75]

Having thus justified resort to equity in terms of the special risks of a jury trial to the nation, it was no surprise that the Court was unsympathetic to counsel's final and perhaps most moving plea—that Debs's contempt conviction violated his constitutional right to trial by jury:

> [T]he power of a court to make an order carries with it the equal power to punish for a disobedience of that order, and the inquiry as to the question of disobedience has been, from time immemorial, the special function of the court. . . . To submit the question of disobedience to another tribunal, be it a jury or another court, would operate to deprive the proceeding of half its efficiency.[76]

In this way, Brewer surmounted one maxim of equity after another and was able to bolster his Commerce Clause analysis by reference to the traditional legal doctrine that allowed courts to order the removal of obstructions to public highways. Yet his job still remained unfinished; the analogy seemed strained. The American Railway Union and the mass action that it spurred were very different from a boulder on a highway, as Brewer well recognized in pointing to the special risk of jury nullification. Something more had to be said to justify the intervention by the judiciary.

---

[74] 158 U.S. at 581.
[75] Ibid., 581–82.

[76] Ibid., 594–95.

Chapter III: *The Maintenance of Public Order*

Sensing this need, Brewer introduced yet a third strand in his analysis: the Civil War. He saw the events in Chicago in 1894 as threatening the union—if not the political union, perhaps the economic one.

In the 1890s the Civil War was still a vibrant memory for the nation. All the justices had lived through it, and two—White and Harlan—had served in the armies (though on opposite sides). There were, of course, many lessons to be drawn from that extraordinary historic event, but Brewer mentioned only two. The first was that military action is sometimes necessary to preserve national interests, and the second, that action may sometimes have to be taken before specific congressional authorization can be obtained. In drawing these lessons from the Civil War experience, Brewer's intent was not to legitimate President Cleveland's use of the troops in Chicago (though that may have been a by-product of this particular discussion and the *Debs* decision as a whole). Rather, the purpose was to shape an argument to justify the power of the attorney general to seek an injunction. Brewer assumed the president could use the army to quell the mobs on the Chicago tracks through the direct application of force. He then drew on the familiar intuition that the greater power includes the lesser and concluded that the application for the injunction was entirely appropriate:

> [I]t is more to the praise than to the blame of the government, that, instead of determining for itself questions of right and wrong . . . and enforcing that determination by the club of the policeman and the bayonet of the soldier, it submitted all those questions to the peaceful determination of judicial tribunals. . . .[77]

A question could be raised about the notion that the injunction is the "lesser" strategy. True, the injunction contemplates a measure of public deliberation that would be absent in a purely military operation; on the other hand, the injunction implicates the courts in the peacekeeping endeavor. That involvement might compromise judicial independence (so treasured by Brewer) or it might lend a degree of legitimacy and authoritativeness to the executive's action otherwise lacking. Brewer's distinction between the greater and lesser is also confounded by the dependence of the injunctive strategy upon the use of arms: Without the military to execute its word, the issuance of the *Debs* injunction would have been—to revert to counsel's example—like "reading a writ to Lee's army." As an abstract matter, the greater may legitimate the lesser, but as a practical matter, the lesser requires the greater. The most serious objection, however, to Brewer's attempt to exploit the Civil War experience goes to his initial assump-

---

[77] Ibid., 583.

tion, namely, that the president could have deployed the military in Chicago without specific congressional authorization.

Brewer was not completely unmindful of the issue of congressional authorization. At an early point in his opinion, Brewer noted the "mass of legislation" establishing and maintaining the post office system, and also regulating the national rail system.[78] These statutes could be read as further evidence of the national commitment to an economic union. They also allowed Brewer to depict the use of troops to quell the Chicago disturbance as wholly consistent with congressional purposes. It was as though he was anticipating Justice Jackson's view in *Youngstown*, affirming the power of the executive branch when it acts in accord with the will of Congress.[79]

There was also the possibility that the executive's action was actually authorized by Congress. A statute on the books since the 1790s did provide that authority, for it specifically allowed the president to use the armed forces when "obstructions, combinations, or assemblages of persons, or rebellion against the authority of the Government of the United States, [make it] impracticable to enforce the laws of the United States . . . by the ordinary course of judicial proceedings."[80] But Brewer never mentioned the statute. Seeing the situation in Chicago as an emergency that put the nation at risk, a threat of the same nature if not the same magnitude as the Civil War, he may have thought statutory authorization for the president's action completely unnecessary: "If the emergency arises, the army of the Nation, and all its militia, are in the service of the Nation to compel obedience to its laws."[81] In his concluding passage, however, he drew back from this more robust view of the presidency and envisioned a coordinated strategy of the legislative and executive branches:

> [T]he powers thus conferred upon the national government are not dormant, but have been assumed and put into practical exercise by the legislation of Congress; that in the exercise of those powers it is competent for the nation to remove all obstructions upon highways, natural or artificial, to the passage of interstate commerce or the carrying of the mail; that while it may be competent for the government (through the executive branch and in the use of the entire executive power of the nation) to forcibly remove all such obstructions, it is equally within its competency to appeal to the civil courts for an inquiry and determination as to the existence and character of any alleged obstructions, and if such

[78] Ibid., 580.

[79] Youngstown Sheet & Tube Co. v. Sawyer, 343 U.S. 579, 637 (Jackson, J., concurring).

[80] An Act to provide for the Suppression of Rebellion against and Resistance to the Laws of the United States, Ch. 25, Sect. 1, 12 Stat. 281, 281 (1861), amending Ch. 36, 1 Stat. 424 (1795).

[81] 158 U.S. at 582.

are found to exist, or threaten to occur, to invoke the powers of those courts to remove or restrain such obstructions. . . .[82]

It should be noted, however, that the word "emergency" does not appear in this final formulation.

IV

The Chicago disturbance started as an ordinary strike but quickly took on extraordinary dimensions. It created a mass disorder, paralyzing the national rail and postal systems and threatening the very idea of an economic union. It occurred in a way and in circumstances that did not allow specific congressional action. The exceptional character of the events in Chicago was recognized at every turn of the Court's opinion. That is why the Court did not confine itself to a review of the formal jurisdictional defect; why it did not rely on the Sherman Act to sustain the injunction; why the Court could invoke and apply to the American Railway Union the doctrine prohibiting interferences with the free flow of commerce; why the attorney general had standing to bring suit even in the absence of showing injury to some pecuniary interest of the United States; why the ordinary processes of the law could not be trusted; and why the executive could speak on behalf of the nation, either through the application for the injunction or the use of bayonets.

The exceptional character of the Chicago events also made Darrow's plea for government neutrality in the class struggle implausible. If the events in Chicago truly threatened the public order, if they were as exceptional as the Court saw them, then it would be hard to expect the legal system to separate the strike and the violence and be content merely to punish the violence after the fact. The law would reach to control and extinguish the cause, even if that meant casting the balance against social change and self-determination. In the face of an incipient revolution the law can be expected, as Brewer said, "to do all that it can." That consists of a lot more than simply waiting for a criminal prosecution of those who happen to commit murder or arson in the course of their revolution.

For the Court, the *Debs* injunction was grounded in the nearly revolutionary character of the Pullman Strike and took its specific historical justification from the extraordinary character of those events. There was, however, a suspicion, nourished by the concluding paragraph of the opinion, that as a precedent the decision would not be so limited. Brewer and his

---

[82] Ibid., 599.

contemporaries saw the Pullman Strike in near-apocalyptic terms, but there was a tendency, so apparent in the Albany speech, to see all strikes in the same way. All involved an appropriation of capital and an interference with the right of workers to engage in productive labor; all contained elements of violence and coercion; all had the potential of threatening the public order, maybe even on the scale of Homestead or Chicago. There was a risk, therefore, that what was acceptable in an extraordinary situation would soon be accepted in the ordinary. In these circumstances the problem with the labor injunction may not be the *Debs* decision itself but rather the failure of the legal system to remember that Chicago in 1894 had been perceived as the equivalent of Fort Sumter.

CHAPTER IV

Pollock—*The Redistributive Function Denied*

HE TURMOIL of the summer of 1894 did not end with the disturbances on the tracks in Chicago. The struggle between labor and capital moved to the legislative halls, and in August 1894 Congress enacted an income tax measure that, because it fell only on the wealthiest, was seen by many as an attack on capital. In the spring of 1895, only weeks after *Debs*, the Supreme Court addressed the statute, and in a case known as *Pollock v. Farmers' Loan & Trust Co.*[1] held the law unconstitutional.

Even more than *Debs*, *Pollock* was a special ceremonial occasion for the Court. The greatest lawyers of the day appeared for both sides. Attorney General Richard Olney, the mastermind of the Pullman strategy, defended the income tax statute.[2] So did James C. Carter, a prominent New York attorney who wrote and lectured widely on a great variety of subjects.[3] Carter represented the Continental Trust Company in its defense of a shareholder suit that was brought to prevent the company from paying the tax

---

[1] 157 U.S. 429 (1895), decision on rehearing, 158 U.S. 601 (1895). For general background on the history of the income tax, the 1894 debate, and the *Pollock* case itself see Sidney Ratner, *Taxation and Democracy in America* (New York: Octagon Books, 1980; originally published as *American Taxation: Its History as a Social Force in Democracy*, New York: W. W. Norton, 1942); Arnold M. Paul, *Conservative Crisis and the Rule of Law: Attitudes of Bar and Bench, 1887–1895* (Ithaca: Cornell University Press, 1960; repr. Gloucester, Mass: Peter Smith, 1976); and Edwin R. A. Seligman, *The Income Tax: A Study of the History, Theory, and Practice of Income Taxation at Home and Abroad* (New York: Macmillan, 1911). See also Elmer Ellis, "Public Opinion and the Income Tax, 1860–1900," *Miss. Valley Hist. Rev.*, 27: 225 (1940), and George Tunell, "The Legislative History of the Second Income-Tax Law," *J. Pol. Econ.*, 3: 311 (1895).

[2] See Gerald G. Eggert, *Richard Olney: Evolution of a Statesman* (University Park: Pennsylvania State University Press, 1974); Gerald G. Eggert, "Richard Olney and the Income Tax Cases," *Miss. Valley Hist. Rev.*, 48: 24 (1961); and Henry James, *Richard Olney and His Public Service* (Boston: Houghton Mifflin, 1923).

[3] See Benjamin R. Twiss, *Lawyers and the Constitution: How Laissez Faire Came to the Supreme Court* (Princeton: Princeton University Press, 1942; repr. New York: Russell & Russell, 1962).

75

(a fact that should give some pause to those inclined to an instrumental account of the era). Joseph Choate, a leading figure in the corporate bar, later appointed ambassador to the Court of St. James's by McKinley, appeared on the other side and led the attack on the statute.[4]

At first, the Court found itself unable to reach a clear decision. Chief Justice Fuller announced that although the Court found certain parts of the statute unconstitutional, it had evenly divided (4 to 4) on whether the other contested portions of the statute were valid and also on whether the statute as a whole should be left standing. One justice, Howell Jackson, did not participate because he was ill at the time of argument.

The failure of the Court to resolve an issue of such public importance was unacceptable to all involved. A second argument was scheduled with the understanding that Jackson would return from his home in Tennessee. Weeks later the second argument was held before the full Court.[5] This time the decision was against the statute in its entirety. The vote was 5 to 4.

The invalidation of any federal statute would be a moment of great public interest. There were, however, several additional factors that heightened the sense of drama in *Pollock*. One was Jackson's vote in favor of the law, which must have seemed odd given his record defending private prop-

---

[4] According to Twiss, Choate was the paradigm of "conservative respectability" (115), "the consummate talker, whose appeal and strength were personal" (175), while Carter was "modest, frugal and serious" (175) and a "thinker" (112).

[5] Carter did not appear for Continental Trust at the rehearing and Ratner surmises from this that Continental Trust did not really want to win and thus that the suit was collusive. "Carter did not appear for the Continental Trust Company [on rehearing] because," Ratner claims, "they were not anxious to have his great talents used in defending the income tax and in winning a victory they did not desire." Ratner, *Taxation and Democracy*, 205. He cites as his evidence two letters from Carter to Olney, but these letters do not in any way support his claim of collusion. The letter of April 27, 1895, merely states that Carter is awaiting communications from Continental Trust as to whether he should appear at the rehearing before the Supreme Court. The letter continues, "I hope you will make as complete an effort as possible, and in every direction, to save the Income Tax." The bulk of the letter rehearses the arguments to support the tax, and then ends, "I shall very much regret if I am not able to join with you in the argument, although I should feel very sorely the want of time for full preparation." Carter to Olney, Apr. 27, 1895, Olney Papers, Library of Congress Manuscript Division. Carter may have thought Olney would be sufficient at the rehearing, especially given his own obligations, or he might have advised Continental Trust that the value added by his appearance at the rehearing would not be worth the expense. The April 30 letter from Carter to Olney begins, "I have your telegram in relation to the income tax case, and it relieves me from what would be a great pressure to me just now, for I am very much occupied with other matters. I hope that a re-consideration may induce a correction of views, but I have but little expectation of it." Carter to Olney, Apr. 30, 1895, Olney Papers. Randolph E. Paul, *Taxation in the United States* (Boston: Little, Brown, 1954), 40, also suggests the possibility of collusion, but gives no evidentiary support.

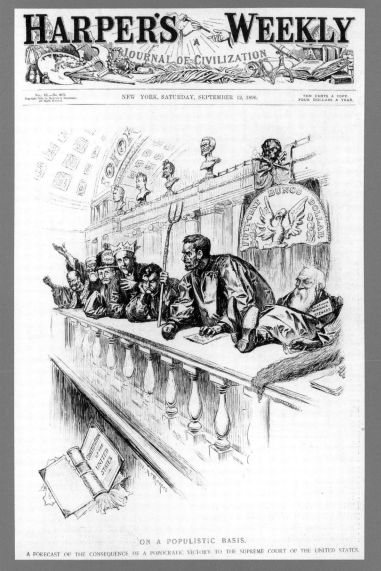

HARPER'S WEEKLY
JOURNAL OF CIVILIZATION

VOL. XL.—No. 2073.
Copyright, 1896, by HARPER & BROTHERS.
All Rights Reserved.

NEW YORK, SATURDAY, SEPTEMBER 12, 1896.

TEN CENTS A COPY.
FOUR DOLLARS A YEAR.

ON A POPULISTIC BASIS.
A FORECAST OF THE CONSEQUENCE OF A POPOCRATIC VICTORY TO THE SUPREME COURT OF THE UNITED STATES.

Cartoon by W. A. Rogers depicting the Supreme Court should William Jennings Bryan win the presidency in 1896. On the bench from the left are prominent figures identified with the Populist-Democratic coalition: Sylvester Pennoyer, governor of Oregon; Jacob S. Coxey, leader of an 1894 march from Ohio to Washington, D.C., supporting job-creating legislation; Eugene V. Debs, head of the American Railway Union and leader of the Pullman strike; Benjamin Ryan Tillman, senator from South Carolina; John Peter Altgeld, governor of Illinois; and William Morris Stewart, senator from Nevada. Above the bench are the busts of Louis Lingg, Adolf Fischer, and August Spies, prosecuted for their roles in the Haymarket riot; and Charles J. Guiteau, President James A. Garfield's assassin. (*Library of Congress*)

Campaign poster for William McKinley's 1896 presidential campaign.
(*Library of Congress*)

Chief Justice Melville Weston Fuller (1833–1910), who served on the
Supreme Court from 1888 until his death. Here about 1905.
(*Library of Congress*)

Associate Justice David Josiah Brewer (1837–1910), who served
on the Supreme Court from 1889 until his death.
Here about 1906.
(*Library of Congress*)

Associate Justice Rufus W. Peckham (1838–1909), who served on the
Supreme Court from 1895 until his death.
Here about 1909.
(*Library of Congress*)

Associate Justice Oliver Wendell Holmes, Jr. (1841–1935), who
served on the Supreme Court from 1902 until his
resignation in 1932.
October 3, 1910.
(*Harvard Law Art Collection*)

The Supreme Court of the United States, 1888. From left to right with dates
of service: Joseph P. Bradley (1870–1892); Stanley Matthews (1881–1889);
Samuel Freeman Miller (1862–1890); Horace Gray (1881–1902); Melville
Weston Fuller (1888–1910); John Marshall Harlan (1877–1911);
Stephen Johnson Field (1863–1897); Samuel Blatchford (1882–
1893); and Lucius Quintus Cincinnatus Lamar (1888–1893).
(*Library of Congress*)

The Supreme Court of the United States, 1894. From left to right with dates
of service: Horace Gray (1881–1902); Howell Edmonds Jackson (1893–1895);
Stephen Johnson Field (1863–1897); Henry Billings Brown (1890–1906);
Melville Weston Fuller (1888–1910); George Shiras, Jr. (1892–1903);
John Marshall Harlan (1877–1911); Edward Douglass White (1894–
1921); and David Josiah Brewer (1889–1910).
(*Library of Congress*)

The Supreme Court of the United States, 1904. From left to right with dates of service: Henry Billings Brown (1890–1906); Oliver Wendell Holmes, Jr. (1902–1932); John Marshall Harlan (1877–1911); Rufus W. Peckham (1895–1909); Melville Weston Fuller (1888–1910); Joseph McKenna (1898–1925); David Josiah Brewer (1889–1910); William R. Day (1903–1922); Edward Douglass White (1894–1921). (*Library of Congress*)

The Supreme Court of the United States, 1907. From left to right with dates of service: Edward Douglass White (1894–1921); William R. Day (1903–1922); John Marshall Harlan (1877–1911); Joseph McKenna (1898–1925); Melville Weston Fuller (1888–1910); Oliver Wendell Holmes, Jr. (1902–1932); David Josiah Brewer (1889–1910); William Henry Moody (1906–1910); and Rufus W. Peckham (1895–1909). (*Library of Congress*)

erty.[6] The other was the final tally. On the first round the Court had evenly divided, voting 4 to 4; Jackson then entered the case, but the side that he joined lost, by 5 to 4. It appeared that one justice—whose identity is still unknown—switched sides the second time around, becoming the fifth and decisive vote to invalidate the tax. Who switched sides? Could it be that Fuller did not correctly tally the votes on the first decision? Did some justice vote strategically the first round in order to necessitate a decision by a full bench?

These questions were the basis for much contemporaneous comment and gave rise to one of the greatest puzzles of Supreme Court history: the enigma of the vacillating justice.[7] There was, more importantly, a substantive issue at stake in *Pollock* that justified all the public attention that the decision received—the permissibility of using federal power to alter the market distribution of wealth. Just as *Debs* was seen as involving not an ordinary strike but rather an incipient revolution, calling forth all the power of government to maintain order, *Pollock* was understood in equally transcendent terms. The income tax of 1894 was not a technical adjustment of the method of taxation but an egalitarian measure intended to put the burden of taxation on the rich. It posed a fundamental question about the nature of the state and its capacity to intervene in the social sphere.

I

For the first century of the American republic, revenues for the federal government were raised largely from tariffs on imported goods. An income tax was enacted during the Civil War after popular sentiment forced the secretary of the treasury to abandon his plan of raising additional

---

[6] As a circuit judge in *In re* Greene, 52 F. 104 (6th Cir. 1892), Jackson restricted the application of the Sherman Act in a way that foreshadowed the Court's reasoning in United States v. E. C. Knight Co., 156 U.S. 1 (1895). See Chapter 5. Jackson concurred in Brewer's dissent in Brass v. North Dakota, 153 U.S. 391, 405 (1894), a case that upheld a statute regulating grain storage. He also wrote the opinion for the Court in Mobile & O. Ry. v. Tennessee, 153 U.S. 486 (1894), which relied on the Contracts Clause to protect a corporate charter. After the initial arguments but before decision was rendered, Jackson wrote to Fuller from Tennessee, expressing regret over his absence. He then added: "In thinking over the subject I have reached the conclusion that the law would be partially sustained and partially declared unconstitutional by the Court." Jackson to Fuller, Apr. 8, 1895, Fuller Papers, Chicago Historical Society.

[7] Although a number of scenarios have been put forward to account for this mysterious voting pattern, the current view (Paul, *Conservative Crisis*, 215-16) is that the two most plausible explanations are: (1) that Justice Gray switched his vote; and (2) that Chief Justice Fuller counted Justice Shiras's original abstention as a sustaining vote, to avoid resting the decision on a 4–3 vote.

needed revenues through a tax on real estate alone. But pressure from business groups, combined with a healthy surplus in the federal treasury, led to the termination of the income tax in 1872. Over the next twenty years more than sixty bills were introduced for the purpose of imposing an income tax, but they all were killed in committee, despite support from southern and western states. It was not until the early 1890s that the movement for a peacetime federal income tax really took hold. Although one justification for the tax was fiscal—to replace the tariff system with a more flexible and economically sounder means of raising government revenues—the egalitarianism associated with the agrarian and labor movements of the early 1890s dominated the debates and was crucial in the process leading to its enactment.

The victory of the Democratic Party in the presidential election of 1892 was interpreted largely as a protest against high tariffs and a mandate for change. If, however, the system of protectionism were to be eliminated, some other method for raising revenue would have to be found. A natural choice was the income tax. It was particularly popular among the farmers of the South and West, who resented the high cost of goods they had to purchase and the regressive character of tariffs (as a tax on consumption). Benton McMillin, congressman from Tennessee, and William Jennings Bryan, then a congressman from Nebraska, pushed to include an income tax clause as a rider to the tariff reform measure in the House. They succeeded, and the entire measure passed the House by a vote of 204 to 140.[8]

The House bill, like the statute eventually enacted, imposed a flat tax of 2 percent. From our perspective that rate looks extraordinarily modest, almost trivial. It was defended by its supporters on these terms, but this defense was not wholly credible. The peacetime income tax was new for America, the revenue needs of the federal government were relatively modest, and the country had just entered an economic depression. Everyone also must have understood that the 2 percent was just a beginning. The significance of the tax was further heightened by the fact that the measure contained an exemption for incomes under $4,000. Given income levels in the 1890s, the practical effect of this exemption was stunning—98 percent of the population would pay no tax.[9] The burden of taxation would be carried almost entirely by the wealthy few. Moreover, according to the terms of the bill, corporations—long the symbol of wealth and privilege and the special subject of populist wrath—would not be allowed the standard $4,000 exemption, while three forms of business organizations identified with the

---

[8] 26 Cong. Rec. 1796–97 (1894).

[9] William Guthrie, who as counsel for Pollock challenged the income tax, stated at oral argument that "[t]he whole burden of the tax falls upon less than two percent of the population of the country." 157 U.S. 442, 444. Extended excerpts from the oral arguments at the first hearing are printed at 157 U.S 442–553.

less privileged economic groups (building and loan associations, mutual savings banks, and mutual insurance companies) were exempted from any taxation at all.[10]

The egalitarianism of the present income tax system is two-sided: a heavier burden is (supposedly) placed on the rich than on the poor in generating revenue, and then some portion of the revenue actually generated is distributed to the poor in the form of welfare programs. The egalitarianism of the 1894 tax had only one side, inasmuch as it placed a heavier burden on the rich. This improved the relative economic position of the poor, and was in that sense redistributive, but there were no welfare programs at the time and they would have been unlikely to come from an administration headed by a Cleveland (or, for that matter, a Harrison or McKinley). On the other hand, welfare programs, such as those then taking root in Europe and arguably foreshadowed by the military pensions of the Civil War, were probably not beyond the contemplation of the sponsors of the tax, like Bryan.[11] To many, the 1894 tax appeared as the indispensable first step toward financing and legitimating the welfare state.

The rhetoric of the sponsors of the tax only underscored these concerns. Representative McMillin declared that "the time has come when the American people ought to impose some of the burdens of taxation upon the accumulated wealth of this country."[12] Bryan, "clad in the armor of a righteous cause" (as he described himself),[13] defended the tax in the name of the poor. He treated as absurd the suggestion that the poor did not favor the tax:

> Why, sir, the gentleman from New York [Mr. Cockran] said that the poor are opposed to this tax because they do not want to be deprived

---

[10] Wilson Tariff Act, Ch. 349, Sect. 27–37, 28 Stat. 509, 553–60 (1894).

[11] On the nineteenth-century antecedents of the welfare state in America, see Stephen Skowronek, *Building a New American State: The Expansion of National Administrative Capacities, 1877–1920* (Cambridge: Cambridge University Press, 1982), and Ann Shola Orloff, "The Political Origins of America's Belated Welfare State," in Margaret Weir, Ann Shola Orloff, and Theda Skocpol, eds., *The Politics of Social Policy in the United States* (Princeton: Princeton University Press, 1988), 37. The local and private aspects of welfarism during this period are discussed in Martin Schiesl, *The Politics of Efficiency: Municipal Administration and Reform in America, 1880–1920* (Berke-

ley: University of California Press, 1977), and Stuart Brandes, *American Welfare Capitalism*, 2d ed. (Chicago: University of Chicago Press, 1976). The European developments were well known to the framers of the 1894 income tax and of special interest to William Jennings Bryan. His biographer notes: "As he did with silver, Bryan steeped himself in the technical lore of the income tax by wading through books and monographs and by soliciting the State Department's help in collecting information abroad on the tax systems of other governments." Louis W. Koenig, *Bryan: A Political Biography of William Jennings Bryan* (New York: G. P. Putnam's Sons, 1971), 130.

[12] 26 Cong. Rec. Appx. 413 (1894).

[13] 26 Cong. Rec. 1655 (1894).

of participation in it, and that taxation instead of being a sign of servitude is a badge of freedom. If taxation is a badge of freedom, let me assure my friend that the poor people of this country are covered all over with the insignia of freemen. [Applause.][14]

He reminded his audience of the modesty of the rate and how similar the proposed income tax, with its exemptions, was to measures in various European countries. The special treatment of corporations also was defended in a revealing way:

> Some gentlemen have accused the committee of showing hostility to corporations. But, Mr. Chairman, we are not hostile to corporations; we simply believe that these creatures of the law, these fictitious persons, have no higher or dearer rights than the persons of flesh and blood whom God created and placed upon his footstool! [Applause.][15]

And he wound up his defense of the measure with the rhetorical eloquence soon to be his trademark:

> And, Mr. Chairman, I desire to here enter my protest against the false political economy taught by our opponents in this debate and against the perversion of language which we have witnessed. They tell us that it is better to consider expediency than equity in the adjustment of taxation. They tell us that it is right to tax consumption, and thus make the needy pay out of proportion to their means, but that it is wrong to make a slight compensation for this system by exempting small incomes from an income tax. They tell us that it is wise to limit the use of necessaries of life by heavy indirect taxation, but that it is vicious to lessen the enjoyment of the luxuries of life by a light tax upon large incomes. They tell us that those who make the load heaviest upon persons least able to bear it are distributing the burdens of government with an impartial hand, but that those who insist that each citizen should contribute to government in proportion as God has prospered him are blinded by prejudice against the rich. They call that man a statesman whose ear is tuned to catch the slightest pulsations of a pocket book, and denounce as a demagogue anyone who dares to listen to the heart-beat of humanity. [Applause.][16]

Cleveland had earlier advocated an income tax on corporations but was against joining the income tax to the tariff bill. He feared that such a move would endanger the success of his promised tariff reform and divide

---

[14] Ibid., 1656.
[15] Ibid., 1655.

[16] Ibid., 1658.

the Democratic Party. The Senate reaction was also mixed. A number of prominent senators denounced the income tax (John Sherman of Ohio called the exemption "a low and mean form of socialism").[17] To complicate matters even further, pressure was brought by various interests to increase the tariffs over those set in the House bill. On July 3 a tariff bill, which included the income tax provision but failed to eliminate the tariff system altogether, passed the Senate by a vote of 39 to 34.[18] Cleveland's prophecy had come true, and he denounced the product as "party perfidy and party dishonor."[19] The House acceded to the Senate amendments, and on August 28, 1894, Cleveland—reluctant to veto the bill because a veto would leave the McKinley tariff in effect—allowed the bill to become law without his signature. The tariffs in the new law were not quite so high as they were under the McKinley Act, but they were sufficiently high to render implausible any claim that the income tax was simply a fiscal substitute for the tariff system.

In the Supreme Court, the egalitarian quality of the statute also stirred passions. Choate denounced the tax as but one step in the "communist march." He espoused a theory of government that denied the state the power to alter the market distribution of wealth by placing a heavier burden on one economic group:

> I have thought that one of the fundamental objects of all civilized government was the preservation of the rights of private property. I have thought that it was the very keystone of the arch upon which all civilized government rests, and that this once abandoned, everything was at stake and in danger.[20]

In speaking of preservation of property as "one of the fundamental objects of all civilized government," Choate echoed Brewer's Albany speech and implicitly drew on the principles enshrined in the social contract tradition.

One of the central tasks for any political theory is to devise some way for both legitimating and limiting government power. Under contractarianism the legitimacy of government is founded on popular consent or, more particularly, on the desire of the citizenry for security. At the same time, however, that democratic element is qualified or limited, because the consent is structured in such a way as to impose limits on what government can do or what the people can demand. As Brewer made clear at Albany, the consent exalted by social contract theory is not one constantly open to revision (as in the electoral process), but rather one that binds over time,

---

[17] 26 Cong. Rec. 6682, 6695 (1894).
[18] 26 Cong. Rec. 7083, 7136 (1894).
[19] Letter of July 2, 1894, from President Cleveland to Congressman William L. Wilson of West Virginia, reprinted at 26 Cong. Rec. 7712–13 (1894).
[20] 157 U.S. at 533.

in the face of changed conditions and changed minds—it is the consent entailed in making a promise on a day past. Even though the government at any one moment might be responsive to the wishes of the current majority, the scope of the government's powers is limited by the terms or promises exchanged at the time of founding and by the pact made at that time among the founders.

The theory of the social contract prevalent in the nineteenth century defined the bargaining relationship among the founders in such a way as to deny government the power to redistribute wealth. For John Locke and the nineteenth-century social contract tradition in America, the contractual negotiations did not occur, to borrow a term from contemporary contract theory, behind a "veil of ignorance."[21] The founders knew who they were, what they had, and what they wanted. It was also assumed that the less wealthy did not insist, or were not in a position to insist, upon a share of the wealth of the others, but instead entered the contract only in order to ensure personal security. As for the rich, they also wanted the state to maintain order, but presumably less intensely than did the unpropertied (they could fend for themselves). Accordingly, they conditioned their consent, so the story went, on an assurance that their holdings would not be taken by the newly established government for the purpose of altering the distribution of wealth.[22]

Reconciling the 1894 tax with this intellectual tradition was not easy. The best justification for the income tax—the declining marginal utility of income, the fact that a dollar taken from the rich hurts less than a dollar taken from the poor—was outside the tradition entirely. Although Carter put forward this justification at oral argument, he and other lawyers supporting the tax did not seem to have their hearts in it; their real hope was to bring the law within the social contract tradition. To do so, they emphasized the provisions regarding corporations, which were defended on the theory that corporations were mere artifacts of the state. Corporations were not present in the "state of nature" and could make no special demands upon the state. They existed at the sufferance of the state and were subject to whatever levy it chose. This line of argument might have been able to save the tax on corporations, as it did years later,[23] but it had no relevance

---

[21] John Rawls, *A Theory of Justice* (Cambridge: Harvard University Press, 1971), 19.
[22] See generally Joshua Cohen, "Structure, Choice, and Legitimacy: Locke's Theory of the State," *Phil. & Pub. Aff.*, 15: 301 (1986).
[23] In 1909 Congress did in fact enact a corporate income tax, Act of Aug. 5, 1909, Ch. 6, Sect. 38, 36 Stat. 112, which

was upheld by the Court in Flint v. Stone Tracy Co., 220 U.S. 107 (1911). The Court read the Constitution to allow Congress to impose "an excise upon the particular privilege of doing business in a corporate capacity," ibid., 151, distinguishing it from a tax on persons "solely because of their general ownership of property." Ibid., 149 (citation and emphasis omitted).

for the provision taxing the income of individuals, which, of course, was the real problem. That provision, too, was defended on contractarian terms, specifically as a form of compensation for the injustices of the past, in this instance, the so-called regressive taxes that were imposed on consumption. The overall structure of this argument is conservative, for it acknowledges, at least as an abstract matter, the sanctity of property: It demands that some property rights be sacrificed, but only to vindicate past violations of those very same rights. Yet it assumes that a consumption tax is unjust and further requires some explanation why the rights of one group (the rich) should be sacrificed to compensate for the wrongs done to another (the poor). Carter's answer was that the rich had gained their wealth unjustly, by using the tax system to their advantage. Such an argument appeals to traditional notions of corrective justice in order to explain why the burden should be placed on the rich, but it also implies that the political system was fundamentally flawed—an implication the Court could hardly accept.

Finally, the Court was urged to see the tax as part of a larger strategy of containment. Carter argued that the 1894 measure, however radical it seemed, might in fact stabilize the political situation. He warned the Court of the dangers of invalidating the statute and thus of holding firm to the contractarian edict against redistribution:

> When the opposing forces of sixty millions of people have become arrayed in hostile political ranks upon a question which all men feel is not a question of law, but of legislation, the only path of safety is to accept the voice of the majority as final. The American people can be trusted not to commit permanent injustice; nor has history yet recorded an instance in which governments have been destroyed by attempts of the many to lay undue burdens of taxation on the few. The teachings of history have all been in the other direction.[24]

This may well have been more than rhetoric. It is plausible that Attorney General Olney supported the income tax not only on fiscal grounds, but also because he was attracted by the idea of containment—as he had been in persuading Charles Perkins and other proponents of the railroad interests to desist from their campaign to abolish the Interstate Commerce Commission.[25] A small concession to egalitarian elements might indeed defuse the discontent of the masses. Invalidating the statute, on the other hand, would not only put the Court in conflict with the other branches of the federal government, but it also would leave "the multitudes," to use Brewer's phrase, without any real incentive to pursue their ends through orderly and formal

---

[24] 157 U.S. at 531–32. | [25] See Chapter I, pp. 13–14.

processes. Constitutional amendment is possible, and indeed in this case it materialized, but looking at the matter prospectively, the burdens of the amending processes were so substantial as to render hollow Brewer's insistence in *Debs* that "the multitudes" leave the streets and turn to the ballot box and the courts.

Choate did not let Carter's plea go unanswered. He was too clever for that:

> If it be true, as my friend said in closing, that the passions of the people are aroused on this subject, if it be true that a mighty army of sixty million citizens is likely to be incensed by this decision, it is the more vital to the future welfare of this country that this court again resolutely and courageously declare, as Marshall did, that it *has* the power to set aside an act of Congress violative of the Constitution, and that it will not hesitate in executing that power, no matter what the threatened consequences of popular or populistic wrath may be.[26]

Choate's response must have been appealing to a justice such as Brewer, who time and time again expressed a daring, or, as we saw in his Albany speech and *Debs* itself, an almost religious faith in the capacity of the judiciary to protect the nation against the onslaught of the masses. But what about the other justices? What Choate said may have only fueled the fears of those who were understandably less confident of their powers and who might well have had a more modest conception of their office. Not everyone was prepared to let the heavens fall.

II

The basic objection to the tax stemmed from its egalitarian character, the singling out of the wealthy few—the 2 percent—to pay the tax. This feature worked a redistribution of wealth to the extent that it decreased, however slightly, the gap between rich and poor. Those who objected to the statute on this ground might have been able to turn to John Locke and his version of the social contract for support; they might even have been able to claim, as the Choates and Brewers of that day did, that property was "the keystone of the arch upon which all civilized government rests." But they could not turn easily to the Constitution for support. There is no constitutional provision that explicitly protects against such egalitarianism. The Constitution contains three protections of property rights, one that prohibits impairing the obligation of contracts, another that prohibits takings of property without just compensation, and a third that prohibits depriva-

---

[26] 157 U.S. at 553.

tions of property without due process. But none seemed especially applicable to the 1894 statute.

Perhaps the Court could have avoided a search for some particular clause or provision guarding against egalitarianism but still have condemned the decision of Congress to tax the rich by finding the Constitution as a whole to imply such a protection. Such an approach has not been unknown to the modern Supreme Court,[27] and it was especially congenial to the justices at the turn of the century. For them, constitutional interpretation was not an exercise in clause-parsing. This was evident in *Debs*, and it will be apparent in almost every major case of the period, including *Lochner*. In fact, in the very term before *Pollock*, Brewer, speaking for a unanimous Court, employed this freewheeling methodology to invalidate a Texas regulation of certain railroad rates on the theory that it violated a federal constitutional right that assured investors some return on capital.[28] In anchoring this right to a fair return in the Constitution, Brewer made a passing reference to the Fourteenth Amendment in general and the Equal Protection Clause in particular. In truth, however, he did not rely on any particular clause of the Constitution but said the right was expressive of "the spirit of common justice."[29] A state law that lowered railroad rates to the point of denying the investors any return on their capital was seen by Brewer and the other members of the Court as a form of economic victimization and on that ground a violation of the constitutional principle that guaranteed all equality before the law.

But the opinion for the majority in *Pollock* was written by Fuller, not Brewer, and perhaps for that reason alone the Court's opinion was not cast in such bold terms.[30] Fuller stuck closer to the text. One clause of the Constitution that deals with the taxing powers of the federal government and

---

[27] See, e.g., Bolling v. Sharpe, 347 U.S. 497 (1954) (establishing a right of equal protection against the federal government), and Shapiro v. Thompson, 394 U.S. 618 (1969) (establishing a right of interstate travel that protected the poor against welfare residency requirements).

[28] Reagan v. Farmers' Loan & Trust Co., 154 U.S. 362 (1894), discussed in Chapter 7.

[29] Ibid., 410. See generally Howard Aaron Gillman, "The Constitution Besieged: The Founding Vision of a Faction-Free Republic, the Intensification of Class Conflict, and Constitutional Ideology During the Lochner Era" (Ph.D. diss., University of California at Los Angeles, 1988). Gillman argues that the Court's commitment to equal treatment of all classes was based on faith that governmental restraint would allow the free market to achieve equality naturally, an expectation that was no longer viable with the emergence of industrial capitalism and class conflict.

[30] After the event, however, Brewer was unrestrained in his praise of Fuller's opinion, calling it "majestic and immortal" and "among the great historic opinions of the court." David J. Brewer, "The Income Tax Cases and Some Comments Thereon," An Address Delivered on the Invitation of the Faculty, Before the Graduating Class of the State University of Iowa, at the Annual Commencement, June 8, 1898 (Iowa City: Iowa State University, 1898), 3–4. No wonder he was Fuller's favorite.

that might have seemed applicable was the one imposing a requirement of "uniformity." Article I, Section 8, reads: "The Congress shall have Power To lay and collect Taxes, Duties, Imposts and Excises, to pay the Debts and provide for the common Defence and general Welfare of the United States; but all Duties, Imposts and Excises shall be uniform throughout the United States." It was not clear, however, that the income tax would qualify as a "Duty," "Impost," or "Excise," inasmuch as those terms seem to refer to tariffs or to taxes on goods. Moreover, the required "uniformity" had a geographic rather than an economic cast. Earlier decisions,[31] as well as the particular words of the provision ("throughout the United States"), suggested that the guarantee of uniformity in Section 8 was aimed at preventing Congress from favoring or singling out one geographic section, or one state or groups of states, over another. "Uniformity" had nothing to do with singling out or favoring one economic class over another.

Although opponents of the tax labored to free the Uniformity Clause from its geographic orientation, they also understood the difficulties of doing so and thus sought to make out a case of geographic discrimination. To do that, they had to move beyond the words of the 1894 statute and look to the actual incidence of the tax. By creating an exemption for incomes under $4,000, the burden of the tax fell on a small portion of the population—the wealthiest 2 percent—and these people were concentrated in a small number of northeastern states (particularly New York, New Jersey, Pennsylvania, and Massachusetts). Opponents argued that, as a result of this disparate impact, the statute violated the constitutional provision that required taxes to be "uniform throughout the United States."

In the final analysis, however, the Court was unsympathetic to this argument. Uncomfortable with a mode of analysis that relied upon an assessment of the actual incidence of a tax, and unattracted by a constitutional guarantee that would do no more than establish a uniform *rate* of taxation and thus still leave the wealthy vulnerable, the justices showed no more interest in this disparate geographic impact than they did in reinterpreting the Uniformity Clause to require uniform treatment of economic groups. The Uniformity Clause dropped out of the case, and the chief justice turned instead to those provisions of the Constitution establishing special rules for so-called direct taxes.

The Constitution does not deny the federal government the power to levy direct taxes. It does, however, require that such taxes (for example, a capitation or head tax) be apportioned according to population, that is, distributed among the states according to their population, so that the most populous states would pay a greater portion of the tax bill than the least populous. One of the provisions of the Constitution requires: "Representa-

---

[31] Head Money Cases, 112 U.S. 580 (1884).

tives and direct Taxes shall be apportioned among the several States which may be included within this Union, according to their respective Numbers."[32] Another provision requires: "No Capitation, or other direct, Tax shall be laid unless in Proportion to the Census or Enumeration herein before directed to be taken."[33] Clearly, the 1894 tax was not apportioned. The amount of the tax to be raised from any particular state was not determined by that state's share of the nation's population. The only question was whether it was a direct tax, comparable to a capitation tax, and thus subject to the apportionment requirement.

In addressing this question, the Court began by positing what might be referred to as the "tracing principle." Under this principle, income does not take on a new constitutional character when it is received by the taxpayer but retains the character given to it by its source. Income that is traceable to state or municipal bonds, for example, retains its particular character (and thus is to be distinguished from wages or income from corporate stocks and bonds) even after this income is in the hands of the recipient. The tracing principle, which was developed in the interstate commerce and intergovernmental tax immunity cases,[34] was implicated in the portion of *Pollock* in which the Court invalidated the tax on income from state and municipal bonds. But the tracing principle was also used in a more innovative way, as part of the Court's analysis of the direct tax issue. The Court segmented the various components of income (wages, dividends, rent, etc.) according to the tracing principle and then asked whether a tax on such a unit of income was or was not a direct tax.

In addressing this issue, Fuller began with a relatively uncontested proposition, namely that a tax on real estate was a direct tax. This proposition did not rest on the specific words of the Constitution (since the only example of a direct tax mentioned in the text is the capitation tax), but it was amply supported by late-eighteenth-century usage and also by dicta in a series of Supreme Court decisions beginning in 1796.[35] All the justices sub-

---

[32] U.S. Const., Art. I, Sect. 2, Cl. 3.

[33] Ibid., Sect. 9, Cl. 4.

[34] The principle can be traced to Brown v. Maryland, 25 U.S. (12 Wheat.) 419, 444 (1827) ("[A] tax on the occupation of an importer is, in like manner, a tax on importation. It must add to the price of the article, and be paid by the consumer, or by the importer himself, in like manner as a direct duty on the article itself would be made. This the State has not a right to do, because it is prohibited by the constitution."), and Weston v. City Council, 27 U.S. (2 Pet.) 449, 468 (1829) ("The right [of a state] to tax

the contract [a loan to the federal government] . . . must operate upon the power to borrow before it is exercised, and have a sensible influence on the contract. . . . To any extent, however inconsiderable, it is a burden on the operations of government.").

[35] Hylton v. United States, 3 U.S. (3 Dall.) 171 (1796); Pacific Ins. Co. v. Soule, 74 U.S. (7 Wall.) 433 (1869); Veazie Bank v. Fenno, 75 U.S. (8 Wall.) 533 (1869); Scholey v. Rew, 90 U.S. (23 Wall.) 331 (1875); Springer v. United States, 102 U.S. 586 (1881).

scribed to the notion that a tax on real estate was a direct tax. What the Court in *Pollock* divided on was the question whether a tax on the *income* from real property (rent) should be treated constitutionally in the same way as a tax on real property itself (which was in fact a tax on the *value* of real property). Attorney General Olney conceded that the income from real estate was a measure of the value of the property, but at the same time he challenged the tracing principle by insisting that once that income had been received it became a form of personal property, analogous to crops or other products of the land. A tax on the value of real estate was a direct tax, the attorney general argued, but a tax on the income of the real estate was not. Obviously, this distinction did not make a great deal of sense from an economic perspective, since the value of a property is the income it can generate. Olney's only response was that "the legal definition of 'direct taxes' in the Constitution is, in truth, not a scientific, but a historical, one."[36]

In the first *Pollock* decision, a majority concluded that a tax on the income from real estate was tantamount to a tax on the land and thus a direct tax. On all the other aspects of the direct tax issue, however, the Court was evenly divided (so Fuller reported). This outcome was something of an anticlimax, in part because it left the fate of the statute as a whole unresolved, and also because the Court seemed to speak only to the easiest issue—if any aspect of the 1894 measure could be labeled a direct tax it was certainly the tax on income from real property. The more difficult issue concerned the status of the income from personal property, especially from corporate stocks and bonds (dividends and interest).

With the first *Pollock* decision on the books, however, the issue concerning the status of dividends and interest must have appeared in a different light; if one of the justices switched sides, this might have been why. The issue no longer was simply whether a tax on income from personal property was a direct tax. Now the question was whether the income from personal property should be considered the same for tax purposes as the income from real property. There were important, legally recognized differences between the two species of property, that is, between real and personal property, but those differences did not in any obvious way make the apportionment guarantee any less appropriate as a protection against an overreaching state.

One difference stemmed from the fact that a tax on personal property bore certain similarities to a tariff, the paradigmatic indirect tax, since the tariff could be viewed as a tax on the importation of personal property. In fact, in a 1796 decision, a majority of justices (there was no single opinion that spoke for the Court) said that a tax on an item of personal property (a carriage) was not a direct tax.[37] But in a constitutional context defined

---

[36] Brief on Behalf of the United States at 22.

[37] Hylton v. United States, 3 U.S. (3 Dall.) 171 (1796).

by the desire to prevent abuses of the power of taxation, it would have seemed anomalous to draw a line between the income from real property and the income from personal property. It would have meant that the power to appropriate an individual's wealth through taxation would be circumscribed by two, quite different guarantees: for a tax on rent, the apportionment requirement; for a tax on dividends or interest, the uniformity requirement. It would have been even more anomalous to deal with dividends or interest by positing the existence of a third type of tax, neither direct nor indirect, for that would have contemplated the existence of a power to appropriate an individual's wealth that was not circumscribed by either protection. The *Pollock* majority decided not to make any of these distinctions or to create this third no-man's-land. Instead, it treated the tax on dividends and interest (income from personal property) the same as it treated a tax on rent (income from real property), that is, as a direct tax that must satisfy the Constitution's apportionment requirement.

In reaching the conclusion that taxes on income from real and from personal property were direct taxes, the Court departed from a number of its precedents that had firmly established only capitation and real estate taxes to be direct taxes within the reach of the Constitution's apportionment requirement. These precedents included the 1796 case upholding a carriage tax and others that followed that case.[38] True, the Court held that a tax on the *income* from personal property was a direct tax while the 1796 decision held that a tax on personal property (a carriage) was not a direct tax. But Fuller's method impeached the earlier decision. He treated property and the income from personal property as the same for purposes of the direct tax provision, and thus implied, contrary to the 1796 decision, that a tax on personal property itself would also be a direct tax. Neverthe-

---

[38] Even if Choate and Fuller were correct in arguing that the facts of these cases concerned taxes on "business, privileges or employments" rather than real or personal property, this technical point at most allowed the Court to avoid overruling explicitly the earlier cases. There was no question that the language of those cases covered much more than taxes on earned income. The Court in *Springer* said that "*direct taxes*, within the meaning of the Constitution, are only capitation taxes, as expressed in that instrument; and taxes on real estate. . . ." 102 U.S. at 602. The two principles most prominent in the seriatim *Hylton* opinions were that "[t]he rule of apportionment is only to be adopted in such cases where it can reasonably apply," 3 U.S. (3 Dall.) at 174, and "the direct taxes contemplated by the Constitution, are only two, to wit, a capitation . . . and a tax on LAND." Ibid., 175 (emphasis in the original). The definition of direct taxes as embracing only land and capitation taxes was also invoked in Pacific Ins. Co. v. Soule, 74 U.S. (7 Wall.) 433 (1869) (various taxes on insurance companies, including income tax), and Veazie Bank v. Fenno, 75 U.S. (8 Wall.) 533 (1869) (tax on state bank notes). Scholey v. Rew, 90 U.S. (23 Wall.) 331, 347–48 (1875) (inheritance tax on real estate) in turn cited *Pacific Insurance* and *Veazie* for the proposition that a direct tax "does not include the tax on income, which cannot be distinguished in principle from a succession tax."

less, there were good reasons for refusing to be bound by the earlier decision. It was announced at a time when taxes on goods—tariffs and excises—were seen as the primary source of revenue for the federal government. The income tax of 1894 represented a wholly new conception of the scope of the federal taxing power and invited a fresh judicial response.

There was one final item that had to be considered in *Pollock*, and that was the tax on wages or earned income—as Fuller put it, income from "business, privileges, or employments"[39] rather than income from "capital."[40] Given the $4,000 exemption, the resolution of the issue probably had little concrete effect one way or the other (the source of an income over $4,000 was more likely to be investments than wages), but this did not reduce the theoretical or constitutional difficulty of the issue. On one hand, a tax on *earned* income seemed to defy contractarian principles even more thoroughly than a tax on the income from real property or a tax on the income from personal property. If a tax on property is direct, so should be a tax on earned income. On the other hand, treating earned income the same as income from property would create problems on another front: stare decisis. Following Choate's lead, the Court had implicitly distinguished away the earlier cases—including the carriage tax case—that had classified various taxes as indirect on the ground that these were not taxes on income from capital but on income from "business, privileges or employments."[41] This suggested that a tax on earned income would be an indirect tax.

The Court managed, however, to avoid a choice between its principles and its precedents by deftly manipulating the order in which the issues were decided. Having concluded in the first *Pollock* decision that the 1894 statute was invalid insofar as it taxed rent, and then having reached a similar conclusion concerning interest and dividends in the second *Pollock* decision,[42] the Court was able to treat the earned income issue solely as a question of statutory interpretation: Could the tax on this item be severed from the provisions of the statute already held invalid? The Court answered that

---

[39] 158 U.S. at 635.

[40] Ibid., 637.

[41] Choate's analysis is not included in the U.S. Reports, but can be found in the record of the case in the United States Supreme Court Records and Briefs, 158 U.S. 601 (1895), "Closing Argument by Mr. Choate, on behalf of Complainants, in support of the contention that the Income Tax Law of 1894 is Unconstitutional," at 38–42. Fuller implicitly adopts Choate's analysis in the second *Pollock* opinion: "We have considered the act only in respect of the tax on income derived from real estate, and from invested personal property, and have not commented on so much of it as bears on gains or profits from business, privileges, or employments, in view of the instances in which taxation on business, privileges, or employments has assumed the guise of an excise tax and has been sustained as such." 158 U.S. at 635.

[42] This aspect of the second *Pollock* decision made redundant the earlier ruling to the effect that interest from state and municipal bonds were immune from federal taxation.

question in the negative. As a practical matter, that meant that regardless of whether a tax on earned income or wages was a direct or indirect tax, that particular tax would have to fall because the other provisions of the statute were unconstitutional.

There was a special cleverness to the way Fuller structured the order of the issues to be resolved. That order enabled him to avoid deciding the constitutional status of a tax on wages and to rest his decision solely on traditional canons of statutory interpretation. As Fuller put it, with his characteristic infelicity: If the provision on earned income were severable, and it alone were sustained, the 1894 statute would be transformed, for "what was intended as a tax on capital would remain in substance a tax on occupations and labor."[43]

III

On one level, the logic of the *Pollock* decision seems coherent. Starting from the tracing principle and the well-established view that a tax on real estate was a direct tax, the conclusion of the case—namely, that a tax on the income from real property and then from personal property is a direct tax—seems plausible enough. What troubles the modern reader is not so much the logic of the decision, nor any of its interstitial premises, but the direct tax provision itself. To us it seems a purely technical requirement, devoid of any great normative significance. Yet Fuller and his brethren saw it in wholly different terms. They viewed the direct tax provision as an important part of the contractual arrangement through which the power of taxation was simultaneously created and limited.

To understand the majority's perspective, one must begin by recalling that the framers, reflecting eighteenth-century practice and their conception of the central government as a government among governments, saw the tariff (variously described as a "Duty," "Impost," or "Excise") as the primary form of federal taxation. A tariff is a tax on goods moving across the boundaries of a political community, and as a consequence, the principal danger of abuse in the imposition of tariffs arose from the possibility that Congress might favor some geopolitical communities over others. In terms of the world at large, Congress is given almost unlimited discretion—it can create preferences for one foreign nation over another—but with respect to the internal political communities, the states, Congress is bounded by a rule that prohibits it from giving a preference to one state over another. America was to be treated as a single economic unit. This constitutional vision is embodied in the Uniformity Clause, which, as noted earlier, provides: "[A]ll Duties, Imposts, and Excises shall be uniform

---

[43] 158 U.S. at 637.

throughout the United States." Two other constitutional provisions have a similar thrust: "No Tax or Duty shall be laid on Articles exported from any State";[44] "No Preference shall be given by any Regulation of Commerce or Revenue to the Ports of one State over those of another."[45]

The power of the central government to tax was not, however, confined to tariffs. The constitutional grant of power is cast in the broadest terms: "The Congress shall have Power To lay and collect Taxes, Duties, Imposts, and Excises, to pay the Debts and provide for the common Defence and general Welfare of the United States." The authority to levy direct taxes would fall within this grant of power but it needed—as did tariffs—some requirement or rule checking it against abuse. For tariffs the check is uniformity; for direct taxes it is apportionment among the states according to population. Direct taxes can be imposed by the federal government, but only if the burden of taxation falls more heavily on those who have the most power to levy that tax. Political power is distributed in the House of Representatives according to population, and the Constitution provides that the burden of direct taxes must be distributed in a similar manner. Tyranny is to be avoided, so it appears, by tying the power to tax to the burden of taxation.[46]

The force of this mechanism appears most clearly in the case of the capitation tax; assuming that the capitation tax charges the same for each person, the burden of taxation will be distributed according to population and thus according to political power as it is constituted in the representative assembly. The most populous states will necessarily have the greatest burden. In the case of a capitation tax the apportionment rule is virtually redundant (head taxes are by necessity distributed according to population), but that is not so with other direct taxes, say a national real estate tax. With respect to them, the apportionment rule, or the linkage of the burden of taxation with the power to tax, could be seen as a check on "the multitudes" (to use, once again, Brewer's phrase), or some kind of assurance that there would be "no taxation without representation." The federal gov-

---

[44] U.S. Const., Art. I, Sect. 9, Cl. 5.

[45] Ibid., Cl. 6. The Port Preference and Uniformity clauses were originally two parts of a single provision, as reported out to the Constitutional Convention by a special committee: "Nor shall any regulation of commerce or revenue give preference to the ports of one state over those of another, or oblige vessels bound to or from any state to enter, clear, or pay duties, in another; and all tonnage, duties, imposts, and excises, laid by the legislature, shall be uniform throughout the United States."

Jonathan Elliot, *Debates on the Adoption of the Federal Constitution* (1888; repr. New York: Burt Franklin, n.d.), 5: 483–84.

[46] Even if the Uniformity Clause were used by the Court to reach the 1894 statute on the theory of a localized impact, it might have seemed less attractive than the Direct Tax Clause as a way of guarding the social contract, because the Uniformity Clause does not link taxation with representation so as to make the burden fall on those with the greatest political power.

Chapter IV: *The Redistributive Function Denied*

ernment could not impose a tax on land unless the tax was somehow structured so as to require the more populous states (that is, the states with more votes in the House) to pay a larger share of the bill. Viewing the matter in these terms, Fuller and the others who joined his opinion saw reason to broaden the reach of the direct tax provision and the apportionment requirement, to enhance its force and sweep, rather than to treat it as a mere technical requirement that could easily be avoided. They saw the direct tax provision, like the social order itself, as a mechanism for reconciling the need to create power and the need to limit it.

The dissenters also understood the need for a check on the power of taxation—they too were part of the same contractarian tradition—but they argued that the apportionment rule was overly cumbersome and a clumsy protection against a tyrannical use of the taxing power. In the case of a real estate tax, for example, the rule of apportionment would, in effect, prohibit Congress from enacting a single tax rate for the nation. The legislature would have to specify the total amount of revenue to be raised, distribute the burden among the states according to population, and then set a rate for each state that would reflect the value of its property and the amount that would have to be raised for that state. The practical difficulties would discourage even the most determined. Moreover, the apportionment rule would introduce inequalities when citizens of different states were compared, that is, would suddenly make state citizenship an important feature of the structure of the national taxing power. In the case of a national real estate tax, for example, the tax bills of two citizens in two different states might be different even if their property were of equal value, if the proportions of landowning citizens in each state were different.

The apportionment rule could also be faulted on the ground that it embodied flawed conceptions of equality and political power. This concern was like Carter's more radical justification of the progressive features of the 1894 tax on grounds of declining marginal utility. Never completely explicit in the dissents, this objection to apportionment operated outside, rather than within, the contractarian tradition, but nonetheless might have led some of the dissenters to construe the direct tax clause narrowly. It was evident that the apportionment rule stressed a formal political power and the necessity of maintaining the political equality of equal numbers of voters. It made no allowance for disparities in wealth among the states considered as political and economic units.

This shortcoming of the apportionment rule can be seen by imagining two states with equal population but grossly unequal wealth (say in land). Under the apportionment rule the tax burden on each state would be equal, even though the tax bill would be a much greater burden on the citizens of the poor state relative to their wealth. Moreover, there would be no reason to assume that the representatives from each state had an equal voice in the national legislative process. Formally their voices would be equal in

93

the Congress, but it is not unreasonable to assume that the effective power of the representatives from the wealthier states would be greater because of the wealth and power of their constituencies.

There was one further difficulty with the apportionment rule as applied to the 1894 statute: It protected against the wrong kind of tyranny because apportionment protected against the victimization of political rather than economic groups. This may not have been a sufficient reason for holding the apportionment rule inapplicable. Apportionment, imperfect or not, was the term of the pact and all that we had to guard against tyranny of the majority, so Fuller might have reasoned. Nevertheless, this difficulty did have the effect of lending a strange element to the Court's decision. Although the apportionment rule served important constitutional purposes, and thus was understandably viewed by the justices, unlike the modern student of constitutional law, as something more than a technical requirement, there still seemed something odd in using it to respond to the 1894 statute and the problem in democratic theory that it raised.

The power of the poor to tax the rich stems from their superior numbers, as is manifest in the fact that only 2 percent of the nation would shoulder the burden of the 1894 tax. The wealthy 2 percent were not, of course, denied a voice in the legislative process that culminated in the adoption of the tax, and in fact their actual power was no doubt well out of proportion to their numbers. Nevertheless, they must have been overwhelmed thoroughly, thus raising the spectre that every theory of democracy must confront: tyranny by the majority. In this instance the alleged tyranny arose because those with political power placed the burden of taxation on others. At first approximation this may seem to be the kind of danger the apportionment rule, linking representation and taxation, was meant to guard against, but there was one important difference. The rule of apportionment involves not a general protection against political victimization but rather a protection against political victimization of a very special kind. The Constitution protects the states qua states from having a taxation burden placed on their citizens in excess of their political power; apportionment is a principle of federalism. The rule of apportionment protects certain kinds of political groups, namely collectivities known as states—it might have been seen as a substitute for the veto states possessed under the Articles of Confederation—while the income tax was a threat to an economic group, the rich.

In making the case turn on the Direct Tax Clause, Fuller might have avoided the difficulties of a more freewheeling, open-ended approach that based the decision on the abstract principle assuring equality before the law. He might have avoided also the difficulties of reinterpreting the Uniformity Clause so as to give it a non-geographic orientation, or, alternatively, to make it sensitive to de facto geographic circumstances (the geographic distribution of the wealthy). In focusing on the Direct Tax Clause, and thus stressing the linkage of taxation and representation, Fuller may have found a more thoroughgoing protection of property rights than the Uniformity Clause would have provided, which guaranteed only equal rates. At the same time, however, the decision to use the Direct Tax Clause left the Court's judgment resting on a provision of the Constitution that was addressed to a problem other than the one raised by the income tax; it meant that the Court did not address frontally and directly the egalitarianism of the 1894 statute, which, of course, was the point of the exercise. The contrived quality of the Court's opinion stemmed not from the Direct Tax Clause itself, on the theory that the clause did not serve any useful purposes, but rather from the fact that the purposes it served were not the ones threatened by the 1894 measure. Relying on the direct tax rationale produced a plausible, if not compelling, decision for Fuller, in the sense that a tax on the income of property is probably as much a direct tax as is a tax on property, but it impoverished the public debate on the tax and, to the extent that these things matter, enhanced the likelihood that the decision would be revised by constitutional amendment.

IV

The early 1890s was a radical period in American politics in which fundamental challenges were posed to the social order and to the capitalist system that underlay that order. Both the Pullman Strike and the 1894 income tax could be seen as creating such challenges. In *Debs* and in *Pollock* the Court spoke to each challenge in turn and thus found itself in the position of using the Constitution to, so to speak, man the barricades. The power of the state to maintain order was affirmed and the power of the state to redistribute wealth denied. Yet *Pollock* strained the institutional resources of the Court and raised, in the profession and maybe beyond, questions about its legitimacy in a way that was not true of *Debs*.

While the Court spoke with one voice in *Debs*, it was divided closely in *Pollock*. Moreover, the division in *Pollock* was accentuated by the initial inability of Fuller to form a majority and then by the phenomenon of the vacillating justice. Of course, at one level, dissent is one of the great institutional features of the Supreme Court, helping to ensure the integrity of the majority position and providing a forum for the expression of ideas that might later control. The right to dissent had secured for itself a venerable place in the institutional practices of the Supreme Court by the 1890s, and there was ample reason to exercise that right in *Pollock*. But division among the justices, especially given the form it took in *Pollock*, also tends to cast doubt on the correctness of the majority's position.

Fuller's judgment reached the public accompanied by a loud and strong statement from four justices—and maybe at one point even five—declaring it to be mistaken. Critics of the decision could invoke the authority and arguments of the dissenters for support. The depth of the division, along with the circumstance of the vacillating justice, could even serve as a basis of rejecting the decision. In his famous 1893 article, Professor Thayer of Harvard argued that acts of Congress should enjoy a presumption of validity and should not be overturned except in the clearest cases.[47] A sharp division among the justices—as in *Pollock*—suggests the absence of the requisite clarity and counsels in favor of letting the statute stand.

There was also the issue of precedent. To reach the judgment in *Debs*, the Court had to extrapolate from precedent, particularly from those cases denying the states the power to interfere with the free flow of commerce. Brewer had to read the dormant Commerce Clause as a prohibition on the American Railway Union and in doing so he had to move by inference. He also had to finesse certain maxims of equity. Yet, unlike Fuller, he did not have to repudiate any previous decisions of the Supreme Court. Fuller also could have brought himself within the terms of stare decisis, if he reasoned directly, as Brewer did in the rate regulation case, from a general theory of property rights and the obligation of the state to treat all equally. But when he chose instead to invoke the Direct Tax Clause, which from one view might have seemed the legally safer strategy, his judgment was brought into a conflict with a number of Supreme Court precedents.

One such precedent, already noted, was the carriage tax case of 1796. It had indicated that only real estate and capitation taxes were direct taxes. Another, of more contemporary significance, sustained an income tax passed during the Civil War.[48] That tax encompassed rents, dividends, and earned income and was necessitated by the disruption of foreign commerce because of the war and the subsequent loss in revenue from tariffs. The Civil War precedent was not readily distinguishable, but Fuller limited it to situations of national emergency.

Fuller was determined to free himself of the force of the earlier decisions, and in so doing he grasped one of the unique and highly commendable features of constitutional adjudication: It enables justices to reach behind earlier interpretation and to ground their decisions on the Constitution pure. Earlier decisions—whether involving the tax on a carriage, or, to take another example, *Plessy v. Ferguson*[49]—are but interpretations of the underlying constitutional text and can be repudiated on the theory that they are mistaken. *Pollock*, like *Brown*, was premised on the view that the Constitution—even as contract—receives its operative meaning from judicial interpretation but nonetheless transcends any of those particular interpretations. Oddly enough, the Constitution, as a legal artifact, both ties us

[47] James B. Thayer, "The Origin and Scope of the American Doctrine of Constitutional Law," *Harv. L. Rev.*, 7: 129 (1893).

[48] Springer v. United States, 102 U.S. 586 (1881).

[49] 163 U.S. 537 (1896). See Chapter 12.

to the past and authorizes bold breaks with the past. It is both conservative and radical.

Although the refusal to be bound by precedent might thus have been wholly justifiable, the fact remains that it put the authority of the Court into question. It divided the Court's use of the past, revering the original pact but disputing the century of accumulated experience under it. To borrow the title of Arnold Paul's book, it provoked a "conservative crisis." It also widened the gap between constitutional and common law adjudication, for in the latter there is no source of authority that stands higher than previous judicial decisions, unless it be reason itself. The repudiation of precedent even lent force and impetus to the charge that the justices simply were writing their own values into law, or using the judicial power to further their class interests; submission to a precedent, no matter how mistaken, appears a form of self-denial, an exercise of discipline and restraint.

Another source of institutional stress created by the *Pollock* decision, distinguishing it from *Debs*, arose from the conflict of the Court with the political branches. As noted in Chapter 3, the emphasis in *Debs* was on the coordination rather than the separation of powers: The Supreme Court spoke only to the injunction, but it implicitly—and maybe not so implicitly—sustained a coordinated strategy of the federal government to restore peace in Chicago. *Pollock*, on the other hand, put the Supreme Court in a confrontational stance vis-à-vis the other branches. It invalidated an act of Congress. Cleveland was no friend of the 1894 measure, but the statute was ardently defended by his attorney general, Richard Olney, and when the Court invalidated this statute, it necessarily rejected the considered position of a coordinate branch.

To engage in conflicts with the political branches is the Court's prerogative and perhaps even its duty under a theory—espoused so clearly by Brewer in Albany—that saw the Court, because of its very independence from the popular pressures, as the safeguard of the nation. On the other hand, each exercise of this prerogative tests the good will of the other branches of government and strains their relationship with the Court. The loss of this good will is nowhere more evident than in the attorney general's petition for rehearing, filed after the initial decision in *Pollock*. It is marked by a biting tone and a bitterness that are indeed startling.[50]

---

[50] Olney's "suggestion on the part of the United States" in response to appellants' petition for rehearing is reported in full at 158 U.S. 605. The tone might also be attributable to Olney's personal involvement in the case and the argument. A month before the hearing, Olney had forced out Solicitor General Lawrence Maxwell, who was supposed to argue *Pollock* for the United States, and had taken over the case himself. One scholar takes a dim view of Olney's motive for this action, arguing that it may have been done "to enhance his own professional standing by participating in a case which he knew would be of major importance" or to "vindicat[e] his own and the Justice Department's reputation" after the *E. C. Knight* case. Eggert, "Richard Olney," 29.

Finally, *Pollock* lacked the directness or explicitness of *Debs*. In *Debs* the Court spoke to the challenge it faced. True, it did not explicitly focus on the breaches of the peace that occurred in Chicago, the individual acts of violence, but instead emphasized the impact of those events on the free flow of commerce. However, that particular mode of analysis was dictated by the need—perceived by all—to locate distinct federal interests that might warrant federal intervention. The use of the Commerce Clause in *Debs* was not contrived—on the contrary. The Pullman Strike threatened the economic union and, for that reason, the Court refused to ground the standing of the United States in something so trivial as the property interest that the government might have in the mails. For similar reasons, it refused to rest its decision on a statute, namely the Sherman Act, but rather spoke at the appropriate level of generality. The Court's opinion was equal to the occasion. The same compliment cannot be paid to *Pollock* and its use of the Direct Tax Clause. Whatever importance the rule of apportionment might have in preventing geopolitical victimization, or preserving one important component of federal structure, it could not persuasively be presented as a guarantee against redistributing wealth from the rich to the poor.

Explicitness and directness are more than issues of style. They are institutional imperatives. The right and power of the Court to thwart popular will, whether it appears on the streets, in legislative halls or in the action of the executive, stems from the duty of the Court to give authoritative expression to the values embodied in the Constitution. This duty devolves on the Court because of its distinctive institutional features—its relative independence, so stressed by Brewer, and its practice of engaging in a public dialogue over the meaning of those values, a practice not mentioned by Brewer but implicit in his celebration of the rationalistic processes of the law. What the chief justice said in *Pollock*—that the income tax is a direct tax and thus invalid because it is not apportioned—may have been sufficient on one level to sustain the judgment of the Court, but it was not responsive to the fundamental question being posed by the political system. A question was being raised regarding the power of government to redistribute wealth, but what the Court said seemed, in the final analysis, somewhat beside the point.

The issues posed by *Debs* and *Pollock* did not, of course, end with the Supreme Court's pronouncements. The first federal response to *Debs* occurred in the Clayton Act of 1914, and there Congress did not deny the injunctive power legitimated by Brewer but instead surrounded it with procedural limitations. The Clayton Act defined the preconditions for the issuance of injunctions and restructured the scope of persons bound by an injunction.[51] In some respects, however, the Clayton Act did break new

---

[51] Ch. 323, Sect. 15–25, 38 Stat. 730, 736–40 (1914). These provisions of the

Clayton Act can be understood as a codification of established principles. Jus-

ground, for example by creating an exemption for labor from the antitrust laws. It also extended the guarantee of trial by jury in criminal contempts. Admittedly, these revisions would have important implications for the labor injunction in the years following 1914, but neither could be seen as a reversal of *Debs*. The *Debs* decision was not predicated on the Sherman Act but on the Commerce Clause and other bodies of law (public nuisance doctrine), and thus to exempt labor from the antitrust law would not in any way bar the *Debs* injunction. Moreover, the jury trial provision did not alter the position the Court took on that issue in *Debs*. The Clayton Act extended trial by jury to contempts where the contemptuous conduct was also a violation of the criminal statute, but it specifically exempted from its scope contempts in cases commenced by the United States.

A generation later the political mood of the nation changed. A demand arose for a more radical revision of the labor injunction. This revision occurred in the Norris-La Guardia Act of 1932,[52] and it is no accident that the most celebrated tract written on behalf of that Act—Frankfurter and Greene's book, *The Labor Injunction* (1930)—began by invoking the plank of the Democratic Party denouncing *Debs*.[53] By this time, at issue was not just *Debs* but the entire program of the Fuller Court—the commitment to liberty and limited government—because it was seen as a threat to President Franklin Roosevelt's recovery program. Even so, the result was not a clear reversal of *Debs*. The Norris-La Guardia Act, which denied the federal courts the power to issue injunctions in "labor disputes," worked a revision of *Debs* only to the extent that what was involved in that case could be deemed a "labor dispute."[54] I have argued that, in its time and in its setting, the Pullman Strike was not a "labor dispute," as that term might normally be understood, but rather a threat to the public order.

The polity's response to *Pollock*, on the other hand, was of an entirely different character. While *Debs* may have been domesticated, *Pollock* was repudiated. It is impossible to know how much that repudiation was due

---

tice Brandeis described the limitation on the scope of persons bound as an "established principle ... of equity jurisdiction," and the same could be said of the rules defining the conditions for an injunction. Chase Nat'l Bank v. Norwalk, 291 U.S. 431, 437 (1934).

[52] Ch. 90, 47 Stat. 70 (1932).

[53] Felix Frankfurter and Nathan Greene, *The Labor Injunction* (New York: Macmillan, 1930), 1.

[54] Despite the broad and unqualified language of the Norris-La Guardia Act, the Court in United States v. United Mine Workers, 330 U.S. 258 (1947), upheld an injunction against a coal strike, where the United States had taken control of the coal mines and the attorney general sought the injunction. The Court said the strike was not a "labor dispute" because the United States was not an ordinary employer. It was exercising a "sovereign function." Ibid., 289. The Court's notion of what sovereignty entailed drew upon the *Debs* notion of "special exigency": "Under the conditions found by the President to exist, it would be difficult to conceive of a more vital and urgent function of the Government than the seizure and operation of the bituminous coal mines." Ibid.

to the various factors I identified as straining the institutional resources of the Court in *Pollock*: the sharp division among the justices; the vacillating justice; the divided attitude toward the past; the conflict with the other branches; and, perhaps, the unwillingness to address the real issue. But whatever the cause, the response to *Pollock* came in a rather blunt form: In 1913 the nation adopted an amendment to the Constitution—the Sixteenth—which simply provides: "The Congress shall have power to lay and collect taxes on incomes, from whatever source derived, without apportionment among the several States, and without regard to any census or enumeration."

Some constitutional amendments may be, in an odd sense, a tribute to the Court and its role in the constitutional system, because a decision of the Court provoked the polity to a new and deeper understanding of its inherited public morality. On one reading, the Eleventh Amendment—the nation's response to *Chisholm v. Georgia*[55]—might be such an instance. One might even venture such a claim about *Dred Scott*[56] and the Civil War amendments. The Sixteenth Amendment was not, however, of that character. It simply removed what appeared to be a technical objection or impediment that *Pollock* had posed to the income tax. The amendment did not deepen the nation's understanding of the issue, nor did it even speak to the egalitarianism that inspired the measure. The Sixteenth Amendment simply "reversed" *Pollock*.[57] In the half-century following its adoption, the progressive income tax became a commonplace feature of contemporary political life and central to the proper functioning of the modern state. Two scholars, Walter Blum and Harry Kalven, Jr., noted this fact in a now classic essay, "The Uneasy Case for Progressive Taxation," and yet found themselves at a loss to explain how the progressive tax made sense in a society that was unwilling to acknowledge and robustly pursue the ideal of economic equality.[58]

---

[55] 2 U.S. (2 Dall.) 419 (1793).

[56] Scott v. Sandford, 60 U.S. (19 How.) 393 (1856). See Chapter 8.

[57] In 1909 several senators proposed the creation of an income tax through statutory amendments to the pending tariff bill, 44 Cong. Rec. 1351, 1420–21 (1909), but it was then decided that a constitutional amendment would be necessary to avoid the force of *Pollock*. Ibid., 1568. The debate in Congress focused on technical issues of constitutional interpretation and congressional authority and only incidentally touched on the grander ideological issues introduced by, for example, Senator Borah, 44 Cong. Rec., 3988 (1909).

[58] Walter J. Blum and Harry Kalven, Jr., "The Uneasy Case for Progressive Taxation," *U. Chi. L. Rev.*, 19: 417, 519–20 (1952) (published in 1953 as a book by the University of Chicago Press).

PART THREE

The Response to Progressivism

D EBS AND POLLOCK established both affirmative and negative limits on state power. In *Debs* the power to maintain order was affirmed, while in *Pollock* the power of the state to redistribute wealth was denied, though in somewhat oblique terms. These limits left the social contract intact, but within them there remained a vast domain within which progressivism operated.

A broad, sprawling movement, progressivism comprised many heterogeneous elements, some in conflict with others. Through the conciliatory processes of politics, however, differences among the contending factions were sometimes buried and coalitions built. The result was a series of statutes and regulatory programs related to antitrust, labor, and the rail industry that I take to be the hallmark of progressivism. These measures addressed problems created by the growth and maturation of industrial capitalism, among them price-fixing, monopolization, price-gouging, and the exploitation of labor.

In this respect, progressivism bore a similarity to reforms advocated by a number of other movements of the time, including populism, socialism, and Bellamy's utopian nationalism. For progressives, as for these other reformers, the primary category of analysis was economic: All spoke of "workers," "consumers," "capital," "labor," "employers," and "employees." But progressivism differed from these other, more leftist movements in the incremental or ameliorative nature of the reforms proposed.

Progressives sought to accomplish their goals through exercises of state power, particularly through legislation, but their reforms were nevertheless consistent with the ideal of limited government that so dominated nineteenth-century America. Progressives did not aim to displace the market as the basic social mechanism, as did populists and socialists, but rather called on the state to eradicate the market's "abuses" or "excesses." In fact, the Sherman Antitrust Act was primarily defended on the ground that it was necessary to preserve the market itself. The essential paradox of antitrust, as Justice White saw it in the 1911 cases, was that freedom had to be curtailed in order to preserve freedom.[1] Statutes imposing ceilings on the number of hours worked or on railroad tariffs constituted more significant departures from the free market, but they were also justified in terms consistent with market ideology. Many insisted that without state intervention the contractual freedom upon which the market was premised would be purely formal.

Fuller and his colleagues were not progressives, no matter how broadly the term is conceived, yet it would be wrong to assume, as previous

---

[1] United States v. American Tobacco Co., 221 U.S. 106, 180 (1911).

accounts have, that the Court's stance toward progressivism was simply one of unqualified hostility. In some instances, progressive measures were struck down—*Lochner* and *Ex parte Young*, one decided in 1905, the other in 1908, are stunning examples of this tendency. *Lochner* held unconstitutional a maximum hours statute; *Ex parte Young* upheld an order holding the attorney general of Minnesota in contempt for enforcing a state statute regulating railroad rates. But in other contexts, such as antitrust, the Court responded differently. Led by Justice Peckham, the very man who wrote *Lochner* and *Ex parte Young*, the Court construed the Sherman Act in a way that laid the foundations for the so-called trust-busting campaign of Theodore Roosevelt's administration.

In responding to progressive reforms, the Court was always suspicious, as it had been in *Pollock*, that state power was being used to take from the rich and give to the poor, favoring one economic class over another and thereby violating the terms of the social contract. The traditionalists within the progressive movement denied that such redistribution of wealth or power was their purpose and defended their reform measures in the most innocuous terms, insisting that they were aimed at nothing more than the protection of health or the promotion of industrial peace. Sometimes the Court accepted the challenged statute or enforcement action on these terms and put its suspicion to one side, but in other instances, recalling Brewer's warning at Albany, the Court was convinced that the seemingly innocent explanation was a sham and acted accordingly. The justices were often of this mind when they reviewed efforts to regulate railroad rates and to fix the terms and conditions of employment, but were less so in antitrust. There, the risk of "legalized thievery" seemed minimal, and as a consequence, the Court looked more favorably on exercises of state power in that domain.

Despite these differences in the Court's response to progressivism, and the checkered pattern of decisions that emerged, all of which will be described in detail in the next three chapters, one factor did exert a unifying force. The Court always had to come to terms with the distinctive mode of state intervention—legislation—so favored by progressives. Statutes were no more nor less coercive than the prohibitions found in the common law (which, at that time, were sometimes backed by criminal as well as civil sanctions), and thus no greater threat to liberty viewed abstractly. Yet they arose from a process that, in the justices' eyes, not only enhanced the risk of redistribution but also raised unique problems of legitimacy.

The common law was judge-made and seen as the embodiment of reason, albeit the "artificial reason"[2] characteristic of the judicial process. The

---

[2] The phrase was used by Sir Edward Coke, sitting on King's Bench in 1607, in *Prohibitions del Roy*, which can be found in vol. 7, pt. 12, p. 65 of the 1777 reprint of his *Reports*.

legitimacy of a common law rule derives from the judiciary's capacity to connect it meaningfully to a set of principles that constitute the underlying values of society, while the legitimacy of a statute stems from the fact that it expresses the desires of the collectivity. In 1901, in a case in which the common law rule against rate discrimination was applied to the interstate telegraph industry, Justice Brewer asked, "What is the common law?" and then turned to, among others, Chancellor Kent, for an answer: "The common law includes those principles, usages and rules of action applicable to the government and security of person and property, which do not rest for their authority upon any express and positive declaration of the will of the legislature."[3]

Today the appeal of legislation as a form of lawmaking stems from the very fact that it expresses the will of the electorate and its presumptive agent, the legislature. At the turn of the century, however, in many constitutional circles, including those that governed in the Supreme Court, the commitment to popular sovereignty was tempered by an even stronger commitment to the social contract tradition. Although contractarianism made consent the touchstone of legitimacy and thus introduced a democratic element, it looked to a more static, historically defined consent. The responsiveness of an agency of the state to the electorate that is presently empowered—"the multitudes" and the "numbers," as Brewer put it in Albany—was seen as more a vice than a virtue.

Progressives knew this and adjusted their strategies accordingly. They sometimes invoked notions of popular sovereignty in defending various statutes before the Court, but by and large they cast the advantages of legislation in more technocratic terms.[4] They emphasized the fact that statutes were more easily revised and enabled the law to keep up with the changing times. Progressives also claimed that legislators could conduct a more thoroughgoing factual inquiry and could achieve a specificity not available through common law rules. Statutes, for example, could prohibit working more than sixty hours a week or set a ceiling of 2 cents per gallon as a rate for shipping milk, rather than simply proscribing an "unreasonable" work week or "discriminatory" rates.

The justices well understood the technical advantages of legislation but nonetheless remained troubled by the fact that it was the embodiment of will rather than of reason. This concern did not lead to a wholesale invalidation of the progressive agenda, but it did result in a determined effort to create and impose limits on the legislative power. Driven by a set of

---

[3] See Western Union Tel. Co. v. Call Publishing Co., 181 U.S. 92, 101 (1901), quoting James Kent's *Commentaries on American Law*, 1st ed. (New York: O. Halsted, 1826), 1: 471.

[4] The debate about statutes is summarized in Roscoe Pound, "Common Law and Legislation," *Harv. L. Rev.*, 21: 383 (1908).

imperatives that they saw rooted in the Constitution, the justices cabined the legislative power by a set of rules that bore a striking similarity to those that constituted the common law: Judge-created, these rules emerged on a case-by-case basis over time and were founded on principle. In this way, legislation increasingly was being transformed into a branch of the common law.

In some instances, as in the promulgation of the "rule of reason" in the 1911 antitrust cases, the limiting principle was read into the statute. In other cases, exemplified by *Lochner* and *Ex parte Young*, the limiting principle was encapsulated in such constitutional rights as "liberty of contract" and "the right of fair return" that were used to mark the outer bounds of state power. Either way, the legislative power was domesticated at the very moment that it was emerging as the predominant form of lawmaking in the modern state, as we were entering what Guido Calabresi has called "the age of statutes."[5]

---

[5] Guido Calabresi, *A Common Law for the Age of Statutes* (Cambridge: Harvard University Press, 1982).

CHAPTER V

The Antitrust Campaign

TODAY WE TEND to view antitrust in technocratic terms. At issue is whether the judiciary should prohibit certain business activity; the standard for resolving that issue is consumer welfare and the method of analysis economic. The judicial task is to predict the likely impact on competition of challenged business practices; the intellectual struggles raised by an antitrust case largely center around those predictions.[1] In the formative era of antitrust, however, the disputes were of another type altogether. They were not technocratic but "constitutional," in the broadest sense of that term. The Sherman Act cases were viewed in much the same way as the modern Court views cases arising under the various civil rights acts.

The antitrust cases were high on the justices' agenda.[2] *Northern Securities*[3] in 1904 was as important to them as the *Pollock* case[4] of 1895 or the *Insular Cases*[5] of 1901. It drew the energy and passion of the justices and sharply divided them, leaving the Court without a majority opinion. Indeed, in terms of the importance the justices assigned to the case and in terms of the conflicts it engendered, *Northern Securities* far surpassed the one response of the Fuller Court to progressivism that we most recall—

---

[1] See, e.g., Robert H. Bork, *The Antitrust Paradox: A Policy at War with Itself* (New York: Basic Books, 1978), and Richard A. Posner, "The Chicago School of Antitrust Analysis," *U. Pa. L. Rev.*, 127: 925 (1979). For a different approach, see Eleanor M. Fox, "The Modernization of Antitrust: A New Equilibrium," *Cornell L. Rev.*, 66: 1140 (1981).

[2] For general works on the history of antitrust during this formative period, see William Letwin, *Law and Economic Policy in America: The Evolution of the Sherman Antitrust Act* (New York: Random House, 1965; repr. Chicago: University of Chicago Press, 1981); Martin J. Sklar, *The Corporate Reconstruction of American Capitalism, 1890–1916: The Market, the Law, and Politics* (Cambridge: Cambridge University Press, 1988); and Hans B. Thorelli, *The Federal Antitrust Policy: Origination of an American Tradition* (London: George Allen & Unwin, 1954).

[3] Northern Sec. Co. v. United States, 193 U.S. 197 (1904).

[4] Pollock v. Farmers' Loan & Trust Co., 157 U.S. 429 (1895); 158 U.S. 601 (1895). See Chapter 4.

[5] Dooley v. United States, 182 U.S. 222 (1901); Armstrong v. United States, 182 U.S. 243 (1901); Downes v. Bidwell, 182 U.S. 244 (1901); Dooley v. United States, 183 U.S. 151 (1901). See Chapter 8.

Lochner v. New York.[6] The antitrust cases were also highly visible public events. Most were initiated by the executive branch and involved the leading figures of the Supreme Court bar. The Court's decisions provoked responses by presidents and Congress and played an important role in the genesis of the Clayton and Federal Trade Commission acts of 1914. The antitrust campaign raised deep and far-reaching questions about the limits of state power, and the method used to resolve those questions was anything but technocratic.

The term "consumer welfare,"[7] as a technical economic concept, had no special significance for the justices. It was not part of their vocabulary. At most one could say that the justices, simply because they were public servants, were concerned with the impact of the Sherman Act on the public welfare in general. It is also fair to say that the justices were committed to the market as the central ordering device of social and economic relationships. But for them—and it is here that the constitutional perspective enters—the market was more a political than an economic construct. It was not a device for achieving the optimum allocation of resources but rather a projection of political and social ideals.[8]

As a political construct, the market offered a vision of a society constituted of atomistic units motivated by considerations of self-interest: Individuals are engaged in a competitive struggle to further their own ends and relate to one another through barter and exchange. It was also assumed that the dynamics of competition would moderate the excesses of individual actors and spur them on to greater progress. Of course, self-interested conduct can take a variety of forms and might well lead businessmen to pursue a course of conduct that can destroy the underlying structure of the market. Atoms may combine; barriers to contractual freedom might be erected; or devices found—like price-fixing or mergers—that provide a measure of relief from the rigors of the competitive struggle. In the early cases, the Court was confronted with business practices that easily could be characterized in such terms and was required to reflect on the meaning of the market as a political construct. Even more, they were forced to clarify the role of the state in this construct.

---

[6] 198 U.S. 45 (1905). See Chapter 6.

[7] Robert Bork has used the term in trying to place a technocratic gloss on the early cases (see "The Rule of Reason and the Per Se Concept: Price Fixing and Market Division," *Yale L.J.*, 74: 775; 75: 373 [1965–66]) and the Sherman Act itself (see "Legislative Intent and the Policy of the Sherman Act," *J.L. & Econ.*, 9: 7 [1966]). Bork's reading of the statute is challenged in Robert Pitofsky, "The Political Content of Antitrust," *U. Pa. L. Rev.*, 127: 1051 (1979), and in Robert H. Lande, "Wealth Transfers as the Original and Primary Concern of Antitrust: The Efficiency Interpretation Challenged," *Hastings L.J.*, 34: 65 (1982). See also the sources cited in note 2, above.

[8] See Pitofsky, "Political Content of Antitrust."

Chapter V: *The Antitrust Campaign*

Traditionally, the state was to operate simply as a background institution to protect property rights and enforce contracts—thus facilitating the operation of the market. But the Sherman Act, enacted in 1890,[9] seemed to contemplate a more robust role for the state. It did not burden the state with the task of promoting "allocative efficiency" or "consumer welfare" understood in some technocratic sense; this not only would have altered the substantive ends of state activity, making them economic rather than political, but also would have made the state into an affirmative instrumentality of public policy and would have constituted a sharp and decisive break with the classical conception of the state.[10] That was far, far from anyone's contemplation. While the Sherman Act enlarged the role of the state, the purpose of state intervention was not to promote efficiency but rather, by curbing business practices that constituted restraints of trade and monopolization, to protect the market from itself. The duty of the Court, in turn, was to decide whether such intervention was constitutionally permissible, an inquiry that raised far-reaching issues about federalism and liberty.

The federalism issue concerned the power of the central government: Was the Sherman Act, or the various enforcement measures under it, within the scope of powers allowed the national government? The Court began its deliberations on this issue with the proposition, central not only to cases like *Debs*[11] and *Pollock* but to the entire contractarian tradition, that the federal government was a government of limited powers. It had no general undefined power to act in the public interest or to further the well-being of the community. To the extent that any such broad power existed, it was the so-called police power and remained with the states. The Constitution enumerated and assigned various powers to the central government, such as the regulation of interstate commerce, and the initial task for the Court was to ascertain whether antitrust fell within one of those enumerated powers or, alternatively, might be an exercise of the police power and thus left to the states.

The liberty issue, on the other hand, arose from the obvious fact that each application of the Sherman Act interfered with the liberty of a businessman to engage in a specific transaction, such as entering into a contract or buying another business. Today we tend to think of the precise entrepreneurial liberties at issue in the early cases—for example, the liberty to enter into a contract to fix prices—as unworthy of any constitutional protection whatsoever: A contract to fix prices is the paradigmatic contract against public policy and, as such, a nullity. But it must be recognized that our per-

---

[9] Sherman Antitrust Act, Ch. 647, Sect. 1, 26 Stat. 209 (1890).
[10] For a different reading, see Sklar, *Corporate Reconstruction*, 43–179.
[11] *In re* Debs, 158 U.S. 564 (1895). See Chapter 3.

spective is colored by almost a hundred years of Supreme Court pronouncements. At the turn of the century, as the antitrust campaign was beginning, claims on behalf of liberties of this type appeared more formidable. Indeed, at that time, the Sherman Act rather than *Lochner* was the primary battlefield of liberty of contract, even when the contract in question fixed prices or set up a cartel.

The Fuller Court did not come to an easy or quick solution to either the federalism or the liberty issue. Its response spanned a twenty-year period that can be divided into four different phases: the beginning—*E. C. Knight* (1895)[12]; a second beginning—*Trans-Missouri* (1897),[13] *Joint Traffic* (1897),[14] and *Addyston Pipe* (1899);[15] the unraveling—*Northern Securities* (1904); and finally, the new synthesis—*Standard Oil* (1911)[16] and *American Tobacco* (1911).[17]

In its first encounter with the Sherman Act, the Court denied enforcement. Using a traditional framework for the analysis of the Commerce Clause, the Court concluded that it was beyond the power of Congress under that clause to reach the transaction in question. In the second phase, the Court, under the leadership of Justice Peckham, managed to use this very same framework to give new life to the statute. The Court broadened the commerce power by demonstrating how activities otherwise assumed to be beyond its scope might be reached; at the same time, it cut liberty of contract back to the bounds of this newly expanded commerce power. If an exercise of power was deemed within the Commerce Clause, then there could be no objection raised to it on the ground that it infringed on constitutionally protected liberty and thus was a denial of substantive due process. In that way the commerce and due process inquiries became coextensive, and due process became the secondary or subordinate category.

The full implications of this position became apparent only in the third stage of doctrinal evolution, in the *Northern Securities* case of 1904, when a majority of five (Brewer, in a separate concurrence, and four dissenters, including Peckham) pulled back from *Trans-Missouri, Joint Traffic*, and *Addyston Pipe*. They perceived a special threat to liberty and federalism in President Roosevelt's effort to undo the effort of James Hill and J. P. Morgan to merge two rail lines and, although the suit was upheld by a slim majority (Brewer and the four who joined Harlan's plurality opinion), the *Northern Securities* decision left the Court without a coherent position on the reach of the Sherman Act. It was not until 1911, in the *Standard*

---

[12] United States v. E. C. Knight Co., 156 U.S. 1 (1895).

[13] United States v. Trans-Missouri Freight Ass'n, 166 U.S. 290 (1897).

[14] United States v. Joint Traffic Ass'n, 171 U.S. 505 (1898).

[15] Addyston Pipe & Steel Co. v. United States, 175 U.S. 211 (1899).

[16] Standard Oil Co. v. United States, 221 U.S. 1 (1911).

[17] United States v. American Tobacco Co., 221 U.S. 106 (1911).

Chapter V: *The Antitrust Campaign*

Oil and *American Tobacco* cases, that White, one of the dissenters in *Northern Securities* and the new chief justice, drew all the pieces together and created the doctrinal edifice that remains to this day. He did so by using an idea he had first articulated in his dissents in *Trans-Missouri* and *Joint Traffic* and that had been put forward more recently by Brewer in his separate concurrence in *Northern Securities*.

The principal instrument of White's synthesis in *Standard Oil* and *American Tobacco* was the rule of reason, which, paralleling a method first employed in *E. C. Knight* on the federalism issue, mooted the constitutional objection based on liberty by inserting the constitutional protection of liberty within the terms of the statute itself. The statute, White said, prohibited only unreasonable restraints of trade, and the constitutional protection of liberty did not reach so far as to allow individuals to engage in activity deemed unreasonable. As originally understood, the concept of reasonableness was to be construed from a constitutional perspective, as a way of protecting what White called the "fundamental right of freedom to trade."[18] But in time that perspective was lost and supplanted by a technocratic one. In the rule of reason White found a method for synthesizing and stabilizing antitrust doctrine, but he also established the foundation for deconstitutionalizing this branch of the law.

I

The populists had little interest in the Sherman Act.[19] They railed against monopolies, but for the most part they did not seek to perfect the market and restore the competitive ethic. Nor did they have the least confidence in the enforcement mechanism of the Sherman Act, relying as it did on the federal courts and suits by the attorney general. Populists feared that the statute would be used, if at all, against their interests, probably to impede the growth of agrarian cooperative enterprises. They were not at all surprised to see the Sherman Act, in both its civil and criminal aspects, used against Debs and his followers. Given the wariness of the oppositional faction, and the natural inclinations of the forces then in control of the Democratic and Republican parties, during the early 1890s enforcement of the Sherman Act was lax and sporadic. The Court had few occasions during this period to confront the constitutional issues presented by the statute.

The first occasion arose in a suit against the Sugar Trust, *United States v. E. C. Knight*, which from the modern perspective involved the crudest of anticompetitive behavior. The American Sugar Refining Company had

---

[18] Ibid., 180.
[19] Tony Powers, "United States v. E. C. Knight: The Problem of the People's Party and the Antitrust Policy" (Yale Law School, 1977; unpublished manuscript on file with author).

embarked on a program to acquire control of all the sugar refineries in America. By 1892, it had about 65 percent of the market. Only five refineries remained outside its empire, four owned and operated by Pennsylvania corporations and one in Boston. In March 1892 the American Sugar Company entered agreements to purchase the stock of the Pennsylvania refineries, a move that would give it 98 percent of the market. Attorney General Richard Olney filed a civil injunctive suit and asked that the stock-purchase agreements, which had been consummated in the interim, be canceled and that the stock be returned to its original owners. In a stunning defeat, the attorney general lost in both the lower court and the Supreme Court—the only vote he won was Harlan's.

To the modern reader, this result is startling, partly because of the extreme degree of industrial concentration—a "stupendous combination," as Justice Harlan said[20]—and partly because the decision was followed only months later by decisions invalidating the income tax (*Pollock*) and sustaining the labor injunction (*Debs*). True, the Court sustained the *Debs* injunction as an enforcement of the Commerce Clause, but it did not in any way disapprove of the lower court's use of the Sherman Act. In fact, the criminal prosecution against Debs, which also was predicated on the Sherman Act, was still pending at the very moment the suit against the Sugar Trust was dismissed. The inference of class justice, fully exploited by Westin and Paul,[21] seemed inescapable.

Not much can be said to deny the coincidence of *Debs*, *Pollock*, and *E. C. Knight*, but it seems to me no more than a fluke of the adjudicatory process. The Court could not control when cases arose, nor could it completely control which ones it would consider. It should be emphasized, however, that *E. C. Knight* was *not* an issue in the election of 1896, although *Debs* and *Pollock* were. Monopolies were denounced by the new Populist-Democratic coalition, but, for reasons already suggested, an antitrust campaign was not seen as the cure. Nor was the Supreme Court's decision in *E. C. Knight*, holding that stopping the merger was not within the commerce power of the Congress, denounced by the left or by any major political force as a distortion of prevailing doctrine.[22] The political reaction might have been different if the Court had stated that the Sherman Act proscribed only "artificial" monopolies, that is, monopolies conferred by government (which is what "monopoly" meant at common law), and not

---

[20] *E. C. Knight*, 156 U.S. at 18 (Harlan, J., dissenting).

[21] Arnold M. Paul, *Conservative Crisis and the Rule of Law: Attitudes of Bar and Bench, 1887-1895* (Ithaca: Cornell University Press, 1960; repr. Gloucester, Mass.: Peter Smith, 1976); Alan F. Wes-

tin, "The Supreme Court, the Populist Movement, and the Campaign of 1896," *J. Politics*, 15: 3 (1953). See the discussion of their work in Chapter 1.

[22] See Powers, "Problem of the People's Party."

"practical" ones. But Fuller was meticulous in avoiding such a ruling or otherwise condoning the conduct of American Sugar. He noted that American Sugar defended its so-called practical monopoly on the ground of greater efficiencies, thereby allowing it to reduce prices. Yet Fuller was also careful to summarize the government's argument, which maintained that, in passing the Sherman Act and outlawing "monopolies," Congress was "not confined to the common law sense of the term."[23]

Refusing to pass on whether the acquisition was a form of monopolization proscribed by the Act, the Court dismissed the suit on commerce grounds. It held that the powers of the central government were limited to regulating the transportation of goods across state and national boundaries and did not embrace processes of production such as manufacturing (here, sugar refining). Some might regard this ruling as not much different from one directly allowing the acquisition—as an instance of class justice in the most striking sense. The fact of the matter is, however, that the Court's position on the scope of the commerce power was wholly congenial to the populists, who feared federal control over other processes of production, such as farming.[24] There was, moreover, ample basis in prevailing doctrine for distinguishing the exertion of federal power in *Debs* (over transportation) from the denial of federal power in *E. C. Knight* (over manufacturing).

Fuller's innovation lay in his reduction of the constitutional issue of national power to an issue of statutory interpretation. He defined his task as one of construing the reach of the statute, rather than the Commerce Clause, although he looked to constitutional doctrine for guidance in this undertaking, since the relevant phrase of the statute, "commerce among the several states," was part of the constitutional text. He posited an intent on the part of Congress to exercise all of its powers under the Commerce Clause and then read the statute in terms of this intent—Congress went to the limits of its power but no further.

Fuller's method had the effect of making the reach of the Sherman Act and the Commerce Clause coextensive, thereby ensuring the constitutionality of the Act insofar as the Commerce Clause was concerned, so that the Act would remain standing even if a particular application was denied. It also meant that the issue of national power would be decided on an as-applied basis; that is, the task of the Court in any antitrust proceeding was to see, on a case-by-case basis, whether the particular transaction or business practice at issue was itself within the scope of congressional power under the Commerce Clause. Thus, the question before the Court in *E. C.*

---

[23] 156 U.S. at 10.
[24] See Lawrence Goodwyn, *Democratic Promise: The Populist Movement in America* (New York: Oxford University Press, 1976), 25–50; Thorelli, *Federal Antitrust Policy*, 231–32; and Powers, "Problem of the People's Party," 19.

Knight was whether Congress had the constitutional power under the Commerce Clause to prevent the American Sugar Company from acquiring the Pennsylvania refinery.

In answering this question in the negative, the Court in *E. C. Knight* relied on two interlocking sets of distinctions, one pertaining to governmental power, the other to economic activity, the latter demarcating the bounds of the former. On the governmental side, the relevant distinction was between the commerce power and the police power. The federal government had no police power, but only a power to regulate interstate commerce. Congress, in other words, was not entitled to pass a statute simply because it would improve the health and welfare of the people (even if all the people of the country were benefited). In starting with this premise, the Court was invoking time-honored, nearly universal nineteenth-century constitutional principles that viewed the federal government as a limited government that existed only for specialized purposes. As noted in the discussion of *Debs* and *Pollock*, the federal government was then conceived of as a government among governments.

The task of setting bounds on the commerce power still remained. For this purpose the Court drew a distinction between two types of economic activity—manufacturing and transportation—and linked the police power with the former and the commerce power with the latter. The Court began with the self-evident proposition that the commerce power was limited to the regulation of "commerce," but then drew on the usage (common in the nineteenth century but perhaps not today) under which "commerce" was not coextensive with business, but instead referred specifically to transportation or, to use Marshall's phrase, "intercourse."[25] Congress was confined to regulating the arteries of interstate transportation—the highways, waterways, and rails—and the movement of goods from one state to another. Manufacturing, on the other hand, was understood as a process of transformation—as Fuller put it, "the fashioning of raw materials into a change of form for use"[26]—and was compared to the more familiar productive activities of the agrarian economy, farming and stock raising. Fuller characterized the refining of sugar as a form of manufacturing and concluded that the monopolization of that economic activity (through the acquisition of stock) was a proper subject of concern for the states, but not for the federal government.

Only Harlan dissented. He seemed to be moved largely by pragmatic considerations. Again and again, he stressed that the Sugar Trust had

---

[25] 156 U.S. at 12, quoting Gibbons v. Ogden, 22 U.S. (9 Wheat.) 1, 189 (1824).

[26] Ibid., 14, quoting Kidd v. Pearson, 128 U.S. 1, 20 (1888), in which Justice Lucius Q. C. Lamar said: "No distinction is more popular to the common mind, or more clearly expressed in economic and political literature, than that between manufacture and commerce."

monopolized a vital foodstuff and insisted that the federal government was the only power equal to the task of curbing this abuse of economic power:

> We have before us the case of a combination which absolutely controls ... the price of all refined sugar in this country. . . . What power is competent to protect the people of the United States against such danger except a national power. . .?[27]

Although the majority left the states free to prosecute monopolies in manufacturing, and although there were some notable state antitrust prosecutions at that time,[28] the power or readiness of any one state to interfere with one of its own industries was limited. The State of Pennsylvania did not alone suffer the consequences of monopolization. Those consequences would be felt throughout the United States, and if Pennsylvania attacked the Sugar Trust, other states might well offer it a safe haven.[29]

Like the majority, Harlan believed that the power of Congress under the Commerce Clause extended only to transportation or intercourse. But while the majority focused on the type of economic activity regulated, and asked whether it was a form or a part of transportation or intercourse, Harlan focused on the *impact* of the regulated activity on transportation or intercourse: "Whatever improperly obstructs the free course of interstate intercourse and trade . . . may be reached by Congress under its authority to regulate commerce among the states."[30] Then he conceptualized monopolistic control as an obstruction or interference with the free flow of the particular good throughout the United States—as though it were a boulder in the highway, to use the *Debs* metaphor. For Harlan, the monopolization of a manufacturing industry could be brought within the reach of Congress because of the impact monopolization would have on the sale of the good throughout the United States.

The majority knew that the sugar refined in Pennsylvania was clearly intended for sale in the national market and that monopoly control over manufacturing ultimately was to be felt in the price of manufactured goods

---

[27] Ibid., 44–45 (Harlan, J., dissenting).

[28] On state antitrust law, see Charles W. McCurdy, "The *Knight* Sugar Decision of 1895 and the Modernization of American Corporation Law, 1869–1903," *Bus. Hist. Rev.*, 53: 304 (1979), and James May, "Antitrust Practice and Procedure in the Formative Era: The Constitutional and Conceptual Reach of State Antitrust Law, 1880–1918," *U. Pa. L. Rev.*, 135: 495 (1987). The simple invocation of the police power did not vitiate all liberty of contract objections, but once the Court had considered and rejected liberty-based arguments in cases challenging the enforcement of the Sherman Act, those arguments had no force against state antitrust laws. See below, note 110.

[29] Professor McCurdy discusses the failure of state antitrust law in "*Knight* Sugar Decision," 336–40.

[30] 156 U.S. at 37 (Harlan, J., dissenting).

sold across state lines. Their error, if any, stemmed not from economic naîveté or a blind formalism, as is usually attributed to them, but rather from a determination to protect the limited character of the central government, as a government among governments, and to do so by using two categories or spheres of economic activity, manufacturing and transportation, to mark the bounds of the commerce power and the police power:

> It is vital that the independence of the commercial power and of the police power, and the delimitation between them, however sometimes perplexing, should always be recognized and observed, for while the one furnishes the strongest bond of union, the other is essential to the preservation of the autonomy of the States as required by our dual form of government; and acknowledged evils, however grave . . . had better be borne, than the risk be run, in the effort to suppress them, of more serious consequences by resort to expedients of even doubtful constitutionality.[31]

In an earlier case, involving state prohibition laws, Fuller had recognized that control over sales could impede the transportation of goods across state lines;[32] in that case he denied a dry state power to prohibit retail sales of liquor imported from sister states on the theory that such regulation of sales would interfere with or obstruct the free flow of goods across state lines. But to characterize the monopolist's power over the price of a good as an obstruction of interstate commerce would have threatened, in the eyes of Fuller and most of the Court, the entire distinction between manufacturing and transportation and thus between the police and commerce powers.

Having a more robust conception of the national power, especially when it came to the legislative branch, Harlan did not share Fuller's fears. On occasion, as in *Adair v. United States*,[33] Harlan found that Congress had exceeded its powers, but the limit he imposed—denying government the power to favor one economic group over another—was as applicable to the state legislatures as to Congress: For Harlan there was only one social contract. He stressed the need for federal intervention in *E. C. Knight*, but he did not try to impose any limit to his theory allowing federal intervention when there was an impact on the flow of goods across state lines. Nor did it seem possible to construct those limits out of the one fact stressed by Harlan again and again, namely that sugar is a foodstuff and a necessity of life. A theory that would vary the reach of congressional power over manufacturing according to the desirability or need of the good manufactured would not yield the sharp distinctions for which the Court was searching.[34] The

---

[31] Ibid., 13.
[32] Leisy v. Hardin, 135 U.S. 100 (1890). See also *In re* Rahrer, 140 U.S.

545 (1891). See Chapter 9.
[33] 208 U.S. 161 (1908). See Chapter 6.
[34] In the prohibition context, the

need or demand for sugar had important implications for the economic power of the monopolist inasmuch as it enhanced its capacity to raise prices, but that capacity did not constitute the kind of obstruction or interference that traditional commerce analysis required.

II

The instrumental accounts of the Fuller Court's encounter with antitrust, such as those offered by Paul and Westin, begin and end with *E. C. Knight* in 1895. That has the effect of linking the Court's stance on the Sherman Act with the Court's decisions in *Debs* and *Pollock* and strengthening the view that treats the entire corpus of the Fuller Court as an extended exercise of class justice. But this linkage is problematic. It is at odds with the fact that the public reception of *E. C. Knight* was quite different from that accorded *Debs* and *Pollock* and ignores whatever reasons might explain that difference. Even more, it ignores the fact that soon after *E. C. Knight* the Court embarked upon a course of decisions that gave life to the Sherman Act and laid the foundations for Theodore Roosevelt's antitrust campaign. The initial step in that direction occurred with the *Trans-Missouri* case decision of 1897, which was affirmed the very next term in *Joint Traffic*; it was soon followed by *Addyston Pipe* in 1901. *Trans-Missouri* and *Joint Traffic* involved railroads and addressed the liberty issue, while *Addyston Pipe* raised issues of federalism as well insofar as that suit, like *E. C. Knight*, involved the application of the Sherman Act to manufacturers. The Court in these cases built on *E. C. Knight*, but in a way that reduced the outcome in that case to a fragile and unrepresentative datum, not a fair indication of what the Court had done in antitrust or what it was about to do.

In this second round of cases (*Trans-Missouri*, *Joint Traffic*, and *Addyston Pipe*), Harlan became part of the majority. It is difficult to believe, however, that the change in the Court's position—if that is what we have—was in any important way due to him. Harlan was passionate in his *E. C. Knight* dissent, but it was a dissent that no one joined and the persuasiveness of which was unlikely to have increased with age.[35] Some might see

---

Court subsequently tried to minimize the damage to principles of economic nationalism by making a distinction in terms of the product. See Clark Distilling Co. v. Western Md. Ry., 242 U.S. 311 (1917), discussed in Chapter 9.

[35] Brewer's statement to the contrary—"They who know his persuasive ways and words appreciate the fact that he is largely responsible for the deci-

sions of the Supreme Court. . . ."—was no doubt the kind of flattery appropriate at testimonials. *Dinner Given by the Bar of the Supreme Court of the United States to Mr. Justice John Marshall Harlan* (New York: Cameron & Bulkeley, 1902), in Alan Westin, ed., *An Autobiography of the Supreme Court* (New York: Macmillan, 1963), 192.

the change in the Court's position as a response to the increasing concentration of economic power that occurred in the late 1890s.[36] This trend did pose new dangers to the integrity of the market, but I doubt that it was sufficiently pervasive or discernible in the interval between 1895 and 1897 to afford a complete explanation for the shift.

A more decisive factor might have been a personnel change. In December 1895, almost a year after *E. C. Knight* but a year before *Trans-Missouri*, Rufus Peckham was appointed to the Court. He brought with him a deep commitment to liberty, previously manifested in his work on the New York Court of Appeals and ultimately to be evidenced in his work on the Supreme Court over the next fifteen years.[37] He also held strong views, perhaps colored by the bitter experiences of the New York rail mergers described in *Chapters of Erie*,[38] about the dangers and abuses posed by an unrestrained capitalism. He came to the Court with a fear of the rapacious tendencies of "combinations of capital."[39] Moreover, unlike Harlan, he seems to have had the ear of those who formed the *E. C. Knight* majority. Throughout this period Peckham played a leadership role on the Court and was assigned by Fuller the task of speaking for the Court in such important cases as *Lochner* and *Ex parte Young*.[40] He spoke for the Court in *Trans-*

---

[36] See Naomi R. Lamoreaux, *The Great Merger Movement in American Business, 1895–1904* (Cambridge: Cambridge University Press, 1985).

[37] On Peckham in general, see William F. Duker, "Mr. Justice Rufus W. Peckham: The Police Power and the Individual in a Changing World," *B.Y.U. L. Rev.*, 1980: 47; "The Fuller Court and State Criminal Process: Threshold of Modern Limitations on Government," *B.Y.U. L. Rev.*, 1980: 275; and "Mr. Justice Rufus W. Peckham and the Case of *Ex Parte Young*: Lochnerizing *Munn v. Illinois*," *B.Y.U. L. Rev.*, 1980: 539.

[38] Charles F. Adams, Jr., and Henry Adams, *Chapters of Erie and Other Essays* (New York: Henry Holt, 1886).

[39] As he later wrote,

In any great and extended change in the manner or method of doing business it seems to be an inevitable necessity that distress and, perhaps, ruin shall be its accompaniment in regard to some of those who were engaged in the old methods. . . . It is wholly different, however, when such changes are effected by combinations of capital, whose purpose in combining is to control the production or

manufacture of any particular article in the market, and by such control dictate the price at which the article shall be sold, the effect being to drive out of business all the small dealers in the commodity and to render the public subject to the decision of the combination as to what price shall be paid for the article. . . . [I]t is . . . unfortunate for the country by depriving it of the services of a large number of small but independent dealers who were familiar with the business and who had spent their lives in it, and who supported themselves and their families from the small profits realized therein.

Trans-Missouri, 166 U.S. at 323.

Bork, offering a technocratic interpretation, can account for Peckham's solicitude for small producers (at the putative expense of consumer welfare) only by calling it a "lapse" (*Antitrust Paradox*, 25), which it most certainly was not. This solicitude was central to Peckham's understanding—and that of the other justices as well—of the market as a political construct.

[40] *Ex parte* Young, 209 U.S. 123 (1908). See Chapter 7.

Chapter V: *The Antitrust Campaign*

Missouri, Joint Traffic, and *Addyston Pipe* and thus emerged as the architect of the new antitrust doctrine.

Trans-Missouri and *Joint Traffic* involved price-fixing contracts among various interstate railroads. Federalism, therefore, was not an issue: Such contracts were clearly within the category of intercourse or transportation as defined in *E. C. Knight*.[41] A number of statutory issues—whether the Commerce Act of 1887 legitimated the joint-tariffs (as they were known at the time of enactment) or preempted the application of the Sherman Act to the rail industry—also were considered, but they too were resolved easily in favor of the government. Like federalism, they appeared to be of secondary importance. The critical issue in *Trans-Missouri* and *Joint Traffic* was one of liberty: whether the enforcement of the antitrust laws was an impermissible interference with liberty of contract, that is, the freedom of the railroads to enter into price-fixing agreements with one another. It was this issue that created the public interest in these cases and that served as the focus of the lawyers (who included James C. Carter, one of the lawyers in *Pollock*, and John Dillon, another prominent figure in the corporate bar). And it was the liberty issue that divided the Court. By the narrowest of margins (5 to 4), the Court upheld the application of the Sherman Act in *Trans-Missouri*, but faced with a professional backlash or, as Peckham described it, "widespread alarm,"[42] the Court found it necessary to return to the problem once again in *Joint Traffic*. The Court adhered to its position, this time 5 to 3 (Field, one of the original dissenters, had resigned in the interim, and McKenna, his replacement, did not participate in the case).

The liberty of contract issue was to haunt the Court in all its encounters with progressivism. It is linked most closely in our minds with *Lochner*, a decision written by Peckham in 1905, almost a decade after *Trans-Missouri* and *Joint Traffic*. It should be noted, however, that just months before *Trans-Missouri*, liberty of contract secured a beachhead in Supreme Court doctrine when, in *Allgeyer v. Louisiana*,[43] the Court invalidated a

---

[41] Peckham's commitment to the *E. C. Knight* framework was evident in the language of *Trans-Missouri* and *Joint Traffic*, as well as in the results in a case decided the same day as *Joint Traffic* and also authored by Peckham—*Hopkins v. United States*, 171 U.S. 578 (1898). In that case the Court ruled that a Sherman Act prosecution against a livestock exchange was outside the scope of interstate commerce. Members of the exchange did not purchase livestock, but merely received them at the stockyards and then arranged for their sale. Peckham wrote: "[I]t is immaterial over how many States the defendants may themselves or by their agents travel in order to thereby secure the business. They do not purchase the cattle themselves; they do not transport them. They receive them at Kansas City, and the complaint made is in regard to the agreements for charges for the services at that point. . . ." Ibid., 590. *Anderson v. United States*, 171 U.S. 604 (1898), was also decided the same day and involved a fact situation similar to *Hopkins*, but Peckham's decision to set aside the Sherman Act prosecution in this case did not rely so clearly on federalism grounds.

[42] *Joint Traffic*, 171 U.S. at 573.

[43] 165 U.S. 578 (1897).

Louisiana law that prohibited contracts with out-of-state insurance companies. It also should be noted that in none of these cases—neither in *Allgeyer* nor in *Lochner* nor in any of the railroad cases—was the claim on behalf of liberty posed in an absolute form.

Everyone recognized that in some instances the state could outlaw or void contracts. The common law did as much. The question was instead more specific—whether the law prohibited *this* contract, recognizing that the referent ("this") could be defined with varying degrees of generality. It might refer to the particular circumstances in which a contract was made or, as the Court saw it in *Trans-Missouri* and *Joint Traffic*, to a type of contract. So formulated, the liberty question in these cases was whether the state could interfere with the liberty of the railroads to enter into contracts to set prices. The Court answered that question in the affirmative and did so in a way that gave the Sherman Act a jolt of life and saved it from the desuetude to which *E. C. Knight* seemed to have consigned it.

The agreement in question was not made in secret; price-fixing through the establishment of joint-tariffs was an open, common, somewhat accepted practice of the railroads of the 1890s. The railroads argued, in terms totally consistent with the Kolko thesis,[44] that the agreement was necessary in order to avoid the "waste" and "horrors" of "ruinous competition"—rate wars would drive many lines into ruin.[45] The rail industry was in a state of decline in the early 1890s, and the railroads claimed that these wars would destroy private investment and leave many communities without rail service. This defense of price-fixing might have been a pretext, but the Court did not pause to inquire into its truthfulness. The Court granted the attorney general relief on the pleadings without any inquiry into the reasons that might have justified the price-fixing agreement. Peckham alluded to the argument of the railroads, that these contracts would avoid "deadly competition so liable to result in the ruin of the roads,"[46] but rather than trying to ascertain whether there was any merit to this argument he read the Sherman Act as prohibiting any price-fixing contracts whatsoever.

This judgment did not rest on any special understanding of the precise words of the Sherman Act or its legislative history. It was instead expressive of a social vision—arguably embodied in the Sherman Act—that claimed for the market a commanding role in ordering social and economic relations and that saw price-fixing agreements as abrogating the cen-

---

[44] See Gabriel Kolko, *Railroads and Regulation, 1877–1916* (Princeton: Princeton University Press, 1965), and *The Triumph of Conservatism: A Reinterpretation of American History, 1900–1916* (New York: Free Press, 1963). For criticism see Chapter 1, note 48.

[45] See Herbert Hovenkamp, "Regulatory Conflict in the Gilded Age: Federalism and the Railroad Problem," *Yale L.J.*, 97: 1017, 1035–44. See generally Chapter 7.

[46] *Trans-Missouri*, 166 U.S. at 333.

tral disciplinary mechanism of that institution: competition. Peckham was willing to sacrifice efficiency so as to avoid the social and political costs of monopoly:

> [B]usiness or trading combinations . . . may even temporarily, or perhaps permanently, reduce the price of the article traded in or manufactured, by reducing the expense inseparable from the running of many different companies for the same purpose. Trade or commerce under those circumstances may nevertheless be badly and unfortunately restrained by driving out of business the small dealers and worthy men whose lives have been spent therein, and who might be unable to readjust themselves to their altered surroundings. Mere reduction in the price of the commodity dealt in might be dearly paid for by the ruin of such a class, and the absorption of control over one commodity by an all-powerful combination of capital.[47]

It was one thing to prevent "combinations" from driving "small dealers and worthy men" out of business and another to allow the railroads to avoid the rigors and ruin that come from free and open competition. For Peckham and the other members of the majority—Fuller, Brewer, Brown, and Harlan—"ruinous competition" was not an excess that might be avoided through private contractual arrangements, but instead an inevitable consequence of the market working to its full.[48]

This total ban on price-fixing contracts prompted a vigorous dissent from Justice White. He argued that the Sherman Act was no more than a procedural emendation of the common law—establishing new kinds of suits for conduct proscribed by the common law—and that the substantive standard of the common law, which proscribed only "unreasonable" restraints of trade, should govern. According to White, a common law court would ask whether a particular contract in restraint of trade was "reasonable," as a price-fixing contract eliminating "ruinous competition" might well be.[49]

Peckham did not explain clearly why he refused to conduct this "reasonableness" inquiry or allow the lower court to do so. In *Trans-Missouri*,

---

[47] Ibid., 323.

[48] Peckham quoted from the dissent at the circuit court level:

Competition, free and unrestricted, is the general rule which governs all the ordinary business pursuits and transactions of life. Evils, as well as benefits, result therefrom. . . . [Y]et balancing the benefits as against the evils, the law of competition remains as a controlling element in the business world.

Ibid., 337, quoting 58 F. 58, 94 (8th Cir. 1893) (Shiras, J., dissenting).

[49] White made the common law much neater than it really was. See Donald Dewey, "The Common-Law Background of Antitrust Policy," *Va. L. Rev.*, 11: 759 (1955); Herbert Hovenkamp, "The Sherman Act and the Classical Theory of Competition," *Iowa L. Rev.*, 74: 1019 (1989).

he simply hid behind the language of the Sherman Act: The statute, he said, proscribed "every" contract in restraint of trade, not just contracts that were unreasonable restraints of trade.[50] But this language hardly compelled the conclusion Peckham sought. "Every" could not really mean *every*, as Peckham later acknowledged in *Joint Traffic*:

> As examples of the kinds of contracts which are rendered illegal by this construction of the act, the learned counsel suggest . . . the formation of a corporation to carry on any particular line of business by those already engaged therein; a contract of partnership or of employment between two persons previously engaged in the same line of business; the appointment by two producers of the same person to sell their goods on commission; the purchase by one wholesale merchant of the product of two producers. . . .[51]

Peckham saw that he needed to qualify the word "every," but rather than going the route White suggested, he borrowed the distinction between "direct" and "indirect," so common in the jurisprudence of the Commerce Clause, and in effect read that distinction into the statute: "[T]he statute applies only to those contracts whose direct and immediate effect is a restraint upon interstate commerce. . . ."[52] A price-fixing contract was a direct restraint; the acquisition of one railroad by another was not.

This distinction between "direct" and "indirect" restraints may have supplied Peckham with the limitation for which he was searching, but it was no more justified by the language of the Sherman Act—or by its legislative history, which was never consulted in any systematic way—than White's distinction between "reasonable" and "unreasonable" restraints. White's invocation of the common law to defend his distinction had no special appeal to Peckham; unlike White, Peckham did not try to argue that his distinction was rooted in the common law. That relieved Peckham from the treacherous task of historical reconstruction, but it also had the effect of sharpening the liberty objection. If the Sherman Act were deemed coextensive with the common law, and if the Court then, as a factual matter, found that the "ruinous competition" defense was wanting and thus the fixing of prices unreasonable, the impingement of contractual liberty inherent in this application of the Sherman Act would be unproblematic. No one would claim that the Constitution protected conduct that was "unreasonable" and thus proscribed by the common law. By contrast, in choosing the path he did, Peckham put himself in the position of having to decide whether the contractual liberty guaranteed by the Constitution could be

---

[50] 166 U.S. at 312.
[51] 171 U.S. at 567.

[52] Ibid., 568.

Chapter V: *The Antitrust Campaign*

constrained in a situation where there was no judgment that the contract was unreasonable.

In resolving the liberty issue, Peckham was moved by two considerations. One minimized the state intervention and thus the infringement of liberty by depicting the Sherman Act as requiring nothing more than the market did: competition. Again and again, Peckham referred to competition as though it were itself a "rule" or a "law." He often spoke of "the general law of competition,"[53] as though the Sherman Act were nothing more or less than the transubstantiation of a law that governed anyway—natural law. The Sherman Act was the "law of competition" made visible and, as such, outlawed all arrangements that tried to abrogate or avoid that law of the marketplace. Seen in this way, however, the Sherman Act would be all-embracing—every contract that constrained competition would fall within its reach—and if upheld on these terms, liberty of contract would be reduced to a virtual nullity. The state could interfere with any contractual activity that adversely affected competition, including, for example, the formation of a partnership. Sensing this weakness in his position, Peckham first alluded to the direct/indirect distinction as a way of building the appropriate limits. But rather than develop this point, he went on to emphasize the special character of the industry—railroading—involved in *Trans-Missouri* and *Joint Traffic*: Railroads were different.

Railroads have always been especially vulnerable to government regulation, and the period of the late nineteenth century was no exception to this rule—quite the contrary. While this was not a Court that was happy with the doctrine of *Munn v. Illinois*,[54] which allowed legislatures to regulate the prices of any "business affected with a public interest," it nonetheless tolerated the regulation of the rates of railroads and did so only because—as suggested by *Debs*—they were seen as the highways of the nation and, as such, performing a distinctly public function. The railroads were delegates or franchisees of the state, performing "a function of government," and thus were subject to regulations, including regulation of their prices, not applied to other wholly private businesses. Of course, the power of the state to regulate rates could be abused, and as Brewer's Albany speech and Peckham's decision in *Ex parte Young* made dramatically clear, the Court was committed to policing the bounds of legislative action so as to guard against confiscation and other abuses. The Court recognized the private, as well as the public, dimension of railroading. However, as Peckham noted in *Joint Traffic*, in the context of the Sherman Act the claim of confiscation was "plainly irrelevant"[55] since the maximum rate was in effect the

[53] See, e.g., ibid., 569.
[54] 94 U.S. 113 (1877). See Chapter 7.

[55] 171 U.S. at 571.

competitive rate. There could be no doubt, Peckham thought, about the power of the state to deny these "grantees of [a] public franchise" the right to form an arrangement that would give them the power to raise their rates above the competitive level:

> We do not think, when the grantees of this public franchise are competing railroads seeking the business of transportation of men and goods from one State to another, that ordinary freedom of contract in the use and management of their property requires the right to combine as one consolidated and powerful association for the purpose of stifling competition among themselves, and of thus keeping their rates and charges higher than they might otherwise be under the laws of competition.[56]

Earlier we saw that the nature of the business was important in *Trans-Missouri* and *Joint Traffic* for disposing of the federalism issue and distinguishing *E. C. Knight*; that earlier decision was limited to manufacturing and did not bar, as a matter of federal power, application of the Sherman Act to railroads. Similarly, even when it came to the liberty issue, Peckham emphasized the character of the regulated business: Railroads are vulnerable to regulation in a way that other industries might not be.[57] While there was thus an undeniable logic to the fact that the first successful applications of the Sherman Act were against railroads, the underlying commitment of *Trans-Missouri* and *Joint Traffic*—to use government power to preserve competition—could not be confined to that industry. It was too strong.

---

[56] Ibid., 570–71.

[57] Instrumentalism dies hard, and those inclined toward that view might see *Trans-Missouri* and *Joint Traffic* as a strategy for forestalling more extensive intervention in the rail industry, under the theory that strong enforcement of the Sherman Act would render more direct forms of intervention unnecessary. The rail industry was a frequent target of populist demands for public ownership. On the state level, the industry already was encumbered with statutes regulating rates; and even on the federal level there was a growing demand for rate regulation. Moreover, at roughly the same time that *Trans-Missouri* and *Joint Traffic* applied the antitrust laws to price-fixing agreements in the rail industry, the Court limited the scope of the Commerce Act of 1887, holding that the Act did not bar long haul/short haul discrimination that was the result of competition (ICC v. Alabama Midland Ry., 168 U.S. 144 [1897]) and that Congress did not intend the Commission established by the Act to have the power to set maximum rates, but only to upset those rates deemed unreasonable on specified statutory grounds, for example, that they were discriminatory (ICC v. Cincinnati, N.O. & Tex. Pac. Ry., 167 U.S. 479 [1897], *aff'g* Cincinnati, N.O. & Tex. Pac. Ry. v. ICC, 162 U.S. 184 [1896]). See Chapter 7. These decisions undoubtedly exacerbated public concern, and some have seen Peckham's revitalization of the Sherman Act as a compensatory strategy. See Michael Lowe, "The Fuller Court and Railroad Regulation" (Yale Law School, 1976; unpublished manuscript on file with author).

Chapter V: *The Antitrust Campaign*

Inevitably, in time the *Trans-Missouri* and *Joint Traffic* ban on price-fixing would be extended to manufacturing, thereby forcing the Court to confront its decision in *E. C. Knight* more directly. This occurred in *Addyston Pipe* in 1901. Peckham was once again the author but, oddly enough, here he was able to achieve a unanimity that eluded him in his first efforts, *Trans-Missouri* and *Joint Traffic*.

The defendants in *Addyston Pipe* were six manufacturers of cast iron pipe. In the past they had sold their product by submitting independent bids to customers, but starting in 1895 they had entered into an elaborate price-fixing scheme. An association or committee of the various firms fixed the price to be offered the customer. An auction was conducted among the firms as to which would get the job, and the winner would be the firm that would pay the highest bonus, which would then be distributed among the firms. The firms that were not designated for a given job would submit high sham bids to customers so as to make the designated bid seem credible. Jobs in large cities were not included in the auction scheme but instead were reserved to individual members, who paid a fixed per-job bonus to the other members. The scheme involved manufacturers who controlled about two-thirds of the market in the South and West. A good number of eastern manufacturers remained outside the agreement, but they were at a competitive disadvantage in that region because of transportation costs. This price-fixing arrangement was considerably more suspect than the joint-tariff arrangements in *Trans-Missouri* and *Joint Traffic*, but nevertheless was defended on the very same grounds—that it was needed to avoid "ruinous competition."[58]

The key to overcoming the federalism objection applied in *E. C. Knight* lay in drawing a distinction between interference with the manufacture of goods and interference with their transport and sale. The majority in *E. C. Knight* adhered rigidly to this distinction and were unprepared to treat an acquisition that strengthened monopoly power as itself an interference with sales. In *Addyston Pipe* the interference with sales—or the transportation of goods across state lines—was clear and direct, as was understood by Taft, then a circuit judge and the author of the opinion of the Court of Appeals in that case.[59] (The panel of the Court of Appeals in *Addyston*

---

[58] Recent commentary has suggested that the claim of "ruinous competition" was justified since competitive equilibrium in the cast-iron pipe industry at the turn of the century was impossible. George Bittlingmayer, "Decreasing Average Cost and Competition: A New Look at the Addyston Pipe Case," *J.L. & Econ.*, 25: 201 (1982); "Price-Fixing and the Addyston Pipe Case," *Res. L. &*

Econ., 5: 57 (1983).

[59] United States v. Addyston Pipe & Steel Co., 85 F. 271 (6th Cir. 1898). Bork writes of this opinion that "given the time at which it was written, *Addyston* must rank as one of the greatest, if not the greatest, antitrust opinions in the history of the law." *Antitrust Paradox*, 26.

Pipe also included Harlan, riding circuit.[60]) Taft quoted Fuller's concession in *E. C. Knight* that "[c]ontracts to buy, sell, or exchange goods to be transported among the several states . . . may be regulated,"[61] and then put the federalism issue to rest:

> The error into which the [trial court] . . . fell, it seems to us, was in not observing the difference between the regulating power of congress over contracts and negotiations for sales of goods to be delivered across state lines, and that over the merchandise, the subject of such sales and negotiations. The goods are not within the control of congress until they are in actual transit from one state to another. But the negotiations and making of sales which necessarily involve in their execution the delivery of merchandise across state lines are interstate commerce, and so within the regulating power of congress even before the transit of the goods in performance of the contract has begun.[62]

Having thus used the distinction between sales and production to meet the federalism objection, one would have expected Taft then to take up what I have referred to as the liberty issue, since state power was being used to restrain entrepreneurial activity. But that question did not engage Taft at all. Like Justice White, Taft claimed that the Sherman Act was, in substance, identical to the common law. To be sure, Taft's understanding of the common law was quite different from White's—Taft argued that the common law proscribed all restraints whose "sole object . . . is merely to restrain competition,"[63] while restraints ancillary to some other purpose were permitted—and in fact yielded an approach that was much closer to Peckham's direct/indirect distinction.[64] But Taft, like White, implicitly relied on the common law to moot the liberty objection: He could not conceive of the Constitution as protecting conduct deemed unlawful under the common law.

---

[60] The final panel member was one of Taft's favorites, Horace Lurton. Lurton was proposed for the Supreme Court by Taft when Taft served as an informal advisor to Roosevelt and finally was appointed to the Court by Taft himself when he became president. See James F. Watts, Jr., "Horace H. Lurton," in Leon Friedman and Fred L. Israel, eds., *The Justices of the United States Supreme Court, 1789–1969: Their Lives and Major Opinions* (New York: Chelsea House, 1969), 3: 1847. Lurton joined White's opinions in *Standard Oil* and *American Tobacco*.

[61] 85 F. at 296 (quoting *E. C. Knight*, 156 U.S. at 13.).

[62] Ibid., 298.

[63] Ibid., 282.

[64] As Bork notes,
Despite their differences in verbalization, Taft's and Peckham's rules . . . are obviously very similar. Taft's non-ancillary restraint is the same thing as Peckham's restraint of trade (or direct restraint)—a cartel agreement. Taft's ancillary restraint was the same thing as Peckham's non-restraint (or indirect restraint)—an agreement eliminating competition only incidentally to the accomplishment of some other purpose sought by the parties.
"Rule of Reason," 799.

Chapter V: *The Antitrust Campaign*

When *Addyston Pipe* reached the Supreme Court, the task of writing the opinion fell, once again, to Peckham. Unlike Taft, Peckham believed the case presented two constitutional issues rather than one—liberty as well as federalism—a perception that ultimately stemmed from the fact that, to Peckham's mind, the Sherman Act and the common law were not coextensive. In *Joint Traffic* he limited the reach of the Sherman Act by holding that it covered only direct restraints, but he did not see that limitation as rooted in the common law. It therefore remained possible for Peckham, but not for Taft, that a prohibition on such constraints interfered with a constitutionally protected liberty and thus violated substantive due process. In *Trans-Missouri* and *Joint Traffic* Peckham had been helped greatly in resolving the liberty objection by the quasi-public character of the business, but the situation in *Addyston Pipe* was different. The defendants were cast-iron manufacturers, not railroads. Thus for Peckham the liberty objection was posed quite sharply, and he began his *Addyston Pipe* opinion by stating that objection: "[The appellants assert] that the Constitution guarantees liberty of private contract to the citizen at least upon commercial subjects, and to that extent the guaranty operates as a limitation on the power of Congress to regulate commerce."[65]

Unable to fall back on *Trans-Missouri* and *Joint Traffic*, and not finding much guidance in Taft's opinion, Peckham needed something new by way of constitutional theory. He found it in the notion of a private government. The theory that Peckham developed in *Addyston Pipe*—and that won the support of the entire Court—transformed the price-fixing contract into the charter of a private government trying to regulate interstate transactions. Peckham described the committee or association of manufacturers established by the price-fixing agreement as though it was a private government empowered to restrain a manufacturer in one state from competing for sales in another state. The term "direct," which in *Trans-Missouri* and *Joint Traffic* had merely a statutory importance, now gained constitutional significance as well. Contracts that "direct[ly] and immediate[ly]"[66] restrained interstate trade were seen as regulations of commerce and thus a usurpation of congressional power: "[C]ertain kinds of private contracts . . . [may] directly, as already stated, limit or restrain, and hence regulate interstate commerce. . . ."[67] Not only did this theory resolve the federalism issue—Congress certainly had the power to interfere with any institution (private governments included) that tried to exercise power reserved to itself—but even more, it also resolved the liberty of contract argument.

As would become evident in *Lochner* (discussed more fully in the next chapter), Peckham and his followers saw liberty of contract as a residual

---

[65] 175 U.S. at 227.
[66] Ibid., 234.

[67] Ibid., 229.

category, consisting of the prerogatives left to the individual after the limits of governmental authority have been exhausted. In the context of *Addyston Pipe*, this view made the Commerce Clause central for resolving the liberty of contract or substantive due process issue, because once it was decided that by virtue of the power vested in it by the Commerce Clause, Congress was entitled to put the price-fixing committee—the usurper—out of business, there could be no protected liberty interest to create the committee in the first place. In a sense, the committee was proscribed by the Commerce Clause itself. As Peckham put it, "[W]e think the provision regarding the liberty of the citizen is, to some extent, limited by the commerce clause of the Constitution. . . ."[68] In saying this, Peckham was assuming that the action of a private association or private government stood on no better footing than the action of the states (or, to put the point in more modern terms, the Commerce Clause had no state action requirement). *Debs* amply supported such an assumption and, in fact, was used by Peckham in *Addyston Pipe*. The committee of manufacturers was treated as the functional equivalent of the American Railway Union.

In contrast to Brewer in *Debs*, Peckham in *Addyston Pipe* relied on the Sherman Act rather than the Constitution, but in truth the doctrinal bases of the two decisions were not so different after all. *Addyston Pipe* was nominally a Sherman Act decision, but at its core was governed by the Commerce Clause. The Commerce Clause had been read into the statute. The Act, he claimed, extended only to contracts or other business arrangements directly and immediately affecting interstate commerce; such arrangements were legitimate subjects of legislation under the Commerce Clause and thus were outside the protection of the Due Process Clause. The Commerce Clause operated as the source of congressional power over the arrangement and as the jurisdictional basis for the Sherman Act. It also limited the reach of the liberty to contract and thus played a crucial role in giving content to the substantive prohibitions of the Act:

> The power to regulate such commerce, that is, the power to prescribe the rules by which it shall be governed is vested in Congress, and when Congress has enacted a statute such as the one in question, any agreement or combination which directly operates, not alone upon the manufacture, but upon the sale, transportation and delivery of an article of interstate commerce, by preventing or restricting its sale, etc., thereby regulates interstate commerce to that extent and to the same extent trenches upon the power of the national legislature and violates the statute.[69]

---

[68] Ibid.

[69] Ibid., 241–42.

Chapter V: *The Antitrust Campaign*

In introducing the private government idea, Peckham thus made an important contribution to the development of the law. He stayed within the theory of the Commerce Clause espoused by Fuller in *E. C. Knight*, but showed how it might be applied to the business of manufacturing. He borrowed Fuller's technique of fusing statute and Constitution, so as to always keep the statute within the bounds of constitutional power, but extended it to the liberty issue. *Trans-Missouri, Joint Traffic*, and *Addyston Pipe* placed the Sherman Act on secure constitutional grounds and declared illegal cartel arrangements fixing the price of interstate transportation or the price of goods sold in national markets.

It was only a matter of time, however, before Peckham's doctrine would be pushed to its limits, forcing the Court to return to the question left open in *E. C. Knight*: Could the Sherman Act properly be used to bar the acquisition of one business by another? The need to address that question arose in the *Northern Securities* case of 1903, and it left the Court deeply divided. There was no majority opinion for the Court. The case produced a dissent by Holmes, more passionate than his famed dissents in *Lochner* and *Abrams*.[70] Even more significantly, it found Brewer and Peckham, the two defenders of liberty, on different sides of the case, with Peckham taking a position that seemed at war with *Trans-Missouri, Joint Traffic*, and *Addyston Pipe*—his own creations.

III

Taken together, *Trans-Missouri, Joint Traffic*, and *Addyston Pipe* seemed to revolve around one idea—the preservation of competition. The Court held in these cases that the purpose of the Sherman Act was to preserve competition, that Congress had the power under the Commerce Clause to preserve competition in national markets, and that the constitutional protection of liberty could not bar an exertion of governmental power needed to preserve competition. From this perspective, the *Northern Securities* case must have seemed the easiest of them all. Indeed, that is how Justice Harlan, who dissented in *E. C. Knight* but who joined *Trans-Missouri, Joint Traffic*, and *Addyston Pipe*, viewed the matter.

Harlan's picture was simple but powerful. The case involved two railroad lines, the Great Northern and the Northern Pacific, which operated parallel routes from the Midwest to the West Coast and were in active competition with one another. Northern Pacific became insolvent and its property passed into the hands of receivers. Before foreclosure, a deal was struck

---

[70] Abrams v. United States, 250 U.S. 616 (1919). See Chapter 11.

between James J. Hill, who controlled the Great Northern, and J. P. Morgan, who acted as the representative of the bondholders of the Northern Pacific: Northern Pacific's creditors would foreclose and then sell half of the stock of the Northern Pacific in exchange for a debt guarantee. In effect, Great Northern would be acquiring control of Northern Pacific. That arrangement was deemed illegal under a statute of Minnesota, the state in which Great Northern was chartered.[71] Hill and Morgan then hit upon a new method for fusing the two companies. They created a "holding company." The Northern Securities Company, a new corporation chartered under the laws of New Jersey, acquired the stock of both Great Northern and Northern Pacific and thereby gained control of both rail lines. The stock of each of the rail companies was exchanged for stock in Northern Securities. The Hill group, which controlled Great Northern, thus acquired 55 percent of the new holding company and the Morgan group the remainder.

Obviously, these transactions ended whatever competition might have existed between the two rail lines. Harlan therefore concluded (in his typically emphatic manner) that the holding company was a combination in restraint of commerce among the several states and thus a violation of the Sherman Act. But his opinion spoke only for four justices—himself, Brown, McKenna, and Day.[72] Four of the remaining five justices— Peckham, Fuller, White, and Holmes—disagreed with Harlan's analysis and conclusion. The fifth justice, Brewer, agreed with Harlan that the arrangement violated the Sherman Act but saw a need to write a separate opinion. Brewer's vote produced a victory for Roosevelt's first and most visible exercise in "trust-busting,"[73] but it was a complicated victory that had the effect of throwing antitrust doctrine into disarray.

The four dissenters lined up behind two opinions, one written by White, the other by Holmes. All the dissenting justices joined both White's and Holmes's opinions (Holmes was a little guarded—"I concur in the main with his [White's] views."[74]), thus blurring the distinctions between the two. On an initial reading, the difference between the two opinions seems primarily related to the source of the law—White's objection was

---

[71] See Pearsall v. Great N. Ry., 161 U.S. 646 (1896).

[72] An odd collection of justices at that. Brown and McKenna later joined *Lochner*, while Harlan and Day dissented there but were in the majority in *Adair*—indeed, Harlan wrote the opinion for the Court in that case. See Chapter 6.

[73] On Roosevelt's antitrust cam-

paign, see Letwin, *Law and Economic Policy*, 195–218; Lewis L. Gould, *The Presidency of Theodore Roosevelt* (Lawrence: University Press of Kansas, 1991), 47–53, 212–18; and Sklar, *Corporate Reconstruction*, 334–364. For a critical view of Roosevelt's antitrust activities, see Kolko, *Triumph of Conservatism*, 61–139.

[74] 193 U.S. at 411.

constitutional while Holmes's was statutory. But on reflection the differences between the two dissents appear deeper and more substantive.

Harlan saw the Hill-Morgan arrangement as destructive of competition and welcomed the strong use of national power to set the deal aside. Treating the case as though it were simply an acquisition of one railroad by another, Harlan viewed the holding company as thoroughly transparent. White, on the other side, agreed that the purpose and probable effect of the holding company was to bring about an acquisition of one line by another, and thus to lessen the competition between the two, but insisted that the form of the transaction had legal—indeed constitutional—significance. Harlan paid no attention to the method by which that result was produced, the formation of the holding company, but for White, it was important *how* things were done, not just why they were done.

This difference in perspective had important ramifications for the justices' treatment of the federalism issue. Seeing *Northern Securities* as a railroad case, Harlan had no doubt as to the power of the federal government to act. Like the price-fixing agreements in *Trans-Missouri, Joint Traffic*, and *Addyston Pipe*, or like the monopolization in *E. C. Knight*, eliminating competition between the two rail lines would have an obvious and direct effect on interstate commerce—for example, on the rate charged for transporting goods from one state to another. It was this impact on transportation that made the Commerce Clause applicable. For White, however, what was relevant was the category or type of economic activity regulated, not the impact of that activity. In this case the regulated activity was incorporation, not railroading. In contrast to Harlan, White focused not on the diminution of competition between the two railroads, but rather on the formation of the holding company whereby the shareholders of Northern Pacific and Great Northern exchanged their stock for shares in Northern Securities. Drawing on a well-established tradition, indeed the very same one that underlay the majority's position in *E. C. Knight*, White insisted that such stock transactions were clearly within the province of the states—more particularly, the state of incorporation (New Jersey)—not within that of Congress.

White recognized that a change of ownership through the exchange of stock could have an impact or effect on interstate commerce (that is, it could reduce the competition between the two rail lines), but he did not believe that such an impact or effect would be sufficient itself to bring that transaction within the scope of the Commerce Clause. If every stock transaction or change of ownership involving a business that operated in national markets were brought within the reach of the commerce power, simply by virtue of its impact on competition, there would be, White feared, virtually no limit to the scope of congressional power. The Tenth Amendment—reserving to the states powers not granted to the central government—would be rendered meaningless. Harlan, on the other hand, did not recoil from the spectre of increasing the power of Congress in this way and thus paid little attention to the *form* of the transaction. What was decisive for him, as in *E. C. Knight*, was the *effect* of the transaction: the diminution of competition. Of course, he insisted that the impact of a business practice be felt in the process of distributing goods across state lines, but at a time when all markets were being nationalized, this was hardly a limitation at all and, in any event, was not nearly so important as the simple pragmatics of the situation, stressed in his *E. C. Knight* dissent and again in *Northern Securities*. He saw the federal government as the only center of power capable of dealing with Hill and Morgan and the other moguls of the new industrial America. Minnesota had the incentive but not the capacity to preserve competition on the Great Northern and Northern Pacific routes. New Jersey had no incentive to do so. Indeed, all the incentives ran the other way. Moved by a desire to increase tax revenues, by the 1890s New Jersey—known as "the traitor state"—had opened its doors to holding companies by specifically authorizing firms incorporated therein to acquire control of firms operating in other states.[75]

This debate between Harlan and White over the characterization of the business transaction—about whether the case concerned stocks or railroads—also had important implications for the liberty issue. Harlan believed in entrepreneurial liberty, yet also acknowledged its limits. To identify those limits he drew on *Trans-Missouri, Joint Traffic,* and *Addyston Pipe*. "[T]his Court," he wrote in *Northern Securities,* "has heretofore adjudged . . . that liberty of contract did not involve a right to deprive the public of the advantages of free competition in trade and commerce."[76] Harlan saw no difference between the combination of the two rail lines in *Northern Securities* and the price-fixing agreements in *Trans-Missouri, Joint Traffic,* and *Addyston Pipe*. At issue in all was the freedom of business to engage in conduct that destroyed competition. Justice White, in contrast, once again focusing on the form of the transaction and the use of the holding company, insisted that the entrepreneurial liberty involved was more absolute than that in *Trans-Missouri, Joint Traffic,* and *Addyston Pipe*. It was the liberty to acquire and own property.

For White, *Trans-Missouri, Joint Traffic,* and *Addyston Pipe* involved agreements between competing businesses that created private governments—artificial constructs that regulated the prices of competitors. The Northern Securities Company, by contrast, was no artificial construct. It

---

[75] Lincoln Steffens, "New Jersey: A Traitor State," *McClure's Magazine,* April, 1905, 41. See McCurdy, "*Knight* Sugar Decision," 315–23. Antitrust was not the only legislative program vulnerable to competition among the states for business. See Harry N. Scheiber, "Federalism and the American Economic Order, 1789–1910," *Law & Soc. Rev.,* 10: 57, 100–118 (1975).

[76] 193 U.S. at 351.

was a company, and as such it had an independent economic existence that transcended the agreement of the incorporators and was the repository of certain property (stock). The liberty issue for White, therefore, was not the freedom to *use* one's property in the way one saw fit, as might have been involved in *Trans-Missouri, Joint Traffic,* and *Addyston Pipe,* but rather the freedom to *acquire* and *own* property, specifically, the right to acquire and own shares in the Northern Securities Company. As White put it in response to the government, "But the case involves the right to *acquire and own,* not the right '*to do.*' "[77]

Harlan saw this as a trivial distinction because he believed both types of liberty—to own and to use property—could be limited in order to protect competition. White agreed that the freedom to use property was limited, and thus could be restricted by government in the name of a public purpose, which presumably included the preservation of competition, but for him the right to own and acquire property was of a different character altogether:

> [T]he general governmental [power], to reasonably control the *use* of property, affords no foundation for the proposition that there exists in government a power to limit the quantity and character of property which may be acquired and owned. The difference between the two is that which exists between a free and constitutional government restrained by law and an absolute government unrestrained by any of the principles which are necessary for the perpetuation of society and the protection of life, liberty and property.[78]

This, it should be remembered, was written at the time *Pollock* governed, but by one of the justices who dissented in that case.

White's view of property was derived, of course, from John Locke and the social contract tradition. According to Locke, property existed in the state of nature and thus prior to the state. White conceded that some types of property were created by the state, for example, charters of incorporation. He also was willing to concede that government had some power over that property. As he saw it, however, such power belonged only to the unit of government that created the property, since the power arose from the right of the creator to impose terms as a condition of creation (an exchange metaphor), or from the right of the creator to control what it created (a parental metaphor). As a result, the power to regulate the government-created property of Northern Securities—the stock, the charter of incorporation, the company—rested with New Jersey, not the United States. Here

---

[77] Ibid., 398 (quoting argument of appellee's counsel). [78] Ibid., 399.

133

federalism was used, as in *Pollock*, to protect freedom understood as the right to acquire and own property.

As suggested earlier, Harlan disputed the absoluteness of the property interest. He placed the right to acquire and own property on the same footing as the contractual right involved in *Trans-Missouri*, *Joint Traffic*, and *Addyston Pipe*—subject to reasonable regulation. The right to acquire and own property could be limited to protect competition. Beyond that, Harlan also denied the reality of Northern Securities as an independent economic enterprise—for him, it was all a sham. In the closing passages of his opinion, Harlan characterized White's analysis as a triumph of form over substance:

> There was no actual investment, in any substantial sense, by the Northern Securities Company in the stock of the two constituent companies. If it was, in form, such a transaction, it was not, in fact, one of that kind.[79]

Harlan saw the holding company as the equivalent of the price-fixing committee in *Addyston Pipe* or the cartels in *Trans-Missouri* and *Joint Traffic*: It had one purpose and one purpose alone, and that was to suppress competition. To support this assertion, Harlan quoted the testimony of J. P. Morgan. When asked, "Why put the stocks of *both* these [constituent companies] into one holding company?" Morgan answered quite frankly, "In the first place, this holding company was simply a question of *custodian*, because it had no other alliances."[80]

Harlan's claim of farce was, in my judgment, decisive in obtaining the crucial vote of Brewer. Of all the justices, Brewer was probably the most sympathetic to the view, articulated in *Northern Securities* by White, that postulated the absoluteness of the right to acquire and own property. He said as much in his Albany speech, he wrote the Court's opinion in *Debs*, he joined the majority in *Pollock*, he later joined *Lochner* and *Adair*, and he wrote *Reagan v. Farmers' Loan & Trust Co.*[81] (which sought to guard against confiscation when the state regulated railroad rates). In fact, in his concurrence in *Northern Securities*, Brewer affirmed his commitment to the general principles articulated by White:

> [T]he general language of the act is . . . limited by the power which each individual has to manage his own property and determine the place and manner of its investment. Freedom of action in these respects is among the inalienable rights of every citizen. If, applying this thought to the present case, it appeared that Mr. Hill was the owner of a majority of

---

[79] Ibid., 353–54.
[80] Quoted ibid., 354.

[81] 154 U.S. 362 (1894). See Chapter 7.

the stock in the Great Northern Railway Company he could not by any act of Congress be deprived of the right of investing his surplus means in the purchase of the stock of the Northern Pacific Railway Company, although such a purchase might tend to vest in him through that ownership a control over both companies.[82]

Brewer was as clear as White about the absoluteness of the right to acquire and own property, yet he reached the opposite conclusion, voting to sustain the government's enforcement action.

In justifying his position, Justice Brewer seemed somewhat at sea. He first emphasized the fact that what was at issue was not the investment of a "single individual" but rather "several individuals."[83] But that seemed an unpromising point of departure: It is hard to understand why Hill should lose his right because Morgan exercised a similar one, even if they acted in concert. Brewer did not explain why the addition of individuals should result in the forfeiture of rights. Instead he moved on, making a distinction between individuals and corporations and the rights they possess: "[A] corporation, while by fiction of law recognized for some purposes as a person and for purposes of jurisdiction as a citizen," he wrote, "is not endowed with the inalienable rights of a natural person."[84] This did not seem promising either: The Northern Securities Company may not have had the "inalienable right" to acquire and own the property of the rail lines, but Hill and Morgan (and the other individual shareholders) arguably still had a right to acquire and own the stock of Northern Securities, and to pay for that stock with the shares they owned in Great Northern and Northern Pacific. The rights of "natural persons" were indeed at issue.

Having sensed the weaknesses of both these leads Brewer came to rest on Harlan's point that the Northern Securities Company was no more than a sham; it had no status as an independent economic organization and was no different from the *Trans-Missouri* and *Joint Traffic* cartels or the price-fixing committee of *Addyston Pipe*. Brewer noted the fictional character of the company's capitalization ("The organizers might just as well have made the nominal stock a thousand millions as four hundred, and the corporation

---

[82] 193 U.S. at 361.

[83] Ibid., 362.

[84] In 1885 the Court was so firmly of the view that corporations were "persons" protected by the Fourteenth Amendment that it declined even to hear argument on that point. Santa Clara County v. S. Pac. R.R., 118 U.S. 394, 396 (1886). A decade later the Court began to shift on that question. See Blake v. McClung, 172 U.S. 239, 259 (1898), and Waters-Pierce Oil Co. v. Texas, 177 U.S. 28, 43 (1900). Brewer's position in *Northern Securities* reflects these later decisions, and subsequently was confirmed when Justice Harlan wrote, "The liberty referred to in [the Fourteenth] Amendment is the liberty of natural, not artificial persons." Northwestern Nat'l Life Ins. Co. v. Riggs, 203 U.S. 243, 255 (1906).

would have been no richer or poorer."[85]), and concluded by equating the price-fixing committee and the holding company:

> In this case [the holding company] was a mere instrumentality by which separate railroad properties were combined under one control. That combination is as direct a restraint of trade by destroying competition as the appointment of a committee to regulate rates.[86]

In this passage, which formed the crux of his opinion, Brewer came to accept Harlan's point about the transparent or farcical status of the holding company and used it to resolve both the liberty and federalism issues. He was, however, even more explicit than Harlan about the factors that drove him to pierce the corporate form and look to the substance of the transaction. One was the realization that individual liberty was as effectively threatened by the then-rampant trust movement as by the growth of government. Part of this concern was especially tied to railroads and the special monopoly power each railroad possessed:

> It must also be remembered that under present conditions a single railroad is, if not a legal, largely a practical, monopoly, and the arrangement by which the control of these two competing roads was merged in a single corporation broadens and extends such monopoly.[87]

He also apparently felt the need to take a stand on the industrial empires of businessmen like Hill and Morgan. If the Sherman Act could not reach holding companies, he feared, these industrial empires would grow and a small number of individuals would achieve power that rivaled the central government's and posed the same threat to liberty. At that point he imagined a constantly pyramiding corporate structure, one holding company being stacked on another, "until," so he wrote, "a single corporation whose stock was owned by three or four parties would be in practical control . . . of the whole transportation system of the country."[88]

Today, such imagery is only the work of humorists like Art Buchwald,[89] but not so when Brewer wrote. In those days, the amalgamation of an entire industry into a single pyramiding corporate structure was a recur-

---

[85] Ibid.

[86] Ibid.

[87] Ibid., 363. Thus Brewer's position on practical monopoly had changed in the decade since *Budd v. New York*, where he had argued that "[a] monopoly of fact any one can break, and there is no necessity for legislative interference." 143 U.S. 517, 550–51 (1892) (Brewer, J., dissenting).

[88] 193 U.S. at 363.

[89] "Everyone Is Merging," *Washington Post*, June 2, 1966, sect. A, p. 21, col. 4.

rent fear, first articulated by Harlan in *E. C. Knight*,[90] but shared by many. It reflected the startling ingenuity of those who hit upon the holding company format and the fluid character of industrial organization at the turn of the century—no one had a clear picture of capitalism's many futures. In adopting an approach that looked beyond, or through, the corporate form, Brewer believed he had found a way of protecting liberty and the market from these disturbing developments.

Enter Holmes. He had been appointed by Theodore Roosevelt the term before. The *Northern Securities* case was launched by Roosevelt during his first years in office and apparently had great significance for the new president; it announced a new stance toward the trusts and identified him with the progressive movement. At first, Roosevelt had talked about public exposure and state prosecutions,[91] but now he was prepared to use the federal power. The *Northern Securities* case also was important to the new justice. By the time Holmes came to the Supreme Court his fame was secure, yet one cannot resist the impression (especially from his "great cases" passage[92] and the uncharacteristically emotional tone of the whole opinion[93]) that the case was important to him as a vehicle for demonstrating his independence from the president who appointed him. Roosevelt's well-known displeasure with Holmes's vote in *Northern Securities*—Roosevelt reportedly commented, "I could carve out of a banana a judge with more back-

---

[90] Harlan wrote:
We have before us the case of a combination which absolutely controls, or may, at its discretion, control the price of all refined sugar in this country. Suppose another *combination*, organized for private gain and to control prices, should obtain possession of all the large flour mills in the United States; another, of all the grain elevators; another, of all the oil territory; another, of all the salt-producing regions; another, of all the cotton mills; and another, of all the great establishments for slaughtering animals, and the preparation of meats.
156 U.S. at 44–45.

[91] See Letwin, *Law and Economic Policy*, 199–200.

[92] "Great cases like hard cases make bad law. For great cases are called great, not by reason of their real importance in shaping the law of the future, but because of some accident in immediate

overwhelming interest which appeals to the feelings and distorts the judgment." 193 U.S. at 400.

[93] That tone is conveyed by his frequent use of the phrase "I repeat," a most uncharacteristic usage for Holmes, and by the intensity of his rhetoric, exemplified by this passage:
The statute of which we have to find the meaning is a criminal statute. The two sections on which the Government relies both make certain acts crimes. That is their immediate purpose and that is what they say. It is vain to insist that this is not a criminal proceeding. The words cannot be read one way in a suit which is to end in fine and imprisonment and another way in one which seeks an injunction. . . . So I say we must read the words before us as if the question were whether two small exporting grocers should go to jail.
193 U.S. at 401–402.

bone than that"[94]—never fazed Holmes. More likely, it was a source of gratification. It reinforced the Olympian image that Holmes so desired—the impartial judge, standing above the fray of ordinary politics, dispassionate and indifferent to the immediate concerns of the day. In much this spirit, Holmes wrote to his intimate friend Ellen Curtis about Roosevelt: "If however his seeming personal regard for us was based on the idea that he had a tool the sooner it is ended the better—we shall see."[95]

As a purely formal matter, Holmes joined White's dissent, but he could not have had much of a taste for White's mode of analysis. White was one of his few companions on the Court,[96] and his willingness to join White's opinion was probably nothing more than a gesture of politeness. White's emphasis on the corporate form and his unwillingness to look behind the holding company was just too formalistic for Holmes.[97] Holmes, unlike White, was prepared to penetrate the facade of the holding company

---

[94] Although the difference of opinion between Roosevelt and Holmes over *Northern Securities* made its way into the newspapers, this quote did not. See "The President and Justice Holmes," *Sun*, Mar. 18, 1904, p. 8; "Have Argued Merger Case Over in Private," *Boston Globe*, Mar. 18, 1904, p. 3; "Roosevelt Angry at Justice Holmes," *World*, Mar. 17, 1904, p. 3; and "Loses Favor," *Boston Globe*, Mar. 17, 1904, p. 6. The quote first appeared in Silas Bent's biography of Justice Holmes, which was published the year of his retirement from the Court. According to Bent, "On hearing that Holmes had written the dissent he exclaimed that he could carve out of a banana a Justice with more backbone than that." Silas Bent, *Justice Oliver Wendell Holmes* (New York: Vanguard Press, 1932), 251. Bent did not cite a source. Bent was a reporter in Louisville, Kentucky, and St. Louis, Missouri, from 1902 to 1911. He later worked in Washington, D.C., including a short stint at the Democratic National Committee, and the story might have been in general circulation in his circles.

[95] Holmes to Curtis, Mar. 8, 1904, Holmes Papers, Harvard Law School Library Manuscript Division. In the same letter, written immediately after *Northern Securities*, Holmes expressed "confidence in [Roosevelt's] great heartedness," and weeks later wrote to another correspondent, "if the Presidt.

has been angry he seems to be getting over it." Holmes to Palfrey, Apr. 1, 1904, Harvard Holmes Papers. But the rift never seems to have healed completely. In a 1912 letter to Lewis Einstein, who was close to both men, Holmes wrote of Roosevelt, "I knew him and liked him personally very much, as much as it was possible to like a man that you knew would throw over the friendship he professed the moment one allowed one's own understanding of one's judicial duty to prevail over what he wanted." Holmes to Einstein, Nov. 24, 1912, in James Bishop Peabody, ed., *The Holmes–Einstein Letters: Correspondence of Mr. Justice Holmes and Lewis Einstein, 1903–1935* (London: Macmillan, 1964), 75. In the same spirit, he wrote to Pollock, "[H]e looked on my dissent to the *Northern Securities* case as a political departure (or, I suspect, more truly, couldn't forgive anyone who stood in his way)." Holmes to Pollock, Feb. 9, 1921, in Mark DeWolfe Howe, ed., *Holmes–Pollock Letters: The Correspondence of Mr. Justice Holmes and Sir Frederick Pollock, 1874–1932* (Cambridge: Harvard University Press, 1941), 2: 63–64.

[96] See Chapter 2, note 58.

[97] On Holmes's pragmatism, see Morton G. White, *Social Thought in America: The Revolt Against Formalism* (New York: Viking Press, 1949; repr. Boston: Beacon Hill Press, 1957), 59–75.

and assume that it was nothing more than an attempt to suppress competition. Holmes also was willing to assume that enough had been done by the parties in furtherance of their intent to destroy competition to constitute what would legally be considered an "attempt," so that if the statute were read as a prohibition on attempts to eliminate competition, the conduct would be illegal. But at a critical and startling turn in his opinion, Holmes denied that the Sherman Act was a measure to protect competition. He rejected the central premise of both Harlan's and Brewer's opinions by trying to sever the connection between the Sherman Act and the preservation of competition: "The law, I repeat, says nothing about competition, and only prevents its suppression by contracts or combinations in restraint of trade, and such contracts or combinations derive their character as restraining trade from other features than the suppression of competition alone."[98]

Holmes's dissent did not rest on any understanding, special or otherwise, of the legislative history of the Sherman Act. It instead purported to be a reading of the "plain language"[99] of the statute. He set his task very modestly—"to read English intelligently."[100] He then proceeded to divide the substantive prohibitions of the Sherman Act into three parts. The first, which prohibited "contracts in restraint of trade," was read to embody the common law rule governing contracts typically formed at the sale of a business: "They are contracts with a stranger to the contractor's business, (although in some cases carrying on a similar one,) which wholly or partially restrict the freedom of the contractor in carrying on that business as otherwise he would."[101] The second prohibition proscribed "combinations or conspiracies in restraint of trade," which Holmes read as a complement to the first: "Combinations or conspiracies in restraint of trade . . . were combinations to keep strangers to the agreement out of the business."[102] Holmes treated Section 2 of the Act—which proscribed monopolies—as the third prohibition. Holmes saw it simply as an adjunct to the prohibition on "combinations in restraint of trade" in Section 1: "It shows that whatever is criminal when done by way of combination is equally criminal if done by a single man."[103]

In this way the Sherman Act was construed as consisting of nothing more than the common law rule against exclusion. It prohibited practices that kept people from entering or conducting a business or trade. According to Holmes, the Sherman Act prohibited exclusion; it did not protect competition. The preservation of competition might be one of the consequences or by-products of the rule that prohibited exclusion; it might even be an underlying rationale or purpose for that rule; but it was not the rule itself.

---

[98] 193 U.S. at 410.
[99] Ibid., 405.
[100] Ibid., 401.

[101] Ibid., 404.
[102] Ibid.
[103] Ibid.

Some of the statutory language seemed at odds with his interpretation, but Holmes easily brushed it to one side and even turned some of the language to his advantage. Section 1 contained the phrase "in the form of trust or otherwise," and Holmes commented:

> The prohibition was suggested by the trusts, the objection to which, as everyone knows, was not the union of former competitors, but the sinister power exercised or supposed to be exercised by the combination in keeping rivals out of the business and ruining those who already were in.[104]

Similarly, Section 7, which created a private right of action for damages, was seized as further support for his theory:

> This cannot refer to the parties to the agreement and plainly means that outsiders who are injured in their attempt to compete with a trust or other similar combination may recover for it.[105]

Finally, carrying his project of "plain reading" to a desperate extreme, Holmes reminded the reader of the title of the statute, which, he insisted, said nothing about competition. The title read: "An act to protect trade and commerce against unlawful restraints and monopolies."[106]

The problem with Holmes's interpretation was not the words of the statute, for they were as congenial to his interpretation as to Harlan's. The real problem was rather the Court's earlier decisions—*Trans-Missouri*, *Joint Traffic*, and *Addyston Pipe*. Although White in his dissent in *Trans-Missouri* and *Joint Traffic* and Taft at the circuit level in *Addyston Pipe* tried to tie the Sherman Act to the common law, for Peckham and the majority he assembled there was no discernible connection between the two. Now in *Northern Securities* Holmes tried to connect the two, though not by the introduction of the word "unreasonable," which never appealed to him,[107] but rather by the way he defined the illegal conduct—the anti-exclusion rule. The problem was, however, that these earlier decisions said nothing about exclusion but instead seemed to revolve around the very idea of competition, an idea which he rejected.

Holmes said, as indeed he had to if he was to gain Peckham's vote (not to mention Fuller's, who had joined Peckham's opinions), that he accepted *Trans-Missouri* and *Joint Traffic* "absolutely, not only as binding upon me, but as decisions which I have no desire to criticize or abridge."[108] It is difficult to know how sincere Holmes was in this affirmation, or why

---

[104] Ibid., 405.
[105] Ibid.
[106] Ch. 647, 26 Stat. 209, 209 (1890), quoted in 193 U.S. at 405.
[107] See sources cited below, note 128.
[108] 193 U.S. at 405.

Eugene V. Debs, head of the American Railway Union, addressing
strikers during the Pullman strike, 1894 (chapter 3).
(*Brown Brothers*)

Two cartoons by W. A. Rogers on the Pullman strike. The one on the left was published on July 14, 1894. The other, published on July 21, 1894, shortly after the strike was broken, depicts Debs leading a vanguard of populist politicians: Sylvester Pennoyer, governor of Oregon; Davis Hanson Waite, governor of Colorado; John P. Altgeld, governor of Illinois; and William Alfred Peffer, senator from Kansas.

(Library of Congress)

Clarence Darrow, on the streets of Chicago, about 1893, shortly before he represented Eugene V. Debs in the proceedings arising from the Pullman strike and began his illustrious career as an attorney for radical causes. (*Chicago Tribune Company*)

William Jennings Bryan, congressman from Nebraska, sponsor of the
1894 federal income tax (chapter 4), and Democratic candidate for
president in 1896, 1900, and 1908. On occasion, he
appeared before the Supreme Court, most notably in
Smyth v. Ames (chapter 7). Here in 1900.
(*Harvard Law Art Collection*)

Joseph H. Choate, prominent attorney and statesman, who appeared
before the Supreme Court to challenge the 1894
federal income tax statute in *Pollock v.*
Farmers' Loan & Trust Co. (chapter 4).
Here in 1895.
(*Library of Congress*)

Richard Olney, attorney general of the United States
from 1893 to 1895. Here in the mid-1890s.
(*Library of Congress*)

Drawing from the New York *Herald*, May 12, 1895, depicting Attorney General
Olney defending the federal income tax before the Supreme
Court in *Pollock v. Farmers' Loan & Trust Co.*
(chapter 4). (*Library of Congress*)

James Coolidge Carter, New York attorney, who appeared before
the Supreme Court on numerous occasions, most notably
to defend the 1894 federal income tax (chapter 4)
and to challenge legislation excluding Chinese
immigrants (chapter 10). Painting by
Irwin Benoni, 1888.
(*Carter, Ledyard & Milburn*)

he did not similarly affirm or even mention *Addyston Pipe*, but the fact remains that his own reading of the Sherman Act was very different from that put forward by Peckham in *Trans-Missouri* and *Joint Traffic* in defense of the broad rule against price–fixing. In the second of those cases Peckham had read the Sherman Act as prohibiting all "direct and immediate" restraints on trade.[109] Holmes might be prepared to apply the Sherman Act to price fixing agreements on the ground that, unlike the arrangement in *Northern Securities*, they were agreements between "strangers" that "wholly or partially restricted [their] freedom in carrying on [their] business," and therefore were in a certain sense exclusionary. But that was his rationale, not Peckham's.

Peckham silently joined Holmes's dissent in *Northern Securities*. So did Fuller. It remained for Brewer, more committed than Harlan to the earlier antitrust decisions, to put the law in order. He did not join Holmes's opinion but, as noted earlier, voted to sustain the suit on the theory that the holding company was a sham and the functional equivalent of the cartels of *Trans-Missouri* and *Joint Traffic* and the price-fixing committee of *Addyston Pipe*. There was no obvious contradiction between his position in *Northern Securities* and the majority opinions in those earlier cases, all of which he joined. Nevertheless, in the face of Holmes's impassioned plea, he pulled back from what he, missing some of Peckham's subtlety, understood to be the rule of those earlier decisions—that the Sherman Act reached every restraint of trade. It was too broad. Brewer wanted the statute to cover some "fusions" or "unions," like the one brought about by the formation of the Northern Securities Company, but not others, like the ordinary partnership (formed by competitors), which was repeatedly mentioned by Holmes to demonstrate the absurdity of the view that the Sherman Act was meant to preserve competition. Ignoring altogether the direct/indirect distinction previously employed by Peckham to deal with this issue and Taft's analogous ancillary/nonancillary distinction, Brewer focused on the reasonable/unreasonable distinction put forward by White in his dissents in *Trans-Missouri* and *Joint Traffic*. According to Brewer, the Sherman Act proscribed only "unreasonable restraints of trade." Thereby adopting the rule of reason previously rejected by Peckham, Brewer's strategy reconnected the Sherman Act with the common law and thus mooted the liberty objection.[110] Brewer spoke for himself in *Northern Securities*, but together with the dissenters who joined Holmes's opinion, his concurrence meant that *Trans-Missouri*, *Joint Traffic*, and *Addyston Pipe* were, in effect, reopened.

---

[109] *Joint Traffic*, 171 U.S. at 568.
[110] Brewer was now in a position to dismiss summarily the liberty of contract objections to state antitrust laws;

see Smiley v. Kansas, 196 U.S. 447, 456 (1905). See also National Cotton Oil v. Texas, 197 U.S. 115 (1905) (McKenna, J.).

Holmes was no friend of the Sherman Act. On many occasions he expressed his dislike and disdain for the statute,[111] an attitude born of Holmes's taste for intellectual rigor and his perception that the Sherman Act had no coherent analytic structure. The preservation of competition might be a hope or desire, but it could not be a rule of law. His effort in *Northern Securities* might be understood as yet another attempt to give the Sherman Act the coherence, purpose, and analytic structure it otherwise lacked.[112] From that perspective, the reference to the common law and its rule against exclusions had no intrinsic importance—it was merely a peg on which to hang an analytic structure and a vehicle for Holmes's rationalism. There was a quality to Holmes's dissent, however, that suggests more was at stake. His dislike of the Sherman Act was more deeply rooted. He seemed to dispute the very power of the state to perpetuate and foster the atomistic conception of society implicit in the classical conception of the market. Reminding the reader of the decisive effect of Brewer's separate concurrence (it deprived Harlan of a majority to support his opinion), Holmes ended his opinion in *Northern Securities* on an extraordinary note:

> I am happy to know that only a minority of my brethren adopt an interpretation of the law which in my opinion would make eternal the *bellum omnium contra omnes* and disintegrate society so far as it could into individual atoms. If that were its intent I should regard calling such a law a regulation of commerce as a mere pretense. It would be an attempt to reconstruct society. I am not concerned with the wisdom of such an attempt, but I believe that Congress was not entrusted by the Constitution with the power to make it and I am deeply persuaded that it has not tried.[113]

Could it be that the Constitution did not enact Herbert Spencer's *Social Statics*, but that it did enact Rousseau's *Social Contract* or Marx's *Capital*? I doubt it. I also doubt that Holmes was simply affirming the ideal of limited government and explaining how that ideal would be undermined

---

[111] See letter from Holmes to Pollock, Apr. 23, 1910, Howe, *Holmes–Pollock Letters*, I: 163 ("I don't disguise my belief that the Sherman Act is a humbug based on economic ignorance and incompetence. . . ."); Holmes to Laski, Mar. 4, 1920, in Mark DeWolfe Howe, ed., *Holmes–Laski Letters: The Correspondence of Mr. Justice Holmes and Harold J. Laski, 1916–1935* (Cambridge: Harvard University Press, 1953), I: 248–49 ("I have been in a minority of one as to the proper administration of the Sherman Act. I hope and believe that I am not influenced by my opinion that it is a foolish law.").

[112] These efforts—by Peckham, Taft, and White as well as Holmes—have parallels in the effort of some to give an analytic structure to the great legislative enactments of our day, the civil rights statutes of the 1960s. See, e.g., Owen M. Fiss, "A Theory of Fair Employment Laws," *U. Chi. L. Rev.*, 38: 235 (1971).

[113] 193 U.S. at 411.

by state intervention on the scale needed to preserve atomistic competition. I suspect rather that this Holmesian outburst was expressive of his peculiar view of history. Holmes was a fatalist and believed in the inevitable,[114] which in this instance consisted of a movement toward industrial cooperation and centralization, indeed, monopolization. Along with many, if not most, academics of the day,[115] Holmes believed that the time of atomistic competition had passed and that capitalism was entering a new phase, one in which the economy would be dominated by new forms of combination and concentration. The economies of scale were irresistible and almost never ending. Holmes also thought it futile and in fact downright absurd (and thus unconstitutional) for the legislature, or for that matter anyone, to try to stop the march of history.

IV

In the years immediately following *Northern Securities*, the Roosevelt administration began two more antitrust suits, one in 1906 against Standard Oil and another in 1907 against American Tobacco. These suits wound their way through the lower courts for the next several years and finally emerged on the Supreme Court docket in 1910, though they were not decided until 1911.[116] These two cases achieved a public visibility and importance equal to, if not greater than, *Northern Securities*. They represented a dramatic final statement for the Fuller Court—although I use that phrase with more than the usual looseness, inasmuch as the position of chief justice had already passed from Melville Fuller to Edward White, and Fuller's two lieutenants, Peckham and Brewer, were gone. These two cases brought together strands of antitrust doctrine that had unraveled during the preceding twenty years, and in so doing they give further insight into the divisions and tensions in antitrust doctrine that emerged during Fuller's tenure. In a well-known book, Hans Thorelli argued that *Northern Securities* "institutionalized" antitrust.[117] In my view, that achievement belongs not to *Northern Securities* but to *Standard Oil* and *American Tobacco*. They charted the future, and they did so by synthesizing the past.

---

[114] See Yosal Rogat, "The Judge as Spectator," *U. Chi. L. Rev.*, 31: 213 (1964), and Edmund Wilson's chapter on Holmes in his *Patriotic Gore: Studies in the Literature of the American Civil War* (New York: Oxford University Press, 1962; repr. New York: Farrar, Straus & Giroux, 1977), 743–96. See also the discussion of Holmes at the close of Chapter 6.

[115] See Letwin, *Law and Economic Policy*, 71–77; Sklar, *Corporate Reconstruction*, 43–86.

[116] See Bruce Bringhurst, *Antitrust and the Oil Monopoly: The Standard Oil Cases, 1890–1911* (Westport, Conn.: Greenwood Press, 1979).

[117] Thorelli, *Federal Antitrust Policy*, 563.

The past largely consisted of *Northern Securities*. It was the most visible antitrust event of the turn of the century, more so than any of the cases that preceded or immediately followed it. It provoked a far-ranging debate among the justices on the Sherman Act and, even more, left many of the questions regarding the Act unresolved. The Court divided with no opinion supported by a majority. The only two cases of note that directly followed *Northern Securities*—*Swift and Co. v. United States* (1905)[118] and the *Danbury Hatters Case* (*Loewe v. Lawlor*, 1908)[119]—did not address the liberty or federalism issue in an illuminating manner. The opinion in the first of those cases was written, oddly enough, given his dissent in *Northern Securities*, by Holmes; the opinion in the second by Fuller. Both are obscure on the liberty and federalism issues, almost intentionally so, perhaps in an effort to minimize the differences among the justices. In *Standard Oil* and *American Tobacco*, however, both objections to the Sherman Act commanded the Court's full attention.

The entrepreneurial activity at issue in the *Standard Oil* and *American Tobacco* suits was strikingly similar to the activity of Hill and Morgan in *Northern Securities*: the construction of corporate empires through the use of the holding company. Only the personalities and industries differed. White, now chief justice, seemed determined to put an end to many of the tensions that were acknowledged and perhaps even inflamed by *Northern Securities*. His strategy was to avoid the full force of Harlan's *Northern Securities* opinion and to construct a position for the Court—for eight of the justices—that roughly coincided with the position Brewer had taken in that case. This left Harlan nearly hysterical.

Both sides in *Northern Securities* suffered attrition through death and resignations. Brown, who joined Harlan's plurality opinion in *Northern Securities*, was gone; so was Brewer, who also voted to sustain the suit. Two of the dissenting justices, Fuller and Peckham, also were no longer on the Court. Some of these changes took place shortly after *Standard Oil* and *American Tobacco* were first argued, and surely the reargument of these cases (a circumstance that only heightened their visibility) must have been prompted by a desire to have a full bench address the issue. As circumstance had it, the full bench included four new justices—Horace H. Lurton (a member of the lower court panel in *Addyston Pipe*), Charles Evans Hughes (the progressive governor of New York), Willis Van Devanter, and Joseph Rucker Lamar—all appointed by Taft, who sat in the White House from 1908 to 1912, and who earlier had written the Court of Appeals opinion upholding the government in *Addyston Pipe*. The justices who participated in *Northern Securities* and who were still on the Court in 1911 were Holmes,

---

[118] 196 U.S. 375 (1905).   [119] 208 U.S. 274 (1908).

Chapter V: *The Antitrust Campaign*

Harlan, McKenna, Day, and, of course, White. White was appointed chief justice by Taft, and that must have placed White in a peculiar position. He had dissented in *Northern Securities*, but now had to forge a position—through compromise if not through persuasion—that simultaneously would (1) be acceptable to a majority of the justices, (2) provoke a minimum of dissents, (3) enhance the strength of the Supreme Court in the public mind, and (4) demonstrate a due regard for the trust and confidence Taft evidenced by appointing him chief justice.

From that perspective, *Standard Oil* and *American Tobacco* were a tour de force. Although White had found himself in dissent seven years earlier in *Northern Securities*, he managed in *Standard Oil* and *American Tobacco* to create a new antitrust doctrine that obtained the support of seven other justices—two of whom, McKenna and Day, had joined Harlan's plurality opinion in *Northern Securities*. Only Harlan remained apart. He subscribed to the results in *Standard Oil* and *American Tobacco*, which, like *Northern Securities*, essentially sustained the enforcement of the statute, but he bitterly complained of the doctrine announced by the Court. The *Standard Oil* and *American Tobacco* cases of 1911 returned Harlan to the position he occupied some fifteen years before in *E. C. Knight*—alone and unhappy with the Court's interpretation of the Sherman Act. He died shortly after the opinions were announced.

In its first encounter with the Sherman Act in *E. C. Knight*, the Supreme Court had transformed the federalism issue regarding the scope of the commerce power into one of statutory interpretation. It was to be decided on a case-by-case basis in light of prevailing constitutional doctrine. If, and only if, the particular exertion of congressional power was authorized by the Commerce Clause would the statute be deemed applicable. This blending of constitutional and statutory interpretation on the federalism issue had persisted throughout the twenty years of Fuller's chief justiceship; it was continued by the 1911 cases and constitutes one of the legacies of *E. C. Knight*. Another aspect of *E. C. Knight* also was implicated in the 1911 cases, but it had a less happy fate. I am referring to the distinction between manufacturing and transportation, and the attempt to structure the scope of the commerce power in terms of the type of economic activity regulated.

Harlan had dissented in *E. C. Knight*, arguing that the bounds of the commerce power should be defined not by the *type* of economic activity regulated but by the *impact* the business had on the flow of goods across state lines. He recognized that the monopolization of a manufacturing industry can have an impact on the process of distributing goods in national markets and insisted only that legislation on the subject of manufacturing be related to that interstate impact. Harlan's impact theory was ignored by the Court in *Trans-Missouri*, *Joint Traffic*, and *Addyston Pipe*, but his plurality opinion in *Northern Securities* reflected it: Prosecuting the Northern

Securities Company under the Sherman Act was a "means . . . germane to the end"[120] of preserving competition in interstate transportation. An even more decisive break with the *E. C. Knight* approach to federalism occurred in 1905 in the *Swift* case, in which Holmes wrote the opinion for a unanimous Court and adopted an approach similar to the one urged by Harlan throughout this period. He treated a price-fixing arrangement among a group of livestock purchasers in Illinois as an interference with the flow of goods across state lines. There was no need for a direct obstruction, like a boulder in the highway; an impact on the "stream of commerce," to change metaphors, was sufficient. Holmes mentioned *E. C. Knight* with a tone of respectful indifference, but it must have been clear to everyone that the distinction between different types of economic activity no longer defined the bounds of the commerce power. Impact was everything.[121] By 1908, Fuller himself applied the Harlan-Holmes theory in the *Danbury Hatters Case* to find that organizing a consumer boycott of a manufacturer in Connecticut violated the Sherman Act. Here the interference with commerce consisted not of a diminution in the competition on the seller's part but of a lessening of demand for the manufactured goods, which were sold to wholesalers throughout the nation:

> If the purposes of the combination were . . . to prevent any interstate transportation at all, the fact that the means operated at one end before physical transportation commenced and at the other end after the physical transportation ended was immaterial.[122]

Thus, although the 1911 cases involved manufacturing, namely the refining of oil and the manufacture of cigarettes, and not transportation, after *Addyston Pipe* (cast-iron pipes) and *Danbury Hatters* (hats), it was now clear that this would not be a bar to the application of the Sherman Act.

There was, however, one aspect of the federalism issue left undisturbed by the impact theory of *Swift* and *Danbury Hatters*, but that had divided the Court in *Northern Securities*: the status of the holding company as a separate economic entity. Although *Northern Securities* involved an arrangement to fuse two interstate railroads, a difficult issue was presented because the suit challenged the formation of a New Jersey corporation that would hold the stock of the railroad companies. In his dissent in *Northern*

---

[120] 193 U.S. at 337.

[121] The outcome in *Swift* was foreshadowed by Montague & Co. v. Lowry, 193 U.S. 38 (1904). *Montague* involved an association of California dealers of tiles, mantels, and grates and their out-of-state manufacturers, who agreed to trade only with association members.

The Court held that even though all sales under the agreement took place within California, the agreement restrained interstate trade because it prevented those not members of the association from being able to purchase goods manufactured out of state.

[122] 208 U.S. at 301.

Chapter V: *The Antitrust Campaign*

Securities, White refused to pierce the corporate veil of the holding company. He insisted that *Northern Securities* was a stock rather than a railroad case and that Congress had no power to regulate the acquisition and ownership of stock. The federalism issue in *Northern Securities* thus turned, at least for White, on a prior question about the economic status of the holding company. The same question was present in *Standard Oil* and *American Tobacco*: Although refined oil and cigarettes moved across state lines in much the same way as the livestock in *Swift* or the hats in *Danbury Hatters*, the suit was aimed not at a collusive action by the producers or sellers but rather at the formation of the holding company that stood at the pinnacle of each industrial empire. What the government attacked in each case was the creation of an industrial empire through the acquisition by a holding company of stock of an endless number of companies. The remedy sought in each case, as in *Northern Securities*, was the dismemberment or dissolution of the holding company.

By the narrowest of margins, a majority in *Northern Securities* penetrated the corporate form and treated the holding company as a mere sham. These five justices were helped in reaching this conclusion by the rather crude and transparent character of the entire scheme—Hill and Morgan had first tried a direct deal between the two lines and created the holding company only after they were blocked in that effort. The Northern Securities Company seemed to be the product of an obvious attempt at evasion. The industrial empires at issue in the 1911 cases, however, were of a somewhat different character. They had been built up over a number of years, and more honorable, or at least more understandable, economic reasons may have been at work; it was difficult to reduce all the underlying transactions to a scheme to evade a bar against mergers or acquisitions. Nevertheless, having taken one step down the reductionist road in *Northern Securities*, the next became almost irresistible, even to one of the dissenters— White. In *Standard Oil*, the first and more important of the two cases, White took that step with remarkable ease. He simply said that the federalism objection to the attack on the holding company—that Congress had no power to regulate stock transactions—was "plainly foreclosed" by earlier decisions, citing *Northern Securities* and a few other cases that seemed to be even less decisive.[123]

After the 1911 cases there was little life left to the federalism objection: As long as the product was sold in national markets, a manufacturer fell

---

[123] 221 U.S. at 68–69. He cited *Danbury Hatters, Swift, Montague*, and Shawnee Compress Co. v. Anderson, 209 U.S. 423 (1908) (sustaining judgment of the Supreme Court of the Territory of Oklahoma that lease of company's entire property and business was a restraint of trade and void, though not specifying whether the result was reached under common law, the Sherman Act, or the Oklahoma statute).

within the regulatory province defined by the Sherman Act.[124] While this rule effectively repudiated the result in *E. C. Knight*, the Court continued the practice, which originated in that case, of treating the federalism issue as one of statutory interpretation. The 1911 cases also continued the trend in cases like *Addyston Pipe, Northern Securities, Swift*, and *Danbury Hatters* that enhanced the power of the national government, but spoke with a new clarity and finality. With respect to the liberty issue, however, the contribution of the 1911 cases was more significant and distinctive, perhaps because it was harder to discern a trend in the prior decisions. On the issue of liberty, the law was in disarray.

In the closing passages of his dissent in *Northern Securities*, Justice White had made—in the most emphatic terms—a sharp distinction between two rights, the right to use property and the right to acquire and own property. The latter was treated as an absolute right, immune from government regulation, while the former was subject to regulation, provided it was reasonable. In *Standard Oil* and again in *American Tobacco*, this distinction between the two rights was quietly abandoned. Now there were no absolute rights; government had the power to restrict the ownership right as well as the use right, provided it prohibited only the unreasonable exercise of these rights.

Having made this concession at the level of constitutional doctrine, White then proceeded to build into the Sherman Act an analytic structure that, at least on a nominal level, automatically would guard against excessive exertions of governmental power. Peckham had tried to achieve a similar result in *Trans-Missouri, Joint Traffic*, and *Addyston Pipe* by construing the Sherman Act as prohibiting only *direct* restraints on trade. In the 1911 cases, however, White chose the rule of reason, first propounded in his dissents in *Trans-Missouri* and *Joint Traffic*, then picked up by Brewer in his concurrence in *Northern Securities*, and now made controlling by *Standard Oil* and *American Tobacco*. After 1911 it was settled that the Sherman Act banned only "unreasonable" restraints of trade, an interpretation of the

---

[124] See, e.g., Standard Sanitary Mfg. Co. v. United States, 226 U.S. 20 (1912) (agreement among enameled ironware manufacturers to restrain trade was prohibited by Sherman Act since New Jersey manufacturer shipped goods out of state); United States v. Patten, 226 U.S. 525, 543 (1913) (conspiracy to corner cotton market, "by its necessary operation . . . directly and materially impede[d] and burden[ed] the due course of trade and commerce among the States."); Straus v. American Publishers' Ass'n, 231 U.S. 222 (1913) (agreement between publishers and booksellers to maintain retail prices restrained interstate commerce in violation of the Sherman Act since Publishers' Association and Booksellers' Association both operated throughout the United States); and Eastern States Retail Lumber Ass'n v. United States, 234 U.S. 600 (1914) (conspiracy to prevent wholesale lumber dealers from selling directly to consumers restrained interstate commerce since the wholesale dealers engaged in the national lumber market).

statute that had the effect of transforming every constitutionally based liberty objection into a claim that the statute was not applicable. Since, according to White, the Constitution protected only reasonable exercises of the right to use or own property, all claims of liberty had to be predicated on the idea that the business practice was reasonable. But if that could be established, then the statute, construed to prohibit only unreasonable restraints of trade, would by its very terms (so to speak) be inapplicable. Conversely, if the businessman could not establish that his conduct was reasonable, the statute would be deemed applicable, and his due process objection to the exertion of government power necessarily would dissolve. Under the rule of reason, the Sherman Act could not, as a matter of logic, interfere with the constitutionally protected zones of individual liberty.[125]

In reading the term "unreasonable" into the Sherman Act, the Court borrowed a technique originally crafted by Fuller in *E. C. Knight*. The limits of the Sherman Act were made to extend no further than the Constitution permitted: Constitutional limits on congressional power—one derived from the Commerce Clause, the other from Due Process—were made terms of the statute. In the case of the federalism objection, this construction of the statute might be regarded as less of an achievement than in the case of liberty. By its very words the Sherman Act was applicable to business practices that restrained "commerce among the states." Fuller had only to conclude that this statutory phrase was to be construed in light of constitutional principle in order to make it coextensive with the grant of power to Congress under the Commerce Clause. In the case of liberty, however, White had to confront the fact that, by its terms, the Sherman Act applied to "every" restraint of trade. The word "unreasonable" had to be, so to speak, inserted into the statute.

In justifying the rule of reason White drew heavily on the common law, which he understood as allowing the businessman only the right—or space—to engage in reasonable practices.[126] The common law also must have been the model for the institutional arrangement that White now con-

---

[125] As White put it,
Many arguments are pressed in various forms of statement which in substance amount to contending that the statute cannot be applied under the facts of this case without impairing rights of property and destroying the freedom of contract or trade, which . . . it is insisted is protected by the constitutional guaranty of due process of law. But the ultimate foundation of all these arguments is the assumption that reason may not be resorted to in interpreting and applying the statute, and therefore that the statute unreasonably restricts the right to contract and unreasonably operates upon the right to acquire and hold property. As the premise is demonstrated to be unsound by the construction we have given the statute, of course the propositions which rest upon the premise need not be further noticed.
Ibid., 69.
[126] See Dewey, "Common-Law Background."

templated for the Sherman Act, that is, one that positioned the courts as arbiters determining which restraints of competition were bad and which were good. The rule of reason gave the judiciary the task of creating the substantive content of the Sherman Act. But White stopped short of transforming the Sherman Act into a branch of the common law as Taft and Holmes counseled.

In *Addyston Pipe* Taft tried to tie the Sherman Act to the common law by confining the statute to arrangements whose sole object was to restrain competition, thereby allowing restraints that were ancillary to legitimate purposes. Commenting on White's opinion in *Standard Oil*, Taft, now president, said, "It was a good opinion. . . . It did not take exactly the line of distinction I have drawn but it certainly approximates it."[127] White also had departed from Holmes's position. At various points in his opinion White used the word "exclusion" in referring to the prohibited practices, but it was clear that he was not reducing the Sherman Act to the rule against exclusion that Holmes had extracted from the common law and insisted upon in *Northern Securities*. Holmes acquiesced in the 1911 cases, but he was not happy. As he wrote to another intimate friend, the Baroness Moncheur, "I don't care about White's hobby of confining the Sherman Act to unreasonable restraints of trade but I backed him in order to get the most moderate results."[128]

In a further departure from the common law, White made it clear that the Sherman Act would reach "practical monopolies" and would not be confined to proscribing "artificial monopolies"—those conferred by government, which, as noted earlier, is what the term "monopoly" had meant in common law.[129] Finally, and most importantly, White emphasized the

---

[127] Taft to Helen Taft, May 16, 1911, W. H. Taft Papers, Library of Congress Manuscript Division.

[128] Holmes to the Baroness Moncheur, May 25, 1911, Harvard Holmes Papers. See also Holmes to Lady Margaret Clifford, June 4, 1911, ibid. ("I am not satisfied with the Standard Oil and Tobacco decisions but I believed that White would get the most moderate result that could be hoped for. . . . White got his way at last in construing the Statute to forbid only contracts and combinations in *unreasonable* restraint of trade—the Statute says 'all contracts &c in restraint of trade.' ").

[129] White noted that the common law originally had not prohibited "the creation of monopoly by an individual" (*Standard Oil*, 221 U.S. at 55) but that

[t]he dread of monopoly as an emanation of governmental power . . . did not serve to assuage the fear as to the evil consequences which might arise from the acts of individuals producing or tending to produce the consequences of monopoly. It resulted that treating such acts as we have said as amounting to monopoly, sometimes constitutional restrictions, again legislative enactments or judicial decisions, served to enforce and illustrate the purpose to prevent the occurrence of the evils recognized in the mother country as consequent upon monopoly, by providing against contracts or acts of individuals or combinations of individuals or corporations deemed to be conducive to such results. Ibid., 57.

constitutional content of the idea of "reasonableness." Just as the statutory phrase "commerce among the states" was to be construed from the perspective of the Commerce Clause, the standard of "reasonableness" was also constitutional.

Because of its vacuity, in later years "reasonableness" suffered a fate unlike "commerce among the states." It lost its constitutional significance and was given a technocratic rather than a constitutional meaning: Only those business practices that interfered with allocative efficiency would be deemed unreasonable.[130] The liberty issue thus dropped from sight. The federalism issue remained, but given the further development of national markets during the twentieth century and the continued vitality of a test for the commerce power that looked to the impact on the stream of goods, the Commerce Clause posed no significant limitations on the application of the Sherman Act. Antitrust became deconstitutionalized. It is important to understand, however, that White's intention was quite different. He adopted the rule of reason to place constitutional limits on the Sherman Act, to assure everyone that liberty of contract would not be infringed. In sorting out which restraints should be allowed and which disallowed, as the rule of reason required, the Court had to determine whether the businessman was exercising his constitutionally protected liberty—in White's words, "the fundamental right of freedom to trade"[131]—not whether he was promoting "allocative efficiency" or "consumer welfare." As White put it, indeed, as inelegantly as the previous chief justice might have,

> [T]he necessity for not departing in this case from the standard of the rule of reason . . . is so plainly required in order to give effect to the remedial purposes which the act under consideration contemplates, and to prevent that act from destroying all liberty of contract and all substantial right to trade, and thus causing the act to be at war with itself by annihilating the fundamental right of freedom to trade which, on the very face of the act, it was enacted to preserve. . . .[132]

Harlan strongly objected in the 1911 cases to the adoption of the rule of reason, and managed to achieve—in his printed opinion and, even more, in the courtroom as the decision was announced—an emotional tone that far surpassed that of his dissents in *Plessy* or *Lochner*.[133] He died a few

---

[130] See, e.g., Continental T.V. v. GTE Sylvania, 433 U.S. 36, 54 (1977).

[131] *American Tobacco*, 221 U.S. at 180.

[132] Ibid.

[133] See David J. Danielski and Joseph S. Tulchin, eds., *The Autobiographical Notes of Charles Evan Hughes* (Cambridge: Harvard University Press, 1973), 170 ("[Harlan] went far beyond his written opinion, launching out into bitter invective, which I thought most unseemly."). See also sources cited in Chapter 2, note 39.

months later, and some of his language, if not a tribute to the sheer length of his tenure (thirty-four years), seemed to anticipate that event. At one point he referred to his "many years of public service at the National Capital,"[134] as though these cases were about to bring them to an end. The tone of his opinion also might have reflected his long-standing feud with White, going back to his service on the Louisiana Commission of 1877,[135] and a growing sense of isolation: He seemed to have returned to the position he had occupied in 1895 in *E. C. Knight*—the only one committed, so he believed, to strong antitrust enforcement. Harlan had lost two of his allies from *Northern Securities*, McKenna and Day, and saw the promise of *Trans-Missouri, Joint Traffic*, and *Addyston Pipe* modified beyond recognition (though the alignments of *Northern Securities* had foreshadowed that modification).[136]

Harlan spoke of the impact that the rule of reason would have on criminal prosecutions under the Sherman Act. It was doubtful, he insisted, that the requirement of the criminal law that the accused act wrongfully or be blameworthy could be satisfied if the statute were read to prohibit only "unreasonable" restraints of trade. Every businessman could defend on the ground that he did not know, and could not have known, in advance that the conduct charged was prohibited. This point was, of course, well taken, and Harlan had good reason to be angry with Holmes for not joining him on this point. In his *Northern Securities* dissent, Holmes had argued for a narrow and precise definition of the action prohibited by the Sherman Act (which he claimed was to be found in his anti-exclusion rule) on the theory that the Sherman Act itself specifically authorized criminal prosecu-

---

[134] *Standard Oil*, 221 U.S. at 105.

[135] Harlan was a member of the commission sent by President Hayes in the spring of 1877 to settle local controversies in Louisiana, while White was the outspoken spokesman for a Louisiana delegation. See Merlo Pusey, *Charles Evans Hughes* (New York: Macmillan, 1951) 1: 277. Disagreements over the colonial issue (see the discussion of *Rassmussen v. United States* in Chapter 8) and the state prohibition cases (see the discussion of *Rhodes v. Iowa* in Chapter 9) did not help matters.

[136] White distinguished *Trans-Missouri, Joint Traffic*, and *Addyston Pipe* by a play on the word "reason." He argued that these cases had only precedential weight because they were "reasoned," which in turn meant that they had adopted his "rule of reason": "As the cases cannot by any possible concep-

tion be treated as authoritative without the certitude that reason was resorted to for the purpose of deciding them, it follows as a matter of course that it must have been held by the light of reason . . . that the assailed contracts or agreements were within the general enumeration of the statute. . . ." *Standard Oil*, 221 U.S. at 64–65. However, White did acknowledge at another point that "general language was made use of, which, when separated from its context, would justify the conclusion that it was decided that reason could not be resorted to for the purpose of determining whether the acts complained of were within the statute." Ibid., 64. In this regard, White's opinion is an improvement over Holmes's dissent in *Northern Securities*, which purported to celebrate those cases.

tions as well as injunctions. Time and time again Holmes insisted that the statute be read with the rigor of the criminal law in mind, although the *Northern Securities* case itself was a civil injunctive proceeding. In joining White's majority opinions in *Standard Oil* and *American Tobacco*, which adopted the rule of reason, Holmes now seemed prepared to read the Sherman Act as only a civil statute. Harlan sensed the compromise.

Harlan's principal objection to the Court's position in the 1911 cases, however, did not arise from the absence of due notice and the difficulty of maintaining criminal prosecutions, but rather concerned the allocation of power effectuated by the adoption of the rule of reason. He protested the flow of power to the judiciary. White responded by insisting that the judicial task under the rule of reason would be no different from what it had been in countless other cases. By way of example, he mentioned "fraud," as well as Peckham's distinction between "direct" and "indirect" restraints on interstate trade.[137] In White's mind (and perhaps mine, too), there is not much of a difference between a judgment attempting to distinguish "direct" from "indirect" restraints and making a determination of "unreasonableness." Harlan, however, was less concerned with the competence of the judiciary to make the judgments contemplated by the rule of reason than with the presumptuousness entailed in entrusting itself with that function. Harlan's point was not one of competence but usurpation. For Harlan, Congress had prohibited "every" restraint of trade; the legislature had clearly expressed its will and he saw in the rule of reason a modification of that will. He saw the judiciary conferring power on itself and denounced the creation of the rule of reason as *"judicial legislation"* (his emphasis).[138] He claimed it was a "usurpation by the judicial branch of the Government of the functions of the legislative department."[139]

The truth of the matter, however, is that the creation of the rule of reason—what Holmes referred to as "White's hobby"—did not represent a usurpation of the legislative function by the judiciary; rather it marked the use of a new rubric for the continuation of a function that the judiciary always had performed—imposing limits on the exercise of legislative power. The rule of reason did not create new restraints upon the legislative will; they were always present, though rooted in and expressed through accepted constitutional doctrines of liberty and limited government to which Harlan fully subscribed. All the 1911 cases did was transform the formal basis of those limits. The limits on the legislature still were to be crafted by the exercise of judicial reason, but now they were said to be part of the legislative will under the theory that Congress meant only to prohibit unreasonable restraints of trade.

---

[137] *Standard Oil*, 221 U.S. at 70.
[138] Ibid., 104.

[139] Ibid., 103.

Harlan complained of this formal transformation, believing that it diminished the power of the legislature. Over the long run, however, the rule of reason may have had the opposite effect. It gave the exercise of legislative power represented by the Sherman Act a new dignity. The Sherman Act was more than the mere assertion of will by "the numbers" (to use Brewer's Albany formulation), for now the legislative power was linked to reason and the common law, and its constitutionality thereby was assured. Even more importantly, the rule of reason brought the limits on the legislative power within the reach of the legislature itself: Congress has greater power over restraints read into a statute than those that remain explicitly rooted in the Constitution.[140] Over time the constitutional origins of these restraints are likely to be either forgotten or ignored, and it will come to be believed that it is for Congress to decide, purely as a matter of public policy, what kinds of restraints of trade are unreasonable.

---

[140] Three years later, Congress responded to the rule of reason cases by proscribing particular anticompetitive practices in the Clayton Act of 1914 and creating an antitrust enforcement agency in the Federal Trade Commission Act, also enacted in 1914. While these statutes were the culmination of a movement that had begun in the first Roosevelt administration to amend the antitrust law, they received an important impetus from the 1911 cases and the reaction those cases produced. However, like the Sherman Act, the 1914 measures did not reflect a fundamental shift of attitude toward the state, but rather once again posited the market as the central ordering device of social and economic relationships. See generally Letwin, *Law and Economic Policy*, 238–78, and Sklar, *Corporate Reconstruction*, 179–332.

CHAPTER VI

Labor Legislation and the Theory of Lochner

A NTITRUST was the primary legal battlefield for progressivism. But the movement had a wide sweep and in time reached the workplace. In response, a number of statutes were enacted that attempted to change various facets of the employment relationship. These laws imposed maximum hours of work; prohibited child labor; outlawed contracts that prevented employees from joining a union (so-called yellow dog contracts); required employers to pay wages in cash rather than scrip; required safety measures in the workplace; and abolished a number of common law defenses, such as the fellow-servant rule, that had the effect of denying recovery for work-related injuries.[1]

These reform measures were not part of a single, comprehensive program in which the enactment of one statute was coordinated closely with another. Most were enacted at the state level, and legislative politics varied considerably from state to state. Taken collectively, however, they represented a striking enlargement of the domain of government power and, as far as the justices were concerned,[2] a sharp break with the past. They challenged the Court's commitment to liberty and culminated in *Lochner v. New York*[3]—a case that stands as the symbol of the Fuller Court's response to progressivism.

---

[1] See generally Robert H. Wiebe, *Businessmen and Reform: A Study of the Progressive Movement* (Cambridge: Harvard University Press, 1962), and Christopher L. Tomlins, *The State and the Unions: Labor Relations, Law, and the Organized Labor Movement in America, 1880–1960* (Cambridge: Cambridge University Press, 1985), 60–95. It was not until around 1910 that the drive for workers' compensation took hold. See James Weinstein, *The Corporate Ideal in the Liberal State, 1900–1918* (Boston: Beacon Press, 1968), 40–61.

[2] Some have argued that extensive government regulation of the economy was a common practice throughout the nineteenth century. See, e.g., Harry N. Scheiber, "The Road to *Munn*: Eminent Domain and the Concept of Public Purpose in the State Courts," in Donald Fleming and Bernard Bailyn, eds., *Law in American History* (Boston: Little, Brown, 1971), 329.

[3] 198 U.S. 45 (1905). For the background of the New York statute, see Paul Kens, *Judicial Power and Reform Politics: The Anatomy of* Lochner v. New York (Lawrence: University Press of Kansas, 1990), 26–78.

Like antitrust, statutes regulating the employment relationship were premised on an acceptance of the capitalist structure of society and constituted a limited and discrete intrusion by the state into the economy. They differed from the Sherman Act, however, in that they were not intended to protect the market against such self-destructive practices as price-fixing. Instead, they were meant only to eliminate certain abuses or excesses, that is, to further a limited number of values that otherwise would elude the typical bargain between worker and employer. Some saw more radical elements in these measures—a repudiation, for example, of the practice of treating labor as a commodity to be sold on the market—but that was the exception. The progressive coalition that brought these labor statutes into being was dominated by middle- and upper-class reformers who sought amelioration, not revolution.[4]

In the context of labor, the amelioration offered by progressivism differed from that of the Sherman Act insofar as the tenets of the social contract were concerned. While measures regulating the employment relationship were defended on universal or seemingly neutral terms (for example, "health" or "industrial peace"), the Court feared that they might have been enacted to serve the narrow interests of some particular economic group such as "workers" or "organized labor" in order to redistribute wealth. As Peckham more diplomatically asserted in *Lochner*, referring to the New York maximum hours statute,

> It is impossible for us to shut our eyes to the fact that many of the laws of this character, while passed under what is claimed to be the police power for the purpose of protecting the public health or welfare, are, in reality, passed from other motives.[5]

Standing guard against the risk of redistribution, the Court scrutinized carefully the statutes in question to make certain that these "other motives" were not present. The need for this scrutiny was perceived to be far greater in labor than in antitrust.

---

[4] Robert H. Wiebe, *The Search for Order, 1877–1920* (New York: Hill & Wang, 1967), 164–95.

[5] The full text reads:
When assertions such as we have adverted to become necessary in order to give, if possible, a plausible foundation for the contention that the law is a "health law," it gives rise to at least a suspicion that there was some other motive dominating the legislature than the purpose to subserve the public health or welfare. . . . It is impossible for us to shut our eyes to the fact that many of the laws of this character, while passed under what is claimed to be the police power for the purpose of protecting the public health or welfare, are, in reality, passed from other motives. We are justified in saying so when, from the character of the law and the subject upon which it legislates, it is apparent that the public health or welfare bears but the most remote relation to the law. 198 U.S. at 62–64.

Moreover, while antitrust cases came to the Court against a background that included the common law doctrine on restraints of trade, many statutes regulating the employment relationship (such as the one involved in *Lochner*, which decreed a maximum workweek of sixty hours for bakers) had no common law antecedents. Now and then the common law became relevant, for example when statutes restricted the contractual rights and duties of various categories of persons such as women and children. But that was the exception, and the common law had only a tangential relationship to the employment regulation being examined. No common law rule existed that placed a ceiling on the number of hours worked, prohibited the employment of children, or outlawed yellow dog contracts.

The absence of common law antecedents might have accounted for the uncertain and jagged quality of the lines the Court tried to draw in the labor context. Without the guiding hand of the common law, the Court was more at sea than in antitrust, allowing some labor statutes while disallowing others. The absence of common law antecedents also may have precluded the interpretive strategies formulated by the Court in such cases as *Standard Oil* and *American Tobacco*.[6] In those cases, the Court read various constitutional constraints into the Sherman Act and thus found it unnecessary ever to declare the statute or its various applications unconstitutional. The situation was different in labor. Even when the Court confronted a federal enactment in the labor context, as in *Adair v. United States*,[7] which held unconstitutional a congressional ban on yellow dog contracts, liberty of contract always remained, so to speak, outside the challenged statute, as an explicit constitutional restraint on the legislative power. The lack of common law antecedents forced the Court to speak more openly and brazenly about the limits on the legislative power, and thus may have been responsible for the preeminence of *Lochner* as the source of the Fuller Court's identity.

I

Lochner has been controlled by its critics. Our understanding of the case has been shaped largely by the quip in Justice Holmes's dissent, surely among the most memorable of all judicial utterances, that "[t]he Fourteenth Amendment does not enact Mr. Herbert Spencer's Social Statics."[8] There are many ways to read this remark, but the one that gives Holmes's

---

[6] These cases are discussed in Chapter 5.

[7] 208 U.S. 161 (1908). *Adair* is discussed in detail later in this chapter.

[8] 198 U.S. at 75 (Holmes, J., dissenting). For a modern appreciation of

Holmes's dissent, and particularly of the rhetorical power of this famous sentence, see Richard A. Posner, *Law and Literature: A Misunderstood Relation* (Cambridge: Harvard University Press, 1988), 281–89.

dissent its greatest power sees Holmes as protesting against judicial inter-ference with the legislature's choice of economic policy.[9] As Holmes him-self said elsewhere in his dissent, "This case is decided upon an economic theory. . . ."[10] In truth, however, the majority opinion, written by Justice Peckham, was not a brief on behalf of a particular economic policy, but rather reflected a particular conception of state authority that had roots in contractarianism—an intellectual tradition far more extensive and entrenched than Holmes's passing reference to Spencer implied.[11] Peck-ham was trying to identify the bounds within which the social contract allowed the legislature to operate, and he invalidated the New York statute because, as he said, those bounds had been "reached and passed."[12]

To help the modern reader understand how Peckham came to that conclusion, it might be helpful to introduce a distinction between two types of authority—one I will call "organic," the other "constitutive." An exam-ple of organic authority can be found in the family, specifically in the authority parents (would like to!) exercise over their children. Another example might be found in the lord–serf relationship. I call this type of authority "organic" because it emerges from the social relationship itself and thus seems natural or intrinsic to it. There are limits on the scope of organic authority, but they are usually few and arise from sources extrane-ous to the processes by which the authority is created. An example of such a limit is the moral principle that prohibits cruelty to one's children. A vio-lation of such a principle is a wrong and strongly condemned, but it does not necessarily throw into question the legitimacy of the parent's authority itself.

Conversely, constitutive authority does not arise naturally nor is it intrinsic to some ongoing relationship. Like that of a club or voluntary asso-ciation, it is artificially or deliberately created to serve discrete ends. This

---

[9] For the accounts of *Lochner* in this vein, see William F. Swindler, *Court and Constitution in the Twentieth Cen-tury: The Old Legality, 1889–1932* (Indi-anapolis: Bobbs-Merrill, 1969); Robert G. McCloskey, *The American Supreme Court* (Chicago: University of Chicago Press, 1960); and Sidney Fine, *Laissez Faire and the General-Welfare State: A Study of Conflict in American Thought, 1865–1901* (Ann Arbor: University of Michigan Press, 1956).

[10] 198 U.S. 75.

[11] For the various accounts of the intellectual sources of the Court's doc-trine, see Chapter 2 and the sources in note 102 of that chapter. See also Clyde L. Jacobs, *Law Writers and the Courts:*

The Influence of Thomas F. Cooley, Christopher G. Tiedeman, and John F. Dillon upon American Constitutional Law (Berkeley: University of California Press, 1954), and David N. Mayer, "The Jurisprudence of Christopher G. Tiede-man: A Study in the Failure of Laissez Faire Constitutionalism," *Mo. L. Rev.*, 55: 93 (1990).

[12] 198 U.S. at 58. For an analysis of Peckham's concept of strictly bounded spheres of power, see Duncan Kennedy, "Toward an Historical Understanding of Legal Consciousness: The Case of Classical Legal Thought in America, 1850–1940," *Res. L. & Soc.*, 3: 3, 9–12 (1980).

form of authority is bounded by principles of morality and thus, like organic authority, has external limits. It is, however, also subject to another set of constraints, which might be called "internal" because they arise from the very reasons for which that authority is created. Internal constraints confine the activities of the association to the specific purposes for which it was created. Violating such a constraint raises not just a question of wrongfulness, as does violating an external restraint, but also one of legitimacy, for such conduct contradicts the very reason for the existence of the authority.

The hallmark of the social contract tradition is that it views political authority as analogous to that of a voluntary association—as though the state were a very special kind of club. The state is an instance of constitutive authority, bound by internal as well as external restraints. This view of the state can be found in many corners of nineteenth-century constitutional law, but nowhere as clearly as in the doctrine of enumerated powers. That doctrine views the federal government as an artificially created instrumentality intended to serve a discrete and finite set of purposes. It assumes that the federal government is limited by fundamental principles of morality such as those embodied in the Bill of Rights, but the function of the doctrine is to place another type of limit on governmental power—what I refer to as internal limits, those derived from the reasons why that power was created in the first place. Such limits require that every exercise of federal power be justified in terms of the ends for which that power was created.

For Justice Peckham, the police power of the state, like the legislative power of the national government, including its power under the Commerce Clause, was a form of constitutive authority. This meant that the state was subject not only to external but also to internal restraints, that is, restraints derived from the reasons for the power's very existence. These internal limits were central to the Court's understanding of liberty and gave specific content to liberty of contract, which was, in the end, not a principle from which limits on state power were derived, but rather the space or area left to the individual after the reasons for the creation of state power were exhausted. Liberty of contract was what remained to the individual after the state reached the outer bounds of its authority.

In Peckham's opinion in *Addyston Pipe & Steel Co. v. United States*,[13] the liberty of contract objection was dissolved once it was determined that the application of the Sherman Act at issue was a proper exercise of the commerce power. In *Lochner*, too, Peckham's emphasis was once again on the scope of authority, not prohibitions. His decision turned on his understanding that it was the limited purposes of government that restricted its authority, rather than any constraints that might be imposed on that

---

[13] 175 U.S. 211 (1899). See Chapter 5.

authority by some abstract or external principle of liberty. Liberty of contract was not an absolute, nor even a guiding principle, but what remained once state authority was exhausted. As he put it in *Lochner*,

> Both property and liberty are held on such reasonable conditions as may be imposed by the governing power of the State in the exercise of [its police] powers, and with such conditions the Fourteenth Amendment was not designed to interfere. . . . The State, therefore, has power to prevent the individual from making certain kinds of contracts, and in regard to them the Federal Constitution offers no protection. If the contract be one which the State, in the legitimate exercise of its police power, has the right to prohibit, it is not prevented from prohibiting it by the Fourteenth Amendment.[14]

For Peckham, the police power was for the states what the commerce power was for the central government.

As an instance of constitutive authority, the first and perhaps most important inquiry about the police power concerns the ends that it might serve. Today we tend to think of the police power as allowing the states to further the general welfare of the community, but that was not how the *Lochner* Court saw the matter. While the formula was general—it allowed the states to further the "safety, health, morals and general welfare of the public"[15]—the Court did not read it as embracing the totality of all social interests. Rather, it treated each term as identifying a discrete and separate public end. "Safety," "health," "morals," and "welfare" were each viewed as a pigeonhole into which the purpose of a statute had to be placed.[16] Moreover, while two of the terms—"morals" and "welfare"—seemed capable of almost infinite expansion, at that time they were in fact carefully bounded by a number of principles.

One such principle, rooted in the general commitment to "equality before the law" and affirmed repeatedly by this Court,[17] denied legislatures the power to redistribute wealth or power from one economic group to another. An exception was made if the group to be treated differently was uniquely disabled and thus entitled to special protection by the state, in which case the legislation would be deemed a "labor law" rather than an exercise of the police power.[18] However, this exception was unavailable in *Lochner*, for the New York statute dealt with the ordinary occupational cat-

---

[14] 198 U.S. at 53 (citations omitted).

[15] 198 U.S. at 53.

[16] As Peckham reasoned, since the law limiting bakers' hours "involves neither the safety, the morals nor the welfare of the public . . . it must be upheld, if at all, as a law pertaining to the health of [bakers]." Ibid., 57.

[17] See the discussion in Chapters 4 and 7 of Reagan v. Farmers' Loan & Trust Co., 154 U.S. 362 (1894).

[18] 198 U.S. at 57. See the discussion later in this chapter of Muller v. Oregon, 208 U.S. 412 (1908).

egory of bakers. This meant that the statute could not be defended in the terms that might seem most plausible and congenial to the contemporary mind, as a measure intended to alter the distribution of power or wealth between employers and their workers. In fact, Peckham began his analysis by making this assumption explicit:

> There is no contention that bakers as a class are not equal in intelligence and capacity to men in other trades or manual occupations, or that they are not able to assert their rights and care for themselves without the protecting arm of the State, interfering with their independence of judgment and of action. They are in no sense wards of the State.[19]

In this passage Peckham closed off the "morals" and "general welfare" categories as permissible ends for the New York maximum hours statute. "Safety" was also dismissed summarily.[20] All that remained was "health." But here, too, Peckham introduced a further refinement insofar as he insisted that the law at issue was concerned with the health of the bakers, not with that of the consumers:

> [The law] does not affect any other portion of the public than those who are engaged in that occupation. Clean and wholesome bread does not depend upon whether the baker works but ten hours a day or only sixty hours a week.[21]

The validity of the statute thereby was made to turn on a judgment on the relation between means and ends—whether there was a sufficient connection between the maximum hours limitation and the health of the bakers.

For the Warren Court, judgments about means–end rationality were frequently made in the context of the Equal Protection Clause and then in terms of the "fit" between means and ends. In the typical equal protection cases of the 1960s, the Court insisted upon a "tight fit" between means and end.[22] For the Fuller Court, the same kind of means–end judgment was made, but in the language of "directness." Borrowing from the constitutional usage of the nineteenth century, already evidenced in *Debs*, *Pollock*, and the antitrust cases, Peckham insisted that the maximum hours statute must have a "direct relation" to health; an "indirect" or "remote" connec-

---

[19] 198 U.S. at 57.

[20] "[W]e think that a law like the one before us involves neither the safety, the morals nor the welfare of the public, and that the interest of the public is not in the slightest degree affected by such an act." Ibid.

[21] Ibid.

[22] See Gerald Gunther, "In Search of Evolving Doctrine on a Changing Court: A Model for a Newer Equal Protection," *Harv. L. Rev.*, 86: 1 (1972), and Owen M. Fiss, "Groups and the Equal Protection Clause," *Phil. & Pub. Aff.*, 5: 107 (1976).

tion would not suffice. He declared:

> The mere assertion that the subject relates though but in a remote degree to the public health does not necessarily render the enactment valid. The act must have a more direct relation, as a means to an end, and the end itself must be appropriate and legitimate, before an act can be held to be valid which interferes with the general right of an individual to be free in his person and in his power to contract in relation to his own labor.[23]

Today we recognize that the adequacy of a means–end connection is largely a matter of degree, turning on *how* direct the connection is. We also understand that such an inquiry implicates certain normative considerations, not just an assessment of the facts. Under equal protection analysis, for example, "strict scrutiny," which requires a very "tight fit" between means and end, is triggered by explicit normative considerations such as the presence of a "suspect classification" (for example, a statute disadvantaging a minority group) or the infringement of some "fundamental right" (for example, the right to vote). In *Lochner*, too, the Court recognized that the judgment about directness was one of degree. The Court assumed that the issue was not dichotomous, that is, whether the connection between means and end was direct or indirect, but rather whether it was sufficiently direct. The Court also understood that the degree of required directness reflected certain normative considerations, specifically the need to preserve a set of limits on the police power. In judging the New York statute, the *Lochner* Court, acting out of a desire to preserve the police power as a form of constitutive authority with readily discernible bounds, insisted that the connection between means and end be very direct.[24]

Peckham did not deny the existence of a possible connection between "health" (the end) and the maximum hours statute (the means). The question for him was whether there was any distinct danger posed to bakers, so that it could be said that a maximum hours regulation of bakers could

---

[23] 198 U.S. at 57–58. For the significance of what Peckham referred to in this passage as the "general right of an individual to be free in his person and in his power to contract in relation to his own labor," see pp. 164, 179.

[24] Peckham wrote:

It must, of course, be conceded that there is a limit to the valid exercise of the police power by the State. There is no dispute concerning this general proposition. Otherwise the Fourteenth Amendment would have no efficacy and the legislatures of the States would have unbounded power, and it would be enough to say that any piece of legislation was enacted to conserve the morals, the health or the safety of the people; such legislation would be valid, no matter how absolutely without foundation the claim might be. The claim of the police power would be a mere pretext— become another and delusive name for the supreme sovereignty of the State to be exercised free from constitutional restraint. Ibid., 56.

be distinguished from a maximum hours statute addressed to any other category of employees. That is why Peckham undertook a long discussion as to whether the trade of a baker was "an unhealthy one."[25] His concern was not equal treatment, that is, whether bakers justifiably could be treated differently from other employees, but rather whether they were within the reach of the legislative power. As he wrote,

> It is unfortunately true that labor, even in any department, may possibly carry with it the seeds of unhealthiness. But are we all, on that account, at the mercy of legislative majorities?[26]

Peckham feared that the police power would be virtually unlimited if the connection between the maximum hours statute and health were deemed sufficient in the case of the bakers:

> A printer, a tinsmith, a locksmith, a carpenter, a cabinetmaker, a dry goods clerk, a bank's, a lawyer's or a physician's clerk, or a clerk in almost any kind of business, would all come under the power of the legislature, on this assumption. No trade, no occupation, no mode of earning one's living, could escape this all-pervading power. . . .[27]

In resisting this "all-pervading power," Peckham did not—to put to rest another misinterpretation of *Lochner* also tied to Holmes's dissent[28]— "find" liberty of contract in the interstices of the Fourteenth Amendment. He instead was trying to preserve the then fairly well recognized limits on the police power as a form of constitutive authority. However, liberty, now understood more abstractly, did play a role in Peckham's analysis. For one thing, it created a hierarchy of means, in much the same way that the contemporary commitment to freedom of speech requires the state to use the least restrictive alternative to accomplish its ends.[29] Although the Court invalidated as beyond the scope of the police power the provision of New York law limiting the rights of laborers and employers to enter certain kinds of contracts (those that provided for a workweek in excess of sixty hours), Peckham spoke approvingly of state laws that authorized state inspections

---

[25] Ibid., 59.
[26] Ibid.
[27] Ibid. Later he added:
Not only the hours of employees, but the hours of employers, could be regulated, and doctors, lawyers, scientists, all professional men, as well as athletes and artisans, could be forbidden to fatigue their brains and bodies by prolonged hours of exercise, lest the fighting strength of the State be impaired.
Ibid., 60–61.

[28] Ibid., 76 (Holmes, J., dissenting) ("I think that the word liberty in the Fourteenth Amendment is perverted when it is held to prevent the natural outcome of a dominant opinion. . . ."). See the text below, at note 91, for the full passage from Holmes's dissent.
[29] Note, "Less Drastic Means and the First Amendment," *Yale L.J.*, 78: 464 (1969); Laurence H. Tribe, *American Constitutional Law*, 2d ed. (Mineola, N.Y.: Foundation Press, 1988), 977–86.

of bakeries and that required improvements in bakeries for the sake of health (washrooms, water closets, proper drainage and painting, adequate ceiling heights, cementing and tiling of floors, etc.).[30] He thought New York could protect the health of the public and presumably the health of bakers through factory inspection and improvement laws, but not through maximum hours statutes. The former interfered with the freedom of employers, but, unlike maximum hours statutes, did not limit or interfere explicitly with the freedom of the parties to bargain—a freedom that was seen as the central dynamic of the market and of the social contract tradition.[31]

Aside from creating this hierarchy of means, the more global concern with liberty entered the *Lochner* analysis as the motive force behind the very idea of constitutive authority and the intellectual tradition of which it was part. Contractarianism was devoted to liberty as the end of all social arrangements and identified the state both as a necessary tool to secure the enjoyment of liberty and as the principal threat to it. Individuals, it was assumed, would justly order their economic and social relationships through exchange; the state would be needed to enforce those bargains and to create the proper conditions of exchange. Legislative majorities might sometimes seek to assign the state more ambitious undertakings, but under the terms of the social contract, fixed once and for all, that option was not available.

It is hard for the modern reader to see New York's maximum hours statute as a wholesale attack upon contractarianism and the particular conception of liberty that it implied. True, Peckham enumerated an endless variety of trades or professions that could be covered by maximum hours statutes if the bakers' law were allowed, but even that would hardly be an occasion for alarm. Peckham's concern had another source, or so it seems to me. It was not the maximum hours statute, either New York's or that of any other state, that bothered him, but rather the conception of state authority implied by this measure. The maximum hours statute was treated by the Court as a prototype, as a representative measure of the entire progressive movement, premised on a police power whose only limits appeared to depend, as Peckham saw it, on the "mercy of legislative majorities."

Like the Sherman Act, or, for that matter, the rate regulation measures to be considered in the next chapter, the New York statute thus

---

[30] 198 U.S. at 61–62.
[31] Peckham wrote:
These various sections [requiring inspections and improvements of bakeries] may be wise and valid regulations, and they certainly go to the full extent of providing for the cleanliness and the healthiness, so far as possible, of the quarters in which bakeries are to be conducted. Adding to all these requirements, a prohibition to enter into any contract of labor in a bakery for more than a certain number of hours a week, is, in our judgment, so wholly beside the matter of a proper, reasonable and fair provision, as to run counter to that liberty of person and of free contract provided for in the Federal Constitution. Ibid., 62.

appeared to pose the most general issue for democracy: Are there any limits to the power of the majority? The Court tried to answer that question in equally grand terms. On this reading, the driving force behind *Lochner* was not a desire to invalidate the New York statute, but rather one to affirm, through a bold act of invalidation, the theory of constitutive authority. *Lochner* sought to say clearly and unequivocally that the legislative power was indeed limited, and to do so during a time when those limits were being called dramatically into question by the progressive movement.

II

The *Lochner* Court was closely divided.[32] Four justices dissented. There were two dissenting opinions. One was by Justice Holmes (which I will take up later), the other by Justice Harlan, joined by Justices Day and White. What is striking about Harlan's opinion is that although it was a dissent, it did not articulate an alternative conception of state authority. Like Peckham, Harlan viewed legislation as a form of constitutive authority. He began his opinion by identifying a narrow set of ends that would be appropriate for judging the statute.[33] For him "health" was the only permissible end to be considered in evaluating the New York statute; the desire to enhance the power or economic position of bakers as a class was not permissible. Harlan also agreed that the connection between the statute and health had to be direct, or, in his words, "real or substantial,"[34] and his test was no different from Peckham's:

> [I]n determining the question of power to interfere with liberty of contract, the court may inquire whether the means devised by the State are germane to an end which may be lawfully accomplished and have a real or substantial relation to the protection of health, as involved in the daily work of the persons, male and female, engaged in bakery and confectionery establishments.[35]

---

[32] Indeed, Charles Henry Butler, the Supreme Court's Reporter of Decisions when *Lochner* was decided, revealed in his memoirs that one of Justice Harlan's sons told him in later years that the initial vote was 5 to 4 to uphold the New York statute. It is not known who might have switched his vote. *A Century at the Bar of the Supreme Court of the United States* (New York: G. P. Putnam's Sons, 1942), 172.

[33] Harlan wrote:

While this court has not attempted to mark the precise boundaries of what is called the police power of the State, the existence of the power has been uniformly recognized, both by the Federal and state courts.

All the cases agree that this power extends at least to the protection of the lives, the health and the safety of the public against the injurious exercise by any citizen of his own rights. Ibid., 65 (Harlan, J., dissenting).

[34] Ibid., 69.

[35] Ibid.

His disagreement with Peckham was limited, turning solely on whether the requisite connection between means and end actually had been demonstrated.

In characterizing Harlan's dissent in these terms, I do not mean to suggest that the differences between Peckham and Harlan rested simply on the facts. As we have seen, judicial review of means–end rationality often reflects larger, more normative considerations. In this instance, the division between Peckham and Harlan may well have reflected widely disparate ideological commitments—a difference in their determination to limit the legislative power or in their assessment of the danger posed to the idea of limited government by the maximum hours statute.[36] But even on this account, it must be stressed that the disagreement between the two was a difference over the application, rather than the theory, of *Lochner*. Like Peckham, Harlan treated the police power as analogous to the commerce power and thus as a form of constitutive authority. That is why Justice White, who just the year before had emphasized the constitutive nature of legislative authority (both federal and state) in his dissent in *Northern Securities Co. v. United States*,[37] was able to join Harlan's dissent in *Lochner*.

Some think Harlan's dissent in *Lochner* was in conflict with his opinion for the majority in *Adair v. United States*,[38] which, only three years later, invalidated a federal labor statute on liberty of contract grounds. But once it is understood that the dispute in *Lochner* was over the application of the theory of constitutive authority, rather than over the theory itself, the apparent conflict dissolves. In *Adair*, Harlan spoke for Peckham and the remaining stalwarts of the Cleveland-Harrison bloc—Fuller, Brewer, and White (Brown had retired earlier)—and in fact used the theory of *Lochner* to set aside another form of labor legislation.

Adair involved the Erdman Act of 1898.[39] This statute was passed by Congress in response to the Pullman Strike of 1894 and was defended by its supporters as a measure to secure labor peace. One section provided for mediation and conciliation of industrial disputes on interstate railways.[40] A second section provided for binding arbitration in such disputes.[41] A third section, the one challenged in *Adair*, prohibited railroads from engaging in certain forms of anti-union conduct.[42] It prohibited railroads from requiring employees as a condition of their employment to enter into yel-

---

[36] Considerations of this nature may have led Harlan to subscribe to the view that doubtful cases should be resolved in favor of a statute's constitutionality. See, e.g., ibid., 68, 72–73.

[37] 193 U.S. 197, 364–400 (1904) (White, J., dissenting). See Chapter 5.

[38] 208 U.S. 161 (1908).

[39] Act of June 1, 1898, Ch. 370, 30 Stat. 424 (1898).

[40] Sect. 2, ibid., 425.

[41] Sect. 3, ibid., 425–26.

[42] Sect. 10, ibid., 428.

low dog contracts in which they promised not to join a union. This same section also prohibited the railroads from discharging employees because of their union activity.[43] The case arose when William Adair, an agent of the Louisville and Nashville Railroad, was prosecuted for firing an employee because of his union membership.[44]

Harlan's principal model for *Adair* was *Lochner*. He quoted at length from Peckham's opinion in *Lochner*, even though the issue in *Adair* was whether the statute was within the power of Congress to enact, rather than that of a state legislature. Harlan also was careful to identify the individual liberty threatened: In *Lochner* it was the freedom to set the terms of employment by agreement; in *Adair*, the liberty to fire any individual for any reason at all, or for no reason.[45] The liberty of *Lochner* belonged to both employer and employee, and, although the freedom of *Adair* seemed more asymmetrical, Harlan thought otherwise. He viewed the employer's liberty to fire for any reason as the reciprocal of the employee's right to quit for any reason (the right upon which Harlan in *Arthur v. Oakes*[46] grounded the right to strike). According to Harlan, both the liberty to fire and the liberty to quit expressed the essentially consensual nature of the employment relationship and both were protected against state interference by the Fourteenth Amendment and against federal interference by the Fifth Amendment:

---

[43] The statute read:
[A]ny employer subject to the provisions of this Act and any officer, agent, or receiver of such employer who shall require any employee, or any person seeking employment, as a condition of such employment, to enter into an agreement, either written or verbal, not to become or remain a member of any labor corporation, association, or organization; or shall threaten any employee with loss of employment, or shall unjustly discriminate against any employee because of his membership in such a labor corporation . . . is hereby declared to be guilty of a misdemeanor, and, upon conviction thereof in any court of the United States of competent jurisdiction in the district in which such offense was committed, shall be punished for each offense by a fine of not less than one hundred dollars and not more than one thousand dollars.
Ibid.
[44] The personalization of the transaction in *Adair*—focusing on the agent and not the railroad—was parallel to the personalization in *Northern Securities*. Perhaps with Brewer's concurrence in that case in mind, Harlan used this personalization as a device for avoiding the question of whether corporate entities possessed the rights protected by the Due Process Clause. He analyzed the case as though only Adair's personal liberty were at stake. 208 U.S. at 172. The employee in *Adair* was named Coppage, but he was not the same person who was the plaintiff in Coppage v. Kansas, 236 U.S. 1 (1915), a later case in the *Adair* line.

[45] 208 U.S. at 174–75. *Adair* was a discharge case, but Harlan also recognized a similar right to hire. Ibid., 172–73, 174–75. This liberty was related more directly to the provision prohibiting yellow dog contracts, which arose in the context of an initial hire.

[46] 63 F. 310 (7th Cir. 1894). The role of Harlan's well-known opinion in *Arthur v. Oakes* in the *Debs* case is noted in Chapter 3.

The right of a person to sell his labor upon such terms as he deems proper is, in its essence, the same as the right of the purchaser of labor to prescribe the conditions upon which he will accept such labor from the person offering to sell it. So the right of the employee to quit the service of the employer, for whatever reason, is the same as the right of the employer, for whatever reason, to dispense with the services of such employee. . . . In all such particulars the employer and the employee have equality of right, and any legislation that disturbs that equality is an arbitrary interference with the liberty of contract which no government can legally justify in a free land.[47]

The protection that Harlan afforded to the individual was not an absolute. As in *Lochner*, it was what remained after state power was exhausted. The liberty to fire, like the liberty to contract, was subject to governmental restraints, but to determine whether the restraint of the Erdman Act was permissible, Harlan had to determine whether the legislature had exceeded the scope of its authority. In *Lochner* the issue was the scope of the police power; in *Adair* the issue was the scope of the commerce power. But this was largely a formal distinction—the substance of the analysis was the same. In both, the violation of substantive due process followed from the conclusion that the legislature had exceeded the scope of its authority. Harlan concluded that the Erdman Act violated the Due Process Clause of the Fifth Amendment only after he determined that Congress had exceeded its authority under the Commerce Clause.[48]

The Erdman Act was limited strictly to railroads engaged in interstate commerce, but according to Harlan that fact alone was not sufficient to bring it within the ambit of the commerce power. It was also necessary to identify the precise purpose served by the Erdman Act and then to ascertain whether there was a sufficiently direct connection between whatever permissible end might exist and the means, the statutory prohibition. The dispute between Peckham and Harlan in *Lochner* largely centered around this last inquiry concerning means–end rationality; the two justices assumed that the purpose of the New York statute was health, but they disagreed over whether there was a sufficiently direct connection between means and end. In *Adair*, however, Harlan never had to decide the means–end issue, for he decided that the end served by the Erdman Act was impermissible. He concluded that the statute was beyond the scope of the commerce power because it sought to achieve an impermissible end.

---

[47] 208 U.S. at 174–75.
[48] Ibid., 179–80. Justice McKenna, in dissent, accused Harlan of the contrary, that is, of establishing that Section 10 was invalid on the basis of the Due Process Clause alone. Ibid., 181–82 (McKenna, J., dissenting).

Chapter VI: *Labor Legislation*

Through all the cases Harlan stood for a very broad conception of the permissible ends of the commerce power. He did not have the narrow conception of "commerce" suggested by the ordinary nineteenth-century meaning of that term so evident in *E. C. Knight*, which reduced "commerce" to "transportation" or "traffic."[49] According to Harlan, Congress was not limited in its purposes to protecting the free flow of goods from state to state, but could regulate conduct that had any *effect* or *impact* upon goods that so moved.[50] In a rare act of modesty, Harlan did not cite his *E. C. Knight* dissent in *Adair*. Instead, he reminded the reader of his general position by referring to the *Lottery Case*[51] and *Northern Securities*, and by discussing the two most recent manifestations of his broad conception of the commerce power. One was *Johnson v. Southern Pacific Co.* (1904),[52] a decision by Fuller that upheld a federal statute requiring automatic couplers as a way of promoting the safety of workers and travelers. The second was the *Employers' Liability Cases* (1908),[53] where the Court, in an opinion by White, virtually said that a congressional act abolishing the fellow-servant rule (which often barred recovery for work-related injuries) would be permissible, provided it was limited by its terms to workers engaged in interstate transportation at the time of the accident.

On the other hand, Harlan did not believe the commerce power to be unlimited. Congress could reach conduct that blocked, impeded, affected, or otherwise interfered with goods moving across state lines, but it could not favor one economic class or group over another any more than could a state legislature. This tenet of contractarianism, an axiom of this Court and the starting point for Peckham's analysis in *Lochner*, proved decisive in *Adair*. Harlan saw the challenged provisions of the Erdman Act as part of a program to facilitate and encourage union organization and thus to alter the distribution of power between worker and employer. Such a purpose, he insisted, was not a permissible one for government. As he put it,

> Labor associations, we assume, are organized for the general purpose of improving or bettering the conditions and conserving the interests of its members as wage-earners—an object entirely legitimate and to be commended rather than condemned. But surely those associations as labor organizations have nothing to do with interstate commerce as such.[54]

---

[49] See Chapter 5.
[50] 208 U.S. at 176–78.
[51] Champion v. Ames, 188 U.S. 321 (1903).
[52] 196 U.S. 1 (1904).

[53] 207 U.S. 463 (1908). The congressional powers hinted at in that case were confirmed in the Second Employers' Liability Cases, 223 U.S. 1 (1912).
[54] 208 U.S. at 178.

Harlan insisted that if it were permissible for government to promote union organization, then union membership could be required as a condition of employment, a result almost unthinkable at that time.[55] Justice Harlan's references to "interstate commerce" in the passage above and elsewhere in his opinion seem to be of no operative significance. Harlan appeared to be making a point about *all* forms of governmental authority, state and federal.

There were two dissents in *Adair*, one by Justice Holmes, the other by Justice McKenna. Each justice spoke only for himself. (Justice Moody, Theodore Roosevelt's attorney general and Justice Brown's replacement, a person likely to be sympathetic to Holmes's position, did not participate.) Holmes might have been accustomed to the dissenter's role, but McKenna was not. Appointed by President McKinley in 1898 to succeed Field, throughout McKenna remained part of the governing coalition of the Fuller Court—he joined the majority in *Lochner*, and, although he now found himself dissenting in *Adair*, he clearly accepted the general structure of Harlan's analysis.

The first question for McKenna, as for Harlan, concerned the permissibility of the end. He, too, subscribed to the principle that denied the state the power to support labor in its struggle with capital, but, in contrast to Harlan, McKenna was able to locate a more benign or universalistic purpose for the Erdman Act. He considered the Act a promoter of labor peace.[56]

Having cleared this hurdle, which had stopped Harlan, McKenna proceeded to examine the relation between the means and the end, and he upheld the Erdman Act as sufficiently related to the protection of industrial peace. With an obvious reference to *Johnson v. Southern Pacific Co.* and the *Employers' Liability Cases*, McKenna insisted:

> A provision of law which will prevent or tend to prevent the stoppage of every wheel in every car of an entire railroad system certainly has as direct influence on interstate commerce as the way in which one car may be coupled to another, or the rule of liability for personal injuries to an employee.[57]

---

[55] Harlan wrote:
If such a power exists in Congress [prohibiting discharges based on union activity] it is difficult to perceive why it might not, by absolute regulation, require interstate carriers, under penalties, to employ in the conduct of its interstate business *only* members of labor organizations, or *only* those who are not members of such organizations—a power which could not be recognized as existing under the Constitution of the United States.
Ibid., 179.

[56] Ibid., 184 (McKenna, J., dissenting).

[57] Ibid., 189.

Chapter VI: *Labor Legislation*

Justice McKenna underscored the fact that the Erdman Act had been enacted in response to the Pullman Strike.[58] He also pointed to the connection between the challenged provision and the other sections of the Erdman Act that provided for mediation and arbitration, as a way of buttressing his claim that its purpose was not to encourage unionization but to promote industrial peace.[59] McKenna's theory was not that each discharge for union activity would cause a strike or other form of industrial unrest, but rather that without the enactment of such a measure the unions would continue to disrupt interstate commerce. The unions demanded the protection provided in the Erdman Act, and Congress acceded to their demand in order to ensure peace.

Harlan agreed that as a general matter it was permissible for Congress to promote industrial peace. Nonetheless, Harlan felt that to uphold the statute on the grounds proposed by McKenna would destroy any limits on the legislative power and also corrupt the law. The validity of a statute would be made to turn on the power of some private interest group to threaten a disturbance of the public order if the legislature did not give it what it wanted.[60] Upholding the statute would be tantamount to surrendering to blackmail, and, with a touch of righteous indignation, always his trademark, Harlan condemned such a conciliatory attitude:

> Will it be said that the provision in question had its origin in the apprehension, on the part of Congress, that if it did not show more consideration for members of labor organizations than for wage-earners who were not members of such organizations, or if it did not insert in the statute some such provision as the one here in question, members of labor organizations would, by illegal or violent measures, interrupt or impair the freedom of commerce among the States? We will not indulge in any such conjectures, nor make them, in whole or in part, the basis of our decision. We could not do so consistently with the respect due to a coordinate department of the Government. We could not do so without imputing to Congress the purpose to accord to one class of wage-earners privileges withheld from another class of wage-earners engaged, it may be, in the same kind of labor and serving the same employer. Nor will we assume, in our consideration of this case, that members of labor organizations will, in any considerable numbers, resort to illegal methods for accomplishing any particular object they have in view.[61]

---

[58] Ibid., 185.
[59] Ibid., 185–86.
[60] Would it have made any difference to Harlan if the peace rationale had focused on the individual discharge (that is, had claimed that a discharge based on union activity would result in strikes)? I think not.
[61] 208 U.S. at 179.

Having rejected McKenna's approach, all that remained for Harlan and the majority was a rather straightforward application of the theory of *Lochner*, although that theory seems to have been brought full circle: *Lochner* involved the police power of the states but turned on a theory of governmental authority that was most clearly expressed in an understanding of the national commerce power as an enumerated power; *Adair*, in turn, applied that theory to the federal government and the commerce power. It therefore was quite fitting for Roscoe Pound in 1909 to begin his classic article, "Liberty of Contract,"[62] with an assault on *Adair*, for that case revealed the true reach of the theory of *Lochner* and was a fair indication of the support it enjoyed on the bench. That theory has been constructed from the words of Peckham, but it was supported by the full spectrum of justices, including, at one point or another, Peckham, Harlan, Brewer, Fuller, White, McKenna, Brown, and Day (and presumably Day's predecessor, Shiras). The theory of *Lochner* unified the Fuller Court and provides the key to understanding its response to the labor measures then being proposed and enacted.

III

In *Lochner* and *Adair* the Court invalidated the labor statutes before it, but that was not the whole of its response to this area of progressive reform. In two other key confrontations of the period involving maximum hours laws, the Court came to the opposite conclusion. This pattern of decision was not whimsical, nor linked to the happenstance of personnel changes on the Court, nor even inconsistent with *Lochner* and its theory of constitutive authority. Indeed, the appeal of the theory here proposed for understanding *Lochner* lies in its ability to accommodate and reconcile the overall pattern of cases: not just the ones in which legislation was invalidated, but also those cases—*Holden v. Hardy*[63] and *Muller v. Oregon*[64]— that upheld similar laws.

The maximum hours law sustained in *Holden v. Hardy* was confined to miners. It was not a statute but a provision of the Utah constitution. Nevertheless, the Court viewed it as an exercise of the police power and treated the measure as though it were a statute, presenting the same danger of tyranny by the majority. But unlike *Lochner*, the challenged provision was

---

[62] *Yale L.J.*, 18: 454 (1909).
[63] 169 U.S. 366 (1898).

[64] 208 U.S. 412 (1908).

upheld by the Court. The majority opinion was written by Justice Brown and announced in 1898. Brown later joined Peckham's opinion in *Lochner*, as did Fuller and McKenna, who both joined Brown's opinion in *Holden v. Hardy*. Peckham and Brewer, the other two justices who later formed the *Lochner* majority, dissented in *Holden v. Hardy*, but in a most uncharacteristic way: without opinion. Since both men were capable of rising to great heights of passion and eloquence in their dissents, their laconic tack in *Holden v. Hardy* suggests to me a degree of indifference on their part, indicating that they saw the decision as close or not especially troubling. The interpretive task, then, is to explain why the *Lochner* majority—Brown, Fuller, and McKenna, and possibly even Peckham and Brewer—came to the opposite conclusion in *Holden v. Hardy*.

The key is the means–end judgment. The purpose of the Utah law was said to be health, as in *Lochner*, but in contrast to that case the majority of justices here concluded that there was a sufficiently direct connection between means and end. In reaching this conclusion some justices might simply have agreed with the factual judgment of the legislature. As far as they were concerned, a workweek in excess of sixty hours might be viewed as more of a threat to the health of miners, confined as they were beneath the ground, than to bakers. On the other hand, as we have seen, this Court's judgment regarding the directness of the connection between means and end inevitably implicated broader normative considerations, above all, the desire to preserve limits on "legislative majorities." From this perspective the Utah provision was less worrisome because mining, in contrast to baking, had a distinct status as an "unhealthful employment."[65]

Utah's brief to the Supreme Court defending the law spoke of the miner's "constant strain of working in the dark . . . breathing the foul gases from powder smoke."[66] This echoed the opinion of the Utah supreme court when it upheld the measure below. After noting the "peculiar hazards and perils" of mining, the Court cautioned that "laws adapted to the protection of such miners . . . should not include other employments not subject" to the same dangers.[67]

There was thus reason to believe that miners were distinguishable from printers, tinsmiths, locksmiths, clerks, and members of the other professions or trades mentioned by Peckham in his parade of horribles in *Lochner* and referred to by Brown in *Holden v. Hardy* as "ordinary employ-

---

[65] 169 U.S. at 386.
[66] Brief for Defendant in Error at 42, 169 U.S. 366.

[67] State v. Holden, 14 Utah 71, 87–88 (1896).

ments."[68] The Court was able to uphold the maximum hours regulation for miners without fearing that it was allowing the legislature to impose such restrictions on all trades and thus undermining the idea of constitutive authority.

Muller v. Oregon, decided three years after *Lochner* but in the very same term as *Adair*, provided, at least at first glance, an even more stunning contrast to *Lochner*. The Court here upheld a statute that limited to ten hours the workday of women "in any mechanical establishment, or factory, or laundry"[69] and, even more startling, its decision was unanimous. The opinion was written by Justice Brewer, who had dissented along with Peckham in *Holden v. Hardy*, joined Peckham's majority opinion in *Lochner*, and, speaking more generally, was Peckham's constant ally.

Brewer did not reaffirm *Lochner* explicitly, nor could he if all the justices were to join his opinion.[70] But such a reaffirmation of *Lochner* seemed especially unnecessary in light of *Adair*, decided just a month before, and in any event Brewer was careful in his *Muller* opinion to protect *Lochner*. He referred the reader to *Lochner*, along with *Holden v. Hardy* and another substantive due process epistle by Peckham, *Allgeyer v. Louisiana*[71] (holding unconstitutional a state statute that barred out-of-state insurance companies). He summarized Peckham's opinion in *Lochner* and in the closing passages disclaimed an intent to question *Lochner* "in any respect."[72] The question then arises, perhaps in even more pronounced form than it did with *Holden v. Hardy*: How could the justices who condemned the maximum hours statute in *Lochner* have embraced one in *Muller*?

---

[68] 169 U.S. at 396. In distinguishing *Holden v. Hardy* in *Lochner*, Peckham stressed the special character of mining:
It was held [in *Holden*] that the kind of employment, mining, smelting, etc., and the character of the employees in such kinds of labor, were such as to make it reasonable and proper for the State to interfere to prevent the employees from being constrained by the rules laid down by the proprietors in regard to labor. The following citation from the observations of the Supreme Court of Utah in that case was made by the judge writing the opinion of this court, and approved: "The law in question is confined to the protection of that class of people engaged in labor in underground mines, and in smelters and other works wherein ores are reduced and refined. This law applies only to the classes subjected by their employment to the peculiar conditions and effects attending underground mining and work in smelters, and other works for the reduction and refining of ores. Therefore it is not necessary to discuss or decide whether the legislature can fix the hours of labor in other employments." . . . There is nothing in *Holden v. Hardy* which covers the case now before us.
198 U.S. at 54–55.

[69] 208 U.S. at 416, quoting 1903 Or. Laws 148.

[70] Justice Brown, part of the *Lochner* majority, was no longer on the Court. He had been replaced by Justice Moody, who might have been viewed as more sympathetic to such exercises of the legislative power.

[71] 165 U.S. 578 (1897).

[72] Ibid., 423.

Chapter VI: *Labor Legislation*

The theory I used to interpret *Lochner* will be helpful in answering this question, though drawing on it involves taking a liberty with Brewer's opinion in *Muller*—perhaps a greater one than that I have already taken with Harlan's opinion in *Adair* or with Brown's in *Holden v. Hardy*, since Brewer himself did not use *Lochner* to shape his opinion in *Muller*. In fact, Brewer did not have much of a theory at all, perhaps reflecting his advanced age at the time of this opinion, his last important one. The volume of the *United States Reports* in which the case appears contains a summary of counsel's arguments, which Brewer probably wrote, and the arguments are in fact structured in terms of *Lochner*, but the Court's opinion itself is rather brief and cryptic on this score. Speculation is necessary to explain the difference between *Lochner* and *Muller*. In that spirit I offer two different explanations, one couched in terms of instrumental rationality, the other in terms of substantive rationality—both of which remain within the framework of a theory that sees the state as a form of constitutive authority.

The first explanation attributes the difference in outcome to the difference in the means–end judgment: The justices in *Muller* were convinced, as they were not in *Lochner*, but were in *Holden v. Hardy*, that there was a sufficiently direct connection between the maximum hours statute and health. In this account, great stress is placed on the famous brief that Louis D. Brandeis filed on behalf of the state of Oregon. The notion is that in *Muller* he had made the factual showing absent in *Lochner*. The "narrow" coverage of the Oregon statute—it was, by its terms, limited to women—had no independent substantive significance but only facilitated the factual demonstration that Brandeis had to make. It reduced Brandeis's task to showing that long hours of work were injurious to women and their families.

This interpretation of *Muller* is supported by portions of Brewer's opinion. It fits easily within the framework of *Lochner* and is, of course, in accord with those theories of history that assign a pivotal role to the individual, although in this instance it seems that the hero was Josephine Goldmark, Publications Secretary of the National Consumers' League and Brandeis's sister-in-law, since it was she who conceived the idea of the brief, involved Brandeis in the case, and did a great deal of the work.[73] In certain respects, however, this interpretation is less than satisfactory. For one thing, Brandeis's brief was anything but a scientific tour de force. Mainly a collection of statutes, statistics, and opinions, it was at best a compilation, but closer to a hodgepodge. Moreover, a similar presentation of facts was before the Court in *Lochner*, or easily available to it; these facts were present in Harlan's dissent, and in a concurring opinion of the New York court

---

[73] Judith Fabricant, "Ideology and Class in *Muller v. Oregon*" (Yale Law School, 1979; unpublished manuscript on file with author), 28, 31.

below, which had upheld the law.[74] Finally, it is hard to imagine Brewer, or any of the other stalwarts of the Fuller Court, moved by such a showing.

The fame of Brandeis's brief largely stems from the odd circumstance that it, unlike any of the briefs in similar cases, was referred to and summarized by Brewer in the Court's opinion.[75] This reference might lend further credence to the reading of *Muller* that celebrates Brandeis's lawyering, but the motives for Brewer's reference are not at all clear to me. The reference might have been intended not as an expression of admiration or as an acknowledgment of an influence, but rather as a distancing technique. Brandeis, already identified with the progressive movement, could not have been a hero of Brewer's. In fact, Brewer's reference to Brandeis's brief was coupled with an often overlooked warning about its significance:

> Constitutional questions, it is true, are not settled by even a consensus of present public opinion, for it is the peculiar value of a written constitution that it places in unchanging form limitations upon legislative action, and thus gives a permanence and stability to popular government which otherwise would be lacking.[76]

Brewer did not treat the brief as demonstrating a factual connection between health and the number of hours worked, but only as evidence "of a widespread belief that woman's physical structure, and the functions she performs in consequence thereof, justify special legislation restricting or qualifying the conditions under which she should be permitted to toil."[77]

It is difficult, then, to explain the difference between *Lochner* and *Muller v. Oregon* in terms of the alleged facts or Brandeis's achievement in demonstrating a connection between the length of the workday and health. It seems more plausible to focus on the limited coverage of the statute—to women—not as a circumstance facilitating the factual demonstration (the connection between means and end), but rather as an independent ground of distinction altogether, related to the legitimacy of ends, or what might be considered substantive rationality. That is, the scope of the *Muller* statute allowed the state to pursue ends that were otherwise denied it, simply because women were not viewed as members of the community that constituted the state.

The idea of constitutive authority, or for that matter the entire social contract tradition, presupposes a community that exists prior to the creation of the state—a gathering of individuals, loosely held together by a network of social and economic relationships and enjoying a set of natural rights. The state is created by the members of that community and owes

---

[74] 198 U.S. 70–71. For the New York opinion, see People v. Lochner, 177 N.Y. 145, 168–74 (1904) (Vann, J., concurring).

[75] 208 U.S. at 419–20.
[76] Ibid., 420.
[77] Ibid.

a special responsibility to them.[78] These persons endow the state with authority and are the source of its legitimacy. By the very act of creating the state they become members of what earlier I have called the constitutional community. Moreover, as a result of their role in the founding of the state, they have special rights against it, including the right to equal treatment. The state thus cannot be used to further the interests of one sector of the constitutional community since it depends on the consent of all for its legitimacy.

Today we are moved by the most universalistic sentiments and tend to view the constitutional community as embracing all adults. We treat with great suspicion the exclusion of any person or group from the political process that directs and controls the state. A denial of the right to vote becomes, in our eyes, a reason for a court to scrutinize a statute with special rigor. Not so for the Court at the turn of the century, when disenfranchisement stood not as a contradiction of some universalistic sentiment, but as evidence that a group was not a member of the constitutional community and as a reason *against* additional judicial scrutiny. Disenfranchisement was a reason for being more tolerant of exercises of state power purportedly on behalf of this group, allowing the state to pursue ends otherwise denied it. The disenfranchised—and only they—could be viewed, to use Peckham's concept, as "wards" of the state.

In the closing paragraphs of *Muller v. Oregon*, Brewer expressed this odd reversal of perspective occasioned by the exclusion of women from the electoral process. He saw disenfranchisement not as an indication that women's interests may not have been adequately taken into account by the maximum hours legislation, but instead as a further expression—proof if you will—that women were different from men in a way that justified a different relationship to the state:

> We have not referred in this discussion to the denial of the elective franchise in the State of Oregon, for while it may disclose a lack of political equality in all things with her brother, that is not of itself decisive. The reason runs deeper, and rests in the inherent difference between the two sexes, and in the different functions in life which they perform.[79]

Brewer's mention of the "inherent difference between the two sexes" and the "different functions in life which they perform" no doubt referred to the domestic and maternal responsibilities of women, including childbirth, but that fact alone was not of any constitutional significance, and Brewer knew it. That fact could achieve such significance only once it was further assumed that, because of this "inherent difference," women and men stand

---

[78] See Stanley N. Katz, "The Strange Birth and Unlikely History of Constitutional Equality," *J. Am. Hist.*, 75: 747 (1988).

[79] 208 U.S. at 423.

in a different relationship to the community that constitutes the state—women are not members, but men are.

It was this lack of status of women in the constitutional community, as they conceived it, that enabled the Court in *Muller* to abandon the stricture against redistribution of *Adair*, and to avoid the first and perhaps most decisive step in the Court's analysis in *Lochner*, which denied that the New York statute was intended to protect the health of workers but instead was a measure to enhance their power. In contrast, the fate of the statute in *Muller* did not have to rest on the health rationale. Women, like children, were viewed as "wards" of the state and thus were the proper subject of "protective" or "paternal" legislation. As Brewer said, "As minors, though not to the same extent, she has been looked upon in the courts as needing especial care that her rights may be preserved."[80] To put the same point in terms of the phrase Peckham used in *Lochner*, women were the appropriate beneficiaries of a "labor law."[81] The redistribution of power was, in the case of women, a permissible end of legislation and was allowed by their very exclusion from the constitutional community.[82]

---

[80] Ibid., 421.

[81] 198 U.S. at 57.

[82] 208 U.S. at 422–23. Oddly, this reading of *Muller* gains support from Justice George Sutherland's majority opinion in Adkins v. Children's Hospital, 261 U.S. 525 (1923), where the Court overturned a minimum wage law for women and thus limited, if not overruled, *Muller*. In explaining why the principles of *Lochner* should now be extended to women, Sutherland emphasized the "revolutionary" changes in the political status of women—most especially the enactment of the Nineteenth Amendment—that had come to pass since *Muller* had been decided:

But the ancient inequality of the sexes, otherwise than physical, as suggested in the *Muller Case*, has continued "with diminishing intensity." In view of the great—not to say revolutionary—changes which have taken place since that utterance, in the contractual, political and civil status of women, culminating in the Nineteenth Amendment, it is not unreasonable to say that these differences have now come almost, if not quite, to the vanishing point. In this aspect of the matter, while the physical differences must be recognized in appropriate cases, and legislation fixing hours or conditions of work may properly take them into account, we cannot accept the doctrine that women of mature age, *sui juris*, require or may be subjected to restrictions upon their liberty of contract which could not lawfully be imposed in the case of men under similar circumstances. To do so would be to ignore all the implications to be drawn from the present day trend of legislation, as well as that of common thought and usage, by which woman is accorded emancipation from the old doctrine that she must be given special protection or be subjected to special restraint in her contractual and civil relationships.

Ibid., 553. Since women were now an acknowledged part of the political community, in Sutherland's view no rationale existed any longer for treating them differently from men when it came to defining the permissible ends of the state. When the Court reversed course on women's equality before the law in West Coast Hotel Co. v. Parrish, 300 U.S. 379 (1937), it again placed them outside the constitutional community, saying that the Fourteenth Amendment did not create a "fictitious equality" between women and men and, quoting *Muller*, that woman is "properly placed in a class by herself." Ibid., 395.

Chapter VI: *Labor Legislation*

Men, of course, needed the helping hand of the state as much as women did. The justices knew that liberty of contract assured only a formal equality that substantively disfavored workers. The difference between *Lochner* and *Muller* did not lie in the domain of social knowledge, or arise from the fact that the Court could see in one, but not the other, the consequence of liberty of contract.[83] The difference instead arose from what was allowed the state under the terms of the social contract. The formal equality that *Lochner* so strenuously insisted upon was a function of the equal citizenship owed those who consented to the state and thereby legitimated its authority. Members, but only members, of the constitutional community stood equal before the law.

IV

The Court had its prophet, and it was Holmes. Like most prophets, he remained aloof and apart from his colleagues. He rejected the theory of *Lochner* thoroughly—not with passion, but with the cutting casualness conveyed by his famous allusion to Herbert Spencer's *Social Statics*.[84] The labors of the majority, or even those of Harlan in dissent, seemed absurd to him. Holmes was not on the Court at the time of *Holden v. Hardy* (1898) and he had no need to speak separately in *Muller v. Oregon*, which, after all, unanimously upheld the challenged statute. Yet in his dissents in *Lochner* and *Adair*—joined by no one—Holmes sounded themes that were to provide the framework for the repudiation of the legacy of the Fuller Court and the eventual triumph of progressivism.

There were two parts to Holmes's approach. The first was to get the Court out of the business of reviewing means–end judgments. For Holmes, the relation between means and end did not have to be direct or substantial; any relation would suffice. The labors of Peckham in *Lochner* were dismissed, and those of Harlan in that case made superfluous, by a single sentence: "A reasonable man might think [the New York statute] a proper measure on the score of health."[85] In *Adair* Holmes made a similar point about the issue that divided McKenna and Harlan:

> It cannot be doubted that to prevent strikes, and, so far as possible, to foster its scheme of arbitration, might be deemed by Congress an important point of policy, and I think it impossible to say that Congress might

---

[83] For a contrasting view, arguing that the difference between the cases was that in *Muller*, but not *Lochner*, the justices were convinced that a sufficient means–end connection had been demonstrated, see Tribe, *American Constitutional Law*, 568–69.

[84] See above, text accompanying note 8. Holmes first alluded to Spencer in "The Path of the Law," *Harv. L. Rev.*, 10: 457, 466 (1897).

[85] 198 U.S. at 76 (Holmes, J., dissenting).

179

not reasonably think that the provision in question would help a good deal to carry its policy along.[86]

The "reasonable man" or "reasonableness" standard is, of course, flexible and, like most common law terms, capable of varying degrees of stringency; but in context, it seems clear that Holmes was using it to indicate a willingness to tolerate virtually any connection between means and end.

The second, and more important, part of Holmes's break with the past concerned the permissibility of ends, or substantive rationality. Holmes embraced the widest conception of permissible ends for state action, believing that legislative power could be used to favor one economic class or social group over another—and thus rejected the very core of the social contract tradition. He was able to join Brewer's opinion in *Muller* because he believed the state was entitled to alter the distribution of power and wealth among various groups, but he would not, in contrast to the rest of the Court, limit that permission to legislation affecting women or other groups that might be deemed "wards" of the state.

Peckham's opinion in *Lochner* began by denying that redistribution was a proper end of the police power and identified "health" as the only permissible end to be served by the statute. All the justices other than Holmes started with the same reading of the New York statute and with the same premises for evaluating it. Holmes was not so clear:

> Men whom I certainly could not pronounce unreasonable would uphold [the New York statute] as a first instalment of a general regulation of the hours of work. Whether in the latter aspect it would be open to the charge of inequality I think it unnecessary to discuss.[87]

In *Adair*, Holmes was more explicit. He said he was willing to accept the Erdman Act as a form of class legislation, that is, as a measure to strengthen the position of labor by protecting union membership.

In his opinion in *Adair*, Holmes first played with the "industrial peace" rationale of McKenna, which was the functional equivalent of "health." To it he applied his lax instrumental standard that would accept as adequate virtually any connection between means and ends. Then he arrived at the larger point, which distinguished him from McKenna (who also dissented) and which put him in direct opposition to Harlan and the other members of the majority. In short, he denied the basic principle that defined the Fuller Court's position toward labor statutes or, for that matter, any legislation whatsoever:

---

[86] 208 U.S. at 191 (Holmes, J., dissenting).

[87] 198 U.S. at 76 (Holmes, J., dissenting).

> But suppose the only effect [of Section 10 of the Erdman Act] really were to tend to bring about the complete unionizing of such railroad laborers as Congress can deal with, I think that object alone would justify the act. I quite agree that the question what and how much good labor unions do, is one on which intelligent people may differ,—I think that laboring men sometimes attribute to them advantages, as many attribute to combinations of capital disadvantages, that really are due to economic conditions of a far wider and deeper kind—but I could not pronounce it unwarranted if Congress should decide that to foster a strong union was for the best interest, not only of the men, but of the railroads and the country at large.[88]

These two notions—that the relation between means and ends need not be direct and that redistribution was a permissible end of legislation—gutted the theory of *Lochner*. They reflect a rejection of the idea of constitutive authority and a willingness to embrace a more organic conception of state authority. On this issue, there is no need to speculate. In a letter written some years earlier to Professor James B. Thayer of Harvard, Holmes spelled out his views and indicated how far he was willing to go:

> There is another principle of *state* constitutional law not within the scope of your discussion which I always had supposed fundamental but which (between ourselves) I infer from the discussions I have had with my brethren does not command their assent—viz. that a state legislature has the power of Parliament, i.e., absolute power, except so far as expressly or by implication it is prohibited by the Constitution—that the question always is where do you find the prohibition—not, where do you find the power—I think the contrary view dangerous and wrong.[89]

Within a decade or so, Holmes's view would predominate. A sense of internal limits on the police power of the state would disappear and the central question would become, in Holmes's terms, not "where do you find the power" but "where do you find the prohibition." Indeed, the Court's about-face in 1937 and its acceptance of the New Deal could be seen as marking the end of the constitutive theory of the state and the triumph of a more organic one, giving the state what Holmes referred to as "absolute power."

In his letter to Thayer, Holmes was willing to acknowledge that the Constitution placed some limits on the state legislative power. Those limits might be vigorously enforced, and if so, Holmes might be read as contemplating a purely formal shift, that is, changing the terms of the inquiry from

---

[88] 208 U.S. at 191–92 (Holmes, J., dissenting).
[89] Holmes to Thayer, Nov. 2, 1893,

Holmes Papers, Harvard Law School Library Manuscript Division.

one of authority to one of prohibition but coming out with the same result. As we learned from the Warren Court era, judicial review dedicated to the enforcement of prohibitions such as those contained in the Bill of Rights and the Fourteenth Amendment can be as thoroughgoing and rigorous as review focusing on the question of authority. But that is not what Holmes had in mind, at least not until his dissent in *Abrams v. United States*[90] more than a decade after *Lochner* and *Adair*, and then only in the limited sphere of free speech. For him violations of external limits—of prohibitions— were largely reducible to the shocking-to-the-conscience or fundamental-fairness standard:

> I think that the word liberty in the Fourteenth Amendment is perverted when it is held to prevent the natural outcome of a dominant opinion, unless it can be said that a rational and fair man necessarily would admit that the statute proposed would infringe fundamental principles as they have been understood by the traditions of our people and our law.[91]

This is what Holmes offered his brethren as a substitute for the theory of constitutive authority, but no one on the Court at the turn of the century was prepared to accept it, for it virtually denied the judicial function as they understood it. In time, however, Holmes's fundamental-fairness standard became the rallying point for the most dedicated apostle of judicial restraint in the modern period: Felix Frankfurter. He picked up where Holmes left off.

Holmes's position cannot be founded on the constitutional text. Indeed, no one—neither Holmes nor Peckham nor Harlan—claimed the authority of some specific clause or provision. In their era, the process of constitutional interpretation was not, as I said earlier, one of parsing the language of some particular provision of the Constitution. In *Holden v. Hardy*, the Court considered the attack on the Utah hours limit as predicated on the Fourteenth Amendment, but no special effort was made to distinguish one particular clause of that amendment from another. *Lochner* was written in a similar spirit. The Due Process Clause was identified more centrally in *Lochner* than in *Holden v. Hardy*, but there was no pretense by Peckham that the result flowed from an interpretation of the "the word liberty," in Holmes's phrase. The result flowed instead from a general conception of state authority. Holmes's proffered substitute was equally general and equally without roots in the words of the Constitution. Instead of an inquiry into the permissibility of the end or the relationship between means and end, the judge was to ascertain whether, once again in Holmes's terms,

---

[90] 250 U.S. 616, 624–31 (1919) (Holmes, J., dissenting). See Chapter 11.

[91] 198 U.S. at 76 (Holmes, J., dissenting).

the statute met "fundamental principles as they have been understood by the traditions of our people and our law."

The Holmesian formula appears informed by a spirit of tolerance, and on that ground might be preferred: Holmes allowed the legislature to have the widest possible discretion in its choice of means and also in its choice of ends. There is some question as to whether such a tolerance is consistent with the judicial function, at least as conceived by Brewer, Peckham, and perhaps all the other justices of the Court at the turn of the century. Holmes's position seemed to deny the Court the power to check excesses of majoritarianism. Even more significantly, a question can be raised whether Holmes's spirit was one truly of tolerance. At times it appeared to be more one of indifference. He allowed the legislature greater prerogatives, but this permissiveness did not appear to flow from a genuine respect for the majority or from a democratic or egalitarian spirit. While Brewer spoke of "the numbers" or "the multitudes," Holmes spoke cynically of "the crowd."[92] No, rather than reflecting a uniquely democratic spirit, Holmes's permissiveness stemmed from a sense of resignation or, to use Yosal Rogat's term, fatalism.[93] Holmes believed that the view embodied in legislation was the "dominant opinion" and thus ultimately, in one form or the other, would prevail. While Brewer and Peckham feared the tyranny of the majority, Holmes accepted it cavalierly, not as just or right, but simply as inevitable.

In that most remarkable closing paragraph of his dissent in *Northern Securities*, Holmes said that there were limits to his permissiveness.[94] He would declare the Sherman Act unconstitutional as beyond the authority of Congress if that statute were given the interpretation urged by the majority, that is, if it were seen as a measure to preserve the system of atomistic competition. In terms of tone and content, this particular plea was hardly an exercise in judicial restraint, nor could it be understood as an assertion, to use Holmes's formula in *Lochner*, of "the fundamental principles as they have been understood by the traditions of our people and our law." Com-

---

[92] In a letter to Harold J. Laski dated January 8, 1917, Mark DeWolfe Howe, ed., *Holmes–Laski Letters: The Correspondence of Mr. Justice Holmes and Harold J. Laski, 1916–1935*, (Cambridge: Harvard University Press, 1953), I: 51–52, Holmes wrote:
On the economic side I am mighty sceptical of hours of labor and minimum wages regulation. . . . [I]t only means shifting the burden to a different point of incidence. . . . If the people who can't get the minimum are to be supported you take out of one pocket to put into the other. I think the courageous thing to say to the crowd, though perhaps the Brandeis school don't believe it, is, you now have all there is—and you'd better face it instead of trying to lift yourselves by the slack of your own breeches.

[93] Yosal Rogat, "The Judge as Spectator," *U. Chi. L. Rev.*, 31: 213, 254 (1964).

[94] See Chapter 5.

munitarianism was not one of the traditions Holmes had in mind. Rather, Holmes's stance in *Northern Securities*, premised as it was on the dominant economic thinking of the day, which declared atomistic competition at an end and which looked to increasing concentration in all industries, probably reflected his ethic of resignation and the belief that such an ethic should govern all branches of government, not just the judiciary. No agency of the state could stop the inevitable march of history. It would be absurd for it even to try.

So formulated, Holmes's position in *Lochner* and *Adair* was not founded on any commitment to democracy, nor on a theory of politics that made him especially distrustful of the judiciary because of its countermajoritarian quality. Instead, he expressed a view—uniquely unappealing as a personal or professional ethic, especially so to someone like Brewer[95]— that mocked the pursuit of any ideal. It is one thing for Holmes to insist that the judge be a spectator, for that entails self-abnegation, a character trait that in some circles might be deemed admirable; but it is quite another thing for him to insist, perhaps with even greater fervor, that legislatures and members of the executive branch—or, for that matter, anyone— should also view social life as a spectacle over which they have no control. Holmes mocked the evolutionary theorists of his day like Herbert Spencer and by implication the American social Darwinist William Graham Sumner, yet he seemed to embody their sense of the inevitable.

---

[95] See Owen M. Fiss, "David J. Brewer, The Judge as Missionary," in Philip J. Bergan, Owen M. Fiss, and Charles W. McCurdy, *The Fields and the Law: Essays* (San Francisco: United States District Court for the Northern District of California Historical Society; New York: Federal Bar Council, 1986), 53.

CHAPTER VII

Rate Regulation:
The Assault on Munn v. Illinois

LIKE ANTITRUST and maximum hours statutes, rate regulation was a volatile issue at the turn of the century. Its roots extend back to the late 1860s and early 1870s, when the Granger movement called for legislation to control the rates of railroads, storage facilities, and other parts of the system for transporting agricultural products.[1] In the early 1890s a similar demand was also voiced by populists, along with their plans for state ownership of railroads.[2] These demands did not fit comfortably within the market ideology that so pervaded the legal establishment, and they remained the subject of heated debate when the call for regulation of railroad rates was taken up by progressives at the turn of the century and became an important part of their program.

Although the initial regulatory measures were enacted by the states, in the late 1880s railroad regulation became a matter of national concern and soon resulted in the enactment of the Commerce Act of 1887. That measure asserted federal jurisdiction over interstate railroading, established the Interstate Commerce Commission, and prohibited pooling and discrimina-

---

[1] The Grange, also known as the Patrons of Husbandry, was a nonpartisan agrarian movement begun in 1867 with the stated aim of organizing farmers for the advancement of agriculture. Its activities were cultural and informational at first, but the movement rapidly gained members and became more politically active during the 1870s as low crop prices and high interest rates caused widespread hardship among farmers. See generally Solon Justus Buck, *The Granger Movement* (Cambridge: Harvard University Press, 1913; repr. Lincoln: University of Nebraska Press, 1963), and D. Sven Nordin, *Rich Harvest: A History of the Grange, 1867–1900* (Jackson: University Press of Mississippi, 1974).

[2] See the Omaha Platform, July 1892, reprinted in George Brown Tindall, ed., *A Populist Reader: Selections from the Works of American Populist Leaders* (New York: Harper & Row, 1966), 93–94, and N. B. Ashby, "The Railroad Problem," excerpted in ibid., 26–36. See generally Lawrence Goodwyn, *Democratic Promise: The Populist Moment in America* (New York: Oxford University Press, 1976).

tion between long hauls and short hauls.[3] The 1887 Act was strengthened by the Elkins Act of 1903, which prohibited railroads from granting secret rebates to favored shippers.[4] But a far more significant development for the history of railroad regulation occurred during Roosevelt's second term with the passage of the Hepburn Act of 1906. That statute gave the Interstate Commerce Commission the power to set minimum and maximum rates on interstate rail trips.[5]

Statutes regulating rates were invariably justified before the Court in the name of the public welfare,[6] but the danger of redistribution—of taking the property of one and giving it to another—and thus breaching the social

---

[3] An Act to Regulate Commerce, Ch. 104, 24 Stat. 379 (1887). "Pooling" refers to informal agreements among competing railroads under which traffic, income, and equipment were shared. The practice grew as competition intensified in the 1870s. The Granger movement, and later the populists, objected to it, and a prohibition of such arrangements became part of the Commerce Act. In exchange, railroad owners won a clause in the new statute that limited the prohibition of discrimination between long hauls and short hauls to cases where hauls were performed under "substantially similar circumstances and conditions." Albro Martin, "The Troubled Subject of Railroad Regulation in the Gilded Age—A Reappraisal," *J. Am. Hist.*, 61: 339, 361–62 (1974); Alfred D. Chandler, Jr., *The Visible Hand: The Managerial Revolution in American Business* (Cambridge: Harvard University Press, 1977), 136–44; Robert L. Rabin, "Federal Regulation in Historical Perspective," *Stan. L. Rev.*, 38: 1189, 1207 (1986).

[4] Ch. 708, 32 Stat. 847 (1903), imposing heavy fines for deviating from the published tariffs filed with the ICC.

[5] Ch. 3591, 34 Stat. 584, 589 (1906). Robert E. Cushman, *The Independent Regulatory Commissions* (New York: Oxford University Press, 1941), 65, described the Hepburn Act as "rescuing the Commission from futility." Rate regulation measures like the Hepburn Act had antecedents in the common law rule requiring the rates of common carriers to be reasonable. See, e.g., Western Union Tel. Co. v. Call Publishing Co., 181 U.S. 92, 95 (1901), and ICC v. Balti-

more & O. R.R, 145 U.S. 263, 275 (1892). See also Walter Chadwick Noyes, *American Railroad Rates* (Boston: Little, Brown, 1905), 32–35. Also, some charters of incorporation fixed rates. See, e.g., Charles River Bridge v. Warren Bridge, 36 U.S. (11 Pet.) 420 (1837). See also B. H. Meyer, "Railway Charters," *Publications Am. Econ. A.* (3d s.), vol. 1, no. 1 at 231 (1900); Noyes, *American Railroad Rates*; and Herbert Hovenkamp, "Technology, Politics, and Regulated Monopoly: An American Historical Perspective," *Tex. L. Rev.*, 62: 1263, 1291, 1303–1304 (1984). Professor Hovenkamp notes that because charters, as opposed to statutory regulation, could not take investors by surprise, "even laissez faire constitutional scholars such as Thomas M. Cooley, who generally opposed statutory rate regulation, and Isaac Redfield, the eminent conservative legal authority on railroad law, believed that it was possible to enforce charter provisions stipulating maximum rates." Herbert Hovenkamp, "Regulatory Conflict in the Gilded Age: Federalism and the Railroad Problem," *Yale L.J.*, 97: 1017, 1060 (1988).

[6] Professor Hovenkamp sees the effort to ensure the profitability of railroads, and thus to avoid competition, to be in the larger interest of the public. He maintains that the maximum rate regulation could prevent monopolistic "rate gouging" in the noncompetitive short-haul markets, and that the minimum rate regulation could prevent "ruinous rate cutting" in the highly competitive long-haul markets. "Regulatory Conflict in the Gilded Age," 1056–58.

contract was manifest. The power to control prices entailed the power to deprive owners of the value of their property, since the precise level of the rate allowed would determine the return on the property and thus its value. This danger led Brewer to denounce rate regulation in his Albany speech in terms he was never tempted to use for the Sherman Act or the progressive measures called into question in *Holden v. Hardy, Lochner v. New York,* and *Adair v. United States*;[7] rate regulation, he said, was tantamount to a legalization of theft, similar to the collective action involved in the Homestead Strike.[8] Brewer feared that "the multitudes" would try to appropriate the property of the industrious, and he pleaded for judicial vigilance even more when it came to rate regulation than in the matter of antitrust or statutes regulating the maximum number of hours worked.

But a countervailing factor—a Supreme Court precedent—greatly modulated the Court's response to this branch of progressivism and lent it a distinctive cast. In *Munn v. Illinois*[9] the Court had upheld a state statute placing a ceiling on the prices charged by grain elevators and more generally legitimated the rate regulation program of the Granger movement. The opinion was written by Chief Justice Morrison Waite and handed down in 1876. Twelve years later the chief justiceship passed from Waite to Fuller, ushering in a new chapter in the history of the Court, but Fuller and the other Cleveland-Harrison appointees who soon joined him on the bench knew that if they were to protect the social contract by limiting the power of the state to regulate rates, they first had to confront and overcome *Munn v. Illinois.* It was clear who would lead the charge. In September 1891 Harlan wrote to Fuller: "Brewer is here, looking well. But *Munn v. Illinois* is still in force, ready to do battle against all the Romans, however able or noble."[10]

In formulating the rule of reason of *Standard Oil* and *American Tobacco* in 1911, the Court arguably also was constrained by its decisions of a decade earlier, particularly *Trans-Missouri, Joint Traffic,* and *Addyston Pipe.*[11] Peckham had maintained in these early decisions that the Sherman Act covered "every" restraint of trade, not only "unreasonable" ones. But, in my view, after the *Northern Securities* decision of 1904 it was clear that a majority of the justices (including Peckham) no longer took that position and that *Trans-Missouri, Joint Traffic,* and *Addyston Pipe* were limited sharply.[12] Similarly, precedent was not much of an obstacle when the

---

[7] These cases are discussed in Chapter 6.

[8] On the Homestead Strike, see the discussion in Chapters 2 and 3.

[9] 94 U.S. 113 (1877).

[10] Harlan to Fuller, Sept. 9, 1891, (postscript to letter of Sept. 8, 1891), Fuller Papers, Library of Congress Manuscript Division.

[11] These cases are discussed in Chapter 5.

[12] See the discussion of *Northern Securities* in Chapter 5.

moment came to decide *Lochner v. New York.* Admittedly, the Court had sustained a maximum hours law in *Holden v. Hardy,* but that decision did not announce an absolute rule, and in any event its precedential force was limited by the special character of the industry involved, namely mining. Moreover, at the time of *Lochner* in 1905, decisions were then on the books—*Allgeyer v. Louisiana*[13] is the one I have most in mind—that invalidated exercises of the police power on liberty of contract grounds and thus created a counterweight to *Holden v. Hardy.*

In the rate regulation cases, however, the situation was wholly different, for *Munn v. Illinois* was, as Harlan put it, "still in force." Although the original decision in *Munn* had divided the Court by a 7 to 2 vote and had aroused an impassioned and well-known dissent by Justice Field, by the 1890s and early 1900s it had achieved the status of a durable and permanent decision. It helped define the established constitutional framework of the era and seemed to interfere unambiguously with any effort to invalidate or even cabin the legislative power to regulate prices and place ceilings on them.

It was not beyond this particular group of justices to repudiate a prior decision. As the income tax decision revealed,[14] the Fuller Court was prepared, when necessary, to overturn long accepted decisions. Indeed, for a brief moment the Court considered directly overruling *Munn v. Illinois.* Its decision in *Chicago, Milwaukee & St. Paul Railway v. Minnesota* in 1890,[15] overturning a regulatory measure on procedural grounds, seemed to set the stage for overruling *Munn* and was construed by the dissenters as "practically" having achieved that result.[16] But when the Court in 1892 returned to the issue of *Munn* in *Budd v. New York,*[17] it announced at the outset that it had decided to adhere to that decision. In contrast to *Pollock,* there could be no claim that the conditions of *Munn* had changed, no hope of limiting it to exceptional circumstances (such as the necessities of financing a war), no possibility of reducing the significance of the case by some interpretive ploy. The justices could not even claim that they were returning to the Constitution pure, for no provision of the Constitution could play quite the role for rate regulation that the Direct Tax Clause played in *Pollock.* The options

---

[13] 165 U.S. 578 (1897) (invalidating a Louisiana statute that barred state citizens from dealing with out-of-state insurance companies not registered in Louisiana).

[14] Pollock v. Farmers' Loan & Trust Co., 157 U.S. 429 (1895); 158 U.S. 601 (1895). As discussed in Chapter 4, *Pollock* was in conflict with a number of Supreme Court precedents, above all Hylton v. United States, 3 U.S. (3 Dall.) 171 (1796), and Springer v. United States, 102 U.S. 586 (1881).

[15] 134 U.S. 418 (1890).

[16] Ibid., 461 (Bradley, J., dissenting).

[17] 143 U.S. 517 (1892).

of the Court were more limited, and as a result the justices took the more conservative tack of revising and confining, rather than repudiating, *Munn*.

Some of the Court's strategies to revise *Munn* were relatively minor. The Court restricted the industries vulnerable to rate regulation essentially to railroads; effectively suspended the power to regulate rates on interstate trips for a twenty-year period; and conferred various procedural rights upon those intent on challenging the rates fixed. The principal revisionist strategy, however, was more far reaching: The Court created a federal constitutional right that assured businessmen a fair rate of return on their capital. This right of a fair return was the creation of Brewer, as Harlan's letter had anticipated. Formulated one year before *Pollock*, it in effect anticipated the outcome and underlying theory of that case by making explicit its edict against redistribution.

Announcing this new substantive right of a fair return did not result in the wholesale invalidation of rate regulation statutes. Instead, it committed the Court to policing the application of the rate-setting power on a case-by-case basis. That commitment in turn led to the Court's highly controversial decision in *Ex parte Young* in 1908,[18] which upheld a federal court injunction barring the attorney general of Minnesota from enforcing a statute of his state that placed a ceiling on railroad rates. The Court's opinion was written by Brewer's constant ally, Justice Peckham, and squarely put the federal equity courts in the business of guarding against confiscation. It also laid the foundation for the civil rights injunction of the Warren Court era. But, ironically enough, Peckham's opinion in *Ex parte Young* provoked a dissent by Justice Harlan, who managed to find within himself almost as much anger as he had expressed in his dissents in the *Civil Rights Cases*[19] and *Plessy v. Ferguson*.[20]

I

One strategy of revision sought to restrict the power legitimated by *Munn v. Illinois* to a narrow group of industries. The Fuller Court made it clear that the rate regulation power did not extend to the entire economy but was confined for the most part to common carriers, primarily railroads. The Court achieved that result largely by formulating reasons for allowing

---

[18] 209 U.S. 123 (1908).
[19] 109 U.S. 3, 26 (1883) (Harlan, J., dissenting).

[20] 163 U.S. 537, 552 (1896) (Harlan, J., dissenting).

states the power to regulate railroad rates that were not easily transferable to other industries.[21]

Munn v. Illinois involved a statute regulating rates charged by grain elevators (only in companion cases was it extended to railroads[22]). Chief Justice Waite used a most expansive verbal formula for bringing grain elevators within the legislature's power. An elevator's rates could be regulated, he said, because it was a business "affected with a public interest."[23] Waite's formula embraced railroads as well as grain elevators but, even more importantly, had the potential of reaching virtually the entire economy. In 1892 with *Budd v. New York*, however, the Fuller Court drew back from the expansive implications of the *Munn* formula. *Budd* upheld a New York statute regulating the rates for the storage and transportation of grain, but the Court avoided Waite's formula and made clear that, even in terms of result, *Munn* was an outer limit rather than a starting point.[24]

The attack on *Munn* was, of course, led by Brewer. He dissented in *Budd* and began his opinion in that case by denouncing the public interest formula of *Munn* as "radically unsound."[25] He urged in its place a principle emphasizing public use:

The vice of the [*Munn*] doctrine is, that it places a public interest in the use of property upon the same basis as a public use of property. Property is devoted to a public use when, and only when, the use is one which the public in its organized capacity, to wit, the State, has a right to create and maintain, and, therefore, one which all the public have a right to demand and share in. The use is public, because the public may create

---

[21] The economic and social importance of the rail industry in the late nineteenth century was enormous. Alfred D. Chandler, Jr., comp. and ed., *The Railroads—The Nation's First Big Business: Sources and Readings* (New York: Harcourt, Brace & World, 1965), 21–40; Albert Fishlow, *American Railroads and the Transformation of the Antebellum Economy* (Cambridge: Harvard University Press, 1965); Robert William Fogel, *Railroads and American Economic Growth: Essays in Econometric History* (Baltimore: Johns Hopkins Press, 1964). But in making the industry the principal target of regulation, the proponents of rate regulation acknowledged implicitly the permissible limits of their demands, just as many of those who sought the abolition of slavery acknowledged (at first) the large extent to which the Constitution legitimated or accepted slavery by limiting their demands to the aboli-

tion of slavery in the territories. See Arthur Bestor, "The American Civil War as a Constitutional Crisis," *Am. Hist. Rev.*, 69: 327 (1964).

[22] See Chicago, B. & Q. R.R. v. Iowa, 94 U.S. 155 (1877); Peik v. Chicago & N.W. Ry., 94 U.S. 164 (1877); and Winona & St. P. R.R. v. Blake, 94 U.S. 180 (1877).

[23] 94 U.S. at 126. See Harry N. Scheiber, "The Road to *Munn*: Eminent Domain and the Concept of Public Purpose in the State Courts," Donald Fleming and Bernard Bailyn, eds., *Law in American History* (Boston: Little, Brown, 1971), 329.

[24] 143 U.S. at 545. The only difference between the Illinois statute sustained in *Munn* and the New York statute sustained in *Budd* was that the latter also regulated rates for the shoveling and trimming of grain.

[25] Ibid., 548

it, and the individual creating it is doing thereby and *pro tanto* the work of the State.[26]

Under the public use doctrine, railroads and a number of other industries would be brought within the scope of rate regulation. But the reasons Brewer offered in support of that conclusion revealed how narrow was the power that he contemplated:

> The creation of all highways is a public duty. Railroads are highways. The State may build them. If an individual does that work, he is *pro tanto* doing the work of the State. He devotes his property to a public use. The State doing the work fixes the price for the use. It does not lose the right to fix the price, because an individual voluntarily undertakes to do the work.[27]

At this point, Brewer would not even concede a power to regulate when there was a so-called practical monopoly, that is, one conferred by economic considerations rather than through the force of law. Such a monopoly was, for him, a form of power created simply by individual effort or economic conditions, rather than a state-conferred privilege.[28] A practical monopoly could and should be remedied, he insisted, by the entrepreneurial activity of other businessmen, not by state regulation of the monopolist's prices.

The view expressed by Brewer in *Budd v. New York*, allowing only the narrowest compass for the rate regulation power, was shared by a number of other justices. Two joined his dissent. One was his uncle, Stephen Field, whose dissent in *Munn* first formulated and propounded the public use doctrine advanced by Brewer in *Budd*.[29] The other was Henry Brown,

---

[26] Ibid., 549.

[27] Ibid.

[28] Ibid., 550–51. On the distinction between artificial and practical monopolies, see Chapter 5, pp. 112–13. An artificial monopoly originates in a grant from the state, while a practical monopoly is attributable to economic circumstance. A natural monopoly occurs where, due to economies of scale, the total costs of production are lower when the entire output is produced by a single firm. This concept of natural monopoly has been used in late-twentieth-century regulatory literature, in particular by Hovenkamp, to reconcile rate regulation with neoclassical economic theory. "Regulatory Conflict in the Gilded Age," 1035–44.

[29] 94 U.S. at 136–54. In his dissent in *Munn*, Justice Field claimed that regulation should be limited to "property dedicated by the owner to public uses, or to property the use of which was granted by the government, or in connection with which special privileges were conferred. Unless the property was thus dedicated, or some right bestowed by the government was held with the property . . . [it] was not affected by any public interest so as to be taken out of the category of property held in private right." 94 U.S. at 139–40. As for the majority's formula, "[i]f this be sound law . . . all property and business in the State are held at the mercy of the majority of its legislature." Ibid., 140.

with whom Brewer also had personal ties.[30] While Field was ending his career on the Court, Brown had just begun his, and over the next fifteen years he would occupy a centrist position on matters of economic regulation. Brown joined Peckham's opinion in *Lochner* but dissented in *Pollock*. He wrote the Court's opinion in *Holden v. Hardy* sustaining a maximum hours law for miners and joined all the opinions of the Court sustaining the enforcement of the Sherman Act.

Field and Brown joined Brewer's dissent in *Budd*. Peckham was not yet on the Court, but there could be no mistaking where he stood. When *Budd* was before the New York Court of Appeals, Peckham, not one to be intimidated by a Supreme Court decision,[31] even one of such standing as *Munn*, voted in dissent to invalidate the New York statute, and justified his position in terms that anticipated much of what Brewer had to say when *Budd* reached the Supreme Court.[32] At the very least, then, in the early 1890s a group of three or four justices (it was hard to know how long Field would hold on) subscribed to a position that openly and explicitly repudiated the *Munn* "public interest" formula. This group was inclined strictly to confine the rate regulation power to railroads, other common carriers, and certain public utilities.

To confound matters, traces of Brewer's position and the public use doctrine also can be found in the majority opinion in *Budd*. That opinion appeared as but a grudging concession to *Munn*, based more on a deference to a venerable precedent than on a belief in the correctness of the public interest doctrine. Justice Samuel Blatchford, the author of the majority opinion, gave lip service to the public interest doctrine, but his real interest lay elsewhere. He noted that the business subject to regulation was "an actual monopoly."[33] Although he also described the business as being "of

---

[30] Brown and Brewer were classmates at Yale, and Brewer apparently owed his appointment in part to the generosity of his recommendation of Brown to the High Court. Lynford A. Lardner, "The Constitutional Doctrines of Justice David Josiah Brewer" (Ph.D. diss., Princeton University, 1938), 4, 15. See also Arnold M. Paul, "David J. Brewer," in Leon Friedman and Fred L. Israel, eds., *The Justices of the United States Supreme Court, 1789–1969: Their Lives and Major Opinions* (New York: Chelsea House, 1969), 2: 1515.

[31] Dean Acheson, who served as Brandeis's private secretary as a young man, recorded in his memoirs the fol-

lowing comment made by Holmes about Peckham:

> A few of [Holmes's] opinions of people stand out in the notes or from memory. "What," I asked, "was Justice Peckham like, intellectually?"
> "Intellectually?" he answered, puzzled. "I never thought of him in that connection. His major premise was, 'God damn it!' But he was a good judge."

Morning and Noon (Boston: Houghton Mifflin, 1965), 65.

[32] People v. Budd, 117 N.Y. 1, 34 (1889) (Peckham, J., dissenting).

[33] 143 U.S. at 545.

a quasi-public character,"[34] he had something else in mind than the public interest notion invoked in *Munn*. For Blatchford, the public character of the business was derived entirely from the fact that it was "incident to the business of transportation and to that of a common carrier."[35] "The elevator at Buffalo," Blatchford emphasized, "is a link in the chain of transportation to the seaboard, and the elevator in the harbor of New York is a like link in the transportation abroad by sea."[36]

Blatchford's new analysis of a question that *Munn* had already answered—the basis of a legislature's power to regulate prices charged by grain elevators—carried an important, negative implication: The rate regulation power extended only to common carriers and to those businesses, presumably few in number, that had important ties or functional links to the common carriers or were analogous to them. Under this reformulation of the rule of *Munn*, the majority's position converged with that of Brewer, and for the next twenty years all the rate regulation cases involved railroads or other industries that fit easily within Brewer's public use doctrine—toll roads, telegraph companies, and public works.[37] Whenever the Court thought it necessary to rationalize or justify that power, the justice who spoke for the Court invoked not the broad *Munn* formula but the theory put forth by Brewer in his *Budd* dissent. This occurred most notably when Harlan—who from the very beginning well understood Brewer's larger ambition—later spoke for a unanimous Court in *Smyth v. Ames* in the late 1890s.[38]

In addition to limiting the industries reached by the rate regulation power, the Court handed down a number of rulings that effectively suspended the power to fix maximum rates on interstate travel. This second strategy for revising *Munn* was implemented in two stages. In the first, the power of state legislatures to regulate rates on interstate rail trips was curtailed sharply and reserved exclusively to Congress. In the second, the

---

[34] Ibid.

[35] Ibid.

[36] Ibid.

[37] See Covington & Cincinnati Bridge Co. v. Kentucky, 154 U.S. 204 (1894) (holding that the state of Kentucky could not regulate toll charges because the traffic across the river was interstate commerce, but that Congress could regulate such fares), and Western Union Tel. Co. v. Call Publishing Co., 181 U.S. 92 (1901) (holding that a telegraph company is a common carrier and has a common law duty to charge reasonable and equal rates to its customers). See also Atkin v. Kansas, 191 U.S. 218 (1903) (holding that the freedom of contract is not infringed by a Kansas statute forbidding public works contractors to require or permit their employees to work in excess of eight hours per day).

[38] 169 U.S. 466 (1898). Although all the justices who participated joined Harlan's opinion, two did not participate: Justice McKenna, who was not a member of the Court when the case was argued, and Chief Justice Fuller.

Court insisted that Congress speak with clarity and specificity if it wished to place ceilings on rates. The effect of these judicial decisions was to free interstate rail trips from rate regulation for two decades, until Congress managed to satisfy the Court's demand for specificity by passing the Hepburn Act in 1906.[39] In practical terms, for twenty years the Court suspended the application of *Munn v. Illinois* to the national rail system.

Munn was primarily a police power case. The principal issue was one of substantive due process, namely whether the legislature had the power to regulate rates, but the Granger movement also put the reach of the Commerce Clause into question: How should the power to regulate rates be allocated between the states and the federal government? In the 1870s the power was exercised largely by the states. In a companion to *Munn*, the Supreme Court approved that allocation, holding that each state had the power to set the rates for trips that (1) were wholly within state borders or (2) either began or ended within that state. This second branch of the Court's ruling might seem dubious since any trip that crossed a state boundary might be regarded as interstate and thus beyond the power of the states, but Waite thought otherwise. He felt that every trip that began or ended in a state was of sufficient concern to the people of the state to bring the trip within the state's jurisdiction.[40]

Over the next decade, a strong nationalistic vision emerged, which ultimately found dramatic expression in *Debs*. The railroads were viewed as the highways of the nation and the Court insisted that they be kept free of all obstructions. The Court saw the United States as a single economic union, constituting a national market, in which goods and people moved freely across state boundaries, and it used the Commerce Clause to nullify all interferences with this free passage. Consistent with this emergent vision, the Supreme Court in the *Wabash* decision of 1886 cut back on its earlier position. *Wabash* involved an Illinois statute prohibiting long-haul/short-haul discrimination and in that case the Court held that a state did not have the power to regulate the rates of trips that extended beyond its borders.[41] Both the origin and destination of the trip had to be within a state's boundaries.

---

[39] The Hepburn Act not only gave the ICC power to establish minimum and maximum rates, but also provided that the Commission's orders were to be effective immediately and remain so until set aside by a court. Ch. 3591, 34 Stat. 584, 589 (1906).

[40] Peik v. Chicago & N.W. Ry., 94 U.S. 177–78.

[41] Wabash, St. L. & P. Ry. v. Illinois, 118 U.S. 557 (1886). Justice Miller held that the Illinois statute prohibiting discrimination between long and short hauls interfered with interstate commerce because the effect of such a statute would be to raise long haul, i.e., interstate, rates. For example, interstate

Chapter VII: *Rate Regulation*

Wabash was one of the final decisions of the Waite Court, but, as noted in Chapter 3 and as will be explored in Chapter 9, the nationalist principles announced by the Court in the late 1880s were endorsed heartily by Fuller and his colleagues. While the power of the states to regulate intrastate trips was fully recognized, even when it had an effect deemed "indirect" or "remote" on interstate rates,[42] the Court's commitment to the negative portion of *Wabash*—denying the states any power over interstate trips— was unqualified. This aspect of *Wabash* was never in doubt in the 1890s or early 1900s, and in fact served as a central premise of much of the Fuller Court's work. Moreover, the Court held that the statute enacted in response to the *Wabash* decision—the Commerce Act of 1887—did not confer upon the federal government the power to set the maximum rates on interstate trips. As a result, when it came to setting maximum rates on such trips, as

competition might indicate a rate of 15 cents per hundred pounds from Peoria to New York City, but the statute would prohibit the railroad from setting such a low rate because of the higher rates being charged on the noncompetitive parts of its lines. Similarly, Justice Miller reasoned that the rate charged for a very short local haul—from Gilman, Illinois, to Sheldon, a distance of twenty-three miles—would determine the minimum rate that could be charged for interstate shipments, even though the cost of loading and unloading represented nearly the total expense of the short hauls, but only a small fraction of the entire cost of the long haul. 118 U.S. at 576. Justice Miller therefore assumed that such a statute would result in a rise in interstate rates and not a drop in intrastate rates. He declined to overrule the Court's earlier decision in the companion to *Munn*, distinguishing it rather unpersuasively as having involved a more "limited" regulation than was at issue in *Wabash*. Miller also noted, more correctly here, that the earlier case did not particularly address the federalism issue but focused on the validity of the power to regulate more generally, which "overshadowed all others." Ibid., 568–69.

[42] Louisville & Nashville R.R. v. Kentucky, 183 U.S. 503 (1902); Minneapolis & St. L. R.R. v. Minnesota, 186

U.S. 257 (1902). Justice Brewer, riding circuit in Nebraska, in Ames v. Union Pac. Ry., 64 F. 165, 189, 170 (C.C.D. Neb. 1894), aff'd sub nom. Smyth v. Ames, 169 U.S. 466 (1898), while invalidating and enjoining the enforcement of a Nebraska statute because the maximum rate it prescribed was so low as to be "unjust and unreasonable," also claimed that a state could prescribe rates charged by a railroad for transportation within its borders, even if the corporation was created by an act of Congress, so long as nothing in that act indicated an intent to remove such corporation from state control. Several commentators noted that state regulation of purely intrastate rates effectively controlled a wide range of interstate rates. See, e.g., Robert Mather, "How the States Make Interstate Rates," *Annals Am. Acad. Soc. & Pol. Sci.*, 32: 102 (1908). In the Minnesota Rate Cases, 230 U.S. 352 (1913), the Court acknowledged the extraterritorial effects of intrastate rate-making and allowed Congress to preempt state rate control when "adequate control of interstate rates cannot be maintained without imposing requirements with respect to . . . intrastate rates which substantially affect the former. . . ." 230 U.S. at 432–33. See generally Hovenkamp, "Regulatory Conflict in the Gilded Age," 1068.

opposed to merely prohibiting discrimination, a "regulatory vacuum" was created.[43]

The Commerce Act of 1887 established the Interstate Commerce Commission. Over time that agency was given the full panoply of regulatory powers and served as the prototype of the independent regulatory agencies of the New Deal,[44] but at the outset the ICC was assigned more limited duties and conceived in almost adjudicatory terms. Aside from the provisions prohibiting pooling, the Commission was charged with enforcing prohibitions aimed at unjust and discriminatory rates. Section 2 of the 1887 Act prohibited "unjust discrimination"; Section 3 prohibited "undue or unreasonable preference"; and Section 4 prohibited railroads from charging more for a short run than for a long run.[45] The Commission would have the power to enforce these prohibitions, that is, to set aside unjust and discriminatory rates, but that power did not authorize the Commission to set rates. The legal mind of the nineteenth century—and maybe even the twentieth—saw all the difference in the world between a negative and a positive duty, between a law prohibiting unreasonable or discriminatory rates and one affirmatively setting a ceiling on the rate to be charged.

This distinction was reflected in the early practices of the Commission. The 1887 Act was read first as specifying in legislation the common law duties of common carriers, not as shifting to the federal government the regulatory power for interstate trips legitimated in the companion to *Munn* and denied by *Wabash*. As Thomas Cooley, the first chairman, wrote to his wife, "The less coercive power we have the greater, I think, will be

---

[43] The quoted phrase comes from Hovenkamp, "Regulatory Conflict in the Gilded Age," 1034, to describe how considerations of federalism, coupled with a general bias against government intervention, hampered a comprehensive program of regulating interstate rail markets. Since the states were able to control only intrastate markets, and the federal government was allowed to control only interstate markets, no one was able to formulate solutions broad enough to solve the problems of the railroad industry. With regard to the setting of rates, the vacuum was not filled until the Hepburn Act of 1906 gave the ICC the power to prescribe maximum rates.

[44] The formative influence of the Interstate Commerce Act on the development of the federal regulatory system is described by Robert Rabin in these terms:

A century ago, when Congress established the Interstate Commerce Commission, it initiated a new epoch in responsibilities of the federal government. For the first time, a national legislative scheme was enacted that provided for wide-ranging regulatory controls over an industry that was vital to the nation's economy—the railroads. Moreover, regulation of the industry was committed to an institutional mechanism that was virtually untested on the national stage, an independent regulatory commission. The modern age of administrative government had begun.

Rabin, "Federal Regulation in Historical Perspective," 1189.

[45] 24 Stat. at 379–80.

our moral influence."[46] In the mid-1890s the Commission became more aggressive and claimed that the power to set maximum rates *was* conferred by the 1887 Act, but the Court proved unaccommodating.[47] In the *Cincinnati, New Orleans* decision of 1897,[48] the so-called *Maximum Rate Case*, the Court ruled that the power to set rates was special, and in order to create such a power, it was necessary for Congress to speak clearly and specifically, which it had not done in the 1887 Act. The original 1887 Act was amended in 1903 by the Elkins Act, but even then Congress did not confer on the ICC the power to set rates. The 1903 statute was an attack only on secret rebates. It was not until 1906, with the passage of the Hepburn Act ten years after *Cincinnati, New Orleans* and fully twenty years after *Wabash*, that Congress, prodded by President Roosevelt,[49] gave the ICC the power to set rates on interstate trips.

The *Cincinnati, New Orleans* opinion was written by Justice Brewer, and for those who subscribe to the instrumental thesis it has a paradoxical relationship with another decision of the same term, *Trans-Missouri*, later affirmed in *Joint Traffic.*[50] In *Trans-Missouri* and *Joint Traffic*, both written by Peckham, the Supreme Court sustained an antitrust action against a price-fixing cartel of the railroads and in so doing severed the connection between the Sherman Act and the common law. To the instrumentalist, who sees the law as a tool of business interests defined in the most concrete

---

[46] Thomas M. Cooley to Mary H. Cooley, Oct. 21, 1888, Cooley Papers, University of Michigan Historical Collection, quoted in Alan Jones, "Thomas M. Cooley and the Interstate Commerce Commission: Continuity and Change in the Doctrine of Equal Rights," *Pol. Sci. Q.*, 81: 602, 615 (1966). Cooley drew a line between deciding cases and affirmatively setting in advance specific rates that the railroads must charge. See also Leonard S. Goodman, "Getting Started: Organization, Procedure and Initial Business of the ICC in 1887," *Transp. L.J.*, 16: 7, 16–20, 29–30 (1987).

[47] In 1896, in Cincinnati, N.O. & Tex. Pac. Ry. v. ICC, 162 U.S. 184 (1896), commonly called the Social Circle Case, the ICC argued that the power to determine the reasonableness of rates necessarily implied the power to fix maximum rates. The Court rejected this argument, claiming that "the reasonableness of the rate, in a given case, depends on the facts" and "if the Commission, instead of withholding judg-

ment in such a matter until an issue shall be made and the facts found, itself fixes a rate, that rate is prejudged by the Commission to be reasonable." 162 U.S. at 196–97. The ICC tried to interpret the Court's holding favorably. *Interstate Commerce Commission Annual Report*, H. Doc. No. 99, 54th Cong., 2d Sess., 21–23 (1896).

[48] ICC v. Cincinnati, N.O. & Tex. Pac. Ry., 167 U.S. 479 (1897).

[49] Theodore Roosevelt, annual message to Congress, Dec. 5, 1905, reprinted in Hermann Hagedorn, ed., *The Works of Theodore Roosevelt* (New York: Charles Scribner's Sons, 1926), 15: 270, 274–82. Senator Foraker, one of only three senators who voted against the bill, attacked the proposed legislation in the opening speech of the Senate debate as "contrary to the spirit of our institutions and of . . . drastic and revolutionary character. . . ." 40 Cong. Rec. 3102–3103, 59th Cong., 1st Sess. (1906).

[50] See Chapter 5.

terms, it might seem odd for the Court to apply the Sherman Act to the rail-roads in this way while denying the ICC the power to regulate their rates. But once we are out from under the instrumental thesis, the coincidence of these rulings is not at all contradictory. The ban on price-fixing affirmed by *Trans-Missouri* and *Joint Traffic* was seen as a way to preserve the market and the system of liberties it supported; so was the limitation on the state's power to regulate prices created by *Cincinnati, New Orleans*, since it too advanced those very same values.

In *Cincinnati, New Orleans* the Court tied the Commerce Act to the common law by reading it as a prohibition of unreasonable rates and by refusing to give the ICC a power no common law court had ever possessed, namely the power to set a specific ceiling on the price an entrepreneur could charge. In this way, the Court removed any threat the statute posed to the market and its central disciplining mechanism, the price system. In another case handed down in the same year, *ICC v. Alabama Midland Railway*,[51] the Court further constricted the powers of the ICC by construing the long-haul/short-haul prohibition of the 1887 Act (the one prohibition of the Act that seemed to have specific content) in a way that emphasized the pro-competition themes of *Trans-Missouri* and *Joint Traffic*. In that case, the Supreme Court held that a differential rate between long hauls and short hauls was not an "unjust discrimination" or otherwise impermissible if the differential reflected competitive conditions. A lower rate for a long haul was permissible if it was required by competition.

A third strategy for revising *Munn* was procedural and related to another development occurring at this time: the shift of the rate regulation power from the legislature to administrative agencies. Although the Fuller Court, like its predecessor, theoretically honored this development, it none-theless imposed procedural restrictions on the administrative agency by linking it to an adjudicatory, rather than a legislative, model. The adminis-trative agency was compelled to adopt procedures that made it seem more like a court and less like a legislature, all for the purpose of lessening the perceived dangers of majoritarianism.

A little remembered aspect of *Munn v. Illinois* is that the rate regula-tion power challenged there was exercised directly by the legislature. The rates were fixed by statute. In the years immediately following *Munn*, a number of state legislatures delegated the rate regulation power to adminis-trative agencies called railroad commissions. By the turn of the century, particularly after the establishment of the ICC and the enlargement of its

---

[51] 168 U.S. 144 (1897).

powers by the Hepburn Act of 1906, the administrative agency had become the central repository of the legislative power to fix rates.[52]

The causes of this development are not wholly clear,[53] but its importance was unmistakable and confronted the Court with several new questions. The most obvious one concerned the placement of the administrative agencies within a scheme of government that emphasized a tripartite division or separation of governmental functions: Where did the administrative agency fit it? Was it a part of the executive or the legislature? Or could it possibly be regarded as part of the judiciary? Oddly enough, these questions did not trouble the Court greatly at that time.[54] The *Railroad Commission Cases*[55] of the mid-1880s held that the states were not under a federal constitutional duty to preserve a strict separation of powers. State legislatures could delegate their powers to administrative agencies. Clearly,

---

[52] By 1886 twenty-four states and the Dakota Territory had commissions that regulated railroads. See the so-called Cullom Report, *Report of the Select Committee on Interstate Commerce*, S. Rep. No. 46, 49th Cong., 1st Sess., Pt. 1, 65–66 (1886). By 1907 the number had increased to forty. *Proc. Nat'l A. Ry. Commissioners, 19th Ann. Convention,* 263–67 (1907). By the end of World War I, all but one state had railroad regulatory commissions. *Proc. Nat'l A. Ry. Commissioners, 29th Ann. Convention,* Table B (1917); *Proc. Nat'l. A. Ry. Commissioners, 30th Ann. Convention,* 2 (1918). Writing at this time, I. Leo Sharfman described the national shift towards rail commissions:

> It had come to be recognized that both the punitive methods of judicial regulation and the spasmodic and inflexible methods of legislative regulation were ineffective. Only through the continuous and constructive activities of administrative commissions could such an adjustment of the relation between the carriers and the people be secured as would afford an adequate protection for private rights and a proper safeguard for public interests. And it had been found necessary to clothe these administrative commissions with plenary powers. Hence the Interstate Commerce Commission and the state railroad

commissions were of the mandatory type. They possessed extensive authority to enforce reasonable rates and to prevent discriminatory practices. I. Leo Sharfman, *The American Railroad Problem* (New York: Century, 1921), 53.

[53] Conventional wisdom explains this allocation in terms of "expertise," but it is not clear why rate regulation called for "expert knowledge," nor why that knowledge would not be accessible to the legislature (or its committees). It seems equally plausible to suggest that rate regulation was either too time consuming or too often in need of readjustment for legislatures to handle. Someone inclined toward the regulatory-capture thesis of Kolko (see Chapter 1) might argue that delegating rate setting to an administrative agency was motivated by a desire to remove the power from public visibility and place it in an institution that the industry could capture more easily.

[54] In that respect, the Court reflected what some think is a distinctively modern perspective. See Peter L. Strauss, "The Place of Agencies in Government: Separation of Powers and the Fourth Branch," *Colum. L. Rev.*, 84: 573, 578–79 (1984).

[55] Stone v. Farmers' Loan & Trust Co., 116 U.S. 307 (1886).

this reasoning could not be used to defeat a similar argument against the ICC—the federal government *had* to respect the separation—but history worked in an odd way to undercut the objection.

The legitimacy of the ICC was established at a time when it was charged with the task of enforcing prohibitions, almost common law in nature, against unjust and unreasonable rates. This required the Commission to perform something very close to a judicial function. Some objected to the absence of Article III protections for commissioners, including the absence of life tenure, but the argument was dismissed by a circuit court in *Kentucky & Indiana Bridge Co. v. Louisville & Nashville Railroad* (1889),[56] which held that the powers of the agency were not quite judicial. The commissioners were compared to "referees or special commissioners, appointed to make preliminary investigation of and report upon matters for subsequent judicial examination and determination."[57] Admittedly, a different kind of issue would be presented once the Commission was given the power to set rates, as it was in the Hepburn Act of 1906, for then it seemed as though the agency was exercising a legislative, rather than a judicial, function. By 1906, however, a kind of reverse-*Bolling v. Sharpe*[58] argument controlled: State railroad commissions were allowed to set rates, and it was unthinkable that the federal government should be denied the power to create an institutional arrangement that was allowed to the states.

Aside from the separation of powers problem, the emergence of the administrative agency created procedural problems and provoked an objection that, in contrast to the separation of powers one, was based on a guarantee unquestionably binding on the states: the duty rooted in the Fourteenth Amendment not to deprive any person of "life, liberty, or property, without due process of law." In the *Chicago, Milwaukee* case of 1890, the Court construed this duty to require that these new institutions conform their procedures to a judicial, rather than a legislative, model as a condition of making the rate established final and conclusive under state law. This

---

[56] 37 F. 567 (C.C.D. Ky. 1889). The opinion was written by Judge Howell Jackson, who was elevated to the Supreme Court four years later. An appeal was taken to the Supreme Court but was dismissed, apparently because the appellant failed to pay the cost of printing the record. 149 U.S. 777 (1893). In ICC v. Brimson, 154 U.S. 447 (1894), the Supreme Court indicated in dicta that it considered the Commission a quasi-judicial body which Congress had full authority to establish. Ibid., at 474. Brewer's dissent in *Brimson* is discussed in Chapter 3.

[57] 37 F. at 613.

[58] 347 U.S. 497 (1954), holding that the Due Process Clause of the Fifth Amendment imposed limitations on the federal government comparable to those imposed on the states in Brown v. Board of Education, 347 U.S. 483 (1954). The Court stated: "In view of our decision [in *Brown*] that the Constitution prohibits the states from maintaining racially segregated public schools, it would be unthinkable that the same Constitution would impose a lesser duty on the Federal Government." 347 U.S. at 500.

procedural requirement was seen as an important modification of *Munn*, provoking comment by the stalwarts of the Waite Court—a separate concurrence by Miller and a dissent by Bradley (joined by Gray and Lamar). Bradley's opinion began: "I cannot agree to the decision of the court in this case. It practically overrules *Munn v. Illinois. . . .*"[59]

The *Chicago, Milwaukee* case had its origin in the State of Minnesota's decision to delegate its rate regulation function to a commission, which was given the power to both set aside "unequal and unreasonable" rates and to prescribe both minimum and maximum rates. The commission declared that a rate of 3 cents a gallon for the shipment of milk was "unequal and unreasonable," and then went on to decide that the maximum reasonable rate was the top amount other shippers charged, 2½ cents. The state attorney general brought a mandamus action to enforce the commission's order. In response, the railroads challenged as an impermissible delegation of legislative power the legislature's decision to establish the commission and to entrust it with the rate regulation power. The railroads also claimed that the 2½-cent rate established by the commission denied investors a fair return on their capital. The rate was, so they argued, unreasonable and tantamount to a confiscation.

The state court found no impermissible delegation and, with specific reference to the confiscation claim, construed the statute in such a way as to deny any court (including itself) the power to inquire into the reasonableness of the maximum rate established by the commission.[60] According to the court's reading of the statute, the judgment of the commission was sufficiently "final" and "conclusive" to block judicial review of the reasonableness of the rate. (The presumption of finality afforded the agency's judgment was, so Justice Bradley later implied in his dissent,[61] the same enjoyed by the rates established by the legislature in *Munn*.)

---

[59] 134 U.S. at 461. One commentator described this case as "highly indecent . . . a most indefensible attempt at judicial legislation" and asserted that it constitutes an "overturning of the fundamental principles upon which all our American governments are founded." "Notes of Recent Decisions," *Am. L. Rev.*, 24: 488, 525, 522 (1890). See also William Draper Lewis, "Editorial Notes," *Am. L. Reg. & Rev.*, 40: 270, 276–80 (1892).

[60] 134 U.S. at 452.

[61] Bradley wrote:

It is complained that the decisions of the board are final and without appeal. So are the decisions of the courts in matters within their jurisdiction. There must be a final tribunal somewhere for deciding every question in the world. Injustice may take place in all tribunals. All human institutions are imperfect—courts as well as commissions and legislatures. Whatever tribunal has jurisdiction, its decisions are final and conclusive unless an appeal is given therefrom. The important question always is, what is the lawful tribunal for the particular case? In my judgment, in the present case, the proper tribunal was the legislature, or the board of commissioners which it created for the purpose.

Ibid., at 465 (Bradley, J., dissenting).

When the *Chicago, Milwaukee* case reached the Supreme Court, Justice Blatchford wrote the opinion for the majority, as he would two years later in *Budd*, but in *Chicago, Milwaukee* he was even more explicit in narrowing the reach of *Munn*. For him, *Munn* determined that the power to regulate rates was within the police power, but it did not preclude a challenge to some specific rate on the ground that the rate was confiscatory.[62] *Munn* did not create an irrebuttable presumption of validity, and states had to provide some means to challenge the rates set.

Underlying Blatchford's analysis was a belief that, whatever *Munn* may have held, the businessman had a right to a fair return on his investment and that it was the responsibility of the judiciary somehow to protect that right. The precise nature of the right of fair return was never made clear. Justice Miller wrote a separate concurrence in *Chicago, Milwaukee* speaking to just that issue, and he put forth a strong substantive conception of the right. For Miller, the right of fair return was grounded on the Due Process Clause of the Fourteenth Amendment, which, in the manner of the substantive due process decisions, was read to protect against arbitrary and unreasonable state action. Miller also assumed that state action that confiscated property or destroyed its value would, almost by definition, be unreasonable and arbitrary. For him, then, the right of fair return was substantive. It was protected, like any federal constitutional right, primarily through an injunctive proceeding in federal court, although sometimes it might be protected through a defense in a state proceeding brought to compel compliance with the regulation or punish a violation.[63] In either case,

---

[62] For this proposition he quoted the more recent *Stone* decision (see above, note 55):

> From what has thus been said, it is not to be inferred that this power of limitation or regulation is itself without limit. This power to regulate is not a power to destroy, and limitation is not the equivalent of confiscation. Under pretense of regulating fares and freights, the State cannot require a railroad corporation to carry persons or property without reward; neither can it do that which in law amounts to a taking of private property for public use without just compensation, or without due process of law.

134 U.S. at 455–56, quoting 116 U.S. at 331. The opinion in *Stone* was written by Chief Justice Waite, the author of *Munn*, but apparently it was Justice Stanley Matthews who insisted that these sentences be added. See John P.

Roche, *Sentenced to Life* (New York: Macmillan, 1974), 226–27, note 36. A precursor to the *Stone* dictum can be found in Waite's opinion in Spring Valley Water Works v. Schottler, 110 U.S. 347, 354 (1884). He there intimated that the Court might review rates themselves if the "authorities do not exercise an honest judgment, or if they fix upon a price which is manifestly unreasonable." Ibid., 354.

[63] Miller insisted that "the proper, if not the only, mode of judicial relief against the tariff of rates established by the legislature or by its commission, is by a bill in chancery asserting its unreasonable character and its conflict with the Constitution of the United States." 134 U.S. at 460 (Miller, J., concurring). He concurred in the judgment because, as noted in the text, he also believed that the businessman should be able to assert his federal claim defensively in a suit brought by the state to enforce the rate.

the question would be: Was the maximum rate so low as to deny investors a fair return on their capital?

Blatchford had, in my view, a much more modest conception of the status of the right he was creating. For him the so-called right, like the property right of *Board of Regents v. Roth*,[64] had only a shadowy existence calling for procedural, rather than substantive, protection. Blatchford's creation was closer to an interest than a right, not itself enforceable directly by an inquiry into the merits of the state's action; rather, it created and imposed certain procedural obligations on the state. The function of the federal courts was, according to Blatchford, not to determine whether the rate allowed a fair return but to enforce procedural guarantees.

Under *Chicago, Milwaukee* the businessman's interest in a fair return entitled him to an adversary hearing on the reasonableness of the rate set, and that hearing had to occur before the rate became final. In this regard, Blatchford found the Minnesota statute wanting:

> No hearing is provided for, no summons or notice to the company before the commission has found what it is to find and declared what it is to declare, no opportunity provided for the company to introduce witnesses before the commission, in fact, nothing which has the semblance of due process of law; and although, in the present case, it appears that, prior to the decision of the commission, the company appeared before it by its agent, and the commission investigated the rates charged by the company for transporting milk, yet it does not appear what the character of the investigation was or how the result was arrived at.[65]

Justice Blatchford did not require the commission to amend its procedure, nor did he order the commission to cure these defects. His strategy instead was to create, through a negative prohibition, strong incentives for such procedural reforms. He denied the state courts the power to enforce orders of the commission without first inquiring fully into the reasonableness of the rate. The Minnesota statute prevented the state courts from conducting this inquiry into reasonableness, and on this ground the statute was held a denial of due process.

Dissenting, Justice Bradley disputed the strong, substantive conception of the right of a fair return articulated by Miller in his concurrence and that some read into Blatchford's majority opinion:

> If not in terms, yet in effect, the present cases are treated as if the constitutional prohibition was, that no state shall take private property with-

---

[64] 408 U.S. 564 (1972) (holding that a nontenured state university professor had an insufficient property interest in his employment contract to justify a pre-termination hearing).

[65] 134 U.S. at 457.

out just compensation. . . . But there is no such clause in the constitution of the United States. The Fifth Amendment is prohibitory upon the federal government only, and not upon the state governments.[66]

The more modest conception of the right I attribute to Blatchford did not make Bradley much happier. Viewing the administrative agency simply as the delegate of the legislature, Bradley could not understand why that agency should be held to a higher procedural standard than was the legislature.

There was also reason to believe that the Court's position was unstable and that it created a dynamic that could lead in only one direction— toward Miller's position and a more serious modification of *Munn*. Bradley feared that Blatchford's federal *interest* in a fair return would soon mature into a federal *right* to a fair return that would be enforceable primarily by federal injunctive suits, where the issue would not be the adequacy of the commission's procedure but the adequacy of the rate. These suits, moreover, could not be confined to railroad commissions: Since the right was wholly federal and substantive, it would operate as a limitation on whatever instrumentality of the state set the rate, whether an administrative agency or the state legislature. The right of fair return would soon become, Bradley feared, a right against the state in the broadest sense of that term. Referring to the majority decision in *Chicago, Milwaukee*, one contemporary commentator lamented, "It is from that decision that I date the flood."[67]

In 1894, a few short years after *Chicago, Milwaukee* and *Budd v. New York*, Bradley's fears were realized in a series of decisions that constituted the most pronounced revision yet of *Munn*. Blatchford's interest in a fair return indeed was transformed into a substantive constitutional right, and the federal courts became fully charged with the duty of actively policing particular exercises of the rate regulation power. Rooted in *Chicago, Milwaukee*, particularly in the separate concurrence of Miller, this revisionist strategy came to final fruition in *Reagan v. Farmers' Loan & Trust Co.* (1894), *Smyth v. Ames* (1898), and perhaps most dramatically, *Ex parte Young* (1908).

II

In 1894, in *Reagan v. Farmers' Loan & Trust Co.*,[68] Brewer completed the radical revision of *Munn v. Illinois* foreshadowed by *Chicago, Milwaukee* and feared by Bradley. Brewer there formulated a doctrine that assured

---

[66] Ibid., 465.
[67] Charles M. Hough, "Due Process of Law—Today," *Harv. L. Rev.*, 32: 218,

228 (1919).
[68] 154 U.S. 362 (1894).

Cartoon by Emil Keppler, published in *Puck*, September 7, 1904,
dramatizing the extent of Standard Oil's influence over government.
One source of Keppler's imagery was probably Frank Norris's
highly popular novel, *The Octopus, A Story of California*,
published in 1901, which chronicled a struggle of wheat
growers against the Railroad Trust. (*Library of Congress*)

William Howard Taft during his tenure as a judge on the United States
Circuit Court of Appeals for the Sixth Circuit (1892–1900). He wrote
the circuit court opinion in the *Addyston Pipe* case (chapter 5),
lauded by a commentator "as one of the greatest, if not the greatest,
antitrust opinions in the history of the law." Robert H. Bork, *The
Antitrust Paradox*, 26. (*Harvard Law Art Collection*)

William Howard Taft during his service in the Philippines (1900–1904).
He served initially as president of the commission to organize the Philippine
civil government, then as the first civil governor. He explained: "I have
some hesitation in saying what I am about to say, for I know there are some
real missionaries in this company, and I may mistake the emotion, but I
sincerely believe I have the missionary spirit. I know I want to do these
people good." Quoted in *Green Bag*, 20: 345 (1908).
(*U.S. Army, Military History Institute*)

William Howard Taft (right) with President Theodore Roosevelt on the day of
Taft's inauguration as president, March 4, 1909. Taft was Roosevelt's choice
to head the Republican ticket in the 1908 election, but Roosevelt soon
became unhappy with many of Taft's policies and decided to run against
him in the 1912 election, thus splitting the Republican vote.
(*Theodore Roosevelt Collection, Houghton Library, Harvard University*)

"A Little Practical Railroading." Cartoon by W. A. Rogers published in the New York *Herald*, May 8, 1906, shortly before Congress passed the Hepburn Act of 1906, strengthening the Interstate Commerce Commission (chapter 7). At right, successfully pushing the administration toward full court review of decisions of the ICC and thus weakening the impact of the bill are John C. Spooner, senator from Wisconsin; Attorney General Philander C. Knox; Joseph B. Foraker, senator from Ohio; and Nelson W. Aldrich, senator from Rhode Island. At left, waving the administration on toward full judicial review is William B. Allison, senator from Iowa. (*Library of Congress*)

The bakery involved in *Lochner v. New York* (chapter 6). The bakery,
owned by Joseph Lochner, second from the right, was located on the
first floor of a building that once stood at 250 South Street,
Utica, New York. Between 1906 and 1909.
(*Anne Marie Lochner Brady, Clinton, New York*)

Louis D. Brandeis, who defended the Oregon maximum-hours law before the Supreme Court in *Muller v. Oregon* (chapter 6). The portrait was inscribed on May 3, 1914, "For Felix Frankfurter, with great appreciation and high hopes." (*Harvard Law Art Collection*)

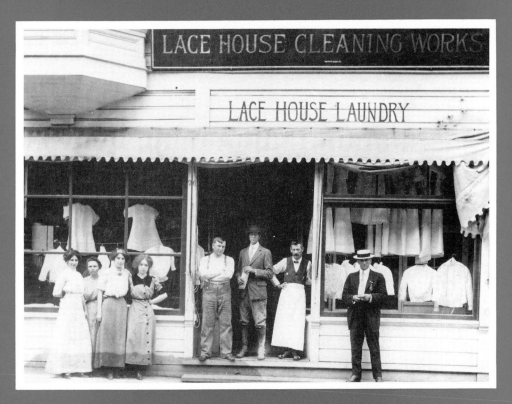

The laundry involved in *Muller v. Oregon*. The owner, Hans Muller, is standing in the doorway with his arms crossed. Between 1890 and 1916. (*Barbara Whisnant, Portland, Oregon*)

Josephine Goldmark, publication secretary of the National Consumers' League. Acting on behalf of the league, she recruited her brother-in-law, Louis D. Brandeis, to represent the State of Oregon in *Muller v. Oregon* and worked with him on the brief he submitted to the Supreme Court. (*Bryn Mawr College Archives*)

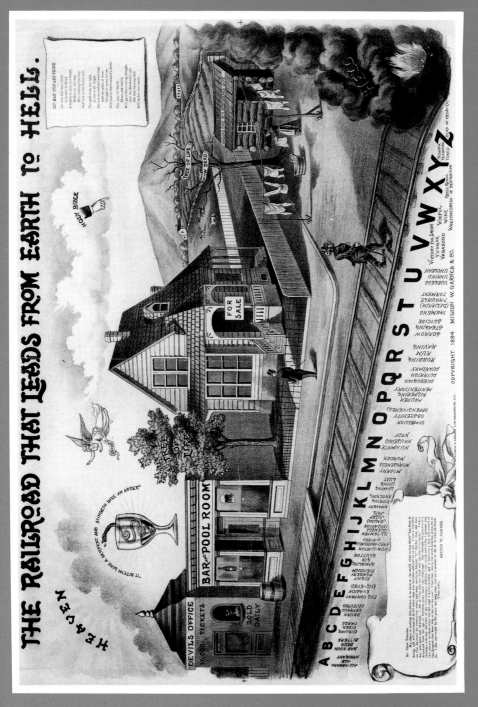

Lithograph by Andrew B. Graham for Milton W. Garnes & Co., 1894, advocating temperance.
(Library of Congress)

the entrepreneur a fair return on his investment. There was no doubt that the right he created—the right to a fair return—was entitled to the full federal protection against invasion by the state governments. By 1894, neither Bradley, Waite, nor any other justice especially committed to *Munn* remained, thus enabling Brewer to speak for a unanimous Court. The succession from the Waite Court to the Fuller Court was complete: Indeed, the unanimous decision of the Court in *Reagan* might be seen as the charter of this new institution. Inspired by the same considerations underlying his opinion in *Debs* and his speech at Albany, Brewer's opinion in *Reagan*, delivered at roughly the same time, reflected fully and forcefully the intellectual tradition that viewed property as the foundation of civilization.

Brewer grounded the right to a fair return and thus the protection against confiscation in "the spirit of common justice."[69] He directly confronted Bradley's earlier objection based on the absence of a Takings Clause in the Fourteenth Amendment (a regulation of the Texas railroad commission was at issue in *Reagan*), by reading the Equal Protection Clause as a protection against takings and thus the source of the right:

> It has always been a part of the judicial function to determine whether the act of one party (whether that party be a single individual, an organized body, or the public as a whole) operates to divest the other party of any rights of person or property. In every constitution is the guarantee against the taking of private property for public purposes without just compensation. The equal protection of the laws which, by the Fourteenth Amendment, no State can deny to the individual, forbids legislation, in whatever form it may be enacted, by which the property of one individual is, without compensation, wrested from him for the benefit of another, or of the public.[70]

In creating this new right Brewer did not deny the rate regulation power altogether, yet the emphasis had shifted decidedly from *Munn*—from a willingness to uphold a state power to a promise to protect against the tyranny of "the multitudes." Like liberty of contract and the rule of reason, doctrines that were to find favor over the next twenty years, Brewer's new right to a fair return placed bounds on the legislative power and was to be given specific content on a case-by-case basis.

In common law adjudication, the first case usually turns out to be the most appealing. It is not surprising, then, that the rate challenged in *Reagan*

---

[69] 154 U.S. at 410.
[70] Ibid., 399. Brewer elaborated on what he referred to as the "sacred and indestructible rights of compensation" in his 1891 commencement address at the Yale Law School. David J. Brewer, "Protection to Private Property from Public Attack" (New Haven: Hoggson & Robinson, 1891), 21.

deprived the railroad of any return at all. The earnings of the railroad were extremely poor—the stockholders never had received a dividend, and for the past three years the railroad had been unable to pay the interest on its debt. The rate set by the Texas commission would only have made things worse. It would have diminished earnings to the point where the railroad would have been unable to pay more than one-half the interest on its bonded debt. In these circumstances, there was no need to ponder the mysteries of how to determine whether a return was in fact "fair," for almost by definition, no return is not a fair one.[71]

In defending the regulation, counsel for Texas tried to justify the absence of any return. He pointed to the decline in prices and the depression affecting the industry and the nation in general; other railroads, he argued, had continued to operate at a loss. He also drew analogies to the postal service, which "not infrequently results in a loss."[72] But Brewer would have none of it. Although he recognized the special and public character of railroads (as opposed to grain elevators), and was for that reason prepared to tolerate state regulation of their rates, he required that the private dimension of the rail industry also be recognized. The investors in railroads, like investors in any business, were entitled to *some* return, said Brewer.

Although business interests won in *Reagan*, the courts were left with no standard for determining what constituted a fair return. Brewer said the investors were entitled to "some return"; but for cases in which there actually was "some return" he provided no guidance for determining whether it was "fair." Did the Constitution require a return of, say, 3, 6, or 12 percent? In any circumstance, this would be a difficult question, but in a setting dominated so thoroughly by the market it appeared downright impossible. In the market there is no "fair return" judged by some independent moral standard, but only the return that competition produces. Some might seek to construct the necessary standard of fairness from an inquiry into the returns from "comparable" investments, but such an inquiry is fraught with difficulties, for it requires choosing an appropriate industry for the comparison. In the case of railroads, those difficulties would be especially pronounced because the entire regulatory scheme was predicated on their special character: performing a unique state function (maintaining a public

---

[71] Brewer stopped short of a per se rule by acknowledging, at least nominally, that there might be some circumstances that would allow the state to regulate at a no-return level: "extravagance and a needless expenditure of money"; "waste in the management"; "enormous salaries"; "material and labor [purchased] at the highest price"; or gross mistakes in the locations of rail lines. 154 U.S. at 412. In another case, he chose a more colorful term to describe the exception to the *Reagan* rule: "rascality." Ames v. Union Pac. Ry., 64 F. 165, 177 (C.C.D. Neb. 1894) (Brewer, Circuit Justice), *aff'd sub nom.* Smyth v. Ames, 169 U.S. 466 (1898).

[72] 154 U.S. at 409.

highway), having a monopoly position, receiving important government subsidies.

Although the question left unresolved by *Reagan*—how to determine whether, as a constitutional matter, a return was in fact fair—was never answered satisfactorily during Fuller's tenure (or beyond), it was not for lack of effort. The issue was presented to the Court again in the late 1890s and resulted in a decision that remains the leading Supreme Court pronouncement on the subject. That case, *Smyth v. Ames*,[73] enlisted a number of prominent lawyers and public figures, including James C. Carter and William Jennings Bryan. A well-known author and leader of the New York bar, Carter appeared before the Court on numerous occasions.[74] Bryan had just lost the presidential election of 1896 but remained the standard-bearer of the Democratic Party and ran again for president in 1900 (and in 1908).

Smyth v. Ames involved a challenge to an 1893 statute of Nebraska. The circuit court invalidated the statute and enjoined its enforcement, and the Supreme Court unanimously affirmed, making only minor modifications. The lower court opinion was written by Brewer,[75] who not only did his share on the Court and lectured widely, but even managed to find time to ride circuit. Harlan was the author of the Supreme Court opinion,[76] but Brewer's influence was evident at every point. The principles announced by Brewer both in his opinion in *Reagan* and in his dissent in *Budd* were reaffirmed by Harlan; Harlan even quoted Brewer's circuit opinion in the case, as did counsel on both sides.[77] The result, however, was largely double-talk. After exhausting every avoidance technique, Harlan finally approached the crucial question, and this is what he had to say:

> The corporation may not be required to use its property for the benefit of the public without receiving just compensation for the services rendered by it. How such compensation may be ascertained, and what are the necessary elements in such an inquiry, will always be an embarrassing question.[78]

Some response.

---

[73] 169 U.S. 466 (1898).

[74] See Chapter 4, notes 3 and 4, Chapter 5, p. 119, and Chapter 10, p. 304.

[75] Ames v. Union Pac. Ry., 64 F. 165 (C.C.D. Neb. 1894). See above, note 71.

[76] Chief Justice Fuller did not participate in the case, and by the time the opinion was delivered—March 1898—Field had resigned. See above, note 38. Harlan was thus the senior justice and presumably assigned himself the opinion. It probably never occurred to Brewer to disqualify himself because of his involvement in the case at the circuit court level.

[77] Harlan primarily located the right of fair return in the Due Process Clause as opposed to the Equal Protection Clause, though the latter also was mentioned by Harlan at various points. Recall that in *Reagan* Brewer had made the Equal Protection Clause the primary textual base of the right.

[78] 169 U.S. at 546.

The primary avoidance technique of *Smyth v. Ames* was to bring the case within the terms of the "some return" rule of *Reagan*. Harlan tried valiantly—it took him almost a year to write the opinion[79]—to show that the investors in *Smyth v. Ames*, like those in *Reagan*, had received no return at all. In order to do so, he estimated what the impact of the rate reduction of the 1893 statute would have been on the earnings of the railroad for 1891, 1892, and 1893, the three fiscal years immediately preceding the enactment. He projected a 29.5 percent reduction in earnings as a result of the statutory rate and then compared the lowered earnings against operating expenses. Although this seemed sufficient to demonstrate that operating expenses were greater than earnings, for good measure he added a 10 percent premium to the operating expenses actually incurred, on the theory that the statute affected only local traffic and that local trips were more expensive to the railroad than through trips (the state had no power to regulate the fares on such trips). Justice Harlan also insisted on segregating the interstate and local aspects of the business, so that the profit on interstate business could not be used to estimate earnings on intrastate operations under the statutory rate. Oddly, he refused to consider the profitability of the business as a whole.[80]

Harlan's elaborate analysis worked for four of the seven railroads affected. Under the Nebraska statute, these four would have received no return at all and thus could claim the benefit of the rule of *Reagan* requiring "some return." With respect to them, the statute was clearly confiscatory.[81] There was some conflict in the evidence as to whether the statute would have forced another of the railroads, the Burlington, to operate at a loss; Harlan was willing to attribute this conflict in evidence to a misunderstanding.[82]

Still, two other railroads remained, the Fremont and the Union Pacific, and for them there was no escape from the fact that there was "some return" on their local business, no matter how hard and elaborately Harlan labored.[83] They forced Harlan to confront the issue left open by *Reagan*,

---

[79] Argued Apr. 5, 6, and 7, 1897; decided Mar. 7, 1898.

[80] 169 U.S. at 528–43.

[81] Ibid., 534–35.

[82] He suggested that the witnesses were talking about different periods and that the estimates of those witnesses claiming a 6 percent return covered a portion of 1892 in which, according to Harlan, "[t]here may have been an unusual amount of business." Ibid., at 539.

[83] Harlan wrote:

It appears, from what has been said, that if the rates prescribed by the act of 1893 had been in force during the years ending June 30, 1891, 1892 and 1893, the Fremont Company, in the years ending June 30, 1891, and June 30, 1893, and the Union Pacific Company, in the years ending June 30, 1892, and June 30, 1893, would each have received more than enough to pay operating expenses. Ibid., 543.

and when he did, he had virtually nothing to say. He ruled that the Nebraska statute could not be applied to these two railroads because the return that would result would be "too small" (his words),[84] but he afforded no insight into how he reached that determination. He did not disclose his standard for measuring fairness and thus left unresolved the central theoretical problem created by the very idea of a right of fair return.

In the closing paragraphs of the opinion in *Smyth v. Ames*, Harlan made a number of well-taken and relevant points, but none clarified the central issue. He argued, for example, that the railroads performed a state function and thus had a duty to the public as well as to private investors. The rights of the public, he claimed, had to be taken into consideration in determining whether a return was fair. He also said that the standard for measuring the value of private investment was the "fair value of the property." The fair value of the property would be used, according to Harlan, as the *base* for determining whether the return was fair.[85] What about the rate of return itself? On that issue, Harlan made a pass but got nowhere. He retreated into a definition of the fair value of the property (as opposed to a fair return) and his definition of fair value turned out to be nothing more than a laundry list—an incomplete one at that—of the factors that must be taken into consideration and be "given such weight as may be just and right in each case." The full text reads:

> We hold, however, that the basis of all calculations as to the reasonableness of rates to be charged by a corporation maintaining a highway under legislative sanction must be the fair value of the property being used by it for the convenience of the public. And in order to ascertain that value, the original cost of construction, the amount expended in permanent improvements, the amount and market value of its bonds and stocks, the present as compared with the original cost of construction, the probable earning capacity of the property under particular rates prescribed by statute, and the sum required to meet operating expenses, are all matters for consideration, and are to be given such weight as may be just and right in each case. We do not say that there may not be other matters to be regarded in estimating the value of the property. What the company is entitled to ask is a fair return upon the value of that which it employs for the public convenience.[86]

It is obvious that, in the end, Harlan had no answer whatsoever to what he referred to as the "embarrassing question": How should a court determine whether a return is fair? Anticipating Justice Potter Stewart's admission of failure in defining hard-core pornography ("I know it when I see

---

[84] Ibid., 547.
[85] Ibid., 544–46.

[86] Ibid., 546–47.

it"[87]), Harlan proclaimed in *Smyth v. Ames*: "Each case must depend upon its special facts."[88]

III

Reagan and the establishment of the right of fair return was the major strategy of the Court for revising and limiting *Munn v. Illinois*. It was the creation of Brewer, and, as already noted, bore a striking resemblance to *Debs*, also written by Brewer and informed by similar fears and concerns. *Debs* legitimated state power while *Reagan* curbed it, but the two decisions were not contradictory, only different manifestations of the same intellectual tradition. The social contract gave the state the duty to preserve the public order so as to ensure the enjoyment of property and simultaneously commanded it not to take or confiscate property. *Reagan* was also analogous to *Debs* inasmuch as it invited and contemplated an enlargement of the federal equity power. This expansion of federal jurisdiction constituted yet another restriction of *Munn*.

Having failed in *Reagan* and again in *Smyth v. Ames* in the impossible task of formulating a yardstick for a fair return, the Court fell back on emphasizing the "facts," a tack that might have accounted for the unanimity of the Court in decisions like *Smyth v. Ames*. This approach also had direct implications for how this new right was to be protected. First, it made it especially risky for the Court to leave the protection of the right to a jury, because it would be difficult for a judge in such a fact-oriented case to direct a verdict or to control juries through the use of instructions. It therefore became imperative in *Reagan* and *Smyth v. Ames*, as it was in *Debs*, to make the injunction available for vindicating the right of fair return: A jury would not sit in cases seeking an injunction against the enforcement of a statute or commission order setting rates. The rate regulation injunction therefore became as central a legal instrument at the turn of the century as the labor injunction, though the latter was more notorious.

Second, the absence of discernible standards and the emphasis upon the facts made it necessary for those asserting the right of a fair return to have some access to the federal trial courts—they had to be able to choose the federal court if they so wished. This view implicitly recognized that state court judges were less likely to invalidate a statute emanating from the political structure of which they were part. Even more, it reflected the difficulty of reviewing factual judgments by appellate courts and thus of ensuring conformity to national norms through federal intervention at the

---

[87] Jacobellis v. Ohio, 378 U.S. 184, 197 (1964) (Stewart, J., concurring).
[88] 169 U.S. at 546, quoting Covington & Lexington Tpke. Rd. Co. v. Sandford, 164 U.S. 578, 597 (1896).

appellate level. Because of its fact-specific quality, the right of fair return could be enforced throughout the nation only if the aggrieved citizen had procedural rights extending beyond an appeal to the Supreme Court. The citizen also needed to have his claim *tried* by a judge who had the independence provided by Article III and who was not an integral part of the political structure that gave rise to the citizen's grievance.

The need for access to a federal trial court was not so great in *Debs* as in *Reagan* because the threat to the substantive federal right involved in *Debs*—the free flow of goods—arose from a private association rather than a state agency. The enemy was the American Railway Union, not Texas or Nebraska. The happenstance of Illinois politics and the role of the national executive in the actual case made the federal courts the natural forum in *Debs*, but it was hard to generalize from that situation. In some situations, labor dominated local politics and controlled the judiciary, but absent such a showing, one could assume that the state courts would provide an adequate and appropriate forum for the labor injunction.[89] However, precisely because it was the state rather than some private party or organization that threatened the right invoked in *Reagan* (the right of a fair return), it also was more difficult for the Court to provide the needed access to federal courts.

In *Debs*, access to the federal equity court was blocked by traditional equity doctrines that remitted the aggrieved citizen to damages or a local prosecution. Equity was available only if these common law remedies were inadequate. This doctrine kept most labor cases in state courts, where common law remedies generally were provided. This doctrine was fully applicable in the *Reagan* context, and in addition, traditional principles of federalism, above all, the Eleventh Amendment, limited access to the federal courts for suits against states. These obstacles had to be surmounted in 1894 in the *Reagan* case itself when Brewer first created the right of fair return, and once again in 1898 in *Smyth v. Ames*, when Brewer, at the circuit court level, and then Harlan, in the Supreme Court, elaborated on that right. But the most dramatic test of the availability of the federal equity court came in 1908 in *Ex parte Young*, where the Court upheld the contempt conviction of the Minnesota attorney general for violating an order of a lower federal court restraining the enforcement of the state's rate statute.[90] Now Fuller turned to Peckham—that other Roman—to speak for the Court and continue the project Brewer had begun: waging battle with *Munn*.

In the rate regulation context, the state appeared in two guises: It threatened the right of fair return, but it also provided a mechanism to chal-

---

[89] On state court labor injunctions, see William E. Forbath, *Law and the Shaping of the American Labor Move-* *ment* (Cambridge: Harvard University Press, 1991), 59–66, 193–98.

[90] 209 U.S. 123 (1908).

lenge the reasonableness of rates. In a proceeding to compel compliance with the prescribed maximum rate, a railroad could, thanks to *Chicago, Milwaukee*, defend itself by attacking as unjust and unreasonable the rate fixed. This opportunity for entrepreneurs to defend themselves in a state court, however, created an obstacle to federal court jurisdiction not present in *Debs*: It enabled the state to insist that the businessman should use his defense in the state court proceeding, rather than the anticipatory federal suit, to protect the right of fair return. Such a demand could be predicated on the traditional equity doctrine that made an injunction unavailable whenever there was an adequate remedy at law.

The Supreme Court's initial response to this line of argument was to confine the inadequate-remedy-at-law doctrine to separate spheres of sovereignty: In judging whether the federal injunction was appropriate, only the remedies at law in the federal system would be considered.[91] The Court also justified the resort to the injunction on the theory that the state remedy (defending in a proceeding brought to enforce the rate) was inadequate. In *Smyth v. Ames*, the emphasis was placed on the ability of the injunction to avoid a multiplicity of suits.[92] In *Ex parte Young*, the emphasis was placed on the speed and the anticipatory quality of the injunction: Relief could be granted without the need for an actual statutory violation and prosecution.[93] Indeed, Justice Peckham, speaking for the Court in *Ex parte Young*, thought the sanctions of the Minnesota statute so "enormous" and "severe" as to render the statute invalid as a denial of due process, wholly apart from its impact on the right of fair return.[94] The promulgation of the rate by the legislature was not preceded by a hearing, and as a practical matter, the severity of the sanction denied the railroad the opportunity of testing the rates' sufficiency by violating the law and inviting prosecution.[95] (This seems an extension of the procedural principles of *Chicago, Milwaukee*, now applied to a legislature.)

It was not, however, the ancient doctrines of equity, but the principles of federalism, particularly the Eleventh Amendment, that presented the

---

[91] As Brewer wrote in *Reagan:*
So that if in any case, there should be any mistaken action on the part of a State, or its commission, injurious to the rights of a railroad corporation, any citizen of another State, interested directly therein, can find in the Federal court all the relief which a court of equity is justified in giving. 154 U.S. at 395.

[92] As Harlan put it, "A court of law could only deal with each separate transaction involving the rates to be charged for transportation." 169 U.S at 518. Harlan was assuming a suit by shippers, but if the state brought suit or was represented in the suit, there would be no reason why the judgment in law would have to be transaction-specific.

[93] 209 U.S. at 145–48.

[94] 209 U.S. at 147.

[95] Using an unaccustomed and striking turn of the word "wonderful," Peckham said: "It would not be wonderful if, under such circumstances, there would not be a crowd of agents offering to disobey the law. The wonder would be that a single agent should be found ready to take the risk." 209 U.S. at 164.

Chapter VII: *Rate Regulation*

more formidable obstacle to granting the federal injunction. The Eleventh Amendment, which by its terms provides that the judicial power of the United States does not extend to cases between a state and the citizens of another state, was construed by the Court in 1890 in *Hans v. Louisiana*[96] to be more than a mere limitation on federal court jurisdiction. According to Justice Bradley, who wrote the Court's opinion in that case, the Eleventh Amendment conferred sovereign immunity on the states, and thus protected a state from a suit brought by its own citizens.

In *Reagan*, Brewer dealt with the Eleventh Amendment issue through two interlocking strategies. The first was to find within the state statutory scheme a waiver of sovereign immunity. One provision of the Texas statute provided that a dissatisfied "railroad company . . . may file a petition in a court of competent jurisdiction in Travis County, Texas, against said commission as defendant."[97] Brewer, in an obvious reach, said that this language was broad enough to embrace the federal trial court: A federal court is "a court of competent jurisdiction in Travis County."[98] This attempt to demonstrate that the state consented to the suit and thus waived its immunity remained problematic because of doubt whether the sovereign immunity created by the Eleventh Amendment was in fact waivable. To avoid resolving that issue, Justice Brewer advanced another argument to overcome the Eleventh Amendment hurdle: The suit to enjoin the enforcement of the Texas regulation was not a suit against the state according to the meaning of the Eleventh Amendment. By way of amplification, Brewer stressed the absence of a pecuniary interest by the state and assumed that the Eleventh Amendment primarily protected the state's treasury. "Not a dollar will be taken from the treasury of the State," he said, "no pecuniary obligation of it will be enforced, none of its property affected by any decree which may be rendered."[99]

In *Smyth v. Ames*, Justice Harlan also had concluded that the federal injunctive suit to protect the right of fair return was not a suit against the state and thus not barred by the Eleventh Amendment. However, Harlan pursued a somewhat different mode of analysis from Brewer's in *Reagan*: Harlan personalized the wrong. A suit against a state officer to enjoin the

[96] 134 U.S. 1 (1890). Modern scholarship tends to take the view that the Eleventh Amendment was meant merely to impose a limit on the Article III grant of federal court jurisdiction over cases between states and citizens of other states and that it was not intended to confer sovereign immunity on the states or otherwise bar federal jurisdiction that arose under the so-called subject matter clauses, such as the clause authorizing federal question jurisdiction. See William A. Fletcher, "A Historical Interpretation of the Eleventh Amendment: A Narrow Construction of an Affirmative Grant of Jurisdiction Rather Than a Prohibition Against Jurisdiction," *Stan. L. Rev.*, 35: 1033 (1983).

[97] 154 U.S. at 392 (quoting 1891 Tex. Gen. Laws 55, 58–59).

[98] Ibid.

[99] Ibid., 390.

enforcement of an unconstitutional statute was not, according to Harlan, a suit against the state but a suit against the state official as an individual to prevent him from committing a trespass. As he put it,

> It is the settled doctrine of this court that a suit against individuals for the purpose of preventing them as officers of a State from enforcing an unconstitutional enactment to the injury of the rights of the plaintiff, is not a suit against the State within the meaning of [the Eleventh] Amendment.[100]

From this perspective, *Ex parte Young* appears to be nothing more than a routine application of the principles established by *Reagan* and *Smyth v. Ames*. Peckham disposed of the Eleventh Amendment objection to the federal injunctive suit under a theory that seemed identical to Harlan's, although he spoke more metaphorically:

> If the act which the state Attorney General seeks to enforce be a violation of the Federal Constitution, the officer in proceeding under such enactment comes into conflict with the superior authority of that Constitution, and he is in that case stripped of his official or representative character and is subjected in his person to the consequences of his individual conduct.[101]

But this decision was perceived as hardly routine. The reaction was strong and stormy.[102] It was denounced in the August 1908 annual meeting of state attorneys general,[103] and one commentator lamented, "Is there any limit to the possible interference by the judiciary?"[104]

Some of this reaction may be attributed to a coincidence of timing: *Ex parte Young* was decided in an extraordinary term—almost a replay of 1895. In the spring of 1895 the Court had handed down *E. C. Knight*, *Debs*, and *Pollock*, and the spring of 1908 produced another stunning threesome: *Adair v. United States*,[105] which held as invalid the provision of the Erdman Act barring yellow dog contracts; the *Danbury Hatters Case*,[106] which applied the Sherman Act to organized labor; and the *Employers' Liability*

---

[100] 169 U.S. at 518–519.

[101] 209 U.S. at 159–160.

[102] See Charles Warren, *The Supreme Court in United States History*, rev. ed. (Boston: Little, Brown, 1926), 2: 716–17.

[103] Report of the meeting of the Association of the Attorneys-General of the United States, *Cent. L.J.*, 67: 265 (1908).

[104] Clifford Thorne, "Will the Supreme Court Become the Supreme Legislature of the United States?," *Am. L. Rev.*, 43: 228, 241 (1909).

[105] 208 U.S. 161 (1908). See Chapter 6.

[106] Loewe v. Lawlor, 208 U.S. 274 (1908).

Chapter VII: *Rate Regulation*

Cases,[107] which invalidated a statute abolishing the fellow-servant rule and other common law defenses for work-related injuries. *Ex parte Young* seemed part of this same general pattern; it enlarged the jurisdiction of the federal courts so as to enable them to review rate regulations of the states in the name of protecting the right of a fair return. Some of the reaction to *Young* also was attributable to political changes then occurring, specifically the ascendancy of the progressive movement. Doctrines that might have been acceptable in the 1890s were especially objectionable in a political culture dominated by Theodore Roosevelt and progressivism. There was in addition the inflammatory spectacle of a federal court holding a state attorney general in criminal contempt for performing what ostensibly was his legal duty, namely enforcing a duly enacted statute of his state.[108] Finally, account should be taken of the innovation in legal doctrine wrought by *Ex parte Young*.[109] It is doubtful whether the public cared greatly about such matters, but doctrinal concerns might explain why Harlan, who joined *Reagan* and authored *Smyth v. Ames*—the primary precedents for *Ex parte Young*—filed a remarkable dissent in that case, one as passionate and yet as lonely as the dissents he filed in the *Civil Rights Cases* and *Plessy*.[110]

To understand Harlan's position and the division in the Court, we must return to the late 1890s and a case called *Fitts v. McGhee*,[111] in which a businessman who owned a toll bridge sought a federal injunction to pro-

---

[107] 207 U.S. 463 (1908). The Court held that Congress had exceeded its powers under the Commerce Clause because the measure was not properly confined to businesses engaged in interstate commerce at the time of injury. As the Court put it, Congress was not allowed to regulate the master–servant relationship "without qualification or restriction as to the business in which the carriers or their employees may be engaged at the time of injury." 207 U.S. at 498. Subsequently, the statute was amended, and the Court upheld it. Second Employers' Liability Cases, 223 U.S. 1 (1912).

[108] Senator Bacon of Georgia put his objection in these terms:

It is utterly inconceivable that it was contemplated in the formation of the Federal Government that a Federal judge could under the Constitution which was being formed, arrest the laws of a State, and put the officer of the State engaged in the enforcement of the laws of the State in the custody of the marshal of the court and fine and imprison him for not obeying its sovereign order! How many States would have ratified the Constitution with such a provision plainly written in it? It is safe to say not one.

42 Cong. Rec. 4853, 60th Cong., 1st Sess. (1908).

[109] See generally William F. Duker, "Mr. Justice Rufus W. Peckham and the Case of *Ex parte Young*: Lochnerizing *Munn v. Illinois*," *B.Y.U. L. Rev.*, 1980: 539, 555.

[110] Even Holmes, the other "great dissenter," joined Peckham's opinion. Referring to "state requirements to carry below cost," Holmes acknowledged, "it is a class of legislation in which I am more ready to interfere than some others." Holmes to Frankfurter, Apr. 16, 1915, Holmes Papers, Harvard Law School Library Manuscript Division.

[111] 172 U.S. 516 (1899).

tect his right of fair return. The suit was dismissed on Eleventh Amendment grounds by the Supreme Court. Writing for a unanimous Court, Harlan distinguished cases like *Reagan* and *Smyth v. Ames* in terms of the generality of the office held by the defendant. *Fitts* was brought against the attorney general of Alabama and the local law enforcement official (the solicitor of the Eleventh Judicial Circuit of the State), while the suits in *Reagan* and *Smyth v. Ames* were brought against officials of the administrative agencies charged specifically with the enforcement of the statute.[112] Harlan emphasized that neither of the state officers named as defendants in *Fitts* held any special relation to the challenged statute. "They were not," he wrote, "expressly directed to see to its enforcement."[113] The defendants in *Smyth v. Ames* and *Reagan* were, on the other hand, "specially charged with the execution of a state enactment alleged to be unconstitutional. . . ."[114]

At the time *Fitts v. McGhee* was announced, the "specially charged" rule of that case might have appeared only as a pleading requirement. As such, it would require that the proper party defendant in a federal injunctive suit should not be the general law enforcement official but the agency charged specifically with the enforcement of the maximum rate law. The issue was simply who should be named defendant in the complaint. To so read *Fitts*, however, one must assume that there was in fact a specially charged official in the enforcement scheme—an assumption that might have been valid in *Fitts* (the reported opinion is unilluminating on this point) but did not hold true in *Ex parte Young*.

In *Ex parte Young* there was no specially charged official; the regulatory scheme of Minnesota did not designate any state official with the duty of enforcing the maximum rate statute.[115] The duty of enforcement fell presumably to the attorney general, as part of his general duties to enforce the law. In discharge of that duty, the Minnesota attorney general brought a mandamus proceeding to compel compliance with the statute and, for that very act, became the subject of the federal injunction.[116] This connection between the attorney general and the state statute was not, according to Harlan, sufficient to satisfy the *Fitts* specially-charged rule because it would destroy the immunity that the Bradley had labored so hard in *Hans v. Louisiana* to create:

---

[112] In *Reagan*, the administrative agency implementing the statute was the Texas railroad commission and in *Smyth v. Ames* it was the Nebraska State Board of Transportation.

[113] 172 U.S. at 530.

[114] Ibid., 529.

[115] Conceivably, the statute's provision for severe criminal sanctions was intended to make it virtually self-executing.

[116] This procedure also was used in *Chicago, Milwaukee* (1890) (see above, note 15), which tends to cast doubt on Duker's evasion thesis—that only after *Fitts* did states seek to avoid lodging enforcement duty in any particular agent or officer. See Duker, "Mr. Justice Rufus W. Peckham," 555.

Chapter VII: *Rate Regulation*

If, because they were law officers of the State, a case could be made for the purpose of testing the constitutionality of the statute, by an injunction suit brought against them, then the constitutionality of every act passed by the legislature could be tested by a suit against the Governor and the Attorney General, based upon the theory that the former as the executive of the State was, in a general sense, charged with the execution of all its laws, and the latter, as Attorney General, might represent the State in litigation involving the enforcement of its statutes. That would be a very convenient way for obtaining a speedy judicial determination of questions of constitutional law which may be raised by individuals, but it is a mode which cannot be applied to the States of the Union consistently with the fundamental principle that they cannot, without their assent, be brought into any court at the suit of private persons. If their officers commit acts of trespass or wrong to the citizen, they may be individually proceeded against for such trespasses or wrong. Under the view we take of the question, the citizen is not without effective remedy, when proceeded against under a legislative enactment void for repugnancy to the supreme law of the land; for, whatever the form of proceeding against him, he can make his defense upon the ground that the statute is unconstitutional and void. And that question can be ultimately brought to this court for final determination.[117]

Harlan's protest was of no consequence. Peckham prevailed, and *Ex parte Young* opened the doors of the federal equity court wider than they had been in *Reagan* or *Smyth v. Ames*. The federal right asserted in *Young* reflected the social contract tradition's concern for property by assuring businessmen a fair return on their investment, but there was no way to confine the federal injunction to the protection of that right alone. It had to extend to the full breadth of the Fourteenth Amendment, and in that way *Young* achieved a more enduring significance. Together with *Debs*, *Ex parte Young* laid the foundation for the civil rights injunction of the 1960s by providing direct access to the federal courts for those attacking the laws of the southern states.[118] It is thus ironic to find Harlan, who largely established his fame by his dissenting opinions in the *Civil Rights Cases* and *Plessy*, also dissenting in *Ex parte Young*, and doing so with such bitterness—and with so little reason.

Harlan believed in the powers of the national government. As we saw in the analysis of his role in antitrust cases discussed in Chapter 5, particularly in his dissent in *E. C. Knight*, Harlan allowed the national legislature wide and sweeping powers. He acknowledged the supremacy of federal law, statutory or constitutional, and as he said in his dissent in *Ex parte Young*

---

[117] 209 U.S. at 192–93 (Harlan, J., dissenting) (entire passage is quoting *Fitts*, 172 U.S. at 530).

[118] See Owen M. Fiss, *The Civil Rights Injunction* (Bloomington: Indiana University Press, 1978), 1–5, 20–25.

itself, he contemplated an important role for the federal courts to adjudicate federal claims; he thought it appropriate for the Supreme Court to have the power to review the validity of state statutes. What he objected to in *Young* was the enhanced role of the federal *trial* courts. Yet that role was predicated on the federal status of the right allegedly infringed and, as a practical matter, was required by basic concerns of remedial efficacy and by the standardless, fact-oriented quality of the rules that he had helped to create. A right such as the one announced in *Smyth v. Ames*, which made everything depend on a determination as to whether a return was "too small," could never become a national right without a heavy reliance on the federal trial courts. The right demanded the remedy.

IV

Over the twenty years of Fuller's chief justiceship, the Court sustained an assault on one of the most venerable precedents of the post–Civil War era: *Munn v. Illinois*. The decision in *Ex parte Young* in 1908 was only the last phase in that process and did no more than create a procedural instrument—the federal injunction—to protect the substantive right that the Court had created in the early 1890s. *Ex parte Young* took on a special significance in the Court's history, however, because a few years later Congress responded to it specifically. Congress enacted Section 17 of the Mann-Elkins Act of 1910, which reconfigured the federal trial bench by requiring three judges, rather than one, to issue injunctions against the enforcement of state statutes.[119]

---

[119] 36 Stat. 539, 557 (1910). For discussion of this section of the Act, see David P. Currie, "The Three-Judge District Court in Constitutional Litigation," *U. Chi. L. Rev.*, 32: 1, 4–8 (1964). The principal purpose of the Mann-Elkins Act was to establish the commerce court, which was given exclusive jurisdiction for reviewing orders of the ICC, subject to review by the Supreme Court. The court was soon abolished. See George E. Dix, "The Death of the Commerce Court: A Study in Institutional Weakness," *Am. J. Legal Hist.*, 8: 238–60 (1964), and Felix Frankfurter and James M. Landis, *The Business of the Supreme Court: A Study in the Federal Judicial System* (New York: Macmillan, 1928), 153–74. The Mann-Elkins Act also modified the Commerce Act of 1887 by tightening the provision regarding long-haul/short-haul discrimination and extending the coverage of the Act to reach telegraph, telephone, and cable companies and express and sleeping-car companies. The ICC was also made self-initiating. The three-judge court provision was inserted at the eleventh hour. The bill that became the Mann-Elkins Act passed the House without any provision limiting the power of the federal courts to issue injunctions. On June 2, 1910, the day before the Senate passed its version of the bill, Senator Overman of

Chapter VII: *Rate Regulation*

The federal injunction legitimated by *Ex parte Young* was not confined to the right of fair return but extended to the full scope of the Fourteenth Amendment. The 1910 provision was written in equally broad terms, covering any federal constitutional challenge to a state statute. In other respects, however, the statute was limited narrowly. For one thing, it only applied to the issuance of interlocutory injunctions, specifically preliminary injunctions, and did not apply to permanent injunctions or temporary restraining orders. This limitation made sense in terms of *Ex parte Young* itself, which involved a preliminary injunction, and could be justified in terms of the procedural shortcomings of those injunctions, which are intended to preserve the status quo during the course of a judicial hearing and are issued without a full adversary hearing. Moreover, the 1910 measure did not bar the issuance of preliminary injunctions against the enforcement of a state statute, but instead required only that they be issued by three federal judges rather than one.[120]

What Congress hoped to gain from increasing the size of the bench from one to three is not clear. Increasing the number of judges might be understood as a way of minimizing the risk of error—three heads are better than one. It might also have been a cosmetic gesture—it was less of an affront to the states to have three judges rather than one enjoin the enforcement of a state statute. But these explanations hardly seem credible. More likely, Congress's decision to increase the number of judges was offered as a political sop to those forces, particularly westerners and southerners, who were offended by the role of the federal courts in enforcing the supremacy of federal law and who sought a more drastic curtailment of their

---

North Carolina proposed an amendment that was to become Section 17 of the Act. 45 Cong. Rec. 7253–54, 61st Cong., 2d Sess. (1910). Senator Sutherland objected to the amendment, although he did express sympathy for the need for such a limitation on the power of the federal courts. He complained that this amendment dealt not only with the railroads, but "all classes of cases." He claimed that such a provision "ought to be considered by itself," and he also noted that such a bill was pending before the Senate and was being received favorably. Ibid., 7254. Nevertheless, the amendment was adopted as part of the railroad bill. When the Sen-

ate amendments were reported back to the House, Congressman Bartlett of Georgia applauded the amendment: "That is something we have insisted on time and time again in this House and in the Senate, and if the bill contained no other provision than that, it is a long stride in an effort to prevent a United States court from destroying the rights of a State. . . ." Ibid., 7575.

[120] The number three was in all likelihood borrowed from the number of judges then on each circuit court of appeals. Circuit Court of Appeals Act, 26 Stat. 826 (1891), described in Chapter 2.

powers.[121] The idea was simply that it would be harder to get three judges than one to agree to issue an injunction.

Although the practical significance of the 1910 measure is hard to gauge,[122] it seems clear that the revision attempted by Congress was slight. The substantive right announced by *Reagan* was not touched; even the limits placed by statute on the procedural right were, despite Harlan's urgent pleas, the least imaginable: an increase in the number of judges from one to three. Indeed, the revision could be seen as being so trivial as to represent an implicit affirmation of the doctrinal regime created by Brewer in *Reagan* and Peckham in *Ex parte Young* to curb the rate regulation power legitimated by *Munn*. As Senator Elkins, one of the sponsors of the 1910 Act, asserted, obviously overstating the matter, "A man should fix the price on property he owns and has for sale, and no one else."[123] In this respect, the requirement in the 1910 Act for a three-judge court bears a striking resemblance to the Clayton Act of 1914, Congress's ambivalent response to the

---

[121] This hostility was long standing. See Tony A. Freyer, "The Federal Courts, Localism, and the National Economy, 1865–1900," *Bus. Hist. Rev.*, 53: 343 (1979). After 1900 it continued unabated and resulted in many proposals, largely from southerners and westerners, to curb the federal courts. See, e.g., 37 Cong. Rec. 151, 58th Cong., 1st Sess. (1903) (Congressman Stephens of Texas); 40 Cong. Rec. 1670, 59th Cong., 1st Sess. (1906) (Senator Patterson of Colorado); 41 Cong. Rec. 329, 59th Cong., 2d Sess. (1906) (Senator Carmack of Tennessee); 42 Cong. Rec. 115, 60th Cong., 1st Sess. (1907) (Congressman Garrett of Tennessee); and ibid., 133–34 (memorial from legislature of Nebraska denouncing "the right of interstate railroad corporations to oppress in the Federal courts, state and other local governments by invoking injunction to prevent the collection of taxes."). After the decisions in *Ex parte Young*, the pace of such proposals accelerated noticeably. See ibid., 4847 (Senator Overman's version of bill S. 3732, the precursor to Section 17 of the Mann-Elkins Act); 44 Cong. Rec. 101, 61st Cong., 1st Sess. (1909) (Congressman Kitchin of North Carolina); ibid., 103 (Congressman Patterson of South Carolina); ibid., 130 (Senator Scott of West Virginia); ibid.,

1363 (Congressman Hardwick of Georgia); and ibid., 4852 (Congressman Henry of Texas).

[122] Putting aside the peculiar history of the Fifth Circuit during the civil rights era (see Jack Bass, *Unlikely Heroes* [New York: Simon & Schuster, 1981; repr. Tuscaloosa: University of Alabama Press, 1990]), I suspect that over time Section 17 had its greatest impact through its limitation on the capacity of the Supreme Court to control its own docket. During much of the modern period, the appeal provisions of the 1910 Act stood as an important exception to the jurisdictional structure that gave the Supreme Court discretion over the cases it reviewed. It should be noted, however, that the direct appeal provisions of the 1910 statute, 36 Stat. at 557, were not a procedural innovation at the time. The Circuit Court of Appeals Act of 1891 (see above, note 120) provided for direct appeals from the trial courts to the Supreme Court in all cases involving constitutional or jurisdictional cases. 26 Stat. at 827–28. See also the Expediting Act of 1903, 32 Stat. 823, and the Criminal Appeals Act of 1907, 34 Stat. 1246, following a similar pattern of direct appeals. See Chapter 2.

[123] 45 Cong. Rec. 6199, 61st Cong., 2d Sess. (1910). Congressman Mann voiced

labor injunction sanctioned by *Debs*,[124] and to the antitrust doctrine promulgated by *Standard Oil* and *American Tobacco*.[125]

Of course, criticism of the Court's actions in the early 1900s was not confined to formal politics—Congress's institutional response was not the whole of the reaction against Brewer's and Peckham's enterprise. Outside the legislative halls, the Court was faulted, and such criticism grew with the progressive movement, becoming ultimately an important factor in the election of 1912.[126] But we can see in the modesty of the 1910 Act, as we saw in the Clayton Act of 1914, broad acceptance by Congress of both the method and many of the values implicit in the Court's decisions. No one disputed the right of a fair return, though many believed that in fact it had been respected by the regulators.[127] One can also see in those muted legislative responses to the Fuller Court's work the ambivalence inherent in progressivism. Progressives were committed to reform but only within the established framework, which, so it turned out, was constructed and legitimated by the very institution they often portrayed as The Enemy.

---

similar sentiments in the debates over the 1910 Act: "Congress cannot take away from the courts a judicial power given to them under the Constitution, and the courts have the power to prevent the legislative body from confiscating the property of the railroad companies, a confiscation that might come through putting the rate so low that the property would be practically confiscated." Ibid., 4572.

[124] See Chapters 3 and 4.
[125] See Chapter 5.
[126] See Chapter 1.
[127] In the Minnesota Rate Cases, 230 U.S. 352 (1913), the Court once again reaffirmed the broad principle that railroad property cannot be placed at the mercy of legislative caprice but must rest secure under the constitutional protection of the right to receive a fair return. Yet at this point the Court began to shift direction. It put a high burden of proof on the railroads and held that for two of the three railroads whose rates were challenged the evidence was insufficient to justify a finding that the rates were confiscatory. As to the third railroad, however, the Court found the rate set was confiscatory.

PART FOUR

The Concept of the Nation

CHAPTER VIII

The American Empire?

W HAT IS THE STATE? Thus far I have viewed the state as an institution brought into being by a community and entrusted with the
coercive power necessary to achieve a number of discrete ends. To invoke
the language of classical liberalism, a language especially fitting for the historical period under consideration, the focus has been primarily on the
relationship between the state and civil society, the state's constituting
body. We have examined the interaction between the Court and the populist and progressive movements and have seen how the Court, in the name
of liberty, tried to limit the power of the state over the individuals and
groups that empowered it. Such a view, however, ignores the relationship
among states, on either a federal or international level. Indeed, once we
consider the American political system as a whole, and locate it within
the world context, we realize that there is not one but many institutions
entrusted with this coercive power and properly entitled to be called "the
state." This multiplicity of states, interacting with one another, creates
a network of relationships that sets bounds upon the power of each.
No state stands alone but each is part of a community of states, and the
power of any state is in part defined by the relationships it has to other
states.

One set of governmental relationships, discussed in the next chapter,
concerns the relationship between the United States, as a single entity, and
the various states of the Union. On this subject, which falls under the rubric
of federalism, the contribution of the Fuller Court was one of consolida-
tion. The overarching development of the nineteenth century, rooted in the
work of the Marshall Court and painfully tested, and ultimately affirmed,
by the Civil War, denied the sovereignty of the states and made the central
government the sole repository of sovereignty. The Fuller Court acknowledged this development and ultimately embraced it: all power to the nation.
With respect, however, to governmental relationships concerning communities that arguably stood outside the Union but were members of the global
community, the contribution of the Fuller Court was more distinctive. That
is the subject of this chapter.

These societies were not at the time, either culturally or politically,
part of the state structure that constitutes the United States. They were sep-

arate cultural and political entities whose dominion was transferred to or acquired by the United States. The question they raised was one not of federalism but of imperialism, specifically whether the United States lawfully could acquire or hold these communities and rule them without intending to make them states. This issue forced the Fuller Court to define the character of the American nation in a way that no other Court has had to, at least not with the same sharpness or exigency. The justices responded in a series of decisions collectively referred to as the *Insular Cases*,[1] decisions that helped shape national identity and secure a unique place in history for the Fuller Court.

America embarked on the Spanish–American War in 1898. The war was short, lasting only a few months. Even more important, victory was decisive. People spoke of the Spanish–American War as "a splendid little war."[2] It was triggered by what appeared to be an attack on the United States battleship *Maine* in Havana harbor, and although at first some pleaded for patience and self-restraint, those voices were soon overwhelmed. The war was extremely popular, bringing news to the American people of Theodore Roosevelt's Rough Riders and Commodore Dewey's spectacular victory over the Spanish armada in Manila Bay. In contrast to the Civil War, or more recently, the Vietnam War, the conduct of the war itself did not provoke great public or legal controversy. But controversy there was—over the spoils of victory.

Throughout the nineteenth century, territorial expansion was an important issue for American politics, and strong forces were arrayed on both sides.[3] The westward expansion seemed to have stopped a decade

---

[1] In De Lima v. Bidwell, 182 U.S. 1, 2 (1901), the Court used the term "Insular Tariff Cases" to refer to that case and the four others argued with it: Dooley v. United States, 182 U.S. 222 (1901); Armstrong v. United States, 182 U.S. 243 (1901); Downes v. Bidwell, 182 U.S. 244 (1901); and Dooley v. United States, 183 U.S. 151 (1901). Two other cases that might be included in this series are Goetze v. United States, 182 U.S. 221 (1901), and Fourteen Diamond Rings v. United States, 183 U.S. 176 (1901). Later the Court pursued the issue of territorial power in Hawaii v. Mankichi, 190 U.S. 197 (1903); Kepner v. United States, 195 U.S. 100 (1904); Dorr v. United States, 195 U.S. 138 (1904); and Rassmussen v. United States, 197 U.S. 516 (1905).

[2] John Hay, ambassador to the Court of St. James's, wrote to then-colonel Theodore Roosevelt: "It has been a splendid little war; begun with the highest motives, carried on with magnificent intelligence and spirit, favored by that Fortune which loves the brave." William Roscoe Thayer, *The Life and Letters of John Hay* (Boston: Houghton Mifflin, 1915), 2: 337. On the war more generally, see Lewis L. Gould, *The Spanish–American War and President McKinley* (Lawrence: University Press of Kansas, 1982), and David F. Trask, *The War with Spain in 1898* (New York: Macmillan, 1981).

[3] See generally Ray A. Billington and Martin Ridge, *Westward Expansion: A History of the American Frontier*, 5th ed.

226

before the Civil War, when the nation reached its present continental boundaries. Alaska was purchased from Russia in 1867, and then no new territories were acquired for some thirty years. Shortly after his inauguration in March 1897, President McKinley pledged that he would oppose "all acquisitions of territory not on the mainland."[4] But with the victory over Spain in hand, McKinley did an about-face—with the aid, he said, of divine guidance.[5]

In the peace treaty of 1898, Spain forfeited all rights to Cuba, and the United States established there an interim military government (dissolved in 1902).[6] In the case of Puerto Rico and the Philippines, however, Ameri-

---

(New York: Macmillan, 1982), and R. W. Van Alstyne, *The Rising American Empire* (New York: Oxford University Press, 1960). For a work on the territorial system focusing on the main subject of this chapter—governmental structure—see Jack E. Eblen, *The First and Second United States Empires: Governors and Territorial Government, 1784–1912* (Pittsburgh: University of Pittsburgh Press, 1968).

[4] Quoted in Samuel E. Morison, Henry S. Commager, and William E. Leuchtenberg, *The Growth of the American Republic*, 7th ed. (New York: Oxford University Press, 1980), 2: 249.

[5] McKinley explained his change of heart this way:

I walked the floor of the White House night after night until midnight; and I am not ashamed to tell you, gentlemen, that I went down on my knees and prayed Almighty God for light and guidance more than one night. And one night late it came to me this way—I don't know how it was, but it came: (1) that we could not give them back to Spain—that would be cowardly and dishonorable; (2) that we could not turn them over to France or Germany—our commercial rivals in the Orient—that would be bad business and discreditable; (3) that we could not leave them to themselves— they were unfit for self-government— and they would soon have anarchy and misrule over there worse than Spain's was; and (4) that there was nothing left for us to do but to take

them all, and to educate the Filipinos, and uplift and civilize and Christianize them, and by God's grace do the very best we could by them as our fellow-men for whom Christ also died. And then I went to bed, and went to sleep and slept soundly.

Quoted in James F. Rhodes, *The McKinley and Roosevelt Administrations, 1897–1909* (New York: Macmillan, 1922), 106–107. On the political history of the period more generally, see Margaret Leech, *In the Days of McKinley* (New York: Harper & Bros., 1959), and H. Wayne Morgan, *William McKinley and His America* (Syracuse: Syracuse University Press, 1963).

[6] The Cuban Constitution of 1902 contained a provision—referred to as the Platt Amendment—that allowed the United States to intervene and to buy or lease land for naval bases. William Everett Kane, *Civil Strife in Latin America: A Legal History of U.S. Involvement* (Baltimore: Johns Hopkins University Press, 1972), 45–46. United States troops returned to Cuba in 1906 to suppress a rebellion and remained in control until 1909, at which time the second Republic was established. Rhodes, *McKinley and Roosevelt Administrations*, 364–66. The United States military intervened in 1912 and again in 1917, to quell uprisings and thus protect American-owned businesses. See Russell H. Fitzgibbon, *Cuba and the United States, 1900–1935* (Menasha, Wis.: George Banta Publishing, 1935), 149–50, 156–61.

can ambitions were more grandiose. These territories were acquired as colonies, thereby raising with new force the question whether the American nation could be transformed into an empire, with all that term implies. In Puerto Rico, the transference of dominion brought to an abrupt end the measure of autonomy Spain had granted to the island in 1897; in the Philippines the insurrection that had begun against Spanish rule was redirected toward the United States. The spoils of victory were a colony and a rebellion.[7] During the same period Hawaii requested, and was granted, annexation by the United States.[8] It was not, however, Hawaii or Alaska or the continental territories but the newly acquired Spanish colonies that presented the question of empire in the most urgent form.[9] Unlike Hawaii and Alaska, they were acquired by conquest; unlike the continental territories, they were not expected to become states. To borrow a memorable phrase from Fuller, one of his very few, each was to be governed like a "disembodied shade."[10]

Much of the debate, in the Court and the body politic, was conducted under the heading: "Does the Constitution follow the flag?"[11] But for the justices—for a Court that rendered decisions such as Lochner,[12] Reagan,[13] Pollock,[14] and Debs[15]—this formulation itself was problematic. The constitutive theory of the state, the governing jurisprudence of the day, could not admit of the possibility of ever separating the flag and the Constitution.

---

[7] See generally Stanley Karnow, *In Our Image: America's Empire in the Philippines* (New York: Random House, 1989), and Richard E. Welch, Jr., *Response to Imperialism: The United States and the Philippine-American War, 1899–1902* (Chapel Hill: University of North Carolina Press, 1979).

[8] See William A. Russ, Jr., *The Hawaiian Revolution (1893–94)* and *The Hawaiian Republic (1894–98) and Its Struggle to Win Annexation* (Selinsgrove, Pa.: Susquehanna University Press, 1959 and 1961).

[9] See generally Robert L. Beisner, *Twelve Against Empire: The Anti-Imperialists, 1898–1900* (New York: McGraw-Hill, 1968; repr. Chicago: University of Chicago Press, 1985); Richard Hofstadter, "Manifest Destiny and the Philippines," in Daniel Aaron, ed., *America in Crisis* (New York: Alfred A. Knopf, 1952), 173; Walter LaFeber, *The New Empire: An Interpretation of American Expansion, 1860–1898* (Ithaca: Cornell University Press, 1963); Ernest R. May, *American Imperialism: A Spec-*ulative Essay (New York: Atheneum, 1968); Ernest R. May, *Imperial Democracy: The Emergence of America as a Great Power* (New York: Harcourt, Brace & World, 1961); Julius W. Pratt, *Expansionists of 1898: The Acquisition of Hawaii and the Spanish Islands* (Baltimore: Johns Hopkins Press, 1936); and William Appleman Williams, *The Tragedy of American Diplomacy*, rev. ed. (New York: Dell, 1972).

[10] Downes v. Bidwell, 182 U.S. 244, 372 (1901) (Fuller, C.J., dissenting).

[11] This phrase originated in the Democratic platform of 1900. Donald B. Johnson, comp., *National Party Platforms*, rev. ed. (Urbana: University of Illinois Press, 1978), 1: 112.

[12] Lochner v. New York, 198 U.S. 45 (1905). See Chapter 6.

[13] Reagan v. Farmers' Loan & Trust Co., 154 U.S. 362 (1894). See Chapter 7.

[14] Pollock v. Farmers' Loan & Trust Co., 157 U.S. 429; 158 U.S. 601 (1895). See Chapter 4.

[15] *In re* Debs, 158 U.S. 564 (1895). See Chapter 3.

Chapter VIII: *The American Empire?*

Flag and Constitution were always and necessarily a unity. The social contract created this unity, for it made the legitimacy of government depend on the consent of its citizenry, conferred at some historical point. But there was nothing consensual about American dominion over the Philippines and Puerto Rico. Nor could the justification be offered that these "territories"—as the colonies were sometimes euphemistically called—were being readied for admission to the Union. If, as one contemporary observer commented, the relationship between the nation and territories expected to become states was analogous to that between parent and child, the colonial relationship was more like that of master to slave.[16]

The political controversy over expansion inflamed by the Spanish–American War did not end with the ratification of the peace treaty in the spring of 1899. Expansion was a major issue in the campaign of 1900, when McKinley ran for reelection. He chose as his running mate war hero Theodore Roosevelt, and together they defended the decision to acquire Puerto Rico and the Philippines. They won, and their victory—no doubt due to a number of factors, including the economy and perhaps even William Jennings Bryan's unsettling personality—could be seen as an affirmation of McKinley's expansionism.[17] Then, in the spring of 1901, just months after McKinley's inaugural, the Supreme Court handed down the *Insular Cases* and refused to impose strict limits on the exercise of the colonial power, much less repudiate the whole idea of empire. This caused the fictional Mr. Dooley of a popular newspaper column of the day to quip, "[N]o matther whether th' Constitution follows th' flag or not, th' Supreme Coort follows th' iliction returns."[18]

---

[16] Responding to Professor Thayer's article "Our New Possessions," *Harv. L. Rev.*, 12: 464 (1899), the prominent Boston lawyer John C. Ropes wrote:

> The true analogy of this subject is like that of the slave-holder's relations to his little children and to his slaves. In both cases his power is supreme, but in the first case the power is exercised only provisionally, and for the purpose of bringing up his children to his own level. In the second case there is a fixed intention never to allow his slaves [to] get upon his own level, and it is the maintenance of this despotic relation which has always been a source of temptation to the slave owner, and a cause of degradation to the slave himself. . . .

John C. Ropes to James B. Thayer, Oct. 14, 1899, Holmes Papers, Harvard Law School Library Manuscript Division.

[17] See generally Thomas A. Bailey, "Was the Presidential Election of 1900 a Mandate on Imperialism?," *Miss. Valley Hist. Rev.*, 24: 43 (1937). Bailey argues that although McKinley's overwhelming victory is often interpreted as a mandate for his imperial policy, a more plausible explanation lies in the general alarm over Bryan's free silver plank and the fear that a Bryan administration would destroy prosperity.

[18] Finley Peter Dunne, *Mr. Dooley at His Best* (New York: Charles Scribner's Sons, 1938; repr. 1969), 77. Dunne's newspaper version was a bit less colorful, using the standard spelling of "election." *Hearst's Chicago American*, June 9, 1901, editorial page.

This remark of Mr. Dooley, certainly his most famous and one of the most memorable cracks about the Supreme Court ever, echoed the instrumental critique advanced against the Court in the early 1890s. Just as the critics of the Court in the 1890s had denounced decisions such as *Debs* and *Pollock* as instruments of class justice, Dooley mocked the Court's compromise of principle, although now the Court was accused of bending the law to serve the electorate rather than some narrowly defined economic interest. Colonialism, Dooley implied, should have been an anathema to a group of justices who equated liberty with limited government founded on consent. By allowing a separation of flag and Constitution, the Court appeared to have succumbed to popular sentiment and to have thrown to the wind the idea of limited government and the entire contractarian tradition upon which it rested.

I

Much of the work of the Fuller Court was informed and shaped by the Civil War, then a recent, violent memory for many Americans. *Debs* bore the imprint of that experience. So did the *Insular Cases*, though in this instance the point of reference was not the war itself but a Supreme Court decision that many understood as one of the causes of the war: *Dred Scott*.[19]

There were two parts to *Dred Scott*. One denied blacks—all blacks, even those living in the North and those set free by their masters—the right ever to be citizens of the United States. This ruling arose in the most technical of contexts, namely in response to the question whether a black assumed to be free could maintain a suit in federal court founded on diversity of citizenship. But the decision had a sweep that knew few limits. Blacks were denied the capacity ever to become members of the political community, even after they had been manumitted or otherwise set free. Although this pronouncement was fundamentally inconsistent with much of what the new nation stood for and seemed to betray its highest ideals, the public reaction to this aspect of *Dred Scott* was muted, and it did not play an important role in the sequence of events leading to the Civil War. Its legal effect was eradicated by the amendments adopted at the end of the war, which formally admitted blacks to the constitutional community.

---

[19] Scott v. Sandford, 60 U.S. (19 How.) 393 (1857). See generally Don E. Fehrenbacher, *The Dred Scott Case: Its Significance in American Law and Politics* (New York: Oxford University Press, 1978), and Robert A. Burt, "What Was Wrong with *Dred Scott*, What's Right about *Brown*," *Wash. & Lee L. Rev.*, 42: 1 (1985). For a response to Burt, see Peter R. Teachout, "The Heart of the Lawyer's Craft," *Wash. & Lee L. Rev.*, 42: 39 (1985).

Chapter VIII: *The American Empire?*

A second aspect of *Dred Scott*, concerning the power of Congress over the territories, was, however, of great importance in the debates preceding the Civil War. It remained of legal consequence even after the adoption of the post-war amendments and was at the core of the *Insular Cases*. Dred Scott based his claim of freedom on the fact that he had been taken into a portion of the Louisiana Purchase (specifically the Minnesota Territory) in which Congress, as part of the Missouri Compromise, had forbidden slavery. He argued that his presence in a "free territory" made him free.

Although the Supreme Court first had determined that there was no jurisdiction in the federal courts to adjudicate Scott's claim of freedom on the ground that even a freed black was not a "citizen" for purposes of diversity jurisdiction, it nevertheless proceeded to what might fairly be regarded as the merits of the suit: Was Scott in fact free?[20] The Court assumed that a slave would be free if brought into a free territory, thereby making Scott's freedom turn on the validity of the congressional measure that banned slavery in the Minnesota Territory. In the 1850s many hoped that an authoritative declaration on this question—on the power of Congress to forbid slavery in the territories—might bring an end to the struggles over slavery and save the nation.

In approaching this question, Chief Justice Roger B. Taney found the Constitution remarkably silent. There was no grant of power to the central government to acquire new territories, nor was there any direction on how the newly acquired territories were to be governed. By the specific terms of the Constitution, Congress was given power to make all "Rules and Regulations respecting the Territory . . . belonging to the United States,"[21] but Taney construed that provision (which, in any event, gave no clue as to the permissible scope of the "Rules" and "Regulations") as inapplicable to the subject of the Missouri Compromise, the Louisiana Purchase. He held that the Territorial Clause applied to no territory other than the Northwest Territory, the one the framers, acting in 1787, anticipated would be ceded to the newly created government.

Having thus put the Territorial Clause to one side, Taney proceeded by inference. He did not deny Congress the power to acquire and govern territories, but he saw that power as a limited one, derived from the power to admit new states:

> There is certainly no power given by the Constitution to the Federal Government to establish or maintain colonies bordering on the United

---

[20] Fehrenbacher argues that Taney saw this question as having jurisdictional significance, that is, as providing additional grounds for the Court's denial of jurisdiction, since a slave would not be a "citizen" for diversity purposes. *Dred Scott Case*, 330–32.

[21] U.S. Const., Art. IV, Sect. 3, Cl. 2.

States or at a distance, to be ruled and governed at its own pleasure; nor to enlarge its territorial limits in any way, except by the admission of new States.[22]

In so grounding the territorial power on the specifically conferred power of Congress to admit new states, Taney was implicitly rejecting a theory of government—in this book it goes by the name "organic"—that saw the power to acquire and rule territories as integral to the idea of nationhood or as a necessary corollary of sovereignty. He appeared more inclined toward a constitutive theory, which depicts the government of the United States as deliberately created to serve a limited number of discrete ends and insists that each power be enumerated. Taney took one small step away from that theory when he inferred congressional power over the territories from the power to admit new states, but he was careful to insist that the congressional power over the territories was limited by the guarantees of the Constitution respecting "person and property."[23]

With these premises in place, Taney next proceeded to examine the Missouri Compromise and found it unconstitutional. In one of the earliest examples of substantive due process jurisprudence, Taney declared the Missouri Compromise a violation of the Fifth Amendment: A law that required slave-owners to relinquish some of their property (their slaves) upon crossing a territorial boundary line—that is, to give up their slaves when they moved north of 36°30′ N—denied them "property" without due process of law. Taney thus invalidated an entire approach to the slavery issue, an effort, born in the spirit of compromise and pragmatism, to deal with slavery in the territories by making some portion of the Louisiana Purchase free and allowing the remainder to decide for itself.

As a purely technical matter, the 1857 *Dred Scott* decision had little operative effect. The 1854 statute creating the Kansas and Nebraska territories from most of the unorganized residue of the Louisiana Purchase allowed these territories to decide the slavery issue for themselves and declared the 1820 Missouri Compromise ban on slavery "inoperative and void."[24] Moreover, by the 1850s the nation had become so polarized over slavery that it was not possible to return to the formula of the Missouri Compromise; the South and the North could no longer agree to ban slavery in territories where slavery might practically be introduced. The signifi-

---

[22] 60 U.S. at 446. Thomas Jefferson, the strictest of all contractarians, initially had thought that any territorial expansion required an amendment. He gave up the notion only when it appeared that the Louisiana Purchase might fall through if he allowed the delay that constitutional scruples would require. See Alexander DeConde, *This Affair of Louisiana* (New York: Charles Scribner's Sons, 1976), 181–85.

[23] 60 U.S. at 450.

[24] Kansas-Nebraska Act, Ch. 54, 10 Stat. 277, 289 (1854).

cance of *Dred Scott* was not, however, strictly limited to the ruling on the Missouri Compromise. While Taney had hoped that by denying Congress the power to ban slavery in the territories he would resolve authoritatively an issue that was dividing the nation, his strategy backfired. His decision caused a realignment of political forces that soon led to the ascendancy of the Republican Party, the election of Lincoln, the secession of the southern states, and finally to the Civil War itself.[25]

The Civil War, of course, put an end to the slavery question once and for all and preserved the Union by denying its constituent members the right to withdraw at will. But it is unlikely that America in 1900, prepared to accept Jim Crow and all it implied, viewed the war in quite the same way as we do today. What must have been uppermost in the minds of most contemporaries were the costs of the war—the violence, the deaths, the destruction.[26] *Dred Scott* and the Court's determination to remove the slavery issue from the domain of political compromise must have struck the justices and the bar as exactly the wrong approach to the question of congressional power. As a purely political matter, *Dred Scott* was their negative example.

II

The Thirteenth Amendment, if not the Union victory itself, deprived Taney's ruling on the territories of any practical significance, for in abolishing slavery the Constitution eradicated that peculiar species of property to which the ruling applied. But neither the war nor the post-war amendments challenged the principle upon which that ruling rested, namely that the power of Congress over the territories was subject to the limitations of the Constitution. It was precisely this principle that was called into question in the initial *Insular Cases*, although at issue was not the due process guarantee of the Fifth Amendment but rather the constitutional provisions governing tariffs. Was Congress's power to impose tariffs on trade with the newly acquired territories limited by the Constitution? Many who defended the empire insisted that congressional power over the territories

---

[25] See David M. Potter, *The Impending Crisis, 1848–1861* (New York: Harper & Row, 1976), 267–96. See generally David M. Potter, *Lincoln and His Party in the Secession Crisis* (New Haven: Yale University Press, 1942). As with the question of jurisdiction (see above, note 20), Fehrenbacher strives for a different perspective on the role of *Dred Scott* in the train of events leading to the Civil War. See *Dred Scott Case*, 417–595.

[26] See, e.g., Henry Adams, *The Education of Henry Adams* (Cambridge: Massachusetts Historical Society, 1918; repr. New York: Modern Library, 1931); William A. Dunning, *Reconstruction, Political and Economic, 1865–1877* (New York: Harper & Bros., 1907); and Robert A. Burt, *Constitution in Conflict* (Cambridge: Harvard University Press, 1992).

was different from that possessed over the states and that Congress should be free to pursue whatever tariff policy it thought best, unfettered by constitutional restrictions.

Congress's power over tariffs was limited by two different provisions of the Constitution. One was the Uniformity Clause, which provides that "all Duties, Imposts and Excises shall be uniform throughout the United States."[27] As we saw in our discussion of *Pollock* in Chapter 4, that clause required the national government, in the exercise of its taxing power, to treat all the constituent communities of the nation on an equal basis—a doctrine obviously incompatible with the spirit of colonialism. The *Insular Cases* also implicated the constitutional provision requiring that "[n]o Tax or Duty shall be laid on Articles exported from any State."[28] Imperialism might be untenable if this provision meant that no tariffs could be imposed on the goods coming into the United States from the colonies, for it was widely feared that free trade between the United States and the Philippines would bankrupt American farmers.

Although the protectionists were concerned primarily with the Philippines and the very practical threat to American producers posed by the importation of goods from that territory, oddly enough it was a tariff on goods from Puerto Rico that gave rise to what came to be regarded as the principal insular case, *Downes v. Bidwell*.[29] This case posed the issue of empire in its most salient form and fully revealed the divisions in the Court.

The tariff in question in *Downes* was a provision of the Foraker Act, the statute that established a territorial government in Puerto Rico. It was less than the tariff then applicable to foreign commerce, and the lower rate was justified in part as a way to help Puerto Rico recover from a severe hurricane that hit the island in August 1899, killing some three thousand people and destroying most of the island's coffee crop. President McKinley lobbied for a measure that would have abolished all tariffs on goods coming from

---

[27] U.S. Const., Art. I, Sect. 8, Cl. 1.

[28] Ibid., Sect. 9, Cl. 5.

[29] 182 U.S. 244 (1901). The other initial insular case involving the constitutional limits of Congress's power over the territories was Dooley v. United States, 183 U.S. 151 (1901). *Dooley* upheld the lower tariff established in the Foraker Act on goods shipped from New York to Puerto Rico over an Export Clause challenge, while *Downes* ruled that the Foraker tariff on goods shipped from Puerto Rico to New York did not violate the Uniformity Clause. In Dooley v. United States, 182 U.S. 222 (1901), followed by Armstrong v. United States, 182 U.S. 243 (1901), the Court decided that the president's power as commander-in-chief to levy a war tariff on goods imported into Puerto Rico from the United States ceased when the peace treaty with Spain was ratified. The remaining initial insular cases treated a statutory question: whether the conquered territories, once ceded, were "foreign" for purposes of the Dingley tariff on goods imported from "foreign countries." This question was answered in the negative both for Puerto Rico, in De Lima v. Bidwell, 182 U.S. 1 (1901), followed by Goetze v. United States, 182 U.S. 221 (1901), and for the Philippines, in Fourteen Diamond Rings v. United States, 183 U.S. 176 (1901).

Chapter VIII: *The American Empire?*

Puerto Rico into the United States, but protectionists managed to force a compromise. As enacted in the spring of 1900, the Foraker Act provided that the tariff for goods coming to the United States from Puerto Rico and vice versa would be 15 percent of the amount levied on like articles imported from foreign countries.[30]

Given *Dred Scott* and its aftermath, it is hardly surprising that a challenge to the Foraker Act found the justices less enthusiastic strictly to limit congressional power over the territories. A closely divided Court voted 5–4 to uphold the Act. Only Brewer, Peckham, and Fuller, a trio that emerged in case after case as the standard-bearers of contractarianism, stood by Taney's insistence that Congress be held to the precise terms of the Constitution.[31] A fourth vote against the Foraker Act was found in Harlan. On the whole he was more permissive than the others in the application of the contractarian tradition, but in the *Insular Cases* it controlled. He explained his vote against the tariff provision of the Foraker Act somewhat defensively, almost as though he had his dissent in *Pollock* in mind:

> It is one thing to give such a latitudinarian construction to the Constitution as will bring the exercise of power by Congress, upon a particular occasion or upon a particular subject, within its provisions. It is quite a different thing to say that Congress may, if it so elects, proceed outside of the Constitution.[32]

For Harlan, as for the other dissenters, flag and Constitution were indivisible: "Congress has no existence . . . outside of the Constitution."[33]

---

[30] The politics of the Foraker Act are described in some detail in Jaime B. Fuster, "The Origins of the Doctrine of Territorial Incorporation and Its Implications Regarding the Power of the Commonwealth of Puerto Rico to Regulate Interstate Commerce," *Revista Juridica de la Universidad de Puerto Rico*, 43: 259, 276–93 (1974). The Act itself is at Ch. 191, 31 Stat. 77 (1900).

[31] Earlier, Fuller had expressed similar views in another territories case, dissenting from the decision to sustain a congressional enactment that effected a forfeiture of most of the real estate of the Mormon Church. Late Corp. of the Church of Jesus Christ of Latter-Day Saints v. United States, 136 U.S. 1, 66 (1890).

[32] 182 U.S. at 380.

[33] Ibid. In contrast to Jefferson (see above, note 22), however, the dissenters allowed territory to be acquired without a constitutional amendment or without forming a new contract. As Fuller put it, "The power of the United States to acquire territory by conquest, by treaty, or by discovery and occupation, is not disputed. . . ." 182 U.S. at 369. There also seemed to be two limited situations where the dissenters permitted a separation of flag and Constitution in the administration of a territory. One pertained to military rule. The four dissenting justices joined the opinion of the Court in Dooley v. United States, 182 U.S. 222 (1901), upholding duties on goods imported into Puerto Rico after its conquest but before the ratification of the peace treaty with Spain. Second, the justices' repeated references to "organized" territories (for example, Fuller described Puerto Rico as "an organized and settled province," *Downes*, 182 U.S. at 372) might be taken as a hint that the Constitution and flag could be separate if the territory were somehow "unorganized."

235

Peckham and Brewer remained unswayed by the warnings contained in the references to *Dred Scott*. The misery of the war was evident, but they were possessed of a certain daring, and at moments an almost unshakable resolve. The temperament of the others—Fuller certainly, and possibly Harlan—who affirmed the sanctity of the contract and insisted upon the unity of flag and Constitution was quite different; they were sensitive to the pragmatic consequences of a decision and quite capable of bending. I doubt they would have taken the stringent view of congressional power that they in fact did in the *Insular Cases* unless they saw important pragmatic differences between slavery and imperialism, between *Dred Scott* and the *Insular Cases*. Invalidating the Foraker Act surely would be an implicit rebuke to President McKinley and his expansionist policies, but Fuller's and maybe Harlan's position must have been premised on the view that invalidating the Foraker Act was not comparable to invalidating the Missouri Compromise and denying Congress the power to bar slavery in the territories. It was not likely to cause a major political realignment.

There was, moreover, one option available to Congress and the president in the *Insular Cases* that was not available in the slavery controversy: deannexation. Even if the Court ruled that Congress was strictly limited by the Constitution in its treatment of the territories, as Taney had in *Dred Scott* and as the dissenters did in the *Insular Cases*, Puerto Rico and the Philippines could always be deannexed—granted independence, or maybe even returned to Spain. While such an arrangement would have dashed the hopes of an American empire, disappointing those who believed that the United States needed an empire to compete in the world arena, it would have relieved the nation of the tasks of colonial government, which, in light of the Philippine insurrection, were becoming more and more burdensome each day. In the slavery controversy, deannexation of the territories might have been a formal option, but it was not considered a viable one, and in any event probably would not have resolved the underlying dispute. What was really at issue was slavery in the southern states, not in the territories, and that would have continued even if Americans had forgone the dream of continental expansion.[34]

At the opposite end of the spectrum to the contractarians stood Justice Brown, who worried openly about the risks of hamstringing the political branches in their effort to construct an American empire. He insisted upon a relatively clear distinction between flag and Constitution and denied that one necessarily followed the other. By affirming a broad and plenary conception of congressional power over the territories, Brown

---

[34] See generally Arthur Bestor, "The American Civil War as a Constitutional Crisis," *Am. Hist. Rev.*, 69: 327 (1964).

repudiated the concept of nation implicit in *Dred Scott*, just as clearly as Fuller, Peckham, Brewer, and Harlan affirmed it.

The core of Brown's opinion in *Downes* was the assertion that the Constitution did not apply in the territories until Congress extended it there. According to this theory of "extension," the power to acquire territory was derived from the treaty-making power. In *De Lima v. Bidwell*, a companion to *Downes*, Brown quoted Article VI for the proposition that treaties "shall be the supreme law of the land,"[35] and then added: "One of the ordinary incidents of a treaty is the cession of territory."[36] Putting the matter this way not only placed Congress's power to acquire territories on secure footing but also disposed of the issue of whether that power was limited by the Constitution. Since most constitutional limitations, including the Uniformity Clause, were, according to Brown, inextricably connected to the process by which the states conferred power on Congress when they ratified the Constitution, these limitations were inapplicable when it came to acquiring or administering a territory, unless, of course, Congress chose to extend the Constitution to that territory:

> The States could only delegate to Congress such powers as they them-selves possessed, and as they had no power to acquire new territory they had none to delegate in that connection. The logical inference from this is, that if Congress had power to acquire new territory, which is con-ceded, that power was not hampered by the constitutional provisions.[37]

The notion of extension propounded by Brown was wholly at odds with the constitutive theory of the dissenters and, of course, with *Dred Scott*. Brown acknowledged that *Dred Scott* "is a strong authority in favor of the plaintiff [who was challenging the Foraker Act], and if the opinion of the Chief Justice [Taney] be taken at its full value it is decisive in his favor."[38] His strategy, however, was to disparage the case. He depicted Taney's treatment of the territorial issue as wholly gratuitous. According to Brown, the decision on jurisdiction made it unnecessary to reach the merits of the territorial issue. As Justice Brown commented, with ironic understatement, "[I]n view of the excited political condition of the country at the time, it is unfortunate that [Taney] felt compelled to discuss the question upon the merits. . . ."[39] Brown was prepared to admit that Taney was motivated by the best of desires, namely, to preserve or restore the "peace and harmony of the country,"[40] but nonetheless emphasized the magnitude of the failure and saw in the sad turn of events an important lesson:

---

[35] 182 U.S. 1, 195 (1901).
[36] Ibid.
[37] *Downes*, 182 U.S. at 285.
[38] Ibid., 273–74.

[39] Ibid., 274.
[40] Ibid., quoting *Dred Scott*, 60 U.S. at 455 (Wayne, J., concurring).

The attempt was not successful. It is sufficient to say that the country did not acquiesce in the opinion, and that the civil war, which shortly thereafter followed, produced such changes in judicial, as well as public sentiment, as to seriously impair the authority of this case.[41]

Brown acknowledged that it would be "an exercise of arbitrary power inconsistent with the underlying principles of a free government"[42] for Congress simultaneously to invite settlers to locate in the territories and to deny them the right to take their property and belongings with them, but he criticized Taney's opinion for refusing to make a distinction "between property in general, and a wholly exceptional class of property,"[43] slaves. He also quoted at length from Senator Benton's tract on the case, which was issued in the midst of the furor over the decision and on the eve of the war. "[T]he great fundamental error of the court, (father of all political errors,)" according to Benton, was "that of assuming the extension of the Constitution to the territories."[44]

At every turn, Brown recoiled from the spectre of confronting the nation with only two choices: either admitting all the territories and their people to full and equal participation in the nation or relinquishing control over the colonies. For Brown, the first alternative would have threatened the cultural integrity of America, while the second would have disadvantaged America in its global competition with the European powers. There had to be some other possibility. Brown believed that the president and, even more, Congress, had to be free in dealing with the so-called territories. Determined to protect the freedom of the political branches, he concluded his exposition of the theory of extension on this glorious note:

Patriotic and intelligent men may differ widely as to the desireableness of this or that acquisition, but this is solely a political question. We can only consider this aspect of the case so far as to say that no construction of the Constitution should be adopted which would prevent Congress from considering each case upon its merits, unless the language of the instrument imperatively demand it. A false step at this time might be fatal to the development of what Chief Justice Marshall called the American Empire. Choice in some cases, the natural gravitation of small bodies towards large ones in others, the result of a successful war in still others, may bring about conditions which would render the annexation of distant possessions desirable. If those possessions are inhabited by alien races, differing from us in religion, customs, law, methods of taxation and modes of thought, the administration of government and justice, according to Anglo-Saxon principles, may for a

---

[41] *Downes*, 182 U.S. at 274.
[42] Ibid., 275.

[43] Ibid.
[44] Ibid., 276.

time be impossible; and the question at once arises whether large concessions ought not to be made for a time, that, ultimately, our own theories may be carried out, and the blessings of a free government under the Constitution extended to them. We decline to hold that there is anything in the Constitution to forbid such action.[45]

Justice Brown was a centrist figure on the Court and over a wide number of cases demonstrated a moderate commitment to the social contract tradition. He dissented in *Pollock* and wrote the majority opinion in *Holden v. Hardy*,[46] but nonetheless joined many of Brewer's and Peckham's strongest denials of the legislative power—for example, he joined Brewer's opinions in *Budd v. New York*[47] and *Reagan*, and Peckham's in *Lochner*. This qualified commitment to liberty was also present in the *Insular Cases*. His theory of extension sought to enlarge the prerogatives of the political branches and thus to accommodate the imperatives of expansionism, but nonetheless recognized two different kinds of limits on congressional power.

The first related to a number of constitutional prohibitions, apparently not connected to the process by which the states delegated power to Congress, but that "go to the very root of the power of Congress to act at all, irrespective of time or place."[48] Examples included the prohibitions on bills of attainder and ex post facto laws, the provision denying the United States the power to confer titles of nobility, and perhaps the First Amendment. The category of such limitations was, of course, limited and did not include the Uniformity Clause, for it did not, according to Brown, deny power altogether but only required uniformity "throughout the United States" (which he then paraphrased as "among or between the several States"[49]).

Brown allowed for a second set of limitations on congressional power by making a distinction between "natural rights"[50] and "artificial or remedial rights." Brown suggested (as he phrased it, "We suggest, without

---

[45] Ibid., 286–87.

[46] 169 U.S. 366 (1898).

[47] 143 U.S. 517, 548 (1892) (Brewer, J., dissenting).

[48] *Downes*, 182 U.S. at 277.

[49] Ibid., 278.

[50] Ibid., 282. Brown continued: Of the former class are the rights to one's own religious opinion and to a public expression of them, or, as sometimes said, to worship God according to the dictates of one's own conscience; the right to personal liberty and individual property; to freedom of speech and of the press; to free access to courts of justice, to due process of law and to an equal protection of the laws; to immunities from unreasonable searches and seizures, as well as cruel and unusual punishments; and to such other immunities as are indispensable to a free government.
Ibid., 282–83. In this passage Brown seems unwittingly to have provided an independent basis for Taney's position, since *Dred Scott* turned on the Due Process Clause; a master's interest in his slave would have been regarded in antebellum America as a form of property.

intending to decide"[51]) that the natural rights would operate as restraints on congressional power in the colonies. Not surprisingly, the Uniformity Clause did not encompass any natural rights. He also excluded from the category of natural rights the right to vote, the right to citizenship (here he seemed prepared to follow *Dred Scott*), and the procedural rights afforded the accused in a criminal trial (which, he was careful to note, "have already been held by the States to be unnecessary to the proper protection of individuals"[52]). In fact, Brown's list of natural rights contained few surprises. It was roughly coextensive with the first eight amendments of the Bill of Rights (though omitting the Second and Third Amendments, the provisions relating to criminal trials in the Fifth and Sixth Amendments, and the civil jury trial guarantee of the Seventh).

In putting forth these views, Brown often spoke of "we," but as it turned out, the invocation of the collective pronoun was sadly misleading. At the conference Brown voted to sustain the tariff provisions of the Foraker Act and was assigned (presumably by Fuller) the task of formulating the Court's position, clearly the most important and most visible assignment of his judicial career.

Brown served on the Court for more than fifteen years, and in no instance was he the architect of any especially noteworthy doctrine or judicial position. He was the author of the Court's opinion in *Plessy v. Ferguson*[53] and *Holden v. Hardy*, but in their day those cases were not subjects of great interest. *Downes v. Bidwell*, on the other hand, was one of the great public occasions for the Fuller Court, attracting attention from newspapers and law reviews. It was comparable in that regard to *Pollock*, and thus Brown must have been especially disappointed in what he was able to achieve. He wrote an opinion in *Downes* that absolutely no one joined. Brown announced the judgment of the Court sustaining the Foraker tariff, but the other four justices who also voted to sustain the measure—White, Gray, Shiras, and McKenna—were unprepared to join his opinion.[54] They rejected Brown's theory of extension and adhered to a theory, first

---

[51] Ibid., 282.
[52] Ibid., 283.
[53] 163 U.S. 537 (1896). See Chapter 12.
[54] Shiras and McKenna joined in White's concurring opinion, while Gray wrote a separate concurrence, "in substance agreeing with the opinion of Mr. Justice White." 182 U.S. at 344. White went so far as to suggest that Brown's opinion, nominally the opinion of the Court, was merely a concurrence:
Mr. Justice Brown, in announcing the judgment of affirmance, has in his opinion stated his reasons for his concurrence in such judgment. In the result I likewise concur. As, however, the reasons which cause me to do so are different from, if not in conflict with, those expressed in that opinion, if its meaning is by me not misconceived, it becomes my duty to state the convictions which control me. 182 U.S. at 287.

advanced in the pages of the *Harvard Law Review* in 1899[55] but developed on the Court by White, that went by the name of incorporation.[56]

Like Brown, White postulated two kinds of territories. While Brown distinguished between territories to which Congress had extended the Constitution and those to which it had not, White divided the class of territories into those that were incorporated into the United States and those that were not, further positing that congressional power was restricted fully by the Constitution only in the case of an incorporated territory. In Brown's theory Congress had to extend the Constitution; in White's, Congress had to incorporate the territory.

Almost needless to say, White did not describe the process of incorporation with complete precision. Chief Justice Fuller quite justifiably complained that the term "incorporation" seemed to have some "occult meaning."[57] The initial emphasis of White's theory, like Brown's, was on the deliberate and highly discretionary quality of the decision to incorporate: Incorporation is a status to be conferred on a territory by Congress; mere acquisition of a territory by military occupation or by treaty is not enough. Congress must assent to incorporation, either by some affirmative act or, in the case where a treaty purports to incorporate a territory, by declining to repudiate the treaty.[58]

This emphasis on Congress's power over incorporation might have been based on a desire to preserve a democratic element in the process of nation-building, for the Constitution does not contemplate a role for the House of Representatives in treaty-making, much less in the decision of military authorities to occupy a territory. But quite close to the surface, another less benign, more chauvinistic or maybe even xenophobic explanation appears. According to Justice White, incorporation occurs only when the people of the United States, speaking through Congress, have decided, in light of their interests and the "fitness of the ceded territory,"[59] that the time has come when it is proper for the territory to "enter into and form a part of the American family."[60]

Although the theory of incorporation contemplated a deliberate and highly discretionary decision by Congress, emphasizing the need for politi-

---

[55] Abbott L. Lowell, "The Status of Our New Possessions—A Third View," *Harv. L. Rev.*, 13: 155 (1899).

[56] 182 U.S. at 287. Given the times, it was not at all surprising to find the term "incorporation" used to describe what was essentially a process by which a community was empowered. See generally Alan Trachtenberg, *The Incorpora-tion of America: Culture and Society in the Gilded Age* (New York: Hill & Wang, 1982).

[57] *Downes*, 182 U.S. at 373.

[58] Ibid., 339.

[59] *De Lima v. Bidwell*, 182 U.S. at 219 (McKenna, J., dissenting, joined by Shiras and White, JJ.).

[60] *Downes*, 182 U.S. at 339.

cal control of the process of entering into "the American family," some elements of the theory limited congressional discretion. For example, while normally any single Congress can repeal the work of its predecessors, the act of incorporation, like the decision to admit a new state, was thought to be irrevocable.[61] This feature of incorporation theory did not readily distinguish it from the theory of extension, for Brown, too, believed that once the Constitution was extended to a territory it could not be withdrawn.[62] White, however, envisioned other limits on congressional discretion that tended—given White's literary powers, one cannot be sure about this—to differentiate the two positions.

One difference was theoretical. Unlike Brown, who argued that the Constitution was not operative in these territories, White insisted that the Constitution *was* operative, but—and here's the catch—some of its provisions did not apply:

> As Congress in governing the territories is subject to the Constitution, it results that all the limitations of the Constitution which are applicable to Congress in exercising this authority necessarily limit its power on this subject. It follows also that every provision of the Constitution which is applicable to the territories is also controlling therein. To justify a departure from this elementary principle by a criticism of the opinion of Mr. Chief Justice Taney in *Scott v. Sandford* appears to me to be unwarranted.[63]

The provisions that did apply in unincorporated territories were those that "withheld all power" from Congress:

> Albeit, as a general rule, the *status* of a particular territory has to be taken in view when the applicability of any provision of the Constitution is questioned, it does not follow when the Constitution has absolutely withheld from the government all power on a given subject, that such an inquiry is necessary. Undoubtedly, there are general prohibitions in the Constitution in favor of the liberty and property of the citizen which are not mere regulations as to the form and manner in which a conceded power may be exercised, but which are an absolute denial of all authority under any circumstances or conditions to do particular acts.[64]

The Uniformity Clause was not such a provision, White concluded.

---

[61] Ibid., 313–15.
[62] Ibid., 270. Brown wrote in a later case, Rassmussen v. United States, 197 U.S. 516 (1905) (discussed below at pp. 248–52) that extension, "once done, in my view, is irrevocable." Ibid., 536.
[63] *Downes*, 182 U.S. at 291 (citation omitted).
[64] Ibid., 294 (emphasis in original).

Chapter VIII: *The American Empire?*

On close inspection, it appears that White's list of limitations on Congress's power over Puerto Rico and the Philippines or any other unincorporated territory is remarkably like Brown's when he spoke of provisions that "go to the very root of the power of Congress to act at all" and thus control regardless of Congress's decision to extend the Constitution. In this respect the two positions are the same, but there is an important difference at the level of theory. While Brown contemplated an act of Congress *extending* the Constitution to the territories, White insisted that the Constitution "[is] the supreme law, and . . . its applicable provisions [are] operative at all times everywhere";[65] the act of incorporating a territory simply triggers the application of additional constitutional provisions. This distinction enabled White to maintain a crucial link to the dissenters and to reconcile his theory of incorporation with contractarianism. Flag and Constitution were, for White, as they were for the dissenters, an analytic unity (though the Constitution itself was not a unity). As Fuller noted, "In the concurring opinion of Mr. Justice White, we find certain important propositions conceded, some of which are denied, or not admitted in the other."[66]

In a second difference from Brown, White expressed unease with the idea of holding a territory that is not eventually to be incorporated. He seemed to agree that "the conception upon which the Constitution proceeds is that no territory as a general rule should be acquired unless the territory may reasonably be expected to be worthy of statehood,"[67] thereby implying that unincorporated or colonial status could only be temporary. Toward the end of his opinion in *Downes* White went even further, declaring that the United States could lawfully hold an unincorporated territory only "if there be obligations of honor and good faith which . . . sacredly bind the United States to terminate the dominion and control, when . . . the situation is ripe to enable it to do so.[68]

The invocation of a sacred duty in this passage of White's opinion imposed obligations on the United States government well beyond those suggested by Brown's concept of extension. White was careful to place the responsibility for carrying out this duty with the Congress—"the determination of when such blessing [of statehood] is to be bestowed is wholly a political question, and the aid of the judiciary cannot be invoked to usurp political discretion"[69]—but the very recognition of the duty put the imperial idea in jeopardy.

Finally, while White left to Congress the decision to incorporate a territory, he nonetheless recognized it was for the judiciary to determine when

---

[65] Hawaii v. Mankichi, 190 U.S. 197, 221 (1903) (White, J., concurring).
[66] *Downes*, 182 U.S. at 371 (Fuller, C.J., dissenting).

[67] Ibid., 312.
[68] Ibid., 343.
[69] Ibid., 312.

such a decision had been made.[70] In the case of Puerto Rico, White decided there had been no incorporation, even though Congress had, through the Foraker Act, imposed tariffs on goods coming from Puerto Rico and established a territorial government. While the statute conferred various rights on the residents of Puerto Rico, White underscored the Senate's decision to reject a provision that would have granted them United States citizenship.[71] For White, the Foraker Act was a mere incident to the acquisition of the colony, a temporary expedient that lacked the affirmative indication that Puerto Rico had "been incorporated into and become an integral part of the United States."[72]

Similarly, Gray's concurrence emphasized the temporary character of the system of special duties established by the Act.[73] The provision giving Puerto Rico a tariff break would expire in two years, or sooner if the government of Puerto Rico became financially self-sufficient. Like White, Gray did not believe that implied incorporation had occurred for Puerto Rico. But by acknowledging the possibility of implied incorporation he created, as did White and those who joined his opinion, a role for the judiciary in the process of incorporation, which inevitably had the effect of restricting congressional discretion. It was for the judiciary to decide—in light of the totality of circumstances—whether a territory had been implicitly incorporated.

In a later case, Brown acknowledged that extension could occur "formally or by implication,"[74] but he preserved a larger element of congressional discretion by narrowing the circumstances under which a court could find extension by implication. Brown insisted upon a specific act of Congress that evidenced a clear intent to extend the Constitution to the territory. "[T]he only true test," said Brown, "was whether Congress intended to apply [the Constitution] or not in the particular case."[75] White's view was broader. He looked to the full panoply of congressional enactments relating to a territory to determine whether it had, in fact, been incorporated. His notion of implication almost permitted inadvertent incorporation.

---

[70] Ibid., 299 (defining the Court's inquiry as whether Puerto Rico had been incorporated).

[71] Ibid., 340–41.

[72] Ibid., 299. White also remarked, with a tone that typified much of his opinion,

> If the treaty-making power can absolutely, without the consent of Congress, incorporate territory, . . . then millions of inhabitants of alien territory, if acquired by treaty, can, without the desire or consent of the people of the United States speaking through Congress, be immediately and irrevocably incorporated into the United States, and the whole structure of the government be overthrown.

Ibid., 312–13.

[73] Ibid., 346–47.

[74] *Rassmussen*, 197 U.S. at 532.

[75] Ibid., 533.

Chapter VIII: *The American Empire?*

Like extension, incorporation was a composite of permissive and restrictive elements as it pertained to congressional power over the territories, but the emphasis was slightly more on the restrictive side. True, the decision to incorporate, like the decision to extend the Constitution, belonged to Congress, but White envisioned a trajectory toward statehood and had a more robust conception of implicit incorporation. Moreover, even before incorporation the Constitution is operative (though not fully applicable). These features of White's theory made no difference to the outcome in *Downes*—under extension or incorporation, the Foraker tariff stood. It was not even clear that they would make a difference in the outcome of any other case, since extension had some restrictive elements, too. But, on the whole, I think it fair to say that the theory of incorporation was closer to the dissenters' position than Brown's and thus more fully consistent with the overall body of doctrine being propounded by the Court at that time.

White's genius for compromise was probably his supreme qualification for his subsequent appointment to the chief justiceship. We saw it manifest in the rule of reason in the antitrust cases of 1911.[76] His insistence on the doctrine of incorporation in *Downes*, however, was disruptive and thus somewhat out of character. It deprived Brown of any support whatsoever. It produced a bitterness among the justices that is evident in the *United States Reports* and left the Court, upon which all eyes were fixed, without a majority opinion. As more than one commentator noted, it resulted in an unseemly spectacle.[77] But there was a synthetic or integrative quality to incorporation much like the rule of reason. The theory simultaneously respected the constitutive theory of *Dred Scott* and accommodated new developments; it allowed Congress freedom and at the same time limited its powers; it both acknowledged the imperial impulse and sought to cabin it. Moreover, like the rule of reason, the balance between permissive and restrictive elements in the theory was to be struck by one's understanding of a process that was never defined with any specificity. Its "occult" quality was not, as Fuller complained, a liability but its supreme virtue and probably assured its eventual victory.

---

[76] See Chapter 5. We will also see it manifest in the state prohibition cases, Chapter 9, and again in the free speech cases, Chapter 11.

[77] See, e.g., Charles E. Littlefield, "The Insular Cases," *Harv. L. Rev.*, 15: 169 (1901). Secretary of War Elihu Root, pressed by reporters for a reaction to the *Insular Cases*, responded: "[A]s near as I can make out the Constitution follows the flag—but doesn't quite catch up with it." Quoted in Philip C. Jessup, *Elihu Root* (New York: Dodd, Mead, 1938; repr. Hamden, Conn: Archon Books, 1964), 1: 348.

III

In 1901 the Supreme Court was divided on the colonial question. A majority of five sustained the Foraker Act, but no single theory achieved majority support. The majority was divided between two theories—extension and incorporation—while the dissenters embraced a third, which I have called contractarianism. In much the manner of all instrumental critiques,[78] Dooley's quip that the Court followed the 1900 election returns focused on the result in *Downes*, but it failed either to capture the division in the Court or to explain the content of the various theories. Even more, it could not account for what happened in 1905, when Justice White became the spokesman for the Court, indeed for a seven-justice majority that included three of the *Downes* dissenters, and then managed to write into law his theory of incorporation.

Between 1901 and 1905, cases arising from the colonies continued to appear on the Supreme Court's docket, though attention shifted from free trade to procedural protections in criminal trials. *Rassmussen v. United States*,[79] the 1905 decision that heralded the triumph of incorporation, involved the permissibility of using a six-person jury for trial of a misdemeanor in the Territory of Alaska. All the justices were prepared to condemn the Alaskan practice, so they said, but there was an important difference in the grounds chosen to support that judgment. Justice Harlan, not known for his flexibility, adhered to the position he announced in the original *Insular Cases*. He simply applied the Constitution to the case at hand, assuming, as did all the other justices, that it guaranteed a common law jury of twelve. With obvious reluctance, Justice Brown also upheld the right to a jury of twelve, but he did so by construing the treaty of cession with Russia. It afforded to all the inhabitants of Alaska the rights of the citizens of the United States (though, of course, it left unresolved the specific question whether the right to trial by jury was one of those rights). Justice White, writing for the others—a solid majority of seven, including Brewer, Peckham, and Fuller—relied on the treaty of cession and a number of subsequent statutes, not as Brown had, but rather to apply his theory of incorporation. White read the treaty and statutes as effectuating an incorporation of Alaska, thus making the constitutional guarantee of trial by jury fully and directly applicable to that territory.

The road from the initial *Insular Cases* of 1901 to *Rassmussen v. United States* in 1905 and the victory of incorporation was not, however, straight. At first, the Court seemed to embrace Brown's extension theory.

---

[78] See, e.g., Marcos A. Ramírez, "Los Casos Insulares: Un Estudio Sobre el Proceso Judicial," *Revista Jurídica de la* *Universidad de Puerto Rico,* 16: 121 (1946).
[79] 197 U.S. 516 (1905).

Chapter VIII: *The American Empire?*

In 1903, in *Hawaii v. Mankichi*,[80] a divided Court sustained a conviction in Hawaii that was rendered by a non-unanimous verdict (9 out of 12) and that was not preceded by a grand jury indictment. Justices Brewer, Fuller, Peckham, and, of course, Harlan dissented. Justice Brown, joined only by Justices Holmes and Day, delivered an opinion that was denominated the "Opinion of the Court," and he was true to the theory he announced in the *Insular Cases*, scrupulously avoiding any mention of incorporation:

> [W]e place our decision of this case upon the ground that the two rights alleged to be violated in this case are not fundamental in their nature, but concern merely a method of procedure which sixty years of practice had shown to be suited to the conditions of the islands, and well calculated to conserve the rights of their citizens to their lives, their property and their well-being.[81]

White was well aware of Brown's craftiness—indeed, he wrote separately to reassert the incorporation theory, and the battle that marked *Downes* flared up once again. Hawaii had not, according to White, been incorporated, and thus the conviction could be upheld despite the constitutional irregularities. Interestingly, White clung to this theory of incorporation even though by the time of the *Hawaii* case in 1903 he had lost two of his original supporters: Justice Gray had been replaced by Holmes, who was appointed to the Court in December 1902; Shiras had been replaced by Day, who was appointed in February 1903, just before the oral argument. In the *Hawaii* case both Holmes and Day sided with Brown and did not join White's concurrence. This meant that in the spring of 1903 there appeared to be only one justice on the Court—McKenna—who had joined White's opinion in the original *Insular Cases* and who, like White, continued to affirm allegiance to the theory expounded therein. The future of the incorporation theory did not appear bright.

Oddly enough, there was also little reason to be optimistic about the future of the extension doctrine. Although Brown's opinion in *Hawaii v. Mankichi* was the "Opinion of the Court," it had the unqualified support of only two other justices, Day and Holmes. Moreover, the freshness of the Holmes and Day appointments should have indicated that their support was tentative. All new appointees go through a period of on-the-job training, as it takes time for them to understand fully the divisions among their colleagues and to formulate positions that they are willing to stand by. This truism seems particularly apt in the case of Day, who joined the Court on February 25, only days before he heard argument and presumably voted on *Hawaii v. Mankichi*. (The opinion was handed down on June 1, but the

---

[80] 190 U.S. 197 (1903).   [81] Ibid., 218.

vote probably occurred in a conference held just days after the argument, which was held on March 4 and 5.) Finally, someone aware of the personal relationship developing between Holmes and White[82]—one of the few Holmes had on the Court—might have foreseen a shift in allegiance.

Holmes never publicly revealed any second thoughts regarding the extension doctrine; Day, however, did. In the spring of 1904, a year after *Hawaii v. Mankichi* but a year before *Rassmussen v. United States*, Day emerged as the spokesman for the Court on the colonial issue; he had been McKinley's secretary of state and for that reason must have seemed to Fuller a natural choice for that role. Day wrote the opinion of the Court in two 1904 cases involving criminal procedure in the Philippines.

In the first, *Kepner v. United States*,[83] it was not necessary to reach the incorporation issue. Congress had passed a statute that Day was able to read as extending to the Philippines the relevant constitutional provision, the Fifth Amendment guarantee against being put twice in jeopardy. The statutory protection against double jeopardy was construed to be coextensive with the Constitution's. In the second case, *Dorr v. United States*,[84] the issue of incorporation was presented more squarely because the case concerned the jury trial right, one of the few constitutional rights not specifically extended to the Philippines by statute. Day concluded that the trial need not be by a jury, a conclusion that could have been reached under either Brown's extension theory or White's incorporation theory (assuming the colony was not yet incorporated). Day did not address the theoretical issue directly, but at a number of points he made reference to the prerogative of Congress to incorporate a territory, thereby indicating substantial movement toward White's view:

> Until Congress shall see fit to incorporate territory ceded by treaty into the United States, we regard it as settled [by *Downes*] that the territory is to be governed under the power existing in Congress to make laws for such territories and subject to such constitutional restrictions upon the powers of that body as are applicable to the situation.[85]

When Justice White was given the privilege of speaking for the Court in *Rassmussen v. United States*, which arose the very next year, he wrote the theory of incorporation into law. He took full advantage of Day's opinion in *Dorr*, but that did not lessen his sense of achievement. Almost gleeful, White told the Court Reporter: "Butler, now [my view] is the opinion of the Court and I want you to make it so appear in your report of this case."[86]

---

[82] See Chapter 2, note 58.
[83] 195 U.S. 100 (1904).
[84] 195 U.S. 138 (1904).
[85] Ibid., 143.

[86] Quoted in Charles H. Butler, *A Century at the Bar of the Supreme Court of the United States* (New York: G. P. Putnam's Sons, 1942), 94.

Chapter VIII: *The American Empire?*

Brown was bitter. While he went along with the result in the case, he was angered by the victory of incorporation. Referring to the earlier divisions in *Downes*, and specifically to White's opinion in that case advancing the incorporation theory, he began his concurrence in *Rassmussen* on this note:

> This, however, was not the opinion of the court; it was certainly not the opinion of the Justice who announced the conclusion and judgment of the court; it was wholly disclaimed by the four dissenting Justices. . . . It was simply the individual opinion of three members of the court. . . . and in my opinion is wholly unnecessary to the disposition of this case.[87]

Brown might have felt trapped: He had joined Day's opinion in *Dorr*, but he apparently had failed to notice the references in Day's opinion to the idea of incorporation. Brown's resentment also might have been fueled by recognition that the final defeat of his extension theory in *Rassmussen* did not stem simply from the personnel changes on the Court between 1901 and 1905. Day and Holmes only replaced two of White's original supporters, Gray and Shiras. White still needed to win over some of the *Downes* dissenters, and as it turned out, he managed to find that crucial support in Fuller, Peckham, and Brewer.[88] Only Harlan held firm.

To some degree, that switch was foreshadowed by *Dorr*. Justice Harlan dissented in that case on the theory that he put forward in *Downes* and in *Hawaii v. Mankichi*. He argued that the Sixth Amendment right to trial by jury was, like every constitutional provision, fully applicable to the territories and to each and every exercise of power by the United States; to hold otherwise, he concluded, would be "utterly revolting."[89] Fuller, Peckham, and Brewer were, however, less faithful to their original view. Peckham wrote an opinion for the three in *Dorr*, and while he reaffirmed the position

---

[87] 197 U.S. at 532. Despite his disappointment, Brown strove for the high ground when he retired the next year:

> I rejoice that I am leaving the court at a time when it has never stood higher in the estimation of the people, nor when more important cases have been, and still are being, presented for its consideration. The antagonisms, sometimes almost fierce, which were developed during the earliest decades of its history, and at one time threatened to impair its usefulness, are happily forgotten; and the now universal acquiescence in its decisions, though sometimes reached by a bare majority of its members, is a magnificent tribute to that respect for the law inherent in the Anglo-Saxon race, and contains within itself the strongest assurance of the stability of our institutions.

Justice Brown's retirement statement, May 28, 1906, at the front of 202 U.S.

[88] Given the personal relationship between Brewer and Brown (see Chapter 7, note 30), Brewer's willingness to support the rival theory must have been especially disappointing to Brown.

[89] *Dorr*, 195 U.S. at 154, 156.

the dissenters took in *Downes*, he acknowledged the precedential force of *Hawaii v. Mankichi* and said that he was concurring out of respect for that decision. While this opinion indicated some movement on his part, and thus implicitly on the part of Brewer and Fuller, the willingness of the three to embrace incorporation in *Rassmussen* the next year constituted a more dramatic, and indeed more puzzling, shift. Neither stare decisis nor a respect for the precedential force of *Hawaii v. Mankichi* can explain that shift, for if *Hawaii v. Mankichi* stood for anything, it was for the victory of Brown's theory and the defeat of White's. Brown's opinion in that case, labeled the "Opinion of the Court," contained no trace of incorporation.

Holmes's appointment might have played some role in Fuller's capitulation, for even by 1905 Holmes had his ear.[90] In addition, as chief justice, Fuller might have been particularly sensitive to institutional imperatives: All that I know about him indicates that he was more than capable of changing his vote just for the sake of formulating a majority position for the Court and ending an unseemly division. But, as plausible as these considerations might be in explaining Fuller's shift in *Rassmussen*, they hold little force for Brewer and Peckham—neither seemed particularly moved by institutional considerations; each was about as independent-minded a justice as there could be; each was far beyond Holmes's sphere of influence and, as far as the evidence shows, had little to do with him.

The key to the change in Peckham's and Brewer's votes, and perhaps Fuller's as well, might be found in *Rassmussen* itself. Since the Court concluded that the territory in question, Alaska, had been implicitly incorporated and that criminal trials were subject to the Bill of Rights, the outcome in *Rassmussen* was wholly agreeable to the *Downes* dissenters. It may have enabled them to see how the incorporation doctrine would serve their overarching theoretical purposes. The theory of incorporation was a skillful blend of permissive and restrictive elements, and the outcome in *Rassmussen*, affirming the applicability of the Constitution to Alaska, might have revealed more clearly, in contradistinction to the original *Insular Cases*, its restrictive side. *Rassmussen* showed Brewer, Peckham, and Fuller that they could safeguard the ideal of liberty and limited government within the framework of the incorporation doctrine itself.[91]

---

[90] See Chapter 2, pp. 27–28.

[91] It should be noted, however, that one of *Rassmussen*'s safeguards was removed by the Taft Court. In *Balzac v. Porto Rico*, the Court rejected the notion that Puerto Rico had been incorporated by implication in the 1917 Jones Act and placed such severe limitations on the idea of implied incorporation itself as almost to make it empty:

Had Congress intended to take the important step of changing the treaty status of Porto Rico by incorporating it into the Union, it is reasonable to suppose that it would have done so by the plain declaration, and would not have left it to mere inference. Before the question became acute at the close of the Spanish War, the distinction between acquisition and incorpora-

Chapter VIII: *The American Empire?*

Another possibility is that the shift of Brewer, Peckham, and Fuller in *Rassmussen* had less to do with the particulars of the case than with the changes in the social context. In the initial *Insular Cases*, the dissenters spoke in the wake of McKinley's victory in November 1900, as the tide of imperialism seemed to be on the rise. By 1905, however, the tide had changed, and the acquisition of colonies seemed less likely. While Roosevelt was determined to protect American economic interests and to keep the European powers out of the hemisphere—this was the gist of the so-called Roosevelt Corollary—he had no intention of establishing new colonies.[92] In fact, in 1904 Roosevelt specifically refused to establish a protectorate over Santo Domingo (now the Dominican Republic). Reflecting a sentiment no doubt forged by an appreciation of the difficulties experienced suppressing the insurrection in the Philippines, Roosevelt said that he had no more desire to acquire Santo Domingo than "a gorged boa constrictor might have to swallow a porcupine wrong-end-to."[93] The Senate was even less interested in annexation, failing to endorse a treaty Roosevelt signed with the government of Santo Domingo giving to the United States certain powers on the island. In this context the threat to liberty and the social contract tradition might have seemed less pressing and the need to insist upon the analytic unity of flag and Constitution less urgent. There was little reason for the contractarians to fear that adopting a more permissive doctrine would cause further colonial expansion. By 1905 the doctrine of incorporation, with all its ambiguities, might have seemed more acceptable.

Such an explanation for the shift in *Rassmussen* obviously assumes a relationship between law and politics, but it is not of the variety contemplated by Dooley and his school. The triumph of incorporation in 1905 may

---

tion was not regarded as important, or at least it was not fully understood and had not aroused great controversy. Before that, the purpose of Congress might well be a matter of mere inference from various legislative acts; but in these latter days, incorporation is not be assumed without express declaration, or an implication so strong as to exclude any other view." 258 U.S. 298, 306 (1922). It is hard to believe that the incorporation of Alaska would have met Taft's test.

[92] See Chapter 2, text accompanying note 79.

[93] Roosevelt to Joseph Bucklin Bishop, Feb. 23, 1904, Elting E. Morison, ed., *The Square Deal, 1903–1905*, vol. 4

of *The Letters of Theodore Roosevelt* (Cambridge: Harvard University Press, 1951), 734. On this episode and Roosevelt's imperial policy more generally, see Howard K. Beale, *Theodore Roosevelt and the Rise of America to World Power* (Baltimore: Johns Hopkins Press, 1956); William H. Harbaugh, *Power and Responsibility: The Life and Times of Theodore Roosevelt* (New York: Farrar, Straus & Cudahy, 1961); George E. Mowry, *The Era of Theodore Roosevelt, 1900–1912* (New York: Harper & Bros., 1958); Edmund Morris, *The Rise of Theodore Roosevelt* (New York: Coward, McCann & Geoghegan, 1979), 565–741; and Lewis L. Gould, *The Presidency of Theodore Roosevelt* (Lawrence: University Press of Kansas, 1991).

not have been born of an impulse to give the electorate what it wanted, as Dooley suggested, but just the opposite. Brewer and Peckham and maybe even Fuller were prepared to give the president and Congress a power earlier denied only after it became clear that the power was one they no longer wanted and were not likely to exercise in any event. It is also conceivable that law, in this instance the doctrines formulated by the justices in *Downes*, played some role in the decline of the imperial impulse and thus contributed to the eventual triumph of the doctrine of incorporation. It was not that the Court followed the "iliction returns," but that the elected representatives followed the Court. No one could have missed the significance of the fact that in the original *Insular Cases* of 1901 only one justice—Brown— was prepared to give the administration all that it wanted.

Of course, the forces that spurred the initial drive toward the establishment of a colonial empire were real and powerful; they were not easily harnessed, much less dissipated, by law or anything else. Yet it was also understood that those very same interests could be satisfied in many different ways, some of which would pose fewer legal problems than did the formal maintenance of "colonies." By 1905 the real question was not whether the Constitution would follow the flag, but whether it would follow the United Fruit Company. Everyone knew the answer to that question.

IV

Just as it would be wrong to think of the *Insular Cases* in exclusively instrumental terms, it would be equally wrong to see them as an utter repudiation of the notion of constitutive authority that lay at the heart of *Lochner v. New York* and so much of the work of the Fuller Court. Such a view would ignore the strong dissents filed by Fuller, Brewer, and Peckham in 1901 and the dissenting position Harlan took throughout the period. These justices advanced the idea that the national government was a constituted authority with no existence outside, or beyond, the Constitution. There were, moreover, important theoretical links between the views of Fuller, Brewer, Peckham, and Harlan and the content of the incorporation doctrine, as the restrictive elements associated with that doctrine no doubt were fashioned with an eye toward meeting the objections of the dissenters and their view of flag and Constitution as an analytic unity. The views of the dissenters lent respectable support to the anti–imperialist movement of the early 1900s and thus might have contributed to the willingness at that time to forsake the idea of an American empire, a development which, as I tried to suggest, might help to explain the victory of incorporation in 1905.

There is a final side, however, to the *Insular Cases*. They may not have represented an unqualified defeat for the idea of constitutive authority, yet they were a defeat of sorts and to that extent were at odds with *Lochner* and its view of the state. Traces of the organic view can be found in the incorporation doctrine and the plenary power it ceded to the nation in the administration of the colonies prior to incorporation. The Constitution was operative but, alas, not applicable. The organic view is reflected as well in the discretionary nature of the decision to incorporate. For both these reasons, the incorporation doctrine should have troubled McKenna, who joined the *Lochner* majority but nonetheless supported incorporation from the outset. Incorporation should have been a problem even for White. True, he dissented in *Lochner*, but he joined Harlan's opinion in *Adair*[94] and by this act, as well as by his own dissenting opinion in *Northern Securities*,[95] revealed his attachment to the contractarian tradition and the general idea of government as a form of constitutive authority. A similar point could be made about Day. But the most puzzling position of all was Brown's, for while he, like McKenna, joined Peckham's opinion in *Lochner*, his opinion in the *Insular Cases* was a paradigmatic expression of the notion of organic authority. Justice Brown recognized certain limits on governmental authority, such as those imposed by natural rights, but for him those limits, like those constraining a parent, were external to the authority itself. In the *Insular Cases*, in contrast to *Lochner*, the central constitutional question for Brown was whether government violated a prohibition, not whether it had the authority. In relation to the colonies, authority was assumed.

To understand these odd reversals and inconsistencies, one must return to the idea used earlier to reconcile *Muller v. Oregon*[96] with *Lochner*: the notion of a constitutional community.[97] Members of such a community are able to make special demands upon the state, treating it strictly as a form of constitutive authority. At the same time, however, membership in the community is seen as limited. Non-members—say women or children—have a radically different relationship to the state. Affective and social ties may be acknowledged, but at the level of constitutional theory the state is allowed to pursue ends otherwise denied to it in its dealings with

---

[94] Adair v. United States, 208 U.S. 161 (1908). See Chapter 6.
[95] Northern Sec. Co. v. United States,

193 U.S. 197 (1904). See Chapter 5.
[96] 208 U.S. 412 (1908).
[97] See Chapter 6.

253

members.[98] Here, asked to decide whether citizens of the colonies were members of the constitutional community, the Court was faced in the *Insular Cases* with a challenge to universalism that was in some respects similar to the question posed by *Muller v. Oregon.*

Justice Brown refused to follow Taney on the question of congressional power, but he did define the constitutional community in an exclusionary way analogous to Taney's treatment of blacks. As already noted, there was no natural right of citizenship. Brown's stance in the *Insular Cases* might have reflected a crude xenophobia, a belief in the otherness and even moral inferiority of the people inhabiting territories that were geographically and culturally distant. Such a view would not be inconsistent with the views Brown had espoused earlier in 1896 in *Plessy v. Ferguson* and, quite frankly, there is more than one passage in his opinion in the *Insular Cases* to confirm such an explanation. Justice Brown was not the least embarrassed to call the inhabitants of the colonies "savages."[99] This may be too harsh or too simplistic a judgment of Brown's character, and history ultimately may find him to have been moved by a more complex set of factors: a desire to accommodate the exertion of power by the political branches of the national government; a belief that without a colonial empire the

---

[98] Before Fuller took his seat, it was well established that Indians stood outside the constitutional community. See Elk v. Wilkins, 112 U.S. 94 (1884) (absent a special treaty or statute, Indians, even those separated from their tribes, are not citizens of the United States). This status held throughout the Fuller Court years. Indeed, Fuller himself openly spoke of the condition of Indians as one of "pupilage or dependency" and acknowledged the absolute character of the power of Congress over their fate. Stephens v. Cherokee Nation, 174 U.S. 445, 485, 488 (1899) (a congressional commission may determine who is a member of a tribe and allot tribal land without regard to treaties). See also Cherokee Nation v. Hitchcock, 187 U.S. 294 (1902) (upholding the authority of the secretary of the interior to grant mineral leases on Cherokee land), and Lone Wolf v. Hitchcock, 187 U.S. 553 (1903) (upholding cession of tribal land to the United States even though it did not comply with treaty requirements and was surrounded by allegations of fraud). In the latter case, the Court, in an opinion by Justice White, denied that a treaty gave rise to any property rights

that might be protected by the Fifth Amendment and then added: "The contention in effect ignores the status of the contracting Indians and the relation of dependency they bore and continue to bear towards the government of the United States." Ibid., 564. See also Chapter 12, text accompanying note 110.

[99] The term appears in this passage:

We are also of opinion that the power to acquire territory by treaty implies not only the power to govern such territory, but to prescribe upon what terms the United States will receive its inhabitants, and what their *status* shall be in what Chief Justice Marshall termed the "American Empire." There seems to be no middle ground between this position and the doctrine that if their inhabitants do not become, immediately upon annexation, citizens of the United States, their children thereafter born, whether savages or civilized, are such, and entitled to all the rights, privileges and immunities of citizens. If such be their status, the consequences will be extremely serious.

Downes, 182 U.S. at 279 (emphasis in original).

Chapter VIII: *The American Empire?*

United States could not effectively compete in the world arena; or the hope of protecting those industrial interests served by the transformation of the American nation into a colonial empire. Speculation regarding his motivation notwithstanding, it cannot be denied that the natural and probable effect of Brown's position was to place the inhabitants of the colonies or, if you will, the territories, outside the constitutional community.

Brown espoused a view that could be interpreted as implanting racial or cultural distinctions into constitutional law. Just as *Muller* could be reconciled with *Lochner* on a theory that gave constitutional force to the exclusion of women from the constitutional community, Brown's position in the *Insular Cases* could be reconciled with *Lochner*—that central, identifying precedent of the Fuller Court—by creating another exclusion from the constitutional community, in this instance one based on racial or cultural distinctions. The psychological dynamic or the materialistic basis of the exclusion may have been different, but at the level of constitutional theory the result was the same.

Given the times and the history of xenophobia in America, such an exclusion may not seem at all remarkable. Yet what is remarkable is how few of the justices were prepared to endorse it. Brown was, but the other justices embraced a theory of governmental authority that rested on a more universalistic conception of the constitutional community. This is clearly true of the four dissenters, Brewer, Peckham, Fuller, and Harlan.[100] It might also be thought to characterize White and those who embraced the theory of incorporation. White, too, spoke of "alien races,"[101] yet tended toward universalism insofar as full incorporation was treated as the aspiration and non-incorporation only a transitional phase.

Of course, some of the justices, maybe all, who subscribed to the more robust contract theory would have been happy to de-annex the territories and disassociate themselves from these communities altogether; they were

---

[100] In *Hawaii v. Mankichi*, Harlan argued vigorously against the proposition that "the protection [of the Constitution] may be claimed by some of the people subject to the authority and jurisdiction of the United States, but cannot be claimed by others equally subject to its authority and jurisdiction[;] . . . that the will of Congress, not the Constitution, is the supreme law of the land only for certain peoples and territories under our jurisdiction." 190 U.S. at 239. Brewer's own brand of universalism is captured in an 1899 speech: "I do not question the capacity of the [Anglo-Saxon] race . . . to well and wisely govern others. I object to it because it antagonizes the principles upon which this government was founded. . . ." "The Spanish War; A Prophecy or an Exception?," Speech Delivered at the Liberal Club, Buffalo, N.Y. (Feb. 16, 1899), 15. Later in the speech, Brewer made reference to slavery, saying that the United States had difficulty incorporating the newly emancipated slaves into the polity because they were not accustomed to freedom, and warned of the problems of trying to incorporate "the savage and semi-civilized races of these islands." Ibid., 31. For the position of these justices on the treatment of blacks and the Chinese, see Chapters 10 and 12.

[101] *Downes*, 182 U.S. at 313.

not singing the songs of brotherhood. But they nevertheless recognized that as long as the United States held on to these distant lands and as long as they were administered by its coercive apparatus, the people of these regions had claims upon the structure of state authority that were equal to the claims of the bakers of New York. These people were also part of the constitutional community. For the dissenters, the *Insular Cases* were essentially similar to *Lochner*, and in this respect radically unlike *Muller*.

The dissenters did not win the day, but their willingness to include the inhabitants of the colonies within the constitutional community was an important statement against racism. Such a limited concession might not be much of an accomplishment, but it shows that—at least on the level of constitutional theory—racism did not fully capture the Court. It also gives us a sobering insight into the depth of sexism. Remembering that *Muller* was a unanimous decision, I think it fair to say of that era that the exclusion of women from the constitutional community was more firmly entrenched and more widely embraced than the exclusion of people of different races and cultures.

CHAPTER IX

Federalism and Liberty

COLONIALISM was a prominent issue in the 1900 election and during the 1900 Term of Court, and it arose in a number of cases over the next several terms; but then it moved to the margin of the Court's agenda. In contrast, the problem of allocating powers between the states and the national government—the federalism issue—has haunted the Supreme Court throughout its history. It has been all pervasive, arising every term and in every kind of case, and the Fuller years were no exception.

In *Debs* the central problem facing the Court, as I saw it, was to justify a role for the national government, as opposed to the State of Illinois, in the restoration of public order.[1] Federalism was also implicated in the Court's income tax decision. The Constitution required an apportionment of direct taxes among the states according to population, and this was seen, at least by the majority in *Pollock*, as an essential feature of the compromise that brought the less populous states into the Union.[2] On the antitrust front, enforcement of the Sherman Act raised important questions about the reach of the national power under the Commerce Clause, whether it embraced manufacturing and on what terms.[3] Similar questions recurred when the Court considered other progressive measures, such as those relating to worker safety[4] and the regulation of railroad rates.[5] Rate regulation began as a purely state phenomenon, but starting with the *Wabash* decision of 1886, the Court limited the power of the states and allocated the rate regulation power between the state and national governments. Finally, considerations of federalism were reflected in the process—which came to a dramatic conclusion in *Ex parte Young* in 1908—of identifying the forum that

---

[1] See Chapter 3.
[2] See Chapter 4.
[3] See Chapter 5.
[4] See The Employers' Liability Cases, 207 U.S. 463 (1908), and Second Employers' Liability Cases, 223 U.S. 1 (1912). These and subsequent cases involving the Employers' Liability Act, and other contemporaneous decisions on the com-

merce power, are discussed in F. D. G. Ribble, *State and National Power over Commerce* (New York: Columbia University Press, 1937), 134–37, and in Bernard C. Gavit, *The Commerce Clause of the United States Constitution* (Bloomington, Ind.: Principia Press, 1932), 218–22.

[5] See Chapter 7.

was to hear federal constitutional challenges to the rate regulations of the states.

Although problems of federalism arose at every turn, it seemed difficult for the justices to find their bearings. Their task was to allocate power between various governmental entities (the nation versus the states), and although any such allocation would have decisive implications for the amount of power possessed by each entity, it was difficult to formulate an allocative rule that always, or even generally, served the ideal of limited government in a simple and straightforward manner. The contractarian tradition spoke to the issue of legitimating government power in general, not to the allocation of power among different levels of government.

From the perspective of individual liberty, the concept that lay at the heart of the social contract, the allocation of power between the nation and the state might seem of no special consequence. A state government is still a government, and its laws are no more nor less coercive than those of the national government. In the eyes of the justices there was no essential difference between the laws involved in *Lochner* and *Adair*; one was as much a threat to liberty as the other.[6] On the other hand, the scale of state government is smaller than that of the nation, and although that difference might not guarantee a protection of individual liberty, it might facilitate the formation of local consensus. While such a social formation might be of special interest to communitarians, which Fuller and his colleagues most assuredly were not, it might also be important to contractarians, who were not just individualists but also rationalists. To a contractarian, liberty was not mere discretion, but rather the power of the individual to set rules for himself—to live his life by his own reasons.[7] When that goal was not attainable, the next best thing might be a political consensus, where the legal rules are those that individuals would have set for themselves had they had the liberty to do so. If an individual cannot be free, he should at least agree with the laws that coerce his conduct.

A view that honored local consensus might have pointed to a resolution of the federalism question that favored the state over the nation. The smallness of scale might facilitate communication among individuals in the polity and permit individuals to move to subdivisions whose values they shared. This indeed might be the theory of the Constitution, as the justices understood it, explaining why the most traditional government functions—those embraced by the police power—were allocated to the states, not the nation. There were, however, two factors that qualified this understanding and thus further complicated the allocative question.

---

[6] See Chapter 6.
[7] See generally Paul W. Kahn, "Reason and Will in the Origins of American Constitutionalism," *Yale L.J.*, 98: 449 (1989).

Chapter IX: *Federalism and Liberty*

One was empirical. The justices understood that the assumptions underlying the theory of local consensus were questionable simply as a matter of fact. Whatever may have been the situation at the founding, by the late nineteenth century the population of each state was becoming diverse and heterogeneous and the burden of moving from one state to another was considerable. The close of the frontier had already been announced. Differences—of ethnicity, class, occupation, religion, or mode of life—that shaped points of view were present within states as well as among them. The assumption of local consensus at the state level must have seemed problematic.

The second factor that complicated the allocative question was more normative. Even if a rule favoring the states might be defended on the basis of local consensus, and thus to some limited extent on the theory of individual liberty, there was another notion—central to *Debs*, *Wabash*, and the later antitrust cases like *Standard Oil* and *American Tobacco*—that pointed in an entirely opposite direction: economic nationalism. This idea, traceable to the work of the Marshall Court, saw national unity as dependent on the formation of the United States into a common market and called for the free movement of goods from state to state. The principal instrument of this theory was the Commerce Clause, or, more precisely, the concept of the "dormant" Commerce Clause, which called for the nullification of all state laws that interfered with the free flow of goods across state lines.

In the antitrust context, the federalism debate centered on the attempt to extend the Sherman Act to manufacturing, and the conflict between economic nationalism and local consensus was at a minimum. If certain states failed to enforce their own antitrust laws, that was because of the trusts' threats and influence, not because their citizens believed in monopoly. In its final resolution, the Court left the regulation of manufacturing and production to the states but held that the federal government could regulate all transactions, including the acquisition of manufacturing firms, that had an impact on intercourse among the states. State laws were not preempted; rather, the Sherman Act was extended. In *Debs*, too, there was little conflict between economic nationalism and local consensus. A variant of the dormant Commerce Clause was applied in that case, but only against the American Railway Union, not the State of Illinois. Although federal intervention was at odds with the position of Governor Altgeld, it was hard to imagine that he was speaking for all the interested citizens of Illinois.

In other domains, however, the conflict between economic nationalism and local consensus was deep and genuine, and thus the federalism question more perplexing. Such was arguably the case in *Wabash* and the other cases discussed in Chapter 7, where the dormant Commerce Clause was used to preempt state regulation of interstate trips. But the conflict there was not nearly so intense as it was in the cases that form the subject of this chapter, those involving regulation by the states of the sale and distribution of intoxicating liquors. At issue in these cases was not state supervision of market conditions but state prohibition of an entire market. The desire of various states to suppress or control the use of intoxicating liquor required not only control over local production, which could have been safely conceded to be within the police power, but also a ban on importation from sister states and abroad. It required the construction of total trade barriers, which was anathema to principles of economic nationalism.

Informed by the history of the Supreme Court over the last twenty years, the contemporary student of constitutional law tends to link conservatism with the enhancement of the power of the states. This view reflects, however, special historical circumstances: Ever since the New Deal the national government has been the principal instrumentality of progressive politics. The Fuller Court has been depicted as a conservative institution because it resisted many of the progressive reforms of the day, and like many contemporary conservatives, did so in the name of individual liberty; but that Court did not translate its general commitment to individual liberty into a comprehensive program favoring state sovereignty. Granted, in situations like *Pollock* the Court curbed the power of the national government and strictly applied to that government a rule that was not applicable to the states. More generally, however, as in the railroad regulation cases, the antitrust area, and *Debs*, the Court curbed the powers of the states and affirmatively strengthened the power of the national government.

The result was the same in the state prohibition cases. Here, there was an especially strong conflict between economic nationalism and local consensus. The justices acknowledged the value of local consensus, insofar as it existed and could be seen as a proxy for individual liberty, and at first made some gestures toward home rule. But in the end the principles of economic nationalism triumphed, and state power was sharply limited. The states were not, on their own authority, allowed to prevent individuals from importing alcohol for personal use or resale. Once authorized by Congress, the states were allowed to prohibit resale, but the Court insisted that there was no power in the states, even with congressional authorization, to prohibit importation for personal use. The temperance movement reacted with fury.

At the turn of the century, antitrust was not the exclusive property of lawyers and economists—thus the special significance of decisions like *Standard Oil* and *American Tobacco*, or, for that matter, *Northern Securities*. Antitrust was a social movement, one of the principal branches of progressivism, debated in elections, and high on the agenda of the president. Antitrust divided the Court, but the trajectory of its decisions—more and more power to the nation—coincided with the demands of the movement. Legal doctrine coincided with the political impulse. The matter of rate regulation was also inspired by broad political considerations, and here an accommodation could be worked out: The states could regulate intrastate trips, the federal government interstate ones (federal legislation regulating the rates of interstate trips was passed in 1887, 1903, and 1906). In *Debs* and the state prohibition cases, however, the position of the Court was more controversial. The Court affirmed principles of economic nationalism, but in doing so it antagonized broad-based popular movements—in one labor, in the other, temperance.

Of the two, the Court's confrontation with the prohibition movement seemed the more perilous. Like antitrust, prohibition drew on the progressive impulse for social betterment, and at the time prohibition seemed a more powerful political force than labor. The decisions in the state prohibition cases also left the Court more exposed institutionally. In *Debs* the Court affirmed principles of economic nationalism by upholding and legitimating strong exercises of power by other branches of the national government—above all by the executive, but perhaps also by Congress, insofar as the injunction against the American Railway Union arguably furthered the intention of Congress as manifest in the Sherman Act. In that sense *Debs* was an exercise in the coordination of powers. In the state prohibition cases, the Court also affirmed principles of economic nationalism but acted without corresponding support from the other branches. In a last-ditch confrontation with Congress the Court acquired the support of President Taft, always the lawyer, but during the late 1890s and early 1900s it acted alone, indeed contrary to the express intention of Congress, and thus confronted the prohibition movement in all its fury. More than in *Debs*, the Court's stance on this issue was especially heroic and especially vulnerable.

I

Some prohibitionists were dedicated to eradicating the consumption of alcohol, and others merely its public use and sale; but all were agreed that the power of government should be brought to bear on those who produced and supplied the drug.[8] Beginning in the mid-nineteenth century,

---

[8] See Norman H. Clark, *Deliver Us from Evil: An Interpretation of American Prohibition* (New York: W. W. Norton, 1976). See also Paul Aaron and David Musto, "Temperance and Prohibition in America: A Historical Overview," in Mark H. Moore and Dean R. Gerstein, eds., *Alcohol and Public Policy: Beyond the Shadow of Prohibition* (Washington, D.C.: National Academy Press, 1981), 127. Two earlier works are D. Leigh Colvin, *Prohibition in the United States: A* *History of the Prohibition Party and of the Prohibition Movement* (New York: George H. Doran, 1926), and Ernest H. Cherrington, *The Evolution of Prohibition in the United States of America: A Chronological History of the Liquor Problem and the Temperance Reform in the United States from the Earliest Settlements to the Consummation of National Prohibition* (Westerville, Ohio: American Issue Press, 1920; repr. Montclair, N.J.: Patterson Smith, 1969).

and then again in the later part of the century, laws were enacted by various states that made it illegal to produce liquor within the state and to sell it on either the wholesale or retail level.[9] In order to stop consumption, however, these exercises of state power required a foreign supplement: The consumer's access to liquor produced in sister states and abroad also had to be blocked. Without such a measure, prohibition of domestic sources alone would put in-state producers out of business, but determined consumers could still get their liquor by importing it.

The purely domestic component of state prohibition laws raised questions of constitutional validity, specifically whether the laws constituted a denial of substantive due process or a takings. But the Court did not formally address these questions when the prohibition issue first reached it in the *License Cases* of 1847—prior to the adoption of the Fourteenth Amendment.[10] Those cases—in which six justices wrote separate opinions—involved challenges to liquor licensing laws in three states: Massachusetts, New Hampshire, and Rhode Island.

The justices were divided on the Commerce Clause issue, that is, on the applicability of these laws to liquor imported from wet states. But all the justices seemed to assume that state statutes that merely prohibited the production of liquor within the state and its sale were an appropriate exercise of the police power. As Chief Justice Taney put it, "nothing in the constitution" prevents a state from aiming its laws at practices it considers "injurious to its citizens, and calculated to produce idleness, vice, or debauchery."[11]

---

[9] The prohibition movement was active between 1840 and 1860, relatively dormant for a generation after the Civil War, and then active again from 1880 to 1920. On prohibition in the nineteenth century, see Ian R. Tyrrell, *Sobering Up: From Temperance to Prohibition in Antebellum America, 1800–1860* (Westport, Conn.: Greenwood Press, 1979), and James Ross Turner, "The American Prohibition Movement, 1865–1897" (Ph.D. diss., University of Wisconsin, 1972). The prohibition movement during the Fuller Court period is covered by the sources cited below in note 73. For a short history of the state prohibition regimes, see Ernest A. Grant, "The Liquor Traffic Before the Eighteenth Amendment," *Annals Am. Acad. Pol. & Soc. Sci.*, 163: 1 (1932). See also Frederick A. Johnson and Ruth R. Kessler, "The Liquor License System—Its Origin and Constitutional Development," *N.Y.U. L.Q. Rev.*, 15: 210–51, 380–424 (1937–38), and Henry C. Black, *A Treatise on the Laws Regulating the Manufacture and Sale of Intoxicating Liquors* (St. Paul, Minn.: West Publishing, 1892).

[10] 46 U.S. (5 How.) 504 (1847). In the famous case of Wynehamer v. People, 13 N.Y. 378 (1856), New York's highest court held that the application of the state prohibition law to liquor existing at the time of the law's passage interfered with vested property rights and therefore violated the state constitution. *Wynehamer* and the other antebellum state liquor cases are discussed in Johnson and Kessler, "Liquor License System," 380–88, and in Tyrrell, *Sobering Up*, 290–93.

[11] 46 U.S. at 577.

Chapter IX: *Federalism and Liberty*

Following the Civil War and the adoption of the Fourteenth Amendment, the constitutional attack on the domestic component of the state prohibition laws acquired a more secure legal foundation.[12] As it turned out, however, when the Court took up the issue in 1873—in *Bartmeyer v. Iowa*,[13] a companion to the *Slaughter-House Cases*[14]—the initial assumption of the *License Cases* was left undisturbed. The Court's decision in *Slaughter-House*, upholding a Louisiana statute that created a monopoly over butchering, provoked passionate dissents by Justices Field and Bradley, but even they voted with the majority in *Bartmeyer*. According to Bradley and Field in the concurring opinions they filed in *Bartmeyer*, the prohibition law fell within the established boundaries of the police power because it did not prevent individuals from participating in a trade open to others, as did the Louisiana statute. Rather, the Iowa law was aimed at the sale of articles "deemed injurious to the safety of society."[15] An additional question— whether Iowa had a duty to compensate property owners whose "vested rights of property"[16] were sacrificed—was deemed moot because of a failure of pleading: The petitioner failed to allege that he owned the property interdicted—a glass of whiskey—prior to the passage of the statute.

Not surprisingly, an effort was soon made—in 1878 in *Beer Co. v. Massachusetts*[17]—to cast the constitutional objection to the domestic component of state prohibition laws in terms that sounded in confiscation. The Takings Clause was unavailable for the same reason as in *Bartmeyer v. Iowa*—the liquor was not in existence at the time the statute was passed— and so counsel turned to the Contracts Clause. He claimed that the Massachusetts statute impaired the obligation of contract, specifically the charter of incorporation previously granted to the beer company. But once again the attack came to naught, failing to pick up even the votes of Bradley and

---

[12] On the development of substantive due process after the Civil War, see generally William F. Swindler, *Court and Constitution in the Twentieth Century: The Old Legality, 1889-1932* (Indianapolis: Bobbs-Merrill, 1969) 18–38, 108–131. See also David N. Mayer, "The Jurisprudence of Christopher G. Tiedeman: A Study in the Failure of Laissez-Faire Constitutionalism," *Mo. L. Rev.*, 55: 93, 94–96 (1990), and Charles W. McCurdy, "The Roots of 'Liberty of Contract' Reconsidered: Major Premises in the Law of Employment, 1867–1937," *Sup. Ct. Hist. Soc'y Y.B.*, 1984: 20–23. On the "domestic" prohibition cases in the Supreme Court, see Charles

Fairman, *Reconstruction and Reunion, 1864–88*, vol. 7 of *History of the Supreme Court of the United States* (New York: Macmillan, 1987), 699–700, 706–707.

[13] 85 U.S. (18 Wall.) 129 (1874).

[14] 83 U.S. (16 Wall.) 36 (1873). The report in *Bartmeyer* states that "[t]he case was submitted on printed arguments some time ago, ... when the *Slaughter-House Cases* ... were argued." 85 U.S. at 131.

[15] 85 U.S. at 136 (Bradley, J., concurring) and 137 (Field, J., concurring).

[16] Ibid.

[17] 97 U.S. 25 (1878).

Field. In fact, Justice Bradley wrote the opinion of the Court. He pointed to a Massachusetts statute of 1809 that gave the legislature the power to repeal all charters of incorporation and that was made a specific term and limitation of the charter of the beer company. Justice Bradley treated the prohibition statute as an implied exercise of the power previously reserved to the legislature by the 1809 statute. He was not content, however, to base his decision only on the peculiarities of the Massachusetts regulatory scheme regarding corporations. According to Bradley, there was no need for the state to reserve to itself the power to repeal the charter of incorporation, because "the legislature cannot, by any contract, divest itself of the [police] power."[18] "All rights," he declared in a way that foreshadowed the final resolution of the question left dangling in *Bartmeyer*, "are held subject to the police power of the State."[19]

In *Mugler v. Kansas*,[20] decided in December 1887, only months before Waite's death and Fuller's appointment, the Court once again took up the validity of domestic liquor regulations.[21] Harlan wrote the opinion for the majority, upholding Kansas's prohibition statute over a dissent that was written by Field alone. This time Joseph Choate appeared before the Court to fight the statute and, almost as a rehearsal for his appearance in *Pollock*, he emphasized the property issue. He insisted that the prohibition statute constituted a taking because it materially destroyed the value of a brewery that had existed before the enactment of the law. Harlan acknowledged the diminution of value but decided that as long as a statute was within the police power of the state, there was no taking of property and no obligation to compensate: "[A]ll property in this country," he said, "is held under the implied obligation that the owner's use of it shall not be injurious to the community."[22] Field, in dissent, argued that Harlan was departing from *Bartmeyer*. He refused to concede "that the legislature, in the exercise of . . . [the] police power, may, without compensation to the owner, deprive him of the use of his brewery for the purposes for which it was constructed under the sanction of the law, and for which alone it is valuable."[23]

Justice Harlan brushed aside the other objections to the Kansas statute as well. He found the state within its rights when, in trying to eradicate

[18] Ibid., 33.
[19] Ibid., 32.
[20] 123 U.S. 623 (1887).
[21] In the interim between *Beer Company* and *Mugler*, the Court decided Foster v. Kansas *ex rel.* Johnston, 112 U.S. 201 (1884), which involved a proceeding to remove a county attorney who refused to prosecute liquor merchants. The attorney defended in part on the basis that the state prohibition law was unconstitutional, but the Court without dissent upheld his removal on the ground that the constitutionality of statutes prohibiting the sale or manufacture of alcohol was "no longer open in this court." Ibid., 206.
[22] 123 U.S. at 665.
[23] Ibid., 678 (Field, J., dissenting in part). Brewer shared Field's sentiment.

consumption, it prohibited production for home use. As for Choate's challenge to the special enforcement mechanism devised by Kansas (injunctive litigation by state agencies and the seizure and destruction of all property used in violation of the statute), which Choate claimed violated procedural due process and the jury trial right, Harlan pointed to the traditional use of injunctions to abate nuisances. Harlan argued that the Kansas legislature legitimately could find a whole class of activities—distilling—to be a nuisance.[24]

On these questions, as on the takings issue, Harlan emphasized that prohibition statutes were within the states' police power. This had been the assumption of the *License Cases*, and as was evident in cases like *Bartmeyer* and *Beer Company*, this reasoning continued to control after the Civil War, despite the rise of substantive due process. Although courts increasingly were willing in other areas to find that legislation exceeded the bounds of the police power, as far as prohibition was concerned, the issue was settled. *Mugler v. Kansas*, coming as the last statement by the Waite Court on this issue, constituted an especially important affirmation of this understanding and in Harlan's hands took on strikingly enthusiastic and revealing formulation:

> [W]e cannot shut out of view the fact, within the knowledge of all, that the public health, the public morals, and the public safety, may be endangered by the general use of intoxicating drinks; nor the fact, established by statistics accessible to every one, that the idleness, disorder, pauperism, and crime existing in the country are, in some degree at least, traceable to this evil.[25]

He was on the Kansas supreme court when it heard *Mugler* and though he agreed to uphold the ban on selling liquor, he voiced a liberty objection to a ban on manufacturing liquor for personal use and then, considering the loss of value that might result from a ban on manufacturing, mused: "If the public good required the destruction of the value of this property, is not prior compensation indispensable?" State v. Mugler, 29 Kan. 252, 274 (1883) (Brewer, J., concurring). Three years later Brewer, now a federal circuit judge, was more decisive when he held that the prohibition amendment to the Kansas state constitution and statutes implementing it were unconstitutional because they deprived the defendants of the use of their brewery without compensation: "Beyond any doubt, the state can prohibit defendants from continuing their business of brewing, but before it can do so it must pay the value of the property destroyed." State v. Walruff, 26 Fed. 178, 200 (C.C.D. Kan. 1886).

[24] A similar procedural challenge to Iowa's prohibition regime was rejected three years after *Mugler* in Eilenbecker v. District Court, 134 U.S. 31 (1890).

[25] 123 U.S. at 662. Field saw no objection to a licensing requirement. Three

II

The Court's decision in *Mugler* may have closed the door, once and for all, on the domestic aspects of prohibition, but that was only half the problem. In order to fulfill their ambitions, dry states had to stop the importation of liquor from abroad and the even greater flow from sister states, and these measures raised important Commerce Clause questions. In the *License Cases*, a majority of the justices, led by Chief Justice Taney, resolved these questions in favor of state prohibition. That ruling did not, however, withstand the force of events, as the Civil War itself and the emergence of a body of judicial decisions sought to forge the United States into a single economic union. These decisions first were announced in the 1870s and 1880s and reached something of a peak with the *Wabash* decision of 1886 and the *Debs* decision of 1895, both of which read the Commerce Clause as embodying principles of economic nationalism and as a mandate to keep the commercial arteries of the nation free and open.[26] This reading of the Commerce Clause had many sources, but Fuller and his contemporaries largely saw it as rooted in an 1827 decision by Chief Justice John Marshall, *Brown v. Maryland*,[27] and they later used that decision to overrule the *License Cases*.

Brown v. Maryland involved neither the prohibition nor even the regulation of imports from sister states, but a state licensing fee imposed on importers of foreign goods. In holding that the license fee violated the Imports Clause and conflicted with the federal statute imposing import taxes, Marshall laid the foundations for the approach that came to fruition in *E. C. Knight*,[28] where the boundaries of state power were defined by the

years after *Mugler*, in upholding a conviction under California's liquor licensing statute, Field wrote for a unanimous Court that "[as the liquor trade] is a business attended with danger to the community it may . . . be entirely prohibited, or be permitted under such conditions as will limit to the utmost its evils." Crowley v. Christensen, 137 U.S. 86, 91 (1890).

[26] On the development of Commerce Clause doctrine in the nineteenth century, see generally Edward S. Corwin, *The Commerce Power Versus States Rights* (Princeton: Princeton University Press, 1936); Felix Frankfurter, *The Commerce Clause under Marshall, Taney and Waite* (Chapel Hill: University of North Carolina Press, 1937); and

Thomas Reed Powell, *Vagaries and Varieties in Constitutional Interpretation* (New York: Columbia University Press, 1956), 49–87, 142–215. See also Ribble, *State and National Power over Commerce*, and Gavit, *Commerce Clause*. The latter work has a chronological appendix abstracting every Commerce Clause decision by the Court up to 1932.

[27] 25 U.S. (12 Wheat.) 419 (1827). An even earlier expression of the dormant Commerce Clause occurred in Gibbons v. Ogden, 22 U.S. (9 Wheat.) 1 (1824), which was also often cited. There, too, it was a dictum, since the state law conflicted with a congressional enactment.

[28] See Chapter 5.

type or category of economic activity regulated. "Any penalty inflicted on the importer, for selling the article, in his character of importer," Marshall wrote, "must be in opposition to the act of congress which authorizes importation."[29] This suggested that a prohibition of imports, as much as the revenue measure itself, would be invalid, although Marshall had hedged on the point earlier in the opinion. Marshall also laid out what came to be known as the "original package" doctrine, holding that the activity of interstate or foreign commerce included not only the importation of goods but also their first resale:

> [W]hen the importer has so acted upon the thing imported, that it has become incorporated and mixed up with the mass of property in the country, it has, perhaps, lost its distinctive character as an import, and has become subject to the taxing power of the State; but while remaining the property of the importer, in his warehouse, in the original form or package in which it was imported, a tax upon it is too plainly a duty on imports to escape the prohibition in the constitution.[30]

Then, almost at the very end of his opinion, Marshall wrote: "It may be proper to add, that we suppose the principles laid down in this case, to apply equally to importations from a sister state."[31]

Since there was no congressional enactment imposing a duty on imports from sister states, the right to import and the right to sell referred to by Marshall in this last sentence could not be implied from the federal statute at issue in *Brown v. Maryland* itself. If one further assumed (as the Court would later hold[32]) that the Imports Clause did not apply domestically, these rights had to come from the Commerce Clause; and if so, Marshall must have read the Commerce Clause to have a preemptive power that would nullify state laws regulating interstate commerce. In Marshall's dictum one thus can find, almost for the first time, the so-called dormant Commerce Clause.

As the attorney general of Maryland, Taney represented the state before the Supreme Court in *Brown v. Maryland*, but by the time of the *License Cases* he had become the chief justice and thus was perfectly positioned to have his revenge on Marshall. Although there was no opinion for the Court—Taney, McLean, Catron, Daniel, Woodbury, and Grier each wrote separate opinions, while Nelson concurred with Taney and Catron—all of the justices agreed that a New Hampshire law regulating the sale of liquor (including domestic and foreign imports) was constitutional. Taney,

---

[29] 25 U.S. at 448.
[30] Ibid., 441–42.
[31] Ibid., 449.

[32] Woodruff v. Parham, 75 U.S. (8 Wall.) 123 (1869). See below, note 37.

Catron, and Woodbury denied any preemptive force to the Commerce
Clause:

> [T]he mere grant of power to the general government cannot, upon any
> just principles of construction, be construed to be an absolute prohibi-
> tion to the exercise of any power over the same subject by the
> States. . . . [T]he State may . . . for the safety or convenience of trade,
> or for the protection of the health of its citizens, make regulations of
> commerce for its own ports and harbours, and for its own territory; and
> such regulations are valid unless they come in conflict with a law of
> Congress.[33]

Daniel disputed the original package doctrine:

> Imports . . . are properly commodities . . . which either have not reached
> their perfect investiture or their alternate destination as property within
> the jurisdiction of the State, or which still are subject to the power of
> the government for a fulfillment of the conditions upon which they have
> been admitted to entrance; as, for instance, goods on which duties are
> still unpaid, or which are bonded or in public warehouses. So soon as
> they are cleared of all control of the government which permits their
> introduction, and have become the complete and exclusive property of
> the citizen or resident, they are no longer imports. . . . I can perceive
> no rational distinction which can be taken upon the circumstance of
> mere quantity, shape, or bulk; or on that of the number of transmissions
> through which a commodity may have passed from the first proprietor,
> or of its remaining still with the latter.[34]

Finally, McLean and Grier both denied Marshall's categorical approach to
commerce questions, arguing that a genuine exercise of the police power
(as determined by the legislature's purpose) was not a "regulation of commerce." As McLean put it in his opinion,

> The State cannot, with a view to encourage its local manufactures, pro-
> hibit the use of foreign articles, or impose such a regulation as shall in
> effect be a prohibition. . . . [But] if the foreign article be injurious to the
> health or morals of the community, a State may, in the exercise of that
> great and conservative police power which lies at the foundation of its
> prosperity, prohibit the sale of it. . . . Such a regulation must be made
> in good faith, and have for its sole object the preservation of the health
> or morals of society.[35]

---

[33] 46 U.S. at 579 (Taney, C.J.). Justice
Wayne seems not to have participated,
although there is no statement to that
effect.
[34] Ibid., 614 (Daniel, J.).
[35] Ibid., 592 (McLean, J.).

Two versions of the same event: At the left, front page of the *New York World*, and at the right, front page of the *New York Journal*, both dated February 17, 1898. *(Library of Congress)*

Drawing for a pamphlet published in 1898 by Arkell Publishing Company, the publisher of *Leslie's Weekly*. (*The Granger Collection*)

Cartoon by Grant Hamilton published in *Judge*, June 11, 1898. It reads: INFORMATION WANTED Uncle Sam—"Now that I've got it, what am I going to do with it?" (*Library of Congress*)

Spokesman for the Supreme Court on the issue of American imperialism (chapter 8):
Edward Douglass White (1845–1921). He served on the Supreme
Court as an associate justice from 1894 to 1910 and as the
chief justice from 1910 until his death.
(*Library of Congress*)

No. 59885

UNITED STATES OF AMERICA.

Certificate of Residence.

Issued to Chinese _Laborer_, under the Provisions of the Act of May 5, 1892.

This is to Certify THAT _Ah Chung_, a Chinese _Laborer_, now residing at _Tucson, Ariz_ has made application No. _85_ to me for a Certificate of Residence, under the provisions of the Act of Congress approved May 5, 1892, and I certify that it appears from the affidavits of witnesses submitted with said application that said _Ah Chung_ was within the limits of the United States at the time of the passage of said Act, and was then residing at _Tucson, Ariz_ and that he was at that time lawfully entitled to remain in the United States, and that the following is a descriptive list of said Chinese _Laborer_ viz.:

NAME: _Ah Chung_ AGE: _37 years_

LOCAL RESIDENCE: _Tucson, Ariz_

OCCUPATION: _Laborer_ HEIGHT: _5 ft 3 7/8 in_ COLOR OF EYES: _D. Brown_

COMPLEXION: _Dark_ PHYSICAL MARKS, OR PECULIARITIES FOR

IDENTIFICATION: _Face pock marked + scar on left jaw_ And as a further means of identification, I have affixed hereto a photographic likeness of said _Ah Chung_

GIVEN UNDER MY HAND AND SEAL this _3rd_ day of _May_, 189_3_ at _____

State of _____

[SEAL.]

L. A. Hughes

Collector of Internal Revenue,

District of _____

2-1498

Certificate of residence required by the Geary Act of 1892 (chapter 10).
(*University of Arizona Special Collection*)

Front page of *The Rocky Mountain News*, June 25, 1905, which
led to a contempt citation that was the subject of
Patterson v. Colorado (chapter 11).
(*Library of Congress*)

Albion Tourgée, attorney for the petitioner in *Plessy v. Ferguson*
(chapter 12), at his home near Chautauqua Lake
in the late 1890s.
(*Chautauqua County Historical Society*)

The author of *Plessy v.
Ferguson*: Henry Billings
Brown (1836–1913). He
served on the Supreme
Court from 1890 until
his resignation in 1906.
Here in the 1890s.
(*Harvard Law Art Collection*)

The dissenter in *Plessy v.
Ferguson*: John Marshall
Harlan (1833–1911). He
served on the Supreme
Court from 1877 until
his death.
Here about 1890.
(*Library of Congress*)

What the future awaited: On July 28, 1917, some ten thousand people
took part in a "Silent Protest Parade" on Fifth Avenue in
New York City. The National Association for the
Advancement of Colored People (begun in 1909) organized
the march, its first, to protest race discrimination
in the wake of the East Saint Louis riot, which had
resulted in the deaths of more than forty blacks.
(*Schomberg Center for Research in Black Culture, The New York Public Library*)

Chapter IX: *Federalism and Liberty*

When taken together, the six opinions in the *License Cases* were a resounding challenge to economic nationalism and an implicit endorsement of the view of federalism that emphasized local consensus.

The *License Cases* were decided in 1847, but only four years later, in another context, the Court apparently changed course again. In *Cooley v. Board of Wardens* the Court used language that appeared to endorse both the dormant Commerce Clause and Marshall's categorical approach: "Whatever subjects of [Congress's commerce power] are in their nature national, or admit only of one uniform system, or plan of regulation, may justly be said to be of such nature as to require exclusive legislation by Congress."[36] Because the state law at issue was upheld, this was dictum, and the Taney Court understood it as such. Nevertheless, the so-called *Cooley* test—invariably cited along with Marshall's dictum in *Brown v. Maryland*—acquired great force after the Civil War. In a series of decisions announced in the 1870s and 1880s, the dormant Commerce Clause was fully embraced and the *Cooley* test became the standard for applying it.[37] It came to be commonly accepted that the interstate movement of goods was a category of economic activity "admit[ting] only of one uniform system" and therefore subject to exclusive congressional control. It was also acknowl-

---

[36] 53 U.S. (12 How.) 299, 319 (1851).

[37] The ascendancy of the *Cooley* test is evident in an 1898 treatise on the Commerce Clause, which commented: "Since the decision of *Cooley v. Port Wardens*, the rule therein laid down has, with one important exception [the interstate application of contract law] . . . been followed in every case in the Supreme Court upon this subject. . . . It is not easy at this time to exaggerate the importance of the case by which this rule was established." E. Parmalee Prentice and John G. Egan, *The Commerce Clause of the Federal Constitution* (Chicago: Callaghan, 1898), 28.

The early post–Civil War cases did not give *Cooley* such weight. In the prohibition context, an important example is Woodruff v. Parham, 75 U.S. (8 Wall.) 123 (1869), which upheld the application of a Mobile, Alabama, sales tax to the sale of out-of-state goods in their original packages. The Court decided that the Imports Clause did not apply domestically; distinguished Marshall's comments in *Brown v. Maryland* about domestic imports as dicta; and dismissed the dormant Commerce Clause challenge in less than a page without mentioning *Cooley*. Ibid., 136–40. The companion case, Hinson v. Lott, 75 U.S. (8 Wall.) 148 (1869), upheld the application of an Alabama state liquor tax on out-of-state, as well as in-state, liquor sales. An instructive contrast with *Woodruff* and *Hinson* is Robbins v. Shelby County Taxing District, 120 U.S. 489 (1887), which was decided at the end of the Waite Court and prohibited the application of a Tennessee license fee to out-of-state traveling salesmen. Justice Bradley, writing for the Court, declared: "The Constitution of the United States having given to Congress the power to regulate commerce . . . that power is necessarily exclusive whenever the subjects of it are national in their character, or admit only of one uniform system, or plan of regulation. This was decided in the case of *Cooley v. Board of Wardens of the Port of Philadelphia* and was virtually involved in the case of *Gibbons v. Ogden* and has been confirmed in many subsequent cases, amongst others, in *Brown v. Maryland* [and in a string of decisions, culminating in *Wabash*]." Ibid., 492 (citations omitted).

edged that a state law could be a police measure, in the sense that it was enacted for the health of the people, yet at the same time be a "regulation of commerce" and thus preempted by the Commerce Clause even in the absence of a national statute. As Justice Miller put it in one case, "Nothing is gained in the argument by calling it the police power."[38]

The significance of these developments for the state prohibition laws and the continued validity of the *License Cases* could hardly be ignored, yet the justices appeared unwilling to leave anything to chance. In the late 1870s, as the *Cooley* test and the *Brown v. Maryland* dictum were becoming more and more authoritative, Justice Bradley, writing for the Court in *Beer Co. v. Massachusetts*, made it known to the bar that the issue of state power resolved in the *License Cases* was open to reconsideration. At the tail end of his opinion in that case, he wrote:

> [W]e do not mean to lay down any rule at variance with what this Court has decided with regard to the paramount authority of the Constitution . . . relating to the regulation of commerce with foreign nations and among the several States. . . . That question does not arise in this case.[39]

While these words might be taken as nothing more than an innocent disclaimer, read in context they seem to have a greater import and to invite a reconsideration of the *License Cases*.

For one thing, the disclaimer was wholly gratuitous. No Commerce Clause questions were involved in *Beer Co. v. Massachusetts*. The case was brought by a Boston brewery on the theory that the Massachusetts prohibition law of 1869 was an impairment of the obligation of contract (the corporate charter). Moreover, since the Court had decided to sustain the Massachusetts law, no one could possibly have thought its decision in *Beer Company* would be "at variance" with the *License Cases*, which, after all, also upheld a state statute—in that case, against a Commerce Clause attack. Justice Bradley cited the *License Cases* in the above passage only to juxtapose that decision to *Brown v. Maryland* and three cases from the mid-1870s that gave Marshall's view of the Commerce Clause the status of law. In this way he made vivid the conflict between Taney and Marshall, and between the *License Cases* and *Brown v. Maryland*.

In the years following *Beer Company*, the Court's attachment to the idea of the United States as a single common market grew. The *Wabash* decision of 1886 constituted an especially dramatic expression of this trend by cutting back on *Munn v. Illinois* (1877)[40] and holding unconstitutional

---

[38] Henderson v. Mayor of New York, 92 U.S. 259, 271 (1876).

[39] 97 U.S. at 33–34.
[40] 94 U.S. 113 (1877). See Chapter 7.

under the Commerce Clause a state statute that sought to prohibit discriminatory rates on interstate trips. Congress immediately filled the void by passing the Commerce Act of 1887 establishing the Interstate Commerce Commission. Then, in March 1888, in the wake of the *Wabash* decision, the Supreme Court returned to the issue framed by Bradley in *Beer Company*: Were the *License Cases* still good law?

The case in question, *Bowman v. Chicago & Northwestern Railway*,[41] had arisen from a railroad's refusal to transport beer from Chicago to Iowa, which was then a dry state. An action was brought against the railroad for breach of its duty as a common carrier, and the railroad defended itself on the basis of the Iowa statute, which prohibited the importation of liquor. The Court rejected this defense, holding the Iowa law to be a regulation of "commerce among the states" and thus unconstitutional.

The Court in *Bowman* was divided, but not over the question whether state regulation of the interstate liquor market was as a general matter a "regulation of commerce." The justices disagreed instead on the question of whether the preemptive power of the Commerce Clause was so strong or extensive as to nullify an appropriate exercise of the police power. *Mugler v. Kansas*, decided only three months before *Bowman*, made it absolutely clear that state prohibition laws were a valid exercise of the police power, and the author of the Court's opinion in *Mugler*—Justice Harlan—wrote the dissent in *Bowman* (joined by Waite and Gray). Although Harlan at points questioned the preemptive force of the Commerce Clause, his main emphasis was to insist that preemption should not work in such a way as to preclude states from exercising their police powers. By way of analogy, Harlan pointed to state inspection and quarantine laws, which everyone assumed were valid; moving even closer to the prohibition issue, he also relied on a sentence in Marshall's opinion in *Brown v. Maryland* that allowed states to regulate the importation of dangerous substances. "The power to direct the removal of gunpowder," Harlan quoted Marshall, obliv-

---

[41] 125 U.S. 465 (1888). Although the Court decided two cases involving state regulation of liquor imports between *Beer Company* and *Bowman*, neither squarely posed the problem raised by the *License Cases* and then again in *Bowman*: reconciling the states' police power with congressional power to regulate interstate commerce. Tiernan v. Rinker, 102 U.S. 123 (1880), and Walling v. Michigan, 116 U.S. 446 (1886), struck down state license taxes that discriminated against the sale of out-of-state liquor. Bradley in *Walling* was willing to assume that the tax there was an exercise of Michigan's police power; but it should have been clear that this justification was implausible, and that the discriminatory state regimes served neither economic nationalism nor even local consensus (since discrimination against out-of-state producers is almost invariably caused by the influence of in-state producers, not by a general understanding that in-state producers should be benefited).

ious to the humor of the analogy, "is a branch of the police power, which unquestionably remains, and ought to remain, with the States."[42]

The majority opinion in *Bowman* was written by Justice Stanley Matthews and joined by Justice Bradley. At various points Matthews tried to shift responsibility from the Commerce Clause to Congress: He said that the failure of Congress to enact a law authorizing a measure like Iowa's indicated an intention that the states not interfere with these interstate transactions. Matthews did not pause to reconcile this reference to congressional silence with the *Cooley* test, which spoke of the need for uniformity. But, in any event, he denied the states the power to enact laws that, either in purpose or effect, interfered with the free flow of goods across state lines. Exceptions to this general rule were duly acknowledged, but while Harlan used these exceptions to build yet another rule—allowing states to exercise their police powers even if they interfered with commerce—Matthews treated these exceptions as narrow pigeonholes into which a state statute had to fit if it were to be saved. One exception was inspection laws. Another was quarantine measures, such as those barring rags infected with yellow fever germs and diseased meat from entering a state; still another actually allowed a state, in keeping with the "sacred law of self-defence," to exclude "convicts, paupers, idiots, and lunatics."[43] The prohibition statute did not fit any of these exceptions, and therefore, even though it may have been an appropriate exercise of the police power, it was preempted.

III

Four days after *Bowman* was handed down, Waite died. When Fuller filled his position he inherited a recently crafted yet inherently unstable body of law: *Mugler*, decided in December 1887, dismissed the due process objections voiced against prohibition laws, but *Bowman*, decided in March 1888, sustained an attack on these laws based on principles of federalism. As a purely formal matter these two decisions were reconcilable, but as a practical matter they were in conflict. As long as liquor could be shipped into a dry state from a sister state or foreign country, the consumption of

---

[42] 125 U.S. at 519 (quoting *Brown v. Maryland*). Harlan also made affirmative use of another Marshall Court decision, Wilson v. Black Bird Creek Marsh Co., 27 U.S. (2 Pet.) 245 (1829) (allowing a dam on a navigable creek to stand) and of a more contemporaneous decision,

Smith v. Alabama, 124 U.S. 465 (1888) (upholding a state licensing requirement for locomotive engineers on trains employed in interstate commerce).

[43] 125 U.S. at 492 (quoting Railroad Co. v. Husen, 95 U.S. 465, 471 [1878]).

liquor would continue. Fuller, demonstrating a resolve especially appropriate for a chief justice, sought to find an acceptable solution. The result was his opinion for the Court in *Leisy v. Hardin*,[44] announced in 1890.

The case involved an Iowa law, which came into effect only several weeks after *Bowman*, that allowed the state to interdict liquor sales following importation. In one respect, *Leisy* was unremarkable, merely finishing the work begun in *Bowman*, formally reaffirming *Brown v. Maryland* and overruling the *License Cases*. *Bowman* had proclaimed a right to transport liquor across state lines, but it did not involve the precise right that was involved in *Brown v. Maryland* and the *License Cases*: the right to sell the imported goods within the state. Under *Bowman*, the states could not prohibit consumers from traveling to the wet states to purchase liquor or from purchasing liquor through mail order and then having it shipped into the state; but a question remained as to whether they could erect a barrier to out-of-state liquor by prohibiting retail sales of such liquor within the state. In his opinion for the Court in *Bowman*, Justice Matthews noted that *Brown v. Maryland* stood for the principle that "the right of importation . . . includes . . . the right of the importer to sell in unbroken packages at the place where the transmit terminates."[45] "But," he continued, "it is not necessary now to express any opinion upon the point, because that question does not arise in the present case."[46] Justice Field wrote separately in *Bowman*, emphasizing, as he had done in *Mugler*, that as far as he was concerned the right of importation affirmed in *Bowman* included the right of sale, even though he recognized that this question was not presented in the case at hand "in a direct way."[47]

There was, however, no escaping this issue in *Leisy*, and Fuller addressed it in terms of the *Cooley* test: "Where the subject matter requires a uniform system as between the States, the power controlling it is vested exclusively in Congress, and cannot be encroached upon by the

---

[44] 135 U.S. 100 (1890). Between *Bowman* and *Leisy* the Court decided Kidd v. Pearson, 128 U.S. 1 (1888), which resolved a question Harlan explicitly had left open in *Mugler*, namely whether a state could prohibit the manufacture of liquor for export. Justice Lamar, writing for a unanimous Court, upheld the state prohibition. *Kidd* can be read as a straightforward application of the categorical approach (as described in Chapter 5, it subsequently was used for that purpose by Fuller in *E. C. Knight*). As Justice Lamar proclaimed, "No distinc-

tion is more popular to the common mind, or more clearly expressed in economic and political literature, than that between manufactures and commerce." Ibid., 20. It is unclear what might have motivated this adherence to the categorical approach, short of placating the prohibitionists, for it neither served economic nationalism nor local consensus: Why should a state stop out-of-staters from consuming liquor?

[45] 125 U.S. at 499.

[46] Ibid.

[47] Ibid., 502.

States. . . ."[48] Fuller then found that interstate liquor transactions were a subject matter calling for uniformity, and he adopted the original package doctrine of *Brown v. Maryland*. He concluded that the right to import included the right to sell the imported liquor in the original package, because the sale was integral to the importation. There was a dissent by Gray, which Harlan and Brewer joined. (Harlan and Gray had dissented in *Bowman*, and Brewer had by then replaced Justice Matthews, the author of *Bowman*.) Recognizing the split among the states on the issue, Justice Gray insisted that the sale of liquor was not a subject that called for uniformity of regulation. Justice Gray even thought it doubtful that Congress had the power to pass a nationwide, uniform law regulating sales.[49]

By overturning the *License Cases*, the *Leisy* Court simply completed a program of economic nationalism that had its roots in the ideas of John Marshall, but which was given a new and decisive impetus in the years following the Civil War and in decisions of the late 1880s such as *Wabash* and *Bowman*. There was, however, another dimension to *Leisy*, one that represented a new departure and—if it had lasted—could thus have constituted a distinctive contribution of Fuller to our understanding of federal structure (comparable, in that respect, to White's doctrine of incorporation). Fuller extended to Congress an invitation to intervene and thus to allow the states to exercise a power denied under the dormant Commerce Clause and *Cooley*.

The talk in *Bowman* about congressional silence could have been similarly construed as an invitation for Congress to step in. In fact, Matthews hinted at such an invitation when he said in passing, "[Existing national statutes] are certainly indications of [Congress's] intention that the transportation of commodities between the States shall be free, except where it is positively restricted by Congress itself, or by the States in particular cases by the express permission of Congress."[50] But *Leisy* did not rely on innu-

---

[48] 135 U.S. at 108–109.

[49] 135 U.S. at 158–59. The companion case to *Leisy* was Lyng v. Michigan, 135 U.S. 161 (1890). Curiously enough, although *Lyng* involved a sales tax that discriminated against out-of-state liquor (so that the police power justification should have been unavailable), the three *Leisy* dissenters here dissented "upon the grounds stated in their opinion in *Leisy*." Ibid., 167.

[50] 125 U.S. at 485. A latent theory of legislative preemption, implicit in references to congressional silence, had long been mentioned in the same breath as the *Cooley* theory of constitutional preemption (see Ribble, *State and National Power over Commerce*, 78–85). But there was no thought that the result in any case would be any different: Congressional silence with respect to a "subject requiring uniformity" was presumed to mean that Congress intended preemption. Matthews formulated the issue in *Bowman* in a way that separated the two theories: "The question . . . may be still considered in each case as it arises, whether the fact that Congress has failed in the particular instance to provide by law a regulation of commerce among the

endo; the difference between *Bowman* and *Leisy* was the difference between a permission and an invitation. In *Leisy* Fuller carefully and deliberately analyzed the Commerce Clause in terms that reserved to Congress the power to lift its preemptive ban and to allow the states to regulate or prohibit liquor imported from sister states or abroad. Fuller began his opinion by saying: "[A] subject matter which has been confided exclusively to Congress by the Constitution is not within the jurisdiction of the police power of the State, unless placed there by congressional action."[51]

In the winter of 1888, in the short period between *Mugler* (decided December 1887) and *Bowman* (decided March 1888), a bill was introduced in the Senate empowering the states to deal with imported liquor. It provided:

[T]he consent of Congress is hereby given, that the laws of the several States relating to the sale of distilled and fermented liquors within the limits of each State may apply to such liquors when they have been imported in the same manner as when they have been manufactured in the United States.[52]

Constitutional objections were immediately raised to this proposal, and the Committee of Finance asked to be discharged of its responsibility for it. The measure was then referred to the Committee on the Judiciary, and a majority of that committee viewed the proposal to confer congressional "consent" on the state trade barriers as constitutionally impermissible.[53] Those barriers were precluded by the Constitution, it was felt, and thus it was not for Congress to decide whether they should be allowed to continue. The congressional maneuvering stopped at that point, with no floor debate. That was in 1888.

States is conclusive of its intention that the subject shall be free from all positive regulation, or that, until it positively interferes, such commerce may be left to be freely dealt with by the respective States." 125 U.S. at 483. Passages such as this led Professor Powell to conclude that *Bowman* "turns the *Cooley* rule from one of constitutional interpretation to one of legislative interpretation." Powell, *Vagaries and Varieties,* 162. However, it was *Leisy* rather than *Bowman* that was perceived at the time to constitute the real break with *Cooley,* as evidenced by the timing and content of the congressional debates on the Wil-

son Act; see below, p. 276.
[51] 135 U.S. at 108.
[52] S. 1067, 50th Cong., 1st Sess. (1888), quoted in S. Rep. No. 610, 50th Cong., 1st Sess. 5 (1888). The bill was introduced on December 21, 1887, by Senator Frye of Maine. 19 Cong. Rec. 142 (1887). In the later debates on the Wilson Act, it was incorrectly stated that Senator Wilson had introduced this earlier bill. 21 Cong. Rec. 4958 (1890).
[53] S. Rep. No. 610, 50th Cong., 1st Sess. 2–4 (1888). The report was ordered to be printed on March 19, 1888. *Bowman* was decided the same day and was not mentioned.

Two years later, immediately following the *Leisy* invitation, Senator Wilson of Iowa renewed the proposal. Little of the ensuing debate focused on the desirability of prohibition or this type of congressional intervention; the debate mainly concerned the constitutionality of the measure.[54] On that issue, Fuller's invitation in *Leisy*—to which frequent reference was made throughout the debate—made all the difference.[55] Indeed, Senator George, the author of the 1888 majority report of the Judiciary Committee that tabled Wilson's original proposal, changed his mind and now supported the bill.[56] Congress accepted the *Leisy* invitation and enacted the Wilson Act, providing

> [t]hat all fermented, distilled, or other intoxicating liquors or liquids transported into any State or Territory or remaining therein for use, consumption, sale or storage therein, shall upon arrival in such State or Territory be subject to the operation and effect of the laws of such State or Territory enacted in the exercise of its police powers, to the same extent and in the same manner as though such liquids or liquors had been produced in such State or Territory, and shall not be exempt therefrom by reason of being introduced therein in original packages or otherwise.[57]

This statute was immediately challenged, but after *Leisy* there could be little doubt as to how the Court would come out. In the *Rahrer* case,[58] the Wilson Act was upheld. The *Leisy* dissenters (Harlan, Gray, and Brewer) concurred in the result; because they did not believe the Constitution barred the state regulation, they could not object to a federal statute that authorized and thus validated those regulations. Fuller, who in *Leisy* invited congressional intervention, was the author of the Court's opinion in *Rahrer*.

One issue he had to address concerned judicial supremacy: How could Congress validate a statute that had been declared unconstitutional

---

[54] On the history of the Wilson Act, see generally Dennis M. Robb, "Legislative History of the Wilson Act" (University of Chicago Law School, 1974; unpublished manuscript on file with author). See also Richard F. Hamm, "Origins of the 18th Amendment: The Prohibition Movement in the Federal System, 1880–1920" (Ph.D. diss., University of Virginia, 1987).

[55] For example, Senator Wilson opened the debate by referring to *Leisy*: "This bill . . . is a response to the suggestion contained in [*Leisy*] . . . , that what-

ever restraint the Constitution may have placed upon this subject, so far as the original action of the State is concerned, Congress can give its permission to the exercise of the restraining power or police power of the State. . . ." 21 Cong. Rec. 4954 (1890).

[56] Ibid., 4957–58.

[57] Wilson Act, Ch. 728, 26 Stat. 313 (1890).

[58] *In re* Rahrer, 140 U.S. 545 (1891). Given the backlog, the Court must have somehow accelerated the case.

by the Court? Fuller might have responded by conceiving of the Wilson Act as a delegation, fully authorized by the Court in *Leisy*, to the states of an authority otherwise belonging to Congress. So conceived, it would be difficult to view the Wilson Act as a usurpation of the Court's rightful role as the supreme arbiter of the Constitution. It turned out, however, that the state law in question in *Rahrer* had been in existence prior to the decision in *Leisy* and had not been reenacted subsequent to the passage of the Wilson Act. This made it difficult for Fuller to conceive of the state statute as the exercise of a delegated power, and for that reason, or because he believed that the commerce power was nondelegable, Fuller conceived the Wilson Act not as a delegation of power to the states but as operating upon the goods themselves:

> No reason is perceived why, if Congress chooses to provide that certain designated subjects of interstate commerce shall be governed by a rule which divests them of that character at an earlier period of time than would otherwise be the case, it is not within its competency to do so.[59]

Fuller thus allowed Congress to define the point in time at which an imported good lost its interstate character. Although, as an abstract matter, Congress might be competent to make such a determination, it is hard to see how this theory was responsive to the issue of judicial supremacy. Under Fuller's theory Congress was making a constitutional decision, and one that sharply differed from the Court's as embodied in *Leisy* and *Bowman*.

The other issue raised in *Rahrer* concerned the assumed need for uniformity, which according to the *Cooley* test was the predicate of preemption and thus the basis of *Leisy*: How could Congress allow the states a home rule option when the predicate for Commerce Clause preemption was a need for a single uniform rule for the nation? A more adventuresome justice might have responded to this conundrum by uncoupling the preemptive effect of the Commerce Clause from the need for uniformity. The power of the Commerce Clause, so it might have been argued, is not derived from Congress's special capacity to produce a single uniform rule, but rather from the fact that Congress constitutes a national forum in which all the interests—would-be importers and prohibitionists alike—could be heard. But that was not Fuller's way. Rather than attempting to forge a new, and perhaps more sensible, rationale for the dormant Commerce Clause, he argued that the uniformity requirement had in fact been satisfied by the Wilson Act:

---

[59] Ibid., 562.

Congress has not attempted to delegate the power to regulate commerce, to exercise any power reserved to the States, or to grant a power not possessed by the States, or to adopt state laws. It has taken its own course and made its own regulation, applying to these subjects of interstate commerce one common rule, whose uniformity is not affected by variations in state laws in dealing with such property.[60]

Whatever Fuller might have had in mind in uttering these words (which, quite frankly, escapes me), the fact remains that the putatively federal regime was no more uniform than a regime of state laws enacted pursuant to a delegated or inherent state power. Whether conceived as a means of honoring local consensus, or simply as a political expedient, this was an exercise in formalism: Uniformity now meant a formally single rule.

Rahrer compromised principles of economic nationalism insofar as it allowed the states to ban out-of-state liquor and thus to complete or perfect their regulatory regimes. The tension between *Mugler* and *Bowman* was resolved in favor of *Mugler*. This result of course greatly pleased the prohibition movement, but there were reasons to doubt the durability of this arrangement. It left individuals in dry states unable to purchase and consume liquor; it frustrated those trying to do business in dry states; and, above all, it threatened—at least with respect to this very special product— the vision of an economic union that underlay the use of federal power in 1894 to break up the Pullman Strike, the *Debs* decision of 1895, and the election of 1896. It was a decision that would not last.

IV

In the years immediately following *Leisy* and *Rahrer* there were significant personnel changes on the Court. Justices Harlan, Gray, and Brewer —the justices who objected to the invalidation of the foreign or interstate component of state prohibition and who thus dissented in *Leisy*— remained, but the majority had begun to crumble. By the late 1890s all the justices who had joined Fuller's opinion in *Leisy* had left the Court, and there were now five new justices who owed their appointments to either Harrison, Cleveland, or McKinley: Brown, Shiras, White, Peckham, and McKenna. In these circumstances, it might not seem so remarkable that a new majority emerged, one that withdrew the *Leisy* invitation and brought this body of doctrine into line with the nationalist principles that underlay decisions such as *Debs* and that were affirmed in the 1896 election. But what was remarkable was that even Fuller changed his mind and now joined the resistance to the Wilson Act. This switch appears to have been

---

[60] Ibid., 561.

Chapter IX: *Federalism and Liberty*

orchestrated by Justice White, who, as we saw in the *Insular Cases* and again in *Standard Oil* and *American Tobacco*, was a master at constructing delicate and intricate compromises. Determined to keep the interstate market free and open, he emerged in 1898 in *Rhodes v. Iowa*[61] as the spokesman for the Court in its battle with the prohibition movement.

White loved to compound categories—he must have subscribed to the reverse of Occam's razor—and his opinion in *Rhodes v. Iowa* is especially evocative of his dissent in *Northern Securities*, which was founded on the distinction between the right to acquire and the right to use.[62] In *Rhodes*, White sharply distinguished the right to import and the right to sell. The right to import was deemed the direct or central right, while the right to sell was seen only as an "incident"[63] of the right to import. Marshall's original package doctrine had sought to unify these rights as a way of limiting state power and thus furthering the goal of economic nationalism. Now White, moved by these same nationalistic sentiments, separated them and thus repudiated the original package doctrine in order to set limits on the power of Congress to authorize the states to pass laws that interfered with the formation and operation of national markets. According to White, Congress could authorize the states, at their option, to interfere with the incidental right, the right to sell, but whether Congress had the additional power to authorize the states to interfere with the right to import was an open question. White also said that the Wilson Act should be construed in a manner that relieved the Court from the necessity of passing on this question. He mooted the constitutional issue by reading the Wilson Act as accomplishing only what he was fully prepared to say Congress had the power to do, which was to authorize the states to interfere with the right to sell. The Wilson Act did not, according to White, intend to authorize the states to interfere with the right to import liquor.

The critical word of the Wilson Act turned out to be "arrival." (To a more limited extent, attention also focused on the statutory phrases "transported into" and "original package.") The Act permitted a state to regulate foreign liquor after its "arrival" in the state and, according to White, liquor did not "arrive" in the state until it was delivered to the person who ordered it (the consignee). As a practical matter, then, the states were able to prohibit the person to whom the liquor was delivered from selling it within the dry state; the states were allowed to outlaw the retail outlet. On the other hand, the states could not intervene prior to delivery to the consignee, even after the liquor crossed the state line. This left the right to import (and, of course, the right to consume that which was imported) essentially unfettered, and like *Bowman* a decade before, *Rhodes* emptied

---

[61] 170 U.S. 412 (1898).
[62] See Chapter 5, p. 133.

[63] 170 U.S. at 424.

279

Mugler of much of its practical effect. Retail outlets were outlawed, only to be replaced by mail order companies.

In moving to this conclusion, White was not driven by the statutory language; to the contrary. In the Wilson Act, Congress used the phrase "upon arrival in such State," but the Court in *Rhodes* construed the phrase to mean "after delivery to the consignee." The original version reported from the Senate Judiciary Committee had used the term "delivery" to mark the boundary of state power, but that bill spoke of "deliver[y] within its own [the state's] limits,"[64] not "delivery to the consignee." One of the opponents of Wilson's proposal, Senator Faulkner, sought to confine the reach of the bill by introducing an amendment—later to be withdrawn—that used the "delivery to the consignee" language.[65]

Although White's reading of the Wilson Act was not faithful to Congress's language, it might have been faithful to congressional intent conceived in more general terms. Congress might have said "arrival" because it wanted to go as far as it could in prohibiting imports. On this reading of the legislative history, it might have been legitimate for the Court to interpose its own judgment about the limits on congressional power, and then read those limits into the Act. But if White was doing in *Rhodes* what he later would do in *Standard Oil* and *American Tobacco*—making the Constitution a term of the statute—then he could not claim, as he did, that his reading of the Wilson Act was based on the standard canon of statutory construction counseling the Court to avoid reaching troublesome constitutional questions. White was not avoiding resolution of a constitutional question but actually was resolving that question when he made the statute coextensive with the Constitution. He said that no "opinion is expressed"[66] on the question whether Congress had the power to authorize the states to abridge the right to import, but his reading of the Wilson Act was, in fact, the expression of his opinion on that question. In a companion case to *Rhodes*, involving not Iowa but South Carolina, White was less guarded: "[U]nder the Constitution of the United States every resident of South Carolina is free to receive for his own use liquor from other States. . . ."[67]

White's deviousness was also evident in his treatment of the precedents. He stressed the fact that the overruling of the *License Cases* had occurred in two steps—first *Bowman* and then *Leisy*—and characterized

----

[64] 21 Cong. Rec. 4954 (1890).
[65] Ibid., 5163.
[66] 170 U.S. at 424.
[67] Vance v. W. A. Vandercook Co., 170 U.S. 438, 452 (1898). South Carolina had established a dispensary system whereby state officers supervised the importation and resale of liquor. The Court ruled that individuals purchasing out-of-state liquor for personal use did not have to submit to the dispensary regulations. Curiously, there was no dissent to this proposition.

one step (*Bowman*) as involving the right to import and the other (*Leisy*) as involving the right to sell. He reminded the reader that the Wilson Act followed *Leisy* rather than *Bowman*, and this sequence was supposed to buttress his claim that the Wilson Act authorized interference only with the right to sell. It also allowed him to claim that *Rhodes* was indeed faithful to *Leisy* and *Rahrer*. *Rahrer*, he insisted, upheld the Wilson Act only insofar as it, like *Leisy* itself, involved the right to sell. This analysis enabled him to pay homage to the principles of stare decisis and give to Fuller, who wrote *Leisy* and *Rahrer*, a cover for joining *Rhodes*.

Admittedly, *Bowman* involved an interference with transportation rather than a sale (the prosecution was specifically aimed at a station agent). But the two-step process of overruling the *License Cases* was due to purely strategic considerations (don't repudiate a prior decision unless you have to) and did not imply, as White claimed, a fundamental distinction between the right to import and the right to sell. The Court thought it best in this first foray to treat the *License Cases* as distinguished rather than overruled, but *Bowman* set the stage for the inevitable next step. Moreover, the fact that the Wilson Act immediately followed *Leisy* rather than *Bowman* did not imply that Congress possessed only the limited intent of lifting the pre-emptive ban imposed by *Leisy* but not that imposed by *Bowman*. The sequence can be explained by noting that the invitation for congressional action was fully and clearly extended only in *Leisy*. The bill that finally culminated in the Wilson Act was introduced shortly before *Bowman*, only to stall because of congressional doubts regarding the constitutionality of such intervention. Those doubts were soon resolved by *Leisy*, but neither the *Leisy* invitation nor *Rahrer*'s subsequent validation of the Wilson Act drew a distinction between the right to import and the right to sell. As a purely factual matter, *Leisy* and *Rahrer* involved sales, but in each Fuller wrote in sweeping terms. He embraced whatever exertions of the congressional power were necessary to make fully effective the promise of *Mugler*.

Gray wrote a dissent in *Rhodes* in which he construed the Wilson Act as adopting the theory of Harlan's dissent in *Bowman*, to the effect that the states could regulate interstate commerce in the exercise of the police power: "[The Wilson Act's] whole object, as appears upon its face, as well as from the circumstances which led to its enactment, is not to define when a particular voyage or transit shall be considered at an end; but to assure to the State, throughout its territorial jurisdiction, the full exercise of its police powers over the subject of intoxicating liquors."[68] Brewer, who had joined Harlan and Gray in *Leisy* and *Rahrer*, was, like Fuller, now in White's camp and henceforth would remain there. The vision of union

---

[68] 170 U.S. at 435.

implicit in *Debs* finally prevailed. Brown had joined Fuller's opinion in *Rahrer* (he was not on the Court at the time of *Leisy*), but in *Rhodes* he switched over to the bloc, consisting of Gray and Harlan, that dissented in *Leisy* and specially concurred in *Rahrer*. He joined Gray's dissent. Harlan did, too. Gray and Harlan were the only two to hold firm to their position, but they did not constitute an especially powerful force within the Court. Gray died in 1902, and his successor, Holmes, was of an entirely different mind.

Rhodes left the right to sell within the ambit of congressional prerogative: Congress could authorize the states to pass laws restricting the right to resell imported liquor. In *Brown v. Maryland* Marshall had claimed that "[n]o goods would be imported, if none could be sold,"[69] and Fuller built his opinion in *Leisy* around this insight. By the time of *Rhodes*, however, the Court might have felt that Marshall's claim was exaggerated and that no great danger to the evolution of national markets would be created if Congress were allowed to do with this right what it wished, either reserve it for itself or institute a home rule policy. Writing fresh, White might have been prepared even to concede to the states the power to regulate the right to sell in the absence of congressional authorization—the right to sell might have been viewed as White had viewed the "chartering of a holding company" in *Northern Securities* or as the majority had viewed "manufacturing" in *E. C. Knight*.[70] But the right to import was an entirely different matter, clearly part of "commerce" or "intercourse," and to allow the dry states to interfere with this right, either directly or under a congressional writ, would be to jeopardize the vision of economic union that lay at the heart of *Debs*.[71] It would, as White subsequently put it, "operate materially to cripple if not destroy that freedom of commerce between the States which

---

[69] 25 U.S. at 439.

[70] In subsequent opinions, Justice White again conceded to the states the power to regulate activities other than importation. In Pabst Brewing Co. v. Crenshaw, 198 U.S. 17 (1905), White upheld Missouri's inspection of out-of-state liquor destined for resale, over a dissent by Brown, Fuller, Brewer, and Day, who claimed that the inspection statute was really a revenue measure. In Delamater v. South Dakota, 205 U.S. 93 (1907), White decided, over Fuller's lone dissent, that the states could impose a licensing fee on traveling salesmen for out-of-state liquor—even those who solicited orders for personal use.

[71] The rhetoric of free trade was largely absent in *Rhodes* itself. Rather than confront the local consensus theory, White in *Rhodes* argued that the application of state law to importation would have "extraterritorial" effects. 170 U.S. at 422. White might have been stressing the fact that out-of-state producers affected by state law were not represented in the state legislature. If so, he would have been objecting to the quality of the state interest—the local consensus was not a consensus of all interested parties. But for a Court concerned with legitimate consensus, the objection could not have much force. The producer profits lost by prohibition that could not have been duplicated in other economic endeavors were likely to have been a consequence of monopoly, and thus probably illegitimate.

it was the great purpose of the Constitution to promote."[72] In *Debs* the Court emphatically affirmed the strong use of the powers of the federal government to preserve the union, and since that vision of economic union was rooted in an understanding of the Constitution itself—in the Commerce Clause, to be legalistic about it—the *Rhodes* Court was not prepared to concede to Congress a power to contradict or even qualify that vision. The *Leisy* invitation was now seen as a mistake and was diplomatically withdrawn.

V

In the early 1900s, prohibition gained greater momentum.[73] The appeal of the movement still lay with the old-stock middle class, but the number of supporters increased and so did the organizational capacities of the movement. Drawing on the rising tide of progressivism and its use of the legislative power to protect health and safety and even morals, the prohibition movement focused its energies on testing the limitation that White and his newly constituted majority "found" in the Wilson Act. The Court refused to buckle and appeared—at least at first—determined to protect and indeed extend the principles of economic nationalism affirmed in *Debs* and elaborated so cunningly in *Rhodes v. Iowa*.

---

[72] American Express Co. v. Iowa, 196 U.S. 133, 144 (1905). See below, note 77. A case decided shortly before *Rhodes* that showed a similar commitment to free trade was Scott v. Donald, 165 U.S. 58 (1897), where the Court struck down an earlier version of the South Carolina dispensary statute involved in *Vandercook* (see above, note 67). Justice Shiras, writing for the Court, saw the law in *Scott* as discriminating against out-of-state liquor and construed the Wilson Act to require nondiscrimination: "[E]quality or uniformity of treatment under state laws was intended [by the Wilson Act]. . . . [T]he State cannot, under the Congressional legislation referred to, establish a system which, in effect, discriminates between interstate and domestic commerce. . . ." Ibid., 100. Brown—who curiously failed to dissent in *Vandercook*—was the lone dissenter here; he viewed the statute as a genuine exercise of the police power and therefore authorized by the Wilson Act.

[73] On the prohibition movement at the turn of the twentieth century, see the general histories cited above, note 9, and Jack S. Blocker, *Retreat from Reform: The Prohibition Movement in the United States, 1890–1913* (Westport, Conn.: Greenwood Press, 1976); K. Austin Kerr, *Organized for Prohibition: A New History of the Anti-Saloon League* (New Haven: Yale University Press, 1985); and James H. Timberlake, *Prohibition and the Progressive Movement, 1900–1920* (Cambridge: Harvard University Press, 1963). An early study by Peter H. Odegard, *Pressure Politics: The Story of the Anti-Saloon League* (New York: Columbia University Press, 1928), addresses the congressional politics of the period. Finally, in addition to the dissertation by Richard Hamm, cited in note 54, there is a master's thesis by Daniel R. Murrell, "Prelude to Prohibition: The Anti-Saloon League and the Webb-Kenyon Act of 1913" (University of Western Ontario, 1974).

This attitude of the Court during the early 1900s was strikingly manifest in *Heyman v. Southern Railway*,[74] a 1906 decision in which the Court went to great lengths to secure the mail order business in liquor that *Rhodes* had protected. Alcohol was carried into a dry state by the Southern Railway and placed in its warehouse. The record did not indicate whether the consignee was notified of its arrival, but in any event there was a delay by the consignee in picking up the liquor and it was seized from the warehouse by state officials. The state supreme court sustained the seizure, reasoning that, in contrast to *Rhodes*, there could be no doubt that the liquor had "arrived" in the state; in *Rhodes* the liquor could have been thought of as still in transit, as it was being moved from the train platform to a freight warehouse six feet away when it was seized. The United States Supreme Court, once again in an opinion by Justice White, refused to limit *Rhodes*, holding in *Heyman* that the seizure of the liquor in the warehouse was unauthorized and thus unprotected by the Wilson Act. White viewed the seizure as a regulation of interstate commerce and thus a violation of the dormant Commerce Clause. This time the decision was unanimous: Both Gray and Brown had left the Court, and the only justice remaining from the dissenting bloc in *Rhodes*—Harlan—for some reason failed to dissent.

In *Heyman*, the delivery-to-the-consignee rule of *Rhodes* was emphatically, almost defiantly, reaffirmed by White. Moreover, in rejecting the claim that delivery was a state law question, White ruled that the issue was largely a matter of federal constitutional rather than statutory law. The Court acknowledged the possibility of constructive delivery if "after notice and full opportunity to receive them [the goods] are designedly left in the hands of the carrier for an unreasonable time."[75] Yet the Court held those facts must be affirmatively alleged and proved, and in the case at hand they had not been. In so ruling, Justice White made it abundantly clear that the Court was determined to construe the Wilson Act so as to keep open the nation's market in alcoholic beverages. Residents of dry states could look to the Supreme Court to defend their access to foreign or out-of-state liquor for purposes of their own consumption.[76]

During this same period, the Court also went out of its way to protect the effort, as embodied in the collect-on-delivery transaction, to bring the mail order and other means of interstate contracting closer and closer to the ordinary retail transaction (in which goods are paid for on receipt). Prohibiting the C.O.D. form of transaction on imported liquor was deemed

---

[74] 203 U.S. 270 (1906).
[75] Ibid., 276.
[76] "[W]e must not be understood as in any way limiting or restricting the ruling made in *Vance* v. *Vandercook Co.* . . . upholding the right of a citizen of one State to bring from another State into the State of his residence, and keep therein, for his personal use, the merchandise referred to in the Wilson Act." Ibid., 277.

an interference with the right to import.[77] The Court even intervened in several cases involving express companies that shipped liquor from out of state to addressees who had not ordered it.[78] Typically, an agent of the company in a state received the package, informed the addressee that it had a package for him, and then, if the addressee consented, delivered it to him C.O.D. Of course, the mail order, even in its most subtle form, was not a perfect substitute for the retail outlet. Reliance on the mails placed some limitation on access to liquor, and the very point of *Leisy* was to remove such a limitation, which was thought sufficiently burdensome to warrant overruling the *License Cases* formally. But as the prohibitionists well knew, the Court's protection of the right to import made liquor readily available in dry states; and as the technology of ordering and transporting out-of-state goods advanced (the nation awaited Lands' End), the effort of dry states to stop the consumption of liquor within their borders must have been increasingly frustrated. The spirit of accommodation that had governed the Court in *Leisy* in the early 1890s had vanished completely.

The prohibition movement naturally turned to Congress for help, as it had done before in securing the Wilson Act. Congress did not immediately respond, but over the next decade, as the interstate business in liquor grew, the prohibition issue became an important part of Congress's agenda, as important, say, as worker safety or the regulation of the rails. In 1909

---

[77] American Express Co. v. Iowa, 196 U.S. 133 (1905); Adams Express Co. v. Iowa, 196 U.S. 147 (1905). Justice White, as usual, wrote for the Court in both cases and Harlan dissented without opinion. The same issue had been before the Court in O'Neil v. Vermont, 144 U.S. 323 (1892). In that case, the Court had allowed O'Neil's sentence—fifty-four years at hard labor, for selling liquor by mail—to stand because of a jurisdictional limitation. The Court concluded, over the dissent of Field, Harlan, and Brewer, that

> [n]o point on the Commerce Clause of the Constitution of the United States was taken in the county court, in regard to the present case, or considered by the Supreme Court of Vermont. . . . The matters thus excepted to were too general to call attention of the state court to the commerce clause. . . .

Ibid., 335. The incorporation of this holding into the headnote angered Field, thus provoking a famous dispute. See Alan F. Westin, "Stephen J. Field

and the Headnote to O'Neil v. Vermont: A Snapshot of the Fuller Court at Work," *Yale L.J.*, 67; 363 (1958). In *American Express* and *Adams Express*, the Iowa supreme court relied on *O'Neil* to sustain the seizure of C.O.D. liquor.

[78] Adams Express Co. v. Kentucky, 206 U.S. 129 (1907); 206 U.S. 138 (1907); American Express Co. v. Kentucky, 206 U.S. 139 (1907). Justice Harlan protested in a short dissent that "[these cases] show only devices or tricks by the express company to evade or defeat the laws of Kentucky relating to the sale" of liquor. 206 U.S. at 141. The majority, in brief opinions by Justice Brewer, reversed the convictions on a technical ground—the indictments failed to allege that the express companies knew they were engaging in illegal sales of liquor. Nevertheless, the language was defiant: "[W]e are not at liberty to recognize any rule which will nullify or tend to weaken the power vested by the Constitution in Congress over interstate commerce." 206 U.S. at 138.

Congress finally responded to *Rhodes* and the situation it created, but the response was measured. The 1909 statute accepted the framework of the Wilson Act as construed by *Rhodes* and sought only to aid the dry states by curbing abuses of the right to import. The statute prohibited the delivery of liquor to any person other than the consignee, unless on written order.[79] The statute also prohibited the collection of the purchase price by the common carrier acting as agent of the buyer or seller (presumably curbing abuses of the C.O.D. form) and required that the label on the outside of the packaged liquor show the name of the consignee and the contents. The 1909 measure was designed to make certain that common carriers were transporters, not disguised retail outlets.

By 1913, however, the legislative response escalated, and something of a turning point came in the Webb-Kenyon Act, which challenged *Bowman* and the very right to import. The states were authorized to intervene before delivery to the consignee and the Court was given no room to maneuver:

> [T]he shipment or transportation [into a state] . . . of any . . . liquor . . . [which] is intended, by any person interested therein, to be received, possessed, sold, or in any manner used, either in the original package or otherwise, in violation of any law of such State . . . is hereby prohibited.[80]

While the Wilson Act authorized the states to regulate interstate shipments of liquor without making the conduct actually prohibited by the states a violation of federal law, the Webb-Kenyon Act actually created a federal prohibition. No penalty was provided for violation of the newly created federal prohibition, and earlier versions of the bill simply divested imported liquor of its interstate character, indicating that this change in the legal structure of the measure was simply a matter of constitutional form.[81] By creating a federal prohibition, defenders of the statute could argue that the statute represented not a delegation of the commerce power to the states, but rather an affirmative exercise of the commerce power by Congress itself, although the power was conditioned upon a decision of the state to prohibit importation.

---

[79] Act of Mar. 4, 1909, Ch. 321, Sect. 238–240, 35 Stat. 1088, 1136–37.

[80] Webb-Kenyon Act, Ch. 90, 37 Stat. 699 (1913).

[81] For the history of the Webb-Kenyon Act see the general references in note 73 as well as Noel T. Dowling and F. Morse Hubbard, "Divesting an Article of Its Interstate Character: An Examination of the Doctrine Underlying the Webb-Kenyon Act," *Minn. L. Rev.*, 5: 253–81 (1921), and Dennis M. Robb, "Legislative History of the Webb-Kenyon Act of March 1, 1913" (University of Chicago Law School, 1975; unpublished manuscript on file with author).

Chapter IX: *Federalism and Liberty*

This notion of a conditional federal prohibition was more elegant, but no less duplicitous, than Fuller's notion in *Rahrer*. It was premised on a distinction between the conditional exercise of a congressional power and a delegation, and the conditional exercise of power was defended on the theory that the greater (a total federal prohibition) included the lesser (a federal prohibition conditioned upon a state prohibition). As Gray made explicit in his dissent in *Leisy*, in the early 1890s there had been considerable doubt as to whether a national prohibition on the sale and distribution of liquor would be a constitutional exercise of the commerce power, but those doubts were considerably reduced after the *Lottery Case* of 1903,[82] which upheld a national ban on the use of interstate facilities for lotteries.

At the time of the Wilson Act, the Court's position was defined by *Leisy*. Now *Rhodes*, founded on strong nationalistic principles, controlled, and despite all the subtle legal strategies, the confrontation between Congress and the Court entailed in the passage of the Webb-Kenyon Act was unmistakable. At this point, the executive branch became involved. Taft was still in the White House when the bill cleared Congress and Attorney General George W. Wickersham advised him that it was "of doubtful constitutionality."[83] Taft himself was, of course, less reserved—one of the risks of having a lawyer as president. He refused to sign the bill because he thought it unconstitutional and, not surprisingly, drew heavily on the body of doctrine crafted by the man he had recently named chief justice, Edward White.

Taft acknowledged that White had never expressed an opinion in *Rhodes* on the specific question whether Congress had the power to authorize the states to abridge the so-called *Bowman* right to import.[84] Nevertheless, Taft found "language"[85] in White's opinion in *Rhodes* and in a number of other precedents that indicated that such a delegation or authorization as contained in the Webb-Kenyon bill would be beyond the power of Congress. Moved by the vision of economic nationalism that underlay *Brown v. Maryland*, *Debs*, and for that matter his own circuit court opinion in *Addyston Pipe*,[86] and by what he considered a proper regard for the role of Congress in the overall structure of government, Taft vetoed the measure. He was horrified by the prospect of "conferring upon Congress the power to amend the Constitution by ignoring or striking out one of its most important provisions."[87]

---

[82] 188 U.S. 321 (1903).
[83] 30 Op. Att'y Gen. 88, 111 (1913).
[84] Veto message of President Taft, Feb. 28, 1913, reprinted in 49 Cong. Rec. 4291 (1913).

[85] Ibid., 4292.
[86] United States v. Addyston Pipe & Steel Co., 85 F. 271 (6th Cir. 1898). See Chapter 5.
[87] 49 Cong. Rec. at 4292.

Congress overrode Taft's veto, and on March 1, 1913, three days before Taft left office, the Webb-Kenyon Act became law.[88] There are many ways of reading that congressional decision, but it did not necessarily evidence a lack of respect for President Taft's analysis of the precedents or his judgment as to how the law would evolve. It could be seen simply as a decision not to frustrate the popular or legislative will until the Supreme Court said in explicit and unmistakable terms that Congress had exceeded its powers—something the Court had not done in *Rhodes* or any of its other decisions. In justifying his veto, Taft insisted that each branch had an independent responsibility to uphold and observe the limits of the Constitution and that a decision to leave the resolution of all constitutional questions to the Court would be inconsistent with his responsibilities as president. He was strengthened in this position by a perceived difference in the standards to be applied by each branch. Like Thayer,[89] he thought the Court ought to invalidate legislation only when it was clearly unconstitutional, but that members of other branches of government should act on a much less restrictive standard and at times refuse to enact or to sign a measure of doubtful constitutionality. President Taft hoped that by taking a constitutional stand he would relieve the Court of the task he thought inevitable—declaring the Webb-Kenyon Act unconstitutional—and thus save the Court from becoming the target of "popular disapproval."[90]

When the Supreme Court finally took up the issue, however, it did not do what Taft thought was inevitable. The validity of the Webb-Kenyon Act was argued twice before the Court—first in May 1915 and then again in November 1916—and finally decided in *Clark Distilling Co. v. Western Maryland Railway*,[91] announced in January 1917. By that time almost all of the *Rhodes* Court was gone; only McKenna and, ironically, White remained. For two decades White had sought to discourage congressional intervention (above all by withdrawing in *Rhodes* the *Leisy* invitation), but now, as chief justice and in a manner most reminiscent of his performance in *Standard Oil* and *American Tobacco*, he assumed the responsibility for formulating a position for the Court that would in one way or another save the Webb-Kenyon Act. Conveniently forgetting his earlier views and the supposed distinction between the right to sell and the right to import, White capitulated to the growing congressional determination to allow home rule.

A substantive due process question was raised to the Webb-Kenyon Act. Although it was based on the Fifth Amendment, White nonetheless

---

[88] See 37 Stat. at 700.
[89] James B. Thayer, "The Origin and Scope of the American Doctrine of Constitutional Law," *Harv. L. Rev.*, 7: 129 (1893).
[90] 49 Cong. Rec. at 4292.
[91] 242 U.S. 311 (1917).

Chapter IX: *Federalism and Liberty*

summarily dismissed it with a reference to the Fourteenth Amendment principles established some thirty years earlier in *Mugler*. Only on one issue—regarding personal use—did a reservation emerge. While Harlan in *Mugler* clearly and emphatically upheld the prohibition on personal use, White in *Clark Distilling* wrote, "Whether the general authority [to prohibit the manufacture and sale of liquor] includes the right to forbid individual use, we need not consider. . . ."[92] Given the disagreement that marked the relationship between White and Harlan in the *Insular Cases* and again in *Standard Oil* and *American Tobacco*, this difference hardly was of any moment, perhaps no moment at all: Even if White were willing to protect personal manufacture, forbidding commercial manufacture would make personal use very, very difficult. In any event, the principal attack on the statute was based on the Commerce Clause, not Due Process, and in engaging this issue White began by reminding the reader of Attorney General Wickersham's opinion and President Taft's veto. These references might have been intended to honor old friends; they might also have been meant as a way of underscoring the difficulty of the question confronting the Court, and perhaps apologizing for what was to follow.

Chief Justice Fuller addressed the Wilson Act in *Rahrer* and the opinion that resulted was almost incoherent; Chief Justice White's effort to deal with the Webb-Kenyon Act did not fare much better. White was able to take advantage of the intervening decisions of the Court that had upheld the power of Congress under the Commerce Clause to deal with what many saw as roughly analogous matters of public morality. One was the decision that upheld the prohibition of lotteries; another dealt with prostitution.[93] White read these cases as indicating that Congress had the power to prohibit interstate trade in alcohol altogether. He viewed the congressional decision to leave it to each state to prohibit such trade as the exercise of a lesser power, and thus, under the now tiresome tenet of this Court, of unquestioned validity. The problem, of course, was that the uniformity requirement—under *Cooley* the key for placing a subject matter within the exclusive jurisdiction of the federal government—seemed very much at odds with the home rule scheme of the Webb-Kenyon Act, just as it had seemed inconsistent with the Wilson Act.

Chief Justice Fuller in *Rahrer* tried to convince his audience of the impossible: that the Wilson Act somehow met the *Cooley* test and the uniformity requirement. In dealing with the Webb-Kenyon Act, White's first instinct was of a similar nature:

---

[92] Ibid., 320.
[93] Lottery Case, 188 U.S. 321 (1903) (Congress can prohibit interstate carriage of lottery tickets); Hoke v. United States, 227 U.S. 308 (1913) (Congress can prohibit interstate transportation of women for prostitution).

So far as uniformity is concerned, there is no question that the act uniformly applies to the conditions which call its provisions into play—that its provisions apply to all the States,—so that the question really is a complaint as to the want of uniform existence of things to which the act applies and not to an absence of uniformity in the act itself.[94]

The uniformity that White spoke of in this sentence, as with Fuller's comments in *Rahrer*, was purely formal and made a sham of *Cooley*. While the *Cooley* test reserved for the exclusive jurisdiction of the federal government subjects that were suitable for a single nationwide rule, White accepted a rule that in fact varied from state to state. At this point, one could only wonder whether there was anything left to the *Cooley* test; and those doubts were reinforced when White continued in the very next sentence,

> But aside from this it is obvious that the argument [against the Act] seeks to engraft upon the Constitution a restriction not found in it, that is, that the power to regulate conferred upon Congress obtains subject to the requirement that regulations enacted shall be uniform throughout the United States.[95]

In this passage, White appears to have repudiated uniformity as a limitation on the commerce power, which may be well and good,[96] but only at the price of leaving *Bowman* and the decisions that built on it, including *Rhodes*, wholly without a rationale. The predicate for exclusive congressional power, and thus for the nullification of state laws, was that the subject required "uniformity of regulation"; if Congress was not bound to regulate uniformly, then there was no sense to that predicate or the exclusion of the states.

Sensing the predicament that he had created, and the incoherence of it all, White's opinion finally took a desperate turn and ended on this high note:

> [T]he exceptional nature of the subject here regulated is the basis upon which the exceptional power exerted must rest and affords no ground for any fear that such power may be constitutionally extended to things which it may not, consistently with the guarantees of the Constitution, embrace.[97]

---

[94] 242 U.S. at 326–27.
[95] Ibid.
[96] Although the Constitution requires national tax, bankruptcy, and naturalization statutes to be "uniform throughout the United States," U.S. Const., Art. I, Sect. 8, there is no explicit uniformity requirement for the Commerce Clause. However, the Port Preference Clause of Section 9 could be interpreted as creating such a requirement, or the requirement could simply be implied.
[97] 242 U.S. at 332.

Chapter IX: *Federalism and Liberty*

No wonder the two dissenters, Van Devanter and Holmes, thought it best not to write an opinion: The points that they might have made were acknowledged already in White's opinion and would only make him feel more uncomfortable. While the motivation for Fuller's opinion in *Rahrer* upholding the Wilson Act might have been ambiguous—was he being politically expedient, or was he simply trying to modulate the demands of economic nationalism to allow a place for local consensus?—there was no ambiguity to White's opinion in *Clark Distilling*. It can be understood only as a concession to the temperance movement.

Clark Distilling constituted an enormous victory for prohibition: The state regulatory regimes finally were perfected. As one might imagine, however, with that victory behind them, prohibitionists were not willing to stop. Measures such as the Webb-Kenyon Act were justified as a way of strengthening the regulatory powers of those states that had adopted a prohibitionist policy. But following *Clark Distilling*, home rule was characterized as "a cowardly yielding to expediency,"[98] and what was sought was, in the words of one senator, a nationwide ban on "an immoral, unhealthful, corrupting, and dangerous traffic."[99] In December 1917, within a year of *Clark Distilling*, Congress responded by passing the Eighteenth Amendment, which was ratified by the states within one month. That amendment embedded the rule against the manufacture and sale of intoxicating beverages in the higher law and substituted a single national rule—uniformity, at last—for the regulations of the various states. Home rule had come to an end.

The Eighteenth Amendment also brought to an end the Court's attempt, first in *Leisy* and *Rahrer* and then some twenty-five years later in *Clark Distilling*, to accommodate, through the idea of congressionally sanctioned home rule, the needs and demands of the temperance movement, even at the expense of the principles of economic nationalism that informed so much of its work. This spirit of accommodation may have been in keeping with the Court's position in the *Insular Cases*, or at least with Mr. Dooley's version of those decisions, but it was uncharacteristic for an institution historically defined by decisions such as *Lochner* and *Pollock*. Progressives often attacked the Fuller Court for its rigidity and intransigence, qualities that were said to flow from its formalism. Decisions such as *Leisy*, *Rahrer*, and *Clark Distilling* were of another character altogether, but when it came time for the nation to formulate a sensible response to the demands of the prohibition movement, itself a branch of progressivism,

---

[98] 56 Cong. Rec. 450 (1917) (statement of Rep. Tillmann).

[99] 55 Cong. Rec. 5552 (1917) (statement of Senator Sheppard). For an account of the post–*Clark Distilling* transformation of the prohibition movement's goal, from home rule to national prohibition, see Hamm, "Prelude to Prohibition," 386–89.

these exercises in accommodationism seem to have been futile or perhaps even counterproductive.

Flexibility comes in many forms. It is conceivable that if the Court in *Leisy, Rahrer,* and *Clark Distilling* had spoken honestly and openly about the virtues of local consensus, the nation might have been saved from the Eighteenth Amendment. Discussion does not necessarily produce restraint, but at least it clarifies the issues and makes the consequences explicit. The Court's use in *Pollock* of the "direct tax" rubric to analyze the 1894 income tax masked or at least skirted the fundamental issues posed by that law and thus impeded rather than facilitated public understanding of the issues. A similar point could be made about the Court's engagement with prohibition in *Leisy, Rahrer,* and *Clark Distilling.* The Court woodenly applied the *Cooley* categories, finding the importation and sale of alcohol to be a matter requiring uniformity, and then found itself forced to engage in legal gyrations in order to fit its result—home rule—within the nationalist doctrine to which it subscribed.

The response to *Pollock*'s indirection was a constitutional amendment, the Sixteenth, that reads like an administrative regulation and is startling in its failure to address the fundamental redistributive issue posed by the income tax. The response to the indirection—perhaps doctrinal incoherence is a less politic but more apt term—of *Leisy, Rahrer,* and *Clark Distilling* was even more problematic. Unlike the Sixteenth Amendment, the Eighteenth made a bold policy statement, but in a way that ill served the federal structure of the Constitution, which seeks to strike a balance between the two competing principles of local consensus and economic nationalism, one founded on the idea of self-governance and the other on the vision of the United States as a common market.[100] In order to satisfy the prohibitionists' conception of the public good, the Eighteenth Amendment sacrificed *both* local consensus and economic nationalism, thereby altering the underlying structure of the Constitution and violating the inherited understanding of the American nation—at least, to borrow a phrase from Chief Justice White, as it pertained to this exceptional subject.

---

[100] No wonder that the Eighteenth Amendment was attacked as unconstitutional. National Prohibition Cases, 253 U.S. 250 (1920).

PART FIVE

Liberty Dishonored

I N ITS ENCOUNTERS with the great social movements of the day, the Court, building on the social contract tradition, developed a body of doctrine that at its heart depicted the state as an authority constituted to serve limited and discrete ends. The state was entrusted with the power to maintain public order, facilitate market exchanges, and preserve the emergent economic union. At the same time, however, the Court drew a sharp distinction between the social and political domains, and the state was denied the authority to alter the distribution of power or wealth in civil society.

This constitutive theory of the state underlies *Debs* and *Pollock*. It also provides a way to understand many of the Court's decisions, *Lochner* included, in which the legislative program of the progressive movement was contested and curbed. The *Leisy* invitation, in which the Court announced its readiness to allow Congress to institute a home rule policy for prohibition, was an exception to this overall pattern. Allowing the states to erect trade barriers in order to perfect an exercise of their police power represented a capitulation to the increasingly strident demands of the prohibition movement. But that exception was short-lived. Soon after *Debs* and the election of 1896, the *Leisy* invitation was withdrawn and the Court reaffirmed its commitment to individual liberty and the principles of economic nationalism.

A more significant exception to the Court's overarching commitment to liberty was its response to the imperialist agenda of the McKinley administration. Granted, the *Insular Cases* and the eventual triumph of the incorporation doctrine should not be understood as an unqualified defeat of the social contract tradition or the idea of constitutive authority: The initial dissents of Justices Brewer, Peckham, Fuller, and Harlan, and even the incorporation doctrine itself, defended the analytic unity of Constitution and flag. Still, significant elements of the incorporation doctrine were at odds with the Court's commitment to the idea of constitutive government, and Justice Brown's position, the extension doctrine, severed the tie between flag and Constitution altogether. The relation between the state and the citizens of Puerto Rico and the Philippines was deemed to be more akin to that of master to slave, or parent to child, or, to account for the odd turn of events in *Muller v. Oregon* in 1908, man to woman.

In three aspects of the Court's work yet to be examined—concerning procedural due process (Chapter 10), free speech (Chapter 11), and racial equality (Chapter 12)—we find a further elaboration of the approach to state authority introduced by Justice Brown in the *Insular Cases*. Here all sense of limits is gone and the relation of state to subject appears more organic than contractual. In two of these areas, racial equality and due process, the continuity between the position of the Court and Brown's position in the *Insular Cases* is striking indeed, for both involved constitutional challenges to state authority by persons who, like the inhabitants of Puerto Rico and the Philippines, might be regarded by the majority as outsiders. *Plessy v. Ferguson* involved the claims of blacks to the kind of liberty guaranteed the bakers in *Lochner*, but the Court, in an opinion by Justice Brown, failed to honor that claim. A similar failure occurred in the realm of procedure, especially as applied to immigrants from China. Admittedly, the 1890s and early 1900s were not a time when the Supreme Court was scrupulous in regard to the dictates of procedural fairness, even in the administration of the criminal justice system.[1] But the Court's jurisprudence took a new and dramatic turn for the worse in cases such as *Fong Yue Ting*.[2] In these, the Court rejected due process claims of Chinese immigrants, who had been excluded by law from the constitutional community and who were subject to remarkably crude and unfair treatment by immigration authorities.

Brown's willingness in the *Insular Cases* to embrace a very strong conception of state power could thus be seen to embody the same spirit that we will encounter in the following three chapters, but with at least one important difference: A remarkable consensus was achieved. In the *Insular Cases*, Justice Brown spoke for himself; but on issues of procedural fairness, free speech, and racial equality, the Court was apparently united in its disregard for the contractarian ideal. Exceptions are notable but limited. Harlan, to his great credit, dissented in *Plessy* and again in the principal free speech case of the period, *Patterson v. Colorado*;[3] Brewer (sometimes with the support of Peckham once he joined the Court, but never with Harlan) spoke out in the cases involving the Chinese. These opinions of Harlan and Brewer were intense and moving, but their tone was unusually shrill. They did not represent divisions in the Court so much as they were attempts to preserve the integrity of the individual justice who disagreed. The majority, which almost always included Fuller, remained solid and unmovable, and the dissents seemed to be written more with an eye to legal posterity than as efforts to move Fuller and his brethren to change their positions.

There is, moreover, no way of explaining this entire body of law in the terms appropriate for the *Insular Cases* or Brown's extension doctrine: Notions of exclusion from the constitutional community may be the key

---

[1] In a chilling and provocative speech, Brewer recommended abolishing appeals as a "remedy" for the increasing number of lynchings—to assure the mob that "justice" would be done swiftly. David J. Brewer, "The Right of Appeal," *The Independent*, 55: 2547, 2548 (1903). See Lawrence M. Friedman, *A History of American Law*, 2d ed. (New York: Simon & Schuster, 1985), 398–403. Describing the procedure followed in the courts of the time, Friedman says it was technical, complex, and at times ultra-persnickety, but hardly a model of fairness.

[2] Fong Yue Ting v. United States, 149 U.S. 698 (1893).

[3] 205 U.S. 454, 463 (1907).

to *Plessy* and *Fong Yue Ting*, but not to *Patterson v. Colorado*.[4] In that case, the editor and publisher of one of Colorado's most respected newspapers—who also happened to be a United States senator—was punished for having published a cartoon and a series of articles criticizing the state supreme court. From the modern perspective, one would have thought that an institution committed to the protection of liberty and limiting the reach of state power also would have found—somehow, somewhere—the energy and power to protect the press in such circumstances. The deplorable failure of the Court to throw its weight behind the Bill of Rights and the Fourteenth Amendment in this case, as well as in cases involving blacks and the Chinese, gave the Fuller Court's activism a jagged and puzzling character. It brought a new question to the fore: How could the Court responsible for *Lochner* also have decided *Patterson*, or, for that matter, *Fong Yue Ting* and *Plessy*?

---

[4] One important free speech case did involve an alleged outsider, John Turner, a British anarchist and labor organizer. United States *ex rel.* Turner v. Williams, 194 U.S. 279 (1904). See Chapter 11.

CHAPTER X

The Chinese Cases: Citizenship and the Claims of Procedure

T HE TURN of the century was a critical phase in the history of immigration in America. The population of the country grew from about 60 million in 1890 to 90 million in 1910, and a considerable portion of the growth—approximately 40 percent—was attributable to immigration.[1] Almost 700,000 people entered the United States each year, most of them from Europe. These waves of European immigration provoked a number of political and social controversies in the nation,[2] but, with a few exceptions,[3] they did not ripen into formal legal or constitutional cases.

While the Fuller Court developed an important body of law on immigration, its engagement with the issue was triggered not by the then current influx of Europeans, but by the presence of a group of people who had come to America much earlier—the Chinese.[4] Most of the Chinese in America

---

[1] This figure of 40 percent represents the growth in population directly attributable to new net immigration. If offspring born in the United States to immigrants who arrived during this period is also taken into account, the figure is of course higher. Richard A. Easterlin, David Ward, William S. Bernard, and Reed Ueda, *Immigration* (Cambridge: Harvard University Press, 1982), 2–4.

[2] See generally John Higham, *Strangers in the Land: Patterns of American Nativism, 1860–1925*, 2d ed. (New York: Atheneum, 1974). The leading work on immigration in this period, Higham's book focuses on European aspects and thus, unfortunately, slights the situation of the Chinese. As Professor Higham explains in the preface to the second edition, "I regarded opposi-

tion to certain non-European people, such as the Chinese and, to a lesser extent, the Japanese, as somewhat separate phenomena, historically tangential to the main currents of American nativism." See also Alan M. Kraut, *The Huddled Masses: The Immigrant in American Society, 1880–1921* (Arlington Heights, Ill.: Harlan Davidson, 1982).

[3] One possible exception is United States *ex rel.* Turner v. Williams, 194 U.S. 279 (1904), discussed in the following chapter.

[4] See generally Gunther Barth, *Bitter Strength: A History of the Chinese in the United States, 1850–1870* (Cambridge: Harvard University Press, 1964); Jack Chen, *The Chinese of America* (San Francisco: Harper & Row, 1980); Stanford M. Lyman, *Chinese Americans* (New York: Random House, 1974); Vic-

298

had come in the middle of the nineteenth century, initially drawn by the gold rush in California, but later to work on the construction of the national rail system. Although many remained here for twenty or thirty years, they never lost their status as immigrants. They were, as Justice Field unabashedly described them in the late 1880s, "strangers in the land."[5]

The cultural barriers between the Chinese and white European settlers, described in touching and disturbing detail by Maxine Hong Kingston,[6] may have contributed to the unusual status of the Chinese in the eyes of the Court. Demography must also have played a role. On a national scale, the Chinese community was relatively small and confined to the West Coast, particularly San Francisco: At the turn of the century, there were roughly 100,000 Chinese in the United States, almost all of them in San Francisco (which then had a population of only 300,000). This concentration prevented the development of social and political ties with other ethnic groups or political factions throughout the country. In the national forum, the Chinese community was truly discrete and insular. The concentration of the Chinese also made their treatment appear to be an issue about which the preferences of the locality should be taken as decisive. Immigration pol-

tor G. Nee and Brett de Bary Nee, *Longtime Californ': A Documentary Study of an American Chinatown* (New York: Pantheon Books, 1973; repr. Stanford: Stanford University Press, 1986); George F. Seward, *Chinese Immigration, in Its Social and Economical Aspects* (New York: Charles Scribner's Sons, 1881); Roger Daniels, "Westerners from the East: Oriental Immigrants Reappraised," *Pac. Hist. Rev.*, 35: 373 (1966); and Kil Young Zo, "Chinese Emigration into the United States, 1850–1880" (Ph.D. diss., Columbia University, 1971). For accounts focusing on the popular response to Chinese immigration, see Mary Roberts Coolidge, *Chinese Immigration* (New York: Arno Press, 1969); Lucile Eaves, *A History of California Labor Legislation* (Berkeley: University of California Press, 1910); Stuart Creighton Miller, *The Unwelcome Immigrant: The American Image of the Chinese, 1785–1882* (Berkeley: University of California Press, 1969); Elmer C. Sandmeyer, *The Anti-Chinese Movement in California* (Urbana: University of Illinois Press, 1973); and Alexander Saxton, *The Indispensable Enemy: Labor and the Anti-Chinese*

Movement in California (Berkeley: University of California Press, 1971). Professor Charles J. McClain, Jr., has written a recent series of articles focusing on the Chinese legal experience in this country: "*In re Lee Sing*: The First Residential Segregation Case," *W. Leg. Hist.*, 3: 179 (1990); "The Chinese Struggle for Civil Rights in 19th Century America: The Unusual Case of *Baldwin v. Franks*," *L. & Hist. Rev.*, 3: 349 (1985); and "The Chinese Struggle for Civil Rights in Nineteenth Century America: The First Phase, 1850–1870," *Cal. L. Rev.*, 72: 529 (1984).

[5] Chae Chan Ping v. United States (The Chinese Exclusion Case), 130 U.S. 581, 595 (1889) ("They remained strangers in the land, residing apart by themselves, and adhering to the customs and usages of their own country. It seemed impossible for them to assimilate with our people or to make any change in their habits or modes of living.").

[6] Maxine Hong Kingston, *The Woman Warrior: Memoirs of a Girlhood among Ghosts* (New York: Alfred A. Knopf, 1976); *China Men* (New York: Alfred A. Knopf, 1980).

icy itself was deemed to rest exclusively with the federal government, and now and then the federal circuit court in San Francisco intervened to protect against the most brutal oppression. There was, however, a general feeling in the nation that the Chinese were a "local problem" and that the local authorities were owed a measure of deference in what was "a difficult situation."[7]

For a considerable period of time, the Chinese systematically were denied the opportunity to become naturalized citizens. Under the first naturalization act, only free white persons could become naturalized citizens;[8] after the Civil War, that statute was amended to allow the naturalization of aliens of African descent, but the Chinese were still excluded.[9] In 1898 the Supreme Court held, in *Wong Kim Ark*,[10] that the Chinese were covered by the provision of the Fourteenth Amendment that conferred citizenship on persons born in the United States and subject to its jurisdiction. Over time, the portion of the Chinese community obtaining citizenship by this means would grow, but at the turn of the century it was relatively small. It is also important to recognize that *Wong Kim Ark* came late, thirty years after the adoption of the Fourteenth Amendment, and that the outcome in the case was hardly a foregone conclusion. Justices Harlan and Fuller dissented, and there is evidence to suggest that writing the majority opinion was not an easy task.[11]

In the years before *Wong Kim Ark*, the Supreme Court developed a case law on the assumption that the Chinese were not citizens and, moreover, could never become so. The Chinese were excluded from the constitutional community and relegated to the status once reserved for blacks by *Dred Scott*[12]—permanent residents who could never become citizens. Many cases of the period, including *Fong Yue Ting*[13] (almost as infamous among the cognoscenti as *Plessy v. Ferguson*[14]), were decided on this basis. Of course, as the constitutional status of the Chinese changed, the measure

---

[7] Eaves, *History of California Labor Legislation*, 105–196. For accounts focusing on the Chinese experience with local officials, see Ralph James Mooney, "Matthew Deady and the Federal Judicial Response to Racism in the Early West," *Or. L. Rev.*, 63: 561 (1984); Lucy Salyer, "Captives of Law: Judicial Enforcement of the Chinese Exclusion Laws, 1891–1905," *J. Am. Hist.*, 76: 91 (1989); and John R. Wunder, "The Chinese and the Courts in the Pacific Northwest: Justice Denied," *Pac. Hist. Rev.*, 52: 191 (1983).

[8] Naturalization Act, Ch. 3, 1 Stat. 103 (1790).

[9] Naturalization Act, Ch. 254, 16 Stat. 254 (1870). Section 7 reads: *"And be it further enacted*, That the naturalization laws are hereby extended to aliens of African nativity and to persons of African descent."

[10] United States v. Wong Kim Ark, 169 U.S. 649 (1898).

[11] The case was argued on March 5 and 8, 1897, but the decision was not rendered until March 28, 1898.

[12] Scott v. Sandford, 60 U.S. (19 How.) 393 (1857). See Chapter 8.

[13] Fong Yue Ting v. United States, 149 U.S. 698 (1893).

[14] 163 U.S. 537 (1896).

of constitutional protection also changed, but always under the burden of a body of decisions that saw the Chinese as forever aliens.

Battles in the law often are fought at the edge of the field, simply because that is the only ground providing room to maneuver. The Chinese cases of the Fuller Court were no exception. Like the early fugitive slave cases,[15] or many of the *Insular Cases*,[16] the decisions of the Court respecting Chinese immigration were, by and large, addressed to procedures used to administer or enforce a government policy; they did not go to the substance of the policy itself, here the substantive criteria for determining who could lawfully be admitted or excluded from the United States. The issue of who may lawfully enter the country might appear of special interest to a group of justices who believed in the free market and rendered decisions like *Lochner v. New York*,[17] but for Fuller and his brethren it was viewed as authoritatively settled.

Beginning in the early 1880s, well before Fuller took his seat, the doors of the nation were closed to most Chinese. Entry was still possible for merchants, professionals, and academics, but in the Chinese Exclusion Act of 1882 Congress barred the entry of Chinese laborers, both skilled and unskilled.[18] On its face, the law announced only a ten-year suspension of Chinese immigration, not a permanent prohibition, but to no one's surprise, at each ten-year interval—in 1892 and then again in 1902—the "suspension" was renewed. The 1882 Act provided that the suspension did not affect Chinese laborers already resident in the United States; they had the right to leave the country and reenter. In 1884 Congress amended that statute so as to make a certificate of reentry issued before departure the *sole* evidence capable of establishing a right of reentry.[19] Then in 1888 a statute was passed revoking all certificates of reentry.[20] In one case, this statute was applied to Chae Chan Ping, who had been resident in the country for twelve years, had obtained a certificate of reentry, but who at the time the revocation was enacted was out of the country for fourteen months on a trip to China. The power of Congress to bar his reentry was fully upheld.[21]

The opinion was written by Justice Field. Although he entitled it "The Chinese Exclusion Case"[22] (Justice Field knew well the power of nam-

---

[15] Prigg v. Commonwealth of Pennsylvania, 41 U.S. (16 Pet.) 539 (1842); Ableman v. Booth, 59 U.S. (18 How.) 476, 479 (1855); 62 U.S. (20 How.) 506 (1858).

[16] Rassmussen v. United States, 197 U.S. 516 (1905); Dorr v. United States, 195 U.S. 138 (1904); Hawaii v. Mankichi, 190 U.S. 197 (1903). See Chapter 8.

[17] 198 U.S. 45 (1905).

[18] Act of May 6, 1882, Ch. 126, 22 Stat. 58.

[19] Act of July 5, 1884, Ch. 220, 23 Stat. 115.

[20] Act of Oct. 1, 1888, Ch. 1064, 25 Stat. 504.

[21] *The Chinese Exclusion Case*, 130 U.S. at 581.

[22] He tried to restyle *Fong Yue Ting* and two related cases as the "Chinese Deportation Cases." 149 U.S. at 744, n. 1.

ing), the case did not in any way put into question the general power to exclude; that power was virtually conceded. The entire opinion was premised on the notion that the power to exclude properly belonged to the national government. As with the power to acquire territories, there was no explicit or direct constitutional provision conferring this power over immigration to the government.[23] But Field, in a way less cautious than Taney in the derivation of the power to acquire and govern territories in *Dred Scott* but perhaps reminiscent of Brown in the early *Insular Cases*, viewed the power to exclude as an essential attribute of national sovereignty.[24] The power to exclude thereby was placed far beyond the kind of substantive constitutional attack that would later triumph in *Lochner* or, for that matter, that earlier had inspired Field's dissent in the *Slaughter-House Cases*.[25] It was only the retroactive aspect of the 1888 statute that troubled Field. In addressing this issue counsel spoke of vested rights and insisted that the 1888 statute could not be applied to someone who left the country under a certificate of reentry before the 1888 statute was passed. But even that objection was dismissed:

> The exercise of these public trusts is not the subject of barter or contract. Whatever license, therefore, Chinese laborers may have obtained, previous to the act of October 1, 1888, to return to the United States after their departure is held at the will of the government, revocable at any time, at its pleasure.[26]

Although the *Chinese Exclusion Case* was handed down very early in Fuller's chief justiceship, before the formation of the coalition that prevailed during most of his tenure, the major premise of the case, conceding to Congress a broad power to exclude, remained unquestioned throughout the period. This was largely because the premise was not new, but merely codified the understanding that evolved on the bench and in Congress during the 1880s, an understanding wholly consistent with contract ideology. The social contract made the consent of the community the touchstone of legitimacy for the state, but, as Peter Schuck and Rogers Smith point out,[27]

---

[23] The effort of the framers to avoid the use of the word "slaves" in the Constitution, even when it came to congressional power to ban the slave trade, might have created a power in Congress over immigration. The Slave-Trade Clause reads: "The Migration or Importation of Such Persons as any of the States now existing shall think proper to admit, shall not be prohibited by the Congress prior to the Year one thousand eight hundred and eight, but a Tax or duty may be imposed on such Importation, not exceeding ten dollars for each Person." U.S. Const., Art. I, Sect. 9, Cl. 1.

[24] See Chapter 8.

[25] 83 U.S. 56, 83 (1872).

[26] 130 U.S. at 609.

[27] Peter M. Schuck and Rogers M. Smith, *Citizenship Without Consent: Illegal Aliens in the American Polity* (New Haven: Yale University Press, 1985), 4.

such an ideology presupposes an almost unqualified power in the community to set the terms of membership. It is thus fair to say that none of the cases the Court considered during the 1890s and 1900s posed any possibility of opening the doors of the nation to a significant number of Chinese. The structure of the immigration policy was set and immune to judicial attack. The cases that arose were intense and hard fought, but they did not concern the substance of the policy, only the method of implementation.

I

The Burlingame Treaty of 1868[28] contemplated free and unlimited immigration by the Chinese, but by the 1880s a new policy was taking shape. In 1880 a supplementary treaty was adopted that gave the United States the right to "regulate, limit or suspend such coming or residence,"[29] and in 1882 the Chinese Exclusion Act was passed. In 1884 Congress legislated once again, subjecting the right of the Chinese to leave and reenter the country to much more rigid procedural requirements: All Chinese seeking reentry had to possess a certificate issued in the United States before departure. In 1888 Congress, moved either by an increase in anti-Chinese sentiment or by abuses of the reentry privilege by forgeries or transfers, denied Chinese the right to reenter altogether. Now the right of Chinese residents to travel, even to their homeland and even for the briefest of periods, could be exercised only on pain of exclusion from America. The 1888 measure also revoked all certificates of return that previously had been issued, and the *Chinese Exclusion Case* of 1889 upheld that provision despite the obvious hardship it inflicted.

In 1892 this exclusionary spiral took a further turn when Congress renewed for another ten years the so-called suspension of immigration initiated in 1882.[30] To strengthen this bar with respect to illegal entrants, Congress provided for punishment of up to one year's hard labor followed by deportation, and stipulated that commissioners (rather than federal judges) would conduct the trials. The law placed the burden of proving lawful entry on the Chinese. But the aspect of the 1892 Act that provoked the greatest controversy pertained not to illegal entrants but to those Chinese who were lawfully resident in the United States at the time. A system of internal controls was established for them that paralleled the pass system of antebellum America, which required all slaves traveling off their plantations to carry passes.[31] The 1892 Act (generally known by the name of its sponsor, Senator

---

[28] July 28, 1868, U.S.–China, 16 Stat. 739.
[29] Treaty Concerning Immigration, Nov. 17, 1880, U.S.–China, 22 Stat. 826.
[30] Act of May 5, 1892, Ch. 60, 27

Stat. 25.
[31] See, e.g., Eugene D. Genovese, *Roll, Jordan, Roll: The World the Slaves Made* (New York: Pantheon Books, 1974), 617–19.

Geary from California) required all Chinese laborers lawfully resident in the United States to be registered and to carry a certificate of residence with them at all times.[32] Anyone found without a certificate one year after the Act came into force would be deemed to be unlawfully in the United States and deported unless (1) that person could establish that the failure to procure a certificate was due to an accident, sickness, or unavoidable cause; and (2) a "credible white witness" testified that the claimant was resident in the United States at the time of the passage of the Act. These determinations were to be made by a federal judge.

Following the enactment of the Geary Act, the Six Companies, a leading organization for Chinese immigrants in San Francisco,[33] engaged three lawyers, James C. Carter, Joseph Choate, and J. Hubley Ashton, to render an opinion on the constitutionality of the registration requirement of the Act.[34] They concluded the provision was unconstitutional, and on the basis of this opinion, as well as instructions from the Six Companies, approximately 85,000 of the 100,000 Chinese residents of San Francisco refused to register by the May 5, 1893 deadline imposed by the Act.[35] On May 15, 1893, the Supreme Court upheld the Act in *Fong Yue Ting v. United States*, a case involving a Chinese laborer who had been a United States resident for fourteen years. He was arrested for failing to have the certificate required by the Act and was subject to deportation despite a federal judge's finding (based on testimony from a Chinese witness) that he was, in fact, a permanent resident of the United States when the Act was passed. In November 1893, after the Supreme Court decision in *Fong Yue Ting*, Congress, moved either by humanitarian sentiments or recognition of the cost of a massive

---

[32] Geary Act, Ch. 60, Sect. 6, 27 Stat. 25, 26 (1892).

[33] The Six Companies was a confederation of *hui kuan*. Each *hui kuan* brought together immigrants who spoke the same dialect, came from the same part of China, or belonged to the same Chinese ethnic group. The *hui kuan* served many immigrant needs, providing, for instance, credit, informal adjudication and resolution of disputes, and representation to the outside world. The *hui kuan* confederated into the Chinese Consolidated Benevolent Association in 1858 and became popularly known as the Six Companies. See Lyman, *Chinese Americans*, 32–37; Stanford M. Lyman, "Conflict and the Web of Group Affiliation in San Francisco's Chinatown, 1850–1910," *Pac. Hist. Rev.*, 43: 473 (1974); Fong Kum Ngon, "The Chinese

Six Companies," *Overland Monthly*, 23: 518 (1894); and *Report of the Special Joint Committee to Investigate Chinese Immigration*, S. Rep. No. 689, 44th Cong., 2d Sess. 124–25, 173–80, 405–406, 446–48 (1877).

[34] For Carter's role in the income tax, antitrust and railroad regulation cases, see Chapter 4, pp. 75, 83, Chapter 5, p. 119, and Chapter 7, p. 207. Choate was also involved in the tax case (see above) and a prohibition case, see Chapter 9, p. 264. Ashton was also a distinguished member of the Supreme Court bar; see the resolution commemorating him, 205 U.S. 553 (1907). He served as counsel for Chinese litigants in many cases challenging the new legislation.

[35] See Eaves, *History of California Labor Legislation*, 194–95, and H.R. Rep. No. 70, 53d Cong., 1st Sess. (1893).

deportation,[36] or both, gave the Chinese a second chance to register by extending the deadline to May 1894.[37] By the new deadline 100,000 Chinese had registered.[38]

The majority opinion in *Fong Yue Ting* was written by Justice Gray. In constructing it he relied heavily upon a decision he had written just one year earlier in the *Nishimura Ekiu*[39] case, in which a Japanese woman was refused admission to the United States on the ground that she was likely to become a public charge. The government's action in that case was based on the general immigration statute of 1891,[40] which established the federal immigration bureaucracy, prescribed minimal standards of admissions (excluding, in the words of the statute, lunatics, paupers, and those likely to become public charges), and made the decisions of executive officers "final." In *Fong Yue Ting*, Justice Gray ignored any possible difference between the long-term Chinese resident threatened with deportation and the immigrant seeking admission for the first time, and he used *Nishimura Ekiu* to dismiss the objections to the procedures of the Geary Act. Since Congress could entrust admissions determinations totally to executive officers, Gray reasoned, the Chinese laborer should be grateful for whatever procedure Congress was gracious enough to confer. It did not matter that the Chinese petitioners were not claiming a right to enter, but only the right to remain in a country they claimed they had lawfully entered and in which they had resided for many years. They were still aliens, and they always would be.

Justice Gray treated the Chinese lawfully resident in the United States as permanent immigrants, forever outside the constitutional community and unable to make constitutional claims on the government. The power to exclude them was absolute and so was the power to expel:

> But they continue to be aliens, having taken no steps toward becoming citizens, and incapable of becoming such under the naturalization laws; and therefore remain subject to the power of Congress to expel them, or to order them to be removed and deported from the country, whenever in its judgment their removal is necessary or expedient. . . .[41]

The government might allow them to stay, but that decision was entirely at its discretion, turning on a judgment as to what was "necessary" or "ex-

---

[36] See H.R. Rep. No. 70, 53d Cong., 1st Sess. (1893) (estimating at $6 million the cost of arresting, prosecuting, and deporting the 85,000 resident Chinese believed liable under the Act).

[37] The McCreary Amendment, Ch. 14, 28 Stat. 7 (1893).

[38] See Sandmeyer, *Anti-Chinese Movement in California*, 105, note 32.

[39] Nishimura Ekiu v. United States, 142 U.S. 651 (1892).

[40] Act of Mar. 3, 1891, Ch. 551, 26 Stat. 1084.

[41] 149 U.S. at 724.

pedient" and subject to whatever conditions it might impose, including a requirement to register. Every moment of their presence in America was dependent on the will of Congress and the continued performance of whatever requirements it might establish. Deportation, from this perspective, was not a punishment for a crime and thus was not subject to the procedural protections surrounding a criminal prosecution; it was merely a means of implementing the will of Congress by removing those who had not fulfilled all the conditions for continued residence:

> The order of deportation is not a punishment for crime. It is not a banishment, in the sense in which that word is often applied to the expulsion of a citizen from his country by way of punishment. It is but a method of enforcing the return to his own country of an alien who has not complied with the conditions upon the performance of which the government of the nation, acting within its constitutional authority and through the proper departments, has determined that his continuing to reside here shall depend.[42]

Gray's affirmation of absolutism is strikingly similar to Field's in the *Chinese Exclusion Case*, and thus it is odd to find Field filing a dissent in *Fong Yue Ting*. He tried to distinguish the two cases on the theory that one involved exclusion while the other concerned expulsion. This distinction, of course, overlooked the fact, partially obscured by the title,[43] that the *Chinese Exclusion Case* was more a deportation than an exclusion case: The petitioner had spent the last twelve years of his life in America and was, after a trip to his homeland, seeking reentry on the basis of a permit authorized by Congress when he left but then revoked by Congress while he was in transit. A more basic incoherence in Field's position arose from the underlying theory of his opinion in the *Chinese Exclusion Case*. In order to respond to the obvious retroactivity of the 1888 statute, Justice Field described a governmental power so broad and so general—the government is entitled to do whatever it concludes is necessary to maintain its independence and protect itself—that it left no room for the distinction that he tried to maintain in *Fong Yue Ting* between expulsion and exclusion.

Field's opinion in the *Chinese Exclusion Case* was largely responsive to the argument of James C. Carter, the most scholarly of the attorneys hired by the Six Companies. As reprinted in the *United States Reports*, Carter's argument was admirable in its logical clarity: (1) With the possible exception of war, there is no constitutional power to expel aliens; (2) the

---

[42] Ibid., 730.
[43] On the detailed attention paid by Field to the precise wording of the official case reports, see Alan F. Westin, "Stephen J. Field and the Headnote to O'Neil v. Vermont: A Snapshot of the Fuller Court at Work," *Yale L.J.*, 67: 363 (1958).

denial of reentry to a longtime resident of the country with a reentry certificate is tantamount to expulsion; (3) therefore the denial of reentry is unconstitutional. Justice Field restated Carter's second premise a number of times but never responded to it directly; he probably could not, given that it aptly described the circumstances of the case. The implication, then, is that the disagreement centered on the first premise, with Field holding that there was power to expel aliens.

For the most part, Field was careful to use the word "exclusion" in the *Chinese Exclusion Case*,[44] but he never drew a sharp distinction in his opinion between "exclusion" and "expulsion," nor did he explain why there might be different sets of rules in the two circumstances. Indeed, Field's affirmation of government power to exclude was so grandiose as to suggest that it embraced the power to expel and thus that he was disputing Carter's initial premise:

> The power of exclusion of foreigners being an incident of sovereignty belonging to the government of the United States, as a part of those sovereign powers delegated by the Constitution, the right to its exercise at any time when, in the judgment of the government, the interests of the country require it, cannot be granted away or restrained on behalf of any one.[45]

Field noted the faint concession to war in Carter's initial premise and fully exploited it. Field's first strategy was to give the concept of war a cultural dimension. "It matters not," Field said, "in what form such aggression and encroachment come, whether from the foreign aggression and encroachment, whether from the foreign nation acting in its national character or from vast hordes of its people crowding in upon us."[46] Then he continued:

> If, therefore, the government of the United States, through its legislative department, considers the presence of foreigners of a different race in this country, who will not assimilate with us, to be dangerous to its peace and security, their exclusion is not to be stayed because at the time there are no actual hostilities with the nation of which the foreigners are subjects. The existence of war would render the necessity of the proceeding only more obvious and pressing.[47]

---

[44] There is one reference to expulsion, in which Field quotes from a communication by Grant's secretary of state, Hamilton Fish, to the U.S. ambassador to France, stating: "The control of the people within its limits, and the right to *expel* from its territory persons who are dangerous to the peace of the State, are too clearly within the essential attributes of sovereignty to be seriously contested." 130 U.S. at 607 (emphasis added).

[45] Ibid., 609.

[46] Ibid., 606.

[47] Ibid.

In defending his initial premise, Carter drew from the debates surrounding the Alien and Sedition Acts of 1798,[48] which sought to expel aliens whom the government considered subversive or disloyal. Many of the leading statesmen of the day, Carter claimed, condemned the Alien and Sedition Acts on the ground that there was no power in the government to expel aliens (with, of course, the possible exception of expulsion in the exigencies of war). At the very end of his opinion in the *Chinese Exclusion Case*, Field once again engaged Carter and took up this precedent, but he quickly dismissed it. Initially, he noted the Alien and Sedition Acts conferred the power on the president to expel dangerous aliens. He did not explain the significance of that observation, which seemed accurate enough, but simply continued,

> There were other provisions, also distinguishing it from the act under consideration. The Act was passed during a period of great political excitement and it was attacked and defended with great zeal and ability. It is enough, however, to say that it is entirely different from the act before us, and the validity of its provision was never brought to the test of judicial decision in the courts of the United States.[49]

In his dissent in *Fong Yue Ting*, however, Justice Field turned around and argued the other side of the case, relying upon the controversy surrounding the Alien and Sedition Acts to support his objection to the Geary Act. According to Field, writing in a new spirit, the debates surrounding the Alien and Sedition Acts indicated that there was no power to expel "friendly aliens."[50]

While the majority's position in *Fong Yue Ting* could draw upon the absolutism of the *Chinese Exclusion Case* and the exclusionary premises of that case—that the Chinese were outside the constitutional community and thus unable to claim the full protection of liberty; they were "strangers in the land"—there was one precedent that introduced a more inclusionary perspective into the law and thus competed with the *Chinese Exclusion Case*. This was *Yick Wo v. Hopkins*,[51] which Field had joined.

---

[48] Alien and Sedition Acts, Ch. 58, 1 Stat. 570 (1798); Ch. 66, 1 Stat. 577 (1798); Ch. 74, 1 Stat. 596 (1798). For general histories of these Acts, see Zechariah Chafee, Jr., *Free Speech in the United States* (Cambridge: Harvard University Press, 1941), and Leonard W. Levy, *Emergence of a Free Press* (New York: Oxford University Press, 1985), revised edition of *The Legacy of Suppression: Freedom of Speech and Press in Early America* (New York: Harper & Row, 1963). See also the discussion of the Acts in Chapter 11 and more generally in New York Times Co. v. Sullivan, 376 U.S. 254 (1964), and in Harry Kalven, Jr., "The New York Times Case: A Note on 'The Central Meaning of the First Amendment,'" *Sup. Ct. Rev.*, 1964: 191.

[49] 130 US. at 610–611.

[50] 149 U.S. at 750.

[51] 118 U.S. 356 (1886).

Chapter X: *The Chinese Cases*

In *Yick Wo*, the Supreme Court invalidated a San Francisco ordinance prohibiting the maintenance of wooden laundries because almost all of the wooden laundries were owned by Chinese. The ordinance did not mention the Chinese by name, but, anticipating a theory of equal protection that awaited the Warren Court era for its full vindication, the Court in *Yick Wo* concluded that the ordinance was, either in effect or intent, a discrimination against the Chinese. In reaching this conclusion, the Court posited a more universalistic conception of the constitutional community. The Chinese were *not* outsiders; as Justice Matthews had put it, "the Fourteenth Amendment . . . is not confined to the protection of citizens" but applies "to all persons within the territorial jurisdiction."[52] Naturally enough, Matthews's decision was used by the lawyers for the Chinese in *Fong Yue Ting* to offset the *Chinese Exclusion Case* and was central to all three dissents filed in *Fong Yue Ting*, including Field's.

The *Fong Yue Ting* majority remained unmoved; they left *Yick Wo* on the books but denied it any operative effect.[53] "The question there," Justice Gray wrote of *Yick Wo*, "was of the power of a State over aliens continuing to reside within its jurisdiction, not the power of the United States to put an end to their residence in the country."[54] Justice Gray was entirely correct in pointing to a difference between the Geary Act and the San Francisco ordinance, but the relevance of the difference was far from clear. Although the sphere of state intervention differed, in each case the claim was that in its interactions with lawfully resident Chinese, the state should be held to the same standard of conduct that applied to its treatment of other groups or persons. The registration system of the Geary Act would have been intolerable if applied to any other group; it effected as crude a form of unequal treatment as the laundry ordinance in *Yick Wo*—even cruder, since Chinese were singled out on the face of the law. True, no formal guarantee of equality appears in the Bill of Rights, but as we have seen

---

[52] Ibid., 369.

[53] Even outside the immigration context, the Fuller Court showed little sympathy to the broad principle of *Yick Wo* and refused to apply it in an analogous case. That occurred in 1905 in Ah Sin v. Wittman, 198 U.S. 500, in which *Yick Wo* was used to challenge a San Francisco ordinance that made it illegal to maintain a gambling table inside a "barred or barricaded house or room." The Court suggested several distinctions from *Yick Wo*: (1) a laundry regulation, as opposed to a gambling regulation, was more suspect; (2) although only Chinese had been prosecuted for violating the gambling ordinance, there was no showing that others violated the law, and thus there was a failure of proof; and (3) there was no reason to believe that the intent or natural tendency of the law was to disadvantage the Chinese. Only Peckham dissented and he did so without an opinion. In this period *Yick Wo* was primarily used in cases involving racial discrimination against blacks, like Williams v. Mississippi, 170 U.S. 213 (1898), but once again, in the end it was distinguished and deprived of much of its promise. See Chapter 12, note 76.

[54] 149 U.S. at 725.

time and time again, especially in the contemporaneous decision in *Reagan v. Farmers' Loan & Trust Co.* (holding unconstitutional a confiscatory regulation of rates as denying equality before the law),[55] Fuller and the members of his Court were wholly at ease with the methods of *Bolling v. Sharpe*.[56] They did not parse clauses but instead acted on the basis of transcendent principle and, for them, equality before the law was such a principle.

Mindful of the prerogatives of a coequal branch, the Supreme Court has now and then exhibited a greater deference to congressional statutes than to municipal ordinances.[57] This attitude might explain the distinction Gray drew in *Fong Yue Ting*, especially given the marked hostility to the Chinese in San Francisco; there was more reason to be suspicious of a San Francisco ordinance than a congressional statute. It seems to me, however, that in distinguishing *Yick Wo*, Justice Gray was not making a point about the different levels of governments, but rather about the subject matter of the two laws. The Geary Act dealt with the Chinese as immigrants, and the Court apparently was prepared to judge the statute on its own premises: Although the registration system applied to those Chinese who were lawfully present in the United States, they retained their status as aliens, as outsiders, and with respect to them—as with women,[58] or arguably the residents of Puerto Rico and the Philippines[59]—the power of the state was complete. By contrast, the ordinance in *Yick Wo* pertained to all laundries; it neither addressed immigration nor sought to regulate the status of the Chinese as immigrants, and as a result the Court seemed prepared to judge the law on the basis of generalized notions of equality. In passing on the San Francisco ordinance, the Chinese were viewed *not* as immigrants, not as "strangers in the land," but more like the bakers of New York.

In 1896, in a case called *Wong Wing v. United States*,[60] this distinction between laws treating the Chinese as members of the community and laws treating them as outsiders received a more explicit recognition. At issue was the provision of the Geary Act that authorized imprisonment at hard labor prior to deportation for those who had not entered the country lawfully. In this instance the expansive notion of community in *Yick Wo* prevailed. The Court was willing to concede that the government had a virtually unlimited power to deport, with no procedural guarantees, those who entered unlawfully, but saw imprisonment at hard labor as a distinct and

---

[55] 154 U.S. 362, 420 (1894). See Chapters 4 and 7.

[56] 347 U.S. 497 (1954), holding the federal government to the equal protection guarantee of the Fourteenth Amendment, as construed in Brown v. Board of Education, 347 U.S. 483 (1954).

[57] Compare Fullilove v. Klutznick, 448 U.S. 448 (1980), with City of Richmond v. J. A. Croson Co., 488 U.S. 469 (1989).

[58] Muller v. Oregon, 208 U.S. 412 (1908). See Chapter 6.

[59] Downes v. Bidwell, 182 U.S. 244 (1901). See above, note 16 and Chapter 8.

[60] 163 U.S. 228 (1896).

separate feature of the regulatory regime, only incidental or indirectly related to the status of the Chinese as immigrants. Because this provision of the Geary Act treated the Chinese more as subjects than as immigrants, the exercises of government power authorized by that provision needed the same procedural protections that were required of exercises of the criminal power; the provision was invalidated, almost surgically, because those protections were lacking. In addition to the majority opinion, there was an incoherent opinion filed by Field (the difficulties of age really began to show). It was labeled as a partial dissent and partial concurrence, and in it Field somehow managed both to express annoyance at the government's argument for an unlimited power and warmly to embrace the principles of *Fong Yue Ting*.[61]

II

David Brewer, as noted, was a nephew of Field born of missionary parents in Asia Minor. He was not on the Court at the time of the *Chinese Exclusion Case*. He joined the Court two years later, in 1891, and almost immediately began to reveal a deep hostility to the exclusionary premises informing that decision. He expressed these views in his first year on the bench in a case (*Quock Ting v. United States*[62]) that presented the question finally resolved by the Court eight years later in *Wong Kim Ark*: Were persons of Chinese ancestry covered by the Fourteenth Amendment provision extending United States citizenship to all those born within its jurisdiction? A majority of the Court in *Quock Ting*, apparently determined to avoid a decision on the broader question as to the reach of the Fourteenth Amendment, discredited the evidence supporting the petitioner's claim of native birth. Brewer refused to become a part of this strategy of avoidance and dissented. He claimed that the majority was operating on the wholly objectionable assumption that a person of Chinese ancestry testifying as to his place of birth was not to be believed. Justice Brewer also dissented in *Nishimura Ekiu*, the 1892 decision that allowed the executive determination of immigrant status to be final. Naturally, Brewer dissented in *Fong Yue Ting* itself, and once again in *Lem Moon Sing*,[63] a decision that upheld the Chandler Act, an 1894 measure broadening the range of cases over which the executive determination would be final.[64]

In all these cases, Brewer was at work building a dissenting tradition that drew on the universalism of *Yick Wo*. The effect of his labors soon was felt on the Court; despite his lack of seniority, Brewer's dissent in *Fong Yue*

---

[61] Ibid., 238–44.
[62] 140 U.S. 417, 422 (1891) (Brewer, J., dissenting).

[63] Lem Moon Sing v. United States, 158 U.S. 538 (1895).
[64] Ch. 301, 28 Stat. 372, 390 (1894).

Ting was printed before the other two dissents in the *United States Reports*, and there are references to it in the other dissents, written by Fuller and Field. Fuller had never shown much sympathy for the constitutional claims of these so-called permanent immigrants.[65] Field's record was more contradictory. He was from California, yet not part of the consensus there that made the life of the Chinese miserable. A number of his circuit court decisions, one anticipating *Wong Kim Ark*,[66] were protective of the rights of the Chinese, but the racist character of Field's opinion in the *Chinese Exclusion Case* was unmistakable, and one does not know quite what to make of the opinion he wrote for the Court in *Quock Ting*. In any event, Brewer's dissent in *Fong Yue Ting* had a passion and a clarity of vision totally lacking in Fuller's or Field's. Brewer invoked *Yick Wo* and then closed his opinion in *Fong Yue Ting* with a truly memorable characterization of the Geary Act: "In view of this enactment of the highest legislative body of the foremost Christian nation, may not the thoughtful Chinese disciple of Confucius fairly ask, Why do they send missionaries here?"[67]

Aside from its rhetorical sweep, Brewer's dissent in *Fong Yue Ting* was distinguished by its understanding of the awkward position the Chinese occupied in the constitutional community. Brewer tried to make sense of their anomalous status by introducing a common law concept—the denizen. A denizen stands between alien and citizen, but nonetheless is able to make legal claims against the government. Quoting from an old English case, Brewer said: "A denizen is in a kind of middle state, between an alien and a natural-born subject, and partakes of both of them."[68] This concept

---

[65] One exception is Fuller's opinion in Lau Ow Bew v. United States, 144 U.S. 47 (1892), in which he allowed reentry to a merchant temporarily absent from the country. But Fuller did join Field's opinions in the *Chinese Exclusion Case* and *Quock Ting*; he joined Gray's opinion in *Nashimura Ekiu*; and he joined Field's opinion in Wan Shing v. United States, 140 U.S. 424 (1891), decided the same year as *Lau Ow Bew*. That decision denied reentry to a merchant without a permit.

[66] *In re* Look Tin Sing, 21 F. 905 (1884). In this case, Field held that children born in the United States of Chinese parents were American citizens. He also made it clear that the 1882 and 1884 Acts did not apply to citizens of the United States: "[N]o citizen can be excluded from this country except in punishment for crime. Exclusion for any other cause is unknown to our laws, and beyond the power of congress."

(Ibid., at 907). Field's unpopularity in California, due in large part to his role on the circuit court, refusing to accept many of the legislative measures hostile to the Chinese, dashed his hopes of obtaining the Democratic nomination for president in 1880 and 1884. See Howard Jay Graham, "Justice Field and the Fourteenth Amendment," *Yale L.J.*, 52: 851, 881–88 (1943), and Carl B. Swisher, *Stephen J. Field: Craftsman of the Law* (Washington, D.C.: Brookings Institution, 1930; repr. Hamden, Conn.: Archon Books, 1963), 282–320.

[67] 149 U.S. at 744 (Brewer, J., dissenting). But see Westin, "Stephen J. Field," 380–83, for an account of Field's campaign to get the decision in *Fong Yue Ting* reversed. This included urging Congress to pass a bill for a rehearing of the case and a court-packing plan. See Chapter 2, note 29.

[68] 149 U.S. at 736 (Brewer, J., dissenting).

provided the intellectual foundation for the next stage in the evolution of the Court's doctrine.

While the majority in *Fong Yue Ting* refused Brewer's offer of a middle status and affirmed the Geary Act as a whole, in 1898 the Court announced a decision that altered the status of the Chinese and moved in the direction Brewer urged. That decision was, of course, *Wong Kim Ark*, which extended the legacy of the Civil War by severing the remaining tie between citizenship and race. The Court finally declared that some members of the Chinese community, those born in the United States, were American citizens by virtue of the Fourteenth Amendment.

The precise number of Chinese who could in 1898 claim citizenship by virtue of birth was indeterminate. Since most Chinese who came to the United States as laborers were males who had left their wives and families in China, the number was probably small. But the impact of *Wong Kim Ark* was not limited to those who were born here. The decision changed the status of all Chinese residents—in effect, making them denizens—by creating the *possibility* that some were citizens. After *Wong Kim Ark*, the Court no longer could assume that a person of Chinese ancestry standing before it was not in fact a citizen. Virtually anyone under forty could claim citizenship on the basis of native birth. The assertion of native birth might be false; but it might be true, and if true the claimant was a citizen. That possibility of citizenship, created by *Wong Kim Ark*, altered the status of the Chinese in the constitutional community and circumscribed the power of government over them.

By recognizing that Chinese people could be citizens, *Wong Kim Ark* implicitly drew into question the principles of the *Chinese Exclusion Case* and many decisions, *Fong Yue Ting* included, that were decided under its framework. It is not clear, however, whether the unsettling implications of *Wong Kim Ark* were fully understood at the moment of decision. The alignment of the justices seemed to belie such an understanding. Gray, the author of the majority opinion in *Fong Yue Ting*, wrote the majority opinion in *Wong Kim Ark*. He was joined by three justices—Brown, Shiras, and White—who had voted with him in *Fong Yue Ting*. Another surprising switch was Fuller. He dissented in *Fong Yue Ting* and yet also dissented in *Wong Kim Ark*, complaining that the majority decision would unsettle precedents that denied to all Chinese various constitutional protections, including due process.[69] Brewer, however, held fast to the position articulated in his dissent in *Fong Yue Ting* and joined Justice Gray's opinion in *Wong Kim Ark*. So did Rufus Peckham, who was not yet on the Court for *Fong Yue Ting*, but once appointed became Brewer's constant ally in the Chinese cases. Justice Field was no longer on the Court at the time of *Wong*

---

[69] 169 U.S. at 706 (Fuller, C.J., dissenting).

Kim Ark, and his replacement, McKenna, also from California, did not participate in the decision.

Justice Harlan dissented in *Wong Kim Ark*, and that was thoroughly consistent with all he had done in this line of cases (though perhaps not with his historical image based on his dissent in *Plessy v. Ferguson*). He joined the Court in the *Chinese Exclusion Case* and *Fong Yue Ting*, and wrote for the Court in two cases that showed a complete disregard for the procedural rights of Asian immigrants. In one, *Lem Moon Sing*, he sustained the finality provisions of the Chandler Act and held that the executive decision to deny admission could not be reexamined in a habeas corpus proceeding. In another, the *Japanese Immigrant Case*,[70] he brushed aside due process objections to an administrative proceeding to exclude or expel a Japanese woman who had been in the United States for two weeks. His opinion contained a notable passage celebrating due process values,[71] but that passage was out of keeping with the general tenor of his opinion.[72] It was also inconsistent with his affirmation of prior decisions such as *Fong Yue Ting*, his comment that the alien's inability to understand the proceedings, conducted wholly in English, was her "misfortune,"[73] and, finally, the outcome—the expulsion was upheld.

---

[70] Yamataya v. Fisher (The Japanese Immigrant Case), 189 U.S. 86 (1903).

[71] The passage reads:
But this court has never held, nor must we now be understood as holding, that administrative officers, when executing the provisions of a statute involving the liberty of persons, may disregard the fundamental principles that inhere in "due process of law" as understood at the time of the adoption of the Constitution. One of these principles is that no person shall be deprived of his liberty without opportunity, at some time, to be heard, before such officers, in respect of the matters upon which that liberty depends,—not necessarily an opportunity upon a regular, set occasion, and according to the forms of judicial procedure, but one that will secure the prompt, vigorous action contemplated by Congress, and at the same time be appropriate to the nature of the case upon which such officers are required to act. Therefore, it is not competent for the Secretary of the Treasury or any executive officer, at any time within the year limited by the statute, arbitrarily to cause an alien, who has entered the country, and has become subject in all respects to its jurisdiction, and a part of its population, although alleged to be illegally here, to be taken into custody and deported without giving him all opportunity to be heard upon the questions involving his right to be and remain in the United States. No such arbitrary power can exist where the principles involved in due process of law are recognized.
189 U.S. at 100–101.

[72] The passage in question comes as a disclaimer directly following Harlan's citations from the three most troubling precedents, *Fong Yue Ting*, *Nishimura Ekiu*, and *Lem Moon Sing*. That is why the passage begins, "But this court has never held, nor must we now be understood as holding. . . ." In fact, Harlan's peroration is part of an exceptionally long paragraph that has a lead sentence pointing in the opposite direction: to justify rather than criticize the disregard for claims of procedural justice.

[73] Here is how Harlan put it:
It is true that [the appellant] pleads a

Chapter X: *The Chinese Cases*

Although *Wong Kim Ark* created unsettling implications for decisions such as *Fong Yue Ting* and the *Chinese Exclusion Case*, the narrow legal issue posed in the case seems, at least in retrospect, relatively easy. The Fourteenth Amendment confers citizenship on persons born in the United States of parents "subject to its jurisdiction." It was conceded by both sides that the children born in the United States of foreign diplomatic personnel, for example, were not citizens by virtue of the Fourteenth Amendment. The question was whether the Chinese were to be treated the same way since, on a reading that emphasized their status as perpetual outsiders, they too were only "visitors." As the dissenters insisted, to be subject to the jurisdiction of the United States means "completely subject," which in turn means "to be in no respect or degree subject to the political jurisdiction of any other government."[74] But recognition was taken of the permanence of their presence and the fact that they were, in any practical sense, subject to the jurisdiction of the United States. Justice Gray, finally grasping the full import of *Yick Wo*, put the point in legal terms: If the Chinese were within the jurisdiction of the United States for equal protection purposes, so must they be for citizenship purposes.

III

Once some members of the Chinese community had, by 1898, become part of the constitutional community, they were able, as were the New York bakers, to invoke the protection of liberty and the tradition committed to limited government. They were part of the contract. Of course, it was still open to the Court to dismiss the claims of the Chinese by repudiating this tradition, at least as far as the Chinese were concerned, or by incorporating a racial distinction into the law; but, contrary to the standard account,[75] I do not believe the Court did either of these. Rather, it struggled against the legacy of the *Chinese Exclusion Case*, modified *Fong Yue Ting*, and

---

want of knowledge of our language; that she did not understand the nature and import of the questions propounded to her; . . . and that she did not, at the time, know that the investigation had reference to her being deported from the country. . . . If the appellant's want of knowledge of the English language put her at some disadvantage . . . that was her misfortune, and constitutes no reason . . . for the intervention of the court by *habeas corpus.*
189 U.S. at 101–102.
[74] 169 U.S. at 725.
[75] See, e.g., William Preston, Jr., *Aliens and Dissenters: Federal Suppression of Radicals, 1903–1933* (New York: Harper & Row, 1966), 11–12.

began in the early 1900s to bring its doctrine in this area more nearly into accord with *Lochner*.

The most important, or perhaps notorious, decisions of this period are *Sing Tuck* (1904)[76] and *Ju Toy* (1905).[77] Each involved a person of Chinese ancestry who, after a short trip to China following extended residence in the United States, had sought reentry. The petitioners in these cases resembled in many respects the claimant in the *Chinese Exclusion Case*, though they were now armed with a wholly new claim: that they were born in the United States and thus, under the terms of *Wong Kim Ark*, were American citizens. The power to exclude remained unquestioned, but, thanks to *Wong Kim Ark*, the procedural questions addressed by the Court in the early 1890s had to be reformulated. Now it was a question of deciding what procedures were acceptable for judging claims of citizenship.

In terms of result alone, *Sing Tuck* was dismal, for the Court imposed an exhaustion requirement on claims of citizenship. The person stopped at the border had to present his claim of citizenship to the secretary of commerce and labor[78] before it was passed on by a court. *Ju Toy* then spoke to the next phase of this process. It held that after exhausting the administrative procedures, the person seeking entry was not entitled to a fresh determination of the merits of the claim by a court. He was entitled only to a review of the secretary's decision, to determine whether the secretary had abused his authority. As might be expected, Brewer dissented in both cases, joined by Peckham and Day.[79] There remained, however, aspects of the majority opinions in *Sing Tuck* and *Ju Toy* that seemed more in line with the dissenting tradition. While neither case offered reasons to rejoice, there was some evidence in both decisions, as well as in the cases that followed, that could be read as an effort by the Court to distance itself from *Fong Yue Ting* and the legacy of the *Chinese Exclusion Case*.

To appreciate why, some account must be taken of a citizenship case that followed *Wong Kim Ark* but immediately preceded *Sing Tuck* and *Ju Toy*. That case, *Chin Bak Kan v. United States*,[80] was pending when Congress renewed the Geary Act and was decided shortly after the renewal. At issue was the authority of commissioners, magistrates lacking Article III

---

[76] United States v. Sing Tuck, 194 U.S. 161 (1904).

[77] United States v. Ju Toy, 198 U.S. 253 (1905).

[78] The responsibility had recently been shifted from the Treasury Department to the new Department of Commerce and Labor, signaling a new perception that immigration was a labor problem. Act of Feb. 14, 1903, Ch. 552, 32 Stat. 825.

[79] Day had replaced Shiras, the author of *Wong Wing*, which was the decision invalidating the provision of the Geary Act authorizing imprisonment.

[80] Chin Bak Kan v. United States, 186 U.S. 193 (1902). It was followed in Chin Ying v. United States, 186 U.S. 202 (1902), which contained the notation that Justices Brewer and Peckham dissented.

status or protections, to determine the merits of the citizenship claim. The Court, in an opinion by the chief justice, sustained their authority, emphasizing that there was a right of appeal from the commissioner to a district court (the appeal had to be received within ten days!). As it turned out, the statutory provision authorizing the appeal was enacted as part of a comprehensive statute intended to implement a treaty that was never ratified, but that omission made no difference to Fuller; he wrote, "[T]his section is in and of itself independent legislation."[81] On a purely technical level, the decision did not reaffirm the *Chinese Exclusion Case*, but the tone of Fuller's opinion was unmistakable: It suggested that the procedural regime legitimated by the underlying principle of the *Chinese Exclusion Case*—a sovereignty without limitations—would be acceptable even for citizenship claims. A number of other decisions (still antedating *Sing Tuck* and *Ju Toy*) confirm this impression. One concluded that the finality provision of the Chandler Act of 1894 did not bar a challenge by the government to an administrative decision to admit a person.[82] Two others gave finality to executive determinations that persons of Chinese descent were abusing the so-called transit privilege, which allowed entry to the United States en route to another country.[83]

Justice Gray was the principal spokesman for the Court in the Chinese cases of the 1890s, and it was perhaps natural for Holmes, his successor, to be assigned the task of speaking for the Court in *Sing Tuck* and *Ju Toy*. Holmes had not participated in any of the earlier Supreme Court decisions concerning this matter, and there is language in his opinion in the first of his Chinese cases, *Sing Tuck*, suggesting an ambivalence toward the earlier precedents: "As to whether or not the act could make the decision of an executive officer final upon the fact of citizenship we leave the question where we find it."[84]

To grasp fully what Holmes might have meant by this sentence, it is important to note that he did not cite *Fong Yue Ting*. That case technically did not involve the finality issue, but it built on the absolutism of the *Chinese Exclusion Case* and so thoroughly undermined any claims of due process as to make it virtually impossible to object to a practice that afforded finality to executive determinations on immigration matters. Holmes did, in fact, cite two cases that spoke directly to the finality issue, but neither involved claims of citizenship. One was *Fok Yung Yo*, which involved the "transit privilege";[85] the other was the *Japanese Immigrant Case*, which made final an executive determination to exclude a Japanese woman (not-

---

[81] 186 U.S. at 201.
[82] Li Sing v. United States, 180 U.S. 486 (1901).
[83] Fok Yung Yo v. United States, 185 U.S. 296 (1902); Lee Gon Yung 185 U.S. 306 (1902).
[84] 194 U.S. at 167.
[85] Ibid.

withstanding certain objectionable features of the administrative process). The one case cited by Holmes that did involve a citizenship claim was the 1902 opinion of Fuller in *Chin Bak Kan*, and that got only a secondary reference. It was preceded by the signal "See. . . ."

Holmes's effort to distance himself from these precedents, all of which easily could have been marshaled in support of his position in *Sing Tuck*, casts that decision in a somewhat more favorable light. So does the manner in which Holmes interpreted the rules or regulations (generally referred to as the Chinese regulations) governing administrative officers when they considered claims of citizenship. One regulation seemed to give the examining officer the power to decide which witnesses would be called; Holmes read it differently: "No right is given to the officer to exercise any control or choice as to witnesses to be heard. . . ."[86] According to Holmes, this particular regulation conferred upon the administrator only the power any trial judge would have, for example to limit duplicative testimony. Another of the so-called Chinese regulations appeared to deny counsel any real opportunity to participate in the administrative process; again, Holmes read the rule differently: "In case of appeal counsel are permitted to examine the evidence . . . and *it is implied* that new evidence, briefs, affidavits and statements may be submitted, all of which can be forwarded with the appeal."[87]

Finally, the harshness of the result in *Sing Tuck* seemed to be mitigated by the fact that Holmes provided an alternative ground of decision. A *mere allegation* of citizenship, Holmes wrote, would not entitle the Chinese to a judicial determination (in a habeas court); this seemed to imply that a more substantiated claim might entitle the claimant to such a hearing, at least after the administrative remedies had been exhausted.[88] In thus establishing a prima facie requirement, Holmes may have been searching for a way to free himself from the dismal body of decisions that he had inherited.

Little of the promise I see in *Sing Tuck* was realized in *Ju Toy*. In that case, the Court held that executive determinations of claims of citizenship would be afforded finality, subject to review only for abuse of authority. Once again, Holmes seemed uncomfortable with the result, and thus I am reluctant to take the decision on face value, and even more reluctant to read it back into *Sing Tuck*. Holmes's unease was manifest in the very composition of his opinion: halting and jerky, unrepresentative of his style in every conceivable way. However, in *Chin Yow*, a case that quickly followed *Ju Toy*, it is clear that a break occurred.[89]

---

[86] 194 U.S. at 170.
[87] Ibid. (emphasis added).
[88] Ibid.

[89] Chin Yow v. United States, 208 U.S. 8 (1908).

Chapter X: *The Chinese Cases*

Chin Yow gave Holmes still another opportunity to address procedural issues surrounding the claim of citizenship, and he used it to make clear that he was not denying the person claiming citizenship the kind of procedural protections we usually associate with judicial process, but only transferring those protections to administrative officers. He ruled that decisions of administrative officials would be deemed final only if they acted in approximate accord with the norms that governed judicial proceedings. Procedural fairness thus became a condition of administrative finality. Holmes was quick to add that "the denial of a [proper] hearing cannot be established by proving that the decision was wrong"[90]—a chilling thought once it is understood that as a practical matter this meant that a citizen (mistakenly held to be a noncitizen) could be expelled—but in other respects Holmes's opinion in *Chin Yow* brought to fruition the promise of revision implicit in *Sing Tuck*.

In *Sing Tuck* Holmes went out of his way to revise, by construction, two of the more offensive Chinese regulations. The one that gave the examining officer control over the witnesses reappeared in *Chin Yow*. Holmes had construed that regulation in *Sing Tuck* as conferring a power analogous to the power exercised by trial judges, but the examining officer in *Chin Yow* did not heed Holmes's cue and excluded a crucial witness. The witness was to testify that the person of Chinese ancestry claiming American citizenship was in fact born in the United States. Holmes never made it entirely clear whether his judgment was predicated on due process or on statutory grounds, but he was unmistakable in his conclusion that the interference by the hearing officer with the choice of witnesses was a sufficient basis for depriving the administrative determination of finality: "The decision of the Department is final, but that is on the presupposition that the decision was after a hearing in good faith, however summary in form."[91]

Having decided that the particular administrative process used in *Chin Yow* was flawed, and therefore could not be considered final, a question still remained as to the remedy. *Ju Toy*'s abuse-of-authority standard expressed a deference to the administrative officer, suggesting that the proper remedy in *Chin Yow* would have been a remand to the administrative officer. Such an arrangement would have given the officer a chance to make the determination.[92] Holmes chose instead to have the citizenship claim tried anew in the federal court, a decision that was inconsistent with *Fong Yue Ting* and all that it implied. "The courts must deal with the matter somehow," Holmes wrote, "and there seems to be no way so convenient

---

[90] Ibid., 13.
[91] Ibid., 12.
[92] As a practical matter, the remand could have been implemented through a conditional issuance of the writ of habeas corpus, directing that the writ be issued unless the administrative official reheard the case.

as a trial of the merits before the judge."[93] At the very end of the opinion, Holmes added a cautionary note, emphasizing that a judicial determination of citizenship would become available only if and when the administrative procedures were inadequate and that a mistaken decision did not necessarily amount to a denial of due process. But these qualifications did not obscure the revisionary elements of *Chin Yow*, highlighted by the fact that the three justices who dissented in *Ju Toy*—Brewer, Peckham, and Day—were able to concur in the Court's decision.

Several months later, in *Liu Hop Fong*,[94] Justice Day took the process of revision initiated by Holmes in *Sing Tuck*, and developed in *Chin Yow*, one step further. While *Chin Yow* confined the finality rule of *Ju Toy* to situations where the administrative procedures were fully adequate, *Liu Hop Fong* confined *Ju Toy* to entry cases and held that there would be no finality to administrative orders concerning deportation. The claimant in *Liu Hop Fong* had entered in 1899 under a student's certificate. He was arrested in 1904 in Nebraska on the ground that he was in fact a laborer, both at the time of his arrest and at the time of entry. He was taken to a commissioner, who ordered his deportation, and this ruling was affirmed by the district court on the basis of the transcript of the hearing before the commissioner. The Supreme Court reversed, directing that the Chinese claimant be released, though "without prejudice to further proceedings."[95]

In reaching this result, the Court held that the student certificate legally entitled the bearer to remain unless there was some competent evidence to overcome or contradict it. In this regard alone, the Court accorded the certificate more weight than it was due under earlier decisions.[96] In flat contradiction of Fuller's earlier decision in *Chin Bak Lin*, the Court also held that the Chinese claimant was entitled to a de novo hearing before the district court. Justice Day, the author of the Court's opinion in *Liu Hop Fong*, reached this result as a matter of statutory interpretation, but he made the general moral or constitutional considerations explicit. Deporting someone without an opportunity for a hearing before a court was, he insisted, "a serious thing."[97] He was not inclined to construe the applicable statute in a way that facilitated deportation or in any way lessened the procedures surrounding such a decision. The applicable statute provided for an appeal from the commissioner to a judge, but did not say that the appeal must be decided on the basis of the transcript before the commissioner, and Justice Day refused to so hold. His view was that access to the courts must be full and complete. Other immigration statutes might not be amenable

---

[93] 208 U.S. at 13.
[94] Liu Hop Fong v. United States, 209 U.S. 453 (1908).
[95] Ibid., 463.

[96] E.g., Li Sing v. United States, 180 U.S. 486 (1901), discussed above in text accompanying note 82.
[97] 209 U.S. at 461.

to Day's sympathetic construction, but even so, *Lin Hop Fong* established a perspective on these matters that seemed inconsistent with *Fong Yue Ting*. The technical issue was the validity of a student certificate, not citizenship, yet the claimant was accorded all the procedures required to assess a claim of citizenship. Brewer, who dissented in *Sing Tuck* and concurred separately in Holmes's opinion in *Chin Yow*, fully joined Day in *Lin Hop Fong*.

The full realization of procedural justice need not be accomplished by a softening of the substantive regime. Indeed, as exemplified by the work of Felix Frankfurter and others who see themselves as part of this same progressive tradition, procedural reform sometimes is undertaken as a way of avoiding the challenge and agony entailed in judging substantive policy. Procedure seems less intrusive because it rests on the values that tend to unify, rather than divide, the legal profession. It is therefore not surprising that at the very moment Holmes in *Sing Tuck* was devising his strategies for enhancing the procedural protections of the Chinese, he rejected an attack upon the substance of the legal regime.

When the Geary Act was renewed in 1902, a provision was added that disclaimed any intent to violate any outstanding treaties. This provision soon became the focal point of a new challenge to the Geary Act, mounted at roughly the same time as *Sing Tuck*. Counsel for the Chinese, Max Kohler, claimed that the registration scheme of the Geary Act and the summary procedures used in its enforcement were inconsistent with a treaty the United States had entered into in 1894—that is, after *Fong Yue Ting*—which contained a most favored nation clause guaranteeing to the Chinese treatment that was equal to the treatment afforded citizens of other nations.[98]

Speaking for the Court in *Ah How v. United States*,[99] Holmes rejected Kohler's argument almost out of hand, treating as boilerplate the disclaimer in the 1902 Act saying that it was not Congress's intent to violate any outstanding treaties. Holmes refused to read that disclaimer as expressing an intent to repeal, abrogate, or in any way modify the registration scheme of the Geary Act. The 1894 treaty had referred specifically to the Geary Act, and China had declared that it would not object to the enforcement of the Act. Once again Brewer dissented, but in contrast to cases involving purely procedural issues, like *Sing Tuck* and *Ju Toy*, where Brewer filed lengthy and urgent dissents, in *Ah How* he, along with Peckham

---

[98] Convention on Emigration, Mar. 17, 1894, U.S.–China, 28 Stat. 1210.

[99] Ah How v. United States, 193 U.S. 65 (1904). In United States v. Lee Yen Tai, 185 U.S. 213 (1902), the Court, in an opinion by Harlan, upheld enforcement of the Geary Act's deportation provision over an objection that it was abrogated by the 1894 treaty.

(but not Day), dissented without an opinion. Even Brewer hesitated to articulate just what was wrong with the substance of the nation's policy toward Chinese immigration.

Over time the Court came to heed Brewer's insistence that American residents of Chinese descent had at least the denizen's claim to the procedural protection of the Constitution, but the substance of the nation's exclusionary policy remained unchanged. That policy drew on xenophobic theories and sentiments whose impact would soon be felt by those initially spared because of their race—white Europeans.[100]

---

[100] See Kraut, *Huddled Masses*, 148–78.

CHAPTER XI

The Early Free Speech Cases

Public discourse in the 1890s and early 1900s was rich and varied. Radicals protested the established order in public meetings and rallies. The newspaper industry, then dominated by such forceful personalities as Joseph Pulitzer and William Randolph Hearst, aggressively searched for scandal and abuse of power, exposing itself to the charge of "yellow journalism."[1] Muckraking magazines such as *McClure's*, *Collier's*, and *Cosmopolitan* flourished, regularly carrying exposes like Ida Tarbell's "History of the Standard Oil Company" and Lincoln Steffens's "Shame of the Cities," both published in 1902.[2] But the judiciary did nothing to encourage these activities nor to protect those who dared participate in them. The Fuller Court was deeply committed to liberty of contract but had no taste whatsoever for freedom of speech or for any of the political liberties we usually associate with that idea.

In a number of cases, the free speech issue was simply ignored.[3] The *Debs* case is perhaps the paramount example.[4] To quell the Pullman Strike

---

[1] On the advent of yellow journalism specifically, see Louis Filler, *The Muckrakers* (University Park: Pennsylvania State University Press, 1976), 29–30. *The Muckrakers* is a new and enlarged edition of Filler's 1939 study, *Crusaders for American Liberalism* (New York: Harcourt, Brace, 1939). See also Edwin Emery and Michael Emery, *The Press and America: An Interpretive History of the Mass Media*, 4th ed. (Englewood Cliffs, N.J.: Prentice-Hall, 1978), 243–55. For a more general overview of the press industry during this time, see Allan Nevins, *American Press Opinion, Washington to Coolidge* (Boston: D. C. Heath, 1928); John Tebbel, *The Compact History of the American Newspaper* (New York: Hawthorn Books, 1969); and Willard G. Bleyer, *Main Currents in the History of American Journalism* (Boston: Houghton Mifflin, 1927; repr. New York: Da Capo Press, 1973).

[2] For the origins and history of muckraking, see Filler, *Muckrakers*; Arthur and Lila Weinberg, eds., *The Muckrakers: The Era in Journalism That Moved America to Reform—The Most Significant Magazine Articles of 1902–1912* (New York: G. P. Putnam's Sons, 1964), xiii–xxiv; and Emery, *Press and America*, 270–74.

[3] In the words of one commentator, in this period "the Court did not address free speech at all. The Court repeatedly denied that cases implicated freedom of expression, and often made no reference to the First Amendment." David M. Rabban, "The First Amendment in Its Forgotten Years," *Yale L.J.*, 90: 514, 542 (1981).

[4] *In re* Debs, 158 U.S. 564 (1885). See Chapter 3.

323

and restore order, the federal court in Chicago prohibited Eugene Debs from issuing directives to his followers. Although the commission that later inquired into the strike saw this feature of the injunction as an interference with freedom of speech,[5] counsel for Debs did not raise the issue and the Court did not address it. The provision of the injunction that silenced Debs does not even appear in the official Supreme Court report of the case.[6] The disregard of the speech issue by the entire Court might not be surprising, since, at least on my reading, the Pullman Strike threatened a breakdown of public order—it was hardly the occasion for reflections on freedom of speech. But in cases lacking any such "special exigency,"[7] to borrow Brewer's phrase, the Court displayed the same attitude of indifference toward freedom of speech.

In 1897, for example, in *Davis v. Massachusetts*,[8] the Court upheld a Boston city ordinance prohibiting public addresses "in or upon any of the public grounds . . . except in accordance with a permit from the mayor,"[9] and did so without explicitly considering the obvious First Amendment issue. In a short and curt opinion, Justice White analyzed the case exclusively in property terms:

> For the legislature absolutely or conditionally to forbid public speaking in a highway or public park is no more an infringement of the rights of a member of the public than for the owner of a private house to forbid it in his house.[10]

The petitioner in *Davis* was no radical labor organizer threatening to subvert the established order, but a minister trying to use the Boston Commons for a Sunday morning sermon; as a matter of principle, he objected to the permit requirement, insisting that it gave the mayor the power of censor-

---

[5] "It is seriously questioned, and with much force, whether courts have jurisdiction to enjoin citizens from 'persuading' each other in industrial or other matters of common interest." United States Strike Commission, *Report on the Chicago Strike of June–July 1894*, S. Exec. Doc. No. 7, 53d Cong., 3d Sess., 40 (1895).

[6] The missing provision of the injunction reads:

And Eugene V. Debs and all other persons are hereby enjoined and restrained from sending out any letters, messages, or communications directing, inciting, encouraging, or instructing any persons whatsoever to interfere with the business or affairs,

directly or indirectly, of any of the railway companies hereinabove named, or from persuading any of the employees of said railway companies while in the employment of their respective companies to fail or refuse to perform the duties of their employment.

Ibid., 180.

[7] 158 U.S. at 592.

[8] 167 U.S. 43 (1897).

[9] Ibid., 44. In a grouping odd to the contemporary mind, the ordinance covered public addresses, the discharge of firearms and cannons, the sale of goods, and all public amusements and shows.

[10] Ibid., 47.

ship, but his plea fell on deaf ears. Similarly, in the same period the Court upheld a flag desecration statute without any discussion at all of free speech[11]—a dramatic contrast to the treatment given the issue today.[12] Obscenity prosecutions, then on the rise, were also unconstrained.[13] At best, the justices were engaged by questions of criminal procedure[14] and now and then intervened to prevent invasions of privacy[15] or clear distortions of legislative intent.[16]

On other occasions, most notably *Turner v. Williams*[17] and *Patterson v. Colorado,*[18] free speech claims were addressed by the Court at greater length, but the results were equally disappointing. The defeat of liberty was striking and complete. In *Turner,* a radical labor organizer from England was deported; in *Patterson,* a publisher was punished for criticizing a court decision. In the latter case, Justice Harlan filed a strong and eloquent dissent on behalf of the publisher:

> It is, I think, impossible to conceive of liberty, as secured by the Constitution against hostile action, whether by the Nation or by the States, which does not embrace the right to enjoy free speech and the right to have a free press.[19]

---

[11] Halter v. Nebraska, 205 U.S. 34 (1907).

[12] Texas v. Johnson, 491 U.S. 397 (1989); United States v. Eichman, 496 U.S. 310 (1990).

[13] Grimm v. United States, 156 U.S. 604 (1895); Rosen v. United States, 161 U.S. 29 (1896); Andrews v. United States, 162 U.S. 420 (1896); Dunlop v. United States, 165 U.S. 486 (1897). These prosecutions were brought under the Comstock Act, Ch. 258, Sect. 2, 17 Stat. 598 (1873), presently codified at 18 U.S.C. Sect. 1461 (1988). That Act, passed in 1873, was designed to restrict circulation of any material considered obscene, as well as information or devices used for contraception or abortion, and barred all such matter from the United States mails. The original Act provided prison sentences of up to ten years and fines of up to $5,000 for senders and recipients of prohibited matter.

[14] In *Rosen,* 161 U.S. at 43, Justice White, joined by Shiras, dissented from a decision that upheld an indictment under the Comstock Act on the ground that the indictment was fatally defective for failing to specify which parts of a publication were alleged to be obscene.

[15] United States v. Chase, 135 U.S. 255 (1890) (construing the original version of the Comstock Act not to reach private letters). In 1888, after the *Chase* prosecution, Congress amended the statute to reach private letters as well as publications, and in the *Andrews* case of 1896 (see above, note 13) the Court gave that amendment full force, upholding a conviction for mailing a personal letter judged obscene without any discussion of the First Amendment.

[16] In Swearingen v. United States, 161 U.S. 446 (1896), the Court held that the Comstock Act could not be used to punish a newspaper publisher for a vituperative attack on a local political figure because the words "obscene, lewd or lascivious," as used in the Act, referred only to "that form of immorality which has relation to sexual impurity." Ibid., at 451.

[17] United States *ex rel.* Turner v. Williams, 194 U.S. 279 (1904).

[18] Patterson v. Colorado, 205 U.S. 454 (1907).

[19] Ibid., 465.

Harlan's record was, however, uneven. He wrote the opinion for the Court in the flag desecration case, decided the very same term, and joined the Court in the deportation case. The record of the rest of the Court, however, did not rise to the level of unevenness; it was uniformly poor.

Aside from an obscure concurrence by Brewer, *Turner* was unanimous, and in *Patterson* Harlan stood virtually alone. Although Brewer also filed a dissent in *Patterson*, he based it on narrow jurisdictional grounds; it lacked the energy of Harlan's and the passion Brewer himself summoned for his dissents in *Budd v. New York*[20] and *Fong Yue Ting*.[21] Even more significantly, Brewer's dissent in *Patterson* failed to gain the support of anyone, not even his natural allies such as Peckham, who, as we well know, had not the slightest reluctance to speak out on behalf of individual liberty when it was conceived in entrepreneurial terms.[22] Why protect one liberty and not the other?

The contrast between the position of the Fuller Court on liberty of contract and liberty of speech is especially puzzling because America did not have to wait for the 1960s for a tradition to emerge in which the judicial power was used affirmatively and aggressively to protect freedom of speech. That tradition has a long and noble history that stretches nearly to the Fuller Court itself.[23] During the 1940s a group of four Roosevelt appointees—Frank Murphy, Wiley Rutledge, Hugo Black, and to a lesser extent William O. Douglas—formed a strong coalition in behalf of free speech. The Court

---

[20] 143 U.S. 517, 548 (1892). See Chapter 7.

[21] Fong Yue Ting v. United States, 149 U.S. 698, 732 (1893). See Chapter 10.

[22] Justice Peckham wrote an opinion for the Court in American School of Magnetic Healing v. McAnnulty, 187 U.S. 94 (1902), denying authority to the postmaster general to stop delivery of payments to a school offering "magnetic healing" treatment. Michael T. Gibson, "The Supreme Court and Freedom of Expression from 1791 to 1917," *Fordham L. Rev.*, 55: 263, 288–99 (1986), regards this decision as a significant First Amendment victory during the *Lochner* period, but in truth, the decision turned on an issue of statutory construction. The relevant statute gave the postmaster general power to prevent fraud but not to intervene because he doubted the efficacy of a treatment. The postmaster general's action was challenged on Fourth and Fifth, not First, Amendment grounds, and the Court made it clear that it was not "deciding . . . or express-ing any opinion upon the various constitutional objections set out in the bill of complainants." 187 U.S. at 111. By contrast, the Court, in an opinion by Fuller (an assignment he hastily took up once Bradley, originally assigned the case, died) upheld the postmaster general's decision to prevent the use of the mails for advertising a lottery. *In re* Rapier, 143 U.S. 110 (1892). In this case, the advertisement was contained in a newspaper, while an earlier decision, *Ex parte* Jackson, 96 U.S. 727 (1877) (Field, J.), allowed the postmaster general to stop advertisements for a lottery in a letter. In *Rapier*, Fuller wrote, "The circulation of newspapers is not prohibited, but the government declines itself to become an agent in the circulation of printed matter which it regards as injurious to the people." 143 U.S. at 134.

[23] See generally Harry Kalven, Jr., *A Worthy Tradition: Freedom of Speech in America*, ed. Jamie Kalven (New York: Harper & Row, 1988).

was also at work building the tradition in the 1930s, when Charles Evans Hughes, then chief justice, used his lawyerly skills to protect speech. Indeed, the origin of the Court's protection of free speech can be traced to Holmes's dissent, joined by Brandeis, in *Abrams v. United States* in 1919.[24]

In that case, a group of left-wing radicals were prosecuted for printing leaflets that condemned the United States for sending troops into Russia following the Bolshevik revolution and called for a general strike. Those leaflets were printed while the nation was at war with Germany, and though Holmes, like the majority, well understood the needs of war and allowed the government every indulgence, he seemed offended by this prosecution. He dissented in especially eloquent and memorable terms:

> Persecution for the expression of opinions seems to me perfectly logical. If you have no doubt of your premises or your power and want a certain result with all your heart you naturally express your wishes in law and sweep away all opposition. To allow opposition by speech seems to indicate that you think the speech impotent, as when a man says that he has squared the circle, or that you do not care whole-heartedly for the result, or that you doubt either your power or your premises. But when men have realized that time has upset many fighting faiths, they may come to believe even more than they believe the very foundations of their own conduct that the ultimate good desired is better reached by free trade in ideas—that the best test of truth is the power of the thought to get itself accepted in the competition of the market, and that truth is the only ground upon which their wishes safely can be carried out. That at any rate is the theory of our Constitution.[25]

Writing more than fifty years later, Harry Kalven, no fan of Holmes, described this passage as having alchemized a "muddled opinion into durable gold."[26]

Almost as soon as Holmes's dissent in *Abrams* was announced, Roscoe Pound, then dean of the Harvard Law School, understood its importance for the law. He immediately wrote to Holmes, congratulating him on it: "It is worthy to stand with your opinion in the *Lochner* case as one of the classics—yes one of the landmarks—of our law."[27] In so linking Holmes's dissents in *Abrams* and *Lochner*, Pound foresaw correctly the future that awaited both opinions. He did not pause long enough, however, to grasp the tension between the two, which mirrors the tension found in the work of figures like Brewer and Peckham. He did not ask why Holmes was able to find the liberty to speak, but not the liberty to contract, in the

---

[24] 250 U.S. 616, 624 (1919).
[25] Ibid., 630.
[26] Kalven, *Worthy Tradition*, 144.

[27] Pound to Holmes, Nov. 26, 1919, Holmes Papers, Harvard Law School Library Manuscript Division.

interstices of the Fourteenth Amendment. Was it that the Fourteenth Amendment enacted the views of John Stuart Mill but not those of Herbert Spencer?

The place of the *Abrams* dissent in the development of the free speech tradition is of special interest because it was part of the same historical era in which Fuller and his brethren systematically rejected or ignored free speech claims. It is of even greater interest because Holmes played a key role in shaping the Fuller Court's First Amendment jurisprudence later repudiated by him so thoroughly in *Abrams*.[28] Holmes joined the Court's opinion in *Turner v. Williams* and, even more importantly, was the spokesman for the Court in *Patterson v. Colorado*. In that case, Holmes gave expression to the narrowest possible conception of the First Amendment, as creating merely a ban on prior restraint as opposed to subsequent punishment. Going beyond that, he voiced some doubt as to whether freedom of speech was a liberty secured from interference by the states. *Turner* and *Patterson* were no flukes. They came at the same time as *Lochner*, when Holmes was at the height of his powers. *Lochner* was decided in 1905, *Turner* in 1904, and *Patterson* in 1907. Moreover, in the 1890s, while still on the Supreme Judicial Court of Massachusetts, Holmes had written the opinion in *Davis*,[29] which was closely followed by his friend-to-be Edward White when that case came up to the Supreme Court on appeal. Holmes gave to a municipal authority the power to forbid all speech in a place so public as the Boston Commons.

We can see in Holmes's stance in *Turner* and *Patterson*, and also in *Davis*, an outlook on free speech fundamentally at odds with *Abrams*. Holmes's position in those cases undercut First Amendment values as

---

[28] The conflict between Holmes's position in *Abrams* and the stance he had taken shortly before in Debs v. United States, 249 U.S. 211 (1919) and in Schenck v. United States, 249 U.S. 47 (1919) has been noted on many occasions. See, e.g., Harry Kalven, Jr., "Professor Ernst Freund and *Debs v. United States*," *U. Chi. L. Rev.*, 40: 235 (1973), and Gerald Gunther, "Learned Hand and the Origins of Modern First Amendment Doctrine: Some Fragments of History," *Stan. L. Rev.*, 27: 719 (1975). In *Debs v. United States*, Holmes wrote an opinion for the Court that sustained the conviction and ten year sentence of Eugene Debs, this time for a speech at a political convention condemning the war and the draft. (Not to be stopped, Debs ran for president the next year on the Socialist ticket while serving his prison term.) In *Schenck v. United States*, Holmes, again writing for the Court, sustained the convictions of persons who had distributed pamphlets urging resistance to the draft.

[29] Commonwealth v. Davis, 162 Mass. 510, 39 N.E. 113 (1895), *aff'd*, 167 U.S. 43 (1897). See above, note 8. In upholding a law banning political activity by policemen, Holmes, sitting on the Supreme Judicial Court of Massachusetts, was responsible for a quip that confounded another branch of First Amendment law. Kalven, *Worthy Tradition*, 301–303. "The petitioner," Holmes said, "may have a constitutional right to talk politics, but he has no constitutional right to be a policeman." McAuliffe v. Mayor of New Bedford, 155 Mass. 216, 220, 29 N.E. 517, 517 (1892).

much as his *Abrams* dissent celebrated them. There is even a more specific point that can be made. At roughly the same time as *Abrams*, he departed from his position in *Patterson* by objecting to the use of the contempt power against a newspaper that had published a cartoon and series of articles criticizing a federal judge.[30] His objection in that case, voiced in another joint dissent with Brandeis, was formally based on a narrow reading of a federal contempt statute so as to require an actual obstruction of justice, but more than likely it was inspired by First Amendment considerations.

The explanation for Holmes's change of outlook on free speech—and perhaps the key to understanding the shift that occurred on the Court as a whole during the 1930s—is not entirely clear, but it might be found in conceptions of state power that had gained a new ascendancy. Holmes never changed the way he viewed the state, but the world eventually came to his view. When *Patterson* and *Turner* were decided, contractarianism was in almost total dominance on the Court.[31] By the time of *Abrams*, however, the powers of the state had grown, and the ultimate triumph of progressivism—symbolized by the appointments to the Court of Hughes in 1910 and Brandeis in 1916—appeared assured. The influence of *Lochner* and its theory of the state started to wane, and as it did, the fundamental constitutional inquiry began to shift from a question of authority to one of prohibition. The issue was no longer whether a state intervention was authorized by the Constitution, but whether it was prohibited.

At the time of *Lochner*, when the emphasis was on the question of authority, the prohibition inquiry was rarely reached. Even for Holmes, there was not much force to it. As he said in his dissent in *Lochner*, only those state actions beyond the bounds of reason were to be condemned. This attitude was reflected amply both in the Court's decisions in *Patterson* and in *Turner* (Holmes wrote one and joined the other). After World War I, however, as the power of *Lochner* began to fade, or at least was called increasingly into question, Holmes—perhaps, to indulge in yet another speculation, with the prodding of Brandeis—saw the need to place some limits on state power by making good on the prohibition question.

For this purpose, free speech seemed an especially appropriate starting point. Once *Lochner* was abandoned, the state would have broad latitude in choosing both means and ends, and in time legislation would supplant the common law as the primary modality of state intervention. Freedom of speech would then become more urgent, for while common law

---

[30] Toledo Newspaper Co. v. United States, 247 U.S. 402, 422 (1918). See also his dissent in Craig v. Hecht, 263 U.S. 255, 280 (1923). *Toledo Newspaper* was decided before *United States v. Debs* and *Schenk v. United States*, and thus tends to confirm the view that the deci-

sions in those two cases were specially tied to the war effort. See Douglas H. Ginsburg, "Ernst Freund and the First Amendment Tradition: Afterword," *U. Chi. L. Rev.*, 40: 243, 246.

[31] See Chapter 6.

is the elaboration of principle, legislation is more an exercise of will. Legislation is an act of a self-governing collectivity and as such presupposes free and open debate. Free speech is, in essence, a procedural limit on the exercise of state power and of ever-increasing importance as the substantive limits on the state dissolve.

Holmes also understood that the vitality of any constitutional prohibition would depend on the development of an independent theory for the liberty that it embraced. Judicial intervention could no longer simply be parasitic on the ideal of limited government. Free speech needed what property already had: its own theory.[32] Thus, what we find in Holmes's dissent in *Abrams*, but totally lacking in *Patterson* and *Turner*, is the development of an independent theory of freedom of speech—what Holmes referred to as "the theory of our Constitution" but which, of course, was nothing more nor less than a projection of his own philosophic outlook.[33]

I

When the Pullman Strike was before the Court, Clarence Darrow, one of the counsel for Debs, compared the effect of issuing the injunction against the American Railway Union with the reading of a writ to Lee's army. His intent was to demonstrate the futility of the action of the federal court in Chicago, but in choosing this imagery he revealed an understanding of the situation that would make the interjection of any free speech claims on behalf of Debs somewhat silly. The First Amendment does not protect a field marshal. The federal strike commission, criticizing the injunction as interference with freedom of speech, might have missed this point, but Darrow did not. His brief in the Supreme Court on behalf of Debs was a wide-ranging analysis of industrial capitalism that described the evolution of the factory system and the role of the sympathetic strike in achieving industrial justice. Darrow's brief did not, however, complain specifically that the injunction forbade Debs from communicating in any way with his followers.[34]

---

[32] See Chapter 3.

[33] On Holmes's philosophy generally, see Chapters 5 and 6. With special reference to his views of free speech, see Robert M. Cover, "The Left, the Right, and the First Amendment: 1918–1928," *Md. L. Rev.*, 40: 349 (1981); Yosal Rogat and James M. O'Fallon, "Mr. Justice Holmes: A Dissenting Opinion—The Speech Cases," *Stan. L. Rev.*, 36: 1349 (1984); and David Cole, "Agon at Agora: Creative Misreadings in the First Amendment Tradition," *Yale L.J.*, 95: 857 (1986).

[34] Conceivably, the silence of the Court on the free speech issue in *In re Debs* was due to Darrow's silence on the issue. But such an explanation seems at odds with the fact that the Court did not take a narrow or technical view of the case—Brewer, the author of the Court's opinion in *Debs*, even eschewed reliance on the Sherman Act in search of broader principles. See Chapter 3.

Chapter XI: *The Early Free Speech Cases*

An odd turn of history occurred in 1904, when Darrow appeared before the Court again, this time to argue *Turner v. Williams*. In that case he broke from the past and began the practice of making free speech a standard part of the radical lawyer's repertoire. Darrow was brought into the case by an organization called the Free Speech League, which had been set up by Emma Goldman specifically to defend Turner.[35] He was assisted by Edgar Lee Masters, later to become one of America's most celebrated writers. Together they wrote a brief stunning in its intellectual range and aspirations—not much about the factory system, but plenty of Kant and Mill. Like Darrow's brief in the original *Debs* case, the Darrow-Masters brief in *Turner* deserves many of the accolades history has reserved for Brandeis's brief in *Muller v. Oregon*. Darrow and Masters were pitted against James McReynolds, then an assistant attorney general, later to become a justice, and one of the central figures defending *Lochner* and the constitutional tradition it represented against the advent of the activist state.

The *Turner* case involved an immigration statute enacted in March 1903.[36] In this measure, a response to the assassination of President McKinley in 1901 by a presumed anarchist and to more general fears of the radical politics then rampant, Congress amended the general immigration statute. The list of people to be excluded from admission to the United States was enlarged to include "anarchists, or persons who believe in or advocate the overthrow by force or violence of the Government of the United States or of all government or of all forms of law, or the assassination of public officials."[37] In October 1903, only months after its enactment, this law was used to deport John Turner, a well-known English anarchist, who was arrested in the course of, or at the end of, a lecture that he gave in New York. Shortly after his arrest, he was taken to Ellis Island, where various administrative officials ordered him deported.

Because the case involved immigration, the Court once again had to address the issues raised in the Chinese cases about the general power of Congress over admissions and exclusions.[38] In this instance, the justices

---

[35] Emma Goldman, *Living My Life* (New York: Alfred A. Knopf, 1931), 1: 346–50. Founded in 1902, eighteen years before the American Civil Liberties Union, the Free Speech League led the fight for free speech prior to World War I. See generally David M. Rabban, "The Free Speech League, the ACLU, and Changing Conceptions of Free Speech in American History" (University of Texas at Austin School of Law, 1992; unpublished manuscript on file with author). Given the developments in the corporate field, it is not surprising that the need for organizations to support constitutional litigation gained increasing recognition at this point in history. The Free Speech League's role in *Turner v. Williams* resembled the National Consumers' League's role in *Muller v. Oregon* (see Chapter 6) and that of the Citizens' Committee to Test the Constitutionality of the Separate Car Law in *Plessy v. Ferguson* (see Chapter 12).

[36] Alien Immigration Act, Ch. 1012, 32 Stat. 1213 (1903).

[37] Ibid., Sect. 2, 32 Stat. at 1214.

[38] See Chapter 10.

acted in a context free of the cultural and racial biases that may have infected their deliberations in the Chinese cases, but the result was essentially the same. Chief Justice Fuller, who wrote the opinion for the Court,[39] simply restated the understanding that had emerged in the 1880s over admissions, an understanding codified in the *Chinese Exclusion Case*[40] and later reaffirmed in *Fong Yue Ting*:

> Whether rested on the accepted principle of international law that every sovereign nation has the power, as inherent in sovereignty and essential to self-preservation, to forbid the entrance of foreigners within its dominions, or to admit them only in such cases and upon such conditions as it may see fit to prescribe; or on the power to regulate commerce with foreign nations, which includes the entrance of ships, the importation of goods, and the bringing of persons into the ports of the United States, the act before us is not open to constitutional objection.[41]

Brewer was obviously disturbed, as he had been in *Fong Yue Ting*, by the reference in this passage to a power "inherent in sovereignty," but he did not quite know how to work himself free of the precedents. His concurrence in *Turner v. Williams* responded to Fuller's opinion only by way of an oblique observation, almost an aside. He invoked the Tenth Amendment and noted that "while undoubtedly the United States as a nation has all the powers which inhere in any nation, Congress is not authorized in all things to act for the nation."[42]

Fuller also drew on the Court's experience with the Chinese immigration cases to dispose of certain procedural objections to the deportation. Turner had been arrested by immigration officers, a hearing was held (apparently the very next day) before an administrative body called the Board of Inquiry, and the United States secretary of commerce and labor, who sat over the Board, reviewed and affirmed the deportation decision. Turner then sought a writ of habeas corpus from a federal circuit court, demanding his release. There was an argument before the circuit court on his habeas petition, but no evidentiary hearing, nor any consideration of his constitutional claims. The circuit court deemed the decision of the secretary as "final" and dismissed Turner's habeas petition.

In the Supreme Court, Darrow and Masters strongly objected to the procedure that had been employed in Turner's case, particularly—and here

---

[39] At one point in his career, Fuller served as an editor of a Democratic newspaper, the *Age*. Willard L. King, *Melville Weston Fuller: Chief Justice of the United States, 1888–1910* (New York: Macmillan, 1950; repr. Chicago: University of Chicago Press, 1967), 30–31. But apparently the experience did not leave him with much of a taste for freedom of the press.

[40] 130 U.S. 581 (1889).

[41] 194 U.S. at 290.

[42] Ibid., 295–96.

comes another irony when *In re Debs* is kept in mind—because of the limitation on the power of the judiciary. Darrow and Masters argued that Turner was entitled to *judicial* determination of the merits of his free speech claim and that it was a mistake for the habeas court to treat the decision of administrative officials as final. The chief justice, on the other hand, saw no objection to the finality rule and invoked the Chinese cases as support.

In the context of those cases, the Fuller Court developed the exception to the finality rule for claims of citizenship: When it came to the issue of whether a person is a citizen, an administrative judgment would not be "final." Citizenship was deemed a jurisdictional fact and would require a judicial inquiry. This development occurred in the early 1900s, but had not yet formally come to fruition at the time of *Turner v. Williams* (which was rendered after *Sing Tuck*[43] and before *Ju Toy*[44]). Nevertheless, Fuller appears to have anticipated it when he said that a rule requiring a judicial determination of citizenship would be of no avail to Turner because, as he noted, "alienage was conceded."[45]

Fuller then went on to consider the issue of finality in the context of free speech claims, but did not create for them any comparable exception to the finality rule. Once the Court found the 1903 Act constitutional on its face, as it was about to do, the application of the Act, and all constitutional issues raised by that application, would be left entirely in the hands of administrative officials. In so ruling, Fuller appeared to be placing free speech on a lower rung of the constitutional ladder than citizenship: Free speech had no jurisdictional significance.[46] A mistaken ruling on a free speech claim would be unfortunate, but it would not deprive the administrative official of the power to deport. There was thus no reason for a court to decide each free speech claim for itself.

Darrow and Masters insisted that Turner's detention on Ellis Island deprived him of still another liberty, the right to move about freely. This deprivation amounted to imprisonment, they argued, and required a judicial hearing. For this argument, they relied on *Wong Wing*,[47] which had invalidated a provision of the Geary Act that authorized commissioners—not courts—to impose a year's imprisonment on illegal entrants. Once again, Fuller was unmoved. He distinguished *Wong Wing* on the theory that Turner's imprisonment was only "[d]etention or temporary confinement as part of the means necessary to give effect to the exclusion or expul-

---

[43] United States v. Sing Tuck, 194 U.S. 161 (1904). See Chapter 10.

[44] United States v. Ju Toy, 198 U.S. 253 (1905). See Chapter 10.

[45] 194 U.S. at 290.

[46] The non-jurisdictional status of the First Amendment claims might also explain why the Court failed to address

free speech in *In re Debs*. Yet, once again, such an explanation seems out of keeping with Brewer's approach in that case. See Chapter 3 and note 34 of this chapter.

[47] Wong Wing v. United States, 163 U.S. 228 (1896). See Chapter 10.

sion."[48] This regular administrative procedure for exclusion and expulsion was contrasted by Fuller with the type of imprisonment at hard labor ("infamous punishment"[49]) that was intended specifically to discourage illegal entry and invalidated in *Wong Wing*.

As with the ruling on congressional power over immigration, Brewer commented on Fuller's disposition of these procedural issues, although the full significance of what he said remains unclear. Brewer's entire comment consisted of two sentences (plus a quotation of the clause prohibiting the suspension of the habeas writ):

> I fully endorse and accentuate the conclusions of the court, as disclosed by the opinion, that, notwithstanding the legislation of Congress, the courts may and must, when properly called upon by petition in *habeas corpus*, examine and determine the right of any individual restrained of his personal liberty to be discharged from such restraint. I do not believe it within the power of Congress to give to ministerial officers a final adjudication of the right of liberty or to oust the courts from the duty of inquiry respecting both law and facts.[50]

While these sentences appear to be fully consistent with Brewer's ideas, proclaimed at Albany and again in *Debs*, depicting the judiciary as the nation's safeguard, it is not clear how their author could have joined Fuller's opinion, which, after all, gave finality to the executive's determination and limited the power of the judiciary. We are left to ponder why Brewer concurred rather than dissented.

Like Harlan, Brewer was not the type to engage in quiet diplomacy; it is hard to conceive of his decision to concur as a strategy intended to limit the negative fallout from the Court's decision. More likely, it was premised on a certain discrepancy between what the Court said and what it did. Fuller announced a general rule affording finality to executive determinations of free speech claims but then went on to consider the merits of Turner's. He rejected Turner's free speech claim on the merits, but in the very act of considering it Fuller afforded Turner the *judicial* determination to which Brewer insisted he was entitled. It mattered not that the hearing was provided by the Supreme Court rather than the circuit court. As to the liberty issue raised by the imprisonment, Brewer may simply have accepted the Court's distinction between "temporary confinement" and "a final adjudication of the right of liberty."

After disposing of these two immigration questions—one going to the general power of Congress to exclude or deport and the other to the finality to be accorded an administrative deportation decision—the Court finally

---

[48] 194 U.S. at 291.
[49] Ibid. (quoting Shiras, J., in *Wong Wing*).
[50] 194 U.S. at 295.

considered Turner's free speech claim and found that it had no merit. In trying to understand that ruling, the temptation is great to emphasize Turner's status as an outsider, as an alien or immigrant, in order to minimize the extent of the First Amendment defeat. Even in the 1970s, long after Holmes's dissent in *Abrams* bore its fruit and gave rise to a vibrant free speech tradition, the Supreme Court allowed the State Department to exclude from the country a well-known Belgian Marxist, Ernest Mandel, who had been invited to lecture at various American universities.[51] At that time, it was fairly well settled that a citizen espousing similar views could not be sanctioned, either directly (through application of the criminal law)[52] or indirectly (say through the loss of employment).[53] But the Court nonetheless concluded that there was no First Amendment violation of Mandel's rights, or those of his would-be listeners, in excluding him from the country. The government was deemed to have special powers over whom to admit, powers so broad and conclusive as to defeat the most elementary free speech claims.

In allowing the government special prerogatives in the context of exclusion, *Mandel* may be correct, and Harlan's willingness to go along with the Court's decision in *Turner v. Williams* may reflect a similar understanding: The government can do what it wishes with outsiders. But it would be a mistake to interpret Fuller's rejection of the free speech claim in that case as based solely on that principle (whatever its merit). *Turner v. Williams* was cited in the *Mandel* case, but *Turner* was a much more resounding defeat for free speech than such a reading would suggest.[54]

To be finicky about it, *Turner*, unlike *Mandel*, was not purely an exclusion case. John Turner was already in the country. He refused to disclose how he had entered, but it was conceded by all that he had been in the United States at least ten days before his arrest. Moreover, six years before the deportation proceeding, Turner had taken out his first papers to become a naturalized citizen. The decision to deport him thus denied Turner the opportunity of ever becoming a citizen. In the case of Ernest Mandel, only a visa for a lecture tour was at stake. Of course, it is not clear that if Turner had not been deported he would have gone through with the naturalization proceeding, or that he was sincere in stating an intention to become a citizen, but Fuller and his colleagues did not consider that. The Court's ruling was conditioned in no way on the view that Turner's attempt to become a citizen was a sham.

Of even greater significance is the fact that the Court's treatment of the First Amendment claim does not reveal even the slightest appreciation

---

[51] Kleindienst v. Mandel, 408 U.S. 753 (1972).
[52] See, e.g., Brandenburg v. Ohio, 395 U.S. 444 (1969).

[53] See, e.g., United States v. Robel, 389 U.S. 258 (1967).
[54] Compare Gibson, "Freedom of Expression," 316.

for the underlying theory of free speech adumbrated by Holmes in *Abrams*: the need for free and open debate on issues of great public importance. Holmes was as sensitive as anyone to the right of the sovereign to maintain public order—had he been on the Court in the early 1890s surely he would have joined *In re Debs*. But later, in a number of cases arising out of the First World War, he tried to accommodate the values that finally were given so forceful an expression in *Abrams* by requiring that the danger of disorder be clear and present.[55] However, the rule that Fuller crafted in *Turner*, then fully supported by Holmes, was of a different character altogether, for it allowed suppression of anarchist speech that was purely philosophical. There was no accommodation between civic freedom and the imperatives of the public order:

> If the word "anarchists" should be interpreted as including aliens whose anarchistic views are professed as those of political philosophers innocent of evil intent, it would follow that [if] Congress was of [the] opinion that the tendency of the general exploitation of such views is so dangerous to the public weal that aliens who hold and advocate them would be undesirable additions to our population, whether permanently or temporarily, whether many or few, and, in the light of previous decisions, the act, even in this aspect, would not be unconstitutional, or as applicable to any alien who is opposed to all organized government.[56]

In this passage and elsewhere, Fuller is careful to identify the speaker as an alien, suggesting that his crabbed reading of the First Amendment was critically dependent on the status of the person seeking to invoke its protection. It is within congressional discretion to decide who "would be undesirable additions to our population." I believe, however, that Turner's alien status was only incidental to Fuller's reasoning and that Fuller was making a more general point, not about immigration, but about the need of the state to maintain public order. Fuller believed, to use a more recent formulation, that Turner's speech was unprotected: The First Amendment does not protect a call to revolution. The discretion he accorded Congress was not simply to decide who would be "undesirable additions to our population," but, more fundamentally, what is "dangerous to the public weal" and how best to protect against that threat—by exclusion, expulsion, or in the case of citizens, imprisonment. The legislature was given broad latitude to decide what kind of speech should be suppressed; it need not wait for an imminent threat of lawlessness or a clear and present danger. The legislature was entirely free to decide for itself when it was appropriate to intervene.

In *Lochner* the Court took a different approach toward legislative discretion. It did not give the legislature much latitude for deciding how it

---

[55] See above, note 28. [56] 194 U.S. at 294.

might best pursue a permissible end: To improve the health of workers, New York could enact factory inspection laws, but it could not limit contractual freedom. It is hard to know what accounted for this difference between *Lochner* and *Turner*—no one stopped to explain it—but it might be attributable to a difference in the substantive end involved, if not the general theories of the state discussed at the outset of this chapter. At issue in *Turner v. Williams*, as opposed to *Lochner*, was not just an end like "health," but one having a more transcendent significance—the public order itself.[57] With a tone he rarely achieved, but that was very much in keeping with Brewer's opinion in *In re Debs* (where the same transcendent end was invoked) Fuller concluded his opinion in *Turner v. Williams* on this note:

> We are not to be understood as depreciating the vital importance of freedom of speech and of the press, or as suggesting limitations on the spirit of liberty, in itself unconquerable, but this case does not involve those considerations. The flaming brand which guards the realm where no human government is needed still bars the entrance; and as long as human governments endure they cannot be denied the power of self-preservation, as that question is presented here.[58]

The early 1900s were not so tumultuous as the early 1890s, but the memories of earlier events—Haymarket, Homestead, Pullman—were fresh in the minds of the justices and made all the more vivid by McKinley's assassination. Fears about "self-preservation" must have seemed more weighty at the beginning of the century than at its close.

Brewer no doubt shared these fears, but he chose to write separately. He understood that Fuller was making a more general statement about freedom of speech itself and was not simply formulating a specialized rule about aliens. In his consideration of the free speech issue, Brewer did not even mention Turner's alien status. But, once again, it is hard to figure out what he thought about this aspect of the case.

At one point in his opinion, Brewer seemed to be expanding the domain of protected speech beyond the limits allowed by Fuller:

> It is not an unreasonable deduction [from the evidence before the Board of Inquiry] that petitioner is an anarchist in the commonly accepted sense of the term, one who urges and seeks the overthrow by force of all government. If that be not the fact, he should have introduced testimony to establish the contrary. It is unnecessary, therefore, to consider what rights he would have if he were only what is called by way of differ-

---

[57] Compare with Fuller's formulation in the *Rapier* case, described above, note 22.

[58] 194 U.S. at 294.

entiation a philosophical anarchist, one who simply entertains and expresses the opinion that all government is a mistake, and that society would be better off without any.[59]

In this passage Brewer makes a distinction, increasingly important to the law after *Abrams*, between the general advocacy of ideas ("entertains and expresses the opinion") and incitement to unlawful conduct ("urges and seeks").[60] Yet the force of that distinction was diluted by Brewer's acceptance of Turner's deportation without inquiring into what sort of an anarchist Turner was.

In explaining his vote, Brewer emphasized Turner's failure to introduce evidence to indicate that he was not "one who urges or seeks the overthrow by force of all government." But that strikes me as a lawyer's trick, for Brewer did not make clear why the burden was Turner's. Given the nature of the charge against Turner, and that Brewer was drawing a line not yet present in the law, Turner's failure of proof hardly could be held against him. At most, it should have led to a remand to the federal habeas court; such a disposition should have been especially appropriate for Brewer, who never tired of celebrating the judiciary and its role in protecting liberty. The record before the Court may not have been complete, but it was sufficient to indicate that he was a union organizer, not a member of a subversive conspiracy.

For six years prior to his arrest in New York, John Turner had been a paid organizer of the retail clerks of Great Britain. He had come to this country to promote the interests of organized labor, and his "crime," if that be the word, was twofold. First, he intended (as revealed in papers found in his possession) to give lectures on the Haymarket Riot of 1886 and to share the platform with Johann (also known as John) Most, whose writings on the manufacture and use of explosives to further revolutionary aims were introduced as evidence against the eight men convicted for the death of the police officers in the riot.[61] Second, he made a public speech in New York that extolled the emancipatory potential of a general strike in the city:

---

[59] Ibid., 296.

[60] See Kalven, *Worthy Tradition*, 119–236.

[61] On the Haymarket Riot, see Chapter 2. Most's connection to the Haymarket Riot is described in Spies v. People, 122 Ill. 1, 59–74, 78–79, 131, 230–35, reported *sub nom*. The Anarchists' Case, 12 N.E. 865, 894–903, 929, 976–79 (1887). In a later brush with the law, Most was convicted, and sentenced to one year's imprisonment, for reprinting in his small German-language newspa-

per a fifty-year-old article calling for the murder of government officials. The article appeared on the very day McKinley was assassinated. People v. Most, 71 A.D. 160, *aff'd* 171 N.Y. 423, 64 N.E. 175 (1902). Earlier, he had been convicted in England for much the same crime: publishing an article hailing the murder of the Russian emperor and lauding it as an example to revolutionists from Constantinople to Washington. The Queen v. Most, 7 Q.B.D. 244 (1881).

Just imagine what a universal tie-up would mean. What would it mean in New York City alone if this idea of solidarity were spread through the city? If no work was being done, if it were Sunday for a week or a fortnight, life in New York would be impossible, and the workers, gaining audacity, would refuse to recognize the authority of their employers and eventually take to themselves the handling of the industries. . . . All over Europe they are preparing for a general strike, which will spread over the entire industrial world. Everywhere the employees are organizing, and to me, at any rate, as an anarchist, as one who believes that the people should emancipate themselves, I look forward to this struggle as an opportunity for the workers to assert the power that is really theirs.[62]

Punishing someone for making such a speech would pose no problem to Fuller, since he drew no distinction between the general advocacy of subversive ideas and the incitement to lawlessness; it should have made a difference to Brewer, however, who emphasized that very distinction in his concurring opinion.

A more satisfactory explanation for Brewer's position might be found in his speech at Albany. There he denounced "force" and "violence" and expanded the ordinary understanding of those categories to embrace the mass strike. Surely he saw the general strike—Turner's "idea of solidarity"—in similar terms, and on that ground he may have justified the deportation in his own mind. It is true that extending his remarks at Albany to cover Turner's case would require blurring or ignoring a distinction between the *expression* of an idea and the *action* that embodies the idea: Turner merely was advocating a general strike, unlike Eugene Debs and Alexander Berkman, who participated in and led such strikes. To the lawyer working in the late twentieth century, this distinction between expression and action is fundamental; it is central to any theory that secures for freedom of speech a privileged position within the realm of human liberty and that gives it special protection from otherwise broad state powers. But for Brewer, who wholeheartedly endorsed *Lochner* and all that it stood for— the protection of liberty by identifying the limits of state authority—such a distinction was not of great importance. Safeguarding the public order comes within those limits, and once within them, there was probably not much difference between a general strike and a speech urging one. Either was a proper subject of state intervention.

---

[62] Quoted at 194 U.S. at 283. Turner's lecture was delivered in New York on   October 23, 1903.

II

Although *Turner v. Williams* approved restrictions on the speech of an alien, the status of the speaker in the constitutional community was not crucial in the Court's thinking. The strong arm of the censor would have been allowed if a citizen had said the same things. The case should be seen as a general statement of the Court's attitude toward free speech; it turned more on a lack of sympathy for the values now associated with the First Amendment than on a belief in the discretion of a community to determine who shall be admitted to membership. This reading of *Turner v. Williams*, sharply distinguishing it from the *Insular Cases*, is reinforced when account is taken of *Patterson v. Colorado*, the other major free speech case of the era. In this instance, the opinion was written by Holmes, and although his opinion in *Patterson* is totally at odds with his *Abrams* dissent, it is consistent with the position he took while on the Supreme Judicial Court of Massachusetts in the Boston Commons case and with his willingness to join Fuller's opinion in *Turner v. Williams*. Without the slightest qualm, Holmes wrote an opinion in *Patterson v. Colorado* that allowed a publisher to be punished for commenting on a number of decisions of the Colorado supreme court.

The Colorado rulings invalidated a highly controversial provision of the state constitution granting home rule to Denver. On the day after the decisions were announced, an article appeared in the *Rocky Mountain News* criticizing the decisions and five members of the court. A number of other articles on the subject followed over the next week. The series also included a political cartoon criticizing the court. Given the journalistic traditions of the day, the tone of the articles and the cartoon was mild, but the message was unmistakable: The decisions of the Colorado supreme court were inconsistent with prior precedents, and the votes of a number of the judges had been influenced improperly by personal considerations. Specifically, the stories and the cartoon suggested that the judges had acted on the basis of their ties to the governor, the Republican Party, and certain corporate interests ("the utilities"), all of whom were opposed to home rule. Immediately after the series ran, the chief judge of the Colorado supreme court directed the attorney general of the state to commence criminal contempt proceedings against the publisher, United States Senator Thomas Patterson, and his publishing company. Both were adjudged in contempt and fined a total of $1,000.

In the Supreme Court of the United States Patterson attacked the contempt conviction on a number of grounds, some of which were unrelated to free speech. One objection, based on due process considerations, focused on the fact that the judges criticized were the same ones who initiated the contempt proceedings and found Patterson in contempt. Patterson complained that he had been denied the right to an impartial tribunal.[63] For Holmes, the answer was simple and obvious (though totally unpersuasive): "[T]he grounds upon which contempts are punished are impersonal."[64] Patterson also claimed that the Colorado supreme court had twisted Colorado law in order to get him. This objection contains elements of due process and equal protection, but at its most fundamental level rests on the principle, so familiar to the Fuller Court, that guaranteed to all an equality before the law. Once again, the answer was obvious to Holmes: "Even if it be true, as the plaintiff in error says, that the Supreme Court of Colorado departed from earlier and well-established precedents to meet the exigencies of this case, whatever might be thought of the justice or wisdom of such a step, the Constitution of the United States is not infringed."[65]

Holmes paused a little longer on the free speech issue, but not much. It, too, was disposed of summarily, indeed with a casualness and sweep that is reminiscent of his opinion in *Lochner*. After analyzing the speech issue, Holmes concluded that all of Patterson's constitutional claims—including the free speech one—were so frivolous, so utterly devoid of merit, as to require dismissing the appeal on the ground that the Supreme Court was without jurisdiction: "We have scrutinized the case, but cannot say that it shows an infraction of rights under the Constitution of the United States, or discloses more than the formal appeal to that instrument in the answer to found the jurisdiction of this court."[66]

Judges are government officials and, from any sensible view of the First Amendment, they should be open to public criticism. Holmes

---

[63] As recently as 1905, two years before the *Patterson* decision, but in a different context, the Court had spoken of "the right of every litigant to an impartial and disinterested tribunal for the determination of his rights. . . ." McGuire v. Blount, 199 U.S. 142, 143 (1905). Later, in his dissent in the *Toledo* case, Holmes wrote, "When it is considered how contrary it is to our practice and ways of thinking for the same person to be accuser and sole judge in a matter which, if he be sensitive, may involve strong personal feeling, I should expect the power to be limited by the necessities of the case 'to insure order and decorum in their presence,' as is stated in *Ex parte Robinson*, 19 Wall. 505." 247 U.S. at 423.

[64] 205 U.S. at 463. He then cited United States v. Shipp, 203 U.S. 563 (1906), which hardly seemed dispositive.

That case, in an opinion by Holmes, cleared the way for contempt proceedings against a sheriff for allowing a mob to lynch a black man who was in the sheriff's custody while his rape conviction was on appeal before the Supreme Court. The sheriff, a deputy, and several members of the lynch mob were later found guilty of contempt. United States v. Shipp, 214 U.S. 386 (1909).

[65] 205 U.S. at 461.

[66] Ibid., 463. Writing to Fuller, Holmes expressed a similar view as to the insubstantiality of the claim: "I infer as you have not returned the Patterson Co.—Contempt No. 223 that you perceive difficulties that I have not seen. I did not expect that any would be felt as this case seemed to be pretty plain." Holmes to Fuller, Mar. 28, 1907, Fuller Papers, Chicago Historical Society.

acknowledged this point inasmuch as he was willing to concede that "courts are subject to the same criticism as other people."[67] On the other hand, he accepted a conception of the contempt power that knew few limits and that easily could be used as a potent instrument for stifling public criticism of the judiciary. While contempt is a familiar tool for maintaining order in the courtroom or for enforcing decrees, at stake in *Patterson* was "constructive contempt"—the punishment of people who are not parties to the proceeding for comments made outside the courtroom.

The potential for abusing this form of the contempt power had been amply demonstrated by an important chapter of American history, the impeachment of Judge James H. Peck. This political controversy, like the Alien and Sedition Acts of 1789, was not resolved authoritatively by a Supreme Court decision, but nonetheless yielded an important "precedent" on freedom of speech.[68] Peck was a federal judge in the 1830s who used the contempt power to punish those who publicly had criticized his decisions. The reaction to this use of the constructive contempt power was strong and immediate; a bill of impeachment against Peck was voted by the House of Representatives. The Senate finally decided not to remove him from office, but the impeachment proceeding itself and the federal statute enacted in response to the controversy, denying the constructive contempt power to federal judges,[69] spoke eloquently of the dangers to a free society posed by the exercise of such a power.

In *Patterson*, Holmes ignored this historical lesson and refused to place any meaningful curbs on the constructive contempt power. He was even willing to accept a conception of the constructive contempt power that allowed judges to punish for truthful statements about their work. Patterson claimed in his answer that the charge of corruption implicit in the articles and cartoon was well founded in fact, but the judges of the Colorado supreme court did not give him a chance to prove that. They entered a judgment on the pleadings alone, and Patterson's pleading admitted only publication, not falsity. Holmes saw no problem in this method of proceeding by the Colorado court. He said that the contempt power "may extend as well to the true as to the false"[70] and explained why truth might be disallowed as a defense:

---

[67] Ibid.

[68] See Arthur J. Stansbury, *Report of the Trial of James H. Peck* (Boston: Hilliard, Gray, 1833); John R. Labovitz, *Presidential Impeachment* (New Haven: Yale University Press, 1978), 47–48; and Walter Nelles and Carol W. King, "Contempt by Publication in the United States," *Colum. L. Rev.*, 28: 401, 423–30 (1928).

[69] Act of Mar. 2, 1831, Ch. 99, 4 Stat. 487, codified as amended at 18 U.S.C. Sect. 401 (1988). See cases cited above, note 30.

[70] 205 U.S. at 462.

Chapter XI: *The Early Free Speech Cases*

> The theory of our system is that the conclusions to be reached in a case will be induced only by evidence and argument in open court, and not by any outside influence, whether of private talk or public print.[71]

Holmes's reference in *Abrams* to "the theory of our Constitution" was supported by mention of the controversy surrounding the Alien and Sedition Acts of 1798; but the strikingly similar reference in *Patterson* to "the theory of our system" was not supported in any way.

Admittedly, there was a long-standing practice that allowed the constructive contempt power to be used to protect juries from "outside influences," that is, to keep them free from any evidence that was not itself introduced at trial, but that practice had no relevance whatsoever in this context. Patterson was not being punished for improperly influencing a jury but for criticizing decisions of the supreme court of Colorado. Moreover, though a power conceived as a means to protect juries might be extended to protect judges from "outside influences," such a power could make no claim to plausibility unless the criticism was directed to a *pending* case. Holmes well understood this point, but sought to avoid its force by allowing the most extended notion of "pendency."

The newspaper articles at issue in *Patterson* were in response to decisions that already had been rendered. The state court acknowledged this embarrassment to its use of the constructive contempt power, but insisted that the cases were still "pending" because the period for filing a motion for rehearing had not expired. The articles in question began to appear the day after the decisions were rendered and continued for a week, and at some point, motions for rehearing had indeed been filed. While the dissent in the Colorado court said that no petition for rehearing had been filed when the articles had been published, the majority said "petitions for rehearing were filed in the causes and undisposed of on the date of the last of said publications."[72] But they did not stress their view of the sequence or use it to limit the idea of pendency. Instead, the majority defined as pending any case that remained subject to reconsideration or modification.

In his brief in the Supreme Court, Patterson pointed out that state law placed no deadline on the period for filing a petition for rehearing—as a purely technical matter, such a petition could be filed at any time. Therefore, accepting the Colorado court's definition of pendency could result in a near-permanent ban on public criticism. In order to be effective, Patterson argued, commentary must be timely, presented when the decision is still news. Holmes brushed these concerns aside in a single sentence:

---

[71] Ibid.
[72] People v. News-Times Publishing Co., 35 Colo. 253, 356, 84 Pac. 912, 945 (1906).

Whether a case shall be regarded as pending while it is possible that a petition for rehearing may be filed, or, if in an appellate court, until the remittitur is issued, are questions which the local law can settle as it pleases without interference from the Constitution of the United States.[73]

By allowing the Colorado court to use any notion of pendency it wished, Holmes enabled it to forge its constructive contempt power into an effective instrument of censorship.

Holmes's casual acceptance of a broad, almost unlimited, use of the constructive contempt power represented an important defeat for free speech, but Justice Harlan in dissent did not seem concerned particularly by Holmes's refusal to place any First Amendment limits on that power. What most troubled Harlan was Holmes's general view of free speech: his casual announcement of two general propositions of constitutional law that seemed to reduce the liberty to speak to about the same level as Holmes saw the liberty to contract.

The first of these propositions limited the First Amendment to a prohibition of prior restraints. Quoting an early Massachusetts decision, Holmes insisted that the main purpose of the amendment was "to prevent all such *previous restraints* upon publications as had been practiced by other governments."[74] The amendment did not prevent "the subsequent punishment of such as may be deemed contrary to the public welfare."[75] The Supreme Court held some twenty-five years later in *Near v. Minnesota*[76] that prior restraints are especially suspect, but a limitation on the First Amendment that would *confine* it to barring prior restraints, as Holmes

---

[73] 205 U.S. at 460. In Craig v. Hecht, 263 U.S. 255 (1923), in much the spirit of the *Toledo* case, Holmes revisited the pendency question with a result opposite to that which he reached in *Patterson. Craig v. Hecht* involved the contempt conviction of the New York City comptroller for writing and printing a letter critical of a federal judge. The comptroller had won his release on a writ of habeas corpus, only to be reversed by the circuit court. The Supreme Court affirmed the circuit court's judgment that the comptroller had used the writ of habeas corpus improperly, and had thereby forfeited his right to any appeal of the contempt conviction. Holmes dissented, saying the sentence for contempt was "wholly void" because "there was no matter pending before the Court in the sense that it must

be to make this kind of contempt possible. It is not enough that somebody may hereafter move to have something done. There was nothing then awaiting decision when the petitioner's letter was published." 263 U.S. at 280 (Holmes, J., dissenting).

[74] 205 U.S. at 462, quoting Commonwealth v. Blanding, 20 Mass. (3 Pick.) 304, 313–14, 15 Am. Dec. 214, 218 (1825) (emphasis in original).

[75] 205 U.S. at 462.

[76] 283 U.S. 697 (1931). The *Davis* case involving the Boston Commons did not suppress a publication, but it can be read as authorizing a prior restraint inasmuch as it involved a permit requirement where the discretion to deny a permit was not subject to any constraint whatsoever.

would, is an entirely different matter. Such a view may have its roots in Blackstone,[77] as Holmes pointed out, but its pedigree should not obscure the fact that it is inconsistent with the position Holmes finally took in *Abrams*, and with the entire tradition that is based on that dissent.[78] It is hard to imagine what freedom of speech in America would be under Blackstone. Harlan understood this and strongly protested this feature of Holmes's opinion:

> I can not assent to [Holmes's] view, if it be meant that the legislature may impair or abridge the rights of a free press and of free speech whenever it thinks that the public welfare requires that to be done. The public welfare cannot override constitutional privileges. . . .[79]

The second general proposition announced by Holmes in *Patterson* appeared to be of even greater concern to Harlan. It seemed to put into question whether the constitutional ideal of liberty offered any protection to freedom of speech when the threat was posed by a state rather than the federal government. In his opinion in *Patterson*, Holmes said: "We leave undecided the question whether there is to be found in the Fourteenth Amendment a prohibition similar to that in the First."[80] On one reading, this sentence appears relatively straightforward and not especially troubling: Holmes simply was identifying a legal question that had not yet been resolved, and would not be until 1925.[81] Harlan, however, read the sentence differently. He saw it as reflecting a measure of skepticism rather than prudence—a skeptical attitude toward liberty, indeed the same skeptical attitude that informed Holmes's famed dissents in *Lochner* and *Adair*. Those two cases involved entrepreneurial, not political, liberty, but as with his opinion in *Patterson*, Holmes's dissents in *Lochner* and *Adair* were premised on a studied indifference to the constitutional ideal of liberty and a willingness to embrace a more organic conception of governmental authority. No doubt, as a purely technical matter, Holmes recognized limits on

---

[77] See Leonard W. Levy, *Emergence of a Free Press* (New York: Oxford University Press, 1985), 12–13; revised edition of *The Legacy of Suppression: Freedom of Speech and Press in Early American History* (New York: Harper & Row, 1963), 14. Levy attributes this view to the framers, though without believing that the Court is bound to follow them. For commentary on Levy's historical thesis, see Walter Berns, "Freedom of the Press and the Alien and Sedition Laws: A Reappraisal," *Sup. Ct. Rev.*, 1970: 109; David A. Anderson, "The Ori-

gins of the Press Clause," *U.C.L.A. L. Rev.*, 30: 455 (1983); and William T. Mayton, "Seditious Libel and the Lost Guarantee of a Freedom of Expression," *Colum. L. Rev.*, 84: 91 (1984).

[78] *Abrams* involved a criminal prosecution, as did *Schenck*, where Holmes explicitly removed the prior restraint limitation. 249 U.S. at 51–52.

[79] 205 U.S. at 465.

[80] Ibid., 462.

[81] See Gitlow v. New York, 268 U.S. 652 (1925).

governmental power; his plea was for a shift of focus, from the question of authority to one of prohibition. Yet Harlan feared that in fact more was at stake: not just a shift in focus, but a diminution in the level of protection.

In part, Harlan's fears arose from the fact that Holmes's reservation on the incorporation of free speech (as the technical issue later came to be known) appeared inconsistent with *United States v. Cruikshank*,[82] a well-known precedent of some thirty years' standing. That case involved a gang of whites who had disrupted a political meeting of black Republicans. The terrorists were prosecuted under a Reconstruction statute that proscribed forceful interference with rights secured by the Constitution. The indictment was dismissed because there was no state involvement in the interference, but by way of dictum the Court seemed to imply that the result would have been different if the state had been involved. The Court also said that the right of the people peaceably to assemble for the purpose of petitioning the federal government for a redress of grievances was in fact an attribute of national citizenship and, as such, was protected even against private interferences.

Harlan read these passages in *Cruikshank* as making a broad statement about the status of freedom of speech in the constitutional order and as authority for the proposition—now thrown into question by Holmes's reservation on incorporation—that such activity was protected from state interferences under the Fourteenth Amendment. According to Harlan,

> [T]he rights of free speech and of a free press are, in their essence, attributes of national citizenship . . . [and] neither Congress nor any State since the adoption of the Fourteenth Amendment can, by legislative enactments or by judicial action, impair or abridge them.[83]

Holmes ignored Harlan's argument and, for that matter, the entire issue of *Cruikshank*.

Getting to an even more fundamental dilemma posed by Holmes's position in *Patterson*, Harlan implicitly invoked that then-vibrant body of decisions that construed the Fourteenth Amendment as protecting liberty to contract and the right to hold property free from state and local interferences. How could entrepreneurial but not political liberties be protected by the Fourteenth Amendment? True, Holmes had dissented from the liberty of contract branch of that body of decisions, but his rejection was never complete; he embraced without qualification decisions such as *Ex parte Young*, which protected property or certain entrepreneurial liberties from

---

[82] 92 U.S. 542 (1876). On the role of *Cruikshank* in *Plessy v. Ferguson*, see Chapter 12, note 29 and accompanying text.

[83] 205 U.S. at 465.

state laws regulating rates.[84] Holmes thus was prepared to give some force to the constitutional ideal of liberty embodied in the Fourteenth Amendment, and from that perspective it was hard for Harlan to understand how Holmes could allow freedom of speech or press to remain unprotected. To Harlan, Holmes had his priorities reversed. Once again, Holmes remained silent.

As the author of the Court's opinion, the anomaly in Holmes's position—a willingness to protect property or certain entrepreneurial liberties from certain state interferences, but a doubt as to "whether there is to be found in the Fourteenth Amendment a prohibition similar to that in the First"—was explicit and clear. The contradiction was, however, in no way confined to him; it was shared by the entire Harrison-Cleveland coalition, specifically, Fuller, White, Peckham, and Brewer, all of whom joined *Patterson*. Indeed, for them the conflict was far more profound. When it came to protecting property or entrepreneurial liberty, Holmes seemed ambivalent—he joined *Ex parte Young* but dissented in *Lochner*. The others, however, were anything but ambivalent. Peckham, for example, was the spokesman for the Court in *Ex parte Young* and *Lochner*. White spoke passionately about the right to acquire property in *Northern Securities* and about freedom of contract in *Trans-Missouri* and *Joint Traffic*,[85] and although he joined Harlan's dissent in *Lochner*, he also joined Peckham's opinion in *Ex parte Young*. Brewer joined *Ex parte Young* and *Lochner*, and wrote the opinion for the Court in *Reagan v. Farmers' Loan & Trust*, which gave the right to fair value Fourteenth Amendment status.[86] He also dissented emphatically in *Budd v. New York*.

There was a dissent by Brewer in *Patterson*, but it was not joined by anyone else and it was disappointing on its own terms. The dissent was very much of a piece with his opinion—a concurrence—in *Turner v. Williams*. Brewer sensed the threat to liberty, and appeared uneasy with Holmes's approach, but he spoke without the clarity or force of which he was capable and that Harlan achieved. Brewer's opinion was brief, focusing on the severity of Holmes's technical conclusion that the federal claims were so frivolous as to warrant dismissal. In objecting to this disposition of the case, Brewer implied some view of the merits—the federal claims were not frivolous—but this was hardly tantamount to the kind of affirmation of liberty that might have been expected of him, especially in a setting so far removed from the concerns and fears expressed in Albany or that may have moved him to concur in *Turner v. Williams*. Moreover, Brewer explicitly disassociated himself from Harlan's dissent in *Patterson* and, in a manner thoroughly uncharacteristic of him, failed to address the merits of the free

---

[84] 209 U.S. 123 (1908). See Chapter 7, note 110.

[85] See Chapter 5.
[86] 154 U.S. 362 (1894). See Chapter 7.

speech issue. Limply justifying his silence, Brewer wrote: "As, however, the court decides that it does not have jurisdiction, and has dismissed the writ of error, it would not be fit for me to express any opinion on the merits of the case."[87]

A more extended discussion by Brewer might have lent a measure of integrity to his commitment to the ideal of liberty and his determination to use the judicial power to vindicate that ideal to the full. Brewer might ultimately have come out against the speech claim—one never knows—but it is also possible that once Brewer embarked on a full consideration of it, he might have grasped the tension between *Patterson* and cases like *Lochner, Ex parte Young*, and *Reagan*. He might have been led to examine his willingness, and that of his colleagues, to focus on the question of authority in such a way and to such an extent as to leave fragile and empty the one prohibition that has played such an important role in the modern understanding of liberty.

III

In 1911 the duty fell on the new chief justice, Edward White, to pull together all the strands of antitrust doctrine that had come unraveled over the twenty years of Fuller's tenure. The challenge was considerable, and the result was *Standard Oil* and *American Tobacco*, no small achievement.[88] Harlan dissented vehemently, but all the other justices went along with White's synthesis, some biting their lips, and as a result White managed to establish the basic framework that has governed antitrust law for most of this century. At approximately the same time, but in a less conspicuous corner of the law, the new chief justice also assumed the responsibility of speaking for the Court in a case involving seditious libel—an issue that implicated what the Court fifty years later would describe as "the central meaning of the First Amendment."[89] Yet White's decision in that case stands on a wholly different plane from *Standard Oil* and *American Tobacco*. There was nothing to synthesize.

The case in question, *United States v. Press Publishing Co.*,[90] stemmed from a series of articles published in December 1908 by the *World*, a New York newspaper owned by Joseph Pulitzer. The articles were about the process by which the United States had acquired the rights to construct the Panama Canal. Those rights were originally in the hands of a private French company organized by Ferdinand de Lesseps, the celebrated engi-

---

[87] 205 U.S. at 466.
[88] See Chapter 5.
[89] New York Times v. Sullivan, 376 U.S. 254, 273 (1964). See Harry Kalven, Jr., "The New York Times Case: A Note on 'The Central Meaning of the First Amendment,' " *Sup. Ct. Rev.*, 1964: 191.
[90] 219 U.S. 1 (1911).

neer of the Suez Canal. In 1894 they were sold to another French company, Compagnie Nouvelle du Canal de Panama, and then in 1902 the United States acquired title for some $40 million.[91] The *World* charged that the assets were worth no more than $12 million and that President Roosevelt had lied to the nation by claiming that the purchase price was paid directly to the French government on behalf of Compagnie Nouvelle, whereas in fact the money went to J. P. Morgan and Company on behalf of an American syndicate that had bought out the troubled French company. Allegedly, that syndicate was composed of friends and relatives of Roosevelt and William Howard Taft.

At the time the articles appeared Taft had just been elected president. He did not claim publicly to have been libeled by the articles. But Roosevelt took a different view of the matter, and he, along with Charles P. Taft (Taft's brother), Elihu Root, and William Nelson Cromwell (who, it was rumored, was about to be made attorney general in the new Taft administration), claimed to have been defamed. They did not file a civil suit, but instead brought pressure on the attorney general to institute, in the name of the United States, a criminal libel in the federal court in New York. McReynolds, developing a First Amendment practice of sorts, once again represented the United States, this time as a special assistant to the attorney general.[92]

A century before, *United States v. Hudson*[93] had abolished the federal common law in criminal cases (that case, like *Press Publishing*, involved a criminal libel). As a result, the prosecution against the *World* was founded on the Assimilative Act of 1898, a federal statute that made applicable to federal reservations the law of the state in which the reservation was located.[94] New York had a criminal libel statute. The newspaper was published in New York City, hardly a federal reservation, but copies of the newspapers were delivered, so the indictment charged, to two federal reservations—the United States Military Academy at West Point and the Post Office Building in Manhattan—which were identified as the places where the assimilated federal crime took place.

Counsel for the *World* conceded that if read literally the Assimilative Act of 1898 would be sufficient to cover the case at bar, but argued that such a construction should be avoided if at all possible:

> According to the theory of the Government, the publication of a single newspaper article might constitute as many distinct crimes as there are

---

[91] On the Panama Canal, see Chapter 2, note 78 and accompanying text.

[92] In 1913, President Wilson appointed McReynolds as attorney general, and the very next year appointed him to the Court.

[93] 11 U.S. (7 Cranch) 32 (1812).

[94] Act of July 7, 1898, Ch. 576, Sect. 2, 30 Stat. 717.

places under the jurisdiction of the United States, in the whole country. It would thus be possible to crush an owner or editor, under an intolerable burden of crime.[95]

The chief justice agreed that such a construction of the Act would be absurd. The purpose of the Assimilative Act was to make sure that crimes committed on federal reservations would not go unpunished for want of jurisdiction, but here New York law was perfectly adequate. Regardless of what transpired at West Point or in the Post Office Building, the "composing and the primary publication"[96] of the allegedly libelous article and its general circulation took place in New York City and could be thus reached by state law. Moreover, White found that it would do violence to New York law to make publishing and circulating a libelous article separate crimes. New York contemplated only a single prosecution for each libelous article, and the Assimilative Act should not be read, White insisted, to frustrate that policy. The indictment should be dismissed.

Press Publishing was White's very first opinion as chief justice. He was nominated by Taft on December 12, 1910, took his seat the next week, and announced his opinion on January 3, 1911. The new chief justice must have been pleased that he was able to get all the justices, including Harlan, to join his opinion. The result, too, gave the press[97] and all those who cared about the First Amendment[98] reason to be pleased, especially when measured against *Patterson* or for that matter White's opinion fifteen years earlier in the Boston Commons case. But in terms of analysis and general perspective there was no warrant for this celebratory mood. *Press Publishing* was not a new beginning for free speech, as some have claimed,[99] but only more of the same.

In *Press Publishing*, White had found a way to stop an obviously contrived use of the federal courts to punish Pulitzer, but he did not take the federal courts out of the seditious libel business. White went out of his way to flag—and then leave unresolved—the question as to what would happen under the Assimilative Act in a case in which the crime was "wholly committed"[100] on a federal reservation. This measure of caution, excessive given the facts, might have reflected an unease (perhaps Harlan's or Hughes's—the latter replaced Brewer in 1910) with the underlying theory of the prosecution, seditious libel pure and simple, but there was nothing

---

[95] 219 U.S. at 6–7.

[96] Ibid., 15.

[97] The decision was welcomed by an editorial of the *World* as "the most sweeping victory won for freedom of speech and of the press in this country since the American people destroyed the Federalist party more than a century ago

for enacting the infamous Sedition law." *World*, Jan. 4, 1911, p. 10.

[98] See, e.g., "The Panama Libel Case," *Bench & Bar*, 24: 43, 48 (1911).

[99] Gibson, "Freedom of Expression," 293. Compare Rabban, "First Amendment in Its Forgotten Years," 540.

[100] 219 U.S. at 17.

reassuring in the opinion on that score. Indeed, the First Amendment never made an appearance in White's opinion; the entire analysis focused on the purpose of the Assimilative Act of 1898 and on the principle of New York law postulating the indivisibility of crime. As a result, no First Amendment restraints of any kind were placed on federal power in *Press Publishing*, and as for state prosecutions for seditious libel and its many cognates, the doors of the state courts were left exactly as White had found them—wide open.

CHAPTER XII

Plessy, *Alas*

F OR THE NEW DEAL GENERATION, Holmes's dissent in *Lochner* was of
the greatest importance, because it repudiated the constitutive theory of state power and made the New Deal constitutionally possible. For
the next generation, defined by its attachment to *Brown*, it was Harlan's
dissent in *Plessy v. Ferguson*[1] that was foundational. That dissent condemned a decision of the Fuller Court that had to be abandoned if justice
was ever to be done. The majority in *Plessy* sustained a Louisiana statute
requiring racial segregation on railways. Harlan denounced that decision
in no uncertain terms, declaring that it would become as infamous as *Dred
Scott*.

After the Civil War, racial segregation became an increasingly pervasive feature of life in the South. It was the social arrangement that replaced
slavery, though its form varied widely. Some institutions, such as juries,
excluded blacks entirely. Others, such as schools, set them apart in separate
facilities that were professed to be equal. Still others gave blacks access only
to inferior levels of accommodation, such as the smoking rooms on trains
or lower decks on steamboats, and denied them admission to first class
facilities.[2] The result was always the same. As historian Eric Foner notes,
"From church services to sporting events, blacks and whites went their separate ways."[3]

At first segregation was a matter of custom only, enforced by social
norms but not backed by law. Then, during the 1880s and early 1890s, this
pattern began to change. Desperate to win the support of discontented
farmers and to hold on to their power in the face of the rising tide of the
populists and the enormous tensions caused by recurrent and prolonged
economic depressions, many southern politicians took up the banner of
white supremacy. They passed laws that segregated employees, requiring
blacks and whites to work in separate rooms and to use separate entrances

---

[1] 163 U.S. 537 (1896).
[2] Eric Foner, *Reconstruction: America's Unfinished Revolution, 1863–1877*
(New York, Harper & Row, 1988),
371–72.
[3] Ibid., 593.

352

and bathrooms. The legislation they enacted also segregated trains, street cars, boarding houses, theatres, hospitals, and amusement parks.[4]

Immediately following the Civil War, the segregation in Louisiana was not so rigid or so all-embracing as in the rest of the South, in part because of the strength of the black community in New Orleans.[5] But by the late 1880s social practices in the state began to conform to the regional norm, and in 1890 Louisiana, following the pattern of her sister states, passed a statute requiring "equal, but separate accommodations" for blacks and whites on all passenger railways. The statute made an exception for street cars and for "nurses attending children of the other race."[6]

The Citizens' Committee to Test the Constitutionality of the Separate Car Law,[7] a black organization in New Orleans, decided to fight the statute in the courts. The committee turned to Albion Tourgée—no Darrow or Brandeis, certainly not a Carter, but a considerable figure in his times. Originally from Ohio, Tourgée fought in the Civil War and settled in Greensboro, North Carolina, in 1865. During Reconstruction he served as a state court judge. Throughout his life he was dedicated to the cause of equal rights, even to the point of becoming embroiled in a fight with the Klan, which of course had the last word. After leaving the bench, Tourgée turned to literary endeavors, and his most famous novel, *A Fool's Errand, by One of the Fools* (1879), was widely acclaimed as the "*Uncle Tom's Cabin* of Reconstruction." In the early 1890s he was living on Chautauqua Lake in western New York, one of the important cultural centers of late-nineteenth-century America.[8] In a column he wrote at that time for a progressive Chi-

---

[4] C. Vann Woodward, *The Strange Career of Jim Crow*, 3d ed. (New York: Oxford University Press, 1974), 82–93, 97–102. Professor Woodward argues that Jim Crow laws appeared at the very end of the nineteenth century, after several decades of fluidity in race relations. Joel Williamson in *The Crucible of Race: Black–White Relations in the American South since Emancipation* (New York: Oxford University Press, 1984), 253, dates the beginning of segregation law at 1882. Two subsequent waves of legislation, one in 1889–93, another in 1897–1907, pertained to public facilities. A third wave, coming in 1913–15, covered factories and urban housing.

[5] Charles A. Lofgren, *The Plessy Case: A Legal-Historical Interpretation* (New York: Oxford University Press, 1987), 16–17.

[6] Act 111, 1890 La. Acts 152, 153.

[7] Lofgren, *Plessy Case*, 29. The Citi-

zens' Committee was the successor to the American Citizens' Equal Rights Association, which fought the bill while it was pending in the legislature.

[8] An adult educational community was founded on Chautauqua Lake in 1874 by a Methodist Sunday School teacher and bishop, John Vincent, and Lewis Miller, a manufacturer. It combined religious study with recreational and cultural pursuits and offered lectures and public readings by such figures as Booker T. Washington, Eugene V. Debs, William Jennings Bryan, and Theodore Roosevelt. See James H. McBath, "The Emergence of Chautauqua as a Religious and Educational Institution, 1874–1900," *Methodist History*, vol. 20, no. 1, p. 3 (1981), and Theodore Morrison, *Chautauqua: A Center for Education, Religion and the Arts in America* (Chicago: University of Chicago Press, 1974).

cago newspaper, the *Inter Ocean*, he criticized the Louisiana statute. He urged his readers to join the civil rights organization he was forming to fight the law and to contribute whatever they could (which surely was not much).[9] Tourgée's brief in the Supreme Court was immortalized by Justice Harlan, who, without attribution, lifted the color-blind metaphor from it ("Our Constitution is color-blind. . . ."[10]). The brief was striking, both eloquent and moving, but in the end, it seemed the work of a legal Don Quixote.

Plessy was Tourgée's second attempt to test the Louisiana statute. The first turned out more favorably to his client, but broke no new legal ground and in fact built on an odd sort of precedent—*Hall v. DeCuir*[11]—an 1878 decision of the Supreme Court invalidating a Louisiana statute that prohibited discrimination. The statute at issue in *Hall*, enacted during the Reconstruction period, required common carriers to make no discrimination on account of race. The common carrier that challenged the statute was operating a steamship under a federally granted coastal license, and a passenger invoked the protection of the Louisiana statute while the ship was on a trip from New Orleans to Vicksburg, Mississippi. The Court held in *Hall* that requiring the carrier to provide accommodations on a non-discriminatory basis constituted an intrusion by the state into a matter left by the Commerce Clause exclusively to Congress.

After the collapse of Reconstruction in 1876, official state policy as represented by the statute at issue in *Hall* reversed itself, but the country's commitment to economic nationalism grew, and the constitutional doctrine that emerged seemed to affirm the nationalist principle underlying

---

[9] Steven Steinbach, "Tourgée and the Road to *Plessy*" (Yale Law School, 1979; unpublished manuscript on file with author), 30–31. Tourgée founded the National Citizens' Rights Association in 1891, the same year that he agreed to participate in the litigation testing the Louisiana statute. Initially, however, Tourgée considered delaying any such challenge until his civil rights organization had generated favorable public opinion. See Otto H. Olsen, *Carpetbagger's Crusade: The Life of Albion Winegar Tourgée* (Baltimore: Johns Hopkins Press, 1965), 312–31. For a biographical sketch of Tourgée, see also John Hope Franklin's preface to the 1961 edition of *A Fool's Errand*, published by Harvard University Press.

[10] 163 U.S. at 559. The full passage reads: "Our Constitution is color-blind, and neither knows nor tolerates classes among citizens. In respect of civil rights, all citizens are equal before the law." Compare with Brief of Plaintiff in Error at 19: "Justice is pictured blind and her daughter, the Law, ought at least to be color-blind." Noting Harlan's use of Tourgée's metaphor, one commentator added: "Several legal historians have wondered what Tourgée's source was. Now I am probably unique in that I have carefully read seven of Tourgée's novels all the way through, and I discovered that Tourgée, like Mozart, was simply repeating himself. These famous words first issued from the mouth of Hesden Le Moyne, the hero of *Bricks Without Straw* [1880]." Bonnie Mathews Wisdom, "The Case of the Crusading Carpetbagger" (New Orleans, 1975; unpublished manuscript on file with author), 25.

[11] 95 U.S. 485 (1878).

Hall and to limit the power of the states to further their ends, now segregation. The *Wabash* decision of 1886,[12] denying the states power to regulate rates on interstate trips, implied that states could not require racial segregation on interstate trips. A question remained, however, as to whether a state's Jim Crow laws could apply to the portion of an interstate trip that was wholly within the state. In 1890 in *Louisville, New Orleans, & Texas Railway v. Mississippi*,[13] the Supreme Court took up that question and, over the dissent of Bradley and Harlan, dismissed a Commerce Clause objection to a Mississippi statute that required all carriers, including those engaged in interstate transportation, to provide separate cars for whites and blacks when operating within the borders of the state.

Writing for the majority in the *Louisville, New Orleans & Texas Railway* case, Justice Brewer acknowledged that the separate car requirement would burden interstate transportation, insofar as it added to the carrier's expenses. But he allowed that burden on the theory that the requirement was no different from "state statutes requiring certain accommodations at depots, compelling trains to stop at crossings of other railroads, and a multitude of other matters confessedly within the power of the state."[14] In order to avoid the force of *Hall v. DeCuir*, Brewer emphasized that the only issue before the Court was the state's power to require railroads to provide separate accommodations on trains operating within the state, and he drew a distinction between the state's power over railroads and its authority to direct where passengers sat. "Obviously," he said, "whether interstate passengers of one race should, in any portion of their journey, be compelled to share their cabin accommodations with passengers of another race, was a question of interstate commerce, and to be determined by Congress alone."[15]

The 1890 Louisiana statute was virtually identical to the Mississippi one.[16] Section 1 required all carriers operating in the state to have separate cars for blacks and whites, while Section 2 required separate seating assignments. Brewer's decision in the Mississippi case foreclosed any Commerce Clause objections to Section 1 of the Louisiana statute, but not with respect to Section 2. As a purely analytic matter, it is hard to see much of a distinction between the two. One provision burdens the interstate carrier, the other the interstate traveler, and if the Commerce Clause allowed the state to burden one, it is hard to understand why it could not burden the other. In purpose and effect the two provisions were identical. Nonetheless, Brewer scrupulously had avoided ruling on the seating provision of the Mississippi statute, and when Tourgée invoked the Commerce Clause in his

---

[12] Wabash, St. L. & P. Ry. v. Illinois, 118 U.S. 557 (1886). See Chapters 7 and 9.

[13] 133 U.S. 587 (1890).

[14] Ibid., 591.

[15] Ibid., 590–91.

[16] Ch. 27, 1888 Miss. Laws 48; Act 111, 1890 La. Acts 153, 153.

first test of the Louisiana statute—*State v. Desdunes*[17]—presumably he was trying to obtain a favorable ruling on that very issue. Despite the suggestion in Brewer's opinion that the essential feature of the law invalidated in *Hall* was its requirement that travelers of different races share accommodations, Tourgée hoped that *Hall* rather than *Louisville, New Orleans & Texas Railway* would control on the theory that Brewer had drawn a distinction between a law regulating railroads and a law regulating passengers, as opposed to a distinction between a law prohibiting discrimination and one requiring it.

Daniel Desdunes, the passenger first chosen to test the Louisiana statute, held a ticket from New Orleans to Mobile, Alabama, and was prosecuted for violating the Louisiana statute. While that case was still pending at the trial level, however, the Supreme Court of Louisiana held in still another case that, under the *Hall* decision, reinforced by *Wabash*, the Louisiana statute could not be applied to interstate passengers: "[E]ither the statute has no application to interstate passengers, or, if it has, . . . it is, as to them, unconstitutional and void."[18] This ruling, soon to be overtaken by decisions of the United States Supreme Court,[19] covered Desdunes and the prosecution against him was soon summarily dismissed.

---

[17] Case No. 18,685, Crim. Dist. Ct., Parish of Orleans, 1892, Supreme Court of Louisiana Collection of Legal Archives, Department of Archives, Manuscripts, and Special Collections, Earl K. Long Library, University of New Orleans. For a description of this case and its relation to *Plessy*, see Lofgren, *Plessy Case*, 32–41.

[18] State *ex rel.* Abbott v. Hicks, 44 La. Ann. 770, 778, 11 So. 74, 76 (1892).

[19] The Supreme Court did not directly decide this issue, but nonetheless crafted a set of rules that subjected black interstate passengers to segregation laws while effectively foreclosing their opportunity to challenge those laws. In Chesapeake & O. Ry. v. Kentucky, 179 U.S. 388 (1900), the Court accepted the state court's construction that its separate car statute had no interstate effect, thereby avoiding the question of whether the state could segregate interstate passengers by race. This was followed by Chiles v. Chesapeake, 218 U.S. 71 (1910), in which an interstate passenger was forced to move to a segregated car when his train entered the state of Kentucky. That case raised the question of the state's power over interstate passengers directly, but the Court

avoided the issue by allowing the railroad to defend its action solely as a matter of its own regulation, disregarding the fact that this regulation was required by Kentucky's separate car law. Finally, in McCabe v. Atchison, Topeka & Santa Fe Ry., 235 U.S. 151 (1914), the Court held that it would not consider the interstate impact of a state's separate car law unless the state court explicitly held that the law had such an impact—a most unlikely event, given these rulings. The opinion in *McCabe* was written by Charles Evan Hughes, Brewer's replacement. In a letter to Holmes, Hughes passionately objected to the failure of the Oklahoma statute there in issue to require the railway to provide blacks with sleeping cars, dining cars or chair cars, describing it as "a bald, wholly unjustified discrimination against a passenger solely on account of race." Hughes to Holmes, Nov. 29, 1914, Holmes Papers, Harvard Law School Library Manuscript Division. Hughes expressed similar sentiments in his opinion, yet he avoided any ruling on that aspect of the statute on the ground that the pleadings did not adequately allege that the plaintiffs had requested and been denied equal accommoda-

Chapter XII: *Plessy*

Desdunes was free, but that was not the point of the exercise. The 1890 Louisiana statute was still in force against persons traveling only within the state; the *Louisville, New Orleans & Texas Railway* decision foreclosed the Commerce Clause objection to separate car requirements; and the Louisiana supreme court decision limiting the seating requirement had no effect outside the state. Jim Crow was very much alive. Accordingly, the Citizens' Committee needed another person to test the statute, this time an intrastate passenger, and for that purpose they turned to Homer A. Plessy, a friend of Desdunes's father. Plessy purchased a ticket from New Orleans to Covington, Louisiana, thereby taking the Commerce Clause out of the case and leaving only the Thirteenth and Fourteenth Amendments as the basis of his claim. Like Desdunes, Plessy was criminally prosecuted for violating the Louisiana statute, but this time around, the charge and the requirements of the 1890 statute as applied to Plessy were upheld by the state courts.

Of the various lines of argument then open to Tourgée in the United States Supreme Court, there was one that was fully consistent with the jurisprudence of the era. It now goes by the name of substantive due process, and at its core appeals to the constitutive theory of the state. By this argument the State of Louisiana would be charged with exceeding the bounds of the police power when it enacted the separate accommodations statute, as New York did when it passed the maximum hours statute overturned in *Lochner*. The claim would be that the Louisiana statute constituted an infringement of liberty, which, as we have seen, was the residue belonging to the individual after the state had been brought to the limits of its authority.

As history would eventually indicate, this line of argument had its difficulties and indeed would ultimately fail, but the approach Tourgée chose was even less likely to succeed. There are many different arguments in Tourgée's brief, including fragments of a substantive due process claim, but for the most part Tourgée, far, far ahead of his time, focused on equality rather than liberty. He called for a new understanding of American citizenship, and in doing so he displayed a talent that belonged more to the poet than the lawyer. Tourgée sensed his limitations—he once wrote to local counsel, James C. Walker, to explain why he was deferring to him on a question of procedure: "A man who has been substantially out of practice for half a dozen years, has no right to an opinion on such points beside one who has been in the traces right along."[20] Unfortunately, Tourgée's conception of citizenship was equally shaky.

---

tions. For a more generous interpretation of *McCabe*, see Alexander M. Bickel and Benno C. Schmidt, Jr., *The Judiciary and Responsible Government, 1910–21*, vol. 9 of *History of the Supreme Court of the United States*

(New York: Macmillan, 1984), 775–84.

[20] Tourgée to Walker, Jan. 14, 1892 (quoted in Lofgren, *Plessy Case*, 40, note 22). The quoted sentence was taken from Tourgée's copybook, Tourgée Papers, Chautauqua County Historical

Before the Civil War the states had been the primary source of the rights and duties of individuals. The war, Tourgée argued, not only put an end to slavery but also altered the significance of state citizenship: It made the individual first and foremost a citizen of the nation and only secondarily a citizen of a state. This change in the nature of citizenship also entailed an expansion of the power of the national government, for it now fell to national institutions to determine the substance of national citizenship— the rights and duties of the citizens of the nation. Referring to the provision of Section 1 of the Fourteenth Amendment conferring citizenship ("any person born in the United States is a citizen of the United States and the State in which he resides"), Tourgée wrote:

> This provision of Section 1 of the Fourteenth Amendment *creates* a *new* citizenship of the United States embracing *new* rights, privileges and immunities derivable in a *new* manner, controlled by *new* authority, having a *new* scope and extent, dependent on national authority for its existence.[21]

Tourgée insisted that this new idea of national citizenship demanded a measure of equality and that it was at odds with Jim Crow, which he depicted as a method of perpetuating the caste structure of slave times. He pointed to the exception for nurses in the statute and explained how it illuminated the underlying purposes of the law:

> In other words, the act is simply intended to promote the comfort and sense of exclusiveness and superiority of the white races. They do not object to the colored person in an inferior or menial capacity—as a servant or dependent, ministering to the comfort of the white race—but only when as a man and a citizen he seeks to claim equal right and privileges on a public highway with the white citizens of the state.[22]

Although Jim Crow laws did not involve the ownership of human beings or, to borrow Tourgée's term, "chattelism,"[23] they nonetheless were a means of reducing blacks to a "condition of utter helplessness and dependence,"[24] which Tourgée believed was "the result and essential concomitant of slavery."[25]

Tourgée's understanding of the social significance of Jim Crow was exceptional. But his notion of national citizenship—his effort to link his sociological insight to legal doctrine—was another matter. However faith-

---

Society, Westfield, New York (microfilmed, Kent State University), and was dated by Professor Lofgren on the basis of references in other correspondence.
[21] Brief of Plaintiff in Error at 12.

[22] Ibid., 31.
[23] Ibid., 33.
[24] Ibid., 32.
[25] Ibid., 33.

ful that idea might have been to the original understanding of the Civil War amendments and to the underlying purposes of Reconstruction,[26] it was completely at odds with major precedents of the era, including the *Civil Rights Cases*.[27] That decision held that the Civil War amendments did not allow Congress to bar private, as opposed to state, discrimination. The regulation of the action of one person against another was the exclusive province of the states, and this view was predicated on the notion that even after the Civil War, the individual's relationship to his or her state remained the primary juridical relationship. State citizenship was paramount, national citizenship subordinate and incidental. This more traditional view of American citizenship was never spelled out fully in the *Civil Rights Cases*, and thus may not have been grasped fully by Tourgée, but the Court had been as explicit as was possible on the point in a case that had figured prominently in Harlan's dissent in *Patterson v. Colorado*.[28] That case was *United States v. Cruikshank*,[29] a precursor to, and an essential building block of, the *Civil Rights Cases*.

Cruikshank, decided in 1876 as Reconstruction collapsed, dismissed a federal indictment against a gang of whites who had disrupted a political meeting of black Republicans. The Court's decision was based on the theory that the federal government was only a government among governments and that it thus had a limited jurisdiction. The national power could intervene when states abused their powers; it could also protect from all interferences, state and private, a circumscribed category of rights that were related to distinctly national functions such as petitioning to Congress. Except in these narrow circumstances, however, states were the sole guardians of their citizens' rights. This was the conception of citizenship upon which the *Civil Rights Cases* was based. That decision did leave room for federal intervention when states actively denied citizens their rights, and Tourgée tried to turn this aspect of the *Civil Rights Cases* to his favor. A state statute was involved and thus the state action requirement was satisfied. However, Tourgée still had to demonstrate that the statute violated the Fourteenth Amendment, and it was for that purpose that he argued for a new conception of citizenship. To his great misfortune, *Cruikshank* and the postulates underlying the *Civil Rights Cases* precluded such an argument, but he faced up to the difficulty. As he confessed, "It is freely admitted that Cruikshank's case is squarely against us."[30]

---

[26] See Foner, *Reconstruction*, 228–80.

[27] 109 U.S. 3 (1883).

[28] 205 U.S. 454, 465 (1907). See Chapter 11, text accompanying note 82.

[29] 92 U.S. 542 (1875).

[30] Brief of Plaintiff in Error at 26. Samuel F. Phillips, who served as co-counsel in *Plessy* in the Supreme Court, and who was solicitor general in the Grant administration, argued and lost *Cruikshank* as well as the *Civil Rights Cases*. Phillips was a friend of Tourgée's from his Greensboro days.

As it turned out, no one on the Court, Harlan included, was prepared to accept Tourgée's approach or willing to overrule *Cruikshank*; in fact, in *Plessy* no one even mentioned that case, indicating how out of touch Tourgée was with the Court's mood. Although Harlan ruled in Tourgée's favor and went so far as to borrow one of his metaphors, he showed no inclination whatsoever toward embracing Tourgée's more radical idea of national citizenship. Harlan had dissented in the *Civil Rights Cases*, but he did not there urge that *Cruikshank* be overruled, nor did his dissent in that case argue for a new conception of citizenship; it was primarily based on his belief that the Thirteenth Amendment gave Congress broad powers to eliminate the badges and incidents of slavery. Nor was there anything radical about Harlan's position in *Plessy*. As we will see, he accepted the framework of the majority, merely applying their principles differently. This is not to deny the significance of Harlan's dissent in *Plessy*, but only to mark an important difference between it and Tourgée's brief, and to underscore the visionary quality of Tourgée's argument and his insistence upon a new understanding of American citizenship.

The majority opinion in *Plessy*, written by Justice Brown, stayed within the traditional contractarian framework. At one point, Brown addressed a property argument that, like everything else, found its way into Tourgée's brief. Homer Plessy was, as the brief put it, "of mixed Caucasian and African blood, in the proportion of one-eighth African and seven-eighths Caucasian."[31] His body was a powerful testament to the absurdity and arbitrariness of a legal regime that sought to classify people according to race.[32] How was the state to decide who was black and who was white? It is possible that Plessy was chosen to test the Louisiana statute to dramatize the impossibility of ever answering that question, and in his brief Tourgée described movingly the plight of an individual of mixed ancestry trying to find his place in a world defined by Jim Crow:

> The crime then, for which he became liable to imprisonment so far as the court can ascertain, was that a person of seven-eighths Caucasian blood insisted in sitting peacefully and quietly in a car the State of Louisiana had commanded the company to set aside exclusively for the white race. Where on earth should he have gone? Will the court hold that a single drop of African blood is sufficient to color a whole ocean of Caucasian whiteness?[33]

---

[31] Ibid., 3.
[32] See Barbara J. Fields, "Ideology and Race in American History," in J. Morgan Kousser, ed., *Region, Race and Reconstruction: Essays in Honor of C. Vann Woodward* (New York: Oxford University Press, 1982), 143, 144. See generally George Fredrickson, *The Black Image in the White Mind: The Debate on Afro-American Character and Destiny, 1817–1914* (New York: Harper & Row, 1971), 71–96.
[33] Brief of Plaintiff in Error at 31.

Chapter XII: *Plessy*

Then he tried to transform Plessy's dilemma—"Where on earth should he have gone?"—into a property argument of sorts, as though Jim Crow constituted a taking. Tourgée—a white man—described the Louisiana statute as conferring upon the "conductor the power to deprive one of the reputation of being a white man, or at least to impair that reputation."[34] Then he categorized this alleged reputational interest as property:

> Probably most white persons if given a choice, would prefer death to life in the United States *as colored persons*. Under these conditions is it possible to conclude that the *reputation of being white* is not property? Indeed, is it not the most valuable sort of property, being the master key that unlocks the golden door of opportunity?[35]

Justice Brown was engaged by this argument (as opposed to the one for national citizenship), but quickly disposed of it in the following terms:

> If he be a white man and assigned to a colored coach, he may have his action for damages against the company for being deprived of his so called property. Upon the other hand, if he be a colored man and be so assigned, he has been deprived of no property, since he is not lawfully entitled to the reputation of a being white man.[36]

So much for the legal mind.

Once the property issue was removed from the case, Justice Brown brushed aside the Thirteenth Amendment argument in Tourgée's brief. He noted that no servitude was involved. Then Brown took up what was for him—and the rest of the Court, though not for Tourgée—the central issue: Did the Louisiana statute deprive Plessy of his liberty? Under established doctrine, the duty of the Court was, first, to ascertain the purpose of the legislation, then to see whether that purpose was allowed the state under the police power, and finally to determine whether the relationship between means and end was sufficiently direct. In his opinion for the Court, Justice Brown honored this doctrine, pursued each of these inquiries, and then concluded that the Louisiana statute was within the police power of the state and thus constitutional.

When this same method was later applied in *Lochner* (which Brown joined), the results were dramatically different. In *Plessy,* however, the Court found no infringement of liberty, as though blacks were not members of the constitutional community and the Civil War and the amendments it produced had never been.[37] Many factors may have accounted for this

---

34 Ibid., 9.
35 Ibid.
36 163 U.S. at 549.
37 Brown's opinion in *Plessy* was superficially different from his opinion in the *Insular Cases*, in which he disavowed the contractarian framework. But, in reality, once account is taken of how the doctrine was applied, the two cases were not very different.

result and the contrast with *Lochner*. One of the less pernicious is tradition. When Jim Crow emerged in legal garb in the 1880s and 1890s, the statutes then enacted, such as the Louisiana one, codified and strengthened existing social practices. The New York statute, in contrast, tried to reverse social practices that were driven by market competition.

Another factor that distinguished *Lochner* and *Plessy* was precedent. While the Court's decision in *Holden v. Hardy*,[38] written by Brown, may have constrained the Court in *Lochner*, that decision was hardly of the same stature as the *Civil Rights Cases*, the precedent that controlled *Plessy*. The *Civil Rights Cases* had declared that regulating the relationship between citizen and citizen was the business of the states, and given the specific ruling of that case—the Supreme Court invalidated a federal equal accommodations statute—there seemed little doubt that it was within the powers of the states to decide whether they wished to have that kind of law or, more realistically, its very opposite. Thus while *Plessy* may have been a test case, the *Civil Rights Cases* rendered its outcome a foregone conclusion. Nowhere in the nation was the decision front page news. The major northern newspapers gave it only the most cursory attention, treating it as page seven railway news.[39] The major southern newspapers were more attentive;[40] so were the newspapers of the black community,[41] but even they did not depict it as a constitutional turning point in the history of race relations. For most, that point had occurred in 1883, in the *Civil Rights Cases*.[42]

Harlan's dissent in *Plessy* was thoroughly consistent with his dissent in the *Civil Rights Cases*—indeed, memories of his defeat in the *Civil Rights Cases* may have engendered the angry and passionate tone of his dis-

---

[38] 169 U.S. 366 (1898). See generally Chapter 6.

[39] The *New York Times*, May 19, 1896, p. 3, covered the ruling under railroad news; the *Washington Post*, May 19, 1896, p. 6, devoted two paragraphs to the majority opinion and one paragraph to the dissent; and the *Chicago Tribune*, May 19, 1896, p. 10, described it only in the briefest terms. See Stephen Good, "A Non-Event: *Plessy v. Ferguson*" (Yale Law School, 1979; unpublished manuscript on file with author), 3–4.

[40] See, e.g., *New Orleans Times-Picayune*, May 19, 1896, p. 4; *Atlanta Constitution*, May 22, 1896, p. 4; and *Richmond Dispatch*, May 21, 1896, p. 4. See Good, "*Plessy v. Ferguson*," 4–5.

[41] See, e.g., *Parson* [Kansas] *Weekly Blade*, May 30, 1896, p. 2; *Cleveland Gazette*, May 30, 1896, p. 2; and *Washington Bee*, May 23, 1896, p. 4. See Otto

H. Olsen, ed., *The Thin Disguise: Turning Point in Negro History—Plessy v. Ferguson, A Documentary Presentation, 1864–1896* (New York: Humanities Press, 1967), and Good, "*Plessy v. Ferguson*," 10–12.

[42] See Loren Miller, *The Petitioners: The Story of the Supreme Court of the United States and the Negro* (Cleveland: World Publishing, 1966), 145. Harold M. Hyman and William M. Wiecek, *Equal Justice under Law: Constitutional Development, 1835–1875* (New York: Harper & Row, 1982), 487–88, identify the Slaughter-House Cases, 83 U.S. 36 (1873), as the first example of the Court's insistence that the authority to define and protect civil rights lay with the states rather than the federal government, though they acknowledge the significance of the decisions occurring during Chief Justice Waite's years.

sent in *Plessy*. But Harlan's opinion in *Plessy*, like Brown's, was primarily an essay on liberty. Harlan took the contractarian framework as seriously in the race cases as elsewhere. "The fundamental objection . . . to the statute," he said, "is that it interferes with the personal freedom of citizens."[43] The specific freedom that Justice Harlan had in mind was the freedom of an individual to travel with whomever he wished. Harlan did not believe that this freedom had an independent existence in the way that property or (as we saw in his *Patterson* dissent) freedom of speech did, but rather that its boundaries or content were derived from the limitations placed on the authority of the state. The state could limit the freedom to travel by using its police power, but he saw the Louisiana statute as exceeding the police power and, thus, as an unconstitutional interference with liberty. Summarizing the principles that reigned supreme during Fuller's tenure, Harlan encapsulated the method that dominated both his opinion and the majority's in *Plessy* in a single sentence: "The adjudged cases in which statutes have been held to be void, because unreasonable, are those in which the means employed by the legislature were not at all germane to the end to which the legislature was competent."[44]

In determining whether a statute was within the police power, Harlan was never much interested in the first part of his test, means–end rationality, but he had no reluctance in overturning statutes once he sensed an impermissible end. In *Lochner*, there was no question about the permissibility of the end postulated for the statute—health—but only a disagreement over the means chosen to further that end. He dissented in *Lochner* because he was willing to allow the legislature a wider latitude on instrumental questions than was the majority. In *Adair*, however, he doubted the permissibility of the end. He thought that in outlawing yellow dog contracts Congress was trying to enhance the power of one group (labor) at the expense of another (capital) and that such a redistributive end was impermissible or, as he might have put it, beyond the competence of the state. Speaking for the majority in *Adair*, he held the Erdman Act unconstitutional because it sought an impermissible end, and in *Plessy* he came to a similar conclusion about the Louisiana statute.

Harlan's dissent in *Plessy* was only an application of the principle of *Adair*, extending it from economic to racial groups. He objected to the Louisiana statute on the ground that its purpose was to favor one group (whites) over another (blacks). Such an end was, Harlan felt, beyond the competence of any state. To define the range of permissible state ends he drew upon the Civil War, the post-war amendments, and above all, the principle requiring all citizens, including blacks, to be treated as equals. As Harlan formulated the principle in another discrimination case decided the same

---

[43] 163 U.S. at 557. | [44] Ibid., 559.

year, "All citizens are equal before the law."[45] The role of the equal-treatment principle in Harlan's dissent in *Plessy*, and the connection between that dissent and his opinion in *Adair*, one applying the principle to economic groups, the other to racial ones, is manifest in the most memorable passage of Harlan's dissent—perhaps the most famous utterance of his entire judicial career: "Our Constitution is color-blind, and neither knows nor tolerates classes among citizens. In respect of civil rights, all citizens are equal before the law."[46]

Justice McKenna argued in *Adair*, by way of dissent, that the purpose of the Erdman Act was industrial peace, not, as Harlan claimed, the enhancement of the power of labor. Similarly, in *Plessy*, Brown disputed Harlan's assessment of the purpose of the Louisiana statute. Brown subscribed to the principle of equal treatment and probably (God only knows) would have agreed that a statute could not stand if its end or purpose were to enhance the power of one class or group over another, whether the opposing groups be labor and capital or whites and blacks. Given Brown's position in the *Insular Cases*, one may doubt whether he genuinely believed blacks were members of the constitutional community, fully entitled to the protection of liberty and all that it implied, but here he spoke for the Court, not himself, and did not dispute Harlan at the level of theory. Rather, like McKenna in *Adair*, he simply denied Harlan's understanding of the purpose of the Louisiana statute.

This was the burden of the most famous—or infamous—passage of Brown's opinion:

> We consider the underlying fallacy of the plaintiff's argument to consist in the assumption that the enforced separation of the two races stamps the colored race with a badge of inferiority. If this be so, it is not by reason of anything found in the act, but solely because the colored race chooses to put that construction upon it.[47]

Brown's point was not to suggest, as some (once including myself) have read this passage, that the perception by blacks of Jim Crow as an insult would be unfounded or gratuitous, but only that racial degradation or the maintenance of white supremacy was not the purpose or end of the statute: That illicit purpose cannot be based on "anything found in the act." Brown, again like McKenna in *Adair*, hypothesized a much more benign purpose for the statute, one that presumably did not transgress the principle of equal treatment. As Brown put it,

---

[45] Gibson v. Mississippi, 162 U.S. 565, 591 (1896).

[46] 163 U.S. at 559.
[47] Ibid., 551.

> In determining the question of reasonableness, [the legislature] is at liberty to act with reference to the established usages, customs and traditions of the people, and with a view to the promotion of their comfort, and the preservation of the public peace and good order.[48]

In this debate over the purpose of the statute, there were no references to legislative history or the politics of Louisiana. Although Brown and Harlan might well have been seeking to determine the actual psychology or intention of the legislators, they confined their inquiry to the statute itself, as though purpose were an attribute of the statute. They agreed that in order for a statute to be a proper exercise of the police power it would have to have a public purpose, but they disagreed as to whether this statute had such a purpose. Harlan insisted, as did Tourgée, that the statute could only be understood or interpreted as a measure to favor one class or group over another. Brown's reference, in the passage just quoted, to "the established usages, customs and traditions of the people" was hardly responsive to Harlan's objection; nor was Brown's remark about promoting their "comfort." Who were "the people"? In both instances, Brown was not so much denying the class purpose of the legislation as he was describing it more indirectly. The customs and comfort Brown spoke about only reified unequal treatment.

The reference to "preservation of the public peace and good order" spoke more to Harlan's concerns. Both Harlan and Brown shared the conviction that the maintenance of peace was, as *Debs* indicated, a public purpose of great urgency, a conviction reinforced by the growth of racial violence in the 1890s.[49] But where Harlan saw segregation as fostering social tension, Brown believed it served to keep the peace. In *Adair*, Harlan denounced McKenna's industrial peace rationale as a species of blackmail,[50] and he similarly felt that Brown's justification of segregation in *Plessy* licensed supremacists to create a public purpose simply by threatening violence if the state did not acquiesce in their demands.

Many have taken the Court's decision in *Brown v. Board of Education* as a vindication of Harlan's position in *Plessy*, and then have read Earl Warren's opinion back into Harlan's dissent. But Harlan worked within the contractarian tradition and analyzed the case in terms of liberty, while for Warren the fundamental issue was one of equality. In saying this I am not making a point about terminology, for as he proved in *Bolling v. Sharpe*,[51] which held school segregation in the District of Columbia a denial of due process, Warren was able to achieve his purposes even under the rubric of

---

[48] Ibid., 550.
[49] See Williamson, *Crucible of Race*, 180–223.

[50] See Chapter 6, p. 171.
[51] 347 U.S. 497 (1954).

liberty—a practice denied to the states, he said, could not be allowed to flourish in the nation's capital. No, the shift in Warren's thinking from liberty to equality represented something far more fundamental: an abandonment of the constitutive theory of the state, and a willingness to judge a statute unconstitutional even if it were within the police powers of the state.

Harlan also spoke of equality in his dissent in *Plessy*, but like Justice Brown and the rest of the *Plessy* Court, he understood that concept within the contractarian framework. Equality was a matter of treating equals equally, and it operated as a "side constraint" (to borrow Robert Nozick's term);[52] that is, it demarcated the range of permissible state purposes. On the other hand, when Warren spoke of equality, he had in mind something quite different. Equality referred to the principle—not so different from that attached to Tourgée's expanded notion of national citizenship—that condemned the creation or maintenance of a caste structure (the hierarchical ordering of various social groups on the basis of ascriptive criteria).[53] Equality was substantive rather than procedural. This principle of substantive equality did not operate as a side constraint—it did not merely place limits on state authority. Rather, it identified the constitutional wrong and thus defined the violation.

Under the theory of *Brown v. Board of Education*, once an inequality was identified a further inquiry would be undertaken to determine whether, to use the balancing metaphor, the deprivation of equality was outweighed by considerations furthered by the measure. In that respect, Harlan's approach in *Plessy* parallels that of the modern civil rights lawyer, for in each there is an examination of the interests served by the statute. There are, however, two differences. In the modern context more emphasis is placed on the justification as opposed to the purpose of the statute; a more objective conception of purpose is used. Moreover, the function of this inquiry into ends is not to determine whether the measure is within the police power of the state, but only to determine whether the violation of the principle of substantive equality might somehow be excused or tolerated. In *Brown*, the evil of Jim Crow was the inequality, or unjustified inequality, understood in substantive terms, not—as it appeared to Harlan in *Plessy*, or for that matter, in *Adair*—an excess of the police power or a transgression by the state into the sphere of liberty belonging to the individual. In *Lochner*, Holmes was prophetic as to both result and theory; for Harlan in *Plessy*, only the result was prophetic.

---

[52] Robert Nozick, *Anarchy, State and Utopia* (New York: Basic Books, 1974), 28.

[53] See Owen M. Fiss, "Groups and the Equal Protection Clause," *Phil. & Pub. Aff.*, 5: 107 (1976).

Chapter XII: *Plessy*

I

Because *Plessy* involved a statute governing seating on a railroad, the restriction on liberty was easily perceived: A public space was divided so as to prevent whites from entering one area and blacks another. This perception was based on the general understanding—reflected in *Debs* and all the rate regulation cases of the era—that railroads were analogous to public highways. Harlan drew on this understanding in *Plessy* and compared the Louisiana statute requiring segregated rail cars to one that divided the public streets, with blacks on one side, whites on the other. Such a state regulation would be puzzling in the extreme, making the question of authority—is the statute within the police power?—hard to answer in the affirmative.

In other settings, however, not involving public places or streets but various state enterprises far more removed from the state of nature hypothesized by social contract theorists, it proves more difficult to locate the liberty interest or to formulate the question about state authority quite so sharply. This difficulty is encountered, for example, in the area of public education, especially during the nineteenth century, when the state not only had to decide which school a child should attend, but also whether there would be state schools at all and if so, whether attending them should be mandatory. In the context of public education—which is, after all, the specific context of *Brown v. Board of Education*—a method of analysis that did no more than put the state to the burden of proving that it was acting within its authority would seem an unpromising foundation for strong exercises of the judicial power. The authority of the state would appear all encompassing, and liberty would shrink to almost nothing.

A test of these generalizations occurred in 1899, only three years after *Plessy*, in *Cumming v. Richmond County Board of Education*,[54] a case involving a Georgia school district that operated on a separate and unequal basis. For whites, the school district operated elementary schools and a high school. For blacks, the board operated only elementary schools. It once had operated a high school for blacks, the Ware High School, but later discontinued the institution. The board denied that black children were barred from a high school, "since for the same charges as were made by this Board for pupilage in the Ware High School they can find this education in three other colored high schools open to the public in the city of Augusta."[55] These other schools, however, were sectarian institutions, and for that reason the plaintiffs protested the decision to close Ware. Plaintiffs were represented by Senator George Edmunds, who, unlike Tourgée, was hardly a

---

[54] 175 U.S. 528 (1899). | [55] Ibid., 534.

quixotic figure,[56] yet the Supreme Court upheld the school board. The decision was unanimous, and the opinion of the Court was, of course, written by "the great dissenter."

Harlan's opinion in *Cumming* was not a retreat from his dissent in *Plessy*,[57] but instead revealed more clearly than ever that his position in *Plessy* was based not on an assessment of the consequences of segregation for the status of blacks, the vision that Earl Warren made law in *Brown*, but rather on a judgment that the state had exceeded the bounds of the police power. The focus of Harlan's opinion was on the board's decision to discontinue the black high school, which he depicted as a model of economic rationality:

> The Board had before it the question of whether it should maintain, under its control, a high school for about sixty colored children or withhold the benefits of education in primary schools from three hundred children of the same race.[58]

In this passage the emphasis was on the numbers—300 students versus 60. Elsewhere Harlan expressed a concern with the content of the educational program—a high school education versus "an opportunity in primary schools to learn the alphabet and to read and write."[59] But under either account, he saw the decision of the board as a trade-off. The board was judging how to best spend its funds, and Harlan viewed this decision, both practically and normatively, as crucially different from, and less reviewable than, a decision to restrict an individual's liberty. As Harlan emphasized, "[I]t is impracticable to distribute taxes equally."[60]

From the perspective of *Brown*, one might focus on the racial element present in the description of the trade-off—the value of *black* elementary schools was being balanced against the value of a *black* high school. The board's decision also could be faulted for the impact it would have on the education of blacks and on their standing in the community. But within a legal framework that stressed liberty rather than equality, neither circumstance seemed especially important. The authority of localities to decide how to spend public funds was, in Harlan's mind, all-embracing, and whatever limits might have existed were not sensitive to the racial character of the options considered or to the effects on blacks of a particular allocation. To make this abundantly clear, and to generalize the conclusion in *Cum-*

---

[56] Edmunds represented the State of Vermont in the United States Senate from 1866 to 1891.

[57] This differs from the interpretation of J. Morgan Kousser, *Dead End: The Development of Nineteenth-Century Lit-* *igation on Racial Discrimination in Schools* (Oxford: Clarendon Press, 1986), 27.

[58] 175 U.S. at 544.

[59] Ibid.

[60] Ibid., 542.

ming beyond the particulars of the case, Harlan closed his opinion by announcing a broad hands-off policy with respect to public education, fully revealing the limits of the received method of protecting liberty and thus also of his *Plessy* dissent:

> We may add that while all admit that the benefits and burdens of public taxation must be shared by citizens without discrimination against any class on account of their race, the education of the people in schools maintained by state taxation is a matter belonging to the respective States, and any interference on the part of Federal authority with the management of such schools cannot be justified except in the case of a clear and unmistakable disregard of rights secured by the supreme law of the land.[61]

Harlan was firm in declaring that Louisiana had exceeded its authority in enacting the Jim Crow statute in *Plessy*, but he was equally emphatic that there had been no similar excess in *Cumming*.

Although I do not see *Cumming* as a retreat from his dissent in *Plessy*, but only as a confirmation of the limits of that dissent, still one can only wonder what Fuller had in mind when he assigned Harlan the responsibility of speaking for the Court. Harlan could not have taken any special pleasure in this assignment, especially given his emotional investment in *Plessy*, and his unease in discharging this responsibility might well account for the technical sparring that characterizes his opinion. At one point, Harlan complained of the plaintiffs' failure to ask for an affirmative injunction compelling the board to establish and operate a high school for blacks. He did not indicate that the result would have been different if they had done so, but only that "different questions might have arisen in the state court."[62] It is hard to figure out, however, what might have been the basis of Harlan's tantalizing suggestion. There is little practical difference between an affirmative injunction and the particular negative injunction actually sought in this case, between a flat ban on funding the white high school and a conditional one forbidding the use of public funds to support a white high school unless and until the Ware High School was reopened.

In a similar vein, Harlan pointed out that no objection had been raised to the segregated character of the school system, and then proceeded to ignore the segregation issue and focus solely on the closing of the Ware High School. But given the majority's position in *Plessy*, and the way Harlan himself treated the school closing issue, it is inconceivable that an objection to the segregated character of the school system would have succeeded. Only with a shift in context from public to private education, where no

---

[61] Ibid., 545.

[62] Ibid.

issue of public finance arose, could the issue of school segregation surface, for only then could an objection based on liberty, the focal point of Harlan's analysis in *Plessy*, acquire any force.

That shift came with *Berea College v. Kentucky*,[63] decided in 1908. The case arose from a prosecution of an integrated school under a Kentucky statute that made it a crime "for any person, corporation, or association of persons to maintain or operate any college, school or institution where persons of the white and negro races are both received as pupils for instruction."[64] Because the school was private, there were no issues of public finance, and thus the state could not invoke, as it had in *Cumming*, the right to devise its own budgets and spend its funds as it chose. Moreover, in this case segregation was being enforced in a way that threatened liberties analogous to those celebrated in *Lochner* and *Adair* (the latter, in fact, was decided the same year as *Berea College*), for the statute interfered with the contractual arrangements between students and teachers. These differences from *Cumming* enabled Harlan to return to his role as the dissenter (this time joined by Day, though not by the other new appointees, Moody and Holmes) and made the task of Justice Brewer, the spokesman for the majority, especially difficult. Brewer had not participated in the *Plessy* case, but he had joined Harlan's opinion in *Cumming* and some years earlier, while sitting on the Kansas supreme court, indicated that he was no friend of the desegregation of the public schools.[65]

In *Berea College*, Brewer returned to a theme he addressed several years earlier in his *Northern Securities* concurrence, in which he had struggled to come to terms with the increasing tide of corporatism.[66] Brewer was one of the staunchest believers in liberty on the Court, but he also believed that liberty belonged to the natural person, not to corporate organizations. Brewer upheld the Kentucky statute in *Berea College* on the theory that it had been applied only to the corporate entity, namely the College. According to Brewer, corporate entities had no place in the state of nature; they were artificially created by the state and thus were without claims against the state, their creator. As a result, the legislature stood in a different and more powerful position with respect to the corporation than with respect to the individual: "In creating a corporation a State may withhold powers which may be exercised by and can not be denied to an individual."[67] In upholding the statute—without any inquiry into its underlying purposes or the relation between means and end—he drew a sharp distinction between the individual and the corporation: "Such a statute may conflict with the Federal Constitution in denying to individuals powers which they

---

[63] 211 U.S. 45 (1908).
[64] 1904 Ky. Acts 181.
[65] Board of Education v. Tinnon, 26 Kan. 1, 23 (1881) (Brewer, J., dissenting).

[66] Northern Sec. Co. v. United States, 193 U.S. 197 (1904). See Chapter 5, note 84.
[67] 211 U.S. at 54.

might rightfully exercise, and yet, at the same time, be valid as to a corporation created by the State."[68]

Although only the corporate entity of Berea College had been prosecuted, the state court had sustained the statute as it applied to both individuals and corporations. Brewer's views about the power of the state over corporations permitted him to uphold the latter portion of the judgment, but left unresolved the matter of the statute as applied to individuals. Rather than confront that issue head on, Brewer decided to sever the corporate and individual aspects of the statute and declined to rule on that portion of the state court judgment upholding the applicability of the statute to individuals. Brewer acknowledged that the Kentucky legislature might have wanted to reach as broadly as possible in enacting this measure, but he thought the legislature nonetheless might have been prepared to have a statute reaching only corporations once it realized that it was approaching the limits of its constitutional powers:

> That the legislature of Kentucky desired to separate the teaching of white and colored children may be conceded, but it by no means follows that it would not have enforced the separation so far as it could do so, even though it could not make it effective under all the circumstances.[69]

While Brewer was careful not to rule on the constitutionality of the statute as applied to individuals, he formulated the issue in such a way as to imply that there would be grave constitutional doubts if the statute were so applied. In so doing, he appeared to be honoring *Lochner* and *Adair*.

Two justices dissented from Brewer's decision: Day, who gave no reason for his opposition; and Harlan, but not because he disagreed with Brewer's denial of the protection of liberty to corporate entities. Like Brewer, Harlan believed that the special relationship between corporation and legislature—the relationship of the creation to the creator—resolved the liberty issue in favor of the state. Harlan's disagreement centered instead on the severability issue. He viewed the statute as a unified whole and insisted that the time was ripe to judge its constitutionality as applied to individuals. Harlan also went on to conclude that this aspect of the statute was unconstitutional, but not in a way that qualified what he said about public education in *Cumming* or that limited the right of the state to make the kind of decisions it had made in that case. In fact, Harlan went out of his way in *Berea College* to preserve his position in *Cumming* by concluding his *Berea College* opinion on this note: "Of course, what I have said has no reference to regulations prescribed for public schools, established at the pleasure of the State and maintained at public expense."[70] The distinction between state and civil society was maintained.

---

[68] Ibid.
[69] Ibid., 55.

[70] Ibid., 69.

Berea College was for Harlan just another police power case. The Kentucky statute constrained the liberties of individuals in how they might teach, and Harlan concluded that, like the railroad statute in *Plessy* and the Erdman Act in *Adair*, the Kentucky statute constituted a denial of substantive due process: "I am of the opinion that in its essential parts the statute is an arbitrary invasion of the rights of liberty and property guaranteed by the Fourteenth Amendment against hostile state action and is, therefore, void."[71] The constitutional evil lay not in the subordination of blacks through the perpetuation of a caste structure but in the fact that the Kentucky legislature had exceeded the bounds of its authority. In a manner that bore witness to Brewer's affectionate crack about Harlan as the justice who went to sleep at night with one hand on the Constitution and the other on the Bible,[72] Harlan formulated his position in *Berea College* in these terms:

> The capacity to impart instruction to others is given by the Almighty for beneficent purpose and its use may not be forbidden or interfered with by Government—certainly not, unless such instruction is, in its nature, harmful to the public morals or imperils the public safety. The right to impart instruction, harmless in itself or beneficial to those who receive it, is a substantial right of property—especially, where the services are rendered for compensation. But even if such right not be strictly a property right, it is, beyond question, part of one's liberty as guaranteed against hostile state action by the Constitution of the United States.[73]

In this passage, Harlan was not so much attacking racial segregation as a denial of substantive equality as he was protecting liberty. He was drawing his inspiration from *Lochner* and *Adair*, rather than from the vision of state and society later to inform *Brown v. Board of Education*.

II

Holmes silently joined the majority opinion in *Berea College*; he was not on the Court at the time of *Plessy* and *Cumming*. Within his first few months on the Court, however, the responsibility fell to him of speaking to the brutal racism of his day. The result—his opinion in *Giles v. Harris*,[74] announced in April 1903—reflected the same philosophic outlook that

---

[71] Ibid., 67.
[72] The quip, that "Justice Harlan retires at eight with one hand on the Constitution and other on the Bible, safe and happy in a perfect faith in justice and righteousness," is attributed to Justice Brewer by Edward F. Waite,

"How 'Eccentric' was Mr. Justice Harlan?," *Minn. L. Rev.*, 37: 173, 180–81 (1953).
[73] 211 U.S. at 67.
[74] 189 U.S. 475 (1903). After Giles lost the injunctive proceeding, he began an

reached climactic expression in his dissent in the *Northern Securities* antitrust case: Law stands impotent before history.[75] In *Northern Securities*, he revealed something special about himself; in *Giles* he spoke for the Court and identified one of the many factors that helped define the Court's position on race during this period.

The 1890s and early 1900s witnessed not only an escalation of racial violence and the use of law to enforce segregation, but also a widespread and systematic effort to exclude blacks from the civic life of their communities by keeping them off juries,[76] and even more powerfully, by denying

---

action for damages in the Alabama courts. He lost that as well and the Supreme Court upheld the decision as resting upon an independent and adequate state ground. *Giles v. Teasley*, 193 U.S. 146 (1904). The opinion in this round was written by Justice Day, who had exhibited humane sentiments in the Chinese immigration cases (see Chapter 10) and who had dissented in *Berea College* and *Hodges*. Day ended his opinion in *Giles v. Teasley* with the following concession: "The Court is not unmindful of the gravity of the statements of the complainant charging violation of a constitutional amendment which is part of the supreme law of the land. . . ." Ibid., 166–67.

[75] See Chapter 5.

[76] Throughout this period, the Court affirmed its commitment to the principle of Strauder v. West Virginia, 100 U.S. 303 (1879), denouncing racial discrimination in jury selection, but it gave virtually no substance to this declaration. The Court promised to look beyond the surface, to make certain that facially innocent laws were not being administered to exclude blacks, but in fact never set aside a conviction on the ground that blacks were excluded from the jury. It simply found no evidence of discriminatory administration. See Smith v. Mississippi, 162 U.S. 592 (1896); Murray v. Louisiana, 163 U.S. 101 (1896); and Martin v. Texas, 200 U.S. 316 (1906). In Thomas v. Texas, 212 U.S. 278, 282 (1909), Chief Justice Fuller went so far as to say:

[Whether] such discrimination was practiced in this case was a question of fact, and the determination of that question adversely to plaintiff in error by the [state courts] was decisive, so

far as this court is concerned, unless it could be held that these decisions constitute such abuse as amounted to an infraction of the Federal Constitution, which cannot be presumed. . . . The Court refused even to consider claims of discriminatory administration in the context of a removal proceeding. See Gibson v. Mississippi, 162 U.S. 565 (1896), *Smith v. Mississippi*, and *Murray v. Louisiana*. It followed the same rule in the habeas context. See In re Wood, 140 U.S. 278 (1891) and Andrews v. Swartz, 156 U.S. 272 (1895). In Williams v. Mississippi, 170 U.S. 213, 223–25 (1898), the Court distinguished Yick Wo v. Hopkins, 118 U.S. 356 (1886) (see Chapter 10), and went on to hold that the discriminatory purpose behind a facially innocent jury statute was irrelevant. *Williams v. Mississippi*, like all the other aforementioned cases, was decided without dissent; and, as it turned out, Harlan wrote the Court's opinion in *In re Wood, Andrews v. Swartz, Gibson v. Mississippi, Smith v. Mississippi,* and *Martin v. Texas*. Every rule has its exception: In Carter v. Texas, 177 U.S. 442 (1900) and Rogers v. Alabama, 192 U.S. 226 (1904), both involving direct appeals, the Court seemed to be engaged by claims of discriminatory administration, but then it did not set aside the convictions. It merely remanded the cases for evidentiary hearings in state court. These two decisions were also unanimous; *Carter v. Texas* was written by Gray and *Rogers v. Alabama* by Holmes. See generally Benno C. Schmidt, Jr., "Juries, Jurisdiction, and Race Discrimination: The Lost Promise of *Strauder v. West Virginia*," *Tex. L. Rev.*, 61: 1401 (1983).

them the right to vote.[77] The endorsement of state power by the *Civil Rights Cases*, it seemed, had to be conditioned on the exercise of political power by blacks. Thus one would have expected that *Giles v. Harris*—the preeminent voting rights case of the period—would have a different result from *Plessy* and the education cases. But Holmes's idiosyncratic approach thwarted that expectation.

Giles v. Harris involved a disenfranchisement program formulated and adopted by the State of Alabama in 1901 at a constitutional convention from which blacks were excluded. The 1901 amendments required voters to have paid a poll tax and to be registered. It then specified two different methods of registration, a permanent plan and a temporary one. The temporary plan applied to persons who registered before January 1, 1903. A person so registered would remain an elector for life, but the term "temporary" was used because the provisions in question applied only to those who registered between 1901 and the end of 1902. Anyone who registered after that time would have to comply with the more stringent requirements of the permanent plan.

The so-called temporary plan provided for the registration of three categories of persons: (1) those who had served in the War of 1812 and in the War with Mexico, and those who had served in the Confederate army (or, as Holmes described it, "those on either side in 'the war between the states'"[78]); (2) the descendants of the aforementioned and descendants of veterans of the Revolution; and (3) "All persons who are of good character and who understand the duties and obligations of citizenship under a republican form of government."[79]

Obviously, few blacks could qualify under the first two categories, although the brief in the Supreme Court for the defendant board of registrars claimed, "These provisions might, and did, in fact, include many citizens of dark color, many of the negro race, and many who had been slaves."[80] The third category appeared more innocent, at least superficially, but it was attacked on the theory that it "invests the registrars with unlimited and arbitrary power."[81] The plaintiff also complained of the way this provision, as well as the entire temporary plan, was administered. It was used as an "engine of discrimination," to borrow a phrase that became

---

[77] See Williamson, *Crucible of Race*, 224–58.

[78] 189 U.S. at 483. Holmes's use of quotation marks for the term "war between the states" may reflect his special sensitivity toward the war, as manifested by his rather bizarre practice of celebrating annually the infliction of the wounds he acquired during the war

(Holmes was wounded three times). See Edmund Wilson, *Patriotic Gore: Studies in the Literature of the American Civil War* (New York: Oxford University Press, 1962), 758.

[79] 189 U.S. at 483.

[80] Ibid., 480.

[81] Ibid., 478.

common when the nation returned to these issues more than a half century later:[82]

> [T]he registrars refused to register qualified negroes for no other reason than their race and color, and required negroes to produce the testimony of white men as to their qualifications and character, and refused to accept the testimony of colored men, while all white men were registered upon their application without further proof of qualification than the oath of the applicant.[83]

Counsel also said that the registrar refused to register "nearly all negroes"[84] under the temporary plan, telling them to come back after January 1903, at which time the so-called permanent plan would govern.

The permanent plan imposed tougher requirements for registration. As Justice Holmes said, it established "tests which might be too severe for many of the whites as well as the blacks."[85] Under the permanent plan a person was entitled to vote if he either could read and write and was regularly employed, or satisfied certain property qualifications (namely owning and living on forty acres or owning real or personal property that had taxes assessed and paid of more than $300). Counsel for Jackson W. Giles, the plaintiff, made only a cursory objection to the permanent plan standing alone; his primary objection to it arose from the fact that, given its terms and the way the temporary plan was administered, the permanent plan provided the only real option for blacks but established tests that most would fail. As counsel put it, the permanent plan was "special class legislation from its inception intended to operate against the negroes of Alabama alone."[86]

Giles, born in 1859, had lived and voted in Montgomery for some thirty years prior to the adoption of the provisions, and in March 1902 he unsuccessfully tried to register under the temporary plan. A suit was filed in September 1902 in federal court, and by way of relief (as described by Holmes) it sought an injunction requiring the defendant board of registrars to enroll Giles and the other qualified blacks who had previously applied for registration. The suit was, as we might put it today, a class action seeking class relief; at the outset of his opinion, Holmes, quoting from the pleadings, described the suit as a "bill in equity brought by a colored man, on behalf of himself 'and on behalf of more than five thousand negroes, citi-

---

[82] See United States v. Alabama, 304 F.2d 583, 586 (5th Cir.), *aff'd* 371 U.S. 37 (1962); Louisiana v. United States, 380 U.S. 145 (1965); and United States v. Mississippi, 380 U.S. 128 (1965). See generally Owen M. Fiss, "Gaston County v. United States: Fruition of the Freezing Principle," *Sup. Ct. Rev.*, 1969: 379.

[83] 189 U.S. at 478.

[84] Ibid., 479.

[85] Ibid., 483.

[86] Ibid., 479.

zens of the county of Montgomery, Alabama, similarly situated and circumstanced as himself'. . . ."[87]

Holmes grasped the significance of the moment. While the overall legal framework for regulating relations between the races had been established in the 1880s and 1890s, the oppression had escalated and Holmes understood that the Court was, as he put it, "dealing with a new and extraordinary situation."[88] In the end, he declared himself powerless before the racism of his day—this "new and extraordinary situation"—but his opinion was especially striking because Holmes seemed almost perversely determined to proclaim his impotence. There were many ways of avoiding this confrontation, but Holmes chose none of them. He seemed bent on reaching the precipice, even to the point of provoking dissents by both Brewer and Harlan. They pleaded with Holmes to stick to the technical issue and to avoid his confession of helplessness, which was, of course, at war with everything the two believed—they were anything but spectators.

In the lower court, a demurrer had been filed by the defendants arguing that there was no federal jurisdiction. The lower court had granted the demurrer, thus dismissing the suit, and had then certified the jurisdictional issue to the Supreme Court. Brewer thought that the circuit court had jurisdiction and counseled a conservative strategy: Answer the certified question in the affirmative and remand the case for a trial on the merits. Brewer's dissent in *Giles* was, as with his dissent in the free speech context, unusually restrained (and lacked the support of Peckham), but he nevertheless explicitly affirmed the power of the judiciary—yes, the nation's safeguard—to give relief in cases of this sort: "That such relief will be given has been again and again affirmed in both National and state courts."[89] Harlan, on the other hand, felt there was a lack of jurisdiction because of a failure to allege the requisite amount in controversy. His opinion was devoted almost entirely to the discussion of the jurisdictional issue, but he then closed on this note:

> As these are my views as to the jurisdiction of this court, upon this record, I will not formulate and discuss my views upon the merits of this case. But to avoid misapprehension, I may add that my conviction is that upon the facts alleged in the bill (if the record showed a sufficient value of the matter in dispute) the plaintiff is entitled to relief in respect of his right to be registered as a voter. I agree with Mr. Justice Brewer that it is competent for the courts to give relief in such cases as this.[90]

---

[87] 189 U.S. at 482.
[88] Ibid., 486.

[89] Ibid., 491.
[90] Ibid., 504.

Although Brewer and Harlan did not elaborate on this issue, they understood that voting was special, different from public education or even public accommodations.

Holmes brushed aside the objection to jurisdiction arising from the absence of an allegation in the complaint of the jurisdictional amount—the right to vote had monetary value, and this defect in the pleading could have been cured by an amendment if there had been a proper objection to the pleadings below, which there had not been. He also noted, but discussed no further, that one of the federal statutes relied upon for jurisdiction did not mention "state constitutions,"[91] although it proscribed deprivation of rights that arose from a "statute, ordinance, regulation, custom, or usage."[92] He treated this as a point that "might be argued with some force,"[93] but never ruled on it. He was, however, very clear that equity jurisdiction did not extend to the protection of voting rights: "The traditional limits of proceedings in equity," he wrote, "have not embraced a remedy for political wrongs."[94] It is not clear whether he truly believed this or was making a concession to some other judge, but in any event he refused to rest his decision on this ground alone. Immediately he added: "But we cannot forget that we are dealing with a new and extraordinary situation, and we are unwilling to stop short of the final consideration which seems to us to dispose of the case."[95]

At an earlier point, Holmes had acknowledged still another way out, but here, too, he seemed determined not to use it. This was not a jurisdictional issue strictly understood, but instead arose from the fact that the suit might be moot. Holmes noted that the bill, which had been filed in September 1902, made reference to the plaintiff's desire to vote in the election that was to be held that November, a time that was long past when the case reached the Supreme Court. In *Mills v. Green*,[96] another voting discrimination suit, the Supreme Court refused to recast the injunction into reparative terms and dismissed the suit—which challenged the exclusion of blacks from an election to choose delegates to a constitutional convention—on the theory that the Court was facing a fait accompli: Both the election and the convention had occurred already. Holmes was, however, too good a judge to hide behind that ruling. He understood that the principal object of Giles's suit was not to vote in any particular election, but to challenge the registration scheme so that the blacks of Montgomery could vote in the future.

---

[91] Ibid., 487.
[92] Ibid., 485, quoting Act of Apr. 20, 1871, Ch. 22, Sect. 1, 17 Stat. 13.
[93] 189 U.S. at 485.

[94] Ibid., 486.
[95] Ibid.
[96] 159 U.S. 651 (1895). See also Wiley v. Sinkler, 179 U.S. 58 (1900).

Once these preliminary matters were disposed of, one would have expected Holmes to speak to the issue he was saving—the final consideration—but he paused once again, this time to muse over a logical dilemma of his own creation: Giles wanted to be registered, but it was not clear how the Court could ever give such relief since the underlying theory of the suit was that the entire registration scheme was invalid. There was, Holmes thought, a simple logical contradiction between attacking a scheme and seeking the benefits of it.

This pause was unworthy of Holmes or, for that matter, any judge who saw through *Mills v. Green*. It is hard to believe that Giles's request for relief was as narrow as Holmes had described, but even if it was, the Court was not strictly confined to it. Equity courts are not bound by the terms of the relief specifically sought in the complaint; an injunction could have been issued against the entire registration scheme, allowing the state to come forward with an arrangement free of discrimination in both its inception and overall design. Or the Court could have pursued a more modest route and ordered the registration of Giles and the class he represented on the assumption that curing this defect in administration would make the plan constitutional. At the end of his discussion of this preliminary point, Holmes gave this latter answer to the logical dilemma he had concocted, and then answered that answer with the most disingenuous of concerns—a fear of creating "a new doctrine in constitutional law."[97] Clearly, Holmes's heart was not in the matter. He seemed to have gone off on a tangent.

There was, in fact, only one point that Holmes wanted to make, and that related to his doubts about whether the jurisdictional statute reached state constitutions and whether equity jurisdiction reached political wrongs, but it differed fundamentally, both in tone and substance, from either of those issues. It had to do with Holmes's own sense of history and the possibilities of practical power. To give some sense of Holmes's extraordinary response to this extraordinary moment, I will quote in full the statement that appears at the very close of his opinion. The entire opinion was a determined, but interrupted, journey to reach this point:

> The bill imports that the great mass of the white population intends to keep the blacks from voting. To meet such an intent something more than ordering the plaintiff's name to be inscribed upon the lists of 1902 will be needed. If the conspiracy and the intent exist, a name on a piece of paper will not defeat them. Unless we are prepared to supervise the voting in that State by officers of the court, it seems to us that all that the plaintiff could get from equity would be an empty form. Apart from damages to the individual, relief from a great political wrong, if done,

---

[97] 189 U.S. at 487.

as alleged, by the people of a State and the State itself must be given by them or by the legislative and political department of the government of the United States.[98]

On one reading, this may seem simply a counsel of prudence—Holmes attempting to save the courts the embarrassment of issuing orders they could not enforce. But the deeper, more cynical message—don't resist the forces of history—becomes clearer when we recall that he expressed the same attitude of helplessness when "the legislative and political department of the government of the United States" was in fact involved. This occurred in *Northern Securities*, decided the very next year, where he denounced the effort of the Roosevelt administration to use the Sherman Act to break up the Morgan-Hill merger or, to put it more grandiosely, to reverse the growing historical trend toward concentration. This same willingness, no, *demand* that we surrender to history may also account for Holmes's decision, just a few years later, to join the Court's decisions in *Hodges v. United States*.[99]

III

In *Giles*, as in *Plessy, Cumming*, and *Berea College*, the power of government was used to create and enforce a system of racial exclusion and segregation. *Hodges v. United States* represented a break from this pattern, for now the power of government—in this instance, the federal government—appeared on the other side of the case. A federal prosecution had been brought against a gang of whites who had tried, through force and intimidation, to have a number of blacks fired from their jobs at a lumber mill in Arkansas. The question for the Court, roughly paralleling the issue in the *Civil Rights Cases*, was whether this action of the federal government was constitutionally permissible. It was almost as though the Court were reconsidering its decisions in the *Civil Rights Cases*, now that the nation understood all that it meant. The attorney general, then William H. Moody, appeared before the Court on behalf of the United States. The argument in *Hodges* occurred in April 1906, and in December of that year—only six weeks after the opinion was handed down—Moody was appointed to the Court by President Roosevelt to fill the position of Brown (of all people).

The particular criminal statute invoked in *Hodges*, prohibiting forcible interferences with rights secured by the Constitution or laws of the United States, was not self-contained. It required reference to some other law, one that established the right that was the subject of the forcible interference. In this case, that second-order statute was one of the early Recon-

---

[98] 189 U.S. at 488.

[99] 203 U.S. 1 (1906).

struction statutes—then referred to as Section 1977—providing blacks with the same right as whites to make and enforce contracts. It was derived from the Civil Rights Act of 1866, which was reenacted in 1870 after the adoption of the Fourteenth Amendment. That statute did not say that the right of blacks to contract was protected against only state interference, and by this omission implied that the right was protected from all interferences, state and private.

The responsibility of speaking for the Court was assigned to Brewer, and in construing Section 1977 he employed a method Fuller had already made familiar in antitrust and that was picked up by White in his treatment of the Wilson Act and in the rule of reason cases:[100] Brewer assumed that Congress wished to go only to the limits of its power and then looked to the Constitution to see whether Congress had the power to regulate the particular transaction before it. The question of statutory interpretation thus was transformed into one of constitutional power: Does Congress have the power to confer on blacks a right to contract that guarded against private interferences?

The attorney general acknowledged the absence of power under the Fourteenth Amendment and relied exclusively on the Thirteenth. That amendment was the basis of Section 1977 when it was first enacted and, unlike the Fourteenth Amendment, did not on its face contain a state action requirement. Slavery, the relationship that the Thirteenth Amendment abolished, was authorized and supported by the states, but it was essentially a relationship between individuals. Moreover, only two years prior to *Hodges*, in the *Clyatt* case,[101] the Court, in an opinion by Brewer, had said that peonage was within the Thirteenth Amendment prohibition against involuntary servitude, thereby strengthening the view that state action was deemed unnecessary for the Thirteenth Amendment. Peonage was defined narrowly, as a condition of compulsory service based on the indebtedness of the peon to the master, but Brewer was clear that there need be no complicity of the state in the scheme: "This amendment denounces a status or condition, irrespective of the manner or authority by which it is created."[102] Moody had also argued *Clyatt*.[103]

---

[100] See Chapters 5 and 9.

[101] Clyatt v. United States, 197 U.S. 207 (1905). Samuel Clyatt, the owner of a still in Georgia, captured two former employees who had since moved to Florida and forced them at gunpoint to return with him to Georgia. Clyatt claimed the workers had left his employ without repaying their debts to him. The Supreme Court remanded the case for a new trial, ruling that the employees had failed to prove that they had been held in or returned to a condition of peonage.

[102] Ibid., 216.

[103] Bickel and Schmidt, *Judiciary and Responsible Government*, 838. The authors report that *Clyatt* and *Hodges* were two of four cases argued by Moody. The others were Swift & Co. v. United States, 196 U.S. 375 (1905) (see Chapter 5), and Cosmopolitan Mining Co. v. Walsh, 193 U.S. 460 (1904). See generally Pete Daniel, *The Shadow of Slavery: Peonage in the South, 1901–1969* (Urbana: University of Illinois Press, 1972), and Paul T. Heffron, "Profile of a Public

Chapter XII: *Plessy*

In trying to use the Thirteenth Amendment in *Hodges*, Moody stressed that the amendment ensured "practical freedom,"[104] not just a formal or legal freedom. By that he meant that Congress had the power under the Thirteenth Amendment to proscribe a practice or pattern of conduct that deprived individuals of certain "*fundamental* rights,"[105] such as the right to labor and to enjoy the fruits of one's work. The attorney general argued that the mob's interference with the freedom of blacks to work, the basis of the indictment in the case, was the functional equivalent of returning blacks to slavery. Slavery denied individuals many liberties; above all, it denied the right to contract and to pursue one's calling.

The position of the government in this case entailed a bold extension of national power, perhaps as bold as the power claimed in *Debs*. To place a limit on what he was advocating, the attorney general stressed the motivation behind the mob's action. It was not just that the right to work of a black was impaired, but that "the motive for such injury, oppression, or interference arises solely from the fact such a laborer is a colored person of African descent."[106] In *Clyatt*, Brewer had been meticulous in defining peonage to avoid including a racial element,[107] even though peonage in fact was used as an instrument of black oppression. Therefore, it was not surprising that in *Hodges* he refused to accept Moody's limiting gesture and indeed appeared to take some offense at it. Although Moody's theory presumably could be understood to cover anyone—not just a black—who was treated as a slave, Brewer accused the attorney general of claiming a special protection for blacks. Turning Tourgée's and Harlan's metaphor around, Brewer insisted on the importance of color-blindness for purposes of marking the bounds of the national legislative power.

Man," *Sup. Ct. Hist. Soc'y Y.B.*, 1980: 30.

[104] 203 U.S. at 11.

[105] Ibid., 10 (emphasis in original).

[106] Ibid., 9.

[107] 197 U.S. at 215. The only mention of the racial status of the peons occurred in Justice Harlan's opinion. Ibid., 223. When the concept of peonage was enlarged in Bailey v. Alabama, 219 U.S. 219 (1911), the racial element was once again excluded. In that case, the Supreme Court struck down an Alabama statute that made breach of contract prima facie evidence of intent to defraud the employer and that prohibited the employee from testifying as to the employee's motive or intent. The Court, in an opinion by Justice Hughes, held that by punishing a person for not working for another to pay off a debt the Alabama statute gave legal sanction to involuntary servitude and thus violated the Thirteenth Amendment, while also abridging the "freedom to labor." Justice Hughes declared, "We at once dismiss from consideration the fact that the plaintiff in error is a black man." Ibid., 231. Similarly, Justice Day's opinion in a third peonage case, United States v. Reynolds, 235 U.S. 133 (1914), avoided any reference to the race of the peon. The Court in *Reynolds* found unconstitutional certain provisions of the Alabama Code that penalized a convict's failure to perform a contract with a surety who had paid the fine and costs that the convict owed to the state. These provisions, the Court ruled, created an "everturning wheel of servitude," in which the convict's original debt, and the period of labor necessary to pay off the debt, were compounded by penalties for breach of contract. Ibid., 146–47. For a discussion of the role of peonage as an instrument of black oppression in the South, see Daniel, *Shadow of Slavery*.

Brewer first explained that it would be unfair to give this protection to blacks but deny it to other disadvantaged groups. Brewer, of course, had the Chinese in mind and reminded the attorney general of the travesty perpetrated by the Court in *Fong Yue Ting*.[108] He referred to the registration requirement of the Geary Act of 1892 and explained that although in slave times free blacks were required to register, no one dreamed of attacking the registration requirement of the Geary Act on Thirteenth Amendment grounds. The fact that blacks had been slaves and the Chinese had not, and thus that blacks might have special claim to the protection of the Thirteenth Amendment, had no relevance for Brewer, a point he awkwardly (and stupidly) expressed by saying: "[N]owhere in the record does it appear that the parties charged to have been wronged by the defendants had ever been themselves slaves, or were the descendants of slaves."[109]

Brewer also found within the established legal structure a deliberate and well-considered judgment by the body politic rejecting the color-conscious strategy he saw the attorney general proposing. At the conclusion of the Civil War, according to Brewer, the nation had available to it three different strategies for dealing with the emancipated slaves: It might have left them in the status of aliens (as *Dred Scott* had treated the free blacks); made them wards of the state (as in the case of the Indians); or made them citizens. The first two strategies were consistent with the kind of special protections he saw the attorney general asking for, but the third—the conferral of citizenship—was not. Conferral of citizenship, according to Brewer, required blacks to "tak[e] their chances with other citizens in the States where they should make their homes."[110] By way of support, Brewer cited the Fifteenth Amendment and the provision of the Fourteenth Amendment conferring citizenship, but in truth he was simply restating the principle of the *Civil Rights Cases*.

The attorney general's attack on the *Civil Rights Cases* was not directed just at the principle behind that decision, but at its specific holding. The Court had struck down the federal statute barring discrimination in public accommodations for failing to satisfy the state action requirement of the Fourteenth Amendment, but that holding necessarily had implications for the Thirteenth Amendment as well. Inspired by the same vision of federalism that underlay its affirmation of the state action requirement of the Fourteenth Amendment—the conviction that the regulation of the relation of citizen to citizen continued to belong to the states—the *Civil Rights Cases* also held that racial discrimination in public accommodations was not a badge or incident of slavery, and thus was not a proper subject of legislation by Congress under the Thirteenth Amendment.

---

[108] See Chapter 10.
[109] 203 U.S. at 18.

[110] Ibid., 20.

Chapter XII: *Plessy*

In trying to distinguish the *Civil Rights Cases*, the attorney general emphasized the economic dimensions of the liberties at issue in *Hodges* and their connection to the institution of slavery. Unlike public accommodations, he argued, these were fundamental liberties. It required no feat of the imagination to say that the infringements of liberty suffered in this case would return blacks to a situation comparable to the one they had suffered as slaves. The attorney general also gave the Court reason to think the result might now be worse: No one had an interest in the material well-being of the free black. A denial of congressional power would leave blacks, the attorney general hypothesized, "in a state made worse by their emancipation by the breaking of the cord of self-interest which bound the slaveholder to take care of his property."[111] Then, almost as though he had *Native Son* in mind, the attorney general spoke to the future in the most alarming terms:

> If the Negro who is in our midst can be denied the right to work, and must live on the outskirts of civilization, he will become more dangerous than the wild beasts, because he has a higher intelligence than the most intelligent beast. He will become an outcast lurking about the borders and living by depredation.[112]

These words are remarkable in themselves, but to find them uttered by one of the most respected lawyers of his day—then the attorney general of the United States and soon to become a justice—is even more so. To be sure, they are the words of a white man who meticulously maintained a distance from the people he was talking about—"the Negro . . . will become more dangerous than the wild beasts." The attorney general was speaking for the nation as a whole, not its black victims. Yet no one could mistake the sense of urgency that Moody felt, nor fail to perceive the parallel with Olney's plea in *Debs*.

Here there was no spectre of revolution—Booker T. Washington had outlined a strategy in the early 1890s for blacks that was fundamentally different from the one Eugene Debs had in mind for the laboring classes.[113] But in a manner that is evocative of *Debs*, the attorney general referred to

---

[111] Ibid., 11.

[112] Ibid., 14.

[113] See Louis R. Harlan, *Booker T. Washington: The Making of a Black Leader, 1856–1901* (New York: Oxford University Press, 1972). Morris K. Jessup, a New York lawyer, wrote to Fuller recommending that income from a certain trust fund they administered be used to purchase 10,000 copies of Washington's *The Future of the American Negro* "for free distribution among the Whites and Blacks in the South." He described the book as "the best statement of facts, together with what is to be done hereafter" that he had read. Jessup to Fuller, Dec. 7, 1900, Fuller Papers, Library of Congress Manuscript Division.

the "exigencies of the public welfare" and spoke of the danger to "civilization." He also focused on the threat to a number of liberties—the liberty to contract, the liberty to work, and the liberty to pursue one's calling—that were then of near-transcendent significance to the justices. The freedom to contract and the freedom to pursue one's calling were not simply social and political rights, as were the liberties implicated in *Plessy, Cumming, Berea College*, or even *Giles*, but instead were freedoms that the Court, time and time again, had declared to be fundamental.

In his Albany speech, Brewer spoke to these freedoms and proclaimed that they should be guarded from all interferences, state or private. These freedoms needed as much protection from mass picketing, a general strike, or a mob as they did from the state. In *Debs* he followed through in his conviction, but not in *Hodges*, where he turned his back on the attorney general and refused to support his effort to protect these fundamental freedoms from the mob. Indeed, *Hodges*—unlike *Plessy, Cumming, Berea College*, and *Giles*—was not an acquiescence in the action of a state, but a *Lochner*-like repudiation of an affirmative act of the national government, and for that reason it may give the true measure of the Fuller Court.

While accepting the attorney general's position in *Hodges* would have required the Court to reconfigure established doctrine, above all the *Civil Rights Cases, Hodges* cannot be explained in purely technical terms. Brewer knew well how to battle the most durable of precedents—recall his systematic attack on *Munn v. Illinois* described in Chapter 7—and the cases here relevant could easily be distinguished, as Moody suggested, in terms of the liberties involved. The result in *Hodges* stemmed rather from the fact that Brewer and his followers—all the justices except Harlan and Day—remained fully committed to the *Civil Rights Cases* and to the allocation of power to the states to deal with relations among the races. For them, that decision was foundational. In *Giles* and *Berea College* Brewer seemed to suggest that the Fourteenth and Fifteenth Amendments might prohibit certain forms of state discrimination, but that was fully consistent with the *Civil Rights Cases*. What he did not want to do was unleash the Thirteenth Amendment as a weapon against private discrimination and accordingly he refused to admit that the Thirteenth Amendment covered anything but servitude narrowly defined. Brewer feared that a broad reading of the amendment—however essential it might have seemed to the nation—would undermine the underlying principles of the *Civil Rights Cases*.

Over the next sixty years, the national power was extended almost as thoroughly over race relations as it had been extended to preserve the economic union in *Debs*. At first, the nation acted within the technical confines of the *Civil Rights Cases*: Discrimination by the states was attacked, time and time again. This process began when shortly after the rule of Fuller, Brewer, and Peckham had come to an end, the Court handed down the

Grandfather Clause Cases[114] invalidating a scheme to disenfranchise blacks. But the full flowering of this process awaited *Brown v. Board of Education* in 1954, for only then did the commitment to racial equality acquire the character of a transcendent imperative, capable of moving mountains.

Throughout the sixties, the principle of substantive equality was enforced repeatedly against the states, first by the Court and then by Congress and the executive, making it clear that the autonomy allowed the states on the issue of race was to be circumscribed severely. For all three branches, the axioms had changed, and as a result the decision in the *Civil Rights Cases* was drained of all normative significance. In 1966 that decision was silently overruled.[115] The Court was no longer prepared to have blacks, to use Brewer's formulation, take "their chances with other citizens in the states where they make their home."

---

[114] Guinn v. United States, 238 U.S. 347 (1915); Myers v. Anderson, 238 U.S. 368 (1915); and United States v. Mosley, 238 U.S. 383 (1915). See above, note 19. On race in the White Court, see Bickel and Schmidt, *Judiciary and Responsible Government*, 725–990, and Randall Kennedy, "Race Relations Law and the Tradition of Celebration: The Case of Professor Schmidt," *Colum. L. Rev.*, 86: 1622 (1986).

[115] Katzenbach v. Morgan, 384 U.S. 641 (1966). See generally Archibald Cox, "Constitutional Adjudication and the Promotion of Human Rights," *Harv. L. Rev.*, 80: 91 (1966).

CONCLUSION

CHAPTER XIII

The End of a Tradition?

LIBERTY was the guiding ideal of the Fuller Court, the notion that gave unity and coherence to its many endeavors. But that ideal has been claimed by all manner of political leaders throughout American history and has as many meanings as it has adherents. For many today, liberty means freedom of speech and personal liberties, including those related to sexual intimacy. We also recognize the state as capable of protecting as well as depriving us of these freedoms. Fuller and his colleagues had something else in mind. The liberty they believed in was shaped by what I have called the social contract tradition.

In this tradition, liberty was conceived of as something that belonged personally to the individual, like a special kind of property or possession. Liberty was something that could be enjoyed even by individuals who lived outside organized society and who met their needs through their own labors and by barter and exchange. In his speech at Albany, and again in his opinion for the Court in *Reagan v. Farmers' Loan & Trust Co.*, Brewer spoke of liberty in just this way and pointed to the importance to the nation of the liberties associated with capitalism: the freedom to contract, to follow one's calling, and to acquire and hold property. As Brewer made clear in *Berea College* and in his concurrence in *Northern Securities*, these liberties belonged only to natural persons, not to corporations or other artificial creations of the state.

The social contract tradition was also defined by its reduction of liberty to a demand for limited government. The state was seen as the natural enemy of freedom, prohibiting individuals from doing whatever they wished, setting limits on their conduct, or requisitioning their property. In cases like *Debs, Joint Traffic, Trans-Missouri, Addyston Pipe*, and even *Northern Securities*, the Court recognized that the state must act boldly sometimes to preserve the public order or to maintain the proper functioning of the market. But the justices were preoccupied mostly with constructing limits on state power, and this concern accounted for their decisions in *Pollock, Reagan, Ex parte Young, Adair*, and, of course, *Lochner*.

In these cases, government power—that of the states as well as the federal government—was held to be limited to the accomplishment of discrete, previously specified ends. As in the fables of classical social contract theory, government was seen as a deliberate contrivance, and the constitutive process that brought the state into being also set the limits on its authority. This understanding was reflected in many branches of nineteenth-century constitutional law, but nowhere so clearly as in the doctrine of enumerated powers. Although this doctrine was technically confined to the federal government, it served as a prism through which the Court saw all manner of state authority. In *Lochner*, for example, Peckham conceptualized the police power of the states as though it were an enumerated power.

This view of governmental power dominated the Court's decisions at a time when contractarianism was beginning to be challenged by reformers, particularly by such leaders of the progressive movement as Theodore Roosevelt. Despite considerable pressure to allow the government to ameliorate the inequities of capitalism and to lessen the significant social and economic stratification that capitalist development had produced, the Court continued to insist that the state had limited authority to interfere. Admittedly, the Court acknowledged the threat to liberty posed by private organizations like the American Railway Union in *Debs*, the price-fixing cartels in *Joint Traffic*, *Trans-Missouri*, and *Addyston Pipe*, and the Hill-Morgan holding company in *Northern Securities*. As Peckham perceived in *Addyston Pipe*, these organizations were acting as private governments wielding powers analogous to those of the state, and they could be controlled only by the countervailing power of the state. But elsewhere the Court responded grudgingly to the new exercises of state power that seemed to jeopardize the entrepreneurial liberties that were celebrated by the social contract tradition and seemed central to the preservation and development of American civilization.

When subsequent generations confronted the Fuller Court and its legacy, the temptation was great to judge that institution in terms of its own premises: to accept the contractarian tradition in general outline but to complain about the way it was applied, particularly the narrow range of liberties protected. The failure of the Fuller Court, some argued, lay not in *Lochner* but rather in decisions like *Patterson* and *Turner*, in which the Court, devoted as it was to protecting the freedom of the market, ignored other liberties, like freedom of speech.

The Fuller Court was criticized also for conceiving the constitutional community too narrowly. When it came to the rights of members of the constitutional community, the Court adamantly held the state to the limits of its authority. But many in the society were not deemed members of the constitutional community. They were outsiders or, in Field's phrase, "strangers in the land"—a category that included not only the Chinese, the group Field had in mind, but also blacks, women, and colonial subjects. With respect to them, the state was conceived as operating almost without limit, more like a master or parent than the agent of a voluntary association. From this perspective, the wrath of the reformers was directed not so much toward *Lochner*, or even *Patterson* or *Turner*, as toward *Plessy*, *Fong Yue Ting*, the *Insular Cases*, and perhaps even *Muller v. Oregon*.

In the years following Fuller's death, the Supreme Court began to broaden the range of protected liberties. In 1919 Holmes reversed the position he had taken a decade earlier in *Patterson* and laid the foundation for strong judicial protection of freedom of speech. In two cases of the 1920s, *Pierce v. Society of Sisters*[1] and *Meyer v. Nebraska*,[2] the Court gave constitutional status to distinctly personal freedoms, such as the freedom to choose a school for one's child. In this early period, the Court also enlarged the community entitled to these liberties. In decisions such as *Truax v. Raich* (1915)[3] and *Adkins v. Children's Hospital* (1923),[4] the Court included aliens and women respectively in the community protected by liberty of contract, and in the *Grandfather Clause Cases*[5] of 1915 it reversed the attitude reflected in such cases as *Giles v. Harris* by striking down state constitutional provisions prohibiting blacks from voting.

In these early efforts at revision, the Court stayed within the bounds of the social contract tradition, broadening both the range of protected liberties and the constitutional community, but it remained committed to limiting the state. In *Pierce* and *Meyer*, as in *Lochner*, liberty was assumed to belong to the individual, and the principal function of the Court was to shield the individual from an overreaching state, though now liberty protected a conception of human fulfillment that was not in any special way tied to the market. These early decisions enriched *Lochner*, but affirmed the underlying commitment of contractarianism to the notion of limited government, and it was this commitment that soon led to constitutional crisis over the New Deal.

The legislative enactments of New Deal Democrats were a blatant challenge to the social contract tradition, for they authorized the most thoroughgoing regulation of market relationships. Trying to honor *Lochner* and all that it stood for, the Court responded by invalidating these measures, and then in 1935 in *Schechter Poultry*[6] held unconstitutional the National Industrial Recovery Act—the centerpiece of early New Deal reforms. Two years later, however, the Court reversed course. In the face of massive popular support for economic reform and for bestowing the government with the authority to carry out such reform, the Court gave its blessing to the

---

[1] 268 U.S. 510 (1925).

[2] 262 U.S. 390 (1923).

[3] 239 U.S. 33 (1915) (holding that a state law that restricted the employment of aliens violated the Equal Protection Clause of the Fourteenth Amendment).

[4] 261 U.S. 525 (1923) (invalidating a minimum wage law for women only on the theory that women have the same liberty of contract as men). See Chapter 6, note 82.

[5] Guinn v. United States, 238 U.S. 347 (1915); Myers v. Anderson, 238 U.S. 368 (1915); United States v. Mosley, 238 U.S. 383 (1915).

[6] A. L. A. Schechter Poultry Co. v. United States, 295 U.S. 495 (1935).

New Deal and thus legitimated its version of the activist state. In 1941 President Franklin Roosevelt included "freedom from want" among his famous Four Freedoms,[7] reflecting the change that the thirties had wrought in our understanding of liberty and the role of the state. The social contract tradition seemed to be at an end.

This new recognition by political leaders and the American people alike that a social condition such as poverty could also be a threat to liberty stripped the status quo of its presumption of legitimacy. It also undermined the conception of the state as a power brought into being to serve discrete, well-defined, and limited ends. Charged with the duty of eradicating social conditions that impaired personal autonomy and fulfillment, the state was required to intervene in social and economic affairs on a broad and continuous basis. No longer a night watchman acting to prevent outbreaks of violence or other lapses in the social order,[8] the state would now have to reconstruct that order and redistribute resources to make freedom possible.

For justices like Brewer and Peckham and all those who continued in their tradition, it was impossible to conceive of the state as a source of freedom. For them liberty was freedom *from* governmental interference. Many defended the activist state on the ground that, on balance, liberty would be furthered by it, because active state intervention would enable more people to live the kind of life they wished than if the state did nothing or acted merely as a watchman. But these calculations, made all the more difficult by class considerations, were controverted by some. Even more significantly, the new forms of state power entailed in the New Deal constituted a concrete and immediate threat to many of the liberties most cherished under contractarianism, including the freedom to set the terms and conditions of work.

The challenge of the New Deal to the contractarian tradition was significantly reinforced by World War II, which, like any war, made state activism a moral imperative of almost transcendent proportions. Then in 1954, in *Brown v. Board of Education*—a case that has inspired my generation and has defined the parameters of this volume—the Court built on the legacy of the New Deal, though there is a dispute as to exactly how. Some see the decisions of the Warren Court as an effort to reconceive the contractarian tradition within the framework of the activist state by extending the bounds of the constitutional community and altering the range of protected

---

[7] "Four Freedoms Speech," annual message to Congress, Jan. 6, 1941. *The Public Papers and Addresses of Franklin D. Roosevelt* (New York: Macmillan, 1941), 9: 663, 672. The other freedoms were "freedom of speech and expression," "freedom of every person to worship God in his own way," and "freedom from fear."

[8] Robert Nozick, *Anarchy, State and Utopia* (New York: Basic Books, 1974), 26.

liberties.[9] For them, the Warren Court, in much the spirit of *Pierce, Meyer,* and the free speech cases of the thirties, gave special protection to interests that were open previously to government regulation—such as rights to bodily integrity and intimate associations and the freedom to engage in political activity. Now, however, liberties tied to the market were readily sacrificed.

But this view understates the significance of *Brown* for the history of constitutional law. In my view, *Brown* did not merely accept the New Deal's charter for the activist state, but rather extended and broadened it to include racism among the social conditions that were to be eliminated. To this end, the Court also indicated its willingness to place limits on the liberty of some in order to achieve equality. Rather than treating racism as Roosevelt did poverty, namely as a threat to self-determination, the Warren Court openly and emphatically defined its role as one of promoting equality, thereby skirting the debate over positive and negative freedom that so dominated discussion about the welfare state in the late 1950s.[10]

This shift from liberty to equality might well have reflected the imperatives of the legal craft and the fact that the Equal Protection Clause, the text upon which the Court based its actions, was couched in terms of equality. But its effect was felt far beyond the law. During the sixties equality became the overarching goal of state activism and as such bore the burden of justifying the sacrifice of many individual liberties, some connected to the market, and others, like the freedom of association, that were not. The emphasis upon equality also threw the individualism of contractarianism into question, for it entailed a reconception of personhood. Individuals were no longer treated by the state as isolated entities but as socially embedded, and it was recognized that their status is vitally dependent on the status of the group with which they are identified.

Not only did the Warren Court broaden our understanding of constitutional ideals to permit a proper consideration of equality, but it also gave us reason to believe that state activism was a constitutional duty. While the Bill of Rights and the Fourteenth Amendment have been treated by many, even the New Deal Court, as a set of prohibitions declaring what the state must not do, *Brown* and its progeny transformed these negative restrictions into affirmative commands. This transformation was in part premised on

---

[9] Bruce Ackerman, *We the People* (Cambridge: Harvard University Press, 1991), 158–59. See also Paul W. Kahn, *Legitimacy and History: The Problem of Self-Government in American Constitutional Theory* (New Haven: Yale University Press, 1992).

[10] Isaiah Berlin, "Two Concepts of Liberty," in *Four Essays on Liberty,* (London: Oxford University Press, 1969), 118–72. This lecture was given in 1958 to inaugurate his professorship at Oxford.

a recognition of the impact of social conditions on the range of choices available to individuals and their standing in the community. Even more, it reflected an appreciation of the responsibility of the state for those conditions.

At first, the state's affirmative obligations were acknowledged in arenas of social activity in which, contrary to Harlan's prescription in *Cumming* and *Berea College*, the role of the state was historically dominant and unmistakable. The affirmative duty of the state to combat racism was first announced in public education. As the Warren Court put it, the state is required to transform dual school systems into unitary, non-racial ones, where schools are considered neither black nor white, but just schools.[11] Similarly, the obligation of the state to compensate for economic inequalities was first announced in the context of the criminal justice system. The Court ruled in *Gideon v. Wainwright*[12] that the provision guaranteeing the right to counsel entailed an affirmative obligation of the state to provide counsel if the accused could not afford one. In time, however, as the state was seen increasingly as responsible for the very basis of our social existence, its affirmative obligations were extended to so-called private arenas like employment or housing. Society was viewed as much a creation of the state as the state was a creation of society. The notion of two separate spheres, state and society, which gave so much life and force to the social contract tradition and to the entire body of law to which it gave rise, came to be treated in the jurisprudence of the Warren Court as an ill-conceived myth.

Analyzed in these terms, much of the history of constitutional law of the twentieth century has an evolutionary quality: *Lochner* enforced the social contract; the decisions of the 1910s and 1920s modified some of the terms of that contract; the New Deal required that the contract be breached; the settlement of 1937 held that breach to be constitutionally permissible; and *Brown* transformed that breach into a constitutional necessity and set the state free to promote equality. But since the mid-1970s, the development of constitutional doctrine has taken a dramatic new turn, making it impossible to continue to speak in evolutionary terms or to picture *Brown* as the culmination of this process.

We are now witnessing an eerie revival of many of the tenets of the contractarian tradition. Under the leadership of William Rehnquist, first as an associate justice and then as chief justice, the Court's doctrine has become increasingly individualistic. Like the Fuller Court before it, the present Court has posited the priority of liberty over equality, treated liberty as little more than a promise of limited government, and as indicated

---

[11] Green v. County School Bd. of New Kent County, 391 U.S. 430, 442 (1968). See also Swann v. Charlotte-Mecklenburg Bd. of Educ., 402 U.S. 1 (1971).

[12] 372 U.S. 335 (1963).

most dramatically in its decisions on state action,[13] has separated state and society into two spheres and treated the social sphere, largely defined by market exchange, as natural and just.

For much of its life, the activism of the Warren Court was haunted by the ghost of *Lochner*. The present Court, cut from the same mold as the one that gave us *Lochner*, now is haunted by the challenge *Brown* poses to the substance of this Court's doctrine: contractarianism redux. In this new dialectic, *Brown* appears not as a negative example but as the embodiment of all that the law might be.

---

[13] See, e.g., Moose Lodge No. 107 v. Irvis, 409 U.S. 163 (1972); Jackson v. Metropolitan Edison Co., 419 U.S. 345 (1974); Flagg Bros. v. Brooks, 436 U.S. 149 (1978); and DeShaney v. Winnebago County Dep't of Social Serv., 489 U.S. 189 (1989). See also Lloyd Corp. v. Tanner, 407 U.S. 551 (1972); Hudgens v. Nat'l Labor Relations Bd., 424 U.S. 507 (1976).

Acknowledgments

PHIL C. Neal first brought me to the University of Chicago and involved me in this project. The firmness of his intellectual judgments was always tempered by a generosity of spirit and I am grateful for all that he did to launch my teaching career. The writing of this book was completed at the Yale Law School and the deans of that institution—Abraham S. Goldstein, Harry H. Wellington, and Guido Calabresi—were always generous in their support. I would also like to express my heartfelt thanks to a large number of students, colleagues, and friends who have made a special contribution to this book and to my understanding of this unusual phase of Supreme Court history: Bruce Ackerman, Natasha A. Adams, Adeno Addis, Matthew D. Adler, José Julian Alvarez Gonzalez, Michael J. Aprahamian, Geoffrey F. Aronow, Eric Bentley, Jr., Nancy Brooks, Jennifer K. Brown, Marc R. Bruner, Marcel A. Bryar, Robert A. Burt, Camille M. Caesar, Guadalupe Chapa, John Michael Clear, Gene P. Coakley, Randall D. Costa, Avidan Y. Cover, Nicole M. J. David, Elizabeth E. deGrazia, Lawrence Douglas, William F. Duker, Peter M. Dwoskin, William N. Eskridge, Jr., Jordan Flyer, William E. Forbath, Brooks R. Fudenberg, Antonio García Padilla, Stephen A. Gardbaum, Allan Gerson, Paul Gewirtz, Sean P. Gugler, Matthew S. Haiken, Jane Hicks Harden, James Hirschhorn, Peter C. Hoffer, Edward Janger, Bruce E. H. Johnson, Paul W. Kahn, Pamela S. Karlan, Stanley N. Katz, Cathy E. Kiselyak, Suzanne Klepper, Jane F. Levey, Michael D. Lowe, Olella Nyiendo, Michele Plescia-Schultz, Walter F. Pratt, Jr., George L. Priest, Valerie Quinn, Dennis Robb, Richard Ross, Kevin K. Russell, Barbara J. Safriet, Robert A. Schapiro, Dana L. Shoenberg, Stephen D. Sowle, Anne P. Standley, Edward E. Steiner, Martin J. Stone, Susan J. Swift, and Yan Yang. Their involvement transformed the writing of this book into a movable seminar that was always informative and always stirring. Finally, I would like to acknowledge the contribution of

397

my secretaries, Sylvia Karjala, Isabel Poludnewycz, and, above all, Lorraine E. Nagle, who kept track of every detail, befriended and aided my many research assistants, calmed me when the light at the end of the tunnel began to flicker, and in other ways too numerous to mention gave themselves to this project with a devotion that is truly remarkable and that will always be remembered.

Table of Cases

Table of Cases

Index

Index

For specific cases see also Table of Cases

Equal Protection Clause (*continued*)
205, 207*n.77*, 391*n.3*, 393
Equity
and Brewer's opinion in *Debs*, 67–69
and labor cases, 211
see also Injunction
Erdman Act of 1898, 166–67, 168, 170,
171, 180, 181, 214, 363
Expansionism. *See* Territorial expansion
Ex parte injunction, 58
see also Injunction
Expediting Act of 1903, 24*n.11*, 220*n.122*
Extension doctrine, 246–47, 248, 295
see also American empire;
Imperialism; Incorporation
doctrine

Fabricant, Judith, 175*n.73*
Fair rate of return, right of, 85, 106,
189, 203–18, 220–21
Faulkner, Charles, 280
Federal government
affirmative obligations of, 394–95
constitutional issues on scope of, 45,
200*n.58*, 229
exclusion powers of, 302
limited powers of, 109, 114, 159, 213*n.96*
New Deal activism, 391–92
police power of, 65–72
rate regulation by states and, 124*n.57*,
194
regulatory controls by, 196*n.44*
revenues, 77–78
see also Congress of the United
States; Federalism; State; State
government
Federalism, 144, 212–13, 225, 257–92
Addyston Pipe and, 117, 125–26
antitrust and, 109, 110, 119*n.41*, 259
Northern Securities and, 131, 134
statutory interpretation of, 145, 146–48
Federal judiciary
structure, 24
three-judge panels, 6*n.19*, 218–20, 221
Federal Trade Commission, 108
Federal Trade Commission Act of 1914,
6, 43, 154*n.140*
Fellow-servant rule, 169, 215
Field, David Dudley, 32
Field, Stephen, 28–30, 32, 35, 119,
207*n.76*, 263–64, 299

Bowman opinion, 273
Chinese Exclusion opinion, 301–02,
306–08
Fong Yue Ting dissent, 308, 312
Look Tin Sing opinion, 312*n.66*
Mugler dissent, 264–65, 266*n.25*
Munn dissent, 188, 191, 192
O'Neil v. Vermont headnote, 285*n.77*
Wong Wing opinion, 311
Fifteenth Amendment, 382, 384
Fifth Amendment, 167, 168, 200*n.58*,
248, 254*n.98*, 288
Fink, Leon, 38
First Amendment, 10, 323*n.3*, 324,
326*n.21*, 328–29, 330, 333*n.46*,
335–36, 341–42, 345, 348, 349, 350, 351
see also Free speech cases
Fish, Hamilton, 307*n.44*
Flag desecration, 325, 326
Fletcher, William, 213*n.96*
Foner, Eric, 352
Foraker, Joseph, 197*n.49*
Foraker Act of 1900, 234*n.29*, 235, 236,
237, 240, 244, 245, 246
Forbath, William, 59*n.40*, 211*n.89*
Four Freedoms, 392, 392*n.7*
Fourteenth Amendment, 85, 162*n.24*,
200, 262, 263, 289, 297, 328, 345,
372, 382, 384, 393
application to corporations, 135*n.84*
application to women, 178*n.82*
citizenship provision, 300, 309,
310*n.56*, 311, 313, 315, 358–59
fair rate of return right and, 217, 219
Holmes's (Oliver Wendell, Jr.) view
of, 157–58, 163*n.28*, 167
liberty to contract in, 163, 167,
346–47, 380
Plessy decision and, 357, 359
see also Due Process Clause; Equal
Protection Clause
Fox, Eleanor, 107*n.1*
Frankfurter, Felix, 9, 24*nn.11, 12*, 34*n.54*,
99, 182, 266*n.26*, 321
Freedoms, fundamental, 384
see also Bill of Rights; Liberty
Free speech cases, 245*n.76*, 323–51
alien subversion, 297*n.4*, 335–39
contractual liberty vs., 326–28
flag desecration, 325, 326
libel, 348–51

Lamar, Joseph Rucker, 144
Lamar, Lucius, 31*n.7*, 114*n.26*, 201, 273*n.44*
Lande, Robert, 108*n.7*
Lardner, Lynford, 192*n.30*
Laski, Harold, 183*n.92*
Law clerks, 30
Legislation
  technical advantages of, 105–06
  see also specific laws
Lesseps, Ferdinand de, 348–49
Letwin, William, 107*n.2*, 130*n.73*, 137*n.91*, 143*n.115*, 154*n.140*
Leuchtenburg, William, 8*n.29*
Levy, Leonard, 308*n.48*, 345
Libel, *Press Publishing* case, 348–51
Liberty, 12–21, 45–46, 389–95
  compatibility of imperialism with constitutional ideal of, 45
  corporations and, 135*n.84*, 370–71, 389
  entrepreneurial, 132–33, 345, 346–47
  and equality, 8, 9, 20–21, 390–91, 392–93, 398
  and federalism, 257–92
  Harlan (John Marshall) on Fourteenth Amendment, 135*n.84*, 167
  Holmes (Oliver Wendell, Jr.) on Fourteenth Amendment, 163*n.28*, 167
  "ordered," 46
  prevailing notions of, 18–19, 389
  and social contract tradition, 258, 389–91, 394–95
  see also Antitrust; Constitutional community; Constitutive authority; Fourteenth Amendment; Freedoms, fundamental; Free speech cases; Liberty of contract; Maximum work hours statutes; Organic authority
Liberty of contract, 106, 157, 159–60, 167, 179, 205, 263, 323, 384
  antitrust laws as interference with, 115*n.28*, 119–29
  and Fourteenth Amendment, 163, 167, 346–47, 380
  liberty of speech vs., 326–28
  Sherman Act and, 109–10, 111, 148–49, 151
  see also Labor
Lindsey, Almont, 58*n.32*, 60

Liquor
  interstate shipment regulation, 6, 286
  state taxation, 269*n.37*, 271*n.41*, 274*n.49*
  see also Prohibition cases
Locke, John, 46, 82, 84, 133
Lofgren, Charles, 353*nn.5, 7*
Looking Backward, 2000—1887
  (Bellamy), 38, 56
Louisiana Commission of 1877, 152
Louisiana Purchase, 232*n.22*
Lowe, Michael, 124*n.57*
Lurton, Horace, 126*n.60*, 144
Lynchings, 296*n.1*, 341*n.64*

Mandel, Ernest, 335
Mann-Elkins Act of 1910, 6*n.19*, 24*n.11*, 218–21
Manufacturing
  price-fixing agreements, 124–29
  transportation vs., 114, 125, 145–46
Marshall, John, 238, 254*n.99*, 272*n.42*, 274, 279, 282
  Brown v. Maryland opinion, 266–69
Marshall Court, 225, 259
Martin, Albro, 14*n.48*, 186*n.3*
Masters, Edgar Lee, 331–34
Master-servant relationship. *See* Labor
Matthews, Stanley
  Bowman opinion, 272, 273, 274, 274–75*n.50*
  Stone opinion, 202*n.62*
  Yick Wo opinion, 309
Maximum work hours statutes, 155–79, 183*n.92*, 193*n.39*
  for bakers, 157, 161, 164
  for miners, 172–74, 188, 192
  for women, 174–78
Maxwell, Lawrence, 97*n.50*
May, James, 115*n.28*
Mayer, David, 158*n.11*, 262*n.12*
McClain, Charles, 299*n.4*
McCurdy, Charles, 29*n.24*, 48*n.102*, 115*nn.28, 29*, 132*n.75*, 263*n.12*
McKenna, Joseph, 35, 36, 119, 172, 193*n.38*, 240, 247, 288
  Adair dissent, 168*n.48*, 179, 364, 365
  appointment and background, 34
  Lochner dissent, 170–71, 173, 253
  Northern Securities opinion, 130, 145, 152
McKinley, William, 34, 35, 40, 227, 229, 234–35, 236, 248, 251, 278, 295, 331

WITHDRAWN